MANAGEMENT

FUNDAMENTALS

SIXTH EDITION

RICKY W. GRIFFIN
Texas A&M University

SOUTH-WESTERN
CENGAGE Learning™

Australia • Brazil • Japan • Korea • Mexico • Singapore • Spain • United Kingdom • United States

SOUTH-WESTERN
CENGAGE Learning

Management Fundamentals
Sixth Edition
Ricky W. Griffin

Vice President of Editorial, Business:
Jack W. Calhoun

Publisher: Melissa Acuña

Executive Editor: Scott Person

Senior Developmental Editor: Julia Chase

Senior Editorial Assistant: Ruth Belanger

Senior Marketing Communications
Manager: Jim Overly

Marketing Coordinator: Julia Tucker

Marketing Director: Clint Kernen

Content Project Management:
PreMediaGlobal

Media Editor: Rob Ellington

Manufacturing Coordinator:
Miranda Klapper

Print Buyer: Arethea Thomas

Production Service/Compositor:
PreMediaGlobal

Senior Art Director: Tippy McIntosh

Internal Design: PreMediaGlobal

Cover Designer: Patti Hudepohl

Photo Credits:

B/W Image: iSockphoto

Cover Image: Shutterstock Images/scantaur

Photography Manager: John Hill

Photo Researcher: PreMediaGlobal

Cengage Learning WebTutor™ is a trademark of Cengage Learning.

Library of Congress Control Number: 2010936308

International Edition:

ISBN-13: 978-1-111-52566-8

ISBN-10: 1-111-52566-8

Cengage Learning International Offices

Asia
www.cengageasia.com
tel: (65) 6410 1200

Australia/New Zealand
www.cengage.com.au
tel: (61) 3 9685 4111

Brazil
www.cengage.com.br
tel: (55) 11 3665 9900

India
www.cengage.co.in
tel: (91) 11 4364 1111

Latin America
www.cengage.com.mx
tel: (52) 55 1500 6000

UK/Europe/Middle East/Africa
www.cengage.co.uk
tel: (44) 0 1264 332 424

Represented in Canada by
Nelson Education, Ltd.
tel: (416) 752 9100/(800) 668 0671
www.nelson.com

Cengage Learning is a leading provider of customized learning solutions with office locations around the globe, including Singapore, the United Kingdom, Australia, Mexico, Brazil, and Japan. Locate your local office at: **cengage.com/global**

For product information: **www.cengage.com/international**
Visit your local office: **www.cengage.com/global**
Visit our corporate website: **www.cengage.com**

Printed in China by China Translation & Printing Services Limited.
1 2 3 4 5 6 7 13 12 11

MANAGEMENT

FUNDAMENTALS

*For my sisters, Donna Goodin
and Cathy Selman*

BRIEF CONTENTS

CONTENTS

PART 2   PLANNING

3 Basic Elements of Planning   57

4 Managing Decision Making and Problem Sovling   87

PART 3   ORGANIZING

PART 4   CONTROLLING

PART 5 LEADING

13 Leadership and Its Impact on Influence Processes · 365

14 The Role of Organizational Communication · 397

15 Teams and Groups · 425

PREFACE

Over the last five decades, hundreds of books have been written for introductory management courses. As the body of material comprising the theory, research, and practice of management has grown and expanded, textbook authors have continued to mirror this expansion of material in their books. Writers have understood the importance of adding new material pertinent to traditional topics, such as planning and organizing, while simultaneously adding coverage of emerging new topics, such as diversity and information technology. As a by-product of this trend, our general survey textbooks have grown longer and longer, making it increasingly difficult to cover all the material in one course.

Another emerging trend in management education is a new focus on teaching in a broader context. That is, introductory management courses are increasingly being taught with less emphasis on theory alone and more emphasis on application of concepts. Teaching students how to apply management concepts successfully often involves focusing more on skills development and the human side of the organization. This trend requires that textbooks cover theoretical concepts within a flexible framework that enables instructors to make use of interactive tools such as case studies, exercises, and projects. It also dictates that a text be as relevant to students as possible. Hence, while this book draws examples and cases from older large firms like Ford, IBM, and Nestle, it also makes extensive use of newer firms such as Google, Abercrombie & Fitch, Facebook, Starbucks, Urban Outfitters, and others.

This textbook represents a synthesis of these trends toward a more manageable and practical approach. By combining concise text discussion, standard pedagogical tools, lively and current content, an emphasis on organizational behavior, and exciting skills-development materials, *Management Fundamentals* answers the need for a new approach to management education. This book provides almost limitless flexibility, a solid foundation of knowledge-based material, and an action-oriented learning dimension unique in the field. Indeed, almost a half million students were introduced to the field of management using the first five editions of this book. This sixth edition builds solidly on the successes of the earlier editions.

ORGANIZATION OF THE BOOK

Most management instructors today organize their course around the traditional management functions of planning, organizing, leading, and controlling. *Management Fundamentals* uses these functions as its organizing framework. The book consists of five parts, with fifteen chapters.

Part One introduces management through two chapters. Chapter 1 provides a basic overview of the management process in organizations, and Chapter 2 introduces students to the environment of management. Part Two covers the first basic management function, planning. Chapter 3 introduces the fundamental concepts of planning and discusses strategic management. Managerial decision making is the topic of Chapter 4. Finally, Chapter 5 covers entrepreneurship and the management of new ventures.

The second basic management function, organizing, is the subject of Part Three. In Chapter 6 the fundamental concepts of organization structure and design are introduced and discussed. Chapter 7 explores organization change and organizational innovation. Chapter 8 is devoted to the management of human resources.

The third management function, controlling, is the subject of Part Four. Chapter 9 introduces the fundamental concepts and issues associated with management of the control process. A special area of control today, managing for total quality, is discussed in Chapter 10.

Many instructors and managers believe that the fourth basic management function, leading, is especially important in contemporary organizations. Thus Part Five consists of five chapters devoted to this management function. Basic concepts and processes associated with individual behavior are introduced and discussed in Chapter 11. Employee motivation is the subject of Chapter 12. Chapter 13 examines leadership and influence processes in organizations. Communication in organizations is the topic of Chapter 14. The management of groups and teams is covered in Chapter 15.

SKILLS-FOCUSED PEDAGOGICAL FEATURES

With this text, it has been possible to address new dimensions of management education without creating a book so long that it is unwieldy. Specifically, each chapter is followed by an exciting set of skills-based exercises. These resources have been created to bring an active and a behavioral orientation to management education by requiring students to solve problems, make decisions, respond to situations, and work in groups. In short, these materials simulate many of the day-to-day challenges and opportunities that real managers face.

Among these skills-based exercises are two different *Building Effective Skills* organized around the set of basic management skills introduced in Chapter 1. The *Skills Self-Assessment Instrument* exercise helps readers learn something about their own approach to management. Finally, an *Experiential Exercise* provides additional action-oriented learning opportunities, usually in a group setting.

New to the sixth edition, each chapter also contains a boxed feature entitled *Tough Times, Tough Choices* or *Ethics in Action*. These features are intended to depart briefly from the flow of the chapter to highlight or extend especially interesting or emerging points and issues related to the tough decisions managers must make in today's business climate or to ethical questions that confront managers today.

In addition to the end-of-the-chapter exercises, every chapter includes important standard pedagogy: learning objectives, a chapter outline, an opening incident, key terms, a summary of key points, questions for review, questions for analysis, and a chapter case with questions that can be found at the end of your textbook.

CHANGES TO THE SIXTH EDITION

The sixth edition of *Management Fundamentals* retains the same basic structure and format as the previous edition. However, within that framework the content of the book has been thoroughly revised and updated. The following changes are illustrative of the new material that has been added:

(1) New topical coverage includes details and references to both domestic and global economic conditions. When the previous edition was published, the

global economic climate was still favorable. But as everyone now knows, the economy began to decline in 2008 and by 2009 was in full recession. By 2010 the economy had begun to stabilize but was still both sluggish and erratic. The implications and impact of these economic fluctuations are now integrated throughout the book.

(2) Since the last edition several new management techniques have been introduced. One of these, for example, is the tiered work force where existing workers are paid at a higher rate than newly hired ones. These new techniques are discussed in several locations in the book.

(3) The latest research findings regarding globalization, strategic management, organizing, motivation, leadership, and control have been incorporated into the text and referenced at the end of the book.

(4) All of the cases and boxed inserts are new to this edition of *Management Fundamentals*. They reflect a wide variety of organizations and illustrate both successful and less successful practices and decisions.

(5) As noted earlier, this book features a rich and diverse array of end-of-chapter materials to facilitate both learning and skill development. For this edition over two-thirds of this material have been replaced or substantially revised.

ACKNOWLEDGMENTS

I would like to acknowledge the many contributions that others have made to this book. My faculty colleagues at Texas A&M University have contributed enormously both to this book and to my thinking about management education. The fine team of professionals at Cengage Learning has also been instrumental in the success of this book. Melissa Acuna, Scott Person, Julia Chase, Melissa Sacco (PreMediaGlobal), Tippy McIntosh, Clint Kernen, Jim Overly, Mardell Glinski Schulz, and Ruth Belanger were instrumental in the production of this edition. Special thanks to Ron Librach.

Many reviewers have played a critical role in the continuous evolution and improvement of this project. They examined my work in detail and with a critical eye. I would like to tip my hat to the following reviewers, whose imprint can be found throughout this text:

Joe Adamo (Cazenovia College), Sally Alkazin (Linfield College), Elizabeth Anne Christo-Baker (Terra Community College), Robert Ash (Santiago Canyon College), Sherryl Berg-Ridenour (DeVry College—Pomona), Alain Broder (Touro College), Murray Brunton (Central Ohio Tech), Sam Chapman (Diablo Valley College), Gary Corona (Florida Community College—Jacksonville), Dr. Anne Cowden (California State University), Thomas DeLaughter (University of Florida), Anita Dickson (Northampton Community College), Joe Dobson (Western Illinois University), Michael Dutch (University of Houston), Norb Elbert (Eastern Kentucky University), Teri Elkins (University of Houston), Jan Feldbauer (Schoolcraft College), Anne Fiedler (Barry University), Eugene Garaventa (College of Staten Island), Phillip Gonsher (Johnson Community College), Patricia Green (Nassau Community College), Joseph S. Hooker, Jr. (North Greenville College), David Hudson (Spalding University), George W. Jacobs (Middle Tennessee State University), Tim McCabe (Tompkins Cortland Community College), Judy Nixon (University of Tennessee—Chatanooga), Ranjna Patel (Bethune–Cookman College), Lisa Reed (University of Portland), Virginia Rich (Caldwell College) Dr. Joan Rivera

(Angelo State University), Roberta B. Slater (Pennsylvania College of Technology), Bob Smoot (Hazard Community College), Howard Stanger (Canisius College), Sheryl A. Stanley (Newman University), Roy Strickland (Ozarks Technical Community College), Mike L. Stutzman (Mt Mercy College and Kirkwood College), Abe Tawil (Baruch University), Barry Van Hook (Arizona State University), Ruth Weatherly (Simpson College), Mary Williams (Community College of Nevada)

My wife, Glenda, and our children, Dustin, Ashley, and Matt, are, of course, due the greatest thanks. Their love, care, interest, and enthusiasm help sustain me in all that I do. I also enthusiastically invite your feedback on this book. If you have any questions, suggestions, or issues to discuss, please feel free to contact me. The most efficient way to reach me is through e-mail. My address is rgriffin@tamu.edu.

R.W.G.

MANAGEMENT FUNDAMENTALS

MANAGING AND THE MANAGER'S JOB

After studying this chapter, you should be able to:

1 Define management, describe the kinds of managers found in organizations, identify and explain the four basic management functions, describe the fundamental management skills, and comment on management as science and art.

2 Justify the importance of history and theory to managers and explain the evolution of management thought through the classical, behavioral, and quantitative perspectives.

3 Identify and discuss key contemporary management perspectives represented by the systems and contingency perspectives and identify the major challenges and opportunities faced by managers today.

In Search of Google

Sergey Brin and Larry Page met at Stanford University in 1995 when both were graduate students in computer science. At the time, Page was working on a software development project designed to create an index of websites by scouring sites for key words and other linkages; he soon recognized Brin as a kindred spirit and invited him to join his fledgling enterprise. Shortly afterward they ran across the description of a business model based on the concept of selling advertising in the form of sponsored links and search-specific ads. They adapted it to their own concept and went into business, eventually building Google into the world's largest search engine, with an index of over 10 billion webpages and a user base of 380 million people per month in 112 different countries.

Following an initial public offering (IPO) in 2004, the company's market capitalization rose steadily and stood at more than $157 billion by 2010, when Google controlled 61.5 percent of the U.S. search market (compared to Yahoo's 29.9 percent and Microsoft's 9.2 percent). Google, however, is much more than a mere search engine. Its services include searches for

> **"I would rather have people think we're confused than let our competitors know what we're going to do."**
>
> —LARRY PAGE, COFOUNDER AND PRESIDENT OF GOOGLE

news, shopping, local businesses, interactive maps, and discussion groups, as well as blogs, web-based e-mail and voice mail, and a digital photo management system. You can access the results of any Google search from the Google website, from your own user's toolbar, from your Windows taskbar, and from wireless devices such as smart phones.

How did two thirty-something computer scientists build this astoundingly successful company, and where will they take it in the future? Neither Brin nor Page has any formal business education, and they sometimes seem naïve in business matters, often rejecting the advice of experienced managers and relying on their own instinctual (and unorthodox) ideas. Interestingly,

AP PHOTO/TED S. WARREN

A key ingredient to Google's success is the firm's ability to recruit talented and creative employees. These software engineers are working in a game room at Google's newest campus in Kirkland, Washington.

however, the duo seems to excel in several managerial areas. First, Brin and Page remain in the forefront of Google's search for technological innovations. They believe in the power of mathematics and have developed unique algorithms for just about every form of activity in the firm. One of the most successful is an algorithm for auctioning advertising placements that ensures the highest possible prices.

Brin and Page have also been remarkably successful in attracting talented and creative employees and then providing them with a work environment and culture that foster the kind of productivity and innovation for which they were hired. At least half of all Google employees are scientists and engineers. Many are recruited from the country's top engineering schools, while others "win" jobs by performing well in online programming contests. Googlers work in small, flexible, self-directed teams, and the company's website reinforces the casual atmosphere: "Work and play," according to Google, "are not mutually exclusive. It is possible to code and pass the puck at the same time." Employees are free to devote 20 percent of the workday to pursuing personal projects, and many of Google's most innovative ideas have sprung from this policy of enlightened self-interest. Pay for performance is standard, and compensation is relatively high. (Brin and Page reward themselves with $1 a year in salary, with no bonuses, stock, or options.)

Finally, although the founders avoid formal strategic planning, they've managed to diversify extensively through acquisitions and key alliances. Typically, Google absorbs an acquired firm and then improves on its technology, thereby adding variety to its own online offerings. Recent acquisitions include YouTube, a leader in online video sharing (2006); Postini, a leader in communications security products (2007); and Double-Click, a leader in online advertising services (2008). Strategic alliances include those with foreign online service providers that offer Google searches on their sites.

For the future, Google plans on doing more of the same, competing head to head with financial service providers for stock information and with iTunes for music and videos. Also committed to the in-house development of new features and services, Google spent $2.1 billion on research and development (R&D) in 2007 (up from $1.2 billion in 2006) and another $1 billion to acquire new information technology (IT) assets. Innovations in the works include an automated universal language translator for translating documents from any language into any other language and personalized home pages for allowing users to design automatic searches and display the results in personal "newspapers."

If there's anything else on the drawing board, nobody knows for sure. In fact, outsiders—notably potential investors—often criticize Google for being a "black box" when they want a few more details about topics of investor interest such as long-range strategy. "We don't talk about our strategy," explains Page, ". . . because it's strategic. I would rather have people think we're confused than let our competitors know what we're going to do."[1]

This book is about managers like Sergey Brin and Larry Page and the work they do. In this chapter, we examine the general nature of management, its dimensions, and its challenges. We explain the basic concepts of management and managers, discuss the management process, and summarize the origins of contemporary management thought. We conclude this chapter by introducing critical challenges and issues that managers are facing now and will continue to encounter in the future.

AN INTRODUCTION TO MANAGEMENT

An **organization** is a group of people working together in a structured and coordinated fashion to achieve a set of goals, which may include profit (Starbucks Corporation), the discovery of knowledge (University of Missouri), national defense (the U.S. Army), the coordination of various local charities (United Way of America), or social satisfaction (a sorority).

organization
A group of people working together in a structured and coordinated fashion to achieve a set of goals

Managers are responsible for using the organization's resources to help achieve its goals. More precisely, **management** can be defined as a set of activities (including planning and decision making, organizing, leading, and controlling) directed at an organization's resources (human, financial, physical, and information), with the aim of achieving organizational goals in an efficient and effective manner. A **manager**, then, is someone whose primary responsibility is to carry out the management process. By **efficient**, we mean using resources wisely, in a cost-effective way. By **effective**, we mean making the right decisions and successfully implementing them. In general, successful organizations are both efficient and effective.[2]

Today's managers face various interesting and challenging situations. The average executive works 60 hours a week; has enormous demands placed on his or her time; and faces increased complexities posed by globalization, domestic competition, government regulation, shareholder pressure, and Internet-related uncertainties. Their job is complicated even more by rapid changes, unexpected disruptions, and both minor and major crises. The manager's job is unpredictable and fraught with challenges, but it is also filled with opportunities to make a difference. Good managers can propel an organization into unprecedented realms of success, whereas poor managers can devastate even the strongest of organizations.[3]

Kinds of Managers

Many different kinds of managers work in organizations today. Figure 1.1 shows how various kinds of managers within an organization can be differentiated by level and by area.

management
A set of activities (including planning and decision making, organizing, leading, and controlling) directed at an organization's resources (human, financial, physical, and information), with the aim of achieving organizational goals in an efficient and effective manner

manager
Someone whose primary responsibility is to carry out the management process

efficient
Using resources wisely in a cost-effective way

effective
Making the right decisions and successfully implementing them

Figure 1.1
Kinds of Managers by Level and Area

Organizations generally have three levels of management, represented by top managers, middle managers, and first-line managers. Regardless of level, managers are also usually associated with a specific area within the organization, such as marketing, finance, operations, human resources, administration, or some other area.

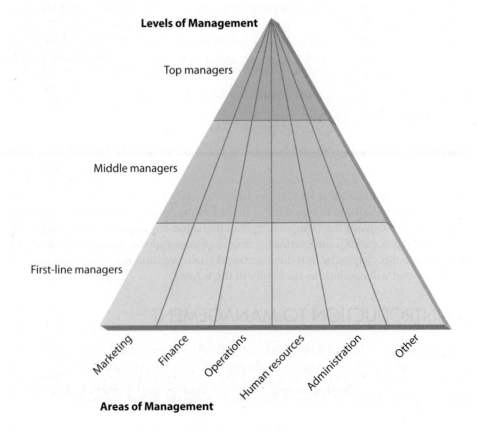

Levels of Management

Top managers

Middle managers

First-line managers

Marketing Finance Operations Human resources Administration Other

Areas of Management

Levels of Management One way to classify managers is in terms of their level in the organization. *Top managers* make up the relatively small group of executives who manage the overall organization. Titles found in this group include president, vice president, and chief executive officer (CEO). Top managers create the organization's goals, overall strategy, and operating policies. They also officially represent the organization to the external environment by meeting with government officials, executives of other organizations, and so forth.

Howard Schultz, CEO of Starbucks, is a top manager, as is Deidra Wager, the firm's executive vice president. Likewise, Sergey Brin, Larry Page, and Alan Mulally are also top managers. The job of a top manager is likely to be complex and varied. Top managers make decisions about activities such as acquiring other companies, investing in R&D, entering or abandoning various markets, and building new plants and office facilities. They often work long hours and spend much of their time in meetings or on the telephone. In most cases, top managers are also very well paid. In fact, the elite top managers of very large firms sometimes make several million dollars a year in salary, bonuses, and stock.[4] In 2009 Ford paid its CEO, Alan Mulally, $2,000,000 in salary. He also earned $1,046,390 in other compensation and $14,641,851 in stock and option awards.[5]

Middle management is probably the largest group of managers in most organizations. Common middle-management titles include plant manager, operations manager, and division head. *Middle managers* are primarily responsible for implementing the policies and plans developed by top managers and for supervising and coordinating the activities of lower-level managers.[6] Jason Hernandez, a regional manager at Starbucks responsible for the firm's operations in three eastern states, is a middle manager.

First-line managers supervise and coordinate the activities of operating employees. Common titles for first-line managers are supervisor, coordinator, and office manager. Positions like these are often the first held by employees who enter management from the ranks of operating personnel. Wayne Maxwell and Jenny Wagner, managers of Starbucks coffee shops in Texas, are first-line managers. They oversee the day-to-day operations of their respective stores, hire operating employees to staff them, and handle other routine administrative duties required of them by the parent corporation. In contrast to top and middle managers, first-line managers typically spend a large proportion of their time supervising the work of their subordinates.

Managing in Different Areas of the Organization Regardless of their level, managers may work in various areas within an organization. In any given firm, for example, these areas may include marketing, financial, operations, human resources, administrative, and others.

Marketing managers work in areas related to the marketing function—getting consumers and clients to buy the organization's products or services (be they Nokia cell phones, Ford automobiles, *Newsweek* magazines, Associated Press news reports, flights on Southwest Airlines, or cups of latte at Starbucks). These areas include new-product development, promotion, and distribution. Given the importance of marketing for virtually all organizations, developing good managers in this area is critical.

Financial managers deal primarily with an organization's financial resources. They are responsible for activities such as accounting, cash management, and investments. In some businesses, especially banking and insurance, financial managers are found in large numbers.

Operations managers are concerned with creating and managing the systems that create an organization's products and services. Typical responsibilities of operations managers include production control, inventory control, quality control, plant layout, and site selection.

Human resources managers are responsible for hiring and developing employees. They are typically involved in human resource planning, recruiting and selecting employees, training and development, designing compensation and benefit systems, formulating performance appraisal systems, and discharging low-performing and problem employees.

Administrative, or general, managers are not associated with any particular management specialty. Probably the best example of an administrative management position is that of a hospital or clinic administrator. Administrative managers tend to be generalists; they have some basic familiarity with all functional areas of management rather than specialized training in any one area.[7]

Many organizations have specialized management positions in addition to those already described. Public relations managers, for example, deal with the public and media for firms such as Philip Morris and the Dow Chemical Company to protect and enhance the image of their organizations. R&D managers coordinate the activities of scientists and engineers working on scientific projects in organizations such as Monsanto Company, NASA, and Merck & Company. Internal consultants are used in organizations such as Prudential Insurance to provide specialized expert advice to operating managers. International operations are often coordinated by specialized managers in organizations like Eli Lilly and Rockwell International. The number, nature, and importance of these specialized managers vary tremendously from one organization to another. As contemporary organizations continue to grow in complexity and size, the number and importance of such managers are also likely to increase.

Basic Management Functions

Regardless of level or area, management involves the four basic functions of planning and decision making, organizing, leading, and controlling. This book is organized around these basic functions, as shown in Figure 1.2.

Figure 1.2
The Management Process

Management involves four basic activities—planning and decision making, organizing, leading, and controlling. Although there is a basic logic for describing these activities in this sequence (as indicated by the solid arrows), most managers engage in more than one activity at a time and often move back and forth between the activities in unpredictable ways (as shown by the dotted arrows).

Planning and Decision Making
Setting the organization's goals and deciding how best to achieve them

Organizing
Determining how best to group activities and resources

Controlling
Monitoring and correcting ongoing activities to facilitate goal attainment

Leading
Motivating members of the organization to work in the best interests of the organization

Planning and Decision Making In its simplest form, **planning** means setting an organization's goals and deciding how best to achieve them. **Decision making**, a part of the planning process, involves selecting a course of action from a set of alternatives. Planning and decision making help maintain managerial effectiveness by serving as guides for future activities. In other words, the organization's goals and plans clearly help managers know how to allocate their time and resources. Part Two of this text is devoted to planning and decision-making activities and concepts.

Organizing Once a manager has set goals and developed a workable plan, the next management function is to organize people and the other resources necessary to carry out the plan. Specifically, **organizing** involves determining how activities and resources are to be grouped. Although some people equate this function with the creation of an organization chart, we will see in Part Three that it is actually much more.

Controlling The final phase of the management process is **controlling**, or monitoring the organization's progress toward its goals. As the organization moves toward its goals, managers must monitor progress to ensure that it is performing in such a way as to arrive at its "destination" at the appointed time. Part Four explores the control function.

Leading The third basic managerial function is leading. Some people consider leading to be both the most important and the most challenging of all managerial activities. **Leading** is the set of processes used to get members of the organization to work together to further the interests of the organization. We cover the leading function in detail in Part Five.

Fundamental Management Skills

To carry out these management functions most effectively, managers rely on a number of different fundamental management skills of which the most important are technical, interpersonal, conceptual, diagnostic, communication, decision-making, and time management skills.[8]

Technical Skills Technical skills are necessary to accomplish or understand the specific kind of work done in an organization. Technical skills are especially important for first-line managers. These managers spend much of their time training their subordinates and answering questions about work-related problems. They must know how to perform the tasks assigned to those they supervise if they are to be effective managers. While Sergey Brin and Larry Page spend most of their time now dealing with strategic and management issues, they also keep abreast of new and emerging technologies that may affect Google.

Interpersonal Skills Managers spend considerable time interacting with people both inside and outside the organization. For obvious reasons, then, they also need **interpersonal skills**—the ability to communicate with, understand, and motivate both individuals and groups. As a manager climbs the organizational ladder, he or she must be able to get along with subordinates, peers, and those at higher levels of the organization. Because of the multitude of roles that managers must fulfill, a manager must also be able to work with suppliers, customers, investors, and others outside the organization.

Conceptual Skills Conceptual skills depend on the manager's ability to think in the abstract. Managers need the mental capacity to understand the overall workings of the organization and its environment, to grasp how all the parts of the organization fit together, and to view the organization in a holistic manner. This ability allows them to think strategically, to

planning
Setting an organization's goals and deciding how best to achieve them

decision making
Part of the planning process that involves selecting a course of action from a set of alternatives

organizing
Determining how activities and resources are to be grouped

controlling
Monitoring organizational progress toward goal attainment

leading
The set of processes used to get members of the organization to work together to further the interests of the organization

technical skills
The skills necessary to accomplish or understand the specific kind of work done in an organization

interpersonal skills
The ability to communicate with, understand, and motivate both individuals and groups

conceptual skills
The manager's ability to think in the abstract

see the "big picture," and to make broad-based decisions that serve the overall organization. The Ethics in Action feature illustrates how some managers use their conceptual skills to help businesses become more "green" while also increasing their profitability.

ETHICS IN ACTION

Performing in the Black (And Green)

"Green," says General Electric CEO Jeffrey Immelt, "is green." He means that a company can support the natural environment—by reducing waste, recycling, using less toxic materials, or cutting back on energy use—and at the same time improve its financial results. One sign that more and more U.S. firms agree with Immelt is the fact that, although the federal government has been cutting back on environmental regulation, many organizations are voluntarily adopting environmentally friendly policies in the interest of higher sales; bigger cost savings; and, ultimately, greater profitability.

Among smaller eco-friendly companies, for example, long-standing efforts are being bolstered. Patagonia, a maker of outdoor clothing, already uses organic fibers and is now encouraging customers to return used clothes for recycling. Other innovative firms have found ways to recycle bamboo and wood window coverings, to manufacture countertops made of recycled glass and concrete, and even to develop reusable fabric diapers with biodegradable inserts.

Among larger more traditionally minded companies, GE promised in 2005 to improve energy efficiency by 4 percent annually and double revenues from "clean" products over the next decade. BP, the English oil and gas giant, created a new alternative energy division, and Walmart, which owns the largest fleet of trucks in the United States, plans to double its fuel efficiency. McDonald's is seeking its first green-building certification, while Starbucks and Whole Foods have both announced that they'll purchase wind energy or wind energy credits to offset their usage of electricity. In addition, when mainstream companies get involved in such projects, they can have a significant impact on other firms with which they do business.

Innovations in batteries, wind turbines, solar devices, and other energy-saving technologies are an important factor in the shift in corporate thinking about the environment. Corning, for example, has developed a "green glass" for use in liquid crystal displays that doesn't contain toxic chemicals. In addition, as green technologies become more affordable, more companies will adopt them. Buyer power is another important element: Collectively, educated customers who demand accountability from the companies they patronize have enough influence to drive change.

Not surprisingly, however, the most crucial factor is the bottom line. Corporate CEOs and other top managers, of course, must answer to shareholders for profitability. When they have the opportunity to increase profits with green methods, they'll naturally do the right thing for their shareholders—which in this case also happens to be the right thing for the rest of the planet. In the midst of the economic turmoil of 2008, for example, GE announced that sales of its so-called ecomagination products would top $17 billion for the year—a jump of 21 percent over the previous year. Thanks in part to the success of its green initiatives, the value of the GE brand went up by 16.9 percent, and CEO Immelt estimates that shareholders gained $0.05 to $0.10 a share. "There is a green lining among the current economic storm clouds," says Immelt, "and GE customers and investors are benefiting."

References: Chip Geller and David Roberts, "The Revolution Begins," Fast Company, March 2006, www.fastcompany.com on December 19, 2008; "Immelt Sees 'Green' Profit for GE," Forbes, May 13, 2005, www.forbes.com on December 19, 2008; Gene C. Marcial, "Corning Turns a Corner," BusinessWeek, April 17, 2006, www.businessweek.com on December 19, 2008; "Green Products Help GE Weather Rough Economic Times," Greenbiz.com, October 22, 2008, www.greenbiz.com on December 9, 2008; and Douglas MacMillan, "The Issue: Immelt's Unpopular Idea," BusinessWeek, March 4, 2008, www.businessweek.com on December 9, 2008.

Diagnostic Skills Successful managers also possess **diagnostic skills**, or skills that enable them to visualize the most appropriate response to a situation. A physician diagnoses a patient's illness by analyzing symptoms and determining their probable cause. Similarly, a manager can diagnose and analyze a problem in the organization by studying its symptoms and then developing a solution.[9]

Communication Skills **Communication skills** refer to the manager's abilities both to effectively convey ideas and information to others and to effectively receive ideas and information from others. These skills enable a manager to transmit ideas to subordinates so that they know what is expected, to coordinate work with peers and colleagues so that they work well together, and to keep higher-level managers informed about what is going on. In addition, communication skills help the manager listen to what others say and to understand the real meaning behind e-mails, letters, reports, and other written communication.

Decision-Making Skills Effective managers also have good decision-making skills. **Decision-making skills** refer to the manager's ability to correctly recognize and define problems and opportunities and to then select an appropriate course of action to solve problems and capitalize on opportunities. No manager makes the right decision *all* the time. However, effective managers make good decisions *most* of the time. And, when they do make a bad decision, they usually recognize their mistake quickly and then make good decisions to recover with as little cost or damage to their organization as possible.

Time Management Skills Finally, effective managers usually have good time management skills. **Time management skills** refer to the manager's ability to prioritize work, to work efficiently, and to delegate work appropriately. As already noted, managers face many different pressures and challenges. It is too easy for a manager to get bogged down doing work that can easily be postponed or delegated to others.[10] When this happens, unfortunately, more pressing and higher-priority work may get neglected.[11]

The Science and the Art of Management

Given the complexity inherent in the manager's job, a reasonable question relates to whether management is a science or an art. In fact, effective management is a blend of both science and art. And successful executives recognize the importance of combining both the science and the art of management as they practice their craft.[12]

The Science of Management Many management problems and issues can be approached in ways that are rational, logical, objective, and systematic. Managers can gather data, facts, and objective information. They can use quantitative models and decision-making techniques to arrive at "correct" decisions. And they need to take such a scientific approach to solving problems whenever possible, especially when they are dealing with relatively routine and straightforward issues. When Starbucks considers entering a new market, its managers look closely at a wide variety of objective details as they formulate their plans. Technical, diagnostic, and decision-making skills are especially important when approaching a management task or problem from a scientific perspective.

diagnostic skills
The manager's ability to visualize the most appropriate response to a situation

communication skills
The manager's abilities both to effectively convey ideas and information to others and to effectively receive ideas and information from others

decision-making skills
The manager's ability to correctly recognize and define problems and opportunities and to then select an appropriate course of action to solve problems and capitalize on opportunities

time management skills
The manager's ability to prioritize work, to work efficiently, and to delegate appropriately

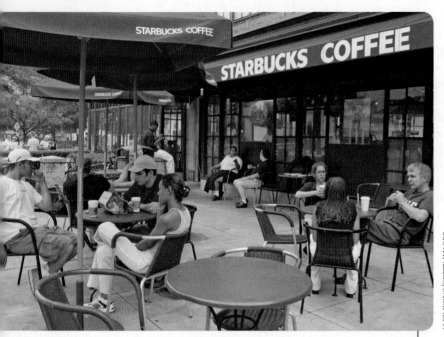

ALEX WONG/GETTY IMAGES

Management involves both art and science. For example, Starbucks managers relied heavily on scientific data when they planned their first stores in New York. But these data actually led the firm to misjudge the coffee drinking tastes of New Yorkers. As a result, Starbucks had to hastily alter its menus and install new equipment. Clearly, then, hard data and facts must be tempered with intuition and personal insight.

The Art of Management

Even though managers may try to be scientific as often as possible, they must frequently make decisions and solve problems on the basis of intuition, experience, instinct, and personal insights. Relying heavily on conceptual, communication, interpersonal, and time management skills, for example, a manager may have to decide among multiple courses of action that look equally attractive. And even "objective facts" may prove to be wrong. When Starbucks was planning its first store in New York City, market research clearly showed that New Yorkers preferred drip coffee to more exotic espresso-style coffees. After first installing more drip coffee makers and fewer espresso makers than in their other stores, managers had to backtrack when the New Yorkers lined up clamoring for espresso. Starbucks now introduces a standard menu and layout in all its stores, regardless of presumed market differences, and then makes necessary adjustments later. Thus, managers must blend an element of intuition and personal insight with hard data and objective facts.[13]

THE EVOLUTION OF MANAGEMENT

Most managers today recognize the importance of history and theory in their work. For instance, knowing the origins of their organization and the kinds of practices that have led to success—or failure—can be an indispensable tool in managing the contemporary organization. Thus, in our next section, we briefly trace the history of management thought. Then we move forward to the present day by introducing contemporary management issues and challenges.

The Importance of Theory and History

Some people question the value of history and theory. Their arguments are usually based on the assumptions that history is not relevant to contemporary society and that theory is abstract and of no practical use. In reality, however, both theory and history are important to all managers today.

theory
A conceptual framework for organizing knowledge and providing a blueprint for action

Why Theory? A theory is simply a conceptual framework for organizing knowledge and providing a blueprint for action.[14] Although some theories seem abstract and irrelevant, others appear very simple and practical. Management theories, used to build organizations and guide them toward their goals, are grounded in reality.[15] Practically any organization that uses assembly lines (such as Daimler AG and Maytag) is drawing on what we describe later in this chapter as *scientific management*. Many organizations, including Best Buy and Texas Instruments, use the behavioral perspective (also introduced later) to improve employee satisfaction and motivation. And naming a large company that does not use one or more techniques from the quantitative management perspective would be difficult. For example, retailers such as Kroger and Target routinely use operations management to determine how many checkout lines they need to have open at any given time. In addition, most managers develop and refine their own theories of how they should run their organizations and manage the behavior of their employees. James Sinegal, founder and CEO of Costco Wholesale, believes that paying his employees well while keeping prices as low as possible are the key ingredients in success for his business. This belief is based essentially on his personal theory of competition in the warehouse retailing industry.

Why History? Awareness and understanding of important historical developments are also important to contemporary managers.[16] Understanding the historical context of management provides a sense of heritage and can help managers avoid the mistakes of others. Most courses in U.S. history devote time to business and economic developments in this country, including the Industrial Revolution, the early labor movement, and the Great Depression, and to captains of U.S. industry such as Cornelius Vanderbilt (railroads), John D. Rockefeller (oil), and Andrew Carnegie (steel). The contributions of those and other industrialists left a profound imprint on contemporary culture.[17]

Many managers are also realizing that they can benefit from a greater understanding of history in general. For example, Ian M. Ross of AT&T's Bell Laboratories cites *The Second World War* by Winston Churchill as a major influence on his approach to leadership. Other books often mentioned by managers for their relevance to today's business problems include such classics as Plato's *Republic*, Homer's *Iliad*, Sun Tzu's *The Art of War*, and Machiavelli's *The Prince*.[18] And new business history books have also been directed at women managers and the lessons they can learn from the past.[19]

Managers at Wells Fargo clearly recognize the value of history. For example, the company maintains an extensive archival library of its old banking documents and records, and even employs a full-time corporate historian. As part of their orientation and training, new managers at Wells Fargo take courses to become acquainted with the bank's history.[20] Similarly, Shell Oil, Levi Strauss, Halliburton, Lloyd's of London, Disney, Honda, and Unilever all maintain significant archives about their pasts and frequently evoke images from those pasts in their orientation and training programs, advertising campaigns, and other public relations activities.

The Historical Context of Management

The practice of management can be traced back thousands of years. The Egyptians used the management functions of planning, organizing, and controlling when they constructed the pyramids. Alexander the Great employed a staff organization to coordinate activities during his military campaigns. The Roman Empire developed a well-defined organizational structure that greatly facilitated communication and control. Socrates discussed management practices and concepts in 400 B.C., Plato described job specialization in 350 B.C., and the Persian scientist and philosopher al-Farabi listed several leadership traits in A.D. 900.[21]

In spite of this history, the serious study of management did not begin until the nineteenth century. Two of its first pioneers were Robert Owen and Charles Babbage. Owen (1771–1858), a British industrialist and reformer, was one of the first managers to recognize the importance of an organization's human resources and to express concern for the personal welfare of his workers. Babbage (1792–1871), an English mathematician, focused his attention on efficiencies of production. He placed great faith in the division of labor and advocated the application of mathematics to such problems as the efficient use of facilities and materials.

The Classical Management Perspective

Early in the twentieth century, the preliminary ideas and writings of these and other managers and theorists converged with the emergence and evolution of large-scale businesses and management practices to create interest and focus attention on how businesses should be operated. The first important ideas to emerge are now called the **classical management perspective**, which actually includes two different viewpoints: scientific management and administrative management.

Scientific Management   Productivity emerged as a serious business problem during the first few years of this century. Business was expanding and capital was readily available, but labor was in short supply. Hence, managers began to search for ways to use existing labor more efficiently. In response to this need, experts began to focus on ways to improve the performance of individual workers. Their work led to the development of **scientific management**. Some of the earliest advocates of scientific management included Frederick W. Taylor (1856–1915), Frank Gilbreth (1868–1924), and Lillian Gilbreth (1878–1972).[22] Taylor played the dominant role.

One of Taylor's first jobs was as a foreman at the Midvale Steel Company in Philadelphia. There he observed what he called **soldiering**—employees deliberately working at a pace slower than their capabilities. Taylor studied and timed each element of the steelworkers' jobs. He determined what each worker should be producing, and then he designed the most efficient way of doing each part of the overall task. Next he implemented a piecework pay system. Rather than paying all employees the same wage, he began increasing the pay of each worker who met and exceeded the target level of output set for his or her job.

After Taylor left Midvale, he worked as a consultant for several companies, including Simonds Rolling Machine Company and Bethlehem Steel. At Simonds he studied and redesigned jobs, introduced rest periods to reduce fatigue, and implemented a piecework pay system. The results were higher quality and quantity of output, and improved morale. At Bethlehem Steel, Taylor studied efficient ways of loading and unloading railcars and applied his conclusions with equally impressive results. During these experiences, he formulated the basic ideas that he called *scientific management*. Figure 1.3 illustrates the basic steps Taylor suggested. He believed that managers who followed his guidelines would improve the efficiency of their workers.[23]

Taylor's work had a major impact on U.S. industry. By applying his principles, many organizations achieved major gains in efficiency. Taylor was not without his detractors, however. Labor argued that scientific management was just a device to get more work from each employee and to reduce the total number of workers needed by a firm. There was a congressional investigation into Taylor's ideas, and evidence suggests that he falsified some of his findings.[24] Nevertheless, Taylor's work left a lasting imprint on business.[25]

Frank and Lillian Gilbreth, contemporaries of Taylor, were a husband-and-wife team of industrial engineers. One of Frank Gilbreth's most interesting contributions was to the craft of bricklaying. After studying bricklayers at work, he developed several procedures

---

classical management perspective
Consists of two distinct branches—scientific management and administrative management

scientific management
Concerned with improving the performance of individual workers

soldiering
Employees deliberately working at a slow pace

Figure 1.3   Steps in Scientific Management

Frederick Taylor developed this system of scientific management, which he believed would lead to a more efficient and productive workforce. Bethlehem Steel was among the first organizations to profit from scientific management and still practices some parts of it today.

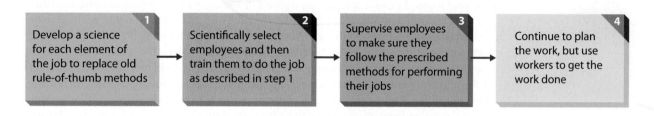

1 Develop a science for each element of the job to replace old rule-of-thumb methods → **2** Scientifically select employees and then train them to do the job as described in step 1 → **3** Supervise employees to make sure they follow the prescribed methods for performing their jobs → **4** Continue to plan the work, but use workers to get the work done

for doing the job more efficiently. For example, he specified standard materials and techniques, including the positioning of the bricklayer, the bricks, and the mortar at different levels. The results of these changes were a reduction from 18 separate physical movements to 5 and an increase in the output of about 200 percent. Lillian Gilbreth made equally important contributions to several different areas of work, helped shape the field of industrial psychology, and made substantive contributions to the field of personnel management. Working individually and together, the Gilbreths developed numerous techniques and strategies for eliminating inefficiency. They applied many of their ideas to their family and documented their experiences raising 12 children in the book and original 1950 movie *Cheaper by the Dozen*.

Administrative Management   Whereas scientific management deals with the jobs of individual employees, **administrative management** focuses on managing the total organization. The primary contributors to administrative management were Henri Fayol (1841–1925), Lyndall Urwick (1891–1983), and Max Weber (1864–1920).

Henri Fayol was administrative management's most articulate spokesperson. A French industrialist, Fayol was unknown to U.S. managers and scholars until his most important work, *General and Industrial Management*, was translated into English in 1930.[26] Drawing on his own managerial experience, he attempted to systematize the practice of management to provide guidance and direction to other managers. Fayol was also the first to identify the specific managerial functions of planning, organizing, leading, and controlling. He believed that these functions accurately reflect the core of the management process. Most contemporary management books (including this one) still use this framework, and practicing managers agree that these functions are a critical part of their jobs.

After a career as a British army officer, Lyndall Urwick became a noted management theorist and consultant. He integrated scientific management with the work of Fayol and other administrative management theorists. He also advanced modern thinking about the functions of planning, organizing, and controlling. Like Fayol, he developed a list of guidelines for improving managerial effectiveness. Urwick is noted not so much for his own contributions as for his synthesis and integration of the work of others.

Although Max Weber lived and worked at the same time as Fayol and Taylor, his contributions were not recognized until some years had passed. Weber was a German sociologist, and his most important work was not translated into English until 1947.[27]

administrative management
Focuses on managing the total organization

Weber's work on bureaucracy laid the foundation for contemporary organization theory, discussed in detail in Chapter 6. The concept of bureaucracy, as we discuss later, is based on a rational set of guidelines for structuring organizations in the most efficient manner.

The Classical Management Perspective Today The classical management perspective provides many techniques and approaches to management that are still relevant today. For example, many of the job specialization techniques and scientific methods espoused by Taylor and his contemporaries are still reflected in the way that many industrial jobs are designed today.[28] Moreover, many contemporary organizations still use some of the bureaucratic procedures suggested by Weber. Also, these early theorists were the first to focus attention on management as a meaningful field of study. Several aspects of the classical perspective are also relevant to our later discussions of planning, organizing, and controlling. And recent advances in areas such as business-to-business (B2B) electronic commerce also have efficiency as their primary goal. On the other hand, the classical perspective focused on stable, simple organizations; many organizations today, in contrast, are changing and complex. They also proposed universal guidelines that we now recognize do not fit every organization. A third limitation of the classical management perspective is that it slighted the role of the individual in organizations. This role was much more fully developed by advocates of the behavioral management perspective.

The Behavioral Management Perspective

Early advocates of the classical management perspective viewed organizations and jobs from an essentially mechanistic point of view; that is, they essentially sought to conceptualize organizations as machines and workers as cogs within those machines. Even though many early writers recognized the role of individuals, their focus tended to be on how managers could control and standardize the behavior of their employees. In contrast, the **behavioral management perspective** placed much more emphasis on individual attitudes and behaviors and on group processes, and recognized the importance of behavioral processes in the workplace.

The behavioral management perspective was stimulated by many writers and theoretical movements. One of those movements was *industrial psychology*, the practice of applying psychological concepts to industrial settings. Hugo Munsterberg (1863–1916), a noted German psychologist, is recognized as the father of industrial psychology. He established a psychological laboratory at Harvard University in 1892, and his pioneering book, *Psychology and Industrial Efficiency*, was translated into English in 1913.[29] Munsterberg suggested that psychologists could make valuable contributions to managers in the areas of employee selection and motivation. Industrial psychology is still a major course of study at many colleges and universities. Another early advocate of the behavioral approach to management was Mary Parker Follett (1868–1933).[30] Follett worked during the scientific management era but quickly came to recognize the human element in the workplace. Indeed, her work clearly anticipated the behavioral management perspective, and she appreciated the need to understand the role of behavior in organizations.

behavioral management perspective
Emphasizes individual attitudes and behaviors and group processes

The Hawthorne Studies Although Munsterberg and Follett made major contributions to the development of the behavioral approach to management, its primary catalyst was a series of studies conducted near Chicago at Western Electric's Hawthorne plant between 1927 and 1932. The research, originally sponsored by General Electric, was conducted by Elton Mayo and his associates.[31] Mayo was a faculty member and consultant at Harvard. The first study involved manipulating illumination for one group of workers and comparing their subsequent productivity with the productivity of another group whose illumination was not changed. Surprisingly, when illumination was increased for the experimental group, productivity went up in both groups. Productivity continued to increase in both groups, even when the lighting for the experimental group was decreased. Not until the lighting was reduced to the level of moonlight did productivity begin to decline (and General Electric withdrew its sponsorship).

Another experiment established a piecework incentive pay plan for a group of nine men assembling terminal banks for telephone exchanges. Scientific management would have predicted that each man would try to maximize his pay by producing as many units as possible. Mayo and his associates, however, found that the group itself informally established an acceptable level of output for its members. Workers who overproduced were branded *rate busters* and underproducers were labeled *chiselers*. To be accepted by the group, workers produced at the accepted level. As they approached this acceptable level of output, workers slacked off to avoid overproducing.

The Hawthorne studies were a series of early experiments that focused on behavior in the workplace. In one experiment involving this group of workers, for example, researchers monitored how productivity changed as a result of changes in working conditions. The Hawthorne studies and subsequent experiments led scientists to the conclusion that the human element is very important in the workplace.

Other studies, including an interview program involving several thousand workers, led Mayo and his associates to conclude that human behavior was much more important in the workplace than had been previously believed. In the lighting experiment, for example, the results were attributed to the fact that both groups received special attention and sympathetic supervision for perhaps the first time. The incentive pay plans did not work because wage incentives were less important to the individual workers than was social acceptance in determining output. In short, individual and social processes played major roles in shaping worker attitudes and behavior.

The Human Relations Movement The **human relations movement**, which grew from the Hawthorne studies and was a popular approach to management for many years, proposed that workers respond primarily to the social context of the workplace, including social conditioning, group norms, and interpersonal dynamics. A basic assumption of the human relations movement was that the manager's concern for workers would lead to increased satisfaction, which would in turn result in improved performance. Two writers who helped advance the human relations movement were Abraham Maslow (1908–1970) and Douglas McGregor (1906–1964).

In 1943 Maslow advanced a theory suggesting that people are motivated by a hierarchy of needs, including monetary incentives and social acceptance.[32] Maslow's hierarchy, perhaps the best-known human relations theory, is described in detail in Chapter 12. Meanwhile, Douglas McGregor's Theory X and Theory Y model best represents the essence of the human relations movement (see Table 1.1).[33] According to McGregor, Theory X and Theory Y reflect two extreme belief sets that different managers have about their workers. **Theory X** is a relatively pessimistic and negative view of workers and is consistent with the views of scientific management. **Theory Y** is

human relations movement
Argued that workers respond primarily to the social context of the workplace

Theory X
A pessimistic and negative view of workers consistent with the views of scientific management

Theory Y
A positive view of workers; it represents the assumptions that human relations advocates make

Table 1.1
Theory X and Theory Y

Douglas McGregor developed Theory X and Theory Y. He argued that Theory X best represented the views of scientific management and Theory Y represented the human relations approach. McGregor believed that Theory Y was the best philosophy for all managers.

Source: D. McGregor and W. Bennis, *The Human Side Enterprise: 25th Anniversary Printing,* 1960, Copyright © 1960 The McGraw-Hill Companies, Inc. Reprinted with permission.

Theory X Assumptions	1. People do not like work and try to avoid it.
	2. People do not like work, so managers have to control, direct, coerce, and threaten employees to get them to work toward organizational goals.
	3. People prefer to be directed, to avoid responsibility, and to want security; they have little ambition.
Theory Y Assumptions	1. People do not naturally dislike work; work is a natural part of their lives.
	2. People are internally motivated to reach objectives to which they are committed.
	3. People are committed to goals to the degree that they receive personal rewards when they reach their objectives.
	4. People will both seek and accept responsibility under favorable conditions.
	5. People have the capacity to be innovative in solving organizational problems.
	6. People are bright, but under most organizational conditions their potential is underutilized.

more positive and represents the assumptions that human relations advocates make. In McGregor's view, Theory Y was a more appropriate philosophy for managers to adhere to. Both Maslow and McGregor notably influenced the thinking of many practicing managers.

Contemporary Behavioral Science in Management Munsterberg, Mayo, Maslow, McGregor, and others have made valuable contributions to management. Contemporary theorists, however, have noted that many assertions of the human relationists were simplistic and provided inadequate descriptions of work behavior. Current behavioral perspectives on management, known as **organizational behavior**, acknowledge that human behavior in organizations is much more complex than the human relationists realized. The field of organizational behavior draws from a broad, interdisciplinary base of psychology, sociology, anthropology, economics, and medicine. Organizational behavior takes a holistic view of behavior and addresses individual, group, and organization processes. These processes are major elements in contemporary management theory.[34] Important topics in this field include job satisfaction, stress, motivation, leadership, group dynamics, organizational politics, interpersonal conflict, and the structure and design of organizations.[35] A contingency orientation also characterizes the field (discussed more fully later in this chapter). Our discussions of organizing (Chapters 6–8) and leading (Chapters 11–15) are heavily influenced by organizational behavior. And, finally, managers need a solid understanding of human behavior as they address diversity-related issues such as ethnicity and religion in the workplace. Indeed, all these topics are useful to help managers better deal with fallout from the consequences of layoffs and job cuts and to motivate today's workers.

organizational behavior
Contemporary field focusing on behavioral perspectives on management

The Behavioral Management Perspective Today The primary contributions of this approach are related to ways in which it has changed managerial thinking. Managers are now more likely to recognize the importance of behavioral processes and to view employees as valuable resources instead of mere tools. On the other hand, organizational behavior is still relatively imprecise in its ability to predict behavior, especially the behavior of a specific individual. It is not always accepted or understood by practicing managers. Hence the contributions of the behavioral school are just beginning to be fully realized.

The Quantitative Management Perspective

The third major school of management thought began to emerge during World War II. During the war, government officials and scientists in England and the United States worked to help the military deploy its resources more efficiently and effectively. These groups took some of the mathematical approaches to management developed decades earlier by Taylor and Gantt and applied these approaches to logistical problems during the war.[36] They learned that problems regarding troop, equipment, and submarine deployment, for example, could all be solved through mathematical analysis. After the war, companies such as DuPont and General Electric began to use the same techniques for deploying employees, choosing plant locations, and planning warehouses. Basically, then, this perspective is concerned with applying quantitative techniques to management. More specifically, the **quantitative management perspective** focuses on decision making, cost effectiveness, mathematical models, and the use of computers. There are two branches of the quantitative approach: management science and operations management.

Management Science   Unfortunately, the term *management science* appears to be related to scientific management, the approach developed by Taylor and others early in the twentieth century. But the two have little in common and should not be confused. **Management science** focuses specifically on the development of mathematical models. A mathematical model is a simplified representation of a system, process, or relationship.

At its most basic level, management science focuses on models, equations, and similar representations of reality. For example, managers at Detroit Edison use mathematical models to determine how best to route repair crews during blackouts. Citizens Bank of New England uses models to figure out how many tellers need to be on duty at each location at various times throughout the day. In recent years, paralleling the advent of the personal computer, management science techniques have become increasingly sophisticated. For example, automobile manufacturers Daimler AG and General Motors use realistic computer simulations to study collision damage to cars. These simulations help them avoid the costs of crashing so many test cars.

Operations Management   Operations management is somewhat less mathematical and statistically sophisticated than management science and can be applied more directly to managerial situations. Indeed, we can think of **operations management** as a form of applied management science. Operations management techniques are generally concerned with helping the organization produce its products or services more efficiently and can be applied to a wide range of problems.

For example, Rubbermaid and Home Depot each use operations management techniques to manage their inventories. (Inventory management is concerned with specific inventory problems, such as balancing carrying costs and ordering costs, and determining the optimal order quantity.) Linear programming (which involves computing simultaneous solutions to a set of linear equations) helps Delta Airlines plan its flight schedules, Consolidated Freightways develop its shipping routes, and General Instrument Corporation plan what instruments to produce at various times. Other operations management techniques include queuing theory, break-even analysis, and simulation. All these techniques and procedures apply directly to operations, but they are also helpful in areas such as finance, marketing, and human resource management.[37]

quantitative management perspective
Applies quantitative techniques to management

management science
Focuses specifically on the development of mathematical models

operations management
Concerned with helping the organization more efficiently produce its products or services

The Quantitative Management Perspective Today Like the other management perspectives, the quantitative management perspective has made important contributions and has certain limitations. It has provided managers with an abundance of decision-making tools and techniques and has increased understanding of overall organizational processes. This perspective has been particularly useful in the areas of planning and controlling. Relatively new management concepts such as supply chain management and new techniques such as enterprise resource planning, both discussed later in this book, also evolved from the quantitative management perspective. Even more recently, mathematicians are using tools and techniques from the quantitative perspective to develop models that might be helpful in the war against terrorism.[38] On the other hand, mathematical models cannot fully account for individual behaviors and attitudes. Some believe that the time needed to develop competence in quantitative techniques retards the development of other managerial skills. Finally, mathematical models typically require a set of assumptions that may not be realistic.

CONTEMPORARY MANAGEMENT PERSPECTIVES

It is important to recognize that the classical, behavioral, and quantitative approaches to management are not necessarily contradictory or mutually exclusive. Even though each of the three perspectives makes very different assumptions and predictions, each can also complement the others. Indeed, a complete understanding of management requires an appreciation of all three perspectives. The systems and contingency perspectives can help us integrate the earlier approaches and enlarge our understanding of all three.

The Systems Perspective

The systems perspective is one important contemporary management perspective. A **system** is an interrelated set of elements functioning as a whole.[39] As shown in Figure 1.4, by viewing an organization as a system, we can identify four basic elements: inputs,

Figure 1.4 The Systems Perspective of Organizations

By viewing organizations as systems, managers can better understand the importance of their environment and the level of interdependence among subsystems within the organization. Managers must also understand how their decisions affect and are affected by other subsystems within the organization.

system
An interrelated set of elements
functioning as a whole

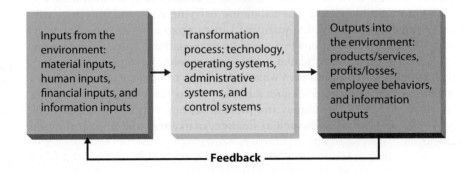

transformation processes, outputs, and feedback. First, inputs are the material, human, financial, and information resources an organization gets from its environment. Next, through technological and managerial processes, inputs are transformed into outputs. Outputs include products, services, or both (tangible and intangible); profits, losses, or both (even not-for-profit organizations must operate within their budgets); employee behaviors; and information. Finally, the environment reacts to these outputs and provides feedback to the system.

Thinking of organizations as systems provides us with a variety of important viewpoints on organizations, such as the concepts of open systems, subsystems, synergy, and entropy. **Open systems** are systems that interact with their environment, whereas **closed systems** do not interact with their environment. Although organizations are open systems, some make the mistake of ignoring their environment and behaving as though their environment is not important.

The systems perspective also stresses the importance of **subsystems**—systems within a broader system. For example, the marketing, production, and finance functions within Mattel are systems in their own right but are also subsystems within the overall organization. Because they are interdependent, a change in one subsystem can affect other subsystems as well. If the production department at Mattel lowers the quality of the toys being made (by buying lower-quality materials, for example), the effects are felt in finance (improved cash flow in the short run owing to lower costs) and marketing (decreased sales in the long run because of customer dissatisfaction). Managers must therefore remember that although organizational subsystems can be managed with some degree of autonomy, their interdependence should not be overlooked. For instance, recent research has underscored the interdependence of strategy and operations in businesses.[40]

Synergy suggests that organizational units (or subsystems) may often be more successful working together than working alone. The Walt Disney Company, for example, benefits greatly from synergy. The company's movies, theme parks, television programs, and merchandise-licensing programs all benefit one another. Children who enjoy Disney movies like *Up* and *Toy Story 3* want to go to Disney World to see the attractions and shows based on the movies and their favorite characters; and when they shop at Target, they see and want to buy stuffed toys and action figures of the same characters. Music from the films generates additional revenues for the firm, as do computer games and other licensing arrangements for lunchboxes, clothing, and so forth. Synergy was also the major objective of Procter & Gamble's acquisition of Gillette—the firm decided it could use its own retailing presence and international distribution networks to substantially increase Gillette's sales. And Gillette's products are natural complements to P&G's existing line of grooming products.[41] Synergy is an important concept for managers because it emphasizes the importance of working together in a cooperative and coordinated fashion.[42]

Finally, **entropy** is a normal process that leads to system decline. When an organization does not monitor feedback from its environment and make appropriate adjustments, it may fail. For example, witness the problems and eventual demise of Studebaker (an automobile manufacturer) and Circuit City (a major retailer). Each of these organizations went bankrupt because it failed to revitalize itself and keep pace with changes in its environment. A primary objective of management, from a systems perspective, is to continually reenergize the organization to avoid entropy.

The Contingency Perspective

Another noteworthy recent addition to management thinking is the contingency perspective. The classical, behavioral, and quantitative approaches are considered **universal perspectives** because they try to identify the "one best way" to manage

open system
A system that interacts with its environment

closed system
A system that does not interact with its environment

subsystem
A system within another system

synergy
Two or more subsystems working together to produce more than the total of what they might produce working alone

entropy
A normal process leading to system decline

universal perspective
An attempt to identify the one best way to do something

organizations. The **contingency perspective**, in contrast, suggests that universal theories cannot be applied to organizations because each organization is unique. Instead, the contingency perspective suggests that appropriate managerial behavior in a given situation depends on, or is contingent on, unique elements in that situation.[43]

Stated differently, effective managerial behavior in one situation cannot always be generalized to other situations. Recall, for example, that Frederick Taylor assumed that all workers would generate the highest possible level of output to maximize their own personal economic gain. We can imagine some people being motivated primarily by money—but we can just as easily imagine other people being motivated by the desire for leisure time, status, social acceptance, or any combination of these (as Mayo found at the Hawthorne plant). In 2000 Cisco Systems had the largest market cap in the world and was growing at a rate of 50 percent per year. A recession and the terrorist attacks in September 2001, however, caused the technology sector to crash, and Cisco's stock dropped in value by 86 percent. Cisco's CEO, John Chambers, had to downsize the company through layoffs and divestitures and transform it into a smaller company. As he went through this process, he also changed his management style. He had previously been an autocratic manager and led Cisco using a command-and-control hierarchy. As a result of the transformation at Cisco, however, Chambers also decided he needed to change his own management style as well. So, he began to adopt a much more democratic approach and to run Cisco using a more democratic organizational structure.[44]

Contemporary Management Issues and Challenges

Interest in management theory and practice has heightened in recent years as new issues and challenges have emerged. No new paradigm has been formulated that replaces the traditional views, but managers continue to strive toward a better understanding of how they can better compete and lead their organizations toward improved effectiveness.

Contemporary Applied Perspectives Several applied authors have significant influence on modern management theory and practice. Among the most popular applied authors today are Peter Senge, Stephen Covey, Tom Peters, Jim Collins, Michael Porter, John Kotter, and Gary Hamel.[45] Their books highlight the management practices of successful firms such as Shell Oil, Ford, IBM, and others, or outline conceptual or theoretical models or frameworks to guide managers as they formulate strategies or motivate their employees. Malcolm Gladwell's books *The Tipping Point*, *Blink*, and *Outliers* have all caught the attention of many contemporary managers. Scott Adams, creator of the popular comic strip *Dilbert*, is also immensely popular today. Adams is a former communications industry worker who developed his strip to illustrate some of the absurdities that occasionally afflict contemporary organizational life. The daily strip is routinely posted outside office doors, above copy machines, and beside water coolers in hundreds of offices.

contingency perspective
Suggests that appropriate managerial behavior in a given situation depends on, or is contingent on, unique elements in a given situation

Contemporary Management Challenges Managers today also face an imposing set of challenges as they guide and direct the fortunes of their companies. Coverage of each of these is thoroughly integrated throughout this book. In addition, many of them are highlighted or given focused coverage in one or more special ways.

One significant challenge is globalization. Managing in a global economy poses many different challenges and opportunities. For example, at a macro level, property ownership arrangements vary widely. So does the availability of natural resources and components of the infrastructure, as well as the role of government in business. Moreover, behavioral processes vary widely across cultural and national boundaries. For example, values, symbols, and beliefs differ sharply among cultures. Different work norms and the role that work plays in a person's life, for example, influence patterns of both work-related behavior and attitudes toward work. They also affect the nature of supervisory relationships, decision-making styles and processes, and organizational configurations. Group and intergroup processes, responses to stress, and the nature of political behaviors also differ from culture to culture.

Another management challenge that has taken on renewed importance is ethics and social responsibility and their relationship to corporate governance. Unfortunately, business scandals involving unethical conduct have become almost commonplace today. For example, the effects of Bernard Madoff's far-reaching pyramid investment scheme continue to be felt. From a social responsibility perspective,

TIMOTHY A. CLARY/AFP/GETTY IMAGES

Ethics remains an ongoing contemporary management challenge. Disgraced Wall Street Bernard Madoff is among the latest high-profile business leaders to fall from grace. Madoff agreed to plead guilty to 11 counts of fraud associated with his pyramid scheme that resulted in losses of billions of dollars to his clients. Madoff is shown here being led from U.S. Federal Court in New York after his sentencing in 2009.

increasing attention has been focused on pollution and business's obligation to help clean up our environment, business contributions to social causes, and so forth. The proper framework for corporate governance is often at the center of these debates and discussions.[46]

Quality also continues to pose an important management challenge today. Quality is an important issue for several reasons. First, more and more organizations are using quality as a basis for competition. Lexus, for example, stresses its high rankings in the J. D. Power survey of customer satisfaction in its print advertising. Second, improving quality tends to increase productivity because making higher-quality products generally results in less waste and rework. Third, enhancing quality lowers costs. Managers at Whistler Corporation once realized that the firm was using 100 of its 250 employees to repair defective radar detectors that had been built incorrectly in the first place.

The shift toward a service economy also continues to be important. Traditionally, most U.S. businesses were manufacturers—using tangible resources like raw materials and machinery to create tangible products like automobiles and steel. And manufacturing is indeed still important in the U.S. economy. The United States remains by far the world's largest manufacturer. Between 1990 and 2009, for example, U.S. manufacturing output grew by nearly $800 billion.[47]

In the last few decades, however, the service sector of the economy has become much more important. Indeed, services now account for well over half of the gross domestic product in the United States and play a similarly important role in many other industrialized nations. Service technology involves the use of both tangible resources (such as machinery) and intangible resources (such as intellectual property) to create intangible services (such as a haircut, insurance protection, or transportation between two cities). Although there are obviously many similarities between managing in a manufacturing and a service organization, there are also many fundamental differences.

The economic recession of 2008–2010 has also created myriad challenges, as well as some opportunities, for managers. Most businesses struggled, and some failed to survive. But some managers also used this period as a framework for reducing their costs, streamlining their operating systems and procedures, and fine-tuning their business strategies. As the economy slowly began to rebound, firms like Ford, Target, and Delia seemed to be well positioned for new growth.

A related challenge for managers is the rapidly changing workplace.[48] Indeed, this new workplace is accompanied by both dramatic challenges and amazing opportunities. Among other things, workplace changes relate in part to both workforce reductions and expansion. For example, many firms hired large numbers of new workers during the economic expansion that was taking place between 2002 and early 2008. But as the recession of 2008–2010 took hold, many of those same firms had to reduce their workforces, while others cut hours and pay and suspended all hiring until conditions showed signs of improvement. But even more central to the idea of workplace change are developments such as workforce diversity and the characteristics of new workers themselves.

The management of diversity continues to be an important organizational opportunity—and challenge—today. The term *diversity* refers to differences among people. Diversity may be reflected along numerous dimensions, but most managers tend to focus on age, gender, ethnicity, and physical abilities and disabilities.[49] For example, the average age of workers in the United States is gradually increasing. An increasing number of women have also entered the U.S. workforce. Fifty years ago, only about one-third of U.S. women worked outside their homes; today, 60 percent of women aged 16 and older are in the workforce. The ethnic composition of the workplace is also changing.

Aside from its demographic composition, the workforce today is changing in other ways as well. During the 1980s, many people entering the workforce were what came to be called yuppies, slang for *young urban professionals*. These individuals were highly motivated by career prospects, sought employment with big corporations, and often were willing to make work their highest priority. Thus, they put in long hours and could be expected to remain loyal to the company, regardless of what happened.

But younger people entering the workforce over the past 20 to 30 years are frequently quite different from their parents and other older workers. Generation X, Generation Y, and the Millennials, as these groups are called, tend to be less devoted to long-term career prospects and less willing to adapt to a corporate mind-set that stresses conformity and uniformity. Instead, they often seek work in smaller, more entrepreneurial firms that allow flexibility and individuality. They also place a premium on lifestyle preferences, often putting location high on their list of priorities when selecting an employer.

Thus, managers are increasingly faced with the challenge of first creating an environment that will be attractive to today's worker; second, managers must address the challenge of providing new and different incentives to keep people motivated and interested in their work. They must build enough flexibility into the organization to accommodate an ever-changing set of lifestyles and preferences. And, of course, as these generations eventually move into top spots of major corporations, there may even be entirely new paradigms for managing that cannot be foreseen today.[50]

Managers must also be prepared to address organization change.[51] This has always been a concern, but the rapid, constant environmental change faced by businesses today has made change management even more critical. Simply put, an organization that fails to monitor its environment and to change to keep pace with that environment is doomed to failure. But more and more managers are seeing change as an opportunity, not a cause for alarm. Indeed, some managers think that if things get too calm in an organization and people start to become complacent, they should shake things up to get everyone energized.

New technology, especially as it relates to information, also poses an increasingly important challenge for managers. Communications advances such as smart phones and other wireless communication networks have made it easier than ever for managers to communicate with one another. At the same time, these innovations have increased the work pace for managers, cut into their time for thoughtful contemplation of decisions, and increased the amount of information they must process. Issues associated with employee privacy have also emerged. For instance, controversies have arisen when businesses have taken action against people for things they do in their personal lives—posting negative comments about their employer on Facebook, for example.

SUMMARY OF LEARNING OBJECTIVES AND KEY POINTS

1. Define management, describe the kinds of managers found in organizations, identify and explain the four basic management functions, describe the fundamental management skills, and comment on management as science and art.

    - Management is a set of activities (planning and decision making, organizing, leading, and controlling) directed at using an organization's resources (human, financial, physical, and information) to achieve organizational goals in an efficient and effective manner.

    - A manager is someone whose primary responsibility is to carry out the management process within an organization.

    - Managers can be classified in terms of level: top managers, middle managers, and first-line managers.

    - Managers can also be classified in terms of area: marketing, finances, operations, human resources, administration, and specialized.

    - The basic activities of the management process include planning and decision making (determining courses of action), organizing (coordinating activities and resources), leading (motivating and managing people), and controlling (monitoring and evaluating activities).

    - Effective managers also tend to have the following skills: technical, interpersonal, conceptual, diagnostic, communication, decision-making, and time management.

    - The effective practice of management requires a synthesis of science and art; that is, it calls for a blend of rational objectivity and intuitive insight.

2. Justify the importance of history and theory to managers and explain the evolution of management thought through the classical, behavioral, and quantitative perspectives.

    - Understanding the historical context and precursors of management and organizations provides a sense of heritage and can also help managers avoid repeating the mistakes of others.

    - The classical management perspective, which paid little attention to the role of workers, had two major branches: scientific management (concerned with improving efficiency and work methods for individual workers) and administrative management (concerned with how organizations themselves should be structured and arranged for efficient operations).

    - The behavioral management perspective, characterized by a concern for individual and group behavior, emerged primarily as a result of the Hawthorne studies. The human relations movement recognized the importance and potential of behavioral processes in organizations but made many overly simplistic assumptions about those processes. Organizational behavior, a more realistic outgrowth of the behavioral perspective, is of interest to many contemporary managers.

- The quantitative management perspective, which attempts to apply quantitative techniques to decision making and problem solving, has two components: management science and operations management. These areas are also of considerable importance to contemporary managers. Their contributions have been facilitated by the tremendous increase in the use of personal computers and integrated information networks.

3. Identify and discuss key contemporary management perspectives represented by the systems and contingency perspectives and identify the major challenges and opportunities faced by managers today.

- There are two relatively recent additions to management theory that can serve as frameworks for integrating the other perspectives: the systems perspective and the contingency perspective.

- The important issues and challenges that contemporary managers face include globalization, ethics and social responsibility, product and service quality, the service economy, the economic recession of 2008–2010, the new workplace, workforce diversity, organization change, and technology.

DISCUSSION QUESTIONS

Questions for Review

1. What are the four basic functions that make up the management process? How are they related to one another?

2. What are the four basic activities that make up the management process? How are they related to one another?

3. Identify several of the important skills that help managers succeed. Give an example of each.

4. Briefly describe the principles of scientific management and administrative management. What assumptions do these perspectives make about workers?

5. Describe the systems perspective. Why is a business organization considered an open system?

Questions for Analysis

1. Recall a recent group project or task in which you have participated. Explain how members of the group displayed each of the managerial skills.

2. The text notes that management is both a science and an art. Recall an interaction you have had with a superior (manager, teacher, group leader, or the like). In that interaction, how did the superior use science? If he or she did not use science, what could have been done to use science? In that interaction, how did the superior use art? If she or he did not use art, what could have been done to use art?

3. Watch a movie that involves an organization of some type. *Harry Potter*, *Avatar*, *Star Trek*, and *Up*

in the Air would all be good choices. Identify as many management activities and skills as you can.

4. Young, innovative, or high-tech firms often adopt the strategy of ignoring history or attempting to do something radically new. In what ways might this strategy help them? In what ways might this strategy hinder their efforts?

5. Can a manager use tools and techniques from several different perspectives at the same time? For example, can a manager use both classical and behavioral perspectives? Give an example of a time when a manager did this and explain how it enabled him or her to be effective.

BUILDING EFFECTIVE TIME MANAGEMENT SKILLS

Exercise Overview

Time management skills refer to the ability to prioritize tasks, to work efficiently, and to delegate appropriately. This exercise allows you to assess your own current time management skills and to gather some suggestions for how you can improve in this area.

Exercise Background

As we saw in this chapter, effective managers must be prepared to switch back and forth among the four basic activities in the management process. They must also be able to fulfill a number of different roles in their organizations, and they must exercise various managerial skills in doing so. On top of everything else, their schedules are busy and full of tasks—personal and job-related activities that require them to "switch gears" frequently throughout the workday.

Stephen Covey, a management consultant and author of *The 7 Habits of Highly Effective People*, has developed a system for prioritizing tasks. First, he divides them into two categories—*urgent* and *critical*. *Urgent* tasks, such as those with approaching deadlines, must be performed right away. *Critical* tasks are tasks of high importance—say, those that will affect significant areas of one's life or work. Next, Covey plots both types of tasks on a grid with four quadrants: A task may be *urgent, critical, urgent and critical*, or *not urgent and not critical*.

Most managers, says Covey, spend too much time on tasks that are *urgent* when in fact they should be focused on tasks that are *critical*. He observes, for example, that managers who concentrate on urgent tasks meet their deadlines but tend to neglect critical areas such as long-term planning. (Unfortunately, the same people are also prone to neglect critical areas of their personal lives.) In short, effective managers must learn to balance the demands of urgent tasks with those of critical tasks by redistributing the amount of time devoted to each type.

Exercise Task

1. Visit the website of FranklinCovey (the firm co-founded by Stephen Covey) at www.franklincovey.com. Click on the tab marked *Effectiveness Zone*, and then select *Assessment Sector*. Now take the "Urgency Analysis Profile," a brief online survey that should take about 10 minutes.

2. Now look over your profile and examine the assessment of your current use of time and the suggestions for how you can improve your time management. In what ways do you agree and disagree with your personal assessment? Explain your reasons for agreeing or disagreeing.

3. Think of a task that you regularly perform and that, if you were being perfectly honest, you could label *not urgent and not critical*. How much time do you spend on this task? What might be a more appropriate amount of time? To what other tasks could you give some of the time that you spend on this *not urgent and not critical* task?

4. What one thing can you do today to make better use of your time? Try it to see if your time management improves.

BUILDING EFFECTIVE DECISION-MAKING SKILLS

Exercise Overview

Decision-making skills include the ability to recognize and define problems or opportunities and then select the appropriate course of action. This exercise will help you develop your own decision-making skills while also underscoring the importance of subsystem interdependencies in organizations.

Exercise Background

You're the vice president of a large company that makes outdoor furniture for decks, patios, and pools. Each product line and the firm itself have grown substantially in recent years. Unfortunately, your success has attracted the attention of competitors, and several have entered the market in the last two years. Your CEO wants you to determine how to cut costs by 10 percent so that prices can be cut by the same amount. She's convinced that the move is necessary to retain market share in the face of new competition.

You've examined the situation and decided that you have three options for cutting costs:

- Begin buying slightly lower-grade materials, including hardwood, aluminum, vinyl, and nylon.

- Lay off a portion of your workforce and then try to motivate everyone who's left to work harder; this option also means selecting future hires from a lower-skill labor pool and paying lower wages.

- Replace existing equipment with newer, more efficient equipment; although this option entails substantial up-front investment, you're sure that you can more than make up the difference in lower production costs.

Exercise Task

With this background in mind, respond to the following questions:

1. Carefully examine each of your three options. In what ways might each option affect other parts of the organization?

2. Which is the most costly option in terms of impact on other parts of the organization, not in terms of absolute dollars? Which is the least costly?

3. What are the primary obstacles that you might face in trying to implement each of your three options?

4. Are there any other options for accomplishing your goal of reducing costs?

SKILLS SELF-ASSESSMENT INSTRUMENT

Self-Awareness

Introduction: Self-awareness is an important skill for effective management. This assessment is designed to help you evaluate your level of self-awareness.

Instructions: Please respond to the following statements by writing a number from the following rating scale in the column. Your answers should reflect your attitudes and behavior as they are now, not as you would like them to be. Be honest. This instrument is designed to help you discover how self-aware you are so that you can tailor your learning to your specific needs.

Rating Scale

6 Strongly agree
5 Agree
4 Slightly agree
3 Slightly disagree
2 Disagree
1 Strongly disagree

____ 1. I seek information about my strengths and weaknesses from others as a basis for self-improvement.

____ 2. When I receive negative feedback about myself from others, I do not get angry or defensive.

____ 3. In order to improve, I am willing to be self-disclosing to others (that is, to share my beliefs and feelings).

____ 4. I am very much aware of my personal style of gathering information and making decisions about it.

____ 5. I am very much aware of my own interpersonal needs when it comes to forming relationships with other people.

____ 6. I have a good sense of how I cope with situations that are ambiguous and uncertain.

_____ 7. I have a well-developed set of personal standards and principles that guide my behavior.

_____ 8. I feel very much in charge of what happens to me, good and bad.

_____ 9. I seldom, if ever, feel angry, depressed, or anxious without knowing why.

_____ 10. I am conscious of the areas in which conflict and friction most frequently arise in my interactions with others.

_____ 11. I have a close relationship with at least one other person with whom I can share personal information and personal feelings.

Source: Developing Management Skills, 2nd ed. by Whetten, Cameron, © 1991. Reprinted with permission of Pearson Education, Inc Upper Saddle River, NJ.

EXPERIENTIAL EXERCISE

Johari Window

Purpose: This exercise has two purposes: to encourage you to analyze yourself more accurately and to start you working on small-group cohesiveness. This exercise encourages you to share data about yourself and then to assimilate and process feedback. Small groups are typically more trusting and work better together, as you will be able to see after this exercise has been completed. The Johari Window is a particularly good model for understanding the perceptual process in interpersonal relationships.

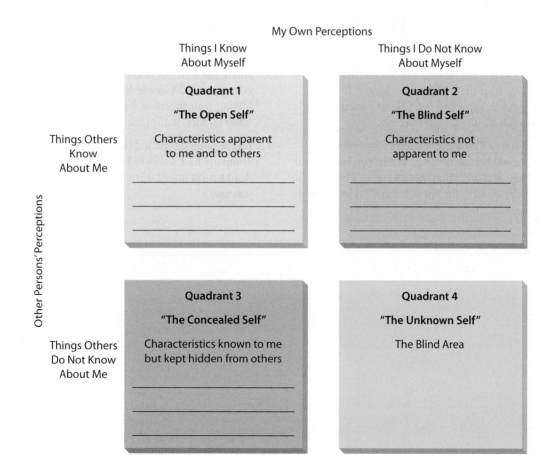

This skill builder focuses on the human resources model and will help you develop your mentor role. One of the skills of a mentor is self-awareness.

Introduction: Each individual has four sets of personality characteristics. One set, which includes such characteristics as working hard, is well known to the individual and to others. A second set is unknown to the individual but obvious to others. For example, in a working situation, a peer group might observe that your jumping in to get the group moving off dead center is appropriate. At other times, you jump in when the group is not really finished, and you seem to interrupt. A third set of personality characteristics is known to the individual but not to others. These are situations that you have elected not to share,

perhaps because of a lack of trust. Finally, there is a fourth set, which is not known to the individual or to others, such as why you are uncomfortable at office parties.

Instructions: Look at the Johari Window on the next page. In quadrant 1, list three things that you know about yourself and that you think others know. List three things in quadrant 3 that others do not know about you. Finally, in quadrant 2, list three things that you did not know about yourself last semester that you learned from others.

Sources: Adapted from Joseph Luft, *Group Processes: An Introduction to Group Dynamics* (Palo Alto, CA: Mayfield, 1970), pp. 10–11; William C. Morris and Marshall Sashkin, *Organizational Behavior in Action* (St. Paul, MN: West, 1976), p. 56.

 YOU MAKE ·THE CALL

In Search of Google

1. You're a Google employee, and Sergey Brin has just stopped by your desk. "I'd like to know," he says, "what you like most and least about working here." How do you think you might respond?

2. You're a major Google stockholder attending the firm's annual board meeting. When you bump into Larry Page at a reception, he asks you, "How do you think we're doing with this company?" How would you respond?

3. You're the founder and owner of a small software company, and Google has indicated an interest in buying your business. In addition to price, what other factors (if any) are important to you?

4. You've been contacted by a marketing research company that wants to know what you like and dislike most about using Google. What would you say?

CHAPTER 2

THE ENVIRONMENT AND CULTURE OF ORGANIZATIONS

LEARNING OBJECTIVES

After studying this chapter you should be able to:

1 Discuss the nature of an organization's environments and identify the components of its general, task, and internal environments.

2 Describe the ethical and social environment of management, including individual ethics, the concept of social responsibility, and how organizations can manage social responsibility.

3 Discuss the international environment of management, including trends in international business, levels of international business activities, and the context of international business.

4 Describe the importance and determinants of an organization's culture, as well as how organization culture can be managed.

FIRST THINGS FIRST

Competition Can Hurt....or Help!

When Starbucks opened a store near It's A Grind, a Long Beach-based independent coffeehouse, locals feared that the giant retailer would put their neighborhood favorite out of business. Natives of San Diego turned out to protest a Starbucks' opening so close to their locally owned coffeehouses. But owners and customers have since found out something surprising about Starbucks stores—sales often increase for all coffeehouses wherever the international chain opens an outlet nearby!

At first glance, customers' qualms appear to be justified. After all, it only makes sense that a huge multinational firm like Starbucks would enjoy advantages in pricing, new-product development, and other areas that would tend to give it an edge. Using size as a competitive weapon has been a common tactic for decades, used by firms ranging from Standard Oil, Sears, and General Motors to the most contemporary example—Wal-Mart. "A big company like Starbucks can come in and lose money for two years until they wipe everybody else out," editorializes the Indianapolis Star, reporting the closing of a local coffeehouse. "It's the old Wal-Mart thing."

Fear of the power of Starbucks has even caused owners to take some extraordinary measures to reduce

> **"Starbucks helped our business, but I don't want to give them any credit for it."**
>
> —JON CATES, CO-OWNER OF
> THE BROADWAY CAFE IN KANSAS CITY

the possibility of head-to-head competition. One owner, Courtney Bates of Kansas City's City Market Coffee Company, required her landlord to sign a clause preventing rental to any other coffeehouse. Another owner was approached by Starbucks about a possible buyout but was too suspicious of the firm to share any store information with it. "I don't think they really wanted to buy it. They just wanted a peek inside my business," claims Jeff Schmidt, owner of Latte Land in Kansas City. One thousand customers in Kansas City signed a petition asking the city to ban Starbucks. Katerina Carson, owner of Katerina's in Chicago, sums up this view when she says tersely, "Starbucks is a corporate monster."

DANIEL ACKER/BLOOMBERG/GETTY IMAGES

Some observers see Starbucks as a threat to independent coffee shops. In reality, though, Starbucks has helped increase awareness of high-quality coffees. This awareness, in turn, often increases sales of other coffeehouses near Starbucks' locations.

But the statistics just do not support the assertion that Starbucks is eliminating competition and slashing profits in the coffeehouse industry. In fact, while Starbucks outlets in the United States have grown from 1,000 in 1997 to almost 7,000 in 2010, independents have also increased from 7,000 to over 11,000 in 2010. And, while the total number of coffeehouses has grown from 8,000 to over 18,000 since 1997, sales have more than doubled, indicating that sales volume per store is also increasing.

Indeed, many coffeehouse owners are now forced to admit that, in spite of their fears, their sales actually increased when a Starbucks located a new store in their vicinity. Jon Cates, coowner of the Broadway Cafe in Kansas City, says, "Starbucks helped our business, but I don't want to give them any credit for it." Some owners have gone further, embracing the entrance of the chain into local markets. "Competition is good," says Norma Slaman, owner of Newbreak Coffee in San Diego, who saw sales rise 15 percent after Starbucks' arrival. Some chains have even adopted the strategy of following Starbucks into a neighborhood. Doug Zell located his Intelligentsia Coffee Roasters store near not just one, but two, Starbucks locations in Chicago. "It's been double-digit growth every year," says Zell.

Starbucks is increasing competitive pressure on independent coffeehouses, yet the independents are prospering right along with their giant competitor. This effect might be because the independents are so fearful of Starbucks that they implement improvements even before the chain arrives. It's A Grind fixed up stores, improving customer service and staff training, too, when a Starbucks opened nearby. The independent's sales have been rising 10 percent or more annually since then. Other independents have been prompted to ban smoking or to roast their own beans, two significant aspects of Starbucks' operations. Focusing on local activities and preferences is another way for independents to compete successfully, through poetry readings, live jazz, works by local artists, and regional food choices.

Starbucks itself, though, hit its own speed bump in 2009 when the firm acknowledged that it had perhaps grown too quickly and would need to do some retrenching. In the aftermath of that announcement Starbucks closed several hundred underperforming stores and severed a few of its licensing arrangements. But the company rebounded quickly and has since begun to open new stores albeit in a more systematic manner. The company also announced that it was going to begin selling its Seattle's Best brand coffee in both Subway and Burger King outlets and launch a new line of flavored coffees to sale in supermarkets. It seems, then, that Starbucks has not merely increased rivalry but also shifted industry dynamics in areas such as customers and new entrants. Although Starbucks and the independent coffeehouses are more profitable than ever, it appears that, for now, the customers are the big winners in this evolving industry.[1]

The business world operates in what can appear to be mysterious ways. Sometimes competition hurts, but sometimes it helps. When Starbucks opens a new store, its closest competitors often benefit. Ford and General Motors compete with each other for consumer dollars but work together to promote the interests of the U.S. auto industry. And CEOs face growing pressure to cut costs and curb their own salaries but grow their businesses. Clearly, the environmental context of business today is changing in unprecedented ways.

THE ORGANIZATION'S ENVIRONMENTS

The **external environment** is everything outside an organization's boundaries that might affect it. There are actually two separate external environments: the **general environment** and the **task environment**. An organization's **internal environment** consists of conditions and forces within the organization.

external environment
Everything outside an organization's boundaries that might affect it

general environment
The set of broad dimensions and forces in an organization's surroundings that determines its overall context

task environment
Specific organizations or groups that affect the organization

internal environment
The conditions and forces within an organization

The General Environment

Each of the following dimensions embodies conditions and events that have the potential to influence the organization in significant ways.

The Economic Dimension The **economic dimension** of an organization's general environment is the overall health and vitality of the economic system in which the organization operates.[2] Particularly important economic factors for business are general economic growth, inflation, interest rates, and unemployment. After several strong years of growth, the U.S. economy fell into recession during 2008. During this period energy and related prices jumped, growth slowed dramatically, and unemployment mushroomed as one struggling business after another made workforce cuts.

As one specific example, beginning in late 2008 and continuing on into 2010 McDonald's U.S. operation has been functioning in an economy characterized by weak growth, high unemployment, and low inflation. These conditions produce paradoxical problems. High unemployment means that fewer people can eat out, but those who do are looking for inexpensive options—like McDonald's. McDonald's can also pay lower wages to attract new employees, since many people are looking for work and fewer opportunities are available than was the case a few years ago. Similarly, low inflation means that the prices McDonald's must pay for its supplies remain relatively constant, but it also is somewhat constrained from increasing the prices it charges consumers for a hamburger or milkshake. The economic dimension is also important to nonbusiness organizations. For example, during weak economic conditions, funding for state universities may drop, and charitable organizations such as the Salvation Army are asked to provide greater assistance at the same time that their incoming contributions dwindle. Similarly, hospitals are affected by the availability of government grants and the number of low-income patients they must treat free of charge. The Tough Times, Tough Choices box highlights many of the issues facing managers in today's turbulent business environment.

The Technological Dimension The **technological dimension** of the general environment is made up of the methods available for converting resources into products or services. Although technology is applied within the organization, the forms and availability of that technology come from the general environment. Computer-assisted manufacturing and design techniques, for example, allow Boeing to simulate the more than three miles of hydraulic tubing that will run through its 787 aircraft currently under development. The results include decreased warehouse needs, higher-quality tube fittings, fewer employees, and major time savings. Although some people associate technology with manufacturing firms, it is also relevant in the service sector. For example, just as an automobile follows a predetermined path along an assembly line as it is built, a hamburger at McDonald's follows a predefined path as the meat is cooked, the burger assembled, and the finished product wrapped and bagged for a customer. The rapid infusion of the Internet into all areas of business is also a reflection of the technological dimension. Another recent advancement is the rapid growth of integrated business software systems. New modes of communication, ranging from social network sites like Facebook to new hardware like the iPad, are also influencing businesses in many different ways.

The Political-Legal Dimension The **political-legal dimension** of the general environment consists of government regulation of business and the relationship between business and government. This dimension is important for three basic reasons. First, the legal system partially defines what an organization can and cannot do. Although the

---

economic dimension
The overall health and vitality of the economic system in which the organization operates

technological dimension
The methods available for converting resources into products or services

political-legal dimension
The government regulation of business and the relationship between business and government

TOUGH TIMES, TOUGH CHOICES

What Goes Around....

It seems like just yesterday. In 2005 the global economy was booming. In the United States, for example, business profits were soaring, jobs were plentiful, and home ownership was at any all-time high. The stock market reached unprecedented highs, pension plans were burgeoning, and new business opportunities were plentiful. And the same held true in Europe, Asia, and much of the rest of the industrialized world.

Now fast forward just five short years to 2010, and things looked a lot different—And actually, things started taking ugly turns in 2008. Business profits are down, hundreds of thousands of jobs have been lost while unemployment claims have soared, and mortgage foreclosures have become the order of the day. The stock market plummeted, pension plans went broke, and it seemed like no one wanted to start a new business. And even when someone had a new business idea, getting loans to start a new enterprise was virtually impossible. Indeed, many historians agree that the economic recession of 2008–2010 was the worst since the Great Depression.

What happened in this short period of time? Economists call it the business cycle. Historically, the U.S. economy has followed long periods of growth and prosperity with periods of cutbacks and retreats. And that's where we were in 2008–2010. During extended periods of prosperity people sometimes think the good times will last forever. They continue to bid up stock prices, for instance, far beyond rational value. They also take on too much debt, save too little money, and spend beyond their means.

Businesses hire too many people, and managers sometimes make operational efficiency and productivity a lower priority. Companies, like people, take on too much debt in their quest to grow and expand. They start awarding increasingly generous bonuses to their prized employees, and they may be a bit too lenient when new labor contracts are negotiated, perhaps unconsciously assuming that revenues and profits will continue to climb. But things have a way of correcting themselves, and that's what happened beginning in 2008.

So what does the future hold? Well, while no one has a real crystal ball, most experts agree that the bad times will run their course and then things will start looking up again. It may take another year, or five. By mid-2010, for example, stock prices were increasing again. Businesses that were bailed out by the U.S. government in 2008–2010 were repaying their debts and some were hiring again. And while hundreds of thousands of employees were still unemployed, there were signs that things were going to start turning around. And one day soon, profits will again start to surge, businesses will embark on ambitious hiring plans, the stock market will surpass all previous highs, and business opportunities will again be plentiful. Until then, though, managers just have to focus on following core business principles and do their best to steer their organizations through today's turbulence.

References: Trade Gap Grows, Driven by Imports," *Wall Street Journal*, April 14, 2010, pp. A1, A14; "The Case for More Stimulus," *Business Week*, April 19, 2010, pp. 32–36; "Not Guilty. Not One Little Bit," *Business Week*, April 12, 2010, pp. 30–38.

United States is basically a free market economy, major regulation of business activity still exits. McDonald's, for example, is subject to a variety of political and legal forces, including food preparation standards and local zoning requirements.

Second, pro- or anti-business sentiment in government influences business activity. For example, during periods of pro-business sentiment, firms find it easier to compete and have fewer concerns about antitrust issues. On the other hand, during a period of anti-business sentiment, firms may find their competitive strategies more restricted and have fewer opportunities for mergers and acquisitions because of antitrust concerns. During the prolonged period of economic growth that ended in 2008, the U.S. government adopted a very "hands-off" approach to business, letting market forces determine business successes and failures. However, as the economy ground to a halt in 2008 and first one and then another industry began to stumble, critics began to point to lack of regulation and oversight as contributing factors. As a result, lawmakers began to take a much more pronounced interest in adopting new and stricter regulations for business.[3]

Finally, political stability has ramifications for planning. No business wants to set up shop in another country unless trade relationships with that country are relatively well defined and stable. Hence, U.S. firms are more likely to do business with England, Mexico, and Canada than with Haiti and Afghanistan. Similar issues are relevant to assessments of local and state governments. A new mayor or governor can affect many organizations, especially small firms that do business in only one location and are susceptible to deed and zoning restrictions, property and school taxes, and the like.

The Task Environment

Because the impact of the general environment is often vague, imprecise, and long term, most organizations tend to focus their attention on their task environment, which includes competitors, customers, suppliers, strategic partners, and regulators. Although the task environment is also quite complex, it provides useful information more readily than the general environment, because the manager can identify environmental factors of specific interest to the organization, rather than having to deal with the more abstract dimensions of the general environment.[4] Figure 2.1 depicts the task environment of McDonald's.

Competitors An organization's **competitors** are other organizations that compete with it for resources. The most obvious resources that competitors vie for are customer dollars. New Balance, Adidas, and Nike are competitors, as are Albertson's, Safeway, and Kroger. McDonald's competes with other fast-food operations, such as Burger King, Wendy's, Subway, and Dairy Queen; it's also taken on Starbucks with its McCafe line of premium coffee products. But competition also occurs between substitute products. Thus Ford competes with Yamaha (motorcycles) and Schwinn (bicycles) for your transportation dollars; and Walt Disney World and Carnival Cruise Lines compete for your vacation dollars. Nor is competition limited to business firms. Universities compete with trade schools, the military, other universities, and the external labor market to attract good students; and art galleries compete with one another to attract the best exhibits.

Customers A second dimension of the task environment is **customers**, or whoever pays money to acquire an organization's products or services. Most McDonald's customers are individuals who buy food. But customers need not be individuals. Schools, hospitals, government agencies, wholesalers, retailers, and manufacturers are just a few of the many kinds of organizations that may be major customers of other organizations. Some institutional customers, such as schools, prisons, and hospitals, also buy food in bulk from restaurants such as McDonald's.

Supplier Suppliers are organizations that provide resources for other organizations. McDonald's buys soft drink products from Coca-Cola; individually packaged servings of ketchup from Heinz; ingredients from wholesale food processors; and napkins, sacks,

competitor
An organization that competes with other organizations for resources

customer
Whoever pays money to acquire an organization's products or services

supplier
An organization that provides resources for other organizations

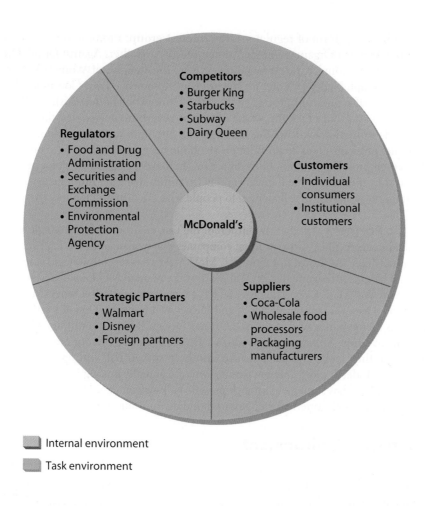

Figure 2.1
McDonald's Task Environment

An organization's task environment includes its competitors, customers, suppliers, strategic partners, and regulators. This figure clearly highlights how managers at McDonald's can use this framework to identify and understand their key constituents.

Internal environment

Task environment

and wrappers from packaging manufacturers. Besides material resources such as these, businesses also rely on suppliers for information (such as economic statistics), labor (in the form of employment agencies), and capital (from lenders such as banks). Some businesses strive to avoid depending exclusively on particular suppliers. Others, however, find it beneficial to create strong relationships with single suppliers.

Regulators Regulators are elements of the task environment that have the potential to control, legislate, or otherwise influence an organization's policies and practices. There are two important kinds of regulators. **Regulatory agencies** are created by the government to protect the public from certain business practices or to protect organizations from one another. Powerful federal regulatory agencies include the Environmental Protection Agency (EPA), the Securities and Exchange Commission (SEC), the Food and Drug Administration (FDA), and the Equal Employment Opportunity Commission (EEOC). Many of these agencies play important roles in protecting the rights of individuals. The FDA, for example, helps ensure that the food is free from contaminants; thus it is an important regulator for McDonald's and Starbucks. At the same time, many managers complain that there is too much government regulation. Most large companies must dedicate thousands of labor hours and hundreds of thousands of dollars a year to complying with government regulations. To complicate the lives of managers even more, different regulatory agencies sometimes provide inconsistent—even contradictory—mandates.

regulator
A body that has the potential to control, legislate, or otherwise influence the organization's policies and practices

regulatory agency
An agency created by the government to regulate business activities

The other basic form of regulator is the **interest group**. Prominent interest groups include the National Organization for Women (NOW), Mothers Against Drunk Driving (MADD), the National Rifle Association (NRA), the League of Women Voters, the Sierra Club, Ralph Nader's Center for the Study of Responsive Law, Consumers Union, and industry self-regulation groups such as the Council of Better Business Bureaus. Although interest groups lack the official power of government agencies, they can exert considerable influence by using the media to call attention to their positions. MADD, for example, puts considerable pressure on alcoholic-beverage producers (to put warning labels on their products), automobile companies (to make it more difficult for intoxicated people to start their cars), local governments (to stiffen drinking ordinances), and bars and restaurants (to refuse to sell alcohol to people who are drinking too much).

Strategic Partners Another dimension of the task environment is **strategic partners** (also called strategic allies)—two or more companies that work together in joint ventures or other partnerships.[5] As shown in Figure 2.1, McDonald's has several strategic partners. For example, it has one arrangement with Wal-Mart whereby small McDonald's restaurants are built in many Wal-Mart stores. The firm also has a long-term deal with Disney: McDonald's will promote Disney movies in its stores, and Disney will build McDonald's restaurants or kiosks in its theme parks. And many of the firm's foreign stores are built in collaboration with local investors. Strategic partnerships help companies get from other companies the expertise they lack. The partnerships also help spread risk and open new market opportunities. Indeed, most strategic partnerships are actually among international firms. For example, Ford has strategic partnerships with Volkswagen (sharing a distribution and service center in South America) and Nissan (building minivans in the United States).

The Internal Environment

Organizations also have an internal environment that consists of their owners, board of directors, employees, and the physical work environment. (Another especially important part of the internal environment is the organization's culture, discussed separately later in this chapter.)

Owners The **owners** of a business are, of course, the people who have legal property rights to that business. Owners can be a single individual who establishes and runs a small business, partners who jointly own the business, individual investors who buy stock in a corporation, or other organizations. McDonald's has 1.11 billion shares of stock, each of which represents one unit of ownership in the firm. The family of McDonald's founder Ray Kroc stills owns a large block of this stock, as do several large institutional investors. In addition, there are thousands of individuals who own just a few shares each. McDonald's, in turn, owns other businesses. For example, it owns several large regional bakeries that supply its restaurants with buns. Each of these is incorporated as a separate legal entity and managed as a wholly owned subsidiary by the parent company. McDonald's is also a partner in some Russian farms that grow potatoes to supply regional restaurants with french fries.

Board of Directors A corporate **board of directors** is a governing body elected by the stockholders and is charged with overseeing the general management of the firm to ensure that it is run in a way that best serves the stockholders' interests. Some boards are relatively passive. They perform a general oversight function but seldom get actively involved in how the company is really run. But this trend is changing, as more and more

interest group
A group organized by its members to attempt to influence organizations

strategic partner
(strategically) An organization working together with one or more other organizations in a joint venture or similar arrangement

owner
Whoever can claim property rights to an organization

board of directors
Governing body elected by a corporation's stockholders and charged with overseeing the general management of the firm to ensure that it is being run in a way that best serves the stockholders' interests

boards are carefully scrutinizing the firms they oversee and exerting more influence over how they are being managed. This trend has been accelerated by numerous recent business scandals. In some cases, board members have been accused of wrongdoing. In other cases, boards have been found negligent for failing to monitor the actions of the firm's executives.[6] At issue is the concept of *corporate governance*—who is responsible for governing the actions of a business. We discuss corporate governance more fully later.

Employees An organization's employees are also a major element of its internal environment. Of particular interest to managers today is the changing nature of the workforce, as it becomes increasingly more diverse in terms of gender, ethnicity, age, and other dimensions. Workers are also calling for more job ownership—either partial ownership in the company or at least more say in how they perform their jobs.[7] Another trend in many firms is increased reliance on temporary workers—individuals hired for short periods of time with no expectation of permanent employment. Employers often prefer to use "temps" because they provide greater flexibility, earn lower wages, and often do not participate in benefits programs. But these managers also have to deal with what often amounts to a two-class workforce and with a growing number of employees who have no loyalty to the organization where they work, because they may be working for a different one tomorrow.[8]

Physical Work Environment Employee safety and health regulations have caused many organizations to pay more attention to their internal environment. This concern, in turn, has also fostered new business opportunities. Rebecca Boenigk, founder and CEO of Neutral Posture, turned a small operation in her garage into an international company selling neutral body posture chairs designed by her father, Dr. Jerome Congleton. A final part of the internal environment is the actual physical environment of the organization and the work that people do. Some firms have their facilities in downtown skyscrapers, usually spread across several floors. Others locate in suburban or rural settings and may have facilities more closely resembling a college campus. Some facilities have long halls lined with traditional offices. Others have modular cubicles with partial walls and no doors. The top hundred managers at Mars, makers of Snickers and Milky Way, all work in a single vast room. The president's desk is located in the very center of the room, while others are arrayed in concentric circles around it. Increasingly, newer facilities have an even more open arrangement, where people work in large rooms, moving among different tables to interact with different people on different projects. Freestanding computer workstations are available for those who need them, and a few small rooms might be off to the side for private business.[9]

IMAGE COPYRIGHT AVAVA, 2009. USED UNDER LICENSE FROM SHUTTERSTOCK.COM

Employee safety and health regulations have caused many organizations to pay more attention to their internal environment. In particular, they want to ensure that their employees have an ergonomically suitable workspace free from safety and/ or health hazards. One innovation being tried by some organizations involves replacing traditional desk chairs with large inflatable balls. These balls, in turn, are reported to help reduce lower back stress in employees who are seated for long periods of time.

THE ETHICAL AND SOCIAL ENVIRONMENT OF MANAGEMENT

The ethical and social environment has become an especially important area for managers in the last few years. In this section we first explore the concept of individual ethics and then describe social responsibility.

Individual Ethics in Organizations

We define **ethics** as an individual's personal beliefs about whether a behavior, action, or decision is right or wrong.[10] Note that we define ethics in the context of the individual—people have ethics; organizations do not. Likewise, what constitutes ethical behavior varies from one person to another. For example, one person who finds a $20 bill on the floor of an empty room believes that it is okay to keep it, whereas another feels compelled to turn it in to the lost-and-found department. Further, although **ethical behavior** is in the eye of the beholder, the term usually refers to behavior that conforms to generally accepted social norms. **Unethical behavior**, then, is behavior that does not conform to generally accepted social norms.

Managerial Ethics   **Managerial ethics** consists of the standards of behavior that guide individual managers in their work.[11] One important area of managerial ethics is the treatment of employees by the organization. It includes, for example, hiring and firing, wages and working conditions, and employee privacy and respect. An example of how different managers might approach this area involves minimum wages. While the U.S. government sets a minimum hourly wage, this amount is often not enough to live above the poverty level in high-cost areas such as New York and San Francisco. Some managers might say that paying only the legal minimum is the right business practice, while others might be inclined to pay a wage more attuned to local conditions.

Numerous ethical issues stem from how employees treat the organization, especially in regard to conflicts of interest, secrecy and confidentiality, and honesty. A *conflict of interest* occurs when an employee's decision potentially benefits the individual to the possible detriment of the organization. To guard against such practices, most companies have policies that forbid their buyers from accepting gifts from suppliers. Divulging company secrets is also clearly unethical. Employees who work for businesses in highly competitive industries—electronics, software, and fashion apparel, for example—might be tempted to sell information about their companies' plans to competitors. A third area of concern is honesty in general. Relatively common problems in this area include activities such as using a business telephone to make personal long distance calls, visiting and updating personal Facebook sites during work hours, stealing supplies, and padding expense accounts. Although most employees are inherently honest, organizations must nevertheless be vigilant to avoid problems with such behaviors.

Managerial ethics also comes into play in the relationship between the firm and its employees with other economic agents. The primary agents of interest include customers, competitors, stockholders, suppliers, dealers, and unions. The behaviors between the organization and these agents that may be subject to ethical ambiguity include advertising and promotions, financial disclosures, ordering and purchasing, shipping and solicitations, bargaining and negotiation, and other business relationships.

ethics
An individual's personal beliefs about whether a behavior, an action, or a decision is right or wrong

ethical behavior
Behavior that conforms to generally accepted social norms

unethical behavior
Behavior that does not conform to generally accepted social norms

managerial ethics
Standards of behavior that guide individual managers in their work

For example, state pharmacy boards are charged with overseeing prescription drug safety in the United States. All told, almost 300 pharmacists serve on such boards. It was recently reported that 72 of these pharmacists were employees of major drugstore chains and supermarket pharmacies. These arrangements, while legal, could create the potential for conflicts of interest, though, because they might give the pharmacist's employers influence over the regulatory system designed to monitor their own business practices.[12]

Another area of concern in recent years involves financial reporting by various e-commerce firms. Because of the complexities inherent in valuing the assets and revenues of these firms, some of them have been very aggressive in presenting their financial position in a highly positive light. And at least a few firms have substantially overstated their earnings projections to entice more investment. Moreover, some of today's accounting scandals in traditional firms have stemmed from similarly questionable practices.[13]

Hilton Hotels recently hired two senior executives away from rival Starwood Hotels. It was later found that the executives took eight boxes of electronic and paper documents; much of the material in the boxes related to plans and details for starting a new luxury-hotel brand. When Hilton announced plans to start such a chain itself, to be called Denizen Hotels, officials at Starwood became suspicious and investigated. When they learned about the theft of confidential materials, which Hilton subsequently returned, Starwood filed a lawsuit against Hilton.[14]

Managing Ethical Behavior Spurred partially by increased awareness of ethics scandals in business and partially by a sense of enhanced corporate consciousness about the distinction between ethical and unethical behaviors, many organizations have reemphasized ethical behavior on the part of employees. This emphasis takes many forms, but any effort to enhance ethical behavior must begin with top management. It is top managers, for example, who establish the organization's culture and define what will and what will not be acceptable behavior. Some companies have also started offering employees training in how to cope with ethical dilemmas. At Boeing, for example, line managers lead training sessions for other employees, and the company has an ethics committee that reports directly to the board of directors. The training sessions involve discussions of different ethical dilemmas that employees might face and how managers might handle those dilemmas. Chemical Bank, Halliburton, and Xerox also have ethics training programs for their managers.

Organizations are also going to greater lengths to formalize their ethical standards. Some, such as General Mills and Johnson & Johnson, have prepared guidelines that detail how employees are to treat suppliers, customers, competitors, and other constituents. Others, such as Whirlpool, Texas Instruments, and Hewlett-Packard, have developed formal **codes of ethics**—written statements of the values and ethical standards that guide the firms' actions. Of course, firms must adhere to such codes if they are to be of value. In one now-infamous case, Enron's board of directors voted to set aside the firm's code of ethics to implement a business plan that was in violation of that code.[15]

Of course, no code, guideline, or training program can truly substitute for the quality of an individual's personal judgment about what is right behavior and what is wrong behavior in a particular situation. Such devices may prescribe what people should do, but they often fail to help people understand and live with the consequences of their choices. Making ethical choices may lead to very unpleasant outcomes—firing, rejection by colleagues, and the forfeiture of monetary gain, to name a few. Thus managers must be prepared to confront their own conscience and weigh the options available when making difficult ethical decisions.

codes of ethics
A formal, written statement of the values and ethical standards that guide a firm's actions

Emerging Ethical Issues

Ethical scandals have become almost commonplace in today's world. Ranging from business and sports to politics and the entertainment industry, these scandals have rocked stakeholder confidence and called into question the moral integrity of our society. At the same time, most women and men today conduct themselves and their affairs in accordance with high ethical standards. Hence, as we summarize several emerging ethical issues in organizations, it is important to remember that one cannot judge everyone by the transgressions of a few.

Ethical Leadership In recent years the media have been rife with stories about unscrupulous corporate leaders. For every unethical senior manager, of course, there are many highly ethical ones. But the actions of such high-profile deposed executives as Dennis Kozlowski (Tyco), Kenneth Lay (Enron), and Bernard Ebbers (WorldCom) have substantially increased the scrutiny directed at all executives. As a direct result, executives everywhere are expected to exhibit nothing but the strongest ethical conduct. This leadership, in turn, is expected to help set the tone for the rest of the organization and to establish both norms and a culture that reinforce the importance of ethical behavior.[16]

The basic premise behind ethical leadership is that because leaders serve as role models for others, their every action is subject to scrutiny. If a senior executive exercises questionable judgment, this sends a signal to others that such actions are acceptable. This signal may, in turn, be remembered by others when they face similar situations. As a result, CEOs such as Aramark's Joseph Neubauer and Costco's James Sinegal are now being held up as the standard against which others are being measured. The basic premise is that CEOs must set their company's moral tone by being honest and straightforward and by taking responsibility for any shortcomings that are identified. To support this view, Congress passed the **Sarbanes-Oxley Act of 2002**, requiring CEOs and CFOs to vouch personally for the truthfulness and fairness of their firms' financial disclosures. The law also imposes tough new measures to deter and punish corporate and accounting fraud and corruption.

James Sinegal, CEO of Costco Wholesale Corporation, has established a strong reputation for himself as an ethical and moral leader. He conducts his business with honesty and sincerity, answers questions in a straightforward and clear manner, and promotes transparency in all of Costco's business practices. As a result, he is increasingly held up as the standard against which other CEOs are measured.

BARRY SWEET/BLOOMBERG/GETTY IMAGES

Sarbanes-Oxley Act of 2002
A law that requires CEOs and CFOs to vouch personally for the truthfulness and fairness of their firms' financial disclosures and imposes tough new measures to deter and punish corporate and accounting fraud and corruption.

Corporate Governance A related area of emerging concern is ethical issues in corporate governance. As discussed earlier, the board of directors of a public corporation is expected to ensure that the business is being properly managed and that the decisions made by its senior management are in the best interests of shareholders and other stakeholders. But many of the recent ethical scandals that we have mentioned have actually started with a breakdown in the corporate governance structure. For instance,

WorldCom's board approved a personal loan to the firm's then—CEO, Bernard Ebbers, for $366 million, when there was little evidence that he could repay it. And Tyco's board approved a $20 million bonus for one of its own members for helping with the acquisition of another firm. Boards of directors are also criticized when they are seen as not being sufficiently independent for senior management.[17]

Ethics and Information Technology A final set of issues that have emerged in recent times involves information technology. Among the specific focal points in this area are individual rights to privacy and the potential abuse of information technology by individuals. Indeed, online privacy has become a hot topic, as companies sort out the related ethical and management issues. DoubleClick, an online advertising network, is one of the firms at the eye of the privacy storm. The company has collected data on the habits of millions of web surfers, recording which sites they visit and which ads they click on. DoubleClick insists that the profiles are anonymous and are used simply to match surfers with appropriate ads. However, after the company announced a plan to add names and addresses to its database, it was forced to back down because of public concerns over the invasion of online privacy.

One way in which management can address these concerns is to post a privacy policy on the company website. The policy should explain exactly what data the company collects and who gets to see the data. It should also allow people a choice about having their information shared with others and indicate how people can opt out of data collection. Disney, IBM, and other companies support this position by refusing to advertise on websites that have no posted privacy policies.

In addition, companies can offer web surfers the opportunity to review and correct information that has been collected, especially medical and financial data. In the offline world, consumers are legally allowed to inspect their own credit and medical records. In the online world, this kind of access can be costly and cumbersome, because data are often spread across several computer systems. Despite the technical difficulties, government agencies are already working on Internet privacy guidelines, which mean that companies will need internal guidelines, training, and leadership to ensure that they are in compliance.

Social Responsibility in Organizations

As we have seen, ethics are associated with individuals and their decisions and behaviors. Organizations themselves do not have ethics, but they relate to their environments in ways that often involve ethical dilemmas and decisions. These situations are generally referred to within the context of the organization's **social responsibility**. Specifically, social responsibility is the set of obligations an organization has to protect and enhance the societal context in which it functions. Some of the more salient arguments on both sides of this contemporary debate are summarized in Figure 2.2 and are further explained in the following sections.

Arguments for Social Responsibility People who argue in favor of social responsibility claim that—because organizations create many of the problems that need to be addressed, such as air and water pollution and resource depletion—organizations should play a major role in solving them. They also argue that, because corporations are legally defined entities with most of the same privileges as private citizens, businesses should not try to avoid their obligations as citizens. Advocates of social responsibility point

social responsibility
The set of obligations an organization has to protect and enhance the societal context in which it functions

Figure 2.2   Arguments for and Against Social Responsibility

Although many people want everyone to see social responsibility as a desirable aim, there are in fact several strong arguments that can be advanced both for and against social responsibility. Hence organizations and their managers should carefully assess their own values, beliefs, and priorities when deciding which stance and approach to take regarding social responsibility.

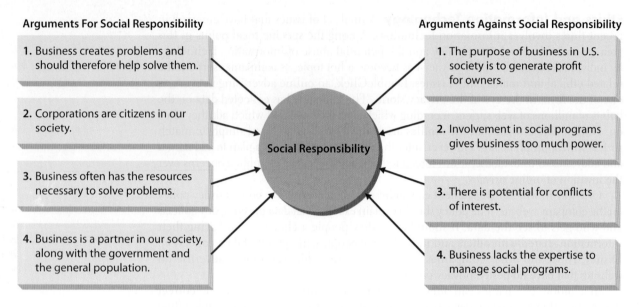

Arguments For Social Responsibility

1. Business creates problems and should therefore help solve them.

2. Corporations are citizens in our society.

3. Business often has the resources necessary to solve problems.

4. Business is a partner in our society, along with the government and the general population.

Social Responsibility

Arguments Against Social Responsibility

1. The purpose of business in U.S. society is to generate profit for owners.

2. Involvement in social programs gives business too much power.

3. There is potential for conflicts of interest.

4. Business lacks the expertise to manage social programs.

out that, whereas governmental organizations have stretched their budgets to the limit, many large businesses often have surplus revenues that could be used to help solve social problems. For example, Dell donates surplus computers to schools, and many restaurants give leftover food to homeless shelters.

Arguments Against Social Responsibility Some people, however, including the famous economist Milton Friedman, argue that widening the interpretation of social responsibility will undermine the U.S. economy by detracting from the basic mission of business: to earn profits for owners. For example, money that Chevron or General Electric contributes to social causes or charities is money that could otherwise be distributed to owners in the form of dividends. Shareholders of Ben & Jerry's Homemade Holdings once expressed outrage when the firm refused to accept a lucrative exporting deal to Japan simply because the Japanese distributor did not have a strong social agenda.[18]

Another objection to increasing the social responsibility of businesses reflects the position that corporations already wield enormous power and that involvement in social programs gives them even more power. Still another argument against social responsibility focuses on the potential for conflicts of interest. Suppose, for example, that one manager is in charge of deciding which local social program or charity will receive a large grant from her business. The local civic opera company (a not-for-profit organization that relies on contributions for its existence) might offer her front-row tickets for the upcoming season in exchange for her support. If opera is her favorite form of music, she may be tempted to direct the money toward the local company, when it might actually be needed more in other areas.[19]

Finally, critics argue that organizations lack the expertise to understand how to assess and make decisions about worthy social programs. How can a company truly know, they ask, which cause or program is most deserving of its support or how money might best be spent?

Managing Social Responsibility

The demands for social responsibility placed on contemporary organizations by an increasingly sophisticated and educated public are probably stronger than ever. As we have seen, there are pitfalls for managers who fail to adhere to high ethical standards and for companies that try to circumvent their legal obligations. Organizations therefore need to fashion an approach to social responsibility in the same way that they develop any other business strategy. In other words, they should view social responsibility as a major challenge that requires careful planning, decision making, consideration, and evaluation. They may accomplish this through both formal and informal dimensions of managing social responsibility.

Formal Organizational Dimensions   Some dimensions of managing social responsibility are a formal and planned activity on the part of the organization. The formal organizational dimensions through which businesses can manage social responsibility include legal compliance, ethical compliance, and philanthropic giving.

Legal compliance is the extent to which the organization conforms to local, state, federal, and international laws. The task of managing legal compliance is generally assigned to the appropriate functional managers. For example, the organization's top human resource executive is responsible for ensuring compliance with regulations concerning hiring, pay, and workplace safety and health. Likewise, the top finance executive generally oversees compliance with securities and banking regulations. The organization's legal department is likely to contribute to this effort by providing general oversight and answering queries from managers about the appropriate interpretation of laws and regulations. Unfortunately, though, legal compliance may not be enough—in some cases, for instance, perfectly legal accounting practices have still resulted in deception and other problems.[20]

Ethical compliance is the extent to which the members of the organization follow basic ethical (and legal) standards of behavior. We noted earlier that organizations have increased their efforts in this area—providing training in ethics and developing guidelines and codes of conduct, for example. These activities serve as vehicles for enhancing ethical compliance. Many organizations also establish formal ethics committees, which may be asked to review proposals for new projects, to help evaluate new hiring strategies, or to assess a new environmental protection plan. They might also serve as a peer review panel to evaluate alleged ethical misconduct by an employee.[21]

Finally, **philanthropic giving** is the awarding of funds or gifts to charities or other worth causes. Target routinely gives a share pre-tax income to charity and social programs. Omaha Steaks gives more than $100,000 per year to support the arts.[22] Giving across national boundaries is also becoming more common. For example, Alcoa gave $112,000 to a small town in Brazil to build a sewage treatment plant. And Japanese firms such as Sony and Mitsubishi make contributions to many social programs in the United States. However, in the current climate of cutbacks, many corporations have also had to limit their charitable gifts over the past several years as they continue to trim their own budgets.[23] And many firms that continue to make contributions are increasingly targeting them to programs or areas where the firm will get something in return. For example, firms today are more likely than they were a few years ago to give money to job training programs rather than to the

legal compliance
The extent to which an organization complies with local, state, federal, and international laws

ethical compliance
The extent to which an organization and its members follow basic ethical standards of behavior

philanthropic giving
Awarding funds or gifts to charities or other worthy causes

arts. The logic is that they get a more direct payoff from the former type of contribution—in this instance, a better-trained workforce from which to hire new employees.[24] And indeed, corporate donations to arts programs declined 5 percent between 2003 and 2008, with further cuts expected in 2009 and 2010 because of economic downturns.[25]

Informal Organizational Dimensions In addition to these formal dimensions of managing social responsibility, there are also informal ones. Leadership, organization culture, and how the organization responds to whistle blowers all help shape and define people's perceptions of the organization's stance on social responsibility.

Leadership practices and organization culture can go a long way toward defining the social responsibility stance an organization and its members will adopt.[26] As described earlier, for example, ethical leadership often sets the tone for the entire organization. For example, Johnson & Johnson executives for years provided a consistent message to employees that customers, employees, communities where the company did business, and shareholders were all important—and primarily in that order. Thus, when packages of poisoned Tylenol showed up on store shelves, Johnson & Johnson employees did not need to wait for orders from headquarters to know what to do: They immediately pulled all the packages from shelves before any other customers could buy them.[27]

Whistle blowing is the disclosure, by an employee, of illegal or unethical conduct on the part of others within the organization.[28] How an organization responds to this practice often indicates its values as they relate to social responsibility. Whistle blowers may have to proceed through a number of channels to be heard, and they may even get fired for their efforts.[29] Many organizations, however, welcome their contributions. A person who observes questionable behavior typically first reports the incident to his or her boss. If nothing is done, the whistle blower may then inform higher-level managers or an ethics committee, if one exists. Eventually, the person may have to go to a regulatory agency or even the media to be heard. Harry Markopolos, a portfolio manager at Rampart Investments, spent nine years trying to convince the Securities and Exchange Commission (SEC) that a money management firm run by Bernard Madoff was falsifying the results it was reporting to investors. Only when the U.S. economy went into recession in 2008 did the truth about Madoff come out.[30] In response, the SEC announced plans to overhaul its whistle blowing system.[31]

THE INTERNATIONAL ENVIRONMENT OF MANAGEMENT

Another important competitive issue for managers today is the international environment. After describing recent trends in international business, we examine levels of internationalization and the international context of business.

Trends in International Business

The stage for today's international business environment was set at the end of World War II. Businesses in war-torn countries such as Germany and Japan had no choice but to rebuild from scratch. Consequently, they had to rethink every facet of their operations, including technology, production, finance, and marketing. Although these countries took many years to recover, they eventually did so, and their economic systems were subsequently poised for growth. During the same era, many U.S. companies grew somewhat complacent. Their customer base was growing rapidly. Increased population, spurred by the baby boom, and increased affluence resulting from the postwar economic boom greatly raised the average person's standard of living and expectations. The U.S. public continually wanted new and better products and services. Many U.S. companies profited greatly from this pattern, but most were also guilty of taking it for granted.

U.S. firms are no longer isolated from global competition or the global market. A few simple numbers help tell the full story of international trade and industry. First of all, the volume of international trade increased more than 3,000 percent between 1960 and 2010. Further, although 153 of the world's largest corporations are headquartered in the United States, there are also 64 in Japan, 39 in France, 37 in Germany, and 34 in Britain.[32] Within certain industries, the preeminence of non-U.S. firms is even more striking. For example, only two of the world's ten largest banks and one of the largest electronics companies are based in the United States. Only two of the ten largest chemical companies are U.S. firms. On the other hand, U.S. firms comprise seven of the nine largest aerospace companies, three of the seven largest airlines, four of the ten largest information technology companies, six of the seven largest diversified financial companies, and six of the ten largest retailers.[33]

U.S. firms are also finding that international operations are an increasingly important element of their sales and profits. For example, in 2008 ExxonMobil realized 69 percent of its revenues and 59 percent of its profits abroad. For Avon, these percentages were 74 percent and 70 percent, respectively.[34] From any perspective, then, it is clear that we live in a truly global economy. Virtually all businesses today must be concerned with the competitive situations they face in lands far from home and with how companies from distant lands are competing in their homelands.

Levels of International Business Activity

Firms can choose various levels of international business activity as they seek to gain a competitive advantage in other countries. The general levels are exporting and importing, licensing, strategic alliances, and direct investment. Table 2.1 summarizes the advantages and disadvantages of each approach.

Table 2.1
Advantages and Disadvantages of Different Approaches to Internationalization

When organizations decide to increase their level of internationalization, they can adopt several strategies. Each strategy is a matter of degree, as opposed to being a discrete and mutually exclusive category. And each has unique advantages that must be considered.

Approach to Internationalization	Advantages	Disadvantages
Importing or Exporting	1. Small cash outlay 2. Little risk 3. No adaptation necessary	1. Tariffs and taxes 2. High transportation costs 3. Government restrictions
Licensing	1. Increased profitability 2. Extended profitability	1. Inflexibility 2. Competition
Strategic Alliances or Joint Ventures	1. Quick market entry 2. Access to materials and technology	Shared ownership (limits control and profits)
Direct Investment	1. Enhanced control 2. Existing infrastructure	1. Complexity 2. Greater economic and political risk 3. Greater uncertainty

Exporting and Importing Importing or exporting (or both) is usually the first type of international business in which a firm gets involved. **Exporting**, or making a product in the firm's domestic marketplace and selling it in another country, can involve both merchandise and services. **Importing** is bringing a good, service, or capital into the home country from abroad. For example, automobiles (Mazda, Ford, Volkswagen, Mercedes-Benz, Ferrari) and stereo equipment (Sony, Bang & Olufsen, Sanyo) are routinely exported by their manufacturers to other countries. Likewise, many wine distributors buy products from vineyards in France, Italy, or the United States and import them into their own country for resale. U.S. sports brands, such as team jerseys and logo caps, have become one of the latest hot exports.[35]

Licensing A company may prefer to arrange for a foreign company to manufacture or market its products under a licensing agreement. Factors that may lead to this decision include excessive transportation costs, government regulations, and home production costs. **Licensing** is an arrangement whereby a firm allows another company to use its brand name, trademark, technology, patent, copyright, or other assets. In return, the licensee pays a royalty, usually based on sales. Franchising, a special form of licensing, is also widely used in international business. Kirin Brewery, Japan's largest producer of beer, wanted to expand its international operations but feared that the time involved in shipping it from Japan would cause the beer to lose its freshness. Thus it has entered into a number of licensing arrangements with breweries in other markets. These brewers make beer according to strict guidelines provided by the Japanese firm and then package and market it as Kirin Beer. They pay a royalty to Kirin for each case sold. Molson produces Kirin in Canada under such an agreement, and the Charles Wells Brewery does the same in England.[36]

Strategic Alliances In a **strategic alliance**, two or more firms jointly cooperate for mutual gain.[37] For example, Kodak and Fuji, along with three other major Japanese camera manufacturers, collaborated on the development of a new film cartridge. This collaboration allowed Kodak and Fuji to share development costs, prevented the advertising war that might have raged if they had developed different cartridges, and made it easier for new cameras to be introduced at the same time as the new film cartridges. A **joint venture** is special type of strategic alliance in which the partners actually share ownership of a new enterprise. Strategic alliances have enjoyed a tremendous upsurge in the past few years.

Direct Investment Another level of commitment to internationalization is direct investment. **Direct investment** occurs when a firm headquartered in one country builds or purchases operating facilities or subsidiaries in a foreign country. The foreign operations then become wholly owned subsidiaries of the firm. Examples include British Petroleum's acquisition of Amoco, Dell Computer's new factory in China, and the new Disney theme park in Hong Kong. And Coca-Cola recently invested $150 million to build a new bottling and distribution network in India. Many U.S. firms are using maquiladoras for the same purpose. **Maquiladoras** are light assembly plants built in northern Mexico close to the U.S. border. The plants are given special tax breaks by the Mexican government, and the area is populated with workers willing to work for very low wages.

The Context of International Business

Managers involved in international business should also be aware of the cultural environment, controls on international trade, the importance of economic communities, and the role of the GATT and WTO.

---

exporting
Making a product in the firm's domestic marketplace and selling it in another country

importing
Bringing a good, service, or capital into the home country from abroad

licensing
An arrangement whereby one company allows another company to use its brand name, trademark, technology, patent, copyright, or other assets in exchange for a royalty based on sales

strategic alliance
A cooperative arrangement between two or more firms for mutual gain

joint venture
A special type of strategic alliance in which the partners share in the ownership of an operation on an equity basis

direct investment
A firm's building or purchasing operating facilities or subsidiaries in a different country from the one where it has its headquarters

maquiladoras
Light assembly plants that are built in northern Mexico close to the U.S. border and are given special tax breaks by the Mexican government

The Cultural Environment One significant contextual challenge for the international manager is the cultural environment and how it affects business. A country's culture includes all the values, symbols, beliefs, and language that guide behavior. Cultural values and beliefs are often unspoken; they may even be taken for granted by those who live in a particular country. Cultural factors do not necessarily cause problems for managers when the cultures of two countries are similar. Difficulties can arise, however, when there is little overlap between the home culture of a manager and the culture of the country in which business is to be conducted. For example, most U.S. managers find the culture and traditions of England relatively familiar. The people of both countries speak the same language and share strong historical roots, and there is a history of strong commerce between the two countries. When U.S. managers begin operations in Vietnam, the People's Republic of China, or the Middle East, however, many of those commonalities disappear.

Cultural differences between countries can have a direct impact on business practice. For example, the religion of Islam teaches that people should not make a living by exploiting the misfortune of others; as a result, charging interest is seen as immoral. This means that in Saudi Arabia, few businesses provide auto-wrecking services to tow-stalled cars to the garage (doing so would be capitalizing on misfortune), and in the Sudan, banks cannot pay or charge interest. Given these cultural and religious constraints, those two businesses—automobile towing and banking—seem to hold little promise for international managers in those particular countries!

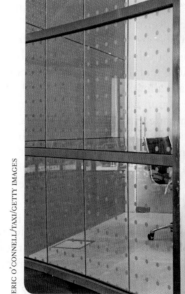

ERIC O'CONNELL/TAXI/GETTY IMAGES

Some cultural differences between countries can be even more subtle and yet have a major impact on business activities. For example, in the United States most managers clearly agree about the value of time. Most U.S. managers schedule their activities very tightly and then try hard to adhere to their schedules. Other cultures do not put such a premium on time. In the Middle East, managers do not like to set appointments, and they rarely keep appointments set too far into the future. U.S. managers interacting with managers from the Middle East might misinterpret the late arrival of a potential business partner as a negotiation ploy or an insult, when it is merely a simple reflection of different views of time and its value.[38]

Language itself can be an important factor. Beyond the obvious and clear barriers posed when people speak different languages,

Virtually all business activity today has international overtones. Cultural differences are among the many elements that affect international business. For instance, a U.S. or Asian manager interacting with an Arab manager has to contend with differences in time zones, work hours, and languages. Cultural differences regarding the importance of time and the values of work schedules and appointments can also come into play.

subtle differences in meaning can also play a major role. For example, Imperial Oil of Canada markets gasoline under the brand name Esso. When the firm tried to sell its gasoline in Japan, it learned that Esso means "stalled car" in Japanese. Likewise, when Chevrolet first introduced a U.S. model called the Nova in Latin America, General Motors executives could not understand why the car sold poorly. They eventually learned, though, that, in Spanish, no va means "it doesn't go." The color green is used extensively in Muslim countries, but it signifies death in some other lands. The color associated with femininity in the United States is pink, but in many other countries yellow is the most feminine color. And when Disney was initially promoting its new theme park in Hong Kong, its print ads featured a family consisting of two parents and two children, failing to consider that the Chinese government limits most families to a single child. As a result, people who saw the ad were confused until Disney relaunched the campaign to show parents and a single child visiting the park.[39]

Controls on International Trade Another element of the international context that managers need to consider is the extent to which there are controls on international trade. These controls include tariffs, quotas, export restraint agreements, and "buy national" laws. A **tariff** is a tax collected on goods shipped across national boundaries. Tariffs can be collected by the exporting country, by countries through which goods pass, or by the importing country. Import tariffs, which are the most common, can be levied to protect domestic companies by increasing the cost of foreign goods. Japan charges U.S. tobacco producers a tariff on cigarettes imported into Japan as a way to keep their prices higher than the prices charged by domestic firms. Tariffs can also be levied, usually by less-developed countries, to raise money for the government.

Quotas are the most common form of trade restriction. A **quota** is a limit on the number or value of goods that can be traded. The quota amount is typically designed to ensure that domestic competitors will be able to maintain a certain market share. Honda is allowed to import 425,000 autos each year into the United States. This quota is one reason why Honda opened manufacturing facilities here. The quota applies to cars imported into the United States, but the company can produce as many other cars within U.S. borders as it wants; such cars are not considered imports. **Export restraint agreements** are designed to convince other governments to limit voluntarily the volume or value of goods exported to or imported from a particular country. They are, in effect, export quotas. Japanese steel producers voluntarily limit the amount of steel they send to the United States each year.

"Buy national" legislation gives preference to domestic producers through content or price restrictions. Several countries have this type of legislation. Brazil requires that Brazilian companies purchase only Brazilian-made computers. The United States requires that the Department of Defense purchase military uniforms manufactured only in the United States, even though the price of foreign uniforms would be only half as much. Mexico requires that 50 percent of the parts of cars sold in Mexico be manufactured inside its own borders.

Economic Communities Just as government policies can either increase or decrease the political risk that international managers face, trade relations between countries can either help or hinder international business. Relations dictated by quotas, tariffs, and so forth can hurt international trade. There is currently a strong movement around the world to reduce many of these barriers. This movement takes its most obvious form in international economic communities.

An international **economic community** is a set of countries that agree to markedly reduce or eliminate trade barriers among member nations. The first (and in many ways still the most important) of these economic communities is the European Union. The **European Union** (or EU, as it is often called) can be traced to 1957 when Belgium,

---

tariff
A tax collected on goods shipped across national boundaries

quota
A limit on the number or value of goods that can be traded

export restraint agreements
Accords reached by governments in which countries voluntarily limit the volume or value of goods they export to or import from one another

economic community
A set of countries that agree to markedly reduce or eliminate trade barriers among member nations (a formalized market system)

European Union (EU)
The first and most important international market system

France, Luxembourg, Germany, Italy, and the Netherlands signed the Treaty of Rome to promote economic integration. Between 1973 and 1986 these countries were joined by Denmark, Ireland, the United Kingdom, Greece, Spain, and Portugal, and the group became known first as the European Committee and then as the European Union. Austria, Finland, and Sweden joined the EU in 1995; twelve additional countries (mostly from the formerly Communist-controlled eastern European region) joined between 2004 and 2007, bringing the EU's membership to 27 countries. For years these countries have followed a basic plan that led to the systematic elimination of most trade barriers. The new market system achieved significantly more potential when most of the EU members eliminated their home currencies (such as French francs and Italian lira) beginning on January 1, 2002, and adopted a new common currency call the euro.

Another important economic community encompasses the United States, Canada, and Mexico. These countries have long been major trading partners with one another; more than 70 percent of Mexico's exports go to the United States, and more than 65 percent of Mexico's imports come from the United States. During the last several years, these countries have negotiated a variety of agreements to make trade even easier. The most important of these, the **North American Free Trade Agreement**, or **NAFTA**, eliminates many of the trade barriers—quotas and tariffs, for example—that existed previously.[40]

The Role of the GATT and WTO The context of international business is also increasingly being influenced by the **General Agreement on Tariffs and Trade (GATT)** and the World Trade Organization (WTO). The GATT was first negotiated following World War II in an effort to avoid trade wars that would benefit rich nations and harm poorer ones. Essentially, the GATT is a trade agreement intended to promote international trade by reducing trade barriers and making it easier for all nations to compete in international markets. The GATT was a major stimulus to international trade after it was first ratified in 1948 by 23 countries; by 1994 a total of 117 countries had signed the agreement.

One key component of the GATT was the identification of the so-called *most favored national* (MFN) principle. This provision stipulates that if a country extends preferential treatment to any other nation that has signed the agreement, then that preferential treatment must be extended to all signatories to the agreement. Members can extend such treatment to non-signatories as well, but they are not required to do so.

The **World Trade Organization**, or **WTO**, came into existence on January 1, 1995. The WTO replaced the GATT and absorbed its mission. The WTO is headquartered in Geneva, Switzerland, and currently includes 140 member nations and 32 observer countries. Members are required to open their markets to international trade and to follow WTO rules. The WTO has three basic goals:

1. To promote trade flows by encouraging nations to adopt nondiscriminatory and predictable trade policies
2. To reduce remaining trade barriers through multilateral negotiations
3. To establish impartial procedures for resolving trade disputes among its members

The WTO is certain to continue to play a major role in the evolution of the global economy. At the same time, it has also become a lightning rod for protesters and other activists, who argue that the WTO focuses too narrowly on globalization issues to the detriment of human rights and the environment.

North American Free Trade Agreement (NAFTA)
An agreement between the United States, Canada, and Mexico to promote trade with one another

General Agreement on Tariffs and Trade (GATT)
A trade agreement intended to promote international trade by reducing trade barriers and making it easier for all nations to compete in international markets

World Trade Organization (WTO)
An organization, which currently includes 140 member nations and 32 observer countries, that requires members to open their markets to international trade and to follow WTO rules

THE ORGANIZATION'S CULTURE

As we noted earlier, an especially important part of the internal environment of an organization is its culture. **Organization culture** is the set of values, beliefs, behaviors, customs, and attitudes that helps the members of the organization understand what it stands for, how it does things, and what it considers important.[41]

The Importance of Organization Culture

Culture determines the "feel" of the organization. A strong and clear culture can play an important role in the competitiveness of a business. At the same time, though, there is no universal culture that will help all organizations. The stereotypic image of Microsoft, for example, is that of a workplace where people dress very casually and work very long hours. In contrast, the image of Bank of America for some observers is that of a formal setting with rigid work rules and people dressed in conservative business attire. And Texas Instruments likes to talk about its "shirtsleeve" culture, in which ties are avoided and few managers even wear jackets. Southwest Airlines maintains a culture that stresses fun and excitement.

Of course, the same culture is not necessarily found throughout an entire organization. For example, the sales and marketing department may have a culture quite different from that of the operations and manufacturing department. Regardless of its nature, however, culture is a powerful force in organizations, one that can shape the firm's overall effectiveness and long-term success. Companies that can develop and maintain a strong culture, such as Starbucks and Procter & Gamble, tend to be more effective than companies that have trouble developing and maintaining a strong culture, such as Kmart.[42]

Organization culture plays a big role in the success of any business. A strong and well-understood culture can play an even bigger role. Many newer businesses have developed cultures based on informality, believing that such a culture helps attract and retain better workers. These employees, for example, are engaged in an important product development meeting. The lack of a conference table promotes equality and collegiality and their informal attire helps maintain a laid-back and casual atmosphere.

RUBBERBALL/JUPITER IMAGES

Determinants of Organization Culture

organization culture
The set of values, beliefs, behaviors, customs, and attitudes that helps the members of the organization understand what it stands for, how it does things, and what it considers important

Where does an organization's culture come from? Typically, it develops and blossoms over a long period of time. Its starting point is often the organization's founder. For example, James Cash Penney believed in treating employees and customers with respect and dignity. Employees at J.C. Penney are still called "associates" rather than "employees" (to reflect partnership), and customer satisfaction is of paramount importance. The impact of Sam Walton, Ross Perot, and Walt Disney is still felt in the organizations they founded.[43] As an organization grows, its culture is modified, shaped, and refined by symbols, stories, heroes, slogans, and ceremonies. And many decisions at Walt Disney Company today are still framed by asking, "What would Walt have done?"

Corporate success and shared experiences also shape culture. For example, Hallmark Cards has a strong culture derived from its years of success in the greeting card industry. Employees speak of "the Hallmark family" and care deeply about the company; many of them have worked there for years. At Kmart, in contrast, the culture is quite weak, the management team changes rapidly, and few people sense any direction or purpose in the company. The differences in culture at Hallmark and Kmart are in part attributable to past successes and shared experiences.

Managing Organization Culture

How can managers deal with culture, given its clear importance but intangible nature? Essentially, the manager must understand the current culture and then decide whether it should be maintained or changed. By understanding the organization's current culture, managers can take appropriate actions. Culture can also be maintained by rewarding and promoting people whose behaviors are consistent with the existing culture and by articulating the culture through slogans, ceremonies, and so forth.

But managers must walk a fine line between maintaining a culture that still works effectively and changing a culture that has become dysfunctional. For example, many of the firms already noted, as well as numerous others, take pride in perpetuating their culture. Shell Oil, for example, has an elaborate display in the lobby of its Houston headquarters that tells the story of the firm's past. But other companies may face situations in which their culture is no longer a strength. For example, some critics feel that General Motors' culture places too much emphasis on product development and internal competition among divisions, and not enough on marketing and competition with other firms. They even argue that this culture was a major contributing factor in the business crisis that GM faced in 2009.

Culture problems sometimes arise from mergers or the growth of rival factions within an organization. For example, Delta recently merged with Northwest Airlines. Combining the two companies led to numerous cases of conflict and operational difficulties because the cultures of the two firms were so different.[44] To change culture, managers must have a clear idea of what they want to create. When Continental Airlines "reinvented" itself a few years ago, employees were invited outside the corporate headquarters in Houston to watch the firm's old policies and procedures manuals set afire. The firm's new strategic direction is known throughout Continental as the "Go Forward" plan, intentionally named to avoid reminding people about the firm's troubled past and to focus on the future instead.

SUMMARY OF LEARNING OBJECTIVES AND KEY POINTS

1. Discuss the nature of an organization's environments and identify and describe the components of its general, task, and internal environments.

   - Managers need to have a thorough understanding of the environment in which they operate and compete. The general environment consists of the economy, technology, and the political-legal climate. The task environment consists of competitors, customers, suppliers, strategic partners, and regulators.

   - The internal environment consists of the organization's owners, board of directors, employees, physical environment, and culture. Owners are those who have claims on the property rights of the organization. The board of directors, elected by stockholders, is responsible for overseeing a firm's top managers. Individual employees are other important parts of the internal environment. The physical environment, yet another part of the internal environment, varies greatly across organizations.

2. Describe the ethical and social environment of management, including individual ethics, the concept of social responsibility, and how organizations can manage social responsibility.

   • The ethical and social environment of management is also quite important. Understanding the differences between ethical and unethical behavior, as well as appreciating the special nature of managerial ethics, can help guide effective decision making. Understanding the meaning of and arguments for and against social responsibility can help a manager effectively address both the formal and the informal dimensions of social responsibility.

3. Discuss the international environment of management, including trends in international business, levels of international business activities, and the context of international business.

   • The international environment of management can be a crucial one. Current trends have resulted in the increasing globalization of markets, industries, and businesses. Organizations seeking to become more international can rely on importing, exporting, licensing (including franchising), strategic alliances, and direct investment to do so. National culture, controls on international trade, economic communities, and the WTO combine to determine the context of international business.

4. Describe the importance and determinants of an organization's culture, as well as how organization culture can be managed.

   • Organization culture is the set of values, beliefs, behaviors, customs, and attitudes that helps the members of the organization understand what it stands for, how it does things, and what it considers important. Organization culture is an important environmental concern for managers. Managers must understand that culture is a key determinant of how well their organization will perform. Culture can be assessed and managed in a number of different ways.

DISCUSSION QUESTIONS

Questions for Review

1. Identify and discuss each major dimension of the general environment and the task environment.

2. Do organizations have ethics? Why or why not?

3. What are the arguments for and against social responsibility on the part of businesses? In your opinion, which set of arguments is more compelling?

4. Describe the basic levels of international business involvement. Why might a firm use more than one level at the same time?

5. Describe various barriers to international trade.

Questions for Analysis

1. Can you think of dimensions of the task environment that are not discussed in the text? Indicate their linkages to those that are discussed.

2. What is the relationship between the law and ethical behavior? Can a behavior be ethical but illegal at the same time?

3. What is your opinion of whistle blowing? If you were aware of criminal activity in your organization but knew that reporting it would probably cost you your job, what would you do?

4. What industries do you think will feel the greatest impact of international business in the future? Are there industries that will remain relatively unaffected by globalization? If so, which ones? If not, explain why not.

5. What is the culture of your college or university? How clear is it? What are its most positive and its most negative characteristics?

BUILDING EFFECTIVE INTERPERSONAL SKILLS

Exercise Overview

Interpersonal skills reflect the manager's ability to communicate with, understand, and motivate individuals and groups. Managers in international organizations must understand how cultural manners and norms affect communication with people in different areas of the world. This exercise will help you evaluate your current level of cultural awareness and develop insights into areas where you can improve.

Exercise Background

As firms become increasingly globalized, they look for managers with international experience or skills. Yet many American college graduates do not have strong skills in foreign languages, global history, or international cultures.

Exercise Task

Take the International Culture Quiz that follows. Then, on the basis of your score, answer the question at the end. In order to make the quiz more relevant, choose your answers from one or more of the ten largest countries in the world. In order, these are China, India, the United States, Indonesia, Brazil, Pakistan, Russia, Bangladesh, Nigeria, and Japan.

The International Culture Quiz

1. Name the major religion practiced in each of the ten largest countries.

2. When greeting a business associate, in which country or countries is it proper to shake hands? to bow? to hug or kiss?

3. In which country or countries should you avoid wearing the color purple?

4. In which country or countries would smiling be considered suspicious?

5. In which country or countries are laughter and smiling often used as a way of covering up feelings of embarrassment or displeasure?

6. Which part of someone else's body should you never touch in Indonesia? in India? Which part of your own body should you never touch in China?

7. In which country or countries would a server or small-business person require that a tip be paid before the service is rendered?

8. In which country or countries would it be an insult to address someone in Spanish?

9. In which country or countries is whistling considered bad luck?

10. In which country or countries is it important to give printed business cards to all business associates?

11. In which country or countries might you be asked your family size or income upon first meeting with a new business associate?

12. In which country or countries should gum not be chewed at work?

Your instructor will provide the answers. Was your score high or low? What does your score tell you about your cultural awareness?

What do you think you could do to improve your score? Share your ideas with the class.

Reprinted by permission of the author Margaret Hill.

BUILDING EFFECTIVE COMMUNICATION SKILLS

Exercise Overview

Communication skills consist of a manager's ability to receive information and ideas from others effectively and to convey information and ideas effectively to others. This exercise will help you develop your communication skills, while also helping you to understand the importance of knowing the customer segments in an organization's task environment.

Exercise Background

Assume that you are a newly hired middle manager in the marketing department of a large food manufacturer. You have just completed your formal study of management and are excited about the opportunity to apply some of those theories to the real-life problems of your firm. One problem in particular intrigues you. Your boss, the marketing vice president, recently developed a consumer survey to solicit feedback about products from customers. The feedback the firm has received varies considerably, ranging from a 2 to a 5 on a scale of 1 to 5, which gives your firm no helpful data. In addition, sales of your company's products have been slowly but steadily declining over time, and the marketing department is under some pressure from upper management to determine why.

You have an idea that the survey is not an accurate reflection of consumer preferences, so you make a suggestion to your boss: "Why don't we gather some information about our customers, in order to understand their needs better? For example, our products are purchased by individual consumers, schools, restaurants, and other organizations. Maybe each type of consumer wants something different from our product." Your boss's response is to stare at you, perplexed, and say, "No. We're not changing anything about the survey." When you ask, "Why?" the boss responds that the product has been a best-seller for years, that "good quality is good quality," and thus that all customers must want the same thing. He then says, "I'll spare you the embarrassment of failure by refusing your request."

Exercise Task

1. With this background in mind, compose a written proposal for your boss, outlining your position. Be sure to emphasize your fundamental concern—that the marketing department must understand the needs of each customer segment better in order to provide products that meet those needs. Consider ways to persuade your boss to change his mind. (Hint: Telling him bluntly that he is wrong is unlikely to be effective.)

2. On the basis of what you wrote in response to Exercise Task 1, do you think your boss will change his mind? If yes, exactly what will persuade him to change his mind? If no, what other actions could you take in a further effort to have your ideas adopted by the firm?

SKILLS SELF-ASSESSMENT INSTRUMENT

Global Awareness

Introduction: As we have noted, the environment of business is becoming more global. The following assessment is designed to help you assess your readiness to respond to managing in a global context.

Instructions: You will agree with some of the following statements and disagree with others. In some cases you may find it difficult to make a decision, but you should force yourself to make a choice. Record your answers next to each statement according to the following scale:

4 Strongly agree
3 Somewhat agree
2 Somewhat disagree
1 Strongly disagree

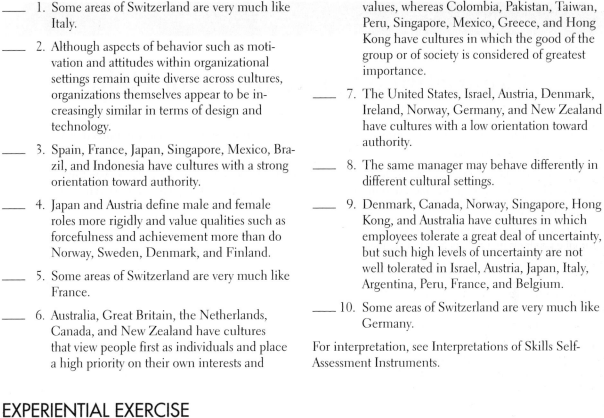

_____ 1. Some areas of Switzerland are very much like Italy.

_____ 2. Although aspects of behavior such as motivation and attitudes within organizational settings remain quite diverse across cultures, organizations themselves appear to be increasingly similar in terms of design and technology.

_____ 3. Spain, France, Japan, Singapore, Mexico, Brazil, and Indonesia have cultures with a strong orientation toward authority.

_____ 4. Japan and Austria define male and female roles more rigidly and value qualities such as forcefulness and achievement more than do Norway, Sweden, Denmark, and Finland.

_____ 5. Some areas of Switzerland are very much like France.

_____ 6. Australia, Great Britain, the Netherlands, Canada, and New Zealand have cultures that view people first as individuals and place a high priority on their own interests and values, whereas Colombia, Pakistan, Taiwan, Peru, Singapore, Mexico, Greece, and Hong Kong have cultures in which the good of the group or of society is considered of greatest importance.

_____ 7. The United States, Israel, Austria, Denmark, Ireland, Norway, Germany, and New Zealand have cultures with a low orientation toward authority.

_____ 8. The same manager may behave differently in different cultural settings.

_____ 9. Denmark, Canada, Norway, Singapore, Hong Kong, and Australia have cultures in which employees tolerate a great deal of uncertainty, but such high levels of uncertainty are not well tolerated in Israel, Austria, Japan, Italy, Argentina, Peru, France, and Belgium.

_____ 10. Some areas of Switzerland are very much like Germany.

For interpretation, see Interpretations of Skills Self-Assessment Instruments.

EXPERIENTIAL EXERCISE

Assessing Organization Culture

Purpose: While organization culture is intangible, it is not difficult to observe. This activity will help you improve your skills in observing and interpreting organization culture, which can help to make you a more effective participant and leader in organizations.

Introduction: Clues to organization culture may be found by observing details that relate to member behavior, traditions or customs, stories, attitudes, values, communication patterns, organization structure, employee dress and appearance, and even office space arrangements. Do members address each other by first names? Are office doors left open or closed? What do members wear? How are achievements recognized? Does the workplace feel energized or laid-back? Do members smile and laugh often? Does seniority or expertise earn more respect?

Instructions: First, observe clues to organization behavior at your school, college, or university. To the extent possible, observe a diversity of members including students, teaching faculty, and non-teaching staff. Write down specific examples. For example, students typically wear blue jeans while instructors usually wear suits. In the cafeteria, freshmen sit mainly with other freshmen. A professor may be referred to as "Doctor" by staff, while she may refer to staff by their first name.

Second, interpret the facts. Use your observations to describe the organization's core values. What does it value most? How did you come to that conclusion?

Third, with the class or in small groups, discuss your facts and interpretations. Focus especially on areas of disagreement. Where individuals disagree about the culture, try to understand why the disagreement occurs. If the facts differ, perhaps the individuals observed two different groups. For example, students majoring in business may be different than students in engineering or education. Or perhaps the organization culture tolerates or encourages lots of differences. If there is agreement on facts but interpretations differ, then perhaps the individuals making the interpretations can explore their differing perceptions.

YOU MAKE THE CALL

Competition Can Hurt ... or Help!

1. Can you identify instances where competition has helped a business near you?

2. Assuming you have convenient access to a Starbucks, are you now more interested in trying other premium coffees? Why or why not?

3. McDonald's recently launched several premium coffee products in a direct effort to take business away from Starbucks. Do you think they will succeed? Why or why not?

4. If McDonald's does succeed, do you think Starbucks should start selling hamburgers? Why or why not?

CHAPTER 3

BASIC ELEMENTS OF PLANNING

LEARNING OBJECTIVES

After studying this chapter, you should be able to:

1 Summarize the planning process and describe organizational goals.

2 Discuss the components of strategy and the types of strategic alternatives.

3 Describe how to use SWOT analysis in formulating strategy.

4 Identify and describe various alternative approaches to business-level strategy formulation.

5 Identify and describe various alternative approaches to corporate-level strategy formulation.

6 Discuss how tactical plans are developed and implemented.

7 Describe the basic types of operational plans used by organizations.

FIRST THINGS FIRST

Recent Developments in Games Theory

Since its start in 1982, Electronic Arts (EA) has been a pioneer in the home computer–games industry. From the outset, EA published games created by outside developers. This strategy offered higher margins and helped keep the new company in close contact with its market. In 1984, having built the largest sales force in the industry, EA generated revenues of $18 million. Crediting its developers as *software artists*, EA regularly gave game creators photo credits on packaging and advertising spreads and, more importantly, developed a generous profit-sharing policy that helped attract some of the industry's best development talent. Most of the best-selling games in the 1980s were developed by independent studios or individual creators, with EA specializing in distribution. By 1986, the company had become the country's largest supplier of entertainment software. It went public in 1989, and net revenue took off in the early 1990s, climbing from $113 million in 1991 to $298 million in 1993, largely because EA had introduced another novel strategy—building its

"EA has tried to commoditize development. We won't absorb [developers] into a big Death Star culture."

—ROBERT KOTICK, CEO, ACTIVISION

JENS WOLF/PICTURE ALLIANCE/PHOTOSHOT

Electronics Arts is one of the world's most successful video game makers. This game player is trying out a new EA product at a trade fair in Germany.

own game cartridges for popular consoles such as Sega's Genesis.

In 1995, EA developed a new strategy based on acquiring other, smaller firms. Under CEO Larry Probst, the company's strategy for acquiring and managing a burgeoning portfolio of studios developed—at least according to its most severe critics—a standard pattern: identify an extremely popular game, buy the developer, delegate the original creative team to churn out sequels until either the team burned out or the franchise fizzled, and then close down or absorb what was left.

EA's other key strategy initiative of the early 2000s seized on the advantages of rolling out products in series. *John Madden Football* had first been published in 1988, and *Franchise Mode*, which allowed users to play multiple seasons, make off-season draft picks, and trade players, was added in 1997. The *Madden* series remains one of the biggest money-making series in videogaming history, and in 2004, EA made the first of numerous sports-licensing deals, an exclusive agreement with the National

Football League. A 15-year arrangement with the cable-TV sports network ESPN followed in 2005, and EA has since reached deals for multiyear sports series such as *FIFA*, *NHL*, *NBA Live*, and *Tiger Woods*. EA has enjoyed similar success with movie-licensed series (notably *Harry Potter*) and other long-running franchises (*Need for Speed*, *Medal of Honor*, and *Battlefield*).

The industry's other big player, Activision, has followed a different path to success. Activision was founded in 1979 by an ex–music-industry executive and four disgruntled programmers from Atari, a pioneer in arcade games and home-videogame consoles. In part, Activision was founded as a haven for game developers who were unhappy with prevailing industry policy. Positioning itself as the industry's first third-party developer, Activision began promoting creators as well as games. The company went public in 1983 and successfully rode the crest of a booming market until the mid-1980s.

The company's struggles began in 1986, when it had an ill-advised merger with Infocom, a software firm founded to develop interactive-fiction games. The relationship was rocky from the first, and Activision closed down Infocom operations in 1989, after three years of mismanagement and escalating losses. Meanwhile, Activision had begun to branch out from video games into other types of software and, to underscore its new commitment to a broader product line, changed its name to Mediagenic. By this time, however, competition in the videogame market had increased substantially, and the decision to expand into areas beyond its distinctive competence turned out to be a major strategic blunder. By 1991, Mediagenic was bankrupt.

This is the point at which Robert Kotick happened on Activision/Mediagenic—"a company," as *Forbes* magazine put it, "with a sorry balance sheet but a storied history." Kotick, a serial entrepreneur with no particular passion for video games, bought one-third of the firm for $440,000 and looked immediately to EA for a survey of best practices in the industry. What he perceived was a company whose culture was disrupted by internal conflict—namely, between managers motivated by productivity and profit and developers driven by independence and imagination. But EA also sold a lot of video games, and to Kotick, the basic tension in EA culture wasn't entirely surprising: Clearly the business of making and marketing video games succeeded when the creative side of the enterprise was supported by financing and distribution muscle, but it was equally true that a steady stream of successful games came from a company's creative people. The key to getting Activision back in the game, Kotick decided, was managing this complex of essential resources better than his competitor did.

So the next year Kotick raised $40 million through a stock offering, moved the company (rechristened Activision) to Los Angeles, and began to recruit people who could furnish the resources that he needed most—creative expertise and a connection with the passion that its customers brought to the videogame industry. Activision, he promised prospective developers, would not manage its human resources the way EA did: EA, he argued, "has commoditized development. We won't absorb you into a big Death Star culture."

Between 1997 and 2003, Kotick proceeded to buy no fewer than nine studios, but his concept of a videogame studio system was quite different from that of EA, which was determined to make production more efficient by centralizing groups of designers and programmers into regional offices. Kotick allows his studios to keep their own names, often lets them stay where they are, and further encourages autonomy by providing seed money for Activision alumni who want to launch out on their own. He conducts market research out of the company's Los Angeles headquarters but doesn't use the results to put pressure on his creative teams; rather, he shares the data with his studios and lets them draw their own conclusions. Each studio draws up its own financial statements and draws on its own bonus pool, and the paychecks of studio heads reflect both companywide profits and losses.

Kotick's strategy has paid off big time. In 1999, Activision's Neversoft studio came up with *Tony Hawks' Pro Skater*, which broke through the monotony of sports games by letting players proceed at their own pace through a virtual landscape. Activision's next blockbuster franchise—the World War II game *Call of Duty*—came in 2003 from a group of developers who'd left EA to found a studio called Infinity Ward. In 2006, Kotick paid $100 million for a company called Harmonix, which had developed a game revolving around a guitar-shaped peripheral: The *Guitar Hero* franchise has revolutionized not only video games but the relationship between video games and popular music and, as of this writing, has generated $2 billion in revenue.

By this time, Activision had built or developed games for every lucrative product category in the market except one—the so-called "massively multiplayer" games in which players pay monthly subscription fees to enter online worlds and build characters over the course of months or even years. The attractiveness of the category is obvious: Whereas a console game might command a one-shot retail price of $40, an online multiplayer game might charge $15 a month to each of several million players. So, Activision recently announced a merger with the game-making unit of the French entertainment conglomerate Vivendi. Vivendi was big, but it had only one blockbuster game—the world's number-one online multiplayer franchise, called *World of Warcraft*. Developed by a Vivendi-owned California studio called Blizzard, *World of Warcraft* had 11 million subscribers and, with $1.1 billion in annual sales, was perhaps the most profitable video game ever invented. The merger, according to Kotick, was Activision's best strategy for making a critical move in an industry increasingly dominated by Internet-based innovations: "We looked every which way to figure out how to participate in what Blizzard had created. We couldn't find a way to duplicate it, but we could acquire the expertise," explained Kotick, who added that acquiring *World of Warcraft* and the know-how of Blizzard had saved Activision another $150 million in development costs.

The new company, known as Activision Blizzard, has now squeezed past EA to become the largest videogame publisher in the world not affiliated with a maker of game consoles (such as Nintendo and Microsoft). Kotick attributed the firm's success to a "focus on a select number of proven franchises and genres where we have proven development expertise. . . . We look for ways to broaden the footprints of our franchises, and where appropriate, we develop innovative business models like subscription-based online gaming."

And what about onetime industry leader EA? Once known for its "bold vision," EA, charged one observer in early 2008, "has stagnated both creatively and financially, reduced to churning out an uninspiring litany of sports sequels and run-and-shoot knockoffs . . . . At Electronic Arts, talent has recently been reduced to a mere ingredient in an MBA's financial soup." CEO John Riccitiello agrees that the company made a critical mistake in trying to develop video games as if it were in the business of developing laundry detergents. "A top-down process that uses a lot of centralized tools to try and build a common brand with a lot of centralized creative calls is just not a good idea," he recently told an industry conference.

First and foremost, Riccitiello intends to give more latitude to the creative side of the product-development process: "Frankly, the core of our business, like any creative business," he admits, "are the guys and women who are actually making the product. You can't just buy people and attempt to apply some-business school synergy to them. It just doesn't work." Paul Lee, president of EA's Worldwide Studios, wants to pump up the proportion of internally created games from 30 percent to 50 percent and to roll out at least one new franchise per year. A new development studio in Montreal, Canada, is dedicated to the development of original titles, and at EA's Los Angeles studio, general manager Neil Young is experimenting with small "cells" of six to eight people, with each cell assigned a special creative task on an important upcoming title. The idea is to encourage developers to make creative contributions at every stage of the project, and to stimulate cross-pollination among cells, weekly breakthroughs are broadcast on flat-panel TV screens located throughout the facility.

"What I'm trying to build," says Young, "is a studio of gamemakers." He has the wholehearted support of his boss, who's committed to changing the way that EA manages its creative and operational resources. "The companies that succeed," acknowledges Riccitiello, "are those that provide a stage for their best people and let them do what they do best, and it's taken us some time to understand that."[1]

Among the most critical concerns for any company in the computer-games market is strategic management. One dominant company in the industry, EA, has flourished by pursuing one strategy, whereas another, Activision, has found success by playing a significant variation on that strategy. Each firm must remain vigilant in monitoring strategic models introduced by newcomers seeking shares of their lucrative market. Firms that effectively plan and manage their own strategies (and keep track of competitors' strategies) are virtually certain to reap rewards, but if either EA or Activision stumbles, it stands to lose millions of dollars in revenues. This chapter discusses how organizations manage strategy and strategic planning. As we note in Chapter 1, planning and decision making comprise the first managerial functions that organizations must address. This chapter is the first of three that explore planning and decision making.

PLANNING AND ORGANIZATIONAL GOALS

The planning process itself can best be thought of as a generic activity. All organizations engage in planning activities, but no two organizations plan in exactly the same fashion. Figure 3.1 is a general representation of the planning process that many organizations attempt to follow. But although most firms follow this general framework, each also has its own nuances and variations.[2]

As Figure 3.1 shows, all planning occurs within an environmental context. If managers do not understand this context, they are unable to develop effective plans. Thus understanding the environment is essentially the first step in planning. The previous chapter covers many of the basic environmental issues that affect organizations and how they plan. With this understanding as a foundation, managers must then establish the organization's mission. The mission outlines the organization's purpose, premises, values, and directions. Flowing from the mission are parallel streams of goals and plans. Directly following the mission are strategic goals. These goals and the mission help determine strategic plans. Strategic goals and plans are primary inputs for developing tactical goals. Tactical goals and the original strategic plans help shape tactical plans. Tactical plans, in turn, combine with the tactical goals to shape operational goals. These goals and the appropriate tactical plans determine operational plans. Finally, goals and plans at each level can also be used as inputs for future activities at all levels.

Organizational Goals

Goals are critical to organizational effectiveness, and they serve a number of purposes. Organizations can also have several different kinds of goals, all of which must be appropriately managed. And a number of different kinds of managers must be involved in setting goals.

Figure 3.1
The Planning Process

The planning process takes place within an environmental context. Managers must develop a complete and thorough understanding of this context to determine the organization's mission and to develop its strategic, tactical, and operational goals and plans.

Purposes of Goals Goals serve four important purposes.[3] First, they provide guidance and a unified direction for people in the organization. Goals can help everyone understand where the organization is going and why getting there is important.[4] Top managers at General Electric (GE) have set a goal that every business owned by the firm will be either number one or number two in its industry. This goal helps set the tone for decisions made by GE managers as it competes with other firms such as Whirlpool and Electrolux.[5] Likewise, Procter & Gamble (P&G) recently announced a goal of doubling its revenues in a ten-year period; this helps everyone in the firm recognize the strong emphasis on growth and expansion that is driving the firm.

Second, goal-setting practices strongly affect other aspects of planning. Effective goal setting promotes good planning, and good planning facilitates future goal setting. For example, the ambitious revenue goal set for P&G demonstrates how setting goals and developing plans to reach them should be seen as complementary activities. The strong growth goal should encourage managers to plan for expansion by looking for new market opportunities, for example. Similarly, they must also always be alert for competitive threats and new ideas that will help facilitate future expansion.

Third, goals can serve as a source of motivation for employees of the organization. Goals that are specific and moderately difficult can motivate people to work harder, especially if attaining the goal is likely to result in rewards.[6] The Italian furniture manufacturer Industrie Natuzzi SpA uses goals to motivate its workers. Each craftsperson has a goal for how long it should take to perform his or her job, such as sewing leather sheets together to make a sofa cushion or building wooden frames for chair arms. At the completion of assigned tasks, workers enter their ID numbers and job numbers into the firm's computer system. If they get a job done faster than their goal, a bonus is automatically added to their paycheck.[7]

Finally, goals provide an effective mechanism for evaluation and control. This means that performance can be assessed in the future in terms of how successfully today's goals are accomplished. For example, suppose that officials of the United Way of America set a goal of collecting $250,000 from a particular small community. If, midway through the campaign, they have raised only $50,000, they know that they need to change or intensify their efforts. If they raise only $100,000 by the end of their drive, they will need to carefully study why they did not reach their goal and what they need to do differently next year. On the other hand, if they succeed in raising $250,000 or more, evaluations of their efforts will take on an entirely different character. In 2009, the Food and Drug Administration (FDA) revealed that it was not meeting the goals it had set for itself for auditing food safety inspection programs. To address the issue, the FDA also announced plans to overhaul its inspection program and to tie individual performance ratings to food safety audits.[8]

mission
A statement of an organization's fundamental purpose

strategic goal
A goal set by and for top management of the organization

tactical goal
A goal set by and for middle managers of the organization

operational goal
A goal set by and for lower-level managers of the organization

Kinds of Goals Goals are set for and by different levels within an organization. An organization's **mission** is a statement of its "fundamental, unique purpose that sets a business apart from other firms of its type and identifies the scope of the business's operations in product and market terms."[9] For instance, Starbucks' mission statement is to be "the premier purveyor of the finest coffee in the world while maintaining our uncompromising principles while we grow." The principles referred to in the mission help managers at Starbucks make decisions and direct resources in clear and specific ways. **Strategic goals** are set by and for top management of the organization. They focus on broad, general issues. For example, Starbucks has a strategic goal of increasing the profitability of each of its coffee stores by 25 percent over the next five years. **Tactical goals** are set by and for middle managers. Their focus is on how to operationalize actions necessary to achieve the strategic goals. To achieve Starbucks' goal of increasing its per-store profitability, managers are working on tactical goals related to company-owned versus licensed stores and the global distribution of stores in different countries. **Operational goals** are set by and for lower-level managers.

Their concern is with shorter-term issues associated with the tactical goals. An operational goal for Starbucks might be to boost the profitability of a certain number of stores in each of the next five years. (Some managers use the words *objective* and *goal* interchangeably. When they are differentiated, however, the term *objective* is usually used instead of *operational goal*.)

Kinds of Organizational Plans

Organizations establish many different kinds of plans. At a general level, these include strategic, tactical, and operational plans.

Strategic Plans   Strategic plans are developed to achieve strategic goals. More precisely, a **strategic plan** is a general plan outlining decisions about resource allocation, priorities, and action steps necessary to reach strategic goals.[10] These plans are set by the board of directors and top management, generally have an extended time horizon, and address questions of scope, resource deployment, competitive advantage, and synergy. We discuss strategic planning further in the next major section.

Tactical Plans   A tactical plan, aimed at achieving tactical goals, is developed to implement specific parts of a strategic plan. Tactical plans typically involve upper and middle management and, compared with strategic plans, have a somewhat shorter time horizon and a more specific and concrete focus. Thus tactical plans are concerned more with actually getting things done than with deciding what to do. Tactical planning is covered in detail in a later section.

Operational Plans   An **operational plan** focuses on carrying out tactical plans to achieve operational goals. Developed by middle and lower-level managers, operational plans have a short-term focus and are relatively narrow in scope. Each one deals with a fairly small set of activities. We cover operational planning in more detail later.

THE NATURE OF STRATEGIC MANAGEMENT

A **strategy** is a comprehensive plan for accomplishing an organization's goals. **Strategic management**, in turn, is a way of approaching business opportunities and challenges—it is a comprehensive and ongoing management process aimed at formulating and implementing effective strategies. Finally, **effective strategies** are those that promote a superior alignment between the organization and its environment and the achievement of strategic goals.[11]

The Components of Strategy

In general, a well-conceived strategy addresses three areas: distinctive competence, scope, and resource deployment. A **distinctive competence** is something the organization does exceptionally well. A distinctive competence of Abercrombie & Fitch is speed in moving inventory. It tracks consumer preferences daily with point-of-sale computers, electronically transmits orders to suppliers in Hong Kong, charters 747s to fly products to the United States, and has products in stores 48 hours later. Because other retailers take weeks or sometimes months to accomplish the same things, Abercrombie & Fitch uses this distinctive competence to remain competitive.[12]

The **scope** of a strategy specifies the range of markets in which an organization will compete. Hershey Foods has essentially restricted its scope to the confectionery business, with a few related activities in other food-processing areas. In contrast, its biggest

strategic plan
A general plan outlining decisions about resource allocation, priorities, and action steps necessary to reach strategic goals

operational plan
A plan that focuses on carrying out tactical plans to achieve operational goals

strategy
A comprehensive plan for accomplishing an organization's goals

strategic management
A comprehensive and ongoing management process aimed at formulating and implementing effective strategies; a way of approaching business opportunities and challenges

effective strategy
A strategy that promotes a superior alignment between the organization and its environment and the achievement of strategic goals

distinctive competence
An organizational strength possessed by only a small number of competing firms

scope
When applied to strategy, it specifies the range of markets in which an organization will compete

competitor, Mars, has adopted a broader scope by competing in the pet food business and the electronics industry, among others. Some organizations, called conglomerates, compete in dozens or even hundreds of markets.

A strategy should also include an outline of the organization's projected **resource deployment**—how it will distribute its resources across the areas in which it competes. General Electric, for example, has been using profits from its highly successful U.S. operations to invest heavily in new businesses in Europe and Asia. Alternatively, the firm might have chosen to invest in different industries in its domestic market or to invest more heavily in Latin America. The choices it makes as to where and how much to invest reflect issues of resource deployment.

Types of Strategic Alternatives

Most businesses today develop strategies at two distinct levels: business level and corporate level. These levels provide a rich combination of strategic alternatives for organizations. **Business-level strategy** is the set of strategic alternatives from which an organization chooses as it conducts business in a particular industry or market. Such alternatives help the organization focus its competitive efforts for each industry or market in a targeted and focused manner.

Corporate-level strategy is the set of strategic alternatives from which an organization chooses as it manages its operations simultaneously across several industries and several markets. As we discuss later, most large companies today compete in various industries and markets. Thus, although they develop business-level strategies for each industry or market, they also develop an overall strategy that helps define the mix of industries and markets that are of interest to the firm.

Drawing a distinction between strategy formulation and strategy implementation is also instructive. **Strategy formulation** is the set of processes involved in creating or determining the strategies of the organization, whereas **strategy implementation** is the methods by which strategies are operationalized or executed within the organization. The primary distinction is along the lines of content versus process: The formulation stage determines what the strategy is, and the implementation stage focuses on how the strategy is achieved.

USING SWOT ANALYSIS TO FORMULATE STRATEGY

The starting point in formulating strategy is usually **SWOT** (strengths, weaknesses, opportunities, and threats) analysis. As shown in Figure 3.2, SWOT analysis is a careful evaluation of an organization's internal strengths and weaknesses as well as its environmental opportunities and threats. In SWOT analysis, the best strategies accomplish an organization's mission by (1) exploiting an organization's opportunities and strengths while (2) neutralizing its threats and (3) avoiding (or correcting) its weaknesses.

Evaluating an Organization's Strengths

Organizational strengths are skills and capabilities that enable an organization to conceive of and implement its strategies. Strengths may include things like a deep pool of managerial talent, surplus capital, a unique reputation and/or brand name, and well-established distribution channels.[13] Sears, for example, has a nationwide network of trained service employees who repair its appliances. Jane Thompson, a Sears executive, conceived

---

resource deployment
How an organization distributes its resources across the areas in which it competes.

business-level strategy
The set of strategic alternatives from which an organization chooses as it conducts business in a particular industry or market

corporate-level strategy
The set of strategic alternatives from which an organization chooses as it manages its operations simultaneously across several industries and several markets

strategy formulation
The set of processes involved in creating or determining the strategies of the organization; it focuses on the content of strategies

strategy implementation
The methods by which strategies are operationalized or executed within the organization; it focuses on the processes through which strategies are achieved

SWOT
An acronym that stands for strengths, weaknesses, opportunities, and threats

organizational strength
A skill or capability that enables an organization to conceive of and implement its strategies

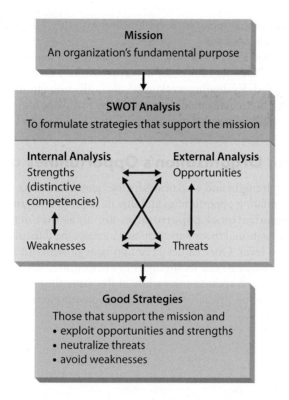

Mission
An organization's fundamental purpose

SWOT Analysis
To formulate strategies that support the mission

Internal Analysis
Strengths
(distinctive
competencies)

Weaknesses

External Analysis
Opportunities

Threats

Good Strategies
Those that support the mission and
• exploit opportunities and strengths
• neutralize threats
• avoid weaknesses

Figure 3.2
SWOT Analysis

SWOT analysis is one of the most important steps in formulating strategy. Using the organization's mission as a context, managers assess internal strengths (distinctive competencies) and weaknesses as well as external opportunities and threats. The goal is then to develop good strategies that exploit opportunities and strengths, neutralize threats, and avoid weaknesses.

of a plan to consolidate repair and home improvement services nationwide under the well-known Sears brand name and to promote them as a general repair operation for all appliances, not just those purchased from Sears. Thus the firm capitalized on existing capabilities and the strength of its name to launch a new operation.

A *distinctive competence*, introduced earlier, is a strength possessed by only a small number of competing firms. Distinctive competencies are rare among a set of competitors. George Lucas's Industrial Light & Magic (ILM), for example, brought the cinematic art of special effects to new heights. Some of ILM's special effects can be produced by no other organization; these rare special effects are thus ILM's distinctive competencies. Indeed, ILM had no real competitor until Peter Jackson formed Weta Digital Effects to help bring *The Lord of the Rings* to the screen. But even so, although ILM and Weta have some of the same competences, each also has proprietary technology that gives it certain unique advantages. Organizations that exploit their distinctive competencies often obtain a *competitive advantage* and attain above-normal economic performance.[14] Indeed, a main purpose of SWOT analysis is to discover an organization's distinctive competencies so that the organization can choose and implement strategies that exploit its unique organizational strengths.

Evaluating an Organization's Weaknesses

Organizational weaknesses are skills and capabilities that do not enable an organization to choose and implement strategies that support its mission. An organization has essentially two ways of addressing weaknesses. First, it may need to make investments to obtain the strengths required to implement strategies that support its mission. Second, it may need

**organizational
weakness**
A skill or capability that does not enable an organization to choose and implement strategies that support its mission

to modify its mission so that it can be accomplished with the skills and capabilities that the organization already possesses.

In practice, organizations have a difficult time focusing on weaknesses, in part because organization members are often reluctant to admit that they do not possess all the skills and capabilities needed. Evaluating weaknesses also calls into question the judgment of managers who chose the organization's mission in the first place and who failed to invest in the skills and capabilities needed to accomplish it.

organizational opportunity
An area in the environment that, if exploited, may generate higher performance

organizational threat
An area that increases the difficulty of an organization performing at a high level

Evaluating an Organization's Opportunities and Threats

Whereas evaluating strengths and weaknesses focuses attention on the internal workings of an organization, evaluating opportunities and threats requires analyzing an organization's environment. **Organizational opportunities** are areas that may generate higher performance. **Organizational threats** are areas that increase the difficulty of an organization performing at a high level. Our "Ethics in Action" box presents an interesting paradox: It shows how a company can use its strengths in environmentally friendly engineering to capitalize on one set of opportunities while at the same time trying to protect future opportunities by fending off threats in the form of pro-environment regulation.

ETHICS IN ACTION

The Hype about Hybrids

In the mid-1990s, Japanese carmakers developed a number of small, innovative, affordable cars, including "hybrids" that run on tandem gas-fueled and electric engines. Toyota's Prius, the world's first mass-produced hybrid vehicle, was introduced in Japan in 1997 and in the United States in 2000. It wasn't much fun to drive, but consumers apparently didn't care: It got better mileage, boasted lower emissions, and retained 57 percent of its value after three years. The second-generation Prius hit the U.S. market in 2003. It was faster and more fashionable and even more fuel efficient and produced even lower emissions. U.S. sales topped 25,000 and then doubled in 2004 and again in 2005. In 2006, *Consumer Reports* ranked the Prius with the Chevy Corvette as the country's "Most Satisfying" cars to own, with even more Prius owners than 'Vette owners saying that they'd buy another one (95 to 93 percent).

In 2007, Prius sales went up a staggering 67 percent and although bound to drop to a more sustainable level actually continued to go up in early 2008, before falling by the end of the year. In fact, after selling more than 90,000 vehicles in the first half of the year, Prius dealers sold fewer than 70,000 in the second half. Why the rollercoaster sales figures? The answer is gasoline prices, which topped $4 per gallon in July but tumbled to an average of $1.62 in December (with second-half figures also reflecting the onset of a global credit crunch that dampened auto sales worldwide).

"At $1.50 a gallon, the American public is not willing to pay for fuel-saving technology," generalizes one U.S. auto executive, who underscores an interesting point about the economics of hybrid cars: While it costs less for fuel to drive a hybrid car, the sticker price reflects the premium that automakers charge for the vehicle's fuel-efficient technology. A comparison of four 2008-model hybrid vehicles and their nonhybrid counterparts revealed an average difference in price—the hybrid premium—of $4,662 and an average improvement in fuel economy of 10 mpg.

Technically, then, you'd be paying a surcharge of $446 per additional mpg for your hybrid vehicle. Obviously, the variables are quite complex, but one reasonable set of calculations estimates that you'd need to drive your hybrid vehicle 15,000 miles a year for ten years before you started to see any savings.

Make no mistake about it, however, you'd be doing a service to the environment. After all, when you burn a gallon of gas, you're emitting 20 pounds of carbon dioxide into the atmosphere, and it shouldn't be surprising that environmental organizations have welcomed the appearance of hybrids and alternative-fuel vehicles that consume less fuel and emit fewer pollutants. The most efficient hybrid vehicles increase fuel economy by 40 to 80 percent, and according to Don MacKenzie, Clean Vehicles Engineer for the Union of Concerned Scientists (UCS), cars such as the Toyota Prius and Toyota Camry hybrid "have the potential to help reduce America's dependence on oil, lessen the impact of . . . high gas prices, and address the automobile's impact on climate change." The UCS, a science-based nonprofit environmental group, also cited Toyota as "the only major automaker to consistently improve global-warming performance since 2001, thanks to hybrids and better conventional technology."

In fall 2007, however, the UCS accused Toyota of "trying to scuttle strong fuel-economy standards" proposed by Congress. What soured the relationship between the environmental group and the environmentally conscious automaker? At issue were the so-called Corporate Average Fuel Economy (CAFE) standards contained in the National Energy and Environmental Security Act of 2007. In its original version, the legislation required U.S. vehicles—including passenger cars, sport-utility vehicles (SUVs), pickups, and vans—to attain an average mpg of 35 by the year 2020. A compromise version of the bill—"a weak, loophole-ridden alternative," according to the UCS—reduced this requirement, calling for an average mpg of 32 to 35 by 2022. The stricter original standards, charged the UCS, would cut 140 percent more oil consumption and 240 percent more global-warming pollution. Toyota, however, had joined with the Big 3 U.S. automakers—GM, Ford, and Chrysler—in lobbying for the passage of the weaker legislation.

Toyota explained its position in a company blog posted by vice president for corporate communications Irv Miller:

Like other major automakers, Toyota is in the business of offering a full lineup of cars and trucks to meet the needs of American motorists. Its success is the result of listening to customers and offering products they want. . . . Like it or not, Americans will continue to want variety, including pickups and SUVs. Nobody forces cars and trucks on consumers. They vote with their wallets.

"Our passenger-car lineup," added Miller, "has the highest CAFE rating in the industry," and the company's critics suggest that its rationale for opposing tougher CAFE standards can be explained by the distinctions that Miller makes among types of vehicles. Toyota sells a lot of passenger cars and a lot of passenger cars with hybrid technology, but history shows that when gas prices get lower, Americans get bigger cars—and not only cars, but SUVs and trucks as well. Since Ford introduced the Escape hybrid in 2004, for example, more hybrid vehicles have been introduced as SUVs than in any other segment. Toyota came out with the Highlander the next year, but its average mpg is a mere 26—a far cry from the 46 mpg offered by the Prius. In 2008, Toyota unveiled its A-BAT hybrid pickup, which, as one might expect, is even less fuel efficient, at 20 mpg.

In short, Toyota needs to grow in the American market for larger vehicles—notably, SUVs and pickups—but it's betting that hybrid technology and fuel economy won't be the critical factors in any success to be had in those markets. As long as hybrids constitute one-quarter of 1 percent of all vehicles on U.S. roads, even a successful effort to bring ratings like those of the Highlander and the A-BAT up to tough fuel-efficiency standards isn't likely to pay off in the kind of growth called for in the company's long-term strategy.

References: Alex Taylor III, "The Birth of the Prius," *Fortune*, March 6, 2006, www.cnnmoney.com on February 16, 2009; Chrissie Thompson, "Hybrid Sales in U.S. Slip 9.9% in 2008," *Automotive News*, January 23, 2009, www.autonews.com on February 16, 2009; Pablo Päster, "Ask Pablo: Should I Buy a Hybrid?" *Triple Pundit*, December 3, 2007, www.triplepundit.com on February 16, 2009; Union of Concerned Scientists, "Hybrid Watchdog: Hybrids' Contribution to Oil Savings," *HybridCenter.org*, 2007, www.hybridcenter.org on February 16, 2009; Irv Miller, "Irv's Sheet: Once More—We at Toyota Want New CAFE Standards!" *Toyota: Open Road Blog*, October 3, 2007, http://blog.toyota.com on February 16, 2009; Union of Concerned Scientists, "Toyota Campaign to Scuttle Stronger Fuel Economy Measures in Energy Bill Undermines Its Green Reputation," press release, October 5, 2007, www.ucsusa.org on February 16, 2009.

FORMULATING BUSINESS-LEVEL STRATEGIES

A number of frameworks have been developed for identifying the major strategic alternatives that organizations should consider when choosing their business-level strategies. Two of the most important ones are Porter's generic strategies and strategies based on the product life cycle.

Porter's Generic Strategies

According to Michael Porter, organizations may pursue a differentiation, overall cost leadership, or focus strategy at the business level.[15] An organization that pursues a **differentiation strategy** seeks to distinguish itself from competitors through the quality (broadly defined) of its products or services. Firms that successfully implement a differentiation strategy are able to charge more than competitors because customers are willing to pay more to obtain the extra value they perceive.[16] Rolex pursues a differentiation strategy. Rolex watches are handmade of precious metals such as gold or platinum and stainless steel, and they are subjected to strenuous tests of quality and reliability. The firm's reputation enables it to charge thousands of dollars for its watches. Coca-Cola and Pepsi compete in the market for bottled water on the basis of differentiation. Coke touts its Dasani brand on the basis of its fresh taste, whereas Pepsi promotes its Aquafina brand on the basis of its purity.[17] Other firms that use differentiation strategies are Lexus, Godiva, Nikon, Mont Blanc, and Ralph Lauren. During the economic meltdown in late 2008, most youth-oriented retailers such as American Eagle Outfitters, Quicksilver, and Aeropostale slashed prices to generate sales. But Abercrombie & Fitch decided to hold firm to standard pricing in an attempt to maintain a differentiated image for its products.[18] Similarly, other firms tried to provide strong differentiation on the basis of outstanding customer service.[19]

An organization implementing an **overall cost leadership strategy** attempts to gain a competitive advantage by reducing its costs below the costs of competing firms. By keeping costs low, the organization is able to sell its products at low prices and still make a profit. Timex uses an overall cost leadership strategy. For decades, this firm has specialized in manufacturing relatively simple, low-cost watches for the mass market. The price of Timex watches, starting around $39.95, is low because of the company's efficient high-volume manufacturing capacity. Poland Springs and Crystal Geyser bottled waters are promoted on the basis of their low cost. Other firms that implement overall cost leadership strategies are Hyundai, BIC, Old Navy, and Hershey. When the economic recession hit in 2008 and 2009, Hershey experienced a jump in sales—during hard times, consumers started cutting back on high-end chocolate products from Godiva but weren't willing to forego chocolate altogether.[20] Likewise, other low-cost producers also benefited as consumers avoided higher-priced brand-name products (that is, those with a differentiation strategy) in favor of lower-priced goods. For instance, both P&G and Colgate saw sales of products such as Tide, Pampers, and Colgate toothpaste decline, whereas sales of lower-priced private-label products jumped.[21]

A firm pursuing a **focus strategy** concentrates on a specific regional market, product line, or group of buyers. This strategy may have either a differentiation focus, whereby the firm differentiates its products in the focus market, or an overall cost leadership focus, whereby the firm manufactures and sells its products at low cost in the focus market. In the watch industry, Tag Heuer follows a focus differentiation strategy by selling only rugged waterproof watches to active consumers. Fiat follows a focus cost leadership strategy by selling its automobiles only in Italy and in selected regions of Europe; Alfa Romeo uses focus differentiation to sell its high-performance cars in these same markets. Fisher-Price uses focus differentiation to

differentiation strategy
A strategy in which an organization seeks to distinguish itself from competitors through the quality of its products or services

overall cost leadership strategy
A strategy in which an organization attempts to gain a competitive advantage by reducing its costs below the costs of competing firms

focus strategy
A strategy in which an organization concentrates on a specific regional market, product line, or group of buyers

sell electronic calculators with large, brightly colored buttons to the parents of preschoolers; stockbroker Edward Jones focuses on small-town settings. General Mills focuses one part of its new-product development on consumers who eat meals while driving—its watchword is "Can we make it 'one-handed'?" so that drivers can safely eat or drink it.

Strategies Based on the Product Life Cycle

The **product life cycle** is a model that shows how sales volume changes over the life of products. Understanding the four stages in the product life cycle helps managers recognize that strategies need to evolve over time. As Figure 3.3 shows, the cycle begins when a new product or technology is first introduced. In this *introduction stage*, demand may be very high and sometimes outpaces the firm's ability to supply the product. At this stage, managers need to focus their efforts on "getting product out the door" without sacrificing quality. Managing growth by hiring new employees and managing inventories and cash flow are also concerns during this stage.

During the *growth stage*, more firms begin producing the product, and sales continue to grow. Important management issues include ensuring quality and delivery and beginning to differentiate an organization's product from competitors' products. Entry into the industry during the growth stage may threaten an organization's competitive advantage; thus strategies to slow the entry of competitors are important.

After a period of growth, products enter a third phase. During this *maturity stage*, overall demand growth for a product begins to slow down, and the number of new firms producing the product begins to decline. The number of established firms producing the product may also begin to decline. This period of maturity is essential if an organization is going to survive in the long run. Product differentiation concerns are still important during this stage, but keeping costs low and beginning the search for new products or services are also important strategic considerations.

product life cycle
A model that portrays how sales volume for products changes over the life of products

$\mathcal{F}igure\ 3.3$ The Product Life Cycle

Managers can use the framework of the product life cycle—introduction, growth, maturity, and decline—to plot strategy. For example, management may decide on a differentiation strategy for a product in the introduction stage and a prospector approach for a product in the growth stage. By understanding this cycle and where a particular product falls within it, managers can develop more effective strategies for extending product life.

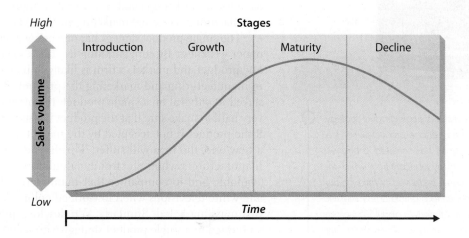

diversification
The number of different businesses that an organization is engaged in and the extent to which these businesses are related to one another

single-product strategy
A strategy in which an organization manufactures just one product or service and sells it in a single geographic market

In the *decline stage*, demand for the product or technology decreases, the number of organizations producing the product drops, and total sales drop. Demand often declines because all those who were interested in purchasing a particular product have already done so. Organizations that fail to anticipate the decline stage in earlier stages of the life cycle may go out of business. Those that differentiate their product, keep their costs low or develop new products or services may do well during this stage.

FORMULATING CORPORATE-LEVEL STRATEGIES

Most large organizations are engaged in several businesses, industries, and markets. Each business or set of businesses within such an organization is frequently referred to as a *strategic business unit* (SBU). An organization such as GE operates hundreds of different businesses, making and selling products as diverse as jet engines, nuclear power plants, and light bulbs. GE organizes these businesses into approximately 20 SBUs. Even organizations that sell only one product may operate in several distinct markets.

Decisions about which businesses, industries, and markets an organization will enter, and how to manage these different businesses, are based on an organization's corporate strategy. The most important strategic issue at the corporate level concerns the extent and nature of organizational diversification. **Diversification** describes the number of different businesses that an organization is engaged in and the extent to which these businesses are related to one another. There are three types of diversification strategies: single-product strategy, related diversification, and unrelated diversification.[22]

Single-Product Strategy

An organization that pursues a **single-product strategy** manufactures just one product or service and sells it in a single geographic market. The WD-40 Company, for example, basically manufactures one product, WD-40 spray lubricant, and for years sold it just in North America. WD-40 has started selling its lubricant in Europe and Asia, but it continues to center all manufacturing, sales, and marketing efforts on one product.

The single-product strategy has one major strength and one major weakness. By concentrating its efforts so completely on one product and market, a firm is likely to be very successful in manufacturing and marketing the product. Because it has staked its survival on a single product, the organization works very hard to make sure that the product is a success. Of course, if the product is not accepted by the market or is replaced by a new one, the firm will suffer. This happened to slide-rule manufacturers when electronic calculators became widely available and to companies that manufactured only black-and-white televisions when low-priced color televisions were first mass-marketed. Similarly, Wrigley long practiced what amounted to a single-product strategy with its line of chewing

SYRACUSE NEWSPAPERS/THE IMAGE WORKS

Some firms pursue a single-product strategy, manufacturing just one product or service. WD-40, for example, has centered its business around the spray lubricant from which the corporate name is derived. While the firm has recently begun to promote a few selected related products, it still derives about 95 percent of its revenue from its well-known lubricant.

gums. But, because younger consumers are buying less gum than earlier generations, Wrigley experienced declining revenues and lower profits. As a result, the Wrigley family eventually sold their business to Mars.[23]

Related Diversification

Given the disadvantage of the single-product strategy, most large businesses today operate in several different businesses, industries, or markets.[24] If the businesses are somehow linked, that organization is implementing a strategy of **related diversification**. Virtually all larger businesses in the United States use related diversification.

Pursuing a strategy of related diversification has three primary advantages. First, it reduces an organization's dependence on any one of its business activities and thus reduces economic risk. Even if one or two of a firm's businesses lose money, the organization as a whole may still survive because the healthy businesses will generate enough cash to support the others.[25] At Disney, a decline in theme park attendance may be offset by an increase in box office and DVD sales of Disney movies.

Second, by managing several businesses at the same time, an organization can reduce the overhead costs associated with managing any one business. In other words, if the normal administrative costs required to operate any business, such as legal services and accounting, can be spread over a large number of businesses, then the overhead costs *per business* will be lower than they would be if each business had to absorb all costs itself. Thus the overhead costs of businesses in a firm that pursues related diversification are usually lower than those of similar businesses that are not part of a larger corporation.[26]

Third, related diversification allows an organization to exploit its strengths and capabilities in more than one business. When organizations do this successfully, they capitalize on synergies, which are complementary effects that exist among their businesses. *Synergy* exists among a set of businesses when the businesses' economic value together is greater than their economic value separately. McDonald's is using synergy as it diversifies into other restaurant and food businesses. For example, its McCafe premium coffee stands in some McDonald's restaurants and investments in Pret A Manger, a European chain of sandwich shops, each allow the firm to create new revenue opportunities while using the firm's existing strengths in food-product purchasing and distribution.

RICHARD WONG/WWW.RWONGPHOTO.COM/ALAMY

For many years Transamerica pursued a strategy of unrelated diversification. Although starting out as a financial services company, at one time Transamerica owned United Artists (a movie distributor), Trans International Airlines, and Budget Rent-a-Car. The Transamerica Pyramid, dominating the skyline of San Francisco, was built to illustrate the firm's power and breadth. In recent years, though, Transamerica has returned to its financial roots, concentrating on insurance, annuities, and retirement services.

Unrelated Diversification

Firms that implement a strategy of **unrelated diversification** operate multiple businesses that are not logically associated with one another. At one time, for example, Quaker Oats owned clothing chains, toy companies, and a restaurant business. Unrelated diversification was a very popular strategy in the 1970s. During this time, several conglomerates such

related diversification
A strategy in which an organization operates in several businesses that are somehow linked with one another

unrelated diversification
A strategy in which an organization operates multiple businesses that are not logically associated with one another

as ITT and Transamerica grew by acquiring literally hundreds of other organizations and then running these numerous businesses as independent entities. Even if there are important potential synergies among their different businesses, organizations implementing a strategy of unrelated diversification do not attempt to exploit them.

In theory, unrelated diversification has two advantages. First, a business that uses this strategy should have stable performance over time. During any given period, if some businesses owned by the organization are in a cycle of decline, others may be in a cycle of growth. Second, unrelated diversification is also thought to have resource allocation advantages. Every year, when a corporation allocates capital, people, and other resources among its various businesses, it must evaluate information about the future of those businesses so that it can place its resources where they have the highest potential for return. Given that it owns the businesses in question and thus has full access to information about the future of those businesses, a firm implementing unrelated diversification should be able to allocate capital to maximize corporate performance.

Despite these presumed advantages, research suggests that unrelated diversification usually does not lead to high performance. First, corporate-level managers in such a company usually do not know enough about the unrelated businesses to provide helpful strategic guidance or to allocate capital appropriately. To make strategic decisions, managers must have complete and subtle understanding of a business and its environment. Because corporate managers often have difficulty fully evaluating the economic importance of investments for all the businesses under their wing, they tend to concentrate only on a business's current performance. This narrow attention at the expense of broader planning eventually hobbles the entire organization.

Second, because organizations that implement unrelated diversification fail to exploit important synergies, they are at a competitive disadvantage compared to organizations that use related diversification. Universal Studios has been at a competitive disadvantage relative to Disney because its theme parks, movie studios, and licensing divisions are less integrated and therefore achieve less synergy.

For these reasons, almost all organizations have abandoned unrelated diversification as a corporate-level strategy. Transamerica sold off numerous businesses and now concentrates on a core set of related businesses and markets. Large corporations that have not concentrated on a core set of businesses have eventually been acquired by other companies and then broken up. Research suggests that these organizations are actually worth more when broken up into smaller pieces than when joined.[27]

Managing Diversification However an organization implements diversification—whether through internal development, vertical integration, or mergers and acquisitions—it must monitor and manage its strategy. **Portfolio management techniques** are methods that diversified organizations use to determine which businesses to engage in and how to manage these businesses to maximize corporate performance. Two important portfolio management techniques are the BCG matrix and the GE Business Screen.

BCG Matrix The **BCG** (Boston Consulting Group) **matrix** provides a framework for evaluating the relative performance of businesses in which a diversified organization operates. It also prescribes the preferred distribution of cash and other resources among these businesses.[28] The BCG matrix uses two factors to evaluate an organization's set of businesses: the growth rate of a particular market and the organization's share of that market. The matrix suggests that fast-growing markets in which an organization has the highest market share are more attractive business opportunities than slow-growing markets in which an organization has small market share. Dividing market growth and market share into two categories (low and high) creates the simple matrix shown in Figure 3.4.

portfolio management techniques
Methods that diversified organizations use to determine which businesses to engage in and how to manage these businesses to maximize corporate performance

BCG matrix
A framework for evaluating businesses relative to the growth rate of their market and the organization's share of the market

CLEAN

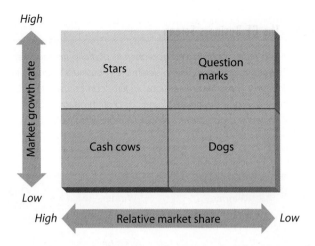

Source: *Perspectives*, No. 66, "The Product Portfolio." Adapted by permission from The Boston Consulting Group, Inc., 1970.

Figure 3.4
The BCG Matrix

The BCG matrix helps managers develop a better understanding of how different strategic business units contribute to the overall organization. By assessing each SBU on the basis of its market growth rate and relative market share, managers can make decisions about whether to commit further financial resources to the SBU or to sell or liquidate it.

The matrix classifies the types of businesses in which a diversified organization can engage as dogs, cash cows, question marks, and stars. *Dogs* are businesses that have a very small share of a market that is not expected to grow. Because these businesses do not hold much economic promise, the BCG matrix suggests that organizations either should not invest in them or should consider selling them as soon as possible. *Cash cows* are businesses that have a large share of a market that is not expected to grow substantially. These businesses characteristically generate high profits that the organization should use to support question marks and stars. (Cash cows are "milked" for cash to support businesses in markets that have greater growth potential.) *Question marks* are businesses that have only a small share of a quickly growing market. The future performance of these businesses is uncertain. A question mark that is able to capture increasing amounts of this growing market may be very profitable. On the other hand, a question mark unable to keep up with market growth is likely to have low profits. The BCG matrix suggests that organizations should invest carefully in question marks. If their performance does not live up to expectations, question marks should be reclassified as dogs and divested. *Stars* are businesses that have the largest share of a rapidly growing market. Cash generated by cash cows should be invested in stars to ensure their preeminent position. For example, BMW bought Rover a few years ago, thinking that its products would help the German automaker reach new consumers. But the company was not able to capitalize on this opportunity, so it ended up selling Rover's car business to a British firm and Land Rover to Ford. Ford couldn't get leverage out of Rover either and ended up selling it (along with Jaguar) to India's Tata Motors.

GE Business Screen Because the BCG matrix is relatively narrow and overly simplistic, GE developed the **GE Business Screen**, a more sophisticated approach to managing diversified business units. The GE Business Screen is a portfolio management technique that can also be represented in the form of a matrix. Rather than focusing solely on market growth and market share, however, the GE Business Screen considers industry attractiveness and competitive position. These two factors are divided into three categories, to make the nine-cell matrix shown in Figure 3.5.[29] These cells, in turn, classify business units as winners, losers, question marks, average businesses, or profit producers.

GE Business Screen
A method of evaluating businesses along two dimensions: (1) industry attractiveness and (2) competitive position; in general, the more attractive the industry and the more competitive the position, the more an organization should invest in a business

Figure 3.5 The GE Business Screen

The GE Business Screen is a more sophisticated approach to portfolio management than the BCG matrix. As shown here, several factors combine to determine a business's competitive position and the attractiveness of its industry. These two dimensions, in turn, can be used to classify businesses as winners, question marks, average businesses, losers, or profit producers. Such a classification enables managers to allocate the organization's resources more effectively across various business opportunities.

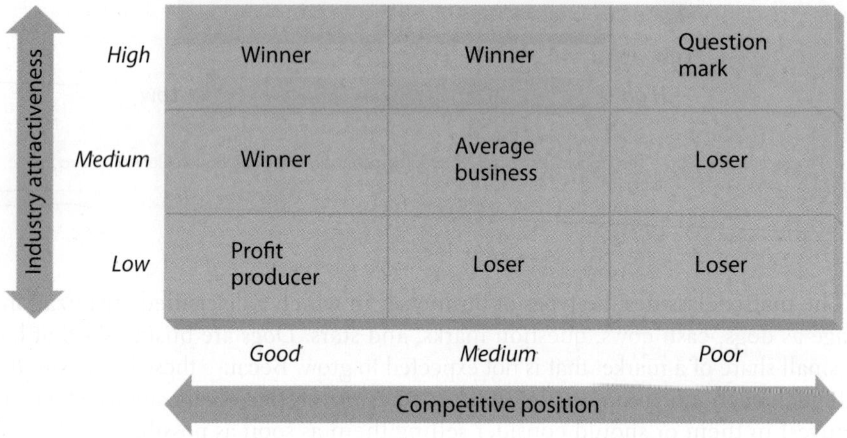

Industry attractiveness	Good	Medium	Poor
High	Winner	Winner	Question mark
Medium	Winner	Average business	Loser
Low	Profit producer	Loser	Loser

Competitive position

Competitive position
1. Market share
2. Technological know-how
3. Product quality
4. Service network
5. Price competitiveness
6. Operating costs

Industry attractiveness
1. Market growth
2. Market size
3. Capital requirements
4. Competitive intensity

Source: From *Strategy Formulation: Analytical Concepts*, 1st edition, by Charles W. Hofer and Dan Schendel. Copyright © 1978. Reprinted with permission of South-Western, a division of Thomson Learning: www.thomsonrights.com.

As Figure 3.5 shows, both market growth and market share appear in a broad list of factors that determine the overall attractiveness of an industry and the overall quality of a firm's competitive position. Other determinants of an industry's attractiveness (in addition to market growth) include market size, capital requirements, and competitive intensity. In general, the greater the market growth, the larger the market, the smaller the capital requirements, and the less the competitive intensity, the more attractive an industry will be. Other determinants of an organization's competitive position in an industry (besides market share) include technological know-how, product quality, service network, price competitiveness, and operating costs. In general, businesses with large market share, technological know-how, high product quality, a quality service network, competitive prices, and low operating costs are in a favorable competitive position.

Think of the GE Business Screen as a way of applying SWOT analysis to the implementation and management of a diversification strategy. The determinants of industry attractiveness are similar to the environmental opportunities and threats in SWOT analysis, and the determinants of competitive position are similar to organizational strengths and weaknesses. By conducting this type of SWOT analysis across several businesses, a diversified organization can decide how to invest its resources to maximize corporate performance. In general, organizations should invest in winners and question marks (where industry attractiveness and competitive position are both favorable), should maintain the market position of average businesses and profit producers (where industry attractiveness and competitive position are average), and should sell losers. For example, Unilever recently assessed its business portfolio using a similar framework and, as a result, decided to sell off several specialty chemical units that were not contributing to the firm's profitability as much as other businesses. The firm then used the revenues from these divestitures and bought more related businesses such as Ben & Jerry's Homemade and Slim-Fast.[30] During the economic recession that started in 2008, many diversified businesses took an especially aggressive approach to selling or closing underperforming businesses. For instance, Japan's Pioneer electronics business sold its television business, Home Depot shut down its Expo home-design stores, and Textron closed a business unit that financed real estate deals.[31]

TACTICAL PLANNING

As we noted earlier, tactical plans are developed to implement specific parts of a strategic plan. You have probably heard the saying about winning the battle but losing the war. **Tactical plans** are to battles what strategy is to a war: an organized sequence of steps designed to execute strategic plans. Strategy focuses on resources, environment, and mission, whereas tactics focus primarily on people and action.[32]

Developing Tactical Plans

Although effective tactical planning depends on many factors, which vary from one situation to another, we can identify some basic guidelines. First, the manager needs to recognize that tactical planning must address a number of tactical goals derived from a broader strategic goal.[33] An occasional situation may call for a stand-alone tactical plan, but most of the time tactical plans flow from and must be consistent with a strategic plan.

For example, top managers at Coca-Cola developed a strategic plan for cementing the firm's dominance of the soft-drink industry. As part of developing the plan, they identified a critical environmental threat—considerable unrest and uncertainty among the independent bottlers that packaged and distributed Coca-Cola's products. To simultaneously counter this threat and strengthen the company's position, Coca-Cola bought several large independent bottlers and combined them into one new organization called "Coca-Cola Enterprises." Selling half of the new company's stock reaped millions in profits while effectively keeping control of the enterprise in Coca-Cola's hands. Thus the creation of the new business was a tactical plan developed to contribute to the achievement of an overarching strategic goal.[34]

Second, although strategies are often stated in general terms, tactics must specify resources and time frames. A strategy can call for being number one in a particular market or industry, but a tactical plan must specify precisely what activities will be undertaken to achieve that goal. Consider the Coca-Cola example again. Another element of its strategic plan involves increased worldwide market share. To facilitate additional sales in Europe, managers developed tactical plans for building a new plant in the south of France to make soft-drink concentrate and for building another canning plant in Dunkirk. The firm

tactical plan
A plan aimed at achieving tactical goals and developed to implement parts of a strategic plan; an organized sequence of steps designed to execute strategic plans

has also invested heavily in India.[35] Building these plants represents a concrete action involving measurable resources (funds to build the plants) and a clear time horizon (a target date for completion).

Finally, tactical planning requires the use of human resources. Managers involved in tactical planning spend a great deal of time working with other people. They must be in a position to receive information from others within and outside the organization, process that information in the most effective way, and then pass it on to others who might make use of it. Coca-Cola executives have been intensively involved in planning the new plants, setting up the new bottling venture noted earlier, and exploring a joint venture with Cadbury Schweppes in the United Kingdom. Each activity has required considerable time and effort from dozens of managers. One manager, for example, crossed the Atlantic 12 times while negotiating the Cadbury deal.

Executing Tactical Plans

Regardless of how well a tactical plan is formulated, its ultimate success depends on the way it is carried out. Successful implementation, in turn, depends on the astute use of resources, effective decision making, and insightful steps to ensure that the right things are done at the right times and in the right ways. A manager can see an absolutely brilliant idea fail because of improper execution.

Proper execution depends on a number of important factors. First, the manager needs to evaluate every possible course of action in light of the goal it is intended to reach. Next, he or she needs to make sure that each decision maker has the information and resources necessary to get the job done. Vertical and horizontal communication and integration of activities must be present to minimize conflict and inconsistent activities. And, finally, the manager must monitor ongoing activities derived from the plan to make sure they are achieving the desired results. This monitoring typically takes place within the context of the organization's ongoing control systems.

OPERATIONAL PLANNING

Another critical element in effective organizational planning is the development and implementation of operational plans. Operational plans are derived from tactical plans and are aimed at achieving operational goals. Thus operational plans tend to be narrowly focused, have relatively short time horizons, and involve lower-level managers. The two most basic forms of operational plans and specific types of each are summarized in Table 3.1.

Organizations develop various operational plans to help achieve operational goals. In general, there are two types of single-use plans and three types of standing plans.

Single-Use Plans

single-use plan
Developed to carry out a course of action that is not likely to be repeated in the future

A **single-use plan** is developed to carry out a course of action that is not likely to be repeated in the future. As Disney planned its newest theme park in Hong Kong, it developed numerous single-use plans for individual rides, attractions, and hotels. The two most common forms of single-use plans are programs and projects.

program
A single-use plan for a large set of activities

Programs A **program** is a single-use plan for a large set of activities. It might consist of identifying procedures for introducing a new product line, opening a new facility, or changing the organization's mission. As part of its own strategic plans for growth, Black & Decker bought

Table 3.1
Types of Operational Plans

Plan	Description
Single-use plan	Developed to carry out a course of action not likely to be repeated in the future
Program	Single-use plan for a large set of activities
Project	Single-use plan of less scope and complexity than a program
Standing plan	Developed for activities that recur regularly over a period of time
Policy	Standing plan specifying the organization's general response to a designated problem or situation
Standard operating procedure	Standing plan outlining steps to be followed in particular circumstances
Rules and regulations	Standing plans describing exactly how specific activities are to be carried out

GE's small-appliance business. The deal involved the largest brand-name switch in history: 150 products were converted from the GE to the Black & Decker label. Each product was carefully studied, redesigned, and reintroduced with an extended warranty. A total of 140 steps were used for each product. It took three years to convert all 150 products to Black & Decker. The total conversion of the product line was a program.

Projects A **project** is similar to a program but is generally of less scope and complexity. A project may be a part of a broader program, or it may be a self-contained single-use plan. For Black & Decker, the conversion of each of the 150 products was a separate project in its own right. Each product had its own manager, its own schedule, and so forth. Projects are also used to introduce a new product within an existing product line or to add a new benefit option to an existing salary package.

Standing Plans

Whereas single-use plans are developed for nonrecurring situations, a **standing plan** is used for activities that recur regularly over a period of time. Standing plans can greatly enhance efficiency by making decision-making routine. Policies, standard operating procedures (SOPs), and rules and regulations are three kinds of standing plans.

Policies As a general guide for action, a **policy** is the most general form of standing plan that specifies the organization's general response to a designated problem or situation. For example, McDonald's has a policy that it will not grant a franchise to an individual who already owns another fast-food restaurant. Similarly, Starbucks has a policy that it will not franchise at all, instead retaining ownership of all Starbucks coffee shops. Likewise, a university admissions office might establish a policy that admission will be granted only to applicants with a minimum SAT score of 1,200 and a ranking in the top quarter of their high school class. Admissions officers may routinely deny admission to applicants

BENJAMIN SKLAR/THE NEW YORK TIMES/REDUX

Rules and regulations are used to govern a variety of activities in organizations. For example, Austin, Texas has one of the toughest and most stringent building codes in the United States. All new buildings are subjected to a detailed energy audit before they can be occupied. John Umphress (right) is inspecting the insulation behind the bathtub of a new home as part of the city's energy audit. Builders who do not follow the city's rules and procedures are subject to fines and their projects may face serious delays.

project
A single-use plan of less scope and complexity than a program

standing plan
Developed for activities that recur regularly over a period of time

policy
A standing plan that specifies the organization's general response to a designated problem or situation

who fail to reach these minimums. A policy is also likely to describe how exceptions are to be handled. The university's policy statement, for example, might create an admissions appeals committee to evaluate applicants who do not meet minimum requirements but may warrant special consideration.

Standard Operating Procedures Another type of standing plan is the SOP. An SOP is more specific than a policy, in that it outlines the steps to be followed in particular circumstances. The admissions clerk at the university, for example, might be told that, when an application is received, he or she should (1) set up an electronic file for the applicant; (2) merge test-score records, transcripts, and letters of reference to the electronic file as they are received; and (3) forward the electronic file to the appropriate admissions director when it is complete. Gallo Vineyards in California has a 300-page manual of SOPs. This planning manual is credited with making Gallo one of the most efficient wine operations in the United States. McDonald's has SOPs explaining exactly how Big Macs are to be cooked, how long they can stay in the warming rack, and so forth.

Rules and Regulations The narrowest of the standing plans, **rules and regulations**, describe exactly how specific activities are to be carried out. Rather than guiding decision making, rules and regulations actually take the place of decision making in various situations. Each McDonald's restaurant has a rule prohibiting customers from using its telephones, for example. The university admissions office might have a rule stipulating that if an applicant's file is not complete two months before the beginning of a semester, the student cannot be admitted until the next semester. Of course, in most organizations a manager at a higher level can suspend or bend the rules. If the high school transcript of the child of a prominent university alumnus and donor arrives a few days late, the director of admissions might waive the two-month rule. Indeed, rules and regulations can become problematic if they are excessive or enforced too rigidly.

Rules and regulations and SOPs are similar in many ways. They are both relatively narrow in scope, and each can serve as a substitute for decision making. An SOP typically describes a sequence of activities, whereas rules and regulations focus on one activity. Recall our examples: The admissions SOP consisted of three activities, whereas the two-month rule related to only one activity. In an industrial setting, the SOP for orienting a new employee could involve enrolling the person in various benefit options, introducing him or her to coworkers and supervisors, and providing a tour of the facilities. A pertinent rule for the new employee might involve when to come to work each day.

Contingency Planning and Crisis Management

Another important type of planning is **contingency planning**, or the determination of alternative courses of action to be taken if an intended plan of action is unexpectedly disrupted or rendered inappropriate.[36] **Crisis management**, a related concept, is the set of procedures the organization uses in the event of a disaster or other unexpected calamity. Some elements of crisis management may be orderly and systematic, whereas others may be more ad hoc and develop as events unfold.

A classic example of widespread contingency planning occurred during the late 1990s in anticipation of what was popularly known as the "Y2K bug." Concerns about the impact of technical glitches in computers stemming from their internal clocks' changing

SOP
A standard plan that outlines the steps to be followed in particular circumstances

rules and regulations
Describe exactly how specific activities are to be carried out

contingency planning
The determination of alternative courses of action to be taken if an intended plan is unexpectedly disrupted or rendered inappropriate

crisis management
The set of procedures the organization uses in the event of a disaster or other unexpected calamity

from 1999 to 2000 resulted in contingency planning for most organizations. Many banks and hospitals, for example, had extra staff available; some organizations created backup computer systems; and some even stockpiled inventory in case they could not purchase new products or materials.[37]

The devastating hurricanes—Katrina and Rita—that hit the Gulf Coast in 2005 dramatically underscored the importance of effective crisis management. For example, inadequate and ineffective responses by the Federal Emergency Management Agency (FEMA) illustrated to many people that organization's weaknesses in coping with crisis situations. On the other hand, some organizations responded much more effectively. Wal-Mart began ramping up its emergency preparedness on the same day when Katrina was upgraded from a tropical depression to a tropical storm. In the days before the storm struck, Wal-Mart stores in the region were supplied with powerful generators and large supplies of dry ice so they could reopen as quickly as possible after the storm had passed. In neighboring states, the firm also had scores of trucks standing by crammed with both emergency-related inventory for its stores and emergency supplies it was prepared to donate—bottled water, medical supplies, and so forth. And Wal-Mart often beat FEMA by several days in getting those supplies delivered.[38]

Seeing the consequences of poor crisis management after the terrorist attacks of September 11, 2001, and the 2005 hurricanes, many firms today are actively working to create new and better crisis management plans and procedures. For example, both Reliant Energy and Duke Energy rely on computer trading centers where trading managers actively buy and sell energy-related commodities. If a terrorist attack or natural disaster such as a hurricane were to strike their trading centers, they would essentially be out of business. Prior to September 11, each firm had relatively vague and superficial crisis plans. But now they and most other companies have much more detailed and comprehensive plans in the event of another crisis. Both Reliant and Duke, for example, have created secondary trading centers at other locations. In the event of a shutdown at their main trading centers, these firms can quickly transfer virtually all their core trading activities to their secondary centers within 30 minutes or less.[39] More recently, many businesses have developed contingency plans for dealing with a potential pandemic such as the H1N1 virus. Unfortunately, however, because it is impossible to forecast the future precisely, no organization can ever be perfectly prepared for all crises.

The mechanics of contingency planning are shown in Figure 3.6. In relation to an organization's other plans, contingency planning comes into play at four action points. At action point 1, management develops the basic plans of the organization. These may include strategic, tactical, and operational plans. As part of this development process, managers usually consider various contingency events. Some management groups even assign someone the role of devil's advocate to ask, "But what if…?" about each course of action. A variety of contingencies is usually considered.

At action point 2, the plan that management chooses is put into effect. The most important contingency events are also defined. Only the events that are likely to occur and whose effects will have a substantial impact on the organization are used in the contingency-planning process. Next, at action point 3, the company specifies certain indicators or signs that suggest that a contingency event is about to take place. A bank might decide that a 2 percent drop in interest rates should be considered a contingency event. An indicator might be two consecutive months with a drop of .5 percent in each. As indicators of contingency events are being defined, the contingency plans themselves should also be developed. Examples of contingency plans

Figure 3.6 **Contingency Planning**

Most organizations develop contingency plans. These plans specify alternative courses of action to be taken if an intended plan is unexpectedly disrupted or rendered inappropriate.

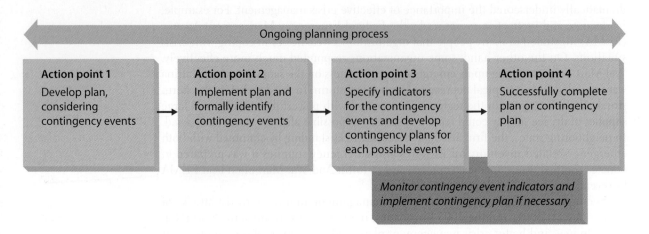

Ongoing planning process

Action point 1
Develop plan, considering contingency events

Action point 2
Implement plan and formally identify contingency events

Action point 3
Specify indicators for the contingency events and develop contingency plans for each possible event

Action point 4
Successfully complete plan or contingency plan

Monitor contingency event indicators and implement contingency plan if necessary

for various situations are delaying plant construction, developing a new manufacturing process, and cutting prices.

After this stage, the managers of the organization monitor the indicators identified at action point 3. If the situation dictates, a contingency plan is implemented. Otherwise, the primary plan of action continues in force. Finally, action point 4 marks the successful completion of either the original or a contingency plan.

Contingency planning is becoming increasingly important for most organizations, especially for those operating in particularly complex or dynamic environments. Few managers have such an accurate view of the future that they can anticipate and plan for everything. Contingency planning is a useful technique for helping managers cope with uncertainty and change. Crisis management, by its very nature, however, is more difficult to anticipate. But organizations that have a strong culture, strong leadership, and a capacity to deal with the unexpected stand a better chance of successfully weathering a crisis than other organizations.[40]

SUMMARY OF LEARNING OBJECTIVES AND KEY POINTS

1. Summarize the planning process and describe organizational goals.

   • The planning process includes understanding the environment, formulating a mission, and creating goals and plans.

   • Goals serve four basic purposes: they provide guidance and direction, facilitate planning,

   inspire motivation and commitment, and promote evaluation and control.

   • With an understanding of the environmental context, managers develop a number of different types of goals and plans, including strategic, tactical, and operational plans.

2. Discuss the components of strategy and types of strategic alternatives.

   - A strategy is a comprehensive plan for accomplishing the organization's goals.

   - Effective strategies address three organizational issues: distinctive competence, scope, and resource deployment.

3. Describe how to use SWOT analysis in formulating strategy.

   - SWOT analysis considers an organization's strengths, weaknesses, opportunities, and threats.

   - Using SWOT analysis, an organization chooses strategies that support its mission, exploit its opportunities and strengths, neutralize its threats, and avoid its weaknesses.

4. Identify and describe various alternative approaches to business-level strategy formulation.

   - A business-level strategy is the plan an organization uses to conduct business in a particular industry or market.

   - Porter suggests that businesses may formulate a differentiation strategy, an overall cost leadership strategy, or a focus strategy.

   - Business-level strategies may also take into account the stages in the product life cycle.

5. Identify and describe various alternative approaches to corporate-level strategy formulation.

   - A corporate-level strategy is the plan an organization uses to manage its operations across several businesses.

   - A firm that does not diversify is implementing a single-product strategy.

   - An organization pursues a strategy of related diversification when it operates a set of businesses that are somehow linked.

   - An organization pursues a strategy of unrelated diversification when it operates a set of businesses that are not logically associated with one another.

   - Organizations manage diversification through the organization structure that they adopt and through portfolio management techniques. The BCG matrix classifies an organization's diversified businesses as dogs, cash cows, question marks, or stars according to market share and market growth rate. The GE Business Screen classifies businesses as winners, losers, question marks, average businesses, or profit producers according to industry attractiveness and competitive position.

6. Discuss how tactical plans are developed and executed.

   - Tactical plans are at the middle of the organization, have an intermediate time horizon, and are moderate in scope.

   - Tactical plans are developed to implement specific parts of a strategic plan.

   - Tactical plans must flow from strategy, specify resource and time issues, and commit human resources.

7. Describe the basic types of operational plans used by organizations.

   - Operational plans are at the lower level of the organization, have a shorter time horizon, and are narrower in scope. They are derived from a tactical plan and are aimed at achieving one or more operational goals.

   - Two major types of operational plans are single-use and standing plans. Single-use plans are designed to carry out a course of action that is not likely to be repeated in the future. Programs and projects are examples of single-use plans. Standing plans are designed to carry out a course of action that is likely to be repeated several times. Policies, SOPs, and rules and regulations are all standing plans.

   - Contingency planning and crisis management are also emerging as very important forms of operational planning.

DISCUSSION QUESTIONS

Questions for Review

1. Describe the nature of organizational goals. Be certain to include both the purposes and the kinds of goals.

2. Identify and describe Porter's generic strategies.

3. What are the basic differences among a single-product strategy, a strategy based on related diversification, and one based on unrelated diversification?

4. What is tactical planning? What is operational planning? What are the similarities and differences between them?

5. What is contingency planning? How is it similar to and different from crisis management?

Questions for Analysis

1. Managers are sometimes criticized for focusing too much attention on the achievement of short-term goals. In your opinion, how much attention should be given to long-term versus short-term goals? In the event of a conflict, which should be given priority? Explain your answers.

2. Which strategy—business or corporate level—should a firm develop first? Describe the relationship between a firm's business- and corporate-level strategies.

3. Volkswagen sold its original Beetle automobile in the United States until the 1970s. The original Beetle was made of inexpensive materials, was built using an efficient mass-production technology, and offered few options. Then, in the 1990s, Volkswagen introduced its new Beetle, which has a distinctive style, provides more optional features, and is priced for upscale buyers. What was Volkswagen's strategy with the original Beetle—product differentiation, low cost, or focus? Which strategy did Volkswagen implement with its new Beetle? Explain your answers.

4. What kind of plan—tactical or operational—should be developed first? Why? Does the order really matter? Why or why not?

5. Cite examples of operational plans that you do or have used or encountered at work, at school, or in your personal life.

BUILDING EFFECTIVE DECISION-MAKING SKILLS

Exercise Overview

Decision-making skills refer to the ability to recognize and define problems and opportunities correctly and then to select an appropriate course of action for solving problems or capitalizing on opportunities. As we noted in this chapter, many organizations use SWOT analysis as part of the strategy-formulation process. This exercise will help you better understand both how managers obtain the information they need to perform such an analysis and how they use it as a framework for making decisions.

Exercise Background

The idea behind SWOT is that a good strategy exploits an organization's opportunities and strengths while neutralizing threats and avoiding or correcting weaknesses.

You've just been hired to run a medium-size company that manufactures electric motors, circuit breakers, and similar electronic components for industrial use. In recent years, the firm's financial performance has gradually eroded, and your job is to turn things around.

At one time, the firm was successful in part because it was able to charge premium prices for top-quality products. In recent years, however, management has tried cutting costs as a means of bringing prices in line with those of new competitors in the market. Unfortunately, the strategy hasn't worked very well, with the effect of cost cutting being primarily a fall off in product quality. Convinced that a new strategy is called for, you've decided to begin with a SWOT analysis.

Exercise Task

Reviewing the situation, you take the following steps:

1. List the sources that you'll use to gather information about the firm's strengths, weaknesses, opportunities, and threats.

2. Then ask yourself: For what types of information are data readily available on the Internet? What categories of data are difficult or impossible to find on the

Internet? (*Note*: When using the Internet, be sure to provide specific websites or URLs.)

3. Next, rate each source that you consult in terms of probable reliability.

4. Finally, ask yourself how confident you would be in basing decisions on the information that you've obtained.

BUILDING EFFECTIVE COMMUNICATION AND INTERPERSONAL SKILLS

Exercise Overview

Interpersonal skills refer to the manager's ability to communicate with, understand, and motivate individuals and groups. Communication skills are used both to convey information to others effectively and to receive ideas and information effectively from others. Communicating and interacting effectively with many different types of individuals are essential skills for planning. This exercise allows you to think through issues of communication and interaction as they relate to an actual planning situation.

Exercise Background

Larger and more complex organizations require greater complexity of planning to achieve their goals. NASA is responsible for the very complex task of managing U.S. space exploration and therefore has very complex planning needs.

In April 1970, NASA launched the Apollo 13 manned space mission, charged with exploration of the lunar surface. On its way to the moon, the ship developed a malfunction that could have resulted in the death of all the crew members. The crew members worked with scientists in Houston to develop a solution to the problem. The capsule was successful in returning to Earth, and no lives were lost.

Exercise Task

1. Watch and listen to the short clip from *Apollo 13*. (This movie was made by Universal Studios in 1995 and was directed by Ron Howard. The script was based on a memoir by astronaut and mission captain Jim Lovell.) Describe the various types of planning and decision-making activities taking place at NASA during the unfolding of the disaster.

2. The biggest obstacles to effective planning in the first few minutes of this crisis were the rapid and unexpected changes occurring in a dynamic and complex environment. List elements of the situation that contributed to dynamism (elements that were rapidly changing). List elements that

contributed to complexity. What kinds of actions did NASA's planning staff take to overcome obstacles presented by the dynamic and complex environment? Suggest any other useful actions the staff could have taken.

3. NASA managers and astronauts did not use a formal planning process in their approach to this situation. Why not? Is there any part of the formal planning process that could have been helpful? What does this example suggest to you about the advantages and limitations of the formal planning process?

SKILLS SELF-ASSESSMENT INSTRUMENT

Self-Assessment
Your Work Life Strengths and Weaknesses

Introduction: The SWOT analysis helps organizations identify their internal capabilities and limitations, as well as significant events and trends from the external environment. The SWOT technique can also be useful in understanding your own personal strengths and weaknesses. The following assessment will help you better understand the SWOT analysis process as well as identify areas for improvement in your readiness for a current or future career.

Instructions: Create two lists, one of your strengths and one of your weaknesses. Judge items as strengths and weaknesses by thinking of them in relation to your current or anticipated future career. For example, creativity may be more valued in a career in marketing, whereas empathy might be more valued in human resource management. If you are having trouble thinking of items or deciding how to classify them, speak to a friend, fellow student, or someone who knows you well. Their insights can be useful.

List the following as strengths:

- Work experience in a similar or related field.

- Formal and informal education. This should include degrees earned or expected, as well as noncredit courses and other types of training.

- Technical skills or knowledge related to your career. This could include, for example, an IT worker's command of programming languages or an accountant's knowledge of audit procedures.

- Generalized skills. Skills that are valued in just about any job would include leadership, teamwork, and communication. Refer to the list of fundamental management skills in Chapter 1 for more ideas.

- Personal characteristics. Again, most careers call for positive personal characteristics such as initiative, creativity, confidence, optimism, self-discipline, energy, and ability to handle stress.

- Job-seeking skills. The ability to present a professional appearance, to network, to mentor others or be mentored, among others, are job-seeking skills that could be an asset in your career.

List the following as weaknesses:

- Lack of any of the aforementioned; for example, no work experience or no degree.

- Areas that are weak or undesirable relative to other job-seekers, such as low GPA or unrelated major, weak skills, little technical knowledge, or negative personal characteristics, that is, poor self-control or an inability to handle criticism.

EXPERIENTIAL EXERCISE

The SWOT Analysis

Purpose: The SWOT analysis provides the manager with a cognitive model of the organization and its environmental forces. By developing the ability to conduct such an analysis, the manager builds both process knowledge and a conceptual skill. This skill-builder focuses on the *administrative management model*. It will help you develop the *coordinator role* of the administrative management model. One of the skills of the coordinator is the ability to plan.

Introduction: This exercise helps you understand the complex interrelationships between environmental

opportunities and threats and organizational strengths and weaknesses. Strategy formulation is facilitated by a SWOT analysis. First, the organization should study its internal operations to identify its strengths and weaknesses. Next, the organization should scan the environment to identify existing and future opportunities and threats. Then, the organization should identify the relationships that exist among these strengths, weaknesses, opportunities, and threats. Finally, major business strategies usually result from matching an organization's strengths with appropriate opportunities or from matching the threats it faces with weaknesses that have been identified.

Instructions: First, read the short narrative of the Trek Bicycle Corporation's external and internal environments, found next.

Second, divide into small group and conduct a SWOT analysis for Trek, based on the short narrative. You may also use your general knowledge and any information you have about Trek or the bicycle manufacturing industry. Then prepare a group response to the discussion questions.

Third, as a class, discuss both the SWOT analysis and the groups' responses to the discussion questions.

Trek's External and Internal Environments

Today in the United States, inflation, cost of materials, and unemployment are fairly low and are not increasing. Emerging economies are growing more rapidly than the U.S. economy in general. Foreign trade is relatively open, so manufacturers face intense international and local competition, with pressure to keep prices low, and also to have the opportunity to utilize low-cost labor and raw materials from around the world. New manufacturing technologies, futuristic materials, and e-commerce are becoming more prevalent and affordable. The political–legal climate is favorable to business in the United States and most developing nations, whereas regulation is higher in the European Union. The standard of living is stable, the population is aging, and ethnic diversity is increasing.

Today in the bicycle manufacturing industry, manufacturers must invest very heavily in research and development (R&D) to compete effectively on a global scale. Domestically, the bicycle manufacturing industry is fragmented, with the largest firm, Trek, controlling just 24 percent of sales. The industry's customers are primarily local, independent bike retailers, a very fragmented group. The Internet, and eBay in particular, provides alternate channels for new and used bike sales.

Discussion Questions:

1. What was the most difficult part of the SWOT analysis?

2. Why do most firms not develop major strategies for matches between threats and strengths?

3. Under what conditions might a firm develop a major strategy around a match between an opportunity and a weakness?

Bike riders, the ultimate purchasers, are interested in style, comfort, and high-tech features, as well as environmental and health issues. Suppliers of many bike components are small, local manufacturers located in developing countries. However, a few suppliers are more powerful, such as Shimano, an internationally known maker of bicycle components and cycling gear. Regulators are not a significant force for bicycle manufacturers, but Trek and others have numerous joint ventures. In one example, Trek teamed with AMD, Nike, and other companies to produce the high-performance cycle used by Lance Armstrong in the Tour de France and other races.

Trek has excellent R&D capability and effectively utilizes low-cost manufacturers in producing the more affordable products in its broad line of bikes. However, its Wisconsin factory produces its high-end lines and can customize a bike to a customer's exact specifications. Trek is beginning to push to improve the customer bike-buying experience. The company will limit the number of retailers it uses and requires retailers to stock a higher percentage of Trek products. In return, it will provide training and funds to improve in-store marketing and increase customer loyalty.

Recent Developments in Games Theory

1. How might a SWOT analysis have helped EA assess its slippage in the videogame market?

2. How might Porter's generic strategies theory help to explain why Activision gained a competitive edge in the videogame market?

3. How would you use the product life cycle to advise Activision on the best way to maintain its leadership in the videogame market?

4. If you ran a small videogame start-up, what would be your strategy for competing with EA and Activision?

5. If you're a videogame player, what aspects of EA's strategy have led to your playing more (or fewer) EA games? How about Activision games? If you're not a videogame player, what aspects of each company's strategy might induce you to try a few of its games?

CHAPTER 4

MANAGING DECISION MAKING AND PROBLEM SOLVING

LEARNING OBJECTIVES

After studying this chapter, you should be able to:

1 Define decision making and discuss types of decisions and decision-making conditions.

2 Discuss rational perspectives on decision making, including the steps involved.

3 Describe the behavioral aspects of decision making.

4 Discuss group and team decision making, including its advantages and disadvantages and how it can be more effectively managed.

FIRST THINGS FIRST

Citi ODs on CDOs

Between November 2006 and November 2008, the market value of Citigroup, the largest financial institution in the United States, fell from $244 billion to slightly more than $20 billion.

> **"[Risk management] has to be independent, and it wasn't independent at Citigroup."**
>
> —FORMER CITIGROUP EXECUTIVE

assets—into bundles for resale to investors. One class of these fixed-income assets is mortgages. A financial institution like Citi might buy mortgages from original lenders (mostly small banks and nonbank lenders), pool the projected revenue (payments to be made in the future by the original home buyers), and sell securities backed by the pooled

Needless to say, the reasons behind such a monumental collapse are extremely complex, but to see what happened, we'll focus on just a few factors—in particular, bad decision making, miscalculated strategy initiatives, and mismanaged tactical policies.

Let's begin with a little background. When Charles O. Prince III took over as Citigroup CEO in October 2003, he inherited a financial-services conglomerate that had been built by acquisition and merger. For a few years, the megabank model worked quite well, with Citi (as the company is collectively known) ringing up handsome profits from an array of services ranging from credit cards to investment advice and asset trading. Unfortunately, says one banking analyst, Citi was also "a gobbledygook of companies that were never integrated. . . . The businesses didn't communicate with each other." In fact, the Citi culture encouraged managers to focus on their own quarterly earnings and revenue targets, and managerial success was measured by short-term earnings and multimillion-dollar bonuses.

To his credit, Prince set out to change this situation. He jettisoned the strategy of growth by acquisition and announced a new strategy based on internal growth. He sold off some of the business units that the bank had accumulated over the years and bolstered consumer-banking operations. He also targeted the bank's trading operations as a source of increased earnings, and this is the point at which our plot starts to thicken. One of the specialties of traders in the financial industry is creating *collateralized debt obligations* or (CDOs): securities that pool various forms or classes of debt—or fixed-income

© TURIKO NAKAO/REUTERS/CORBIS

When Charles Prince was handed the reins of Citi, one of the world's largest financial services businesses, the firm was considered to be a financially sound and well-managed enterprise. A series of poor decisions, though, brought Citi to the brink of bankruptcy and led to Prince's resignation.

revenue. In return for the promise to redeem the securities at interest, the bank that issues them takes fees of up to 2.5 percent of the amount of the securities sold.

In the heady days of the housing boom, there was a lot of money to be made in CDOs, and between 2003 and 2005, Citi tripled the volume of CDOs that it issued—from $6.28 billion to more than $20 billion. In 2005, its trading operations generated $500 million in fees, and in that year, Prince made a concerted effort to produce even more revenue from the group responsible for trading high-growth fixed-income assets through CDOs and similar instruments. He bulked up the unit, recruited key personnel from competitors, and doubled and tripled bonuses for traders. Randall H. Barker, who oversaw the buildup in the department, received $20 million a year in compensation, and Thomas G. Maheras, who headed it, took home $30 million.

Now, CDOs may be profitable, but they can also be tricky. Mortgages became a popular component of CDOs because of the housing boom that lasted from the mid-1990s to mid-2006, but CDOs typically contain several different classes of fixed-income assets—from mortgages and credit-card loans to junk bonds to aircraft leases and movie revenues. Because the risk entailed by each class of assets may depend on very different factors, overall risk can be quite difficult to determine.

Charles Prince was aware of the risks entailed by investment in fixed-asset securities, but as one former Citigroup executive puts it, "he didn't know a CDO from a grocery list." Like any responsible manager, he thus sought advice, turning to Robert E. Rubin, a onetime Wall Street executive and Secretary of the Treasury in the Clinton administration, who had chaired Citi's executive committee for years. As Treasury secretary, Rubin had helped relax federal oversight of exotic financial instruments such as CDOs, and according to the same former executive, he "had always been an advocate of being more aggressive in the [trading] arena. He would say, 'You have to take more risk if you want to earn more.'" At the time, the housing market was going strong, and as traders invented newer and more profitable types of fixed-asset securities, the CDO market was still expanding. So Prince and Rubin endorsed a strategy that called for taking greater risks in the interest of expanding business and generating higher profits.

In retrospect, analysts believe that, at least in part, Citi's decision to become the biggest player in the CDO market reflected uncritical—even naïve—confidence in the standard risk assessments offered by credit-rating agencies. Like bonds and many other debt instruments, CDOs are issued with grade ratings—independent measurements of relative credit risk. Typically, ratings from agencies such as Moody's and Standard & Poor's (S&P) assess the possibility that the debt entailed by an instrument will not be honored and indicate the probability that a financial loss will be suffered if it's not. S&P, for example, uses a scale of AAA to D, with AAA denoting the most stable and reliable debt issuer and D the issuer most likely to default. CDOs are divided into three classes or "tranches" according to default risk: senior (rated AAA), mezzanine (AA to BB), and junior (unrated). Because they carry the highest risk of default, junior tranches also carry the highest interest rates.

A study released in mid-2008 by the Securities and Exchange Commission was highly critical of the policies and practices by which major agencies determined ratings for CDOs between 2002 and 2007. In particular, rating agencies tended to give their blessings to CDOs despite the fact that they consisted of extremely risky assets, such as junk bonds and subprime mortgages. The problem was particularly troublesome because rating agencies often worked with banks and other financial firms to divide CDOs into the most profitable tranches. "It's important to understand," says one consultant who has worked with Citigroup, Bank of America, and other major banks, "that in the [CDO] market, the rating agencies run the show. This is not a passive process. . . . This is a financial-engineering business."

Flash forward to mid-2007. Housing prices had started to drop in 2006 and refinancing had become more difficult. Initial terms on adjustable-rate mortgages (ARMs) were expiring, higher interest rates were taking effect, and now 16 percent of all subprime ARMs were delinquent or in foreclosure proceedings. In September, when Charles Prince met with Citigroup executives in the library next to his office, he learned that the bank was sitting on $43 billion in mortgage-related assets. As he had for months, Thomas Maheras, head of the trading unit, assured Prince that the bank was not facing big losses. To be on the safe side, Prince dispatched a risk management team to take a closer look at Citi's mortgage-related holdings. What they discovered was that it was too late to be on the safe side. Four months later, Citi announced a fourth-quarter loss of nearly $10 billion.

By the beginning of 2009, losses would total $65 billion—more than half of which stemmed from the mortgage-related securities for which Maheras had vouched back in September 2007. To say the least, Citi—indeed, the banking industry as a whole—had misjudged the risk that it had been taking in the CDO market. Why were CDOs so much riskier than most investment managers thought? Because so many of the mortgages that backed them were much riskier than they cared to believe.

What's more, as we've already seen, credit-rating agencies were no better than banks in assessing the risks entailed by CDOs backed by more than $1 trillion in subprime and other higher-rate loans. In the aftermath of the so-called subprime meltdown, regulators have criticized Citi and other banks for relying too heavily on rating agencies. Says John C. Dugan, head of the Office of the Comptroller of the Currency, the government's main bank regulator, "There's really no excuse for institutions that specialize in credit risk assessment, like commercial banks, to rely solely on credit ratings in assessing credit risk."

At Citi, the problem was further exacerbated by a breakdown in internal risk management practices. Normally, risk managers carefully monitor the activities of managers in lending and trading units to guard against excessive risk taking. Clearly, Thomas Maheras's trading unit had taken huge risks in saddling

the bank with $43 billion in mortgage-related assets, but as we've seen, when CEO Charles Prince wanted to know if those risks were excessive, he asked Maheras. Maheras, whose unit was generating immense profits (and hefty bonuses) from CDO trading, said no.

Apparently, Prince was no better served by David C. Bushnell, his senior risk officer and the manager responsible for putting the brakes on potentially dangerous trading activities. Maheras and Bushnell were longtime friends, having climbed the Citi corporate ladder together, and some insiders at the bank report that the boundaries between their two units weren't as rigorous as they should have been. Risk management, says one, "has to be independent, and it wasn't independent at Citigroup, at least when it came to [trading]." In fact, at one point, risk managers responsible for overseeing trading activities reported to Maheras as well as Bushnell, thus giving the trading unit leverage over the very same managers who were supposed to be keeping an eye on the activities of traders.

Maheras and Bushnell were eventually fired, Prince resigned, and Citigroup received $45 billion in cash infusions from the federal government. The bank has a new CEO, who has announced plans to divide it into two separate parts, and a new chief risk officer, who has promised to see that Citi "takes the lessons learned from recent events and makes critical enhancements to its risk-management framework. A change in culture," he adds, "is required at Citi."[1]

Making effective decisions, as well as recognizing when a bad decision has been made and quickly responding to mistakes, is a key ingredient in organizational effectiveness. Indeed, some experts believe that decision making is the most basic and fundamental of all managerial activities.[2] Thus we discuss it here, in the context of the first management function, planning. Keep in mind, however, that although decision making is perhaps most closely linked to the planning function, it is also part of organizing, controlling, and leading.

We begin our discussion by exploring the nature of decision making. We then describe rational perspectives on decision making. Behavioral aspects of decision making are then introduced and described. We conclude with a discussion of group and team decision making.

THE NATURE OF DECISION MAKING

In late 2009, managers at Disney made the decision to buy Marvel Comics for $4.3 billion.[3] At about the same time, the general manager of the Ford dealership in Bryan, Texas, made a decision to sponsor a local youth soccer team for $200. Each of these examples reflects a decision, but the decisions differ in many ways. Thus, as a starting point in understanding decision making, we must first explore the meaning of decision making as well as types of decisions and conditions under which decisions are made.[4]

Decision Making Defined

Decision making can refer to either a specific act or a general process. **Decision making** is the act of choosing one alternative from among a set of alternatives. The decision-making process, however, is much more than this. One step of the process, for example, is that the person making the decision must both recognize that a decision is necessary and identify the set of feasible alternatives before selecting one. Hence, the **decision-making process** includes recognizing and defining the nature of a decision situation, identifying alternatives, choosing the "best" alternative, and putting it into practice.[5]

The word *best*, of course, implies effectiveness. Effective decision making requires that the decision maker understands the situation driving the decision. Most people would consider an effective decision to be one that optimizes some set of factors, such as profits, sales, employee welfare, and market share. In some situations, though, an effective decision may be one that minimizes loss, expense, or employee turnover. It may even mean selecting the best method for going out of business, laying off employees, or terminating a strategic alliance.

We should also note that managers make decisions about both problems and opportunities. For example, making decisions about how to cut costs by 10 percent reflects a problem—an undesirable situation that requires a solution. But decisions are also necessary in situations of opportunity. Learning that the firm is earning higher-than-projected profits, for example, requires a subsequent decision. Should the extra funds be used to increase shareholder dividends, reinvest in current operations, or expand into new markets?

Of course, it may take a long time before a manager can know if the right decision was made. For example, in late 2008 and early 2009 government leaders made the decision to invest billions of dollars in failing financial institutions and other businesses. It will be years—or perhaps decades—before economists and other experts will know if those were sound decisions or if the United States would have been better off by allowing those businesses to fail.

Types of Decisions

Managers must make many different types of decisions. In general, however, most decisions fall into one of two categories: programmed and nonprogrammed.[6] **Programmed decisions** are relatively structured or recur with some frequency (or both). Starbucks uses programmed decisions to purchase new supplies of coffee beans, cups, and napkins, and its employees are trained in exact procedures for brewing coffee. Likewise, the Bryan Ford dealer made a decision that he will sponsor a youth soccer team each year. Thus, when the soccer club president calls, the dealer already knows what he will do. Many decisions regarding basic operating systems and procedures and standard organizational transactions are of this variety and can therefore be programmed.[7]

Nonprogrammed decisions, on the other hand, are relatively unstructured and occur much less often than programmed decisions. Disney's decision to buy Marvel was a nonprogrammed decision. Managers faced with such decisions must treat each one as unique, investing enormous amounts of time, energy, and resources into exploring the situation from all perspectives. Intuition and experience are major factors in nonprogrammed decisions. Most of the decisions made by top managers involving strategy (including mergers, acquisitions, and takeovers) and organization design are nonprogrammed. So are decisions about new facilities, new products, labor contracts, and legal issues.

decision making
The act of choosing one alternative from among a set of alternatives

decision-making process
Recognizing and defining the nature of a decision situation, identifying alternatives, choosing the best alternative, and putting it into practice

programmed decision
A decision that is relatively structured or recurs with some frequency (or both)

nonprogrammed decision
A decision that is relatively unstructured and occurs much less often than a programmed decision

Decision-Making Conditions

Just as there are different kinds of decisions, there are also different conditions under which decisions are made. Managers sometimes have an almost perfect understanding of conditions surrounding a decision, but at other times they have few clues about those conditions. In general, as shown in Figure 4.1, the circumstances that exist for the decision maker are conditions of certainty, risk, or uncertainty.[8]

Decision Making under Certainty When the decision maker knows with reasonable certainty what the alternatives are and what conditions are associated with each alternative, a **state of certainty** exists. Suppose, for example, that managers at Singapore Airlines make a decision to buy five new jumbo jets. Their next decision would be from whom to buy them. Because there are only two companies in the world that make jumbo jets, Boeing and Airbus, Singapore Airlines knows its options exactly. Each has proven products and will guarantee prices and delivery dates. The airline thus knows the alternative conditions associated with each. There is little ambiguity and relatively little chance of making a bad decision.

Few organizational decisions, however, are made under conditions of true certainty. The complexity and turbulence of the contemporary business world make such situations rare. Even the airplane purchase decision we just considered has less certainty than it appears. The aircraft companies may not be able to really guarantee delivery dates, so they may write cost increase or inflation clauses into contracts. Thus the airline may be only partially certain of the conditions surrounding each alternative.

Decision Making under Risk A more common decision-making condition is a state of risk. Under a **state of risk**, the availability of each alternative and its potential payoffs and costs are all associated with probability estimates.[9] Suppose, for example, that a labor contract negotiator for a company receives a "final" offer from the union right before a strike deadline. The negotiator will have two alternatives: to accept or to

Figure 4.1   Decision-Making Conditions

Most major decisions in organizations today are made under a state of uncertainty. Managers making decisions in these circumstances must be sure to learn as much as possible about the situation and approach the decision from a logical and rational perspective.

state of certainty
A condition in which the decision maker knows with reasonable certainty what the alternatives are and what conditions are associated with each alternative

state of risk
A condition in which the availability of each alternative and its potential payoffs and costs are all associated with probability estimates

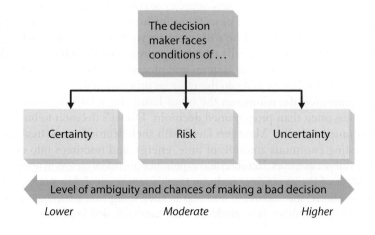

reject the offer. The risk centers on whether the union representatives are bluffing. If the company negotiator accepts the offer, she avoids a strike but commits to a relatively costly labor contract. If she rejects the contract, she may get a more favorable contract if the union is bluffing, but she may provoke a strike if it is not.

On the basis of past experiences, relevant information, the advice of others, and her own judgment, she may conclude that there is about a 75 percent chance that union representatives are bluffing and about a 25 percent chance that they will back up their threats. Thus she can base a calculated decision on the two alternatives (accept or reject the contract demands) and the probable consequences of each. When making decisions under a state of risk, managers must reasonably estimate the probabilities associated with each alternative. For example, if the union negotiators are committed to a strike if their demands are not met, and the company negotiator rejects their demands because she guesses they will not strike, her miscalculation will prove costly.

As indicated in Figure 4.1, decision making under conditions of risk is accompanied by moderate ambiguity and chances of a bad decision. For instance, like many other automobile companies, Ford laid off thousands of workers during 2008. But toward the

state of uncertainty
A condition in which the decision maker does not know all the alternatives, the risks associated with each, or the likely consequences each alternative

end of the year, Ford executives noted that as fuel prices were dropping, demand for its new F-150 pickup was increasing. So, the firm rehired 1,000 of its former workers to help build more pickups. The risk was that if gas prices had surged unexpectedly and/or demand for the F-150 had cooled, Ford would have been in the embarrassing position of having recalled workers and then once again terminating them. But the upside was that Ford's assessment that it would generate new revenues and more profits was correct.[10] Likewise, executives at Porsche have made several recent decisions under conditions of risk, starting with the question of whether it should join most of the world's other automakers and build sport-utility vehicles (SUVs) (and potentially earn higher revenues) or maintain its focus on high-performance sports cars. Although the additional revenue is almost certain, the true risk in the firm's ultimate decision to build its Cayenne SUV is that the brand may lose some of its cachet among its existing customers. And now the firm is facing additional risky decisions regarding potential new products, including a four-door coupe, a smaller SUV, and even a minivan.[11] The "Ethics in Action" box shows how one manager at a major pharmaceutical company turned the willingness to make riskier decisions into a key factor in the company's ability to develop new products more efficiently and (for the most part) more effectively.

Decision Making under Uncertainty Most of the major decision making in contemporary organizations is done under a **state of uncertainty**, where the decision maker does not know all the

AP PHOTO/TED S. WARREN

Most negotiations between management and labor unions are carried out under a condition of risk. Each side, for instance, has information about what it will and will not accept as part of a labor contract, but can only assign probabilities to what the other side might or might not agree to. The negotiation taking place here was between executives at Boeing and representatives of the 22,000-member Society of Professional Engineering Employees in Aerospace.

ETHICS IN ACTION

Prescribing Doses of R&D

More than companies in most industries, pharmaceutical firms have to deal with a basic paradox in the product development process. On the one hand, they have to ensure that products work—which in the pharmaceuticals business means that they've been thoroughly tested and proven both effective and safe. On the other hand, they also have to take certain risks. If they don't, the new-product pipeline dries up—an especially important consideration in an industry in which profitability depends on patents that eventually expire.

Robert Ruffolo took over as executive vice president for R&D operations at Wyeth, a major U.S. supplier of pharmaceuticals and over-the-counter healthcare products, in 2002. Charged by CEO Robert Essner to "rattle the cage," he was determined to spark innovation, but to set controls on the entire new-product process, he first announced a review of every product currently in development. Ruffolo was surprised to find that his plan didn't meet with the wholehearted approval of his staff of 70 research scientists, some of whom expressed concern that it would actually stifle personal productivity. In fact, recalls researcher Steven Projan, "there was a lot of fear and loathing about going through that [review] process."

Why the unexpected resistance? Ruffolo discovered why when he sat down to assess probable outcomes on a project-by-project basis. During the course of his review, he ran across a curious phenomenon: Projects that appeared to be failing—and were least likely to pay off—often received an inordinate share of available resources. Ruffolo quickly came to the conclusion that Wyeth scientists were willing to reroute resources from more promising projects to those which, for a variety of reasons, they wanted to rescue despite low probabilities of success. "Everybody was convinced," confirms Projan, "that [the review] was a tool to kill off their favorite project."

Ruffolo instituted a policy of annual reviews aimed at evaluating projects according to factors such as development costs, likelihood of success, and expected sales. He also set firm targets for how many products should move forward at each stage of the new-product development process, which in the pharmaceutical industry is usually measured in testing stages. The tactic immediately began to bear results. When Ruffolo first got to Wyeth, for example, the so-called "discovery" team—which creates compounds to be passed along to other groups for further development—was turning out a mere four drugs per year. Ruffolo set a new target of 12, which had to be met with no increase in personnel or resources. The group met the new target in every year between 2001 and 2006, when it was bumped to 15.

Not everybody, however, agrees that such targets are a good idea in the pharmaceuticals industry. Quotas, argues one former Wyeth researcher, can seduce researchers into "overlooking problems" to make their numbers. By 2006, Wyeth had in fact begun experiencing problems with increased failure rates during human testing and clinical trials, and the problem became more serious in 2007, when the U.S. Food and Drug Administration withheld approval of three major drugs that Wyeth deemed crucial to its plans for future growth. It's unreasonable, however, to lay such setbacks at the feet of Robert Ruffolo, who points out that the decision to advance products from development to testing stages is made at Wyeth by a council consisting of scientists, regulatory experts, and marketing executives, not by researchers laboring under quota requirements. In recent years, moreover, the entire drug industry has not only encountered increasing difficulties in developing new products, but has been forced to operate in an increasingly risk-averse regulatory environment.

Robert Ruffolo stepped down in 2008, and in January 2009, Wyeth announced that it would be purchased for $68 billion by Pfizer, the world's largest research-based pharmaceuticals firm.

References: Amy Barrett, "Cracking the Whip at Wyeth," *BusinessWeek*, February 6, 2006, www.businessweek.com on February 20, 2009; Matthew Herper, "Wyeth's Worries," Forbes, August 13, 2007, www.forbes.com on February 20, 2009; Ed Silverman, "Wyeth's R&D Chief Bob Ruffolo Retires," *Pharmalot.com*, April 30, 2008, www.pharmalot.com on February 20, 2009; Henry I. Miller, "Pfizer Weds Wyeth," Forbes, January 27, 2009, www.forbes.com on February 20, 2009.

alternatives, the risks associated with each, or the likely consequences of each alternative. This uncertainty stems from the complexity and dynamism of contemporary organizations and their environments. The emergence of the Internet as a significant force in today's competitive environment has served to increase both revenue potential and uncertainty for most managers.

To make effective decisions in these circumstances, managers must acquire as much relevant information as possible and approach the situation from a logical and rational perspective. Intuition, judgment, and experience always play major roles in the decision-making process under conditions of uncertainty. Even so, uncertainty is the most ambiguous condition for managers and the one most prone to error.[12] Indeed, many of the problems associated with the downfall of Arthur Andersen resulted from the firm's apparent difficulties in responding to ambiguous and uncertain decision parameters regarding the firm's moral, ethical, and legal responsibilities.[13]

RATIONAL PERSPECTIVES ON DECISION MAKING

Most managers like to think of themselves as rational decision makers. And, indeed, many experts argue that managers should try to be as rational as possible in making decisions.[14] This section highlights the fundamental and rational perspectives on decision making.

The Classical Model of Decision Making

The **classical decision model** is a prescriptive approach that tells managers how they should make decisions. It rests on the assumptions that managers are logical and rational and that they make decisions that are in the best interests of the organization. Figure 4.2 shows how the classical model views the decision-making process.

1. Decision makers have complete information about the decision situation and possible alternatives.
2. They can effectively eliminate uncertainty to achieve a decision condition of certainty.
3. They evaluate all aspects of the decision situation logically and rationally.

As we see later, these conditions rarely, if ever, actually exist.

classical decision model
A prescriptive approach to decision making that tells managers how they should make decisions; assumes that managers are logical and rational and that their decisions will be in the best interests of the organization

Figure 4.2   **The Classical Model of Decision Making**

The classical model of decision making assumes that managers are rational and logical. It attempts to prescribe how managers should approach decision situations.

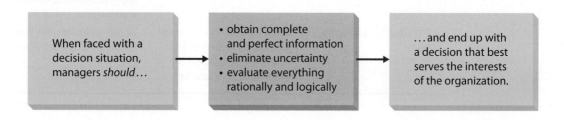

When faced with a decision situation, managers *should*...

- obtain complete and perfect information
- eliminate uncertainty
- evaluate everything rationally and logically

...and end up with a decision that best serves the interests of the organization.

Steps in Rational Decision Making

A manager who really wants to approach a decision rationally and logically should try to follow the **steps in rational decision making**, listed in Table 4.1. These steps in rational decision making help keep the decision maker focused on facts and logic and help guard against inappropriate assumptions and pitfalls.

Recognizing and Defining the Decision Situation The first step in rational decision making is recognizing that a decision is necessary—that is, there must be some stimulus or spark to initiate the process. For many decisions and problem situations, the stimulus may occur without any prior warning. When equipment malfunctions, the manager must decide whether to repair or replace it. Or, when a major crisis erupts, as described in Chapter 3, the manager must quickly decide how to deal with it. As we already note, the stimulus for a decision may be either positive or negative. A manager who must decide how to invest surplus funds, for example, faces a positive decision situation. A negative financial stimulus could involve having to trim budgets because of cost overruns.

Inherent in problem recognition is the need to define precisely what the problem is. The manager must develop a complete understanding of the problem, its causes, and its relationship to other factors. This understanding comes from careful analysis and thoughtful consideration of the situation. Consider the situation currently being faced in the international air travel industry. Because of the growth of international travel related to business, education, and tourism, global carriers such as Singapore Airlines, KLM, JAL, British Airways, and American Airlines need to increase their capacity for international travel. Because most major international airports are already operating at

steps in rational decision making
Recognize and define the decision situation; identify appropriate alternatives; evaluate each alternative in terms of its feasibility, satisfactoriness, and consequences; select the best alternative; implement the chosen alternative; and follow up and evaluate the results of the chosen alternative

Table 4.1
Steps in the Rational Decision-Making Process

Although the presumptions of the classical decision model rarely exist, managers can still approach decision making with rationality. By following the steps of rational decision making, managers ensure that they are learning as much as possible about the decision situation and its alternatives.

Step	Detail	Example
1. Recognizing and defining the decision situation	Some stimulus indicates that a decision must be made. The stimulus may be positive or negative.	A plant manager sees that employee turnover has increased by 5 percent.
2. Identifying alternatives	Both obvious and creative alternatives are desired. In general, the more important the decision, the more alternatives should be generated.	The plant manager can increase wages, increase benefits, or change hiring standards.
3. Evaluating alternatives	Each alternative is evaluated to determine its feasibility, its satisfactoriness, and its consequences.	Increasing benefits may not be feasible. Increasing wages and changing hiring standards may satisfy all conditions.
4. Selecting the best alternative	Consider all situational factors and choose the alternative that best fits the manager's situation.	Changing hiring standards will take an extended period of time to cut turnover, so increase wages.
5. Implementing the chosen alternative	The chosen alternative is implemented into the organizational system.	The plant manager may need permission from corporate headquarters. The human resource department establishes a new wage structure.
6. Following up and evaluating the results	At some time in the future, the manager should ascertain the extent to which the alternative chosen in step 4 and implemented in step 5 has worked.	The plant manager notes that, six months later, turnover dropped to its previous level.

or near capacity, adding a significant number of new flights to existing schedules is not feasible. As a result, the most logical alternative is to increase capacity on existing flights. Thus Boeing and Airbus, the world's only manufacturers of large commercial aircraft, recognized an important opportunity and defined their decision situation as how to best respond to the need for increased global travel capacity.[15]

Identifying Alternatives Once the decision situation has been recognized and defined, the second step is to identify alternative courses of effective action. Developing both obvious, standard alternatives and creative, innovative alternatives is generally useful.[16] In general, the more important the decision, the more attention is directed to developing alternatives.[17] If the decision involves a multimillion-dollar relocation, a great deal of time and expertise will be devoted to identifying the best locations. JCPenney spent two years searching before selecting the Dallas–Fort Worth area for its new corporate headquarters. If the problem is to choose a color for the company softball team uniforms, less time and expertise will be brought to bear.

Although managers should seek creative solutions, they must also recognize that various constraints often limit their alternatives. Common constraints include legal restrictions, moral and ethical norms, authority constraints, available technology, economic considerations, and unofficial social norms. Boeing and Airbus identified three different alternatives to address the decision situation of increasing international airline travel capacity: They could independently develop new large planes, they could collaborate in a joint venture to create a single new large plane, or they could modify their largest existing planes to increase their capacity.

Evaluating Alternatives The third step in the decision-making process is evaluating each of the alternatives. Figure 4.3 presents a decision tree that can be used to judge different alternatives. The figure suggests that each alternative be evaluated in terms of its *feasibility*, its *satisfactoriness*, and its *consequences*. The first question to ask is whether an alternative is feasible. Is it within the realm of probability and practicality? For a small, struggling firm, an alternative requiring a huge financial outlay is probably out of the question. Other alternatives may not be feasible because of legal barriers. And limited human, material, and information resources may make other alternatives impractical.

When an alternative has passed the test of feasibility, it must next be examined to see how well it satisfies the conditions of the decision situation. For example, a manager searching for ways to double production capacity might initially consider purchasing an existing plant from another company. If more detailed analysis reveals that the new plant would increase production capacity by only 35 percent, this alternative may not be satisfactory. Finally, when an alternative has proven both feasible and satisfactory, its probable

AP PHOTO/JANE HWANG

JCPenney spent two years evaluating alternatives before announcing plans to move its world headquarters away from downtown New York to this campus in Plano, a Dallas suburb. A variety of factors including cost, the local labor market, and access to transportation all played a role in the decision. Nevertheless, while some employees welcomed the news, many others decided to resign rather than relocate.

Figure 4.3 Evaluating Alternatives in the Decision-Making Process

Managers must thoroughly evaluate all the alternatives, which increases the chances that the alternative finally chosen will be successful. Failure to evaluate an alternative's feasibility, satisfactoriness, and consequences can lead to a wrong decision.

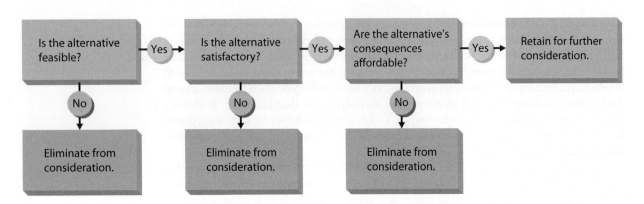

consequences must still be assessed. To what extent will a particular alternative influence other parts of the organization? What financial and nonfinancial costs will be associated with such influences? For example, a plan to boost sales by cutting prices may disrupt cash flows, require a new advertising program, and alter the behavior of sales representatives because it requires a different commission structure. The manager, then, must put "price tags" on the consequences of each alternative. Even an alternative that is both feasible and satisfactory must be eliminated if its consequences are too expensive for the total system. Airbus felt it would be at a disadvantage if it tried to simply enlarge its existing planes, because the Boeing 747 was already the largest aircraft being made and could readily be expanded to remain the largest. Boeing, meanwhile, was seriously concerned about the risk inherent in building a new and even larger plane, even if it shared the risk with Airbus as a joint venture.

Selecting the Best Alternative Even though many alternatives fail to pass the triple tests of feasibility, satisfactoriness, and affordable consequences, two or more alternatives may remain. Choosing the best of these is the real crux of decision making. One approach is to choose the alternative with the optimal combination of feasibility, satisfactoriness, and affordable consequences. Even though most situations do not lend themselves to objective, mathematical analysis, the manager can often develop subjective estimates and weights for choosing an alternative.

Optimization is also a frequent goal. Because a decision is likely to affect several individuals or units, any feasible alternative will probably not maximize all of the relevant goals. Suppose that the manager of the Kansas City Royals needs to select a new outfielder for the upcoming baseball season. Bill hits .350 but has difficulty catching fly balls, Joe hits only .175 but is outstanding in the field, and Sam hits .290 and is a solid but not outstanding fielder. The manager would probably select Sam because of the optimal balance of hitting and fielding. Decision makers should also remember that finding multiple acceptable alternatives may be possible; selecting just one alternative and rejecting all the others might not be necessary. For example, the Royals's manager might decide that Sam will start each game, Bill will be retained as a pinch hitter, and Joe will be retained as a defensive substitute. In many hiring decisions, the candidates remaining after evaluation are ranked. If the top candidate rejects the offer, it may be automatically extended to the number-two candidate and, if necessary, to the remaining candidates in order. For the reasons noted earlier, Airbus proposed a joint venture with Boeing. Boeing, meanwhile, decided that its best course of action was to modify its existing 747 to increase its capacity. As a result, Airbus then decided to proceed on its own to develop and manufacture a new jumbo jet. Boeing, however, also decided that in addition to modifying its 747, it would also develop a new plane to offer as an alternative, albeit one not as large as the 747 or the proposed Airbus plane.

Implementing the Chosen Alternative   After an alternative has been selected, the manager must put it into effect. In some decision situations, implementation is fairly easy; in others, it is more difficult. In the case of an acquisition, for example, managers must decide how to integrate all the activities of the new business, including purchasing, human resource practices, and distribution, into an ongoing organizational framework. For example, when Hewlett-Packard made the decision to buy Compaq Computer, managers estimated that it would take at least a year to integrate the two firms into a single one. Operational plans, which we discussed in Chapter 3, are useful in implementing alternatives.

Managers must also consider people's resistance to change when implementing decisions. The reasons for such resistance include insecurity, inconvenience, and fear of the unknown. When JCPenney decided to move its headquarters from New York to Texas, many employees resigned rather than relocate. Managers should anticipate potential resistance at various stages of the implementation process. (Resistance to change is covered in Chapter 7.) Managers should also recognize that even when all alternatives have been evaluated as precisely as possible and the consequences of each alternative weighed, unanticipated consequences are still likely. Any number of factors—unexpected cost increases, a less-than-perfect fit with existing organizational subsystems, or unpredicted effects on cash flow or operating expenses, for example—could develop after implementation has begun. Boeing set its engineers to work expanding the capacity of its 747 from 416 passengers to as many as 520 passengers by adding 30 feet to the plane's body. The company has also been developing its new plane intended for international travel, the Boeing 787 Dreamliner. Airbus engineers, meanwhile, spent years developing and constructing its new jumbo jet, the A380, equipped with escalators and elevators, and capable of carrying 655 passengers. Airbus's development costs alone are estimated to be more than $12 billion.

Following Up and Evaluating the Results   The final step in the decision-making process requires that managers evaluate the effectiveness of their decision—that is, they should make sure that the chosen alternative has served its original purpose. If an implemented alternative appears not to be working, the manager can respond in several ways. Another previously identified alternative (the original second or third choice, for instance) could be adopted. Or the manager might recognize that the situation was not correctly defined to begin with and start the process all over again. Finally, the manager might decide that the original alternative is in fact appropriate but has not yet had time to work or should be implemented in a different way.[18]

Failure to evaluate decision effectiveness may have serious consequences. The Pentagon once spent $1.8 billion and eight years developing the Sergeant York antiaircraft gun. From the beginning, tests revealed major problems with the weapon system, but not until it was in its final stages, when it was demonstrated to be completely ineffective, was the project scrapped.

At this point, both Boeing and Airbus are still learning about the consequences of their decisions. Airbus's A380 has been placed in commercial service. However, the plane has suffered numerous mechanical problems. Moreover, because the weakened economy has dealt a blow to large international airlines, some of them—such as Qantas Airways and Emirates Airlines—deferred or cancelled orders for the plane. Airbus estimated that it needs to sell 420 A380s before it starts making a profit. Current projections suggest that sales of the plane may not hit that target until at least 2020.[19] Meanwhile, it appeared for awhile that Boeing's commitment to the new 787 might prove to be the best decision of all. A key element of the new plane is that it is much more fuel efficient than other international airplanes. Given the dramatic surge in fuel costs in recent years, a fuel-efficient option like the 787 is likely to be an enormous success. However, the 787 has suffered from numerous manufacturing problems and it may not be available for passenger service until 2011, so its real impact will not be known for a few more years.[20]

BEHAVIORAL ASPECTS OF DECISION MAKING

If all decision situations were approached as logically as described in the previous section, more decisions might prove to be successful. Yet decisions are often made with little consideration for logic and rationality. Some experts have estimated that U.S. companies use rational decision-making techniques less than 20 percent of the time.[21] And, even when organizations try to be logical, they sometimes fail. For example, when Starbucks opened its first coffee shop in New York, it relied on scientific marketing research, taste tests, and rational deliberation in making a decision to emphasize drip over espresso coffee. However, that decision still proved wrong, as New Yorkers strongly preferred the same espresso-style coffees that were Starbucks mainstays in the West. Hence, the firm had to hastily reconfigure its stores to better meet customer preferences.

On the other hand, sometimes when a decision is made with little regard for logic, it can still turn out to be correct.[22] An important ingredient in how these forces work is the behavioral aspect of decision making. The administrative model better reflects these subjective considerations. Other behavioral aspects include political forces, intuition and escalation of commitment, risk propensity, and ethics.

administrative model
A decision-making model that argues that decision makers (1) use incomplete and imperfect information, (2) are constrained by bounded rationality, and (3) tend to "satisfice" when making decisions

The Administrative Model

Herbert A. Simon was one of the first experts to recognize that decisions are not always made with rationality and logic.[23] Simon was subsequently awarded the Nobel Prize in economics. Rather than prescribing how decisions should be made, his view of decision making, now called the **administrative model**, describes how decisions often actually are made. As illustrated in Figure 4.4, the model holds that decision makers (1) use

Figure 4.4   **The Administrative Model of Decision Making**

The administrative model is based on behavioral processes that affect how managers make decisions. Rather than prescribing how decisions should be made, it focuses more on describing how they are made.

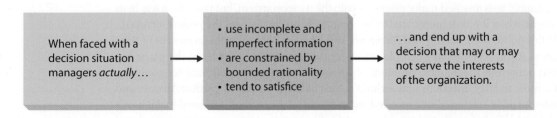

When faced with a decision situation managers *actually*…

- use incomplete and imperfect information
- are constrained by bounded rationality
- tend to satisfice

…and end up with a decision that may or may not serve the interests of the organization.

incomplete and imperfect information, (2) are constrained by bounded rationality, and (3) tend to "satisfice" when making decisions.

Bounded rationality suggests that decision makers are limited by their values and unconscious reflexes, skills, and habits. They are also limited by less-than-complete information and knowledge. Bounded rationality partially explains how U.S. auto executives allowed Japanese automakers to get such a strong foothold in the U.S. domestic market. For years, executives at GM, Ford, and Chrysler compared their companies' performance only to one another's and ignored foreign imports. The foreign "threat" was not acknowledged until the domestic auto market had been changed forever. If managers had gathered complete information from the beginning, they might have been better able to thwart foreign competitors. Essentially, then, the concept of bounded rationality suggests that although people try to be rational decision makers, their rationality has limits.

Another important part of the administrative model is **satisficing**, which suggests that rather than conducting an exhaustive search for the best possible alternative, decision makers tend to search only until they identify an alternative that meets some minimum standard of sufficiency. A manager looking for a site for a new plant, for example, may select the first site she finds that meets basic requirements for transportation, utilities, and price, even though further search might yield a better location. People satisfice for a variety of reasons. Managers may simply be unwilling to ignore their own motives (such as reluctance to spend time making a decision) and therefore not be able to continue searching after a minimally acceptable alternative is identified. The decision maker may be unable to weigh and evaluate large numbers of alternatives and criteria. Also, subjective and personal considerations often intervene in decision situations.

Because of the inherent imperfection of information, bounded rationality, and satisficing, the decisions made by a manager may or may not actually be in the best interests of the organization. A manager may choose a particular location for the new plant because it offers the lowest price and best availability of utilities and transportation. Or she may choose the location because it is located in a community where she wants to live.

In summary, then, the classical and administrative models paint quite different pictures of decision making. Which is more correct? Actually, each can be used to better understand how managers make decisions. The classical model is prescriptive: It explains how managers can at least attempt to be more rational and logical in their approaches to decisions. The administrative model can be used by managers to develop a better understanding of their inherent biases and limitations.[24] In the following sections, we describe more fully other behavioral forces that can influence decisions.

Political Forces in Decision Making

Political forces are another major element that contributes to the behavioral nature of decision making. Organizational politics is covered in Chapter 13, but one major element of politics, coalitions, is especially relevant to decision making. A **coalition** is an informal alliance of individuals or groups formed to achieve a common goal. This common goal is often a preferred decision alternative. For example, coalitions of stockholders frequently band together to force a board of directors to make a certain decision.

When General Motors (GM) decided to launch Saturn as a new automobile company, the idea had the full backing and support of its CEO Roger Smith. Saturn was to have its own factories, design teams, and dealer networks and was to compete directly with high-quality foreign imports such as Toyota and Honda. Just as the first Saturn cars were being introduced, however, Smith retired. As it turned out, there was a coalition of senior GM executives who had opposed the Saturn concept but had been unable to do anything about it since Smith was

bounded rationality
A concept suggesting that decision makers are limited by their values and unconscious reflexes, skills, and habits

satisficing
The tendency to search for alternatives only until one is found that meets some minimum standard of sufficiency

coalition
An informal alliance of individuals or groups formed to achieve a common goal

such a powerful product champion. When Smith left GM, though, the coalition managed to divert resources intended for Saturn to other GM brands. As a result, new Saturn products were delayed, the brand received weak marketing support, and it never lived up to expectations.[25]

The impact of coalitions can be either positive or negative. They can help astute managers get the organization on a path toward effectiveness and profitability, or they can strangle well-conceived strategies and decisions. Managers must recognize when to use coalitions, how to assess whether coalitions are acting in the best interests of the organization, and how to constrain their dysfunctional effects.[26]

Intuition and Escalation of Commitment

Two other important decision processes that go beyond logic and rationality are intuition and escalation of commitment to a chosen course of action.

Intuition Intuition is an innate belief about something, without conscious consideration. Managers sometimes decide to do something because it "feels right" or they have a "hunch." This feeling usually is not arbitrary, however. Rather, it is based on years of experience and practice in making decisions in similar situations.[27] An inner sense may help managers make an occasional decision without going through a full-blown rational sequence of steps. For example, the New York Yankees once contacted three major athletic shoe manufacturers—Nike, Reebok, and Adidas—and informed them that they were looking to make a sponsorship deal. While Nike and Reebok were carefully and rationally assessing the possibilities, managers at Adidas quickly realized that a partnership with the Yankees made a lot of sense for them. They responded very quickly to the idea and ended up hammering out a contract while the competitors were still analyzing details.[28] Of course, all managers, but most especially inexperienced ones, should be careful not to rely too heavily on intuition. If rationality and logic are continually flouted for "what feels right," the odds are that disaster will strike one day.

Escalation of Commitment Another important behavioral process that influences decision making is **escalation of commitment** to a chosen course of action. In particular, decision makers sometimes make decisions and then become so committed to the courses of action suggested by those decisions that they stay with them, even when the decisions appear to have been wrong.[29] For example, when people buy stock in a company, they sometimes refuse to sell it even after repeated drops in price. They chose a course of action—buying the stock in anticipation of making a profit—and then stay with it even in the face of increasing losses. Moreover, after the value drops, they rationalize that they can't sell now because they will lose money.

For years Pan American World Airways ruled the skies and used its profits to diversify into real estate and other businesses. But, with the advent of deregulation, Pan Am began to struggle and lose market share to other carriers. When Pan Am managers finally realized how ineffective their airline operations had become, experts today point out that the "rational" decision would have been to sell off the remaining airline operations and concentrate on the firm's more profitable businesses. But because they still saw the company as being first and foremost an airline, they instead began to slowly sell off the firm's profitable holdings to keep the airline flying. Eventually, the company was left with nothing but an ineffective and inefficient airline, and then it had to sell off its more profitable routes before being taken over by Delta. Had Pan Am managers made the more rational decision years earlier, chances are the firm could still be a profitable enterprise today, albeit one with no involvement in the airline industry.[30]

intuition
An innate belief about something, without conscious consideration

escalation of commitment
A decision maker's staying with a decision even when it appears to be wrong

In contrast, a group of investors licensed the use of Hard Rock logos and trademarks for a large theme park—Hard Rock Park—to be built in South Carolina. After six years of planning and construction and an investment of over $400 million, the park in Myrtle Beach opened to dismal reviews and poor attendance. Rather than increasing their investment and trying to increase attendance, owners decided after only nine months to shut down the park and sell off its assets.[31]

Thus decision makers must walk a fine line. On the one hand, they must guard against sticking too long with an incorrect decision. To do so can bring about financial decline. On the other hand, they should not bail out of a seemingly incorrect decision too soon, as Adidas once did. Adidas had dominated the market for professional athletic shoes. It subsequently entered the market for amateur sports shoes and did well there also. But managers interpreted a sales slowdown as a sign that the boom in athletic shoes was over. They thought that they had made the wrong decision and ordered drastic cutbacks. The market took off again with Nike at the head of the pack, and Adidas never recovered. Fortunately, a new management team has changed the way Adidas makes decisions, and the firm is again on its way to becoming a force in the athletic shoe and apparel markets.

Risk Propensity and Decision Making

The behavioral element of **risk propensity** is the extent to which a decision maker is willing to gamble when making a decision. Some managers are cautious about every decision they make. They try to adhere to the rational model and are extremely conservative in what they do. Such managers are more likely to avoid mistakes, and they infrequently make decisions that lead to big losses. Other managers are extremely aggressive in making decisions and

risk propensity
The extent to which a decision maker is willing to gamble when making a decision

are willing to take risks.[32] They rely heavily on intuition, reach decisions quickly, and often risk big investments on their decisions. As in gambling, these managers are more likely than their conservative counterparts to achieve big successes with their decisions; they are also more likely to incur greater losses.[33] The organization's culture is a prime ingredient in fostering different levels of risk propensity.

Ethics and Decision Making

As we introduced in Chapter 2, individual ethics are personal beliefs about right and wrong behavior. Ethics are clearly related to decision making in a number of ways. For example, suppose that, after careful analysis, a manager realizes that his company could save money by closing his department and subcontracting with a supplier for the same services. But to recommend this course of action would result in the loss of several jobs, including his own. His own ethical standards will clearly shape how he proceeds.[34] Indeed, each component

M. TIMOTHY O'KEEFE/ALAMY

Investors licensed the use of Hard Rock logos and trademarks for a new theme park—Hard Rock Park—to be located in South Carolina. Despite six years of planning and an investment of over $400 million, the park received poor reviews and attracted few visitors. One option would have been for the owners to invest more money to upgrade the park and attract more visitors. But instead, the owners decided to cut their losses and close the park after nine months.

of managerial ethics (relationships of the firm to its employees, of employees to the firm, and of the firm to other economic agents) involves a wide variety of decisions, all of which are likely to have an ethical component. Thus a manager must remember that, just as behavioral processes such as politics and risk propensity affect the decisions he makes, so, too, do his ethical beliefs.[35]

GROUP AND TEAM DECISION MAKING IN ORGANIZATIONS

In more and more organizations today, important decisions are made by groups and teams rather than by individuals. Examples include the executive committee of Abercrombie & Fitch, product design teams at Texas Instruments, and marketing planning groups at Red Lobster. Managers can typically choose whether to have individuals or groups and teams make a particular decision. Thus knowing about forms of group and team decision making and their advantages and disadvantages is important.[36]

Forms of Group and Team Decision Making

The most common methods of group and team decision making are interacting groups, Delphi groups, and nominal groups. Increasingly, these methods of group decision making are being conducted online.[37]

Interacting Groups or Teams **Interacting groups or teams** is the most common form of decision-making group. The format is simple—either an existing or a newly designated group or team is asked to make a decision. Existing groups or teams might be functional departments, regular work teams, or standing committees. Newly designated groups or teams can be ad hoc committees, task forces, or newly constituted work teams. The group or team members talk among themselves, argue, agree, form internal coalitions, and so forth. Finally, after some period of deliberation, the group or team makes its decision. An advantage of this method is that the interaction among people often sparks new ideas and promotes understanding. A major disadvantage, though, is that political processes can play too big a role.

Delphi Groups A **Delphi group** is sometimes used to arrive at a consensus of expert opinion. Developed by the Rand Corporation, the Delphi procedure solicits input from a panel of experts who contribute individually. Their opinions are combined and, in effect, averaged. Assume, for example, that the problem is to establish an expected date for a major technological breakthrough in converting coal into usable energy. The first step in using the Delphi procedure is to obtain the cooperation of a panel of experts. For this situation, experts might include various research scientists, university researchers, and executives in a relevant energy industry. At first, the experts are asked to anonymously predict a time frame for the expected breakthrough. The persons coordinating the Delphi group collect the responses, average them, and ask the experts for another prediction. In this round, the experts who provided unusual or extreme predictions may be asked to justify them. These explanations may then be relayed to the other experts. When the predictions stabilize, the average prediction is taken to represent the decision of the group of experts. The time, expense, and logistics of the Delphi technique rule out its use for routine, everyday decisions, but it has been successfully used for forecasting technological breakthroughs at

interacting group or team
A decision-making group or team in which members openly discuss, argue about, and agree on the best alternative

Delphi group
A form of group decision making in which a group is used to arrive at a consensus of expert opinion

Boeing, market potential for new products at GM, research and development patterns at Eli Lilly, and future economic conditions by the U.S. government.[38] Moreover, although the Delphi method originally relied on paper-and-pencil responses obtained and shared through the mail, modern communication technologies such as e-mail and the Internet have enabled Delphi users to get answers much more quickly than in the past.

Nominal Groups   Another useful group and team decision-making technique that is occasionally used is the **nominal group**. Unlike the Delphi method, in which group members do not see one another, nominal group members are brought together in a face-to-face setting. The members represent a group in name only, however; they do not talk to one another freely like the members of interacting groups. Nominal groups are used most often to generate creative and innovative alternatives or ideas. To begin, the manager assembles a group of knowledgeable experts and outlines the problem to them. The group members are then asked to individually write down as many alternatives as they can think of. The members then take turns stating their ideas, which are recorded on a flip chart or board at the front of the room. Discussion is limited to simple clarification. After all alternatives have been listed, more open discussion takes place. Group members then vote, usually by rank, ordering the various alternatives. The highest-ranking alternative represents the decision of the group. Of course, the manager in charge may retain the authority to accept or reject the group decision.[39]

Advantages of Group and Team Decision Making

The advantages and disadvantages of group and team decision making relative to individual decision making are summarized in Table 4.2. One advantage is simply that more information is available in a group or team setting—as suggested by the old axiom, "Two heads are better than one." A group or team represents a variety of education, experience, and perspective. Partly as a result of this increased information, groups and teams typically can identify and evaluate more alternatives than can one person.[40] The people involved in a group or team decision understand the logic and rationale behind it, are more likely to accept it, and are equipped to communicate the decision to their work group or department.[41] Finally, research evidence suggests that groups may make better decisions than individuals.[42]

nominal group
A structured technique used to generate creative and innovative alternatives or ideas

Table 4.2
Advantages and Disadvantages of Group and Team Decision Making

To increase the chances that a group or team decision will be successful, managers must learn how to manage the process of group and team decision making. Federal Express and IBM are increasingly using groups and teams in the decision-making process.

Advantages	Disadvantages
More information and knowledge are available.	The process takes longer than individual decision making, so it is costlier.
More alternatives are likely to be generated.	Compromise decisions resulting from indecisiveness may emerge.
More acceptance of the final decision is likely.	One person may dominate the group.
Enhanced communication of the decision may result.	Groupthink may occur.
Better decisions generally emerge.	

Disadvantages of Group and Team Decision Making

Perhaps the biggest drawback of group and team decision making is the additional time and hence the greater expense entailed. The increased time stems from interaction and discussion among group or team members. If a given manager's time is worth $50 an hour, and if the manager spends two hours making a decision, the decision "costs" the organization $100. For the same decision, a group of five managers might require three hours of time. At the same $50-an-hour rate, the decision "costs" the organization $750. Assuming the group or team decision is better, the additional expense may be justified, but the fact remains that group and team decision making is more costly.

Group or team decisions may also represent undesirable compromises.[43] For example, hiring a compromise top manager may be a bad decision in the long run because he or she may not be able to respond adequately to various subunits in the organization nor have everyone's complete support. Sometimes one individual dominates the group process to the point where others cannot make a full contribution. This dominance may stem from a desire for power or from a naturally dominant personality. The problem is that what appears to emerge as a group decision may actually be the decision of one person.

Finally, a group or team may succumb to a phenomenon known as **groupthink**, which occurs when the desire for consensus and cohesiveness overwhelms the goal of reaching the best possible decision.[44] Under the influence of groupthink, the group may arrive at decisions that are made not in the best interests of either the group or the organization, but rather to avoid conflict among group members. One of the most clearly documented examples of groupthink involved the space shuttle *Challenger* disaster. As NASA was preparing to launch the shuttle, numerous problems and questions arose. At each step of the way, however, decision makers argued that there was no reason to delay and that everything would be fine. Shortly after its launch, the shuttle exploded, killing all seven crew members.

groupthink
A situation that occurs when a group or team's desire for consensus and cohesiveness overwhelms its desire to reach the best possible decision

SSPL/GETTY IMAGES

NASA scientists, engineers, and managers must often make crucial decisions under tight time constraints and with incomplete or limited information. When these situations arise, those best prepared to make the decision quickly discuss their options and then make a timely decision. These engineers, for example, are making a decision about recalibrating the orbital path of an important NASA satellite.

Managing Group and Team Decision-Making Processes

Managers can do several things to help promote the effectiveness of group and team decision making. One is simply being aware of the pros and cons of having a group or team make a decision to start with. Time and cost can be managed by setting a deadline by which the decision must be made final. Dominance can be at least partially avoided if a special group is formed just to make the decision. An astute manager, for example, should know who in the organization may try to dominate and can either avoid putting that person in the group or put several strong-willed people together.

To avoid groupthink, each member of the group or team should critically evaluate all alternatives. So that members present divergent viewpoints, the leader should not make his or her own position known too early. At least one member of the group or team might be assigned the role of devil's advocate. And, after reaching a preliminary decision, the group or team should hold a follow-up meeting wherein divergent viewpoints can be raised again if any group members wish to do so.[45] Gould Paper Corporation used these methods by assigning managers to two different teams. The teams then spent an entire day in a structured debate presenting the pros and cons of each side of an issue to ensure the best possible decision.

SUMMARY OF LEARNING OBJECTIVES AND KEY POINTS

1. Define decision making and discuss types of decisions and decision-making conditions.

    *   Decision making is the act of choosing one alternative from among a set of alternatives.

    *   The decision-making process includes recognizing and defining the nature of a decision situation, identifying alternatives, choosing the "best" alternative, and putting it into practice.

    *   Two common types of decisions are programmed and nonprogrammed.

    *   Decisions may be made under states of certainty, risk, or uncertainty.

2. Discuss rational perspectives on decision making, including the steps involved.

    *   Rational perspectives on decision making rest on the classical model.

    *   This model assumes that managers have complete information and that they will behave rationally. The primary steps in rational decision making are
        *   recognizing and defining the situation
        *   identifying alternatives
        *   evaluating alternatives
        *   selecting the best alternative
        *   implementing the chosen alternative
        *   following up and evaluating the effectiveness of the alternative after it is implemented

3. Describe the behavioral aspects of decision making.

    *   Behavioral aspects of decision making rely on the administrative model.

    *   This model recognizes that managers use incomplete information and that they do not always behave rationally.

    *   The administrative model also recognizes the concepts of bounded rationality and satisficing.

    *   Political activities by coalitions, managerial intuition, and the tendency to become increasingly committed to a chosen course of action are all important.

    *   Risk propensity is also an important behavioral perspective on decision making.

    *   Ethics also affect how managers make decisions.

4. Discuss group and team decision making, including its advantages and disadvantages and how it can be more effectively managed.

    *   To help enhance decision-making effectiveness, managers often use interacting, Delphi, or nominal groups or teams.

    *   Group and team decision making in general has several advantages and disadvantages relative to individual decision making.

    *   Managers can adopt a number of strategies to help groups and teams make better decisions.

DISCUSSION QUESTIONS

Questions for Review

1. Describe the difference between programmed and nonprogrammed decisions. What are the implications of these differences for decision makers?

2. What are the different conditions under which decisions are made?

3. Describe the behavioral nature of decision making. Be certain to provide some detail about political forces, risk propensity, ethics, and commitment in your description.

4. What is meant by the term *escalation of commitment*? In your opinion, under what conditions is escalation of commitment likely to occur?

5. Explain the differences between three common methods of group decision making—interacting groups, Delphi groups, and nominal groups.

Questions for Analysis

1. Was your decision about what college or university to attend a rational decision? Did you go through each step in rational decision making? If not, why not?

2. Most business decisions are made under conditions of either risk or uncertainty. In your opinion, is it easier to make a decision under a condition of risk or a condition of uncertainty? Why?

3. Recall a decision that you recently made that had ethical implications. Did these implications make the decision easier or harder?

4. In what ways are escalation of commitment and decision making under conditions of risk related to one another?

5. Consider the following list of business decisions. Which decisions would be handled most effectively by group or team decision making? Which would be handled most effectively by individual decision making? Explain your answers.

   - A decision about switching pencil suppliers

   - A decision about hiring a new CEO

   - A decision about firing an employee for stealing

   - A decision about calling 911 to report a fire in the warehouse

   - A decision about introducing a brand new product

BUILDING EFFECTIVE CONCEPTUAL SKILLS

Exercise Overview

Conceptual skills refer to the manager's ability to think in the abstract. This exercise will aid you in understanding the effect that nonrational biases and risk propensity can have on decision making.

Exercise Background

Two psychologists, Amos Tversky and Daniel Kahneman, conducted much of the research that led to our knowledge of decision-making biases. Tversky and Kahneman found that they could understand individuals' real-life choices by presenting experimental subjects with simulated decisions in a laboratory setting. They developed a theory called *prospect theory*, which uses behavioral psychology to explain why individuals are nonrational when making economic decisions. Their work has contributed a great deal to the developing discipline of behavioral economics. In fact, Kahneman won the 2002 Nobel Prize in Economics for development of these concepts. (Tversky could not share in the award because the Nobel Prize cannot be given posthumously.)

Tversky and Kahneman's most important finding was that an individual's *perception* of gain or loss in a situation is more important than an objective measure of gain or loss. Thus individuals are nonrational—that is, they do not make decisions based purely on rational criteria.

Related to this conclusion, Tversky and Kahneman found that humans think differently about gains and losses. This is called *framing*. Another finding is that people allow their perceptions to be skewed positively or negatively, depending on information they receive. Later, when new information becomes available, people have a hard time letting go of their initial perceptions, even if the new information contradicts their original impressions. This effect is referred to as anchoring and adjustment.

To answer the following questions, you must be able to calculate an expected value. To calculate an expected value, multiply each possible outcome value by the probability of its occurrence, and then sum all the results. Here is a simple example: You have a 50 percent chance of earning 80 points on an exam and a 50 percent chance of earning 70 points. The expected value can be calculated as $(.5 \times 80) + (.5 \times 70)$, or a .5 chance of 80 points (equal to 40 points) plus a .5 chance of 70 points (equal to 35 points). Therefore, the expected value of your exam is 75 points.

Exercise Task

1. Answer the list of brief questions that your professor provides to you. No answer is correct or incorrect; simply choose your most likely response. Then, when the professor asks, share your answers with the class.

2. Discuss the answers given by the class. Why do students' answers differ?

3. What have you learned about decision-making biases and risk propensity from these experiments?

BUILDING EFFECTIVE TECHNICAL SKILLS

Exercise Overview

Technical skills are the skills necessary to accomplish or understand the specific kind of work being done in an organization. This exercise will enable you to practice technical skills in using the Internet to obtain information for making a decision.

Exercise Background

Assume that you are a business owner seeking a location for a new factory. Your company makes products that are relatively "clean"—that is, they do not pollute the environment, nor will they produce any dangerous waste products. Thus most communities would welcome your plant.

You are seeking a place that has a stable and well-educated workforce, as well as ample affordable housing, access to quality health care, and a good educational system. You have narrowed your choice to the following towns.

1. Santa Cruz, California

2. Madison, Wisconsin

3. Manhattan, Kansas

4. College Station, Texas

5. Amherst, Massachusetts

6. Athens, Georgia

Exercise Task

With this background information as context, do the following:

1. Use the Internet to research each of these cities.

2. Rank-order the cities on the basis of the criteria noted.

3. Select the best city for your new factory.

SKILLS SELF-ASSESSMENT INSTRUMENT

Decision-Making Styles

Introduction: Decision making is clearly important. However, individuals differ in their decision-making style, or the way they approach decisions. The following assessment is designed to help you understand your decision-making style.

Instructions: Respond to the following statements by indicating the extent to which they describe you. Circle the response that best represents your self-evaluation.

1. Overall, I'm _____ to act.

    1. quick   2. moderately fast   3. slow

2. I spend _____ amount of time making important decisions as/than I do making less important ones.

    1. about the same   2. a greater   3. a much greater

3. When making decisions, I _____ go with my first thought.

    1. usually   2. occasionally   3. rarely

4. When making decisions, I'm _____ concerned about making errors.

    1. rarely   2. occasionally   3. often

5. When making decisions, I _____ recheck my work more than once.

    1. rarely   2. occasionally   3. usually

6. When making decisions, I gather _____ information.

    1. little   2. some   3. lots of

7. When making decisions, I consider _____ alternatives.

    1. few   2. some   3. lots of

8. I usually make decisions _____ before the deadline.

    1. way   2. somewhat   3. just

9. After making a decision, I _____ look for other alternatives, wishing I had waited.

    1. rarely   2. occasionally   3. usually

10. I _____ regret having made a decision.

    1. rarely   2. occasionally   3. often

Source: Adapted from Robert N. Lussier, Supervision: A Skill-Building Approach, *2nd ed., 1994, pp. 122–123, © 1994 by Richard D. Irwin, Inc. Reproduced with permission of The McGraw-Hill Companies.*

EXPERIENTIAL EXERCISE

Decision Making with Journaling and Affinity Diagrams

Purpose: This exercise gives you practice in using both journaling and affinity diagrams, both of which are tools for effective decision making. These techniques can be used to help expand and improve your decision making in many areas of your life, both personal and professional.

Introduction: The chemist Linus Pauling, winner of Nobel Prizes in both Chemistry and Peace, said, "The best way to have a good idea is to have a lot of ideas." Journaling is one technique to increase the quantity of ideas generated in response to a decision situation. Affinity diagrams can be used alone or in conjunction with journaling or other idea-generation techniques.

Affinity diagrams help you to interpret and organize a quantity of diverse ideas. The diagrams are particularly useful in decision situations that involve lots of ideas, where the ideas are very different from each other and the relationships between the ideas are not well understood, and where the underlying questions seem overwhelming or too complex to analyze rationally.

Instructions:

1. Have on hand a number of index cards or sticky notes, at least 50. Or use several sheets of paper cut into at least 50 smaller slips. Set aside 30 minutes or so of quiet time. Assume that graduation day is

approaching and you are faced with the decision about where to live. Assume that your options are broad and that the decision will be for at least five years but would not necessarily commit you for the rest of your life. You could choose to live in an urban, suburban, or rural community. You could choose a large or small community, various regions of the country or world, and many different types of social and economic settings.

2. Think about the qualities you desire for your future hometown. Briefly jot qualities that you desire, putting one quality on each piece of paper. Relax and visualize your ideal community, and then commit the ideas to paper. For example, your ideas might include "ethnic diversity" or "upscale suburb." Or something quite different might be important to you. Allow the answers to just "come to" you. Don't try to force your thinking along any one path. Don't edit yourself or criticize your thoughts at this point in the process. It's okay to have some ideas that don't seem rational, that are duplicates, or even that seem meaningless.

 If you can, work quickly and without interruption. Try to generate at least 25 ideas. If that number comes easily to you, generate some more. Stop when you feel that you've exhausted your supply of ideas. This process is one way to use the technique known as *journaling*.

3. Lay out the slips of paper so you can see all of them and then read them. Begin to move the slips of paper into groups of ideas that are similar to each other.

Gradually, as you rearrange the slips, patterns of ideas will emerge. Again, don't try to be critical or rational at this point, simply consider the relationships between the ideas. Keep moving the slips into different combinations until you find a set of groups that "feels right."

 Then assign each of these groups a theme that identifies the common element. For example, you might group the ideas *green housing*, *good public transportation*, and *vegetarian restaurants* into a theme called *environmentally conscious*. Or you might group *good public transportation*, *short commute to work*, and *walk to restaurants and stores* into a theme called *convenience*. The finished project, a grouping of a diverse set of ideas into related themes, is called an *affinity diagram*.

Follow-up Questions:
1. Did the techniques of journaling and affinity diagramming help you generate more ideas and better see the connections between ideas? If so, explain how. If not, what technique(s) would have worked better?

2. Note that both techniques explicitly encourage the behavioral aspects of decision making, especially intuition. Do you think this is appropriate when making this type of decision? Or would a more rational approach be more effective?

3. How might a manager use these techniques at work? What situations would not be appropriate for the use of these techniques?

 YOU MAKE THE CALL

Citi ODs on CDOs

1. Summarize the *state of risk* as it stood at Citigroup in 2005 to 2008. What were the payoffs and costs that should have been considered in making risk assessment estimates?

2. Identify the specific decisions made at Citi by Charles Prince. In your opinion, which single decision contributed most to the breakdown in risk management at the bank?

3. Sometimes ambiguity complicates the task of making a good decision under conditions of risk.

How did ambiguity affect some of the factors that the Citi management team needed to consider?

4. To what extent was the Citi management team operating under a *state of uncertainty*?

5. Take advantage of hindsight: What should the Citi management team have done, and when? What might have been the outcome had Prince and his managers followed this course of action?

CHAPTER 5

MANAGING STRATEGY AND STRATEGIC PLANNING

LEARNING OBJECTIVES

After studying this chapter, you should be able to:

1 Discuss the nature of entrepreneurship.

2 Describe the role of entrepreneurship in society.

3 Understand the major issues involved in choosing strategies for small firms and the role of international management in entrepreneurship.

4 Discuss the structural challenges unique to entrepreneurial firms.

5 Understand the determinants of the performance of small firms.

FIRST THINGS FIRST

Facebook Faces the Problem of Booking Revenues

Do you Facebook? An estimated 175 million people in the United States do, and almost half are college students. The immensely popular social-networking website was started by Harvard sophomore Mark Zuckerberg in February 2004. Zuckerberg noticed that while each Harvard dorm had a directory of residents, there was no college-wide listing—a severe limitation to serious socializing. "I've always enjoyed building things and puttering around with computer code," recalls Zuckerberg, a computer prodigy who turned down a $1 million job offer at Microsoft after high school, "so I sat down and in about a week I had produced the basic workings of the site."

As Facebook grew, more and more universities were added, and by November 2004, the site boasted 1 million users. A mere 18 months later, membership had ballooned to 7 million members at 2,100 colleges and 22,000 high schools. When it began accepting nonstudents in October 2006, membership doubled from 12 million to 24 million in just 8 months. Today, Facebook.com is one of the most visited sites on the Internet, running neck-and-neck with Google among U.S. college students. The total number of worldwide Facebook users passed 400 million in 2010.

Although Facebook began as a noncommercial enterprise,

> **"We're not doing this to cash in. We're doing this to build something cool."**
>
> —MARK ZUCKERBERG, FOUNDER OF FACEBOOK

it wasn't long before it needed money to grow. PayPal cofounder Peter Thiel invested $500,000 in 2004, and substantial investments of additional venture capital followed. The new company lost $3.6 million in fiscal 2005, but with projected revenues of $150 million in 2007, Microsoft paid $240 million for a 1.6 percent stake in the company, pushing its valuation to $15 billion. Bear in mind that Facebook is not a publicly traded company—its stock can't be purchased on the open market. It's all privately held, and that $15 billion figure reflects the prices being paid at the time for the company's

AP PHOTO/PAUL SAKUMA

Facebook, the social networking site, has become a worldwide phenomenon. Mark Zuckerberg, founder of Facebook, has used his entrepreneurial skills to help transform his start-up operation into a business worth an estimated $15 billion.

preferred stock by Microsoft and other major investors. At the end of 2008, Facebook common stock was being bought and sold in private transactions at a rate that would place the company's valuation at $3.7 billion. Whatever its actual value, Zuckerberg claims that, at least at the beginning, Facebook was more about the entrepreneurial adventure than the money, and he's already turned down several offers to buy his brainchild (including a reported $900 million offer from Yahoo!). "We're not really looking to sell the company," he's said. "We're not looking to IPO any time soon.… We're not doing this to cash in. We're doing this to build something cool."

Facebook, of course, is a business, and money is an issue with any business—especially one that's growing at the rate of Zuckerberg's. Approximately 85 percent of the company's total revenue comes from advertising (about $210 million in 2008), with another $35 million to $50 million coming from sales of virtual gifts—those little icons that pop up in certain Facebook programs and that users can exchange for about $1. In 2008, Facebook sold about $3 million worth of virtual gifts every month, but revenues for the year—about $260 million—fell short of the company's $300 million projection. It was time to get serious about profit.

If we sort through these numbers, we notice an interesting phenomenon: User rates and revenues aren't going in the same direction. Since its inception, Facebook has had a problem with monetization—how to make a profit. It's a problem that Facebook shares with MySpace, which still commands most of the income from social networking. The solution, of course, is ad revenue—user fees are negligible, and even $3 million a month in virtual-gift sales won't begin to cover server costs. When they first appeared on the Internet scene, social networks seemed like turbocharged revenue generators, but both Facebook and MySpace have found that selling spots on webpages dedicated to personal profiles and group interchanges isn't as easy as it seemed.

Facebook took its first step in establishing relationships with advertisers in 2007, when it invited thousands of technology companies and programmers to contribute "social applications"—games, photo- and music-sharing tools, and other new features—to its Facebook Platform initiative. The idea was not only to

jumpstart additional activity on the site but also to allow developers to build their own businesses on a platform supported by Facebook. "You can build a real advertising business on Facebook," Zuckerberg promised interested developers at a special company-sponsored event. "If you don't want to run ads, you can sell something. We encourage you to do both." By October, the Facebook site had been flooded with more than 4,000 social apps, and the wave of attention—coupled with an upsurge in the number of Facebook users—sealed the investment deal with Microsoft.

Having promised that it would soon introduce a system whereby advertisers could access Facebook and its user base, the company launched part two of its "social applications" initiative—a plan characterized as "social advertising"—in November 2007. Called Beacon, the new feature consisted of ads in which a user's photo appeared in conjunction with a commercial message promoting a product that the user had either bought or expressed an opinion about. Ads were sent automatically to all the user's Facebook "friends"—the accumulated network of people with whom a user shares comments, photos, and profiles. After all, explained Zuckerberg, "nothing influences a person more than a recommendation from a trusted friend," and Facebook users were already in the habit of telling friends about things they liked and/or bought. The only difference with Beacon was that advertisers were also communicating with the user's friends. Advertisers responded quite favorably to the Beacon initiative, and marketers from several companies—including Blockbuster, Condé Nast, and Coke—announced that they intended to make spending on social-networking sites a priority. The numbers on Facebook, said one, "speak for themselves—their numbers are staggering." Moreover, added Zuckerberg, "on Facebook we know exactly what gender someone is and exactly what age they are."

The Beacon process called for getting the user's permission to broadcast a commercial message to all his or her friends—but not for consulting those friends, who were unable to avoid any commercial messages. Not surprisingly, critics of the initiative quickly expressed concern about privacy issues, and within a month, the company was presented with a petition containing the names of 50,000 users who objected to its tactics in rolling out the advertising plan. For one thing, it seems that Facebook didn't actually *ask* users' permission to piggyback ads on their personal messages. Rather, it posted less-than-conspicuous notices of its intent to do so and then proceeded to assume that everyone who ignored them was giving tacit permission. In addition, Facebook neglected to inform advertisers that users had to take overt action to opt out of Beacon. "I'm not proud of the way we've handled this situation," blogged a penitent Zuckerberg, "and I know we can do better." Facebook declined to offer a universal opt-out for Beacon but did agree to treat a nonresponse as a no.

Facebook's "social-advertising" strategy has since evolved into a process called *hypertargeting*, which allows advertisers to select an audience—say, Florida college students who watch the cable TV sports network ESPN—and target simple ads at its members. In February 2009, Facebook announced an initiative called Engagement Ads, which is designed to attract

advertisers to the site's potential for market research rather than sales.

Critics point out, however, that Facebook users aren't very good candidates for survey responses. In particular, they tend to use the site strictly for the activities that attracted them to it in the first place—commenting on friends' photos, leaving wall posts, and adding the applications that they want. "Social networks are some of the stickiest sites out there," says advertising consultant Andrew Chen. "They have very low click-through rates." In other words, users stick to the site and don't click on the ads. In fact, while 79 percent of all Internet users click through, only 57 percent of users on sites such as Facebook and MySpace leave the lively interactive environments of the host sites. It's a proclivity that doesn't bode well for monetization in the online social-networking business. The business model, adds Chen, "has to mature significantly before any sort of real revenue or value can be created."[1]

Just like Mark Zuckerberg, thousands of people all over the world start new businesses each year. Some of them succeed and many, unfortunately, fail. Some of the people who fail in a new business try again, and sometimes it takes two or more failures before a successful business gets underway. Henry Ford, for example, went bankrupt twice before succeeding with Ford Motor Company.

This process of starting a new business or business venture, sometimes failing and sometimes succeeding, is part of what is called *entrepreneurship*, the subject of this chapter. We begin by exploring the nature of entrepreneurship. We then examine the role of entrepreneurship in the business world and discuss strategies for entrepreneurial organizations. We then describe the structure and performance of entrepreneurial organizations.

THE NATURE OF ENTREPRENEURSHIP

entrepreneurship
The process of planning, organizing, operating, and assuming the risk of a business venture

entrepreneur
Someone who engages in entrepreneurship

Entrepreneurship is the process of planning, organizing, operating, and assuming the risk of a business venture. An **entrepreneur**, in turn, is someone who engages in entrepreneurship. Mark Zuckerberg, as highlighted in our opening incident, fits this description. He put his own resources on the line and took a personal stake in the success or failure of Facebook. Business owners who hire professional managers to run their businesses and then turn their attention to other interests are not true entrepreneurs. Although they are assuming the risk of the venture, they are not actively involved in organizing or operating it. Likewise, professional managers whose job is running someone else's business are not entrepreneurs, for they assume less-than-total personal risk for the success or failure of the business.

Entrepreneurs start new businesses. We define a **small business** as one that is privately owned by one individual or a small group of individuals and has sales and assets that are not large enough to influence its environment. A small, two-person software development company with annual sales of $100,000 would clearly be a small business, whereas Microsoft Corporation is just as clearly a large business. But the boundaries are not always this clear-cut. For example, a regional retailing chain with 20 stores and annual revenues of $30 million may sound large but is really very small when compared to giants such as Wal-Mart and Sears.

THE ROLE OF ENTREPRENEURSHIP IN SOCIETY

The history of entrepreneurship and of the development of new businesses is in many ways the history of great wealth and of great failure. Some entrepreneurs have been very successful and have accumulated vast fortunes from their entrepreneurial efforts. For example, when Microsoft Corporation first sold its stock to the public in 1986, Bill Gates, then just 30 years old, received $350 million for his share of Microsoft.[2] Today his holdings—valued at over $40 billion—make him the richest person in the United States and one of the richest in the world.[3] Many more entrepreneurs, however, have lost a great deal of money. Research suggests that the majority of new businesses fail within the first few years of founding.[4] Many that last longer do so only because the entrepreneurs themselves work long hours for very little income.

As Figure 5.1 shows, most U.S. businesses employ fewer than 100 people, and most U.S. workers are employed by small firms. For example, Figure 5.1(a) shows that approximately 89.2 percent of all U.S. businesses employ fewer than 20 people; another 8.89 percent employ between 20 and 99 people. In contrast, only about 1.5 percent employ between 100 and 499 workers, and another 0.3 percent employ 500 or more workers. Figure 5.1(b) shows that 18 percent of all U.S. workers are employed by firms with fewer than 20 people; another 17 percent work in firms that employ between 20 and 99 people. The vast majority of these companies are owner operated.[5] Figure 5.1(b) also shows that 14 percent of U.S. workers are employed by firms with 100 to 499 employees, and another 49 percent work for businesses that employ 500 or more employees.

On the basis of numbers alone, then, small business is a strong presence in the economy, which is also true in virtually all of the world's mature economies. In Germany, for example, companies with fewer than 500 employees produce two-thirds of the nation's gross national product, train nine of ten apprentices, and employ four of every five workers. Small businesses also play major roles in the economies of Italy, France, and Brazil. In addition, experts agree that small businesses will be quite important in the emerging economies of countries such as Russia and Vietnam. The contribution of small business can be measured in terms of its effects on key aspects of an economic system. In the United States, these aspects include job creation, innovation, and importance to big business.

Job Creation

In the early 1980s, a widely cited study suggested that small businesses are responsible for creating eight of every ten new jobs in the United States. This contention touched off considerable interest in the fostering of small business as a matter of public policy. As we will see, though, relative job growth among businesses of different sizes is not easy to determine. But it is clear that small business—especially in certain industries—is an important source

small business
A business that is privately owned by one individual or a small group of individuals and has sales and assets that are not large enough to influence its environment

$\mathcal{F}igure\ 5.1$ The Importance of Small Business in the United States

Over 89 percent of all U.S. businesses have fewer than 20 employees. The total number of people employed by these small businesses is approximately 18 percent of the entire U.S. workforce. Another 17 percent work for companies with fewer than 100 employees.

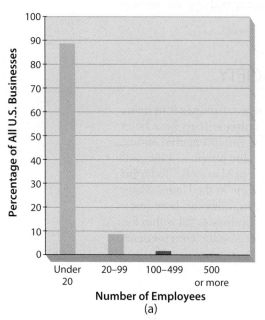

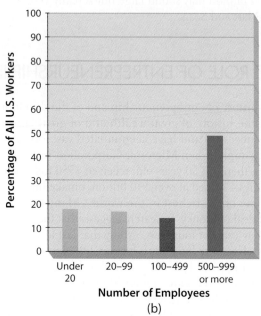

Source: U.S. Census Bureau, *Statistical Abstract of the United States: 2009* (Washington, D.C.: Government Printing Office, 2009).

of new (and often well-paid) jobs in the United States. According to the Small Business Administration (SBA), for example, seven of the ten industries that added the most new jobs in 2007 were in sectors dominated by small businesses. Moreover, small businesses currently account for over one-third of all jobs in high-technology sectors of the economy.[6]

Note that new jobs are also being created by small firms specializing in international business. For example, Bob Knosp operates a small business in Bellevue, Washington, that makes computerized sign-making systems. Knosp gets over half his sales from abroad and has dedicated almost 75 percent of his workforce to handling international sales. Indeed, according to the SBA, small businesses account for 92 percent of all U.S. exporters.[7]

It is important to note, though, that tracking job gains and losses is very complicated and somewhat imprecise. For instance, suppose a business eliminates one full-time job but later replaces it with two part-time jobs. Some statistics would count this as a loss of one job followed by a gain of two jobs. Similarly, the jobs within a company can fluctuate when it acquires or sells a business unit. In Figure 5.2, for instance, Halliburton is shown to have cut 53,000 jobs. But in reality, these "losses" actually came when the firm sold its largest subsidiary, KBR. Only a handful of jobs were actually eliminated; instead, over 50,000 jobs were simply moved to a new firm.

At least one message is clear: Entrepreneurial business success, more than business size, accounts for most new job creation. Whereas successful retailers such as Wal-Mart and Best Buy have been growing and adding thousands of new jobs, struggling chains

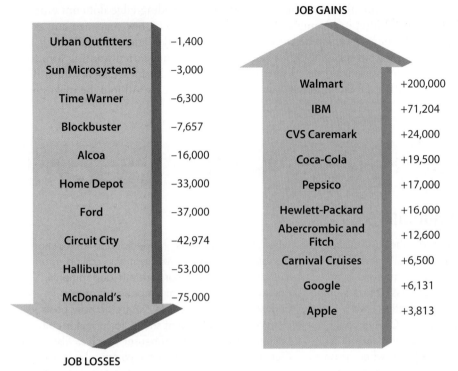

JOB GAINS

Urban Outfitters	–1,400
Sun Microsystems	–3,000
Time Warner	–6,300
Blockbuster	–7,657
Alcoa	–16,000
Home Depot	–33,000
Ford	–37,000
Circuit City	–42,974
Halliburton	–53,000
McDonald's	–75,000

Walmart	+200,000
IBM	+71,204
CVS Caremark	+24,000
Coca-Cola	+19,500
Pepsico	+17,000
Hewlett-Packard	+16,000
Abercrombie and Fitch	+12,600
Carnival Cruises	+6,500
Google	+6,131
Apple	+3,813

JOB LOSSES

Figure 5.2
Representative Jobs Created and Lost Between 2007 and 2008

All businesses create and eliminate jobs. Because of their size, the magnitude of job creation and elimination is especially pronounced in bigger businesses. This figure provides several representative examples of job creation and elimination at several big U.S. businesses between the years 2007 and 2008. For example, while Ford cut 37,000 jobs and McDonald's cut 75,000 jobs, Walmart created 200,000 jobs during this same period.

such as Kmart have been eliminating thousands. Hence, most firms, especially those in complex and dynamic environments, go through periods of growth when they add new jobs but also have periods when they cut jobs.

The reality, then, is that jobs are created by entrepreneurial companies of all sizes, all of which hire workers and all of which lay them off. Although small firms often hire at a faster rate than large ones, they are likely to eliminate jobs at a far higher rate. Small firms are also usually the first to hire in times of economic recovery, whereas large firms are generally the last. Conversely, however, big companies are also the last to lay off workers during economic downswings.

Innovation

History has shown that major innovations are as likely to come from small businesses (or individuals) as from big businesses. For example, small firms and individuals invented the personal computer, the stainless-steel razor blade, the transistor radio, the photocopying machine, the jet engine, and the self-developing photograph. They also gave us the helicopter and power steering, automatic transmissions and air conditioning, cellophane, and the disposable ballpoint pen. Today, says the SBA, small businesses consistently supply over half of all "innovations" introduced into the U.S. marketplace each year.[8]

Not surprisingly, history is repeating itself with increasing rapidity in the age of computers and high-tech communication. For example, much of today's most innovative software is being written at relatively new start-up companies. Yahoo! and Netscape brought the Internet into the average U.S. living room, and online companies such as Amazon.com, eBay, and Google are using it to redefine our shopping habits. MySpace, Facebook, and Twitter have changed how we interact with one another.[9] Each of these firms started out as a small business.

Of course, not all successful new start-ups are leading-edge dot-com enterprises. Take Sacha White, for example. He moved to Oregon a few years ago and got a job as a bicycle messenger. He began to tinker with his bike, and eventually built himself a custom one from scratch. Other riders took note, and started wanting him to build bikes for them as well. White eventually started his own business called *Vanilla Bicycles*. He handcrafts each one and has a waiting list of four years. All told, he makes between

MANAGEMENT TECH

How to Dial Up a Human

Submitted for your consideration: the frustration associated with customer-service call centers and automated phone menus—interminable waits, unannounced hang-ups, and endless transfers. Upon even the most casual recollection, two contradictory facts should emerge: On the one hand, a company's marketing department will pay you good money to talk to them, whereas on the other, the same company's customer-service department treats you as if the staff were being paid to drive you into the arms of the competition.

It's a paradox that is by no means lost on the humanitarian website www.gethuman.com, where technology entrepreneur Paul English poses a simple question—one that might appear in the short-answer section of your Marketing 101 final: "Which do you think will result in companies learning how to improve their products and services and getting more customer revenue? Spending a hundred million dollars on market research and advertising or loving your existing customers?" "I'm not anti-computer," avows English. "I've been a programmer for 20 years. I'm not anti-capitalist. I'm on my fifth start-up. But I am anti-arrogance. Why do the executives who run these call centers think they can decide when I deserve to speak to a human being and when I don't?"

A lot of people, of course, complain about corporate call centers, but most of us mutter under our breath, put our faith in the redial function, and prepare to be reasonably civil to the next voice we hear. We have, however, neither Paul English's tech skills nor his industry credibility. First, he started castigating customer call centers in his blog, and

when that didn't work, he decided to take action. Conducting his own investigations, calling upon friends who work in corporate IT departments, and collecting tips from simpatico strangers, English set up his website, where he now posts an alphabetized "cheat sheet" for popular call centers, ranging from Anheuser Busch to Xbox. The Get Human list tells you how you can bypass an automated phone system and talk to a live service representative. All you have to know is how to press the buttons on your phone. Can't get served by CompuServe? Press 1211 without waiting for the prompts. Getting zero satisfaction from NetZero? Try # # #, then 32.

Granted, a company that's really bent on universal frustration could respond by making its phone system even more complex and difficult to use. Companies that require customers, on the other hand, could take the advice of Jim Kelly, head of customer service at ING Direct. Kelly has made his bank's online system so easy to use that customers call to complain only 1.6 times annually. And those callers get to hear the sound of a human voice every time. The thing to do, advises Kelly, is simply "eliminate most of the problems and complaints. [Then] the only reason for people to call is to do business. And those are calls you're eager to take."

References: Fuze Digital Solutions, "Gethuman.com Survey Results Reveal Significant Consumer Expectations for Online Customer Support" (press release), *PRWeb*, October 21, 2008, www.prweb.com on June 9, 2009; Christopher Null, "How to Get a Human on the Phone," *Yahoo! Tech*, February 11, 2008, http://tech.yahoo.com on June 9, 2009; Burt Helm, "Building Good Web Buzz," *BusinessWeek*, April 17, 2006, www.singlearticles.com on June 9, 2009; William C. Taylor, "Your Call Should Be Important to Us, but It's Not," *New York Times*, February 26, 2006, www.nytimes.com on June 9, 2009.

40 and 50 bikes per year; about 40 percent of these bikes are sold domestically, the rest to international customers. The average price of each of his custom bikes is around $7,000.[10] Entrepreneurs have also achieved success in diverse fields such as specialized dog training, handcrafted musical instruments, and delicate fly-fishing reels.

Importance to Big Business

Most of the products made by big manufacturers are sold to consumers by small businesses. For example, the majority of dealerships selling Fords, Chevrolets, Toyotas, and Kias are independently owned and operated. Moreover, small businesses provide big businesses with many of the services, supplies, and raw materials they need. Likewise, Microsoft relies heavily on small businesses in the course of its routine business operations. For example, the software giant outsources much of its routine code-writing functions to hundreds of sole proprietorships and other small firms. It also outsources much of its packaging, delivery, and distribution to smaller companies. Dell Computer uses this same strategy, buying most of the parts and components used in its computers from small suppliers around the world.

STRATEGY FOR ENTREPRENEURIAL ORGANIZATIONS

One of the most basic challenges facing an entrepreneurial organization is choosing a strategy. The three strategic challenges facing small firms, in turn, are choosing an industry in which to compete, emphasizing distinctive competencies, and writing a business plan.[11]

Choosing an Industry

Not surprisingly, small businesses are more common in some industries than in others. The major industry groups that include successful new ventures and small businesses are services, retailing, construction, finance and insurance, wholesaling, transportation, and manufacturing. Obviously, each group differs in its requirements for employees, money, materials, and machines. In general, the more resources an industry requires, the harder it is to start a business and the less likely that the industry is dominated by small firms. Remember, too, that *small* is a relative term: The criteria (number of employees and total annual sales) differ from industry to industry and are often meaningful only when compared with businesses that are truly large. Figure 5.3 shows the distribution of all U.S. businesses employing fewer than 20 people across industry groups.

Services Primarily because they require few resources, service businesses are the fastest-growing segment of small-business enterprise. In addition, no other industry group offers a higher return on time invested. Finally, services appeal to the talent for innovation typified by many small enterprises. As Figure 5.3 shows, 39.5 percent of all U.S. businesses with fewer than 20 employees are services.

Small-business services range from shoeshine parlors to car rental agencies, from marriage counseling to computer software, from accounting and management consulting to professional dog walking. In Dallas, for example, Jani-King has prospered by selling commercial cleaning services to local companies. In Virginia Beach, Virginia, Jackson Hewitt Tax Services has found a profitable niche in providing computerized tax preparation and electronic tax-filing services. Great Clips, Inc. is a fast-growing family-run chain of hair salons headquartered in Minneapolis.

Figure 5.3 Small Business (businesses with fewer than 20 employees) by Industry

Small businesses are especially strong in certain industries, such as retailing and services. On the other hand, there are relatively fewer small businesses in industries such as transportation and manufacturing. The differences are affected primarily by factors such as the investment costs necessary to enter markets in these industries. For example, starting a new airline would require the purchase of large passenger aircraft and airport gates, and hiring an expensive set of employees.

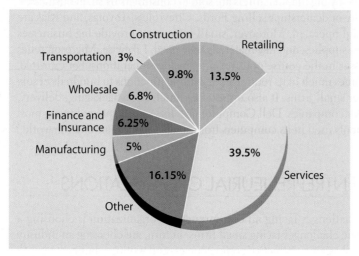

Source: U.S. Census Bureau, *Statistical Abstract of the United States: 2009* (Washington, D.C.: Government Printing Office, 2009).

David Flanary, Richard Sorenson, and Michael Holloway recently established an Internet-based long-distance telephone service in Austin, Texas, called PointOne Telecommunications. The basic idea was hatched during a tennis match. Recalls Sorenson, "We started getting excited, volleying at the net, and then finally we put the rackets down and went to the side to talk." The firm is off to a great start. Currently, it acts as a wholesale voice carrier, but as soon as its network is completed, PointOne will start signing up its own commercial customers. Investors agree that the company will soon be a major force in telecommunications.[12]

Retailing A retail business sells directly to consumers products manufactured by other firms. There are hundreds of different kinds of retailers, ranging from wig shops and frozen yogurt stands to automobile dealerships and department stores. Usually, however, people who start small businesses favor specialty shops—for example, big-men's clothing or gourmet coffees—which let them focus limited resources on narrow market segments. Retailing accounts for 13.5 percent of all U.S. businesses with fewer than 20 employees.

John Mackey, for example, launched Whole Foods out of his own frustration at being unable to find a full range of natural foods at other stores. He soon found, however, that he had tapped a lucrative market and started an ambitious expansion program. Today, with 276 outlets scattered across 40 states and Washington, D.C., Whole Foods is the largest natural-foods retailer in the United States, three times larger than its biggest competitor.[13] Likewise, when Olga Tereshko found it difficult to locate just the right cloth diapers and breast-feeding supplies for her newborn son, she decided to start selling them herself. Instead of taking the conventional retailing route, however, Tereshko set up shop on the

Internet. Her business, called Little Koala, has established a customer base of over 10,000 loyal customers.

Construction About 9.8 percent of businesses with fewer than 20 employees are involved in construction. Because many construction jobs are relatively small, local projects, local construction firms are often ideally suited as contractors. Many such firms are begun by skilled craftspeople who start out working for someone else and subsequently decide to work for themselves. Common examples of small construction firms include home builders, wood finishers, roofers, painters, and plumbing, electrical, and roofing contractors.

For example, Marek Brothers Construction in College Station, Texas, was started by two brothers, Pat and Joe Marek. They originally worked for other contractors but started their own partnership in 1980. Their only employee is a receptionist. They

SUSAN LAW CAIN, 2010/USED UNDER LICENSE FROM SHUTTERSTOCK.COM

Almost 10 percent of businesses with fewer than 20 people are involved in construction. Local companies are ideally suited to handle relatively small, local construction projects such as building a new home, restaurant, or retail outlet. These workers, for example, are laying the brick for walls of a new Lowe's home improvement store in California.

manage various construction projects, including new-home construction and remodeling, subcontracting out the actual work to other businesses or to individual craftspeople. Marek Brothers has an annual gross income of about $5 million.

Finance and Insurance Finance and insurance businesses comprise about 6.25 percent of all firms with fewer than 20 employees. In most cases, these businesses either are affiliates of or sell products provided by larger national firms. Although the deregulation of the banking industry has reduced the number of small local banks, other businesses in this sector are still doing quite well.

Typically, for example, local State Farm Mutual offices are small businesses. State Farm itself is a major insurance company, but its local offices are run by 16,500 independent agents. In turn, agents hire their own staff, run their own offices as independent businesses, and so forth. They sell various State Farm insurance products and earn commissions from the premiums paid by their clients. Some local savings and loan operations, mortgage companies, and pawnshops also fall into this category.

Wholesaling Small-business owners often also do very well in wholesaling; about 6.8 percent of businesses with fewer than 20 employees are wholesalers. A wholesale business buys products from manufacturers or other producers and then sells them to retailers. Wholesalers usually buy goods in bulk and store them in quantity at locations that are convenient for retailers. For a given volume of business, therefore, they need fewer employees than manufacturers, retailers, or service providers.

They also serve fewer customers than other providers—usually those who repeatedly order large volumes of goods. Wholesalers in the grocery industry, for instance, buy packaged food in bulk from companies such as Del Monte and Campbell's and then sell it to both large grocery chains and smaller independent grocers. Luis Espinoza has found a promising niche for Inca Quality Foods, a Midwestern wholesaler that imports and distributes Latino foods for consumers from Mexico, the Caribbean, and Central America. Partnered with the large grocery store chain Kroger, Espinoza's firm continues to grow steadily.[14]

Transportation Some small firms—about 3 percent of all U.S. companies with fewer than 20 employees—do well in transportation and transportation-related businesses. Such firms include local taxi and limousine companies, charter airplane services, and tour operators. In addition, in many smaller markets, bus companies and regional airlines subcontract local equipment maintenance to small businesses.

Consider, for example, some of the transportation-related small businesses at a ski resort like Steamboat Springs, Colorado. Most visitors fly to the town of Hayden, about 15 miles from Steamboat Springs. Although some visitors rent vehicles, many others use the services of Alpine Taxi, a small local operation, to transport them to their destinations in Steamboat Springs. While on vacation, they also rely on the local bus service, which is subcontracted by the town to another small business, to get to and from the ski slopes each day. Other small businesses offer van tours of the region, hot-air balloon rides, and helicopter lifts to remote areas for extreme skiers. Still others provide maintenance support at Hayden for Continental, American, and United aircraft that serve the area during ski season.

Manufacturing More than any other industry, manufacturing lends itself to big business—and for good reason. Because of the investment normally required in equipment, energy, and raw materials, a good deal of money is usually needed to start a manufacturing business. Automobile manufacturing, for example, calls for billions of dollars of investment and thousands of workers before the first automobile rolls off the assembly line. Obviously, such requirements shut out most individuals. Although Henry Ford began with $28,000, it has been a long time since anyone started a new U.S. car company from scratch.

Research has shown that manufacturing costs often fall as the number of units produced by an organization increases. This relationship between cost and production is called an *economy of scale*.[15] Small organizations usually cannot compete effectively on the basis of economies of scale. As depicted in Figure 5.4(a), organizations with higher levels of production have a major cost advantage over those with lower levels of production. Given the cost positions of small and large firms when there are strong economies of scale in manufacturing, it is not surprising that small manufacturing organizations generally do not do as well as large ones.

Interestingly, when technology in an industry changes, it often shifts the economies-of-scale curve, thereby creating opportunities for smaller organizations. For example, steel manufacturing was historically dominated by a few large companies, which owned several huge facilities. With the development of mini-mill technology, however, extracting economies of scale at a much smaller level of production became possible. This type of shift is depicted in Figure 5.4(b). Point A in this panel is the low-cost point with the original economies of scale. Point B is the low-cost point with the economies of scale brought on by the new technology. Notice that the number of units needed for low costs is considerably lower for the new technology. This has allowed the entry of numerous smaller firms into the steel industry. Such entry would not have been possible with the older technology.

This is not to say that there are no small-business owners who do well in manufacturing—about 5 percent of businesses with fewer than 20 employees are involved in some aspect of manufacturing. Indeed, it is not uncommon for small manufacturers to outperform big business in innovation-driven industries such as chemistry, electronics, toys, and computer software. Some small manufacturers prosper by locating profitable

Figure 5.4 Economies of Scale in Small-Business Organizations

Small businesses sometimes find it difficult to compete in manufacturing-related industries because of the economies of scale associated with plant, equipment, and technology. As shown in (a), firms that produce a large number of units (that is, larger businesses) can do so at a lower per-unit cost. At the same time, however, new forms of technology occasionally cause the economies-of-scale curve to shift, as illustrated in (b). In this case, smaller firms may be able to compete more effectively with larger ones because of the drop in per-unit manufacturing cost.

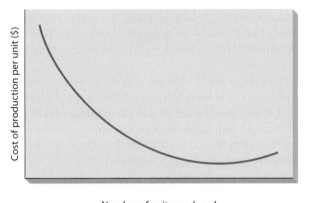

(a) Standard economies-of-scale curve

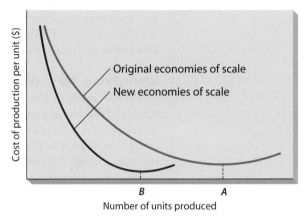

(b) Change in technology that shifts economies of scale and may make small-business manufacturing possible

niches. For example, brothers Dave and Dan Hanlon and Dave's wife Jennie recently started a new motorcycle-manufacturing business called Excelsior-Henderson. (Excelsior and Henderson are actually names of classic motorcycles from the early years of the twentieth century; the Hanlons acquired the rights to these brand names because of the images they evoke among motorcycle enthusiasts.) The Hanlons started by building 4,000 bikes in 1999 and will soon have annual production of 20,000 per year. So far, Excelsior-Henderson motorcycles have been well received (the top-end Excelsior-Henderson Super X sells for about $18,000), and many Harley-Davidson dealers have started to sell them as a means of diversifying their product line.[16]

Emphasizing Distinctive Competencies

As we defined in Chapter 3, an organization's distinctive competencies are the aspects of business that the firm performs better than its competitors. The distinctive competencies of small business usually fall into three areas: the ability to identify new niches in established markets, the ability to identify new markets, and the ability to move quickly to take advantage of new opportunities.

Identifying Niches in Established Markets An **established market** is one in which several large firms compete according to relatively well-defined criteria. For example, throughout the 1970s, several well-known computer-manufacturing companies, including IBM, Digital Equipment, and Hewlett-Packard, competed according to three product criteria: computing power, service, and price. Over the years, the computing power and quality of service delivered by these firms continued to improve, while prices (especially relative to computing power) continued to drop.

established market
A market in which several large firms compete according to relatively well-defined criteria

Enter Apple Computer and the personal computer. For Apple, user-friendliness, not computing power, service, or price, was to be the basis of competition. Apple targeted every manager, every student, and every home as the owner of a personal computer. Apple's major entrepreneurial act was not to invent a new technology (indeed, the first Apple computers used all standard parts taken from other computers), but to recognize a new kind of computer and a new way to compete in the computer industry.

Apple's approach to competition was to identify a new niche in an established market. A **niche** is simply a segment of a market that is not currently being exploited. In general, small entrepreneurial businesses are better at discovering these niches than are larger organizations. Large organizations usually have so many resources committed to older, established business practices that they may be unaware of new opportunities. Entrepreneurs can see these opportunities and move quickly to take advantage of them.[17]

Identifying New Markets Successful entrepreneurs also excel at discovering whole new markets. Discovery can happen in at least two ways. First, an entrepreneur can transfer a product or service that is well established in one geographic market to a second market. This is what Marcel Bich did with ballpoint pens, which occupied a well-established market in Europe before Bich introduced them to the United States. Bich's company, Société Bic, eventually came to dominate the U.S. market.

Second, entrepreneurs can sometimes create entire industries. Entrepreneurial inventions of the dry paper-copying process and the semiconductor have created vast new industries. Not only have the first companies into these markets been very successful (Xerox and National Semiconductor, respectively), but also their entrepreneurial activity has spawned the development of hundreds of other companies and hundreds of thousands of jobs. Again, because entrepreneurs are not encumbered with a history of doing business in a particular way, they are usually better at discovering new markets than are larger, more mature organizations.

First-Mover Advantages A **first-mover advantage** is any advantage that comes to a firm because it exploits an opportunity before any other firm does. Sometimes large firms discover niches within existing markets or new markets at just about the same time small entrepreneurial firms do, but are not able to move as quickly as small companies to take advantage of these opportunities.

There are numerous reasons for this difference. For example, many large organizations make decisions slowly because each of their many layers of hierarchy has to approve an action before it can be implemented. Also, large organizations may sometimes put a great deal of their assets at risk when they take advantage of new opportunities. Every time Boeing decides to build a new model of a commercial jet, it is making a decision that could literally bankrupt the company if it does not turn out well. The size of the risk may make large organizations cautious. The dollar value of the assets at risk in a small organization, in contrast, is quite small. Managers may be willing to "bet the company" when the value of the company is only $100,000. They might be unwilling to "bet the company" when the value of the company is $1 billion.

Writing a Business Plan

Once an entrepreneur has chosen an industry to compete in and determined which distinctive competencies to emphasize, these choices are usually included in a document called a business plan. In a **business plan**, the entrepreneur summarizes the business

niche
A segment of a market not currently being exploited

first-mover advantage
Any advantage that comes to a firm because it exploits an opportunity before any other firm does

business plan
A document that summarizes the business strategy and structure

strategy and how that strategy is to be implemented. The very act of preparing a business plan forces prospective entrepreneurs to crystallize their thinking about what they must do to launch their business successfully and obliges them to develop their business on paper before investing time and money in it. The idea of a business plan is not new. What is new is the growing use of specialized business plans by entrepreneurs, mostly because creditors and investors demand them for use in deciding whether to help finance a small business.[18]

The plan should describe the match between the entrepreneur's abilities and the requirements for producing and marketing a particular product or service. It should define strategies for production and marketing, legal aspects and organization, and accounting and finance. In particular, it should answer three questions: (1) What are the entrepreneur's goals and objectives? (2) What strategies will the entrepreneur use to obtain these goals and objectives? (3) How will the entrepreneur implement these strategies?

Business plans should also account for the sequential nature of much strategic decision making in small businesses. For example, entrepreneurs cannot forecast sales revenues without first researching markets. The sales forecast itself is one of the most important elements in the business plan. Without such forecasts, it is all but impossible to estimate intelligently the size of a plant, store, or office, or to determine how much inventory to carry or how many employees to hire.

Another important component of the overall business plan is financial planning, which translates all other activities into dollars. Generally, the financial plan is made up of a cash budget, an income statement, balance sheets, and a breakeven chart. The most important of these statements is the cash budget because it tells entrepreneurs how much money they need before they open for business and how much money they need to keep the business operating.

Entrepreneurship and International Management

Although many people associate international management with big business, many smaller companies are finding expansion and growth opportunities in foreign countries. For example, Fuci Metals, a small but growing enterprise, buys metal from remote locations in areas such as Siberia and Africa and then sells it to big automakers such as Ford and Toyota. Similarly, California-based Gold's Gym is expanding into foreign countries and has been especially successful in Russia. And Markel Corporation, a small Philadelphia-based firm that manufactures tubing and insulated wiring, derives 40 percent of its annual revenues (currently around $32 million) from international sales. Although such ventures are accompanied by considerable risks, they give entrepreneurs new opportunities and can be a real catalyst for success.

STRUCTURE OF ENTREPRENEURIAL ORGANIZATIONS

With a strategy in place and a business plan in hand, the entrepreneur can then proceed to devise a structure that turns the vision of the business plan into a reality. Many of the same concerns in structuring any business are also relevant to small businesses. For example, entrepreneurs need to consider organization design and develop job descriptions, organization charts, and management control systems.

ANDREW OLNEY/GETTY IMAGES

The Internet has clearly rewritten the rules for starting and operating a small business. The Internet makes it easier to gather information and to launch and to run a new business. But it also increases competition since other entrepreneurs have the same opportunities. These small-business employees are moving into their new offices and making Internet access one of their highest priorities.

The Internet, of course, has virtually rewritten all the rules for starting and operating a small business. Getting into business is easier and faster than ever before, there are many more potential opportunities than at any other time in history, and the ability to gather and assimilate information is at an all-time high. Even so, would-be entrepreneurs must still make the right decisions when they start. They must decide, for example, precisely how to get into business. Should they buy an existing business or build from the ground up? In addition, would-be entrepreneurs must find appropriate sources of financing and decide when and how to seek the advice of experts.

Starting the New Business

The first step in starting a new business is the individual's commitment to becoming a business owner. Next comes choosing the goods or services to be offered—a process that means investigating one's chosen industry and market. Making this choice also requires would-be entrepreneurs to assess not only industry trends but also their own skills. Like the managers of existing businesses, new business owners must also be sure that they understand the true nature of the enterprise in which they are engaged.

Buying an Existing Business After choosing a product and making sure that the choice fits their own skills and interests, entrepreneurs must decide whether to buy an existing business or to start from scratch. Consultants often recommend the first approach. Quite simply, the odds are better: If successful, an existing business has already proved its ability to draw customers at a profit. It has also established working relationships with lenders, suppliers, and the community. Moreover, the track record of an existing business gives potential buyers a much clearer picture of what to expect than any estimate of a new business's prospects. Around 30 percent of the new businesses started in the past decade were bought from someone else. For example, the McDonald's empire was started when Ray Kroc bought an existing hamburger business and then turned it into a global phenomenon. Likewise, Starbucks was a struggling mail-order business when Howard Schultz bought it and turned his attention to retail expansion.

Starting from Scratch Some people, however, prefer the satisfaction that comes from planting an idea, nurturing it, and making it grow into a strong and sturdy business. There are also practical reasons to start a business from scratch. A new business does not suffer the ill effects of a prior owner's errors. The start-up owner is also free to choose lenders, equipment, inventories, locations, suppliers, and workers, unbound by a predecessor's commitments and policies. Of the new businesses begun in the past decade, 64 percent were started from scratch.

Not surprisingly, though, the risks of starting a business from scratch are greater than those of buying an existing firm. Founders of new businesses can make only predictions and projections about their prospects. Success or failure thus depends heavily on identifying a genuine business opportunity—a product for which many customers will pay well but which is currently unavailable to them. To find openings, entrepreneurs must study markets and answer the following questions: (1) Who are my customers? (2) Where are they? (3) At what price will they buy my product? (4) In what quantities will they buy? (5) Who are my competitors? (6) How will my product differ from those of my competitors?

Finding answers to these questions is a difficult task even for large, well-established firms. But where can the new business owner get the necessary information? Other sources of assistance are discussed later in this chapter, but we briefly describe three of the most accessible here. First, the best way to gain knowledge about a market is to work in it before going into the business in it. For example, if you once worked in a bookstore and now plan to open one of your own, you probably already have some idea about the kinds of books people request and buy. Second, a quick scan of the local Yellow Pages or an Internet search will reveal many potential competitors, as will advertisements in trade journals. Personal visits to these establishments and websites can give you insights into their strengths and weaknesses. And, third, studying magazines, books, and websites aimed specifically at small businesses can be of help, as can hiring professionals to survey the market for you.

Financing the New Business

Although the choice of how to start is obviously important, it is meaningless unless a new business owner can obtain the money to set up shop. Among the more common sources for funding are family and friends, personal savings, banks and similar lending institutions, investors, and government agencies. Lending institutions are more likely to help finance the purchase of an existing business than a new business because the risks are better understood. Individuals starting up new businesses, on the other hand, are more likely to have to rely on their personal resources.

Personal Resources According to a study by the National Federation of Independent Business (NFIB), an owner's personal resources, not loans, are the most important source of money. Including money borrowed from friends and relatives, personal resources account for over two-thirds of all money invested in new small businesses and one-half of that invested in the purchase of existing businesses. John Mackey started Whole Foods with a $10,000 loan from his father. Fred Smith used $4 million he had inherited from his father to launch FedEx. And Rebecca Boenigk started Neutral Posture, an ergonomic chair company, with personal savings and loans from several family members.

Strategic Alliances Strategic alliances are also becoming a popular method for financing business growth. When Steven and Andrew Grundy decided to launch an Internet CD-exchange business called Spun.com, they had very little capital and thus made extensive use of alliances with other firms. They partnered, for example, with wholesaler Alliance Entertainment Corporation as a CD supplier. Orders to Spun.com actually go to Alliance, which ships products to customers and bills Spun.com directly. This setup has allowed Spun.com to promote a vast inventory of labels without actually having to buy inventory. All told, the firm created an alliance network that has provided the equivalent of $40 million in capital.[19]

Lenders Although banks, independent investors, and government loans all provide much smaller portions of start-up funds than the personal resources of owners, they are important in many cases. Getting money from these sources, however, requires some extra effort. Banks and private investors usually want to see formal business plans—detailed

Venture capital companies are groups of investors seeking to make profits on companies with rapid growth potential. These investors provide funding in return for equity ownership. John Doerr, partner with Kleiner Perkins Caufield & Byers (KPCB), recently announced that KPCB is doubling the venture capital of its iFund to $200 million. iFund provides venture capital for entrepreneurs and companies that create applications for Apple's iPhone OS family of products, including iPhone, iPod touch, and iPad.

AP PHOTO/MARCIO JOSE SANCHEZ

outlines of proposed businesses and markets, owners' backgrounds, and other sources of funding. Government loans have strict eligibility guidelines.

Venture Capital Companies Venture **capital companies** are groups of small investors seeking to make profits on companies with rapid growth potential. Most of these firms do not lend money: They invest it, supplying capital in return for stock. The venture capital company may also demand a representative on the board of directors. In some cases, managers may even need approval from the venture capital company before making major decisions. Of all venture capital currently committed in the United States, around 25 percent comes from true venture capital firms.[20] In 2008, venture capital firms invested $18 billion in new start-ups in the United States. SoftBank Capital is a venture capital firm that has provided funds to over 300 web companies, including Yahoo! and E*Trade.

As noted earlier, Fred Smith used his inheritance to launch FedEx. Once he got his business plan developed and started service, though, he needed an infusion of substantial additional capital. All told, he raised about $80 million in venture capital to buy his first small fleet of planes. Our opening case also provided details of the importance of venture capital in the growth of Facebook. And Twitter has raised over $50 million in venture capital.

Small-Business Investment Companies Taking a more balanced approach in their choices than venture capital companies, small-business investment companies (SBICs) seek profits by investing in companies with potential for rapid growth. Created by the Small Business Investment Act of 1958, SBICs are federally licensed to borrow money from the SBA and to invest it in or lend it to small businesses. They are themselves investments for their shareholders. Past beneficiaries of SBIC capital include Apple Computer, Intel, and Federal Express. In addition, the government has recently begun to sponsor minority enterprise small-business investment companies (MESBICs). As the name suggests, MESBICs specialize in financing businesses that are owned and operated by minorities.

SBA Financial Programs Since its founding in 1953, the SBA has offered more than 20 financing programs to small businesses that meet standards of size and independence. Eligible firms must also be unable to get private financing at reasonable terms. Because of these and other restrictions, SBA loans have never been a major source of small-business financing. In addition, budget cutbacks at the SBA have reduced the number of firms benefiting from loans. Nevertheless, several SBA programs currently offer funds to qualified applicants.

venture capital company
A group of small investors seeking to make profits on companies with rapid growth potential.

For example, under the SBA's guaranteed loans program, small businesses can borrow from commercial lenders. The SBA guarantees to repay 75 to 85 percent of the loan amount, not to exceed $750,000. Under a related program, companies engaged in international trade can borrow up to $1.50 million. Such loans may be made for as long as 15 years. Most SBA lending activity flows through this program.

Sometimes, however, both desired bank and SBA-guaranteed loans are unavailable (perhaps because the business cannot meet stringent requirements). In such cases, the SBA may help finance the entrepreneur through its immediate participation loan program. Under this arrangement, the SBA and the bank each puts up a share of the money, with the SBA's share not to exceed $150,000. Under the local development companies (LDCs) program, the SBA works with a corporation (either for-profit or nonprofit) founded by local citizens who want to boost the local economy. The SBA can lend up to $500,000 for each small business to be helped by an LDC.

Spurred in large part by the boom in Internet businesses, both venture capital and loans are in general becoming easier to get. Most small businesses, for example, report that it became increasingly easier to obtain loans between 1995 and 2005. And firms such as Facebook and Twitter are being offered so much venture capital that they are turning down part of it to keep from unnecessarily diluting their ownership. Unfortunately, the credit crunch that began in 2008 has made it harder for most entrepreneurs to obtain funds, but experts believe this is only a short-term problem.[21]

Sources of Management Advice

Financing is not the only area in which small businesses need help. Until World War II, for example, the business world involved few regulations, few taxes, few records, few big competitors, and no computers. Since then, simplicity has given way to complexity. Today, few entrepreneurs are equipped with all the business skills they need to survive. Small-business owners can no longer be their own troubleshooters, lawyers, bookkeepers, financiers, and tax experts. For these jobs, they rely on professional help. To survive and grow, however, small businesses also need advice regarding management. This advice is usually available from four sources: advisory boards, management consultants, the SBA, and networking.

Advisory Boards   All companies, even those that do not legally need boards of directors, can benefit from the problem-solving abilities of advisory boards. Thus some small businesses create boards to provide advice and assistance. For example, an advisory board might help an entrepreneur determine the best way to finance a plant expansion or to start exporting products to foreign markets.

Management Consultants   Opinions vary widely about the value of management consultants—experts who charge fees to help managers solve problems. They often specialize in one area, such as international business, small business, or manufacturing. Thus they can bring an objective and trained outlook to problems and provide logical recommendations. They can be quite expensive, however, as some consultants charge $1,000 or more for a day of assistance.

Like other professionals, management consultants should be chosen with care. They can be found through major corporations that have used their services and that can provide references and reports on their work. Not surprisingly, they are most effective when the client helps (for instance, by providing schedules and written proposals for the work to be done).

The Small Business Administration Even more important than its financing role is the SBA's role in helping small-business owners improve their management skills. It is easy for entrepreneurs to spend money; SBA programs are designed to show them how to spend it wisely. The SBA offers small businesses four major management-counseling programs at virtually no cost.

A small-business owner who needs help in starting a new business can get it free through the Service Corps of Retired Executives (SCORE). All SCORE members are retired executives, and all are volunteers. Under this program, the SBA tries to match the expert to the need. For example, if a small-business owner needs help putting together a marketing plan, the SBA will send a SCORE counselor with marketing expertise.

Like SCORE, the Active Corps of Executives (ACE) program is designed to help small businesses that cannot afford consultants. The SBA recruits ACE volunteers from virtually every industry. All ACE volunteers are currently involved in successful activities, mostly as small-business owners themselves. Together, SCORE and ACE have more than 12,000 counselors working out of 350 chapters throughout the United States. They provide assistance to some 140,000 small businesses each year.

The talents and skills of students and instructors at colleges and universities are fundamental to the Small Business Institute (SBI). Under the guidance of seasoned professors of business administration, students seeking advanced degrees work closely with small-business owners to help solve specific problems, such as sagging sales or rising costs. Students earn credit toward their degree, with their grades depending on how well they handle a client's problems. Several hundred colleges and universities counsel thousands of small-business owners through this program every year.

Finally, the newest of the SBA's management counseling projects is its Small Business Development Center (SBDC) program. Begun in 1976, SBDCs are designed to consolidate information from various disciplines and institutions, including technical and professional schools. Then they make this knowledge available to new and existing small businesses. In 1995, universities in 45 states took part in the program.

Networking More and more, small-business owners are discovering the value of networking—meeting regularly with one another to discuss common problems and opportunities and, perhaps most important, to pool resources. Businesspeople have long joined organizations such as the local chamber of commerce and the NFIBs to make such contacts.

ISTOCKPHOTO.COM

Networking has become an increasingly important tool for small business owners and entrepreneurs. Building relationships with other people can be helpful in terms of learning new information, building a client base, becoming aware of new business opportunities, and as a source of peer support. Networks and contacts can also be very helpful in determining what a firm's competitors are doing and how to compete with them more effectively.

Today, organizations are springing up all over the United States to facilitate small-business networking. One such organization, the Council of Smaller Enterprises of Cleveland, boasts a total membership of more than 10,000 small-business owners, the largest number in the country. This organization offers its members not only networking possibilities but also educational programs and services tailored to their needs. In a typical year, its 85 educational programs draw more than 8,500 small-business owners.

In particular, women and minorities have found networking to be an effective problem-solving tool. The National Association of Women Business Owners (NAWBO), for example, provides a variety of networking forums. The NAWBO also has chapters in most major cities, where its members can meet regularly. Increasingly, women are relying more on other women to help locate venture capital, establish relationships with customers, and provide essential services such as accounting and legal advice. According to Patty Abramson of the Women's Growth Capital Fund, all these tasks have traditionally been harder for women because, until now, they have never had friends in the right places. "I wouldn't say this is about discrimination," adds Abramson. "It's about not having the relationships, and business is about relationships."

Franchising

The next time you drive or walk around town, be on the alert for a McDonald's, Taco Bell, Subway, Denny's, or KFC restaurant; a 7-Eleven or Circle K convenience store; a RE/MAX or Coldwell Banker real estate office; a Super 8 or Ramada Inn motel; a Blockbuster Video store; a Sylvan Learning educational center; an Express Oil Change or Precision Auto Wash service center; or a Supercuts hair salon. What do these businesses have in common? In most cases, they are franchised operations, operating under licenses issued by parent companies to local entrepreneurs who own and manage them.

As many would-be businesspeople have discovered, **franchising agreements** are an accessible doorway to entrepreneurship. A franchise is an arrangement that permits the *franchisee* (buyer) to sell the product of the *franchiser* (seller, or parent company). Franchisees can thus benefit from the selling corporation's experience and expertise. They can also consult the franchiser for managerial and financial help.

For example, the franchiser may supply financing. It may pick the store location, negotiate the lease, design the store, and purchase necessary equipment. It may train the first set of employees and managers and provide standardized policies and procedures. Once the business is open, the franchiser may offer franchisees savings by allowing them to purchase from a central location. Marketing strategy (especially advertising) may also be handled by the franchiser. Finally, franchisees may benefit from continued management counseling. In short, franchisees receive—that is, invest in—not only their own ready-made business but also expert help in running it.

Franchises offer many advantages to both sellers and buyers. For example, franchisers benefit from the ability to grow rapidly by using the investment money provided by franchisees. This strategy has enabled giant franchisers such as McDonald's and Subway to mushroom into billion-dollar concerns in a brief time.

For the franchisee, the arrangement combines the incentive of owning a business with the advantage of access to big-business management skills. Unlike the person who starts from scratch, the franchisee does not have to build a business step by step. Instead, the business is established virtually overnight. Moreover, because each franchise outlet is probably a carbon copy of every other outlet, the chances of failure are reduced. McDonald's, for example, is a model of consistency—Big Macs taste the same everywhere.

franchising agreement
A contract between an entrepreneur (the franchisee) and a parent company (the franchiser); the entrepreneur pays the parent company for the use of its trademarks, products, formulas, and business plans

Of course, owning a franchise also involves certain disadvantages. Perhaps the most significant is the start-up cost. Franchise prices vary widely. Fantastic Sams hair salon franchise fees are $25,000 to $30,000. Extremely profitable or hard-to-get franchises are much more expensive, though. A McDonald's franchise costs at least $900,000 to $1,740,000, and a professional sports team can cost several hundred million dollars. Franchisees may also have continued obligations to contribute percentages of sales to the parent corporation.

Buying a franchise also entails less tangible costs. For one thing, the small-business owner sacrifices some independence. A McDonald's franchisee cannot change the way its hamburgers or milkshakes are made. Nor can franchisees create an individual identity in their community; for all practical purposes, the McDonald's owner is anonymous. In addition, many franchise agreements are difficult to terminate.

Finally, although franchises minimize risks, they do not guarantee success. Many franchisees have seen their investments—and their dreams—disappear because of poor location, rising costs, or lack of continued franchiser commitment. Moreover, figures on failure rates are artificially low because they do not include failing franchisees bought out by their franchising parent companies. An additional risk is that the chain itself could collapse. In any given year, dozens—sometimes hundreds—of franchisers close shop or stop selling franchises.

THE PERFORMANCE OF ENTREPRENEURIAL ORGANIZATIONS

The formulation and implementation of an effective strategy play major roles in determining the overall performance of an entrepreneurial organization. This section examines how entrepreneurial firms evolve over time and the attributes of these firms that enhance their chances of success. For every Henry Ford, Walt Disney, Mary Kay Ash, or Bill Gates—people who transformed small businesses into major corporations—there are many small-business owners and entrepreneurs who fail.

Figure 5.5 illustrates recent trends in new business start-ups and failures. As you can see, new business start-ups have generally run between around 150,000 and 200,000 per year. Business failures have generally run between 50,000 and 100,000 per year. In this section, we look first at a few key trends in small-business start-ups. Then we examine some of the main reasons for success and failure in small-business undertakings.

Trends in Small-Business Start-ups

Thousands of new businesses are started in the United States every year. Several factors account for this trend, and in this section we focus on four of them.

Emergence of E-Commerce Clearly, one of the most significant recent trends in small-business start-ups is the rapid emergence of electronic commerce. Because the Internet has provided fundamentally new ways of doing business, savvy entrepreneurs have been able to create and expand new businesses faster and more easily than ever before. Leading-edge firms such as Facebook, Google, and eBay, for example, owe their very existence to the Internet. At the same time, however, many would-be Internet entrepreneurs have gone under in the last few years, as the so-called dot-com boom quickly

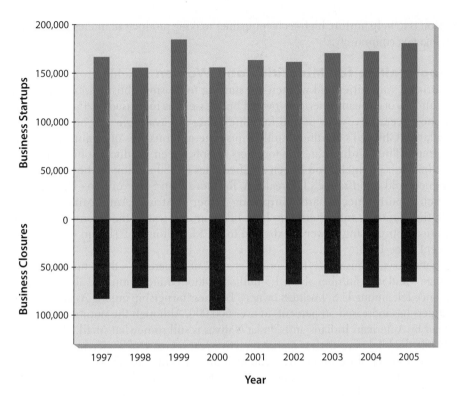

Figure 5.5
**Business Start-Up Successes
and Failures**

*Over the most recent ten-
year period for which data
are available, new business
startups numbered between
150,000 and 200,000 per
year. Business failures during
this same period, meanwhile,
ranged from about 50,000 to
nearly 100,000 per year.*

Source: U.S. Census Bureau,
*Statistical Abstract of the United
States* (Washington, D.C.:
U.S. Census Bureau, 2009).

faded. In 2008, online retail sales exceeded $200 billion, an increase of 17 percent from the previous year.

Indeed, it seems as if new ideas emerge virtually every day. Andrew Beebe, for example, is scoring big with Bigstep, a web business that essentially creates, hosts, and maintains websites for other small businesses. So far, Bigstep has signed up 75,000 small-business clients. Beebe actually provides his basic services for free but earns money by charging for the so-called premium services such as customer billing. Karl Jacob's Keen. com is a web business that matches people looking for advice with experts who have the answers. Keen got the idea when he and his father were struggling to fix a boat motor and did not know where to turn for help. Keen.com attracted 100,000 subscribers in just three months.[22]

Crossovers from Big Business   It is interesting to note that increasingly more businesses are being started by people who have opted to leave big corporations and put their experience and know-how to work for themselves. In some cases, these individuals see great new ideas they want to develop. Often, they get burned out working for a big corporation. Sometimes they have lost their jobs, only to discover that working for themselves was a better idea anyway.

Cisco Systems CEO John Chambers is acknowledged as one of the best entrepreneurs around. But he spent several years working first at IBM and then at Wang Laboratories before he set out on his own. Under his leadership, Cisco has become one of the most important technology companies in the world. In a more unusual case, Gilman Louie recently left an executive position at Hasbro toy company's online group to head up a Central Intelligence Agency (CIA)-backed venture capital firm called In-Q-It. The firm's mission is to help nurture high-tech companies making products of interest to the nation's intelligence community.[23]

Opportunities for Minorities and Women In addition to big-business expatriates, minorities and women are starting more small businesses. For example, the number of African American–owned businesses has increased by 45 percent during the most recent five-year period for which data are available and now totals about 1,150,000. Chicago's Gardner family is just one of thousands of examples illustrating this trend. The Gardners are the founders of Soft Sheen Products, a firm specializing in ethnic hair products. Soft Sheen attained sales of $80 million in the year before the Gardners sold it to France's L'Oréal S.A. for more than $160 million. The emergence of such opportunities is hardly surprising, either to African American entrepreneurs or to the corporate marketers who have taken an interest in their companies. African American purchasing power is expected to hit $1 trillion by 2012, an increase of 188 percent since 1998.

Latino-owned businesses have grown at a rate of 31 percent—three times the national average—and now number about 1.5 million. Other ethnic groups are also making their presence felt among U.S. business owners. Business ownership among Asians and Pacific Islanders has increased 56 percent, to over 600,000. Although the number of businesses owned by American Indians and Alaska Natives is still somewhat small, at slightly over 200,000, the total nevertheless represents a five-year increase of 87 percent.

The number of women entrepreneurs is also growing rapidly. Celeste Johnson, for example, left a management position at Pitney Bowes to launch Obex, Inc., which makes gardening and landscaping products from mixed recycled plastics. Katrina Garnett gave up a lucrative job at Oracle to start her own software company, Crossworlds Software. Laila Rubenstein closed her management-consulting practice to create Greeting Cards. com, Inc., an Internet-based business selling customizable electronic greetings.

There are now 10.1 million businesses owned by women—about 40 percent of all businesses in the United States. Combined, they generate nearly $4 trillion in revenue a year—an increase of 132 percent since 1992. The number of people employed nationwide at women-owned businesses since 1992 has grown to around 27.5 million—an increase of 108 percent.[24]

Better Survival Rates Finally, more people are encouraged to test their skills as entrepreneurs because the failure rate among small businesses has been declining in recent years. During the 1960s and 1970s, for example, less than half of all new start-ups survived more than 18 months; only one in five lasted for ten years. Now, however, new businesses have a better chance of surviving. Of new businesses started in the 1980s, for instance, over 77 percent remained in operation for at least three years. Today, the SBA estimates that at least 50 percent of all new businesses can expect to survive for at least five years. For the reasons discussed in the next section, small businesses suffer a higher mortality rate than larger concerns. Among those that manage to stay in business for six to ten years, however, the survival rate levels off.

Reasons for Failure

Unfortunately, 64 percent of all new businesses will not celebrate a tenth anniversary. Why do some succeed and others fail? Although no set pattern has been established, four general factors contribute to new business failure. One factor is managerial incompetence or inexperience. Some would-be entrepreneurs assume that they can succeed through common sense, overestimate their own managerial acumen, or think that hard work alone will lead to success. But if managers do not know how to make basic business decisions or understand the basic concepts and principles of management, they are unlikely to be successful in the long run.

Second, neglect can also contribute to failure. Some entrepreneurs try either to launch their ventures in their spare time or to devote only a limited amount of time to a new business. But starting a new business requires an overwhelming time commitment. Entrepreneurs who are not willing to put in the time and effort that a business requires are unlikely to survive.

Third, weak control systems can lead to serious problems. Effective control systems are needed to keep a business on track and to help alert entrepreneurs to potential trouble. If control systems do not signal impending problems, managers may be in serious trouble before more visible difficulties alert them.

Finally, insufficient capital can contribute to new business failure. Some entrepreneurs are overly optimistic about how soon they will start earning profits. In most cases, however, it takes months or years before a business is likely to start turning a profit. Amazon.com, for example, has still not earned a profit. Most experts say that a new business should have enough capital to operate for at least six months without earning a profit; some recommend enough to last a year.[25]

Reasons for Success

Similarly, four basic factors are typically cited to explain new business success. One factor is hard work, drive, and dedication. New business owners must be committed to succeeding and be willing to put in the time and effort to make it happen. Having positive feelings and a good outlook on life may also play an important role.[26] Gladys Edmunds, a single teenaged mother in Pittsburgh, washed laundry, made chicken dinners to sell to cab drivers, and sold fire extinguishers and Bibles door to door to earn money to launch her own business. Today, Edmunds Travel Consultants employs eight people and earns about $6 million in annual revenues.[27]

Second, careful analysis of market conditions can help new business owners assess the probable reception of their products in the marketplace. This will provide insights about market demand for proposed products and services. Whereas attempts to expand local restaurants specializing in baked potatoes, muffins, and gelato have been largely unsuccessful, hamburger and pizza chains continue to have an easier time expanding into new markets.

Third, managerial competence also contributes to success. Successful new business owners may acquire competence through training or experience or by using the expertise of others. Few successful entrepreneurs succeed alone or straight out of college. Most spend time working in successful companies or partner with others to bring more expertise to a new business.

Finally, luck also plays a role in the success of some firms. For example, after Alan McKim started Clean Harbors, an environmental cleanup firm based in New England, he struggled to keep his business afloat. Then the U.S. government committed $1.6 billion to toxic waste cleanup—McKim's specialty. He was able to get several large government contracts and put his business on solid financial footing. Had the government fund not been created at just the right time, McKim may well have failed. Similarly, when several major retailers closed their doors in 2009, others firms that specialize in liquidating inventories of bankrupt companies flourished and most saw a big jump in revenues and profits.[28]

SUMMARY OF LEARNING OBJECTIVES AND KEY POINTS

1. Discuss the nature of entrepreneurship.

   - Entrepreneurship is the process of planning, organizing, operating, and assuming the risk of a business venture.

   - An entrepreneur is someone who engages in entrepreneurship. In general, entrepreneurs start small businesses.

2. Describe the role of entrepreneurship in society.

   - Small businesses are an important source of innovation.

   - Small businesses create numerous jobs.

   - Small businesses contribute to the success of large businesses.

3. Understand the major issues involved in choosing strategies for small firms and the role of international management in entrepreneurship.

   - In choosing strategies, entrepreneurs have to consider the characteristics of the industry in which they are going to conduct business.

   - Small businesses generally have several distinctive competencies that they should exploit in choosing their strategy. They are usually skilled at identifying niches in established markets, identifying new markets, and acting quickly to obtain first-mover advantages.

   - Small businesses are usually not skilled at exploiting economies of scale.

   - Once an entrepreneur has chosen a strategy, the strategy is normally written down in a business plan. Writing a business plan forces an entrepreneur to plan thoroughly and to anticipate problems that might occur.

4. Discuss the structural challenges unique to entrepreneurial firms.

   - With a strategy and business plan in place, entrepreneurs must choose a structure to implement them.

   - In addition, the entrepreneur has some unique structural choices to make. For example, the entrepreneur can buy an existing business or start a new one.

   - In determining financial structure, an entrepreneur has to decide how much personal capital to invest in an organization, how much bank and government support to obtain, and whether to encourage venture capital firms to invest.

   - Entrepreneurs can also rely on various sources of advice.

5. Understand the determinants of the performance of small firms.

   - Several interesting trends characterize new business start-ups today.

   - There are several reasons why some new businesses fail and others succeed.

DISCUSSION QUESTIONS

Questions for Review

1. Describe the similarities and differences between entrepreneurial firms and large firms in terms of their job creation and innovation.

2. What characteristics make an industry attractive to entrepreneurs? Based on these characteristics, which industries are most attractive to entrepreneurs?

3. Describe recent trends in new business start-ups.

4. What are the different sources of advice for entrepreneurs? What type of information would an entrepreneur be likely to get from each source? What are the drawbacks or limitations for each source?

5. What are the basic reasons why small businesses succeed and what are the basic reasons they fail?

Questions for Analysis

1. Entrepreneurs and small businesses play a variety of important roles in society. If these roles are so important, do you think that the government should do more to encourage the development of small business? Why or why not?

2. Consider the four major reasons for new business failure. What actions can entrepreneurs take to minimize or avoid each cause of failure?

3. The U.S. automotive industry is well established, with several large and many small competitors. Describe the unexploited niches in the U.S. auto industry and tell how entrepreneurs could offer products that fill those niches.

4. List five entrepreneur-owned businesses in your community. In which industry does each business compete? Based on the industry, how do you rate each business's long-term chances for success? Explain your answers.

5. Using the information about managing a small business presented in this chapter, analyze whether you would like to work in a small business—either as an employee or as a founder. Given your personality, background, and experience, does working in or starting a new business appeal to you? What are the reasons for your opinion?

BUILDING EFFECTIVE DIAGNOSTIC SKILLS

Exercise Overview

Diagnostic skills enable a manager to visualize the most appropriate response to a situation. This exercise is designed to develop your diagnostic skills by asking you to think about your chances of becoming an entrepreneur.

Exercise Background

Scholars of entrepreneurship are naturally interested in the reasons why some people choose to start new businesses while other people—indeed, most people—don't. Researchers have surveyed thousands of individuals, both entrepreneurs and nonentrepreneurs, in efforts to identify some of the factors that distinguish between individuals in the two groups. Out of these hundreds of studies some consensus has emerged. The results tell us that the following types of individuals are most likely to become entrepreneurs:

- Parents, children, spouses, or siblings of entrepreneurs

- Immigrants to the United States or the children of immigrants

- Members of the Jewish or Protestant faiths

- Professional degree holders in fields such as medicine, law, or engineering

- People who've recently experienced life-changing events, such as getting married, having a child, moving to a new city, or losing a job

Exercise Task

Considering the information above, do the following:

1. Choose one of the above categories and explain why this particular factor might make an individual more likely to become a business owner.

2. Being sure to choose a category other than the one that you discussed for question 1, select one of these categories that applies to *you*. In your opinion, does that factor make it more likely that you'll become an entrepreneur? Why or why not? If none of the above categories applies to you, discuss whether that fact itself makes it *less* likely that you'll become an entrepreneur.

BUILDING EFFECTIVE CONCEPTUAL SKILLS

Exercise Overview

Conceptual skills require you to think in the abstract. This exercise will help you apply your conceptual skills to an analysis of certain criteria for successful entrepreneurship.

Exercise Background

Now that you're about to graduate, you've decided to open a small business in the local community where you've been attending college. We won't ask where you got them, but we'll assume that you have enough funds to start a business without having to worry about finding investors.

Based solely on your personal interests, list five businesses that you might want to open and operate. For the moment, forget about technicalities such as market potential or profitability. If, for example, you like riding your bicycle, think about opening a shop that caters to cyclists.

Next, *without regard for any personal interest you might have in them*, list five businesses that you might want to open and operate. In this case, your only criteria are market opportunity and profitability. What types of businesses might be profitable in your chosen community? Use the Internet to gather information on factors such as population, local economic conditions, local competition, and franchising opportunities.

Finally, evaluate the prospects for success of each of the ten businesses that you've listed and jot down some notes to summarize your conclusions.

Exercise Task

Reviewing your lists, the information that you've gathered, and the conclusions that you've drawn, do the following:

1. Form a small group of four or five classmates and discuss your respective lists. Look for instances in which the same type of business appears on either both of your lists or one of your lists and one of a classmate's lists. Also look for cases in which the same business appears on one or more than one list with either similar or dissimilar prospects for success.

2. At this point, how important do you regard personal interest as a factor in small-business success?

3. How important do you regard market potential as a factor in small-business success?

SKILLS SELF-ASSESSMENT INSTRUMENT

An Entrepreneurial Quiz

Introduction: Entrepreneurs are starting ventures all the time. These new businesses are vital to the economy. The following assessment is designed to help you understand your readiness to start your own business—to be an entrepreneur.

Instructions: Place a checkmark or an X in the box next to the response that best represents your self-evaluation.

1. Are you a self-starter?
   - ❏ I do things on my own. Nobody has to tell me to get going.
   - ❏ If someone gets me started, I keep going all right.
   - ❏ Easy does it. I don't push myself until I have to.

2. How do you feel about other people?
   - ❏ I like people. I can get along with just about anybody.
   - ❏ I have plenty of friends—I don't need anybody else.
   - ❏ Most people irritate me.

3. Can you lead others?
   - ❏ I can get most people to go along when I start something.
   - ❏ I can give orders if someone tells me what we should do.
   - ❏ I let someone else get things moving. Then I go along if I feel like it.

4. Can you take responsibility?
   - ❏ I like to take charge of things and see them through.
   - ❏ I'll take over if I have to, but I'd rather let someone else be responsible.
   - ❏ There are always eager beavers around wanting to show how smart they are. I let them.

5. How good an organizer are you?
   - ❏ I like to have a plan before I start. I'm usually the one to get things lined up when the group wants to do something.
   - ❏ I do all right unless things get too confused. Then I quit.
   - ❏ You get all set and then something comes along and presents too many problems. So I just take things as they come.

6. How good a worker are you?
   - ❏ I can keep going as long as I need to. I don't mind working hard for something I want.
   - ❏ I'll work hard for a while, but when I've had enough, that's it.
   - ❏ I can't see that hard work gets you anywhere.

7. Can you make decisions?
   - ❏ I can make up my mind in a hurry if I have to. It usually turns out okay, too.
   - ❏ I can if I have plenty of time. If I have to make up my mind fast, I think later I should have decided the other way.
   - ❏ I don't like to be the one who has to decide things.

8. Can people trust what you say?
   - ❏ You bet they can. I don't say things I don't mean.
   - ❏ I try to be on the level most of the time, but sometimes I just say what's easiest.
   - ❏ Why bother if the other person doesn't know the difference?

9. Can you stick with it?
   - ❏ If I make up my mind to do something, I don't let *anything* stop me.
   - ❏ I usually finish what I start—if it goes well.
   - ❏ If it doesn't go well right away, I quit. Why beat your brains out?

10. How good is your health?
    - ❏ I *never* run down!
    - ❏ I have enough energy for most things I want to do.
    - ❏ I run out of energy sooner than most of my friends.

Total the checks or Xs in each column here _____.

Source: From Business Startup Basics by Donald Dible, pp. 9–10, © 1978. Adapted by permission of Prentice-Hall, Inc., Upper Saddle River, N.J.

EXPERIENTIAL EXERCISE

Negotiating a Franchise Agreement

Step 1: Assume that you are the owner of a rapidly growing restaurant chain. To continue your current level of growth, you are considering the option of selling franchises for new restaurants. Working alone, outline the major points of most concern to you that you would want to have in a franchising agreement. Also note the characteristics you would look for in potential franchisees.

Step 2: Assume that you are an individual investor looking to buy a franchise in a rapidly growing restaurant chain. Again working alone, outline the major factors that might determine which franchise you elect to buy. Also note the characteristics you would look for in a potential franchiser.

Step 3: Now form small groups of four. Randomly select one member of the group to play the role of the franchiser; the other three members will play the roles of potential franchisees. Role-play a negotiation meeting. The franchiser should stick as closely as possible to the major points developed in Step 1. Similarly, the potential franchisees should try to adhere to the points they developed in Step 2.

Follow-up Questions

1. Did doing both Step 1 and Step 2 in advance help or hinder your negotiations?

2. Can a franchising agreement be so one-sided as to damage the interests of both parties? How so?

 YOU MAKE THE CALL

Facebook Faces the Problem of Booking Revenues

1. If you use Facebook (or any other social-networking site), which of its features are most attractive to you? If you don't use any social-networking site, what features are most likely to cause you to try one out?

2. Identify the primary factors in Facebook's success in attracting users over the course of its brief lifetime.

3. Why is Facebook's user base so valuable an asset? In what ways has Facebook tried to turn that asset into a profitable resource? What strategy would you recommend that Facebook use to generate more revenue, whether from advertising or some other source?

4. What do you see as the most serious threats to Facebook?

5. Would you be willing to invest in Facebook? Why or why not?

CHAPTER 6

MANAGING ORGANIZATION STRUCTURE AND DESIGN

LEARNING OBJECTIVES

After studying this chapter, you should be able to:

1 Identify the basic elements of organizations.

2 Describe the bureaucratic perspective on organization design.

3 Identify and explain key situational influences on organization design.

4 Describe the basic forms of organization design that characterize many organizations.

5 Identify and describe emerging issues in organization design.

Promoting Brand Loyalty at Abercrombie & Fitch

Abercrombie & Fitch (A&F) is one of the largest specialty retailers catering to young adults ages 18 to 22. Look around your college classroom and you'll probably spy at least one A&F item—a cap, a shirt, a pair of jeans. A&F, a line of "casual luxury" apparel and other products, is actually one of five brands owned by Ohio-based A&F Corporation. The company's other brands include abercrombie ("classic cool" for preteens), Hollister ("SoCal" for teenagers), RUEHL No.925 (a higher-priced brand for postcollegiates ages 22 to 30), and Gilly Hicks (Australian-themed lounge and underwear for women). Obviously, A&F's businesses are related, and its overall corporate strategy is best characterized as one of *related diversification* (see Chapter 5). Most firms that use this strategy have a form of organization design based on divisions—one division for each major product or product group. Interestingly, however, A&F relies instead on a different kind of organization design centered around functional departments (groups responsible for specific company functions). Why does A&F run counter to most other organizations? Basically, A&F wants an employee to develop highly specialized skills within a functional area. In addition, the functional design is more

"Abercrombie's biggest weakness is that it's all about Mike."

—ROBERT BUCHANAN,
INVESTMENT ANALYST, A.G. EDWARDS & SONS

effective in coordinating activities within a function.

The company's history also accounts in part for its choice of a functional structure. From its founding in 1892 until a bankruptcy in 1977, A&F was a high-end sporting-goods retailer. In 1978, Oshman's, a Houston-based sporting-goods chain, purchased the company brand and trademark and for 11 years operated a combination retail chain and catalog company selling an eclectic line of products ranging from tweed jackets to exercise machines. Limited Brands purchased the

Abercrombie & Fitch is one of the nation's most successful retailers. The firm uses a functional organization design in order to maintain tight control over operations and to help employees identify with specific business functions.

brand in 1988, putting it on preppy, upscale clothing for young adults. Nine years later, Limited sold 16 percent of the company through a public stock sale. When the remaining shares were sold to the public in 1998, A&F became an independent company. In its current incarnation, then, A&F started out as a division of a larger firm, and so it makes sense that its structure might remain that of one division in a multidivisional corporation.

It's also interesting to note that, even before the spin-off from Limited, A&F had begun to establish its own culture and its own pattern of growth. Michael Jeffries, a retail-industry veteran, became president in 1992 and undertook to transform the company into the retailer of choice for younger consumers. Jeffries quickly managed to attach the brand to an "ideal" lifestyle, emphasizing apparel that complemented youth, good looks, and good times. The transformation turned out to be highly profitable, with sales increasing from $85 million in 1992 to $165 million in 1994. During the same period, the number of stores in the chain grew from 36 to 67, and in 1999, with 212 stores nationwide, A&F topped $1 billion in sales. In the same year, A&F started its abercrombie division for children and preteens, and a year later, it launched Hollister, the first of its "lifestyle" chains. By the end of 2002, the multi-division company was running 485 A&F stores, 144 abercrombie shops, and 32 Hollister outlets. Sales for the year were just under $1.4 billion. RUEHL opened in 2004 and Gilly Hicks in 2008. Today, A&F Corporation operates 1,059 stores, including 6 stores across Canada and 2 in London. Stores are slated for Paris and other European cities starting in 2011.

And yet, A&F is still organized as if it were one big company with one big brand. The main advantage of this choice can be explained as a desire to exercise top-down control over each brand by separating and controlling all the functions on which every brand—that is, every store type—depends. However A&F is organized and otherwise managed, one thing is clear: It's the way it is because that's the way CEO Jeffries wants it. Jeffries took over a company that was losing $25 million a year, declared that survival depended on becoming a "young, hip, spirited company," and engineered a reversal of fortunes by turning it into something completely new—a retailer that celebrates what one observer calls "the vain, highly constructed

male" (A&F has had much less influence on women's fashion). And Jeffries himself, suggests Benoit Denizet-Lewis, demonstrates his own brand of brand loyalty by gleefully playing the role of the vain, highly constructed male. At 63, he dyes his hair blond and dresses for work in torn A&F jeans, A&F muscle polo shirts, and A&F flip-flops. And the outfit is more or less a uniform among employees at the company's "campus" in New Albany, Ohio, where Jeffries has designed everything to foster what Denizet-Lewis characterizes as "a cultlike immersion in his brand identity."

By the end of fiscal 2009, Jeffries had also delivered increased revenues in 57 out of the previous 60 quarters. "To me," says investment analyst Robert Buchanan, "it's the most amazing record . . . in U.S. retailing, period." The A&F brand may be a direct extension of Jeffries' eccentric image of the contemporary young American male, but as Denizet-Lewis puts it, Jeffries has made it "the most dominant and imitated lifestyle-based brand for young men in America." The key to his success seems to be his determination to control every aspect of his brands and his business. Jeffries spends much of the time in his office (which is actually a conference room with big windows from which he can see the whole campus) discussing new products and new ideas with designers and much of the time outside his office overseeing the details of store layouts, down to the fixtures and mannequins. "How does a store look? How does it feel? How does it smell? That's what I'm obsessed with," admits Jeffries. On the Ohio campus, there are models of all five A&F store types, and it's not unusual to find Jeffries making sure that everything is just the way he wants it. When it is, pictures are taken and sent to stores so that everything can be perfectly replicated. "It's so rare to find someone who's brilliant at both the creative and the business sides," says a former coworker at Jeffries' previous employer. "But Jeffries is both. He's good at thinking in broad terms, but he's also obsessed with details."

As the company's earnings record suggests, there doesn't seem to be much that's wrong with the way A&F is run, but it stands to reason that, given the thoroughness of his hands-on approach, Michael Jeffries must be held responsible for the firm's debits as well as its credits. A.G. Edwards's Buchanan, though impressed by Jeffries' streak of revenue increases, goes so far as to say that

"Abercrombie's biggest weakness is that it's all about Mike." Jeffries' 16-year tenure, though distinguished by outstanding financial success, has in fact been marred by controversy. Parents' groups have long complained about A&F's sex-infused image and the advertising used to convey it. Catalogs and store walls, for example, are dominated by pictures of scantily clad models often engaged in suggestive activities. In February 2008, police in Virginia, prompted by customer complaints, raided a local A&F store and stripped the walls of promotional photos, citing a law banning "obscene materials in a business that is open to juveniles."

Perhaps more serious, at least from a strictly business standpoint, is the controversy stirred by some of Jeffries' actions among A&F shareholders. In particular, investigations of shareholder complaints have indicated possible problems with Jeffries' control over his board of directors. In 2005, for instance, a suit filed by shareholders charged that Jeffries' pay was excessive. Although no one admitted any wrongdoing, Jeffries agreed to cut in half (from $12 million to $6 million), a bonus for staying in his job, along with some stock options. He also agreed to add more outside directors to the board; at the time, two of the board's six outside members, including the head of the compensation committee, were receiving substantial fees for business conducted with the company. In addition, he agreed to make the heads of the firm's five retail divisions presidents of their respective divisions (up until then they'd been executive or senior vice presidents). In January 2009, Jeffries reached an agreement to remain as chairman and CEO until 2014. His compensation remains pretty much the same: an annual base salary of $1.5 million plus bonuses up to a maximum of 240 percent of base salary.

A&F's net income for fiscal 2008 was $272.3 million—down 42 percent from $475.7 in 2007. In the fourth quarter alone, which Jeffries called "a catastrophe for the retail industry," net profit plummeted by 68 percent. Over the course of the year, the company's stock had lost 74 percent of its value, and although the global economy is obviously the primary factor, as of this writing, analysts and investors are questioning the wisdom of Jeffries' refusal both to discount prices and to engage in high-profile promotional activity as a means of countering the plunge in consumer spending. One analyst, for example, disagrees strongly with "Jeffries' stubborn position not to run sales promotions in the midst of the worst retail environment in decades": "With the entire retail world (including the top luxury retailers and brands) promoting fiercely to free up cash and keep market share, Mr. Jeffries seems to believe that any hint of promotional activity . . . will tarnish A&F's . . . [brand] positioning forever." Jeffries replies that "promotions are a short-term solution with dreadful long-term effects" and has insisted on avoiding any strategy that would compromise the long-term value of the company's brands.

Jeffries had taken the same stance during the post-9/11 economic slump of 2001–2002 and the recession of 2008–2009, emerging with his streak of increasingly profitable quarters intact and confirming his conviction that A&F's customers would pay premium prices for the brands they regarded as worth the money. "I don't care what anyone other than our target customer thinks," says Jeffries, but this time around, his target customers appear to be thinking more about the value of their money than that of their apparel. In February 2009, A&F sales dropped 28 percent from 2008, and same-store sales declined by 30 percent. With price points 2.1 times those of American Eagle and 3.2 times those of Aéropostale, A&F has found itself losing customers to its main rivals.[1]

One of the major ingredients in managing any business is the creation of an organization design to link the various elements that comprise the organization. There is a wide array of alternatives that managers in any given organization might select for its design. As we noted earlier, for instance, A&F uses a functional design but could also use a divisional design if Michael Jeffries chose to do so. This chapter, the first of three devoted to organizing, discusses many of the critical elements of organization structure and design that managers can control. We first identify and describe the various elements of organizing. Next we explore how those elements can be combined to create an overall design for the organization. Next we introduce situational factors and how they impact organization design. We conclude by presenting emerging issues in organization design.

THE BASIC ELEMENTS OF ORGANIZING

The term *organization structure and design* refers to the overall set of elements that can be used to configure an organization. This section introduces and describes these elements: job specialization, departmentalization, reporting relationships, distribution of authority, and coordination.

Job Specialization

The first building block of organization structure is job specialization. **Job specialization** is the degree to which the overall task of the organization is broken down and divided into smaller component parts. For example, when Walt Disney started his company, he did everything himself—wrote cartoons, drew them, added character voices, and then marketed them to theaters. As the business grew, though, he eventually hired others to perform many of these same functions. As growth continued, so, too, did specialization. For example, as animation artists work on Disney movies today, they may specialize in generating computer images of a single character or doing only background scenery. Others provide voices, and marketing specialists develop promotional campaigns. And today, the Walt Disney Company has literally thousands of different specialized jobs. Clearly, no one person could perform them all. The "Tough Times, Tough Choices" box introduces the relatively new management specialty of chief ethics officer.

Benefits and Limitations of Specialization   Job specialization provides four benefits to organizations.[2] First, workers performing small, simple tasks will become very proficient at each task. Second, transfer time between tasks decreases. If employees perform several different tasks, some time is lost as they stop doing the first task and start doing the next. Third, the more narrowly defined a job is, the easier it is to develop specialized equipment to assist with that job. Fourth, when an employee who performs a highly specialized job is absent or resigns, the manager is able to train someone new at relatively low cost. Although specialization is generally thought of in terms of operating jobs, many organizations have extended the basic elements of specialization to managerial and professional levels.[3]

On the other hand, job specialization can have negative consequences. The foremost criticism is that workers who perform highly specialized jobs may become bored and dissatisfied. The job may be so specialized that it offers no challenge or stimulation. Boredom and monotony set in, absenteeism rises, and the quality of the work may suffer. Furthermore, the anticipated benefits of specialization do not always occur. For example, a classic study conducted at Maytag found that the time spent moving work in process from one worker to another was greater than the time needed for the same individual to change from job to job.[4] Thus, although some degree of specialization is necessary, it should not be carried to extremes because of the possible negative consequences. Managers must be sensitive to situations in which extreme specialization should be avoided. And indeed, several alternative approaches to designing jobs have been developed in recent years.

job specialization
The degree to which the overall task of the organization is broken down and divided into smaller component parts

TOUGH TIMES, TOUGH CHOICES

"The Organization Shall…"

The position of "ethics officer" first became popular in both for-profit and nonprofit organizations because other members of the executive hierarchy wanted to stay out of jail. Okay, that's not *exactly* true. The position did, however, begin appearing on organization charts in the early 1990s in response to the establishment of the U.S. Sentencing Commission in 1984. The Commission was authorized by Congress to establish the U.S. Sentencing Guidelines for Organizations and the U.S. Sentencing Guidelines for Individuals to ensure uniformity in the sentencing of parties convicted of violating federal law.

To recommend good corporate citizenship as a means of complying with the law, the Commission's Guidelines for Organizations (issued in 1991) took into consideration not only the relative seriousness of an organization's crime but also the degree of its culpability. The Guidelines laid out seven elements of an "Effective Compliance and Ethics Program"; they are, in effect, guidelines by which organizations can deal proactively with the factors that will be considered by the courts in assessing culpability and handing down sentences for violations. Like most federal statutes, they're far too complicated to summarize in adequate detail, but we'll provide a brief rundown: The organization shall

1. "exercise due diligence to prevent and detect criminal conduct";
2. "promote an organizational culture that encourages ethical conduct and a commitment to compliance with the law";
3. "use reasonable efforts" to exclude from its management ranks anyone who has acted illegally or in ways "inconsistent with an effective compliance and ethics program";
4. "take reasonable steps to communicate" the "standards and procedures" of its program;
5. "take reasonable steps" to see that its program is followed, to evaluate its effectiveness, and to publicize ways in which employees can take advantage of it;

6. promote its program by offering incentives to conform to it and establishing "appropriate disciplinary measures" to deal with violations; and
7. "take reasonable steps to respond appropriately" to any detected criminal conduct.

The guidelines also define the main activities for which the organization's "ethics officer" or "compliance and ethics officer" is responsible. A survey conducted by the Ethics Resource Center (ERC), a Washington, D.C.–based nonprofit dedicated to research on organizational ethics, reveals that, despite latitude in the language of the Guidelines and differences in the needs of various organizations, the position tends to feature certain core responsibilities:

a. overseeing the ethics function of organizational activities;
b. collecting and analyzing ethics-related data;
c. developing and interpreting ethics-related policy;
d. developing and administering ethics education and training;
e. overseeing ethics investigations.

Ethics officers, according to the Ethics and Compliance Officer Association (ECOA), a nonprofit organization serving practitioners in the field, are responsible for "integrating their organizations' ethics and values initiatives, compliance activities, and business-conduct practices into the decision-making processes at all levels of the organization."

Organizations such as the ERC and the ECOA agree that while ethics and compliance standards and procedures must be institutionalized in organization-wide efforts, all levels of an organization are not equal when it comes to ensuring that programs are effective. They emphasize that effectiveness depends on a close working relationship between the ethics officer and *high-level* management. As the ERC points out, the federal Sentencing Guidelines, as revised in 2002 and 2004, encourage organizations to take a closer look at the clause that makes an organization's "governing authority" and "high-level personnel" responsible for its ethics and compliance program. At a large corporation, the "governing authority" is the board of directors, but the term "high-level personnel" must be interpreted much more broadly: It includes not only directors but executives, any individuals in charge of business or functional units, and even individuals with substantial ownership interests. All these people are responsible for seeing that the organization's program is *effective*, and one or more of these individuals must be assigned ultimate and overall responsibility.

Although they must report to appropriate "high-level personnel," ethics officers themselves do not have to be among an organization's high-level personnel. As a practical matter, however, many organizations have found that the key function of an ethics program—effectiveness—is better served when the head of the program is in fact a high-level executive. For one thing, the presence of a high-level ethics officer underscores the organization's commitment to the program. For another, it makes much more sense to empower an ethics officer with the authority of high-level management if he or she is a member of high-level management. At the American Arbitration Association, for example, the post of ethics officer has been a senior-level job since its inception. Current ethics officer Jennifer Coffman reports directly to the CEO and makes regular presentations to the board of directors, and she adds that both the CEO and the board regard it as crucial that she be included in "critical and key decision-making discussions" of all organizational activities at the highest level.

"We believe," states the ERC, "that an ethics officer who has direct and unfettered access to the highest authorities within an organization can most effectively impact an ethical culture and contribute substantively to the ethical integrity of an organization." Unfortunately, adds the ERC, "ethics officers in many companies have become removed from top-level managers and directors, severing a critical link between senior management and line supervisors."

According to Alex Brigham, director of the Ethisphere Institute, an international think tank concerned with best practices in business ethics and corporate social responsibility, such a separation between the office responsible for ethical oversight and at least one department that needed it occurred

in 2006 at AIG, the giant U.S. insurance company that suffered huge losses in the so-called "subprime crisis" and that (as of this writing) is slated to receive $173 billion in government "bailout" funds. Compliance officer Dennis W. St. John, charges Brigham, was explicitly barred from meetings by John Cassano, head of AIG Financial Products, the group largely responsible for losses amounting to more than $1 billion in 2008–2009. St. John's testimony to Congress in 2008 backs up the allegation. According to St. John, Cassano had excluded him from meetings "because [in Cassano's words] 'I was concerned that you would pollute the process.'" "My belief," explained St. John, "is that the 'pollution' Mr. Cassano was concerned about was the transparency I brought to the … process…. I resigned because … Mr. Cassano took actions that I believed were intended to prevent me from performing the job duties for which I was hired."

Steve Priest, president of the consulting firm Ethical Leadership Group, suggests that similar scenarios—coupled with laxity on the part of ethics officers themselves—occurred in the offices of banks and other mortgage lenders whose lax lending standards eventually saddled them with too many bad loans and too little capital, leading to the collapse in 2008 of Wall Street institutions such as Bears Stearns and Merrill Lynch and a taxpayer bailout of (again, as of this writing) $3.8 trillion. As a result, says Priest, "investors don't trust the companies they're investing in. They don't trust the financial statements, they don't trust the audits, they don't trust the bond ratings agencies." Another result is that millions of Americans have also lost at least one-fourth of their retirement savings and millions more have lost their jobs.

References: United States Sentencing Commission, 2005 Federal Sentencing Guideline Manual, November 1, 2005, www.ussc.gov on March 9, 2009; Ethics Resource Center, "What Is an Ethics Officer?" Ethics Today Online, October 2004, www.ethics.org on March 8, 2009; American Society of Association Executives, "Should You Hire an Ethics Officer?" Executive Update Magazine, 2008, www.asaecenter.org on March 8, 2009; Wyche Burgess Freeman and Parham, U.S. Sentencing Commission Amends Guidelines for Corporate Compliance and Ethics Programs, August 4, 2004, www.abanet.org on March 8, 2009; Alexander F. Brigham and Stefan Linssen, "How a Mirror Can Help in a Crisis," What Went Wrong Ethically in the Economic Collapse, December 31, 2008, http://ethisphere.com on March 10, 2009; Joseph W. St. John, Letter to House of Representatives Committee on Oversight and Government Reform, October 4, 2008, http://oversight.house.gov on March 10, 2009; Claudia Parsons, "From Madoff to Merrill Lynch, 'Where Was Ethics Officer?'" International Herald Tribune, January 29, 2009, www.iht.com on March 7, 2009.

Alternatives to Specialization To counter the problems associated with specialization, managers have sought other approaches to job design that achieve a better balance between organizational demands for efficiency and productivity and individual needs for creativity and autonomy. Five alternative approaches are job rotation, job enlargement, job enrichment, job characteristics approach, and work teams.[5]

Job rotation involves systematically moving employees from one job to another. A worker in a warehouse might unload trucks on Monday, carry incoming inventory to storage on Tuesday, verify invoices on Wednesday, pull outgoing inventory from storage on Thursday, and load trucks on Friday. Thus the jobs do not change, but instead, workers move from job to job. Unfortunately, for this very reason, job rotation has not been very successful in enhancing employee motivation or satisfaction. Jobs that are amenable to rotation tend to be relatively standard and routine. Workers who are rotated to a "new" job may be more satisfied at first, but satisfaction soon wanes. Although many companies (among them American Cyanamid, Bethlehem Steel, Ford, Prudential Insurance, TRW, and Western Electric) have tried job rotation, it is most often used today as a training device to improve worker skills and flexibility.

Job enlargement was developed to increase the total number of tasks workers perform. As a result, all workers perform a wide variety of tasks, which presumably reduces the level of job dissatisfaction. Many organizations have used job enlargement, including IBM, Detroit Edison, AT&T, the U.S. Civil Service, and Maytag. At Maytag, for example, the assembly line for producing washing-machine water pumps was systematically changed so that work that had originally been performed by six workers, who passed the work sequentially from one person to another, was performed by four workers, each of whom assembled a complete pump.[6] Unfortunately, although job enlargement does have some positive consequences, they are often offset by some disadvantages: (1) training costs usually increase, (2) unions have argued that pay should increase because the worker is doing more tasks, and (3) in many cases the work remains boring and routine even after job enlargement.

A more comprehensive approach, **job enrichment**, assumes that increasing the range and variety of tasks is not sufficient by itself to improve employee motivation.[7] Thus job enrichment attempts to increase both the number of tasks a worker does and the control the worker has over the job. To implement job enrichment, managers remove some controls from the job, delegate more authority to employees, and structure the work in complete, natural units. These changes increase subordinates' sense of responsibility. Another part of job enrichment is to continually assign new and challenging tasks, thereby increasing employees' opportunity for growth and advancement. AT&T, Texas Instruments, IBM, and General Foods are among the firms that have used job enrichment. This approach, however, also has disadvantages. For example, work systems need to be analyzed before enrichment, but this seldom happens, and managers rarely ask for employee preferences when enriching jobs.

The **job characteristics approach** is an alternative to job specialization that does take into account the work system and employee preferences.[8] As illustrated in Figure 6.1, the job characteristics approach suggests that jobs should be diagnosed and improved along five core dimensions:

1. *Skill variety*, the number of things a person does in a job
2. *Task identity*, the extent to which the worker does a complete or identifiable portion of the total job
3. *Task significance*, the perceived importance of the task

---

job rotation
An alternative to job specialization that involves systematically moving employees from one job to another

job enlargement
An alternative to job specialization that increases the total number of tasks workers perform

job enrichment
An alternative to job specialization that attempts to increase both the number of tasks a worker does and the control the worker has over the job

job characteristics approach
An alternative to job specialization that suggests that jobs should be diagnosed and improved along five core dimensions, taking into account both the work system and employee preferences

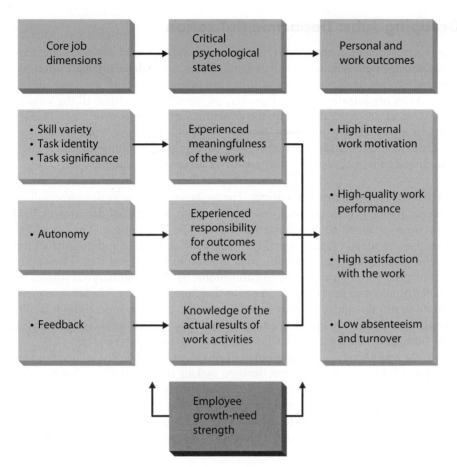

Figure 6.1
The Job Characteristics Approach

The job characteristics approach to job design provides a viable alternative to job specialization. Five core job dimensions may lead to critical psychological states that, in turn, may enhance motivation, performance, and satisfaction while also reducing absenteeism and turnover.

Source: J. R. Hackman and G. R. Oldham, "Motivation through the Design of Work: Test of a Theory," *Organizational Behavior and Human Performance,* 1976, Vol. 16, pp. 250–279. © Academic Press, Inc. Reprinted by permission of Academic Press and the authors.

4. *Autonomy,* the degree of control the worker has over how the work is performed
5. *Feedback,* the extent to which the worker knows how well the job is being performed

Increasing the presence of these dimensions in a job presumably leads to higher motivation, higher-quality performance, higher satisfaction, and lower absenteeism and turnover. A large number of studies have been conducted to test the usefulness of the job characteristics approach. The Southwestern Division of Prudential Insurance, for example, used this approach in its claims division. Results included moderate declines in turnover and a small but measurable improvement in work quality. Other research findings have not supported this approach as strongly. Thus, although the job characteristics approach is one of the most promising alternatives to job specialization, it is probably not the final answer.

Another alternative to job specialization is **work teams**. Under this arrangement, a group is given responsibility for designing the work system to be used in performing an interrelated set of tasks. In the typical assembly-line system, the work flows from one worker to the next, and each worker has a specified job to perform. In a work team, however, the group itself decides how jobs will be allocated. For example, the work team assigns specific tasks to members, monitors and controls its own performance, and has autonomy over work scheduling.[9]

work team
An alternative to job specialization that allows an entire group to design the work system it will use to perform an interrelated set of tasks

Grouping Jobs: Departmentalization

The second element of organization structure is the grouping of jobs according to some logical arrangement. The process of grouping jobs is called **departmentalization**. When organizations are small, the owner-manager can personally oversee everyone who works there. As an organization grows, however, personally supervising all the employees becomes more and more difficult for the owner-manager. Consequently, new managerial positions are created to supervise the work of others. Employees are not assigned to particular managers randomly. Rather, jobs are grouped according to some plan. The logic embodied in such a plan is the basis for all departmentalization.[10]

Functional Departmentalization   The most common base for departmentalization, especially among smaller organizations, is by function. **Functional departmentalization** groups together those jobs involving the same or similar activities. (The word *function* is used here to mean organizational functions such as finance and production, rather than the basic managerial functions, such as planning or controlling.) This approach, which is most common in smaller organizations, has three primary advantages. First, each department can be staffed by experts in that functional area. Marketing experts can be hired to run the marketing function, for example. Second, supervision is facilitated because an individual manager needs to be familiar with only a relatively narrow set of skills. And, third, coordinating activities inside each department is easier.

On the other hand, as an organization begins to grow in size, several disadvantages of this approach may emerge. For one, decision making tends to become slower and more bureaucratic. Employees may also begin to concentrate too narrowly on their own unit and lose sight of the total organizational system. Finally, accountability and performance become increasingly difficult to monitor. For example, determining whether a new product fails because of production deficiencies or a poor marketing campaign may not be possible.

Product Departmentalization   Product departmentalization, a second common approach, involves grouping and arranging activities around products or product groups. Most larger businesses adopt this form of departmentalization for grouping activities at the business or corporate level. Product departmentalization has three major advantages. First, all activities associated with one product or product group can be easily integrated and coordinated. Second, the speed and effectiveness of decision making are enhanced. Third, the performance of individual products or product groups can be assessed more easily and objectively, thereby improving the accountability of departments for the results of their activities.

Product departmentalization also has two major disadvantages. For one, managers in each department may focus on their own product or product group to the exclusion of the rest of the organization. For example, a marketing manager may see his or her primary duty as helping the group rather than helping the overall organization. For another, administrative costs rise because each department must have its own functional specialists for areas such as market research and financial analysis.

Customer Departmentalization   Under **customer departmentalization**, the organization structures its activities to respond to and interact with specific customers or customer groups. The lending activities in most banks, for example, are usually tailored to meet the needs of different kinds of customers (business, consumer, mortgage, and agricultural loans). The basic advantage of this approach is that the organization is able to

departmentalization
The process of grouping jobs according to some logical arrangement

functional departmentalization
Grouping jobs involving the same or similar activities

product departmentalization
Grouping activities around products or product groups

customer departmentalization
Grouping activities to respond to and interact with specific customers or customer groups

use skilled specialists to deal with unique customers or customer groups. It takes one set of skills to evaluate a balance sheet and lend $500,000 for operating capital and a different set of skills to evaluate an individual's creditworthiness and lend $20,000 for a new car. However, a fairly large administrative staff is required to integrate the activities of the various departments. In banks, for example, coordination is necessary to make sure that the organization does not over-commit itself in any one area and to handle collections on delinquent accounts from a diverse set of customers.

Location Departmentalization   Location departmentalization groups jobs on the basis of defined geographic sites or areas. The defined sites or areas may range in size from a hemisphere to only a few blocks of a large city. Transportation companies, police departments (precincts represent geographic areas of a city), and the Federal Reserve Bank all use location departmentalization. The primary advantage of location departmentalization is that it enables the organization to respond easily to unique customer and environmental characteristics in the various regions. On the negative side, a larger administrative staff may be required if the organization must keep track of units in scattered locations.

Establishing Reporting Relationships

The third basic element of organizing is the establishment of reporting relationships among positions. The purpose of this activity is to clarify the chain of command and the span of management.

Chain of Command   Chain of command is an old concept, first popularized in the early years of the twentieth century. For example, early writers about the **chain of command** argued that clear and distinct lines of authority need to be established among all positions in an organization. The chain of command actually has two components. The first, called unity of command, suggests that each person within an organization must have a clear reporting relationship to one and only one boss (as we see later in Chapter 13, newer models of organization design routinely—and successfully—violate this premise). The second, called the scalar principle, suggests that there must be a clear and unbroken line of authority that extends from the lowest to the highest position in the organization. The popular saying "The buck stops here" is derived from this idea—someone in the organization must ultimately be responsible for every decision.

Span of Management   Another part of establishing reporting relationships is determining how many people will report to each manager. This defines the **span of management** (sometimes called the *span of control*). For years, managers and researchers sought to determine the optimal span of management. Today we recognize that the span of management is a crucial factor in structuring organizations but that there are no universal, cut-and-dried prescriptions for an ideal or optimal span.[11]

Tall versus Flat Organizations   In recent years, managers have begun to focus attention on the optimal number of layers in their organizational hierarchy. Having more layers results in a taller organization, whereas having fewer layers results in a flatter organization. What difference does it make whether the organization is tall or flat? One early study at Sears found that a flat structure led to higher levels of employee morale and productivity.[12] Researchers have also argued that a tall structure is more expensive (because of the larger number of managers involved) and that it fosters more communication problems (because of the increased number of people through whom information must

location departmentalization
Grouping jobs on the basis of defined geographic sites or areas

chain of command
A clear and distinct line of authority among the positions in an organization

span of management
The number of people who report to a particular manager

pass). On the other hand, a wide span of management in a flat organization may result in a manager having more administrative responsibility (because there are fewer managers) and more supervisory responsibility (because there are more subordinates reporting to each manager). If these additional responsibilities become excessive, the flat organization may suffer.[13]

Many experts agree that businesses can function effectively with fewer layers of organization than they currently have. The Franklin Mint, for example, reduced its number of management layers from 6 to 4. At the same time, the CEO increased his span of management from 6 to 12. The British firm Cadbury PLC, maker of Cadbury Dairy chocolates, Trident gum, and other confectionary products, recently eliminated a layer of management separating the CEO and the firm's operating units. The specific reasons for the change were to improve communication between the CEO and the operating unit heads and to speed up decision making.[14] One additional reason for this trend is that improved communication technologies such as e-mail and text messaging allow managers to stay in touch with a larger number of subordinates than was possible even just a few years ago.[15]

Distributing Authority

authority
Power that has been legitimized by the organization

delegation
The process by which a manager assigns a portion of his or her total workload to others

Another important building block in structuring organizations is the determination of how authority is to be distributed among positions. **Authority** is power that has been legitimized by the organization.[16] Two specific issues that managers must address when distributing authority are delegation and decentralization.[17]

The Delegation Process Delegation is the establishment of a pattern of authority between a superior and one or more subordinates. Specifically, **delegation** is the process by which managers assign a portion of their total workload to others.[18] In theory, the delegation process involves three steps. First, the manager assigns responsibility or gives the subordinate a job to do. The assignment of responsibility might range from telling a subordinate to prepare a report to placing the person in charge of a task force. Along with the assignment, the individual is also given the authority to do the job. The manager may give the subordinate the power to requisition needed information from confidential files or to direct a group of other workers. Finally, the manager establishes the subordinate's accountability—that is, the subordinate accepts an obligation to carry out the task assigned by the manager. For instance, the CEO of AutoZone will sign off for the company on financial performance only when the individual manager responsible for each unit has certified his or her own results as being accurate. The firm believes that this high level of accountability will help it avoid the kind of accounting scandal that has hit many businesses in recent times.[19]

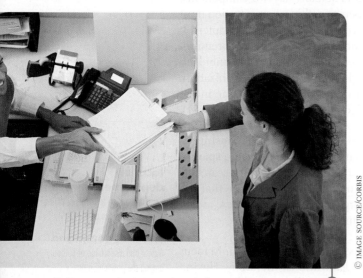

© IMAGE SOURCE/CORBIS

Delegation is the process by which managers assign tasks to their subordinates. This manager, for example, needs the worker on the left to complete a new project. She is shown here giving him a file with important information. The worker, in turn, is now accountable to her to complete the project as assigned.

Decentralization and Centralization Just as authority can be delegated from one individual to another, organizations also develop patterns of authority across a wide variety of positions and departments. **Decentralization** is the process of systematically delegating power and authority throughout the organization to middle and lower-level managers. It is important to remember that decentralization is actually one end of a continuum anchored at the other end by **centralization**, the process of systematically retaining power and authority in the hands of higher-level managers. Hence, a decentralized organization is one in which decision-making power and authority are delegated as far down the chain of command as possible. Conversely, in a centralized organization, decision-making power and authority are retained at the higher levels of management.

What factors determine an organization's position on the decentralization–centralization continuum? One common determinant is the organization's external environment. Usually, the greater the complexity and uncertainty of the environment, the greater is the tendency to decentralize. Another crucial factor is the history of the organization. Firms have a tendency to do what they have done in the past, so there is likely to be some relationship between what an organization did in its early history and what it chooses to do today in terms of centralization or decentralization. The nature of the decisions being made is also considered. The costlier and riskier the decisions, the more pressure there is to centralize. In short, managers have no clear-cut guidelines for determining whether to centralize or decentralize. Many successful organizations, such as General Electric and Johnson & Johnson, are quite decentralized. Equally successful firms, such as McDonald's and Wal-Mart, have remained centralized.

IBM has recently undergone a transformation from using a highly centralized approach to a much more decentralized approach to managing its operations. A great deal of decision-making authority was passed from the hands of a select group of top executives down to six product and marketing groups. The reason for the move was to speed up the company's ability to make decisions, introduce new products, and respond to customers. In contrast, Royal Dutch Shell, long operated in a highly decentralized manner, has recently gone through several major changes all intended to make the firm more centralized. New CEO Peter Voser went so far as to note that "fewer people will make strategic decisions."[20] Yahoo Inc. has also initiated a change to become more centralized.[21]

Coordinating Activities

The fifth major element of organizing is coordination. As we discussed earlier, job specialization and departmentalization involve breaking jobs down into small units and then combining those jobs into departments. Once this has been accomplished, the activities of the departments must be linked—systems must be put into place to keep the activities of each department focused on the attainment of organizational goals. This is accomplished by **coordination**—the process of linking the activities of the various departments of the organization.[22]

The Need for Coordination   The primary reason for coordination is that departments and work groups are interdependent—they depend on one another for information and resources to perform their respective activities. The greater the interdependence between departments, the more coordination the organization requires if departments are to be able to perform effectively. There are three major forms of interdependence: pooled, sequential, and reciprocal.[23]

Pooled interdependence represents the lowest level of interdependence. Units with pooled interdependence operate with little interaction—the output of the units is pooled

decentralization
The process of systematically delegating power and authority throughout the organization to middle and lower-level managers

centralization
The process of systematically retaining power and authority in the hands of higher-level managers

coordination
The process of linking the activities of the various departments of the organization

pooled interdependence
When units operate with little interaction; their output is pooled at the organizational level

at the organizational level. Gap clothing stores operate with pooled interdependence. Each store is considered a "department" by the parent corporation. Each has its own operating budget, staff, and so forth. The profits or losses from each store are "added together" at the organizational level. The stores are interdependent to the extent that the final success or failure of one store affects the others, but they do not generally interact on a day-to-day basis.

In **sequential interdependence**, the output of one unit becomes the input for another in a sequential fashion. This creates a moderate level of interdependence. At Nissan, for example, one plant assembles engines and then ships them to a final assembly site at another plant, where the cars are completed. The plants are interdependent in that the final assembly plant must have the engines from engine assembly before it can perform its primary function of producing finished automobiles. But the level of interdependence is generally one way— the engine plant is not necessarily dependent on the final assembly plant.

Reciprocal interdependence exists when activities flow both ways between units. This form is clearly the most complex. Within a Marriott hotel, for example, the reservations department, front-desk check-in, and housekeeping are all reciprocally interdependent. Reservations has to provide front-desk employees with information about how many guests to expect each day, and housekeeping needs to know which rooms require priority cleaning. If any of the three units does not do its job properly, all the others will be affected.

Structural Coordination Techniques Because of the obvious coordination requirements that characterize most organizations, many techniques for achieving coordination have been developed. Some of the most useful devices for maintaining coordination among interdependent units are the managerial hierarchy, rules and procedures, liaison roles, task forces, and integrating departments.[24]

Organizations that use the hierarchy to achieve coordination place one manager in charge of interdependent departments or units. In Wal-Mart distribution centers, major activities include receiving and unloading bulk shipments from railroad cars and loading other shipments onto trucks for distribution to retail outlets. The two groups (receiving and shipping) are interdependent in that they share the loading docks and some equipment. To ensure coordination and minimize conflict, one manager is in charge of the whole operation.

Routine coordination activities can be handled through rules and standard procedures. In the Wal-Mart distribution center, an outgoing truck shipment has priority over an incoming rail shipment. Thus, when trucks are to be loaded, the shipping unit is given access to all of the center's auxiliary forklifts. This priority is specifically stated in a rule. But, as useful as rules and procedures often are in routine situations, they are not particularly effective when coordination problems are complex or unusual.

As a device for coordination, a manager in a liaison role coordinates interdependent units by acting as a common point of contact. This individual may not have any formal authority over the groups but instead simply facilitates the flow of information between units. Two engineering groups working on component systems for a large project might interact through a liaison. The liaison maintains familiarity with each group as well as with the overall project. She can answer questions and otherwise serve to integrate the activities of all the groups.

A task force may be created when the need for coordination is acute. When interdependence is complex and several units are involved, a single liaison person may not be sufficient. Instead, a task force might be assembled by drawing one representative from each group. The coordination function is thus spread across several individuals, each of whom has special information about one of the groups involved. When the project is completed, task force members return to their original positions. For example, a college

sequential interdependence
When the output of one unit becomes the input for another in a sequential fashion

reciprocal interdependence
When activities flow both ways between units

overhauling its degree requirements might establish a task force made up of representatives from each department affected by the change. Each person not only retains his or her regular departmental affiliation and duties but also serves on the special task force. After the new requirements are agreed on, the task force is dissolved.

Integrating departments are occasionally used for coordination. These are somewhat similar to task forces but are more permanent. An integrating department generally has some permanent members as well as members who are assigned temporarily from units that are particularly in need of coordination. One study found that successful firms in the plastics industry, which is characterized by complex and dynamic environments, used integrating departments to maintain internal integration and coordination.[25] An integrating department usually has more authority than a task force and may even be given some budgetary control by the organization.

Electronic Coordination Advances in information technology are also providing useful mechanisms for coordination. E-mail, for example, makes it easier for people to communicate with one another. This communication, in turn, enhances coordination. Similarly, many people in organizations today use electronic scheduling, at least some of which is accessible to others. Hence, if someone needs to set up a meeting with two colleagues, he can often check their electronic schedules to determine their availability, making it easier to coordinate their activities.

Local networks, increasingly managed by hand-held electronic devices, are also making it easier to coordinate activities. Bechtel, for example, now requires its contractors, subcontractors, and suppliers to use a common web-based communication system to improve coordination among their myriad activities. The firm estimates that this improved coordination technology routinely saves it thousands of dollars on every big construction project it undertakes.

DENNIS MACDONALD/ALAMY

Electronic coordination has become almost a standard business practice in organizations today. Electronic scheduling programs synched with smart phones and similar gadgets make it easier than ever before to check schedules, set meetings, and verify attendance. This manager, for instance, is verifying her schedule as shown on her PDA with the schedule on her e-mail system.

THE BUREAUCRATIC MODEL OF ORGANIZATION DESIGN

Max Weber, an influential German sociologist, was a pioneer of classical organization theory. At the core of Weber's writings was the bureaucratic model of organizations.[26] The Weberian perspective suggests that a **bureaucracy** is a model of organization design based on a legitimate and formal system of authority. Many people associate bureaucracy with "red tape," rigidity, and passing the buck. For example, how many times have you heard people refer disparagingly to "the federal bureaucracy"? And many U.S. managers believe that bureaucracy in the Chinese government is a major impediment to U.S. firms' ability to do business there.

bureaucracy
A model of organization design based on a legitimate and formal system of authority

Weber viewed the bureaucratic form of organization as logical, rational, and efficient. He offered the model as a framework to which all organizations should aspire—the "one best way" of doing things. According to Weber, the ideal bureaucracy exhibits five basic characteristics:

1. The organization should adopt a distinct division of labor, and each position should be filled by an expert.
2. The organization should develop a consistent set of rules to ensure that task performance is uniform.
3. The organization should establish a hierarchy of positions or offices that creates a chain of command from the top of the organization to the bottom.
4. Managers should conduct business in an impersonal way and maintain an appropriate social distance between themselves and their subordinates.
5. Employment and advancement in the organization should be based on technical expertise, and employees should be protected from arbitrary dismissal.

Perhaps the best examples of bureaucracies today are government agencies and universities. Consider, for example, the steps you must go through and the forms you must fill out to apply for admission to college, request housing, register each semester, change majors, submit a degree plan, substitute a course, and file for graduation. Even when paper is replaced with electronic media, the steps are often the same. The reason these procedures are necessary is that universities deal with large numbers of people who must be treated equally and fairly. Hence, rules, regulations, and standard operating procedures are needed. Large labor unions are also usually organized as bureaucracies.[27]

Some bureaucracies, such as the U.S. Postal Service, have been trying to portray themselves as less mechanistic and impersonal. The strategy of the Postal Service is to become more service oriented as a way to fight back against competitors such as FedEx and UPS.

A primary strength of the bureaucratic model is that several of its elements (such as reliance on rules and employment based on expertise) do, in fact, often improve efficiency. Bureaucracies also help prevent favoritism (because everyone must follow the rules) and make procedures and practices very clear to everyone. Unfortunately, however, this approach also has several disadvantages. One major disadvantage is that the bureaucratic model results in inflexibility and rigidity. Once rules are created and put in place, making exceptions or changing them is often difficult. In addition, the bureaucracy often results in the neglect of human and social processes within the organization.

SITUATIONAL INFLUENCES ON ORGANIZATION DESIGN

situational view of organization design
Based on the assumption that the optimal design for any given organization depends on a set of relevant situational factors

The **situational view of organization design** is based on the assumption that the optimal design for any given organization depends on a set of relevant situational factors. In other words, situational factors play a role in determining the best organization design for any particular circumstance.[28] Four basic situational factors—technology, environment, size, and organizational life cycle—are discussed here.

Core Technology

technology
Conversion process used to transform inputs into outputs

Technology consists of the conversion processes used to transform inputs (such as materials or information) into outputs (such as products or services). Most organizations use multiple technologies, but an organization's most important one is called its *core* *technology*. Although most people visualize assembly lines and machinery when they think of technology, the term can also be applied to service organizations. For example, an investment firm like Fidelity uses technology to transform investment dollars into income in much the same way that Union Carbide uses natural resources to manufacture chemical products.

The link between technology and organization design was first recognized by Joan Woodward.[29] Woodward studied 100 manufacturing firms in southern England. She collected information about aspects such as the history of each organization, its manufacturing processes, its forms and procedures, and its financial performance. Woodward expected to find a relationship between the size of an organization and its design, but no such relationship emerged. As a result, she began to seek other explanations for differences. Close scrutiny of the firms in her sample led her to recognize a potential relationship between technology and organization design. This follow-up analysis led Woodward to first classify the organizations according to their technology. Three basic forms of technology were identified by Woodward:

1. *Unit or small-batch technology*. The product is custom-made to customer specifications or produced in small quantities. Organizations using this form of technology include a tailor shop specializing in custom suits, a printing shop that produces business cards and company stationery, and a photography studio.
2. *Large-batch or mass-production technology*. The product is manufactured in assembly-line fashion by combining component parts into another part or finished product. Examples include automobile manufacturers like Subaru, appliance makers like Whirlpool Corporation, and electronics firms like Philips.
3. *Continuous-process technology*. Raw materials are transformed to a finished product by a series of machine or process transformations. The composition of the materials themselves is changed. Examples include petroleum refineries like ExxonMobil and Shell, and chemical refineries like Dow Chemical and Hoechst AG.

These forms of technology are listed in order of their assumed levels of complexity. In other words, unit or small-batch technology is presumed to be the least complex and continuous-process technology the most complex. Woodward found that different configurations of organization design were associated with each technology.

Specifically, Woodward found that the two extremes (unit or small-batch and continuous-process) tended to have very little bureaucracy, whereas the middle-range organizations (large-batch or mass-production) were much more bureaucratic. The large-batch and mass-production organizations also had a higher level of specialization.[30] Finally, she found that organizational success was related to the extent to which organizations followed the typical pattern. For example, successful continuous-process organizations tended to have less bureaucracy, whereas less-successful firms with the same technology tended to be more bureaucratic.

Environment

Environmental elements and organization design are specifically linked in a number of ways.[31] The first widely recognized analysis of environment–organization design linkages was provided by Tom Burns and G. M. Stalker.[32] Like Woodward, Burns and Stalker worked in England. Their first step was identifying two extreme forms of organizational environment: stable (one that remains relatively constant over time) and unstable (subject to uncertainty and rapid change). Next they studied the designs of organizations in each type of environment. Not surprisingly, they found that organizations in stable environments tended to have a different kind of design than organizations in unstable environments. The two kinds of design that emerged were called mechanistic and organic organization.

A **mechanistic organization**, quite similar to the bureaucratic or System 1 model, was most frequently found in stable environments. Free from uncertainty, organizations structured their activities in rather predictable ways by means of rules, specialized jobs, and centralized authority. Mechanistic organizations are also quite similar to bureaucracies. Although no environment is completely stable, A&F and Wendy's use mechanistic designs. Each A&F store, for example, has prescribed methods for store design and merchandise-ordering processes. Little or no deviation is allowed from these methods. An **organic organization**, on the other hand, was most often found in unstable and unpredictable environments, in which constant change and uncertainty usually dictate a much higher level of fluidity and flexibility. Motorola (facing rapid technological change) and Apple (facing both technological change and constant change in consumer tastes) both use organic designs. A manager at Motorola, for example, has considerable discretion over how work is performed and how problems can be solved.

These ideas were extended in the United States by Paul R. Lawrence and Jay W. Lorsch.[33] They agreed that environmental factors influence organization design but believed that this influence varies between different units of the same organization. In fact, they predicted that each organizational unit has its own unique environment and responds by developing unique attributes. Lawrence and Lorsch suggested that organizations could be characterized along two primary dimensions.

One of these dimensions, **differentiation**, is the extent to which the organization is broken down into subunits. A firm with many subunits is highly differentiated; one with few subunits has a low level of differentiation. The second dimension, **integration**, is the degree to which the various subunits must work together in a coordinated fashion. For example, if each unit competes in a different market and has its own production facilities, they may need little integration. Lawrence and Lorsch reasoned that the degree of differentiation and integration needed by an organization depends on the stability of the environments that its subunits face.

Organizational Size and Life Cycle

The size and life cycle of an organization may also affect its design.[34] Although several definitions of size exist, we define **organizational size** as the total number of full-time or full-time-equivalent employees. A team of researchers at the University of Aston in Birmingham, England, believed that Woodward had failed to find a size–structure relationship (which was her original expectation) because almost all the organizations she studied were relatively small (three-fourths had fewer than 500 employees).[35] Thus they decided to undertake a study of a wider array of organizations to determine how size and technology both individually and jointly affect an organization's design.

Their primary finding was that technology did in fact influence structural variables in small firms, probably because all their activities tend to be centered on their core technologies. In large firms, however, the strong technology-design link broke down, most likely because technology is not as central to ongoing activities in large organizations. The Aston studies yielded a number of basic generalizations: When compared to small organizations, large organizations tend to be characterized by higher levels of job specialization, more standard operating procedures, more rules, more regulations, and a greater degree of decentralization. Wal-Mart is a good case in point. The firm expects to continue its dramatic growth for the foreseeable future, adding several thousand new jobs

mechanistic organization
Similar to the bureaucratic or System 1 model, most frequently found in stable environments

organic organization
Very flexible and informal model of organization design, most often found in unstable and unpredictable environments

differentiation
Extent to which the organization is broken down into subunits

integration
Degree to which the various subunits must work together in a coordinated fashion

organizational size
Total number of full-time or full-time-equivalent employees

in the next few years. But, as it grows, the firm acknowledges that it will have to become more decentralized for its first-line managers to stay in tune with their customers.[36]

Of course, size is not constant. As we noted in Chapter 5, for example, some small businesses are formed but soon disappear. Others remain as small, independently operated enterprises as long as their owner-manager lives. A few, such as Dell Computer, JetBlue, and Starbucks, skyrocket to become organizational giants. And occasionally large organizations reduce their size through layoffs or divestitures. For example, Navistar is today far smaller than was its previous incarnation as International Harvester Company.

Although no clear pattern explains changes in size, many organizations progress through a four-stage **organizational life cycle**.[37] The first stage is the *birth* of the organization. The second stage, *youth*, is characterized by growth and the expansion of organizational resources. *Midlife* is a period of gradual growth evolving eventually into stability. Finally, *maturity* is a period of stability, perhaps eventually evolving into decline.

Managers must confront a number of organization design issues as the organization progresses through these stages. In general, as an organization passes from one stage to the next, it becomes bigger, more mechanistic, and more decentralized. It also becomes more specialized, devotes more attention to planning, and takes on an increasingly large staff component. Finally, coordination demands increase, formalization increases, organizational units become geographically more dispersed, and control systems become more extensive. Thus an organization's size and design are clearly linked, and this link is dynamic because of the organizational life cycle.[38]

BASIC FORMS OF ORGANIZATION DESIGN

Because technology, environment, size, and life cycle can all influence organization design, it should come as no surprise that organizations adopt many different kinds of designs. Most designs, however, fall into one of four basic categories. Others are hybrids based on two or more of the basic forms.

Functional (U Form) Design

The **functional design** is an arrangement based on the functional approach to departmentalization. This design has been termed the *U form* (for unitary).[39] Under the U form arrangement, the members and units in the organization are grouped into functional departments such as marketing and production.

For the organization to operate efficiently in this design, there must be considerable coordination across departments. This integration and coordination are most commonly the responsibility of the CEO and members of senior management. Figure 6.2 shows the U form design applied to the corporate level of a small manufacturing company. In a U form organization, none of the functional areas can survive without the others. Marketing, for example, needs products from operations to sell and funds from finance to pay for advertising. The WD-40 Company, which makes a popular lubricating oil, and the McIlhenny Company, which makes TABASCO sauce, are both examples of firms that use the U form design. As we noted earlier, A&F also uses the U form design.

In general, this approach shares the basic advantages and disadvantages of functional departmentalization. Thus it allows the organization to staff all important positions with functional experts and facilitates coordination and integration. On the other hand,

organizational life cycle
Progression through which organizations evolve as they grow and mature

functional design
Based on the functional approach to departmentalization

Figure 6.2 Functional (U form) Design for a Small Manufacturing Company

The U form design is based on functional departmentalization. This small manufacturing firm uses managers at the vice presidential level to coordinate activities within each functional area of the organization. Note that each functional area is dependent on the others.

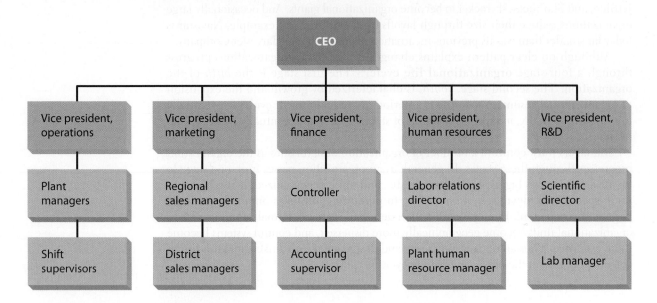

it also promotes a functional, rather than an organizational, focus and tends to promote centralization. Functionally based designs are most commonly used in small organizations because an individual CEO can easily oversee and coordinate the entire organization. As an organization grows, the CEO finds staying on top of all functional areas increasingly difficult.

Conglomerate (H Form) Design

Another common form of organization design is the *conglomerate*, or *H form* (for holding, as in holding company), approach.[40] The **conglomerate design** is used by an organization made up of a set of unrelated businesses. Thus the H form design is essentially a holding company that results from unrelated diversification.

This approach is based loosely on the product form of departmentalization. Each business or set of businesses is operated by a general manager who is responsible for its profits or losses, and each general manager functions independently of the others. Samsung Electrics Company, a South Korean firm, uses the H form design. As illustrated in Figure 6.3, Samsung consists of four basic business groups. Other firms that use the H form design include General Electric (aircraft engines, appliances, medical equipment, financial services, lighting products, plastics, and other unrelated businesses) and Tenneco (pipelines, auto parts, financial services, and other unrelated businesses).

In an H form organization, a corporate staff usually evaluates the performance of each business, allocates corporate resources across companies, and shapes decisions about buying and selling businesses. The basic shortcoming of the H form design is the complexity associated with holding diverse and unrelated businesses. Managers usually find comparing and integrating activities across a large number of diverse operations difficult. Research suggests that many organizations following this approach achieve only

conglomerate design
Used by an organization made up of a set of unrelated businesses

Figure 6.3   **Conglomerate (H form) Design at Samsung**

Samsung Electronics Company, a South Korean firm, uses the conglomerate form of organization design. This design, which results from a strategy of unrelated diversification, is a complex one to manage. Managers find that comparing and integrating activities among the dissimilar operations are difficult. Companies may abandon this design for another approach, such as the M form design.

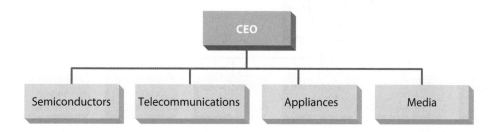

average-to-weak financial performance.[41] Thus, although some U.S. firms are still using the H form design, many have abandoned it for other approaches.

Divisional (M Form) Design

In the **divisional design**, which is becoming increasingly popular, a product form of organization is also used; in contrast to the H form, however, the divisions are related. Thus the *divisional design*, or *M form* (for multidivisional), is based on multiple businesses in related areas operating within a larger organizational framework. This design results from a strategy of related diversification.

Some activities are extremely decentralized down to the divisional level; others are centralized at the corporate level.[42] For example, as shown in Figure 6.4, Hilton Hotels uses this approach. Each of its divisions is headed by a president or executive vice president and operates with reasonable autonomy, but the divisions also coordinate their activities as is appropriate. Other firms that use this approach are the Walt Disney Company (theme parks, movies, and merchandising units, all interrelated) and Hewlett-Packard (computers, printers, scanners, electronic medical equipment, and other electronic instrumentation).

The opportunities for coordination and shared resources represent one of the biggest advantages of the M form design. Hilton's market research and purchasing departments are centralized. Thus a site selector can visit a city and look for possible locations for different Hilton brands and a buyer can purchase bed linens for multiple Hilton brands from the same supplier. The M form design's basic objective is to optimize internal competition and cooperation. Healthy competition for resources among divisions can enhance effectiveness, but cooperation should also be promoted. Research suggests that the M form organization that can achieve and maintain this balance will outperform large U form and all H form organizations.[43]

Matrix Design

The **matrix design**, another common approach to organization design, is based on two overlapping bases of departmentalization.[44] The foundation of a matrix is a set of functional departments. A set of product groups, or temporary departments, is then superimposed

divisional design
Based on multiple businesses in related areas operating within a larger organizational framework

matrix design
Based on two overlapping bases of departmentalization

Figure 6.4 **Multidivisional (M Form) Design at Hilton Hotels**

Hilton Hotels uses the multidivisional approach to organization design. Although each unit operates with relative autonomy, all units function in the same general market. This design resulted from a strategy of related diversification. Other firms that use M form designs include PepsiCo and the Walt Disney Company.

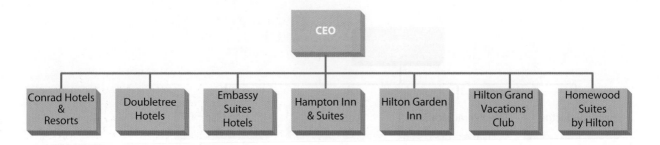

across the functional departments. Employees in a matrix are simultaneously members of a functional department (such as engineering) and of a project team.

Figure 6.5 shows a basic matrix design. At the top of the organization are functional units headed by vice presidents of engineering, production, finance, and marketing. Each of these managers has several subordinates. Along the side of the organization are a number of positions called *project manager*. Each project manager heads a project group composed of representatives or workers from the functional departments. Note from the figure that a matrix reflects a *multiple-command structure* — any given individual reports to both a functional superior and one or more project managers.

The project groups, or teams, are assigned to designated projects or programs. For example, the company might be developing a new product. Representatives are chosen from each functional area to work as a team on the new product. They also retain membership in the original functional group. At any given time, a person may be a member of several teams as well as a member of a functional group. Ford used this approach in creating its popular Focus automobile. It formed a group called "Team Focus" made up of designers, engineers, production specialists, marketing specialists, and other experts from different areas of the company. This group facilitated getting a very successful product to the market at least a year earlier than would have been possible using Ford's previous approaches.

Martha Stewart also uses a matrix organization for her lifestyle business. The company was first organized broadly into media and merchandising groups, each of which has specific product and product groups. Layered on top of this structure are teams of lifestyle experts organized into groups such as cooking, crafts, and weddings. Each of these groups is targeted toward specific customer needs, but they work as necessary across all of the product groups. For example, a wedding expert might contribute to an article on wedding planning for a *Martha Stewart Living* magazine, contribute a story idea for a cable TV program, and supply content for a Martha Stewart website. This same individual might also help select fabrics suitable for wedding gowns for retailing.[45]

The matrix form of organization design is most often used in one of three situations.[46] First, a matrix may work when there is strong pressure from the environment. For example, intense external competition may dictate the sort of strong marketing thrust that is best spearheaded by a functional department, but the diversity of a company's products may argue for product departments. Second, a matrix may be appropriate when large amounts of information need to be processed. For example, creating lateral relationships by means of a matrix is one effective way to increase the organization's capacity for processing

$\mathcal{F}igure\ 6.5$ **A Matrix Organization**

A matrix organization design is created by superimposing a product form of departmentalization on an existing functional organization. Project managers coordinate teams of employees drawn from different functional departments. Thus a matrix relies on a multiple-command structure.

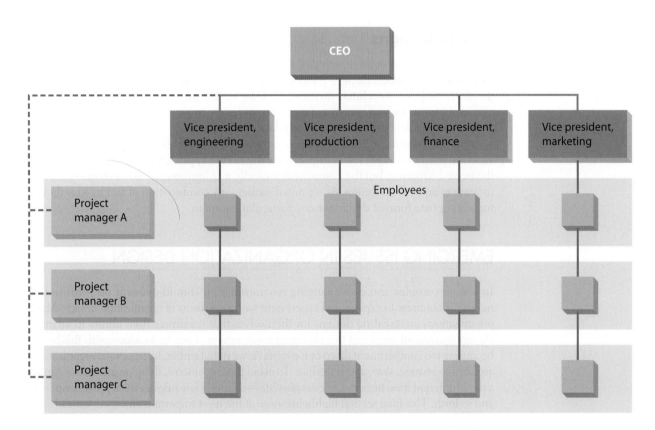

information. Third, the matrix design may work when there is pressure for shared resources. For example, a company with ten product departments may have resources for only three marketing specialists. A matrix design would allow all the departments to share the company's scarce marketing resources.

Both advantages and disadvantages are associated with the matrix design. Researchers have observed six primary advantages of matrix designs. First, they enhance flexibility because teams can be created, redefined, and dissolved as needed. Second, because they assume a major role in decision making, team members are likely to be highly motivated and committed to the organization. Third, employees in a matrix organization have considerable opportunity to learn new skills. Fourth, the matrix design provides an efficient way for the organization to take full advantage of its human resources. Fifth, team members retain membership in their functional unit so that they can serve as a bridge between the functional unit and the team, enhancing cooperation. Sixth, the matrix design gives top management a useful vehicle for decentralization. Once the day-to-day operations have been delegated, top management can devote more attention to areas such as long-range planning.

On the other hand, the matrix design also has some major disadvantages. Employees may be uncertain about reporting relationships, especially if they are simultaneously assigned to a functional manager and to several project managers. To complicate matters, some managers see the matrix as a form of anarchy in which they have unlimited freedom. Another set of problems is associated with the dynamics of group behavior. Groups take longer than individuals to make decisions, may be dominated by one individual, and may compromise too much. They may also get bogged down in discussion and not focus on their primary objectives. Finally, in a matrix, more time may also be required for coordinating task-related activities.[47]

Hybrid Designs

Some organizations use a design that represents a hybrid of two or more of the common forms of organization design.[48] For example, an organization may have five related divisions and one unrelated division, making its design a cross between an M form and an H form. Indeed, few companies use a design in its pure form; most firms have one basic organization design as a foundation for managing the business but maintain sufficient flexibility so that temporary or permanent modifications can be made for strategic purposes. Ford, for example, used the matrix approach to design the Focus and the newest Mustang, but the company is basically a U form organization showing signs of moving to an M form design. As we noted earlier, any combination of factors may dictate the appropriate form of design for any particular company.

EMERGING ISSUES IN ORGANIZATION DESIGN

In today's complex and ever-changing environment, it should come as no surprise that managers continue to explore and experiment with new forms of organization design. Many organizations are creating designs for themselves that maximize their ability to adapt to changing circumstances and to a changing environment. They try to accomplish this by not becoming too compartmentalized or too rigid. As we noted earlier, bureaucratic organizations are hard to change, slow, and inflexible. To avoid these problems, then, organizations can try to be as different from bureaucracies as possible—relatively few rules, general job descriptions, and so forth. This final section highlights some of the most important emerging issues.[49]

The Team Organization

Some organizations today are using the **team organization**, an approach to organization design that relies almost exclusively on project-type teams, with little or no underlying functional hierarchy. Within such an organization, people float from project to project as necessitated by their skills and the demands of those projects. At Cypress Semiconductor, T. J. Rodgers refuses to allow the organization to grow so large that it cannot function this way. Whenever a unit or group starts getting too large, he simply splits it into smaller units. Consequently, all units within the organization are small. This allows them to change direction, explore new ideas, and try new methods without dealing with a rigid bureaucratic organizational context. Although few organizations have actually reached this level of adaptability, Apple Computer and Xerox are among those moving toward it.[50]

The Virtual Organization

Closely related to the team organization is the **virtual organization** that has little or no formal structure. Such an organization typically has only a handful of permanent employees and a very small staff and administrative headquarters facility. As the needs of the organization change, its managers bring in temporary workers, lease facilities, and

team organization
An approach to organization design that relies almost exclusively on project-type teams, with little or no underlying hierarchy

virtual organization
One that has little or no formal structure

outsource basic support services to meet the demands of each unique situation. As the situation changes, the temporary workforce changes in parallel, with some people leaving the organization and others entering. Facilities and the services subcontracted to others change as well. Thus the organization exists only in response to its needs. And, increasingly, virtual organizations are conducting most—if not all—of their businesses online.[51]

For example, Global Research Consortium is a virtual organization. GRC offers research and consulting services to firms doing business in Asia. As clients request various services, GRC's staff of three permanent employees subcontracts the work to an appropriate set of several dozen independent consultants and researchers with whom it has relationships. At any given time, therefore, GRC may have several projects under way and 20 or 30 people working on projects. As the projects change, so, too, does the composition of the organization.

Virtual organizations have little or no structure and a very small staff. Interactions among members at different locations are handled via technology. Stephen Lewis, for example, is a geophysicist at British Petroleum Exploration, Alaska. He is shown here in the firm's virtual work room. He and his colleagues from around the world can interact in virtual space as they collaborate on potential drilling targets and strategies.

AP PHOTO/AL GRILLO

The Learning Organization

Another recent approach to organization design is the so-called learning organization. Organizations that adopt this approach work to integrate continuous improvement with continuous employee learning and development. Specifically, a **learning organization** is one that works to facilitate the lifelong learning and personal development of all its employees while continually transforming itself to respond to changing demands and needs.[52]

Although managers might approach the concept of a learning organization from a variety of perspectives, improved quality, continuous improvement, and performance measurement are frequent goals. The idea is that the most consistent and logical strategy for achieving continuous improvement is by constantly upgrading employee talent, skill, and knowledge. For example, if each employee in an organization learns one new thing each day and can translate that knowledge into work-related practice, continuous improvement will logically follow. Indeed, organizations that wholeheartedly embrace this approach believe that only through constant learning by employees can continuous improvement really occur.[53]

In recent years, many different organizations have implemented this approach. For example, Shell Oil purchased an executive conference center north of its headquarters in Houston. The center boasts state-of-the-art classrooms and instructional technology, lodging facilities, a restaurant, and recreational amenities such as a golf course, a swimming pool, and tennis courts. Line managers at the firm rotate through the Shell Learning Center, as the facility has been renamed, and serve as teaching faculty. Such teaching assignments last anywhere from a few days to several months. At the same time, all Shell employees routinely attend training programs, seminars, and related activities, all the while learning the latest information they need to contribute more effectively to the

learning organization
One that works to facilitate the lifelong learning and personal development of all its employees while continually transforming itself to respond to changing demands and needs

firm. Recent seminar topics have ranged from time management, to implications of the Americans with Disabilities Act, to balancing work and family demands, to international trade theory. The idea is that by continuously immersing people in shared learning experiences, the firm will promote an organic design populated by people with common knowledge, goals, and expectations.

SUMMARY OF LEARNING OBJECTIVES AND KEY POINTS

1. Identify the basic elements of organizations.
   - Organizations are made up of a series of elements:
     - designing jobs
     - grouping jobs
     - establishing reporting relationships
     - distributing authority
     - coordinating activities
     - differentiating between positions

2. Describe the bureaucratic perspective on organization design.
   - The bureaucratic model attempted to prescribe how all organizations should be designed.
   - It is based on the presumed need for legitimate, logical, and formal rules, regulations, and procedures.

3. Identify and explain key situational influences on organization design.
   - The situational view of organization design is based on the assumption that the optimal organization design is a function of situational factors.
   - Four important situational factors are the following:
     - technology
     - environment
     - size
     - organizational life cycle

4. Describe the basic forms of organization design that characterize many organizations.
   - Many organizations today adopt one of four basic organization designs:
     - functional (U form)
     - conglomerate (H form)
     - divisional (M form)
     - matrix
   - Other organizations use a hybrid design derived from two or more of these basic designs.

5. Identify and describe emerging issues in organization design.
   - Three emerging issues in organization design are the following:
     - team organization
     - virtual organization
     - learning organization

DISCUSSION QUESTIONS

Questions for Review

1. What is job specialization? What are its advantages and disadvantages?

2. What is departmentalization? What are its most common forms?

3. Distinguish between centralization and decentralization and comment on their relative advantages and disadvantages.

4. Describe the basic forms of organization design. What are the advantages and disadvantages of each?

5. Compare and contrast the matrix organization and the team organization, citing their similarities and differences.

Questions for Analysis

1. How is specialization applied in settings such as a hospital, restaurant, and church?

2. Learn how your school or business is organized. Analyze the advantages and disadvantages of this form of departmentalization, and then comment on how well or how poorly other forms of organization might work.

3. Identify five ways in which electronic coordination affects your daily life.

4. Each of the organization designs is appropriate for some firms but not for others. Describe the characteristics that a firm using the U form should have.

Then do the same for the H form, the M form, and the matrix design. For each item, explain the relationship between that set of characteristics and the choice of organization design.

5. What are the benefits of using the learning organization approach to design? Now consider that, to learn, organizations must be willing to tolerate many mistakes because it is only through the effort of understanding mistakes that learning can occur. With this statement in mind, what are some of the potential problems with the use of the learning organization approach?

BUILDING EFFECTIVE CONCEPTUAL SKILLS

Exercise Overview

Conceptual skills require you to think in the abstract. In this exercise, you'll use your conceptual skills in analyzing organizational structure.

Exercise Background

Looking at its organization chart allows you to understand a company's structure, including its distribution of authority, its divisional breakdown, its levels of hierarchy, and its reporting relationships. The reverse is also true: When you understand the elements of a company's structure, you can draw up an organization chart to reflect it. In this exercise, that's just what you'll do: You'll use the Internet to research a firm's structure and then draw an appropriate organization chart.

Exercise Task

1. Alone or with a partner, go online to research a publicly traded U.S. firm in which you're interested. Focus on information that will help you understand the company's structure. If you research Ford Motor Company, for example, you should look for information about different types of vehicles, different regions in which Ford products are sold, and different functions that the company performs.

(*Hint:* The firm's annual report is usually available online and typically contains a great deal of helpful information. In particular, take a look at the section containing an editorial message from the chairman or CEO and the section summarizing financial information. In many cases, "segment" data reveal a lot about divisional structure.)

2. Draw an organization chart based on your research.

3. Share your results with another group or with the class as a whole. Be prepared to explain and justify the decisions that you made in determining the firm's structure.

BUILDING EFFECTIVE TECHNICAL SKILLS

Exercise Overview

Technical skills are necessary to understand or perform the specific kind of work that an organization does. This exercise asks you to use your technical skills to understand the impact of an organization's strategy on its structure.

Exercise Background

You're a manager in a firm that has developed an innovative new system of personal transportation, much like the Segway HT but different enough to get you a patent.

(If you're not familiar with Segway products, go to the website at www.segway.com.)

Exercise Task

Each of the following items provides you with a hypothetical direction for your firm's corporate-level strategy. Combining this information about your strategy with your knowledge of your Segway-like product, choose an appropriate form of organization structure for your company.

1. Your corporate-level strategy calls for continued production of a limited line of similar products for sale in the United States. What would be the most appropriate organization structure for your firm?

2. Your corporate-level strategy calls for continued production of your core product only, but you intend to sell it in Asia and Europe as well as in North America. What would be the most appropriate organization structure for your firm?

3. Your corporate-level strategy calls for you to move into areas related to your core product, integrating the design innovations that you developed for that product into several other products. What would be the most appropriate organization structure for your firm?

4. Your corporate-level strategy calls for you to exploit your expertise in personal ground transportation to move into other areas, such as personal air or personal water transport. What would be the most appropriate organization structure for your firm?

5. Your corporate-level strategy calls for you to invest the revenue generated by core-product sales in industries unrelated to that product. What would be the most appropriate organization structure for your firm?

6. Review your responses to each of the five strategies. Explain precisely how a given strategy influenced your choice of a given organizational design.

SKILLS SELF-ASSESSMENT INSTRUMENT

Delegation Aptitude Survey

Purpose: To help students gain insight into the process of and the attitudes important to delegation.

Introduction: Delegation has a number of advantages for managers, workers, and organizations, but it also presents challenges. Managers who understand the benefits of delegation, who trust their subordinates, and who have the emotional maturity to allow others to succeed are more likely to be effective delegators.

Instructions:

1. Complete the following Delegation Aptitude Survey. You should think of work-related or group situations in which you have had the opportunity to delegate responsibility to others. If you have not had such experiences, try to imagine how you would respond in such a situation. Circle the response that best typifies your attitude or behavior.

2. Score the survey according to the directions that follow. Calculate your overall score.

3. Working with a small group, compare individual scores and prepare group responses to the discussion questions.

4. Calculate a class-average score. Have one member of the group present the group's responses to the discussion questions.

Delegation Aptitude Survey

Statement	Strongly Agree	Slightly Agree	Not Sure	Slightly Disagree	Strongly Disagree
1. I don't think others can do the work as well as I can.	1	2	3	4	5
2. I often take work home with me.	1	2	3	4	5
3. Employees who can make their own decisions tend to be more efficient.	5	4	3	2	1
4. I often have to rush to meet deadlines.	1	2	3	4	5
5. Employees with more responsibility tend to have more commitment to group goals.	5	4	3	2	1
6. When I delegate, I always explain precisely how the task is to be done.	1	2	3	4	5
7. I always seem to have too much to do and too little time to do it in.	1	2	3	4	5
8. When employees have the responsibility to do a job, they usually do it well.	5	4	3	2	1
9. When I delegate, I make clear the end results I expect.	5	4	3	2	1
10. I usually only delegate simple, routine tasks.	1	2	3	4	5
11. When I delegate, I always make sure everyone concerned is so informed.	5	4	3	2	1
12. If I delegate, I usually wind up doing the job over again to get it right.	1	2	3	4	5
13. I become irritated watching others doing a job I can do better.	1	2	3	4	5
14. When I delegate, I feel I am losing the control I need.	1	2	3	4	5
15. When I delegate, I always set specific dates for progress reports.	5	4	3	2	1
16. When I do a job, I do it to perfection.	1	2	3	4	5
17. I honestly feel that I can do most jobs better than my subordinates can.	1	2	3	4	5
18. When employees make their own decisions, it tends to cause confusion.	1	2	3	4	5
19. It's difficult for subordinates to make decisions because they don't know the organization's goals.	1	2	3	4	5
20. When employees are given responsibility, they usually do what is asked of them.	5	4	3	2	1

Discussion Questions

1. In what respects do the survey responses agree or disagree?
2. What might account for some of the differences in individual scores?
3. How can you make constructive use of the survey results?

Source: Linda Morable, *Exercises in Management*, 8th ed., pp. 82–84. © 2005.

EXPERIENTIAL EXERCISE

Purpose: Organization design refers to the overall set of elements used to configure an organization. The purpose of this exercise is to give you insights into how managers must make decisions within the context of creating an organization design.

Introduction: Whenever a new enterprise is started, the owner must make decisions about how to structure the organization. For example, he or she must decide what functions are required, how those functions will be broken down into individual jobs, how those jobs will be grouped back together into logical departments, and how authority and responsibility will be allocated across positions.

Instructions: Assume that you have decided to open a handmade chocolate business in your local community. Your products will be traditional bars and novelty shaped chocolates, truffles, other chocolate products such as ice cream, and gift baskets and boxes featuring chocolates. You have hired a talented chef and believe that her expertise, coupled with your unique designs and high-quality ingredients, will make your products very popular. You have also inherited enough money to get your business up and running and to cover about one year of living expenses (in other words, you do not need to pay yourself a salary).

You intend to buy food items including chocolate, cocoa, white chocolate, nuts, and fruit from suppliers who deliver to your area. Your chef will then turn those ingredients into luscious products that will then be attractively packaged. Local grocery store owners and restaurant chefs have seen samples of your products and indicated a keen interest in selling them. You know, however, that you will still need to service accounts and keep your customers happy. At the present time, you are trying to determine how many people you need to get your business going and how to group them most effectively into an organization. You

realize that you can start out quite small and then expand as sales warrant. However, you also worry that if you are continually adding people and rearranging your organization, confusion and inefficiency may result.

Under each of the following scenarios, decide how best to design your organization. Sketch a basic organization chart to show your thoughts.

- Scenario 1—You will design and sell the products yourself, as well as oversee production. You will start with a workforce of five people.
- Scenario 2—You intend to devote all of your time to sales to increase revenues, leaving all other functions to others. You will start with a workforce of nine people.
- Scenario 3—You do not intend to handle any one function yourself but will instead oversee the entire operation and will start with a workforce of 15 people.

1. After you have created your organization chart, form small groups of four to five people each. Compare your various organization charts, focusing on similarities and differences.

2. Working in the same group, assume that five years have passed and that your business has been a big success. You have a large factory for making your chocolates and are shipping them to 15 states. You employ almost 500 people. Create an organization design that you think fits this organization best.

Discussion Questions

1. How clear (or how ambiguous) were the decisions about organization design?

2. What are your thoughts about starting out too large to maintain stability, as opposed to starting small and then growing?

3. What basic factors did you consider in choosing a design?

 YOU MAKE THE CALL

Promoting Brand Loyalty at A&F

1. If you were hired to advise Michael Jeffries on A&F's current organizational design, what weaknesses and potential threats would you identify? What strengths and opportunities?

2. What kind of organizational design do you think would be best suited to Jeffries' managerial style?

3. What's the current status of A&F in the organizational life cycle? In what ways is it typical of its current stage? In which ways does it appear to be atypical?

4. It seems that mergers, acquisitions, and divestitures are currently business as usual in the retailing

sector. Following such an event, does it make more sense to retain the current organizational design for a while or to modify it right away? Why?

5. What differences might you expect to see between the organizational designs of traditional retailers such as A&F and American Eagle and those at online retailers such as Amazon.com and eBay?

6. Assuming that you wanted a career in retailing, would you want to work for A&F? Why or why not?

MANAGING ORGANIZATION CHANGE AND INNOVATION

LEARNING OBJECTIVES

After studying this chapter, you should be able to:

1 Describe the nature of organization change, including forces for change and planned versus reactive change.

2 Discuss the steps in organization change and how to manage resistance to change.

3 Identify and describe major areas of organization change and discuss the assumptions, techniques, and effectiveness of organization development (OD).

4 Describe the innovation process, forms of innovation, the failure to innovate, and how organizations can promote innovation.

FIRST THINGS FIRST

The Science of the Deal

In 2000, OSI Pharmaceuticals, a small biotechnology company based on Long Island, New York, was looking for a partner to share in the development of a newly invented drug for the treatment of lung and pancreatic cancer. The drug, which used small molecules to inhibit the activity of certain enzymes, was extremely promising, and with 42 companies in the bidding, the OSI deal was the year's most competitive in the pharmaceutical industry. The winner was San Francisco–based Genentech, a highly successful pioneer in the biotech field. To lock up the deal, Genentech and its largest shareholder, the Swiss pharmaceutical

> *"The way you maximize the value of the [biotech] business is by leveraging the resources of partners in manufacturing and development."*
>
> —JOE MCCRACKEN, VICE PRESIDENT OF BUSINESS DEVELOPMENT, GENENTECH

company Roche Holding, each purchased $35 million in OSI stock and offered upfront fees totaling another $117 million.

The commercialized drug, called Tarceva®, was released in November 2004 and quickly acquired blockbuster status. U.S. sales for 2005 hit $275 million and continued to climb, reaching $457 million just three years later. Worldwide sales were $860 million in 2007 and topped $1 billion in 2008. Tarceva is an extremely profitable product, and it's a good thing for OSI, inasmuch as it's the company's only marketed drug. In the second quarter of 2008, for example, OSI

Managing organization change and innovation are important to all organizations. But dealing with change and innovation as effectively as possible is especially important to businesses like Genentech.

reported total revenues of $96 million. Of that amount, $52 million came from sales of Tarceva in conjunction with Genentech and $35 million in Tarceva royalties from Roche. One analyst who recommended that investors sell OSI stock suggested that the firm, though profitable, had become "a one-trick pony with a small pipeline."

For Genentech, on the other hand, Tarceva is just one of four billion-dollar cancer drugs. In February 2009, Genentech announced the results of late-stage trials in which one of those drugs, Avastin™, had been combined with Tarceva. Tests had demonstrated that patients with advanced lung cancer lived longer without the disease getting worse. The announcement alone pushed up the value of Genentech shares by 2 percent and those of OSI by nearly 11 percent. The results of Genentech's successful trials, said one Wall Street observer, "will have a profound impact on Tarceva use" and could in fact spur a "second leg of growth for the product." Analysts forecasted Tarceva sales of $2 billion by 2013 and estimated that OSI would enjoy about $200 million in added revenue for several years.

At Genentech—at least according to Joe McCracken—deals like the one with OSI are mostly about the science and the organizational processes that transform scientific resources into profitable products. He's performed a similar role in a Big Pharma environment (for seven years at French chemical and pharmaceutical giant Rhône-Poulenc-Rorer and its successor, Aventis, between two stints at Genentech), but he's much happier in the more focused environment of biotechnology. At Genentech, he says, "we emphasize scientific rationale and probability of approval much more than we emphasize market size. A strong underlying scientific rationale or a probability of approval will trump market size any time."

In January 2007, for instance, McCracken negotiated a deal with a biotech firm called Seattle Genetics Inc. to partner in the commercialization of a cancer drug known as SGN-40. Under the terms of the arrangement, Genentech agreed to an upfront payment of $60 million and to pay for future research, development, and manufacturing through "milestone" payments of more than $800 million based on Genetics' clinical and regulatory progress in developing the drug. Genentech made a first milestone payment of $12 million in December of the same year, when Genetics started a clinical trial in which SGN-40 was combined with a Genentech drug called Rituxan®, which

was already the best-selling cancer drug in the world. In 2008, Genetics reported the results of the trial, which showed that the combination of the two drugs enhanced certain cancer therapies beyond what either drug could achieve alone.

It was an expensive deal (although the market isn't exactly small—more than 60,000 Americans are diagnosed with one target disease every year). McCracken, however, is confident that he made the right move: "[F]or us to do these larger deals," he explains, "we have to believe we have synergies we can exploit in maximizing the development of [the products]. In this case, we really believe we have some good insights and expertise in basic research and in development and manufacturing that we can leverage." "This product," he adds, "has the opportunity to address an important disease that we don't have anything else in our pipeline to address. We put a big premium on that."

Recruited by Genentech in 1983 to conduct research on drug therapies for animals, McCracken (who's trained as a veterinarian) switched to the business end of the company when Genentech decided to sell off its animal-therapeutics division. In fact, his first assignments in "business development" involved selling off more and more pieces of the company. Concerned about the company's direction and lack of opportunities, he left in 1993 to make deals for Rhône-Poulenc-Rorer, where he stayed until 2000, when he abandoned Big Pharma (the world of pharmaceutical giants that boast $3 billion in annual revenues) for a return to medical biotech (companies that settle for smaller incomes from medical technology based on simple molecules and genetically altered microorganisms). Not surprisingly, what McCracken didn't like about Big Pharma was the habit of letting commercial needs drive the science rather than vice versa.

Fortunately, the Genentech to which he returned was a much different company from the one he'd left. For one thing, it was now focused on acquiring technologies rather than divesting them, and as head of business development, McCracken has been responsible for helping grow the company through deal making ever since. In the pharmaceutical industry, in addition to the usual run of joint ventures and mergers and acquisitions (M&As), deals come in a variety of forms. *In-licensing* ventures, for example, are partnerships between firms with shared goals, strategies, or fields of interest; like Genentech's deals with OSI and Seattle

Genetics, they're often created to share the costs of developing products from which both partners can profit. *Out-licensing* refers to ventures in which a firm seeks a partner to continue development of a product that's previously been developed internally. Back in 1996, for example, Genentech had taken a drug called Raptiva through preclinical and mid-stage clinical trials but was too financially strapped to go any further. So it out-licensed the drug to a small biotech company called Xoma, which used its familiarity with similar antibodies to complete the development process ("better, faster, and cheaper," according to McCracken). Raptiva, a therapy for psoriasis, came out in 2003 and returned $56 million in revenue for Genentech the next year.

"Never underestimate the value of a small company that has a singular focus," advises McCracken, who points out that all the while Genentech was strapped for both the necessary "human resources and management attention," Raptiva was Xoma's "most important project." In the long run, reasons McCracken, this approach to deal making means that "we have all these opportunities and [we] manage our internal growth. The way you maximize the value of the [biotech] business is by leveraging the resources of partners in manufacturing and development." Interestingly, McCracken's approach leaves little room for acquisition as a deal-making option; in fact, Genentech has only made one acquisition in its entire 33-year history. "We haven't had to do them to drive growth," he explains. "We've been able to sustain growth with our internal pipeline. We've been able to get access to the technologies and products that we needed through licensing activities."

In early 2004, McCracken was given additional responsibilities as head of a new unit called Strategic Pipeline Development. The new function was part of a major reorganization in Genentech's Development, Commercial, and Manufacturing activities. Among the goals of the reorganization was focusing the efforts of top managers on product innovation and the firm's product pipeline—the flow of new-product concepts through the process that transforms them into products available to end users. Susan D. Hellmann, who'd been the vice president for Development and Product Operations, was promoted to president of a new Product Development unit, which would focus on activities such as Business Development, Alliance Management, and Pipeline Planning Support. As vice president of Business Development, McCracken would continue to report directly to Hellmann, but his new responsibilities included heading up a team to advise Hellmann on the expansion of the company's product pipeline.

In the next few years, McCracken's team would negotiate anywhere from 40 to 50 deals annually, but hooking up with partners, according to McCracken, now takes up only about 20 percent of his time. The rest, he says, is spent working with what he calls "my customers"—the people *inside* Genentech who conduct the research necessary to develop products in the pipeline and who know where the pipeline is running thin and where it isn't. He's able to divide his time this way, says McCracken, "because business development here is so integrated with our internal customers in research [and] development." Under the reorganization, for instance, McCracken's Business Development unit was divided into three areas—oncology, immunology, and tissue growth and repair—that mirror precisely the three areas of the company's Research activities.

Genentech's relationship with Roche Holding began in 1990, when the Swiss company bought a 60 percent stake in Genentech for $2.1 billion. As a result of additional stock purchases and sell-offs, Roche (now the Roche Group) owned about 56 percent of Genentech in 2008, when it launched an effort to buy the rest of the company. Following some negotiations over price, a friendly takeover agreement was reached in March 2009, with Roche paying $46.8 billion ($95 per share) to complete the buyout. At the time, Genentech was the world's largest biotech company in terms of stock value and the second-largest (after Amgen) in revenue. The agreement created the seventh-largest U.S. pharmaceutical company in terms of market share. For Roche, the merger was an opportunity to further exploit the potential of what CEO Severin Schwan called "a pharma–biotechnology partnership." Roche announced that Genentech's research and early development activities would be conducted at the biotech firm's San Francisco facilities by an independent unit within Roche. Genentech's scientific talent would be retained, and as Roche chairman Franz Humer assured analysts, the new owners would "do everything in our power to make sure [that the] innovative culture in Genentech gets maintained."[1]

Managers at Genentech are keeping the firm at the forefront of its industry through the astute management of innovation. In particular, the company relies on the development of innovative products to grow and prosper. At a broader lever, Genentech also embraces change. As we will see, understanding when and how to implement change is a vital part of management. This chapter describes how organizations manage change. We first examine the nature of organization change and identify the basic issues of managing change. We then identify and describe major areas of change, including business process change, a major type of change undertaken by many firms recently. We then examine organization development and conclude by discussing organizational innovation as a vital form of change.

THE NATURE OF ORGANIZATION CHANGE

Organization change is any substantive modification to some part of the organization.[2] Thus change can involve virtually any aspect of an organization: work schedules, bases for departmentalization, span of management, machinery, organization design, people themselves, and so on. It is important to keep in mind that any change in an organization may have effects extending beyond the actual area where the change is implemented. For example, when Northrop Grumman recently installed a new automated production system at one of its plants, employees were trained to operate new equipment, the compensation system was adjusted to reflect new skill levels, the span of management for supervisors was altered, and several related jobs were redesigned. Selection criteria for new employees were also changed, and a new quality control system was installed.[3] In addition, it is quite common for multiple organization change activities to be going on simultaneously.[4]

Forces for Change

Why do organizations find change necessary? The basic reason is that something relevant to the organization either has changed or is likely to change in the foreseeable future. The organization therefore may have little choice but to change as well. Indeed, a primary reason for the problems that organizations often face is failure to anticipate or respond properly to changing circumstances. The forces that compel change may be external or internal to the organization.[5]

External Forces External forces for change derive from the organization's general and task environments. For example, two energy crises, an aggressive Japanese automobile industry, floating currency exchange rates, and floating international interest rates—all manifestations of the international dimension of the general environment—profoundly influenced U.S. automobile companies. New rules of production and competition forced them to dramatically alter the way they do business. In the political area, new laws, court decisions, and regulations affect organizations. The technological dimension may yield new production techniques that the organization needs to explore. The economic dimension is affected by inflation, the cost of living, and money supplies. The sociocultural dimension, reflecting societal values, determines what kinds of products or services will be accepted in the market.

Because of its proximity to the organization, the task environment is an even more powerful force for change. Competitors influence an organization through their price

organization change
Any substantive modification to some part of the organization

structures and product lines. When Dell lowers the prices it charges for computers, Gateway may have little choice but to follow suit. Because customers determine what products can be sold at what prices, organizations must be concerned with consumer tastes and preferences. Suppliers affect organizations by raising or lowering prices or changing product lines. Regulators can have dramatic effects on an organization. For example, if OSHA rules that a particular production process is dangerous to workers, it can force a firm to close a plant until it meets higher safety standards. Unions can force change when they have the clout to negotiate for higher wages or if they go on strike.[6]

Internal Forces A variety of forces inside the organization may cause change. If top management revises the organization's strategy, organization change is likely to result. A decision by an electronics company to enter the home computer market or a decision to increase a ten-year product sales goal by 3 percent would occasion many organization changes. Other internal forces for change may be reflections of external forces. As sociocultural values shift, for example, workers' attitudes toward their job may also shift—and workers may demand a change in working hours or working conditions. In such a case, even though the force is rooted in the external environment, the organization must respond directly to the internal pressure it generates.[7]

Planned versus Reactive Change

Some change is planned well in advance; other change comes about as a reaction to unexpected events. **Planned change** is designed and implemented in an orderly and timely fashion in anticipation of future events. **Reactive change** is a piecemeal response to circumstances as they develop. Because reactive change may be hurried, the potential for poorly conceived and executed change is increased. Planned change is almost always preferable to reactive change.[8]

Georgia-Pacific, a large forest products business, is an excellent example of a firm that went through a planned and well-managed change process. When A. D. Correll became CEO, he quickly became alarmed at the firm's high accident rate—9 serious injuries per 100 employees each year, and 26 deaths during the most recent five-year period. Although the forest products business is inherently dangerous, Correll believed that the accident rate was far too high and set out on a major change effort to improve things. He and other top managers developed a multistage change program intended to educate workers about safety, improve safety equipment in the plant, and eliminate a long-standing part of the firm's culture that made injuries almost a badge of courage. As a result, Georgia-Pacific achieved the best safety record in the industry, with relatively few injuries.[9]

On the other hand, Caterpillar was caught flat-footed by a worldwide recession in the construction industry, suffered enormous losses, and took several years to recover. Had managers at Caterpillar anticipated the need for change earlier, they might have been able to respond more quickly. Similarly, Kodak had to cut 12,000 jobs in reaction to sluggish sales and profits.[10] Again, better anticipation might have forestalled those job cuts. The importance of approaching change from a planned perspective is reinforced by the frequency of organization change. Most companies or divisions of large companies implement some form of moderate change at least every year and one or more major changes every four to five years.[11] Managers who sit back and respond only when they have to are likely to spend a lot of time hastily changing and rechanging things. A more effective approach is to anticipate forces urging change and plan ahead to deal with them.[12]

planned change
Change that is designed and implemented in an orderly and timely fashion in anticipation of future events

reactive change
A piecemeal response to circumstances as they develop

MANAGING CHANGE IN ORGANIZATIONS

Organization change is a complex phenomenon. A manager cannot simply wave a wand and implement a planned change like magic. Instead, any change must be systematic and logical to have a realistic opportunity to succeed.[13] To carry this off, the manager needs to understand the steps of effective change and how to counter employee resistance to change.[14]

Steps in the Change Process

Researchers have over the years developed a number of models or frameworks outlining steps for change.[15] The Lewin model was one of the first, although a more comprehensive approach is usually more useful in today's complex business environment.

The Lewin Model Kurt Lewin, a noted organizational theorist, suggested that every change requires three steps.[16] The first step is *unfreezing*—individuals who will be affected by the impending change must be led to recognize why the change is necessary. The second step is the *implementation* of the change itself. The third step is *refreezing*, which involves reinforcing and supporting the change so that it becomes a part of the system.[17] For example, one of the changes Caterpillar faced in response to the recession noted earlier involved a massive workforce reduction. The first step (unfreezing) was convincing the United Auto Workers (UAW) to support the reduction because of its importance to long-term effectiveness. After this unfreezing was accomplished, 30,000 jobs were eliminated (implementation). Then it worked to improve its damaged relationship with its workers (refreezing) by guaranteeing future pay hikes and promising no more cutbacks. As interesting as the Lewin model is, it unfortunately lacks operational specificity. Thus a more comprehensive perspective is often needed.

A Comprehensive Approach to Change The comprehensive approach to change takes a systems view and delineates a series of specific steps that often leads to successful change. This expanded model is illustrated in Figure 7.1. The first step is recognizing the need for change. Reactive change might be triggered by employee complaints, declines in productivity or turnover, court injunctions, sales slumps, or labor strikes. Recognition may simply be managers' awareness that change in a certain area is inevitable. For example, managers may be aware of the general frequency of organizational change undertaken by most organizations and recognize that their organization should probably follow the same pattern. The immediate stimulus might be the result of a forecast indicating new market potential, the accumulation of a cash surplus for possible investment, or an opportunity to achieve and capitalize on a major technological breakthrough. Managers might also initiate change today because indicators suggest that it will be necessary in the near future.[18]

Second, managers must set goals for the change. To increase market share, to enter new markets, to restore employee morale, to settle a strike, and to identify investment opportunities—all might be goals for change. Third, managers must diagnose what brought on the need for change. Turnover, for example, might be caused by low pay, poor working conditions, poor supervisors, or employee dissatisfaction. Thus, although turnover may be the immediate stimulus for change, managers must understand its causes to make the right changes.

The next step is to select a change technique that will accomplish the intended goals. If turnover is caused by low pay, a new reward system may be needed. If the cause is poor supervision, interpersonal skills training may be called for. (Various change techniques

Figure 7.1   **Steps in the Change Process**

Managers must understand how and why to implement change. A manager who, when implementing change, follows a logical and orderly sequence like the one shown here is more likely to succeed than a manager whose change process is haphazard and poorly conceived.

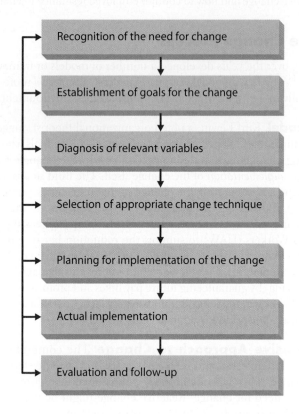

Recognition of the need for change

Establishment of goals for the change

Diagnosis of relevant variables

Selection of appropriate change technique

Planning for implementation of the change

Actual implementation

Evaluation and follow-up

are summarized later in this chapter.) After the appropriate technique has been chosen, its implementation must be planned. Issues to consider include the costs of the change, its effects on other areas of the organization, and the degree of employee participation appropriate for the situation. If the change is implemented as planned, the results should then be evaluated. If the change was intended to reduce turnover, managers must check turnover after the change has been in effect for a while. If turnover is still too high, other changes may be necessary.[19]

Understanding Resistance to Change

Another element in the effective management of change is understanding the resistance that often accompanies change.[20] Managers need to know why people resist change and what can be done about their resistance. When Westinghouse first provided all its managers with personal computers, most people responded favorably. One manager, however, resisted the change to the point where he began leaving work every day at noon! It was some time before he began staying in the office all day again. Such resistance is common for a variety of reasons.[21]

Uncertainty Perhaps the biggest cause of employee resistance to change is uncertainty. In the face of impending change, employees may become anxious and nervous. They may worry about their ability to meet new job demands, they may think that their job security is threatened, or they may simply dislike ambiguity. Nabisco was once the target of an extended and confusing takeover battle, and during the entire time, employees were nervous about the impending change. The *Wall Street Journal* described them this way: "Many are angry at their leaders and fearful for their jobs. They are swapping rumors and spinning scenarios for the ultimate outcome of the battle for the tobacco and food giant. Headquarters staffers in Atlanta know so little about what's happening in New York that some call their office 'the mushroom complex,' where they are kept in the dark."[22]

TIM BOYLE/GETTY IMAGES

When Nabisco, then an independent company, was the target of unwanted takeover attempts, the firm's staffers complained about being kept in the dark and not knowing what was going on. But now that Nabisco has become part of Kraft Foods, lines of communication have been improved and employees know much more about what is going on in the firm.

Threatened Self-Interests Many impending changes threaten the self-interests of some managers within the organization. A change might diminish their power or influence within the company, so they fight it. Managers at Sears once developed a plan calling for a new type of store. The new stores would be somewhat smaller than a typical Sears store and would not be located in large shopping malls. Instead, they would be located in smaller strip centers. They would carry clothes and other "soft goods," but not hardware, appliances, furniture, or automotive products. When executives in charge of the excluded product lines heard about the plan, they raised such strong objections that the plan was cancelled.

Different Perceptions A third reason that people resist change is due to different perceptions. A manager may make a decision and recommend a plan for change on the basis of her own assessment of a situation. Others in the organization may resist the change because they do not agree with the manager's assessment or perceive the situation differently.[23] Executives at 7-Eleven battled this problem as they attempted to enact a major organizational change. The corporation wanted to take its convenience stores a bit "upscale" and begin selling fancy fresh foods to go, the newest hardcover novels, some gourmet products, and higher-quality coffee. But many franchisees balked because they saw this move as taking the firm away from its core blue-collar customers.

Feelings of Loss Many changes involve altering work arrangements in ways that disrupt existing social networks. Because social relationships are important, most people resist any change that might adversely affect those relationships. Other intangibles threatened by change include power, status, security, familiarity with existing procedures, and self-confidence.

Overcoming Resistance to Change

Of course, a manager should not give up in the face of resistance to change. Although there are no surefire cures, there are several techniques that at least have the potential to overcome resistance.[24]

Participation Participation is often the most effective technique for overcoming resistance to change. Employees who participate in planning and implementing a change are better able to understand the reasons for the change. Uncertainty is reduced, and self-interests and social relationships are less threatened. Having had an opportunity to express their ideas and assume the perspectives of others, employees are more likely to accept the change gracefully. A classic study of participation monitored the introduction of a change in production methods among four groups in a Virginia pajama factory.[25] The two groups that were allowed to fully participate in planning and implementing the change improved significantly in their productivity and satisfaction, relative to the two groups that did not participate. 3M Company recently attributed several millions in cost savings to employee participation in several organization change activities.

Education and Communication Educating employees about the need for and the expected results of an impending change should reduce their resistance. If open communication is established and maintained during the change process, uncertainty can be minimized. Caterpillar used these methods during many of its cutbacks to reduce resistance. First, it educated UAW representatives about the need for and potential value of the planned changes. Then management told all employees what was happening, when it would happen, and how it would affect them individually.

Facilitation Several facilitation procedures are also advisable. For instance, making only necessary changes, announcing those changes well in advance, and allowing time for people to adjust to new ways of doing things can help reduce resistance to change.[26] One manager at a Prudential regional office spent several months systematically planning a change in work procedures and job design. He then became too impatient, coming in over the weekend with a work crew and rearranging the office layout. When employees walked in on Monday morning and saw what he had done, they were hostile, anxious, and resentful. What was a promising change became a disaster, and the manager had to scrap the entire plan.

Force-Field Analysis Although force-field analysis may sound like something out of a *Star Trek* movie, it can help overcome resistance to change. In almost any change situation, forces are acting for and against the change. To facilitate the change, managers start by listing each set of forces and then trying to tip the balance so that the forces facilitating the change outweigh those hindering the change. It is especially important to try to remove or at least minimize some of the forces acting against the change. Suppose, for example, that General Motors (GM) is considering a plant closing as part of a change. As shown in Figure 7.2, three factors are reinforcing the change: GM needs to cut costs, it has excess capacity, and the plant has outmoded production facilities. At the same time, there is resistance from the UAW, concern for workers being put out of their jobs, and a feeling that the plant might be needed again in the future. GM might start by convincing the UAW that the closing is necessary by presenting profit and loss figures. It could then offer relocation and retraining to displaced workers. And it might shut down the plant and put it in "mothballs" so that it can be renovated later. The three major factors hindering the change are thus eliminated or reduced in importance.[27]

Figure 7.2 Force-Field Analysis for Plant Closing at General Motors

A force field analysis can help a manager facilitate change. A manager able to identify forces acting both for and against a change can see where to focus efforts to remove barriers to change (such as offering training and relocation to displaced workers). Removing the forces against the change can at least partially overcome resistance.

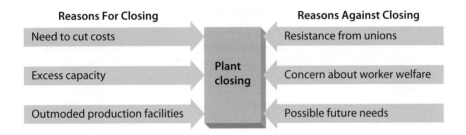

Reasons For Closing	Plant closing	Reasons Against Closing
Need to cut costs		Resistance from unions
Excess capacity		Concern about worker welfare
Outmoded production facilities		Possible future needs

AREAS OF ORGANIZATION CHANGE

We noted earlier that change can involve virtually any part of an organization. In general, however, most change interventions involve organization structure and design, technology and operations, or people. The most common areas of change within each of these broad categories are listed in Table 7.1. In addition, many organizations have gone through massive and comprehensive business process change programs.

Changing Organization Structure and Design

Organization change might be focused on any of the basic components of organization structure or on the organization's overall design. Thus the organization might change the way it designs its jobs or its bases of departmentalization. Likewise, it might change reporting relationships or the distribution of authority. For example, we noted in Chapter 6, the trend toward flatter organizations. Coordination mechanisms and line-and-staff configurations are also subject to change. On a larger scale, the organization might change its overall design. For example, a growing business could decide to drop its functional design and adopt a divisional design. Or it might transform itself into a matrix. Changes in culture usually involve the structure and design of the organization as well (recall that we discussed changing culture back in Chapter 2). Finally, the organization might change any part of its human resource management system, such as its selection criteria, its performance appraisal methods, or its compensation package.[28]

Changing Technology and Operations

Technology is the conversion process used by an organization to transform inputs into outputs. Because of the rapid rate of all technological innovation, technological changes are becoming increasingly important to many organizations. Table 7.1 lists several areas where technological change is likely to be experienced. One important area of change today revolves around information technology. The adoption and institutionalization of information technology innovations is almost constant in most firms. Sun Microsystems,

Table 7.1 Areas of Organization Change

Organization change can affect any part, area, or component of an organization. Most change, however, fits into one of three general areas: organization structure and design, technology and operations, and people.

Organization Structure and Design	Technology and Operations	People
Job design	Information technology	Abilities and skills
Departmentalization	Equipment	Performance
Reporting relationships	Work processes	Perceptions
Authority distribution	Work sequences	Expectations
Coordination mechanisms	Control systems	Attitudes
Line-staff structure	Enterprise resource planning	Values
Overall design		
Culture		
Human resource management		

for example, adopted a very short-range planning cycle to be best prepared for environmental changes.[29] Another important form of technological change involves equipment. To keep pace with competitors, firms periodically find that replacing existing machinery and equipment with newer models is necessary.

A change in work processes or work activities may be necessary if new equipment is introduced or new products are manufactured. In manufacturing industries, the major reason for changing a work process is to accommodate a change in the materials used to produce a finished product. Consider a firm that manufactures battery-operated flashlights. For many years flashlights were made of metal, but now most are made of plastic. A firm might decide to move from metal to plastic flashlights because of consumer preferences, raw materials' costs, or other reasons. Whatever the reason, the technology necessary to make flashlights from plastic differs importantly from that used to make flashlights from metal. Work process changes may occur in service organizations as well as in manufacturing firms. As traditional barbershops and beauty parlors are replaced by hair salons catering to both sexes, for example, the hybrid organizations have to develop new methods for handling appointments and setting prices.

A change in work sequence may or may not accompany a change in equipment or a change in work processes. Making a change in work sequence means altering the order or sequence of the workstations involved in a particular manufacturing process. For example, a manufacturer might have two parallel assembly lines producing two similar sets of machine parts. The lines might converge at one central quality-control unit, where inspectors verify tolerances. The manager, however, might decide to change to periodic rather than final inspection. Under this arrangement, one or more inspections are established farther up the line.

Work sequence changes can also be made in service organizations. The processing of insurance claims, for example, could be changed. The sequence of logging and verifying claims, requesting checks, getting countersignatures, and mailing checks could be altered in several ways, such as combining the first two steps or routing the claims through one person while another handles checks. Organizational control systems may also be targets of change.[30] For example, a firm attempting to improve the quality of its products might develop and implement a set of more rigorous and comprehensive quality-control procedures.

Finally, many businesses have been working to implement technological and operations change by installing and using complex and integrated software systems. Such systems—called *enterprise resource planning* (ERP)—link virtually all facets of the business, making it easier for managers to keep abreast of related developments. **ERP** is a large-scale information system for

Changes in work sequence and/or work processes are common in manufacturing and service organizations. Assembly lines, for example, were once rigidly structured in ways that made them difficult and expensive to modify. But most manufacturers today have adopted much more flexible assembly-line arrangements that make it easier and less expensive to modify them. Robotics, computer-managed assembly processes, and more flexible work forces have all contributed to this trend.

AP PHOTO/CARLOS OSORIO, FILE

integrating and synchronizing the many activities in the extended enterprise. In most cases, these systems are purchased from external vendors who then tailor their products to the client's unique needs and requirements. Companywide processes—such as materials management, production planning, order management, and financial reporting—can all be managed through ERP. In effect, these are the processes that cut across product lines, departments, and geographic locations.

Developing the ERP system starts by identifying the key processes that need critical attention, such as supplier relationships, material flows, or customer order fulfillment. The system could result, for instance, in sales processes being integrated with production planning and then integrating both of these into the firm's financial accounting system. For example, a customer in Rome can place an order that is to be produced in Ireland, schedule it to be shipped through air cargo to Rome, and then have it picked up by a truck at the airport and delivered to the customer's warehouse by a specified date. All of these activities are synchronized by activities linkages in one massive database.

The ERP integrates all activities and information flows that relate to the firm's critical processes. It also keeps updated real-time information on their current status, reports recent past transactions and upcoming planned transactions, and provides electronic notices that action is required on some items if planned schedules are to be met. It coordinates internal operations with activities by outside suppliers and notifies business partners and customers of current status and upcoming deliveries and billings. It can integrate financial flows among the firm, its suppliers, its customers, and commercial bank deposits for up-to-the-minute status reports that can be used to create real-time financial reports at a moment's notice, rather than in the traditional one-month (or longer) time span for producing a financial statement. ERP's multilanguage capabilities also allow real-time correspondence in various languages to facilitate international transactions.

enterprise resource planning (ERP)
A large-scale information system for integrating and synchronizing the many activities in the extended enterprise

Changing People, Attitudes, and Behaviors

A third area of organization change has to do with human resources. For example, an organization might decide to change the skill level of its workforce. This change might be prompted by changes in technology or by a general desire to upgrade the quality of the workforce. Thus training programs and new selection criteria might be needed. The organization might also decide to improve its workers' performance level. In this instance, a new incentive system or performance-based training might be in order. *Reader's Digest* has attempted to implement significant changes in its workforce. For example, the firm eliminated 17 percent of its employees, reduced retirement benefits, and took away many of the "perks" (perquisites, or job benefits) that employees once enjoyed. Part of the reason for the changes was to instill in the remaining employees a sense of urgency and the need to adopt a new perspective on how they do their jobs.[31] Similarly, Saks Fifth Avenue recently changed its entire top management team as a way to breathe new life into the luxury retailer.[32]

Perceptions and expectations are also a common focus of organization change. Workers in an organization might believe that their wages and benefits are not as high as they should be. Management, however, might have evidence that shows the firm is paying a competitive wage and providing a superior benefit package. The change, then, would be centered on informing and educating the workforce about the comparative value of its compensation package. A common way to do this is to publish a statement that places an actual dollar value on each benefit provided and compares that amount to what other local organizations are providing their workers. Change might also be directed at employee attitudes and values. In many organizations today, managers are trying to eliminate adversarial relationships with workers and to adopt a more collaborative relationship. In many ways, changing attitudes and values is perhaps the hardest thing to do.

Changing Business Processes

Many organizations today have also gone through massive and comprehensive change programs involving all aspects of organization design, technology, and people. Although various descriptions are used, the terms currently in vogue for these changes are **business process change**, or **reengineering**, which is the radical redesign of all aspects of a business to achieve major gains in cost, service, or time.[33] ERP, as described earlier, is a common platform for changing business processes. However, business process change is a more comprehensive set of changes that goes beyond software and information systems.

Corning, for example, has undergone major reengineering over the last few years. Whereas the 150-year-old business once manufactured cookware and other durable consumer goods, it has transformed itself into a high-tech powerhouse making products such as the ultra-thin screens used in products like Palm Pilots and laptops.[34] Similarly, the dramatic overhauls of Kodak away from print film to other forms of optical imaging, of Yellow into a sophisticated freight delivery firm, and of UPS into a major international delivery giant all required business process changes throughout these organizations.

The Need for Business Process Change Why are so many organizations finding it necessary to undergo business process change? We noted in Chapter 1 that all systems, including organizations, are subject to entropy—a normal process leading to system decline. An organization is behaving most typically when it maintains the status quo, does not change in synch with its environment, and starts consuming its own resources to survive. In a sense, that is what happened to Kmart. In the early and mid-1970s, Kmart was in such a high-flying growth mode that it passed first JCPenney and then Sears to become

business process change (reengineering)
The radical redesign of all aspects of a business to achieve major gains in cost, service, or time

the world's largest retailer. But then the firm's managers grew complacent and assumed that the discount retailer's prosperity would continue and that they need not worry about environmental shifts, the growth of Wal-Mart, and so forth—and entropy set in. The key is to recognize the beginning of the decline and immediately move toward changing relevant business processes. Major problems occur when managers either do not recognize the onset of entropy until it is well advanced or are complacent in taking steps to correct it.

Approaches to Business Process Change Figure 7.3 shows general steps in reengineering. The first step is setting goals and developing a strategy for the changes. The organization must know in advance what new business processes are supposed to accomplish and how those accomplishments will be achieved. Next, top managers must begin and direct the reengineering effort. If a CEO simply announces that business process change is to occur but does nothing else, the program is unlikely to be successful. But, if the CEO is constantly involved in the process, underscoring its importance and taking the lead, business process change stands a much better chance of success.

Most experts also agree that successful business process change is usually accompanied by a sense of urgency. People in the organization must see the clear and present need for the changes being implemented and appreciate their importance. In addition, most successful reengineering efforts start with a new, clean slate. In other words, rather than assuming that the existing organization is a starting point and then trying to modify it, business process change usually starts by asking questions such as how customers are best

Figure 7.3 The Reengineering Process

Reengineering is a major redesign of all areas of an organization. To be successful, reengineering requires a systematic and comprehensive assessment of the entire organization. Goals, top management support, and a sense of urgency help the organization recreate itself and blend both top-level and bottom-up perspectives.

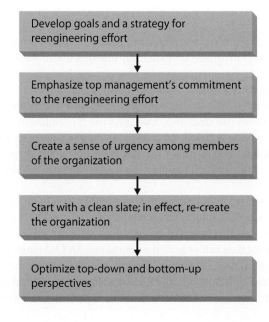

Develop goals and a strategy for reengineering effort

Emphasize top management's commitment to the reengineering effort

Create a sense of urgency among members of the organization

Start with a clean slate; in effect, re-create the organization

Optimize top-down and bottom-up perspectives

served and competitors best neutralized. New approaches and systems are then created and imposed in place of existing ones.

Finally, business process change requires a careful blend of top-down and bottom-up involvement. On the one hand, strong leadership is necessary, but too much involvement by top management can make the changes seem autocratic. On the other hand, employee participation is also important, but too little involvement by leaders can undermine the program's importance and create a sense that top managers do not care. Thus care must be taken to carefully balance these two countervailing forces. Our next section explores more fully one related but distinct approach called *organization development* (OD).

Organization Development

We noted in several places the importance of people and change. Beyond those change interests discussed earlier, a special area of interest that focuses almost exclusively on people is OD.

OD Assumptions OD is concerned with changing attitudes, perceptions, behaviors, and expectations. More precisely, **OD** is a planned effort that is organization-wide, and managed from the top, intended to increase organizational effectiveness and health through planned interventions in the organization's process, using behavioral science knowledge.[35] The theory and practice of OD are based on several very important assumptions. The first is that employees have a desire to grow and develop. Another is that employees have a strong need to be accepted by others within the organization. Still another critical assumption of OD is that the total organization and the way it is designed will influence the way individuals and groups within the organization behave. Thus some form of collaboration between managers and their employees is necessary to (1) take advantage of the skills and abilities of the employees and (2) eliminate aspects of the organization that retard employee growth, development, and group acceptance. Because of the intense personal nature of many OD activities, many large organizations rely on one or more OD consultants (either full-time employees assigned to this function or outside experts hired specifically for OD purposes) to implement and manage their OD program.[36]

OD Techniques Several kinds of interventions or activities are generally considered part of OD.[37] Some OD programs may use only one or a few of these; other programs use several of them at once.

- *Diagnostic activities.* Just as a physician examines patients to diagnose their current condition, an OD diagnosis analyzes the current condition of an organization. To carry out this diagnosis, managers use questionnaires, opinion or attitude surveys, interviews, archival data, and meetings to assess various characteristics of the organization. The results of this diagnosis may generate profiles of the organization's activities, which can then be used to identify problem areas in need of correction.
- *Team building.* Team-building activities are intended to enhance the effectiveness and satisfaction of individuals who work in groups or teams and to promote overall group effectiveness. Given the widespread use of teams today, these activities have taken on increased importance. An OD consultant might interview team members to determine how they feel about the group; then an off-site meeting could be held to discuss the issues that surfaced and iron out any problem areas or member concerns. Caterpillar used team building as one method

organization development (OD)
A planned effort that is organization-wide, and managed from the top, intended to increase organizational effectiveness and health through planned interventions in the organization's process, using behavioral science knowledge

for changing the working relationships between workers and supervisors from confrontational to cooperative. An interesting new approach to team building involves having executive teams participate in group cooking classes to teach them the importance of interdependence and coordination.[38]

- *Survey feedback.* In survey feedback, each employee responds to a questionnaire intended to measure perceptions and attitudes (for example, satisfaction and supervisory style). Everyone involved, including the supervisor, receives the results of the survey. The aim of this approach is usually to change the behavior of supervisors by showing them how their subordinates view them. After the feedback has been provided, workshops may be conducted to evaluate results and suggest constructive changes.

- *Third-party peacemaking.* Another approach to OD is through third-party peacemaking, which is most often used when substantial conflict exists within the organization. Third-party peacemaking can be appropriate on the individual, group, or organizational level. The third party, usually an OD consultant, uses a variety of mediation or negotiation techniques to resolve any problems or conflicts among individuals or groups.

- *Process consultation.* In process consultation, an OD consultant observes groups in the organization to develop an understanding of their communication patterns, decision-making and leadership processes, and methods of cooperation and conflict resolution. The consultant then provides feedback to the involved parties about the processes he or she has observed. The goal of this form of intervention is to improve the observed processes. A leader who is presented with feedback outlining deficiencies in his or her leadership style, for example, might be expected to change to overcome them.

- *Life and career planning.* Life and career planning helps employees formulate their personal goals and evaluate strategies for integrating their goals with the goals of the organization. Such activities might include specification of training needs and plotting a career map. General Electric has a reputation for doing an outstanding job in this area.

- *Coaching and counseling.* Coaching and counseling provide nonevaluative feedback to individuals. The purpose is to help people develop a better sense of how others see them and learn behaviors that will assist others in achieving their work-related goals. The focus is not on how the individual is performing today; instead, it is on how the person can perform better in the future.

The Effectiveness of OD Given the diversity of activities encompassed by OD, it is not surprising that managers report mixed results from various OD interventions. Organizations that actively practice some form of OD include American Airlines, Texas Instruments, Procter & Gamble, and BF Goodrich. Goodrich, for example, has trained 60 persons in OD processes and techniques. These trained experts have subsequently become internal OD consultants to assist other managers in applying the techniques.[39] Many other managers, in contrast, report that they have tried OD but discarded it.[40]

OD will probably remain an important part of management theory and practice. Of course, there are no sure things when dealing with social systems such as organizations, and the effectiveness of many OD techniques is difficult to evaluate. Because all organizations are open systems interacting with their environments, an improvement in an organization after an OD intervention may be attributable to the intervention, but it may also be attributable to changes in economic conditions, luck, or other factors.[41]

ORGANIZATIONAL INNOVATION

innovation
The managed effort of an organization to develop new products or services or new uses for existing products or services

A final element of organization change that we address is **innovation**, which is the managed effort of an organization to develop new products or services or new uses for existing products or services. Innovation is clearly important because, without new products or services, any organization will fall behind its competition.[42] Our "First Things First" highlighted the importance of innovation in the growth of the biotech firm Genentech. The "Management Tech" box takes a close look at the role of innovation in the start-up and development of a smaller company called Sportvision.

MANAGEMENT TECH

The Diehards Whined but They Still Watched

Football fans: Where were you on September 27, 1998? It was a Sunday, so you were probably watching a couple of National Football League (NFL) games, perhaps an otherwise less-than-memorable matchup between the Baltimore Ravens and Cincinnati Bengals. Fans in the stands didn't see anything out of the ordinary, but TV viewers got their first look at a remarkable innovation in sports telecasting: the virtual first-and-ten line—that bright-yellow line that appears on your TV screen to show you where the offensive team needs to go to keep the football. The biggest innovation in sports coverage since slo-mo and the instant replay debuted in the 1960s, it's a product of Chicago-based Sportvision Inc., which has since become a pipeline of innovative technologies for revolutionizing TV sports from golf to NASCAR.

The seed for Sportvision was planted in 1995, when chief technology officer Stan Honey and Sports CEO David Hill got together to brainstorm ideas for tricking out sports coverage on Fox TV. At the top of the agenda were sluggish ratings for the network's coverage of National Hockey League (NHL) games, to which Fox had recently acquired the rights. At some point, Honey and Hill came up with idea of electronically enhancing the puck—the three-inch black disc that hurtles across the ice at speeds reaching 100 miles an hour. They decided to give the puck a red comet-like tail and introduced the innovation (called Fox Trax) for the 1996 NHL All-Star Game. "The diehards whined,"

recalls Honey, "but they still watched," and ratings improved.

The little red comet disappeared when Fox and the NHL parted company three years later, but it had already inspired Honey to start up a promising new business. Sportvision was launched in 1998, and it quickly developed its 1st & Ten Line™ computer system to project the virtual first-down line during football broadcasts. In 1999, with surveys showing that 92 percent of football fans wanted it for every game, ABC, Fox, and ESPN signed a deal to feature the virtual line in more than 100 NFL and college football games broadcast over the next two years. A decade later, according to one ESPN executive, "it's become so much a part of the fabric [of football on TV] that if people don't see it, their reaction is that the telecast is substandard."

Before long, Sportvision had added kick and pass trackers to the virtual first-down line to enhance the coverage of football and turned its attention to other major sports. Today, K-Zone projects a virtual strike zone and PITCHf/x tracks the arc of pitches in a baseball game. GOLFf/x features virtual shot trails, course flyovers, and simulated putting zones. RACEf/x treats motor-sports fans to virtual dashboards and simulated flags to identify cars, and an in-car electronic device gathers and relays data on speed, RPMs, and track position. There are also applications tailored to horse racing, soccer, bowling, Olympic competition, and extreme sports. StroMotion™, which reveals an athlete's movements over time, is applicable to the presentation of multiple sports.

Sportvision works with some pretty big clients, including sports organizations such as the NFL, Major League Baseball, NASCAR, the PGA Tour, and the National Basketball Association, and TV broadcasters such as ESPN, Fox Sports, and Turner Sports. Seventy percent of its revenues come from licensing its technology to the networks that broadcast the sporting events. Fox, for example, will pay about $12,000 in fees for a basic package to broadcast regular NFL games and ESPN about $25,000 for a deluxe package of bells and whistles on *Monday Night Football*. These may seem like handsome sums, but they come with built-in ceilings: TV networks know that sports fans will or won't tune in to an event regardless of whatever flashy new technology Sportvision brings to the show, and so the tech provider has few options when it comes to upping its prices. Recent ventures with foreign broadcasters yield similarly slim margins.

Sportvision's revenues grew by an average of 33 percent annually between 2003 and 2007 (as of this writing, the last year for which data were available). Revenues for 2007 reached $25 million, but earnings amounted to just $3.5 million. "There's a big difference," admits CEO Hank Adams, "between serving a dozen clients versus serving a million customer subscribers," and the company has turned to Internet subscriptions as a more promising source of revenue. Currently, for example, more than 100,000 auto-racing fans pay $80 a year to subscribe to RaceCast, a joint venture in which ESPN showcases Indy Racing League events and

Sportvision permits viewers to track drivers in real time and even enjoy cockpit views from any car. Similar subscription products include TrackPass, a collaboration with NASCAR.com and Turner Sports New Media, and TOURCast, a venture with IBM and PGATOUR.com.

Having been founded to capitalize on an innovative idea, Sportvision has always been an innovative company. Indeed, it bills itself as "the nation's premier innovator of sports and entertainment products for fans, media, and marketers," and *SportsBusiness Journal* credits the company with 10 of the 20 greatest innovations in sports broadcasting. That's why Sportvision engineers are working on their latest innovative technology—one that the firm hopes will help it score better in the race for more revenue. Not surprisingly, the new project also involves a partnership with NASCAR: To further blur the increasingly fine line between real and virtual sports, Sportvision is currently developing a new generation of computer video games that will use real-time data to put racing fans in the driver's seat, barreling around the oval at Daytona and bumping fenders with the likes of Dale Earnhardt Jr.

References: "Company Overview," "Management Team," "Products and Services," Sportvision website, www.sportvision.com on March 25, 2009; Mark Hyman, "Stan Honey: Virtual Virtuoso," BusinessWeek, October 31, 2005, www.businessweek.com on March 25, 2009; Dan Williams, "Sportvision Enhances Fan Experiences and Provides New Revenue Streams," Sport and Technology, July 2003, www.sportandtechnology.com on April 16, 2006; Jeff Borden, "Second and 10 for Sportvision," BusinessWeek, February 29, 2008, www.businessweek.com on March 25, 2009; "Goal Oriented: How Hank Adams Applied Technology to Sports to Make Sportvision a Winner," Smart Business, July 2008, www.sbonline.com on March 25, 2009; Jeffrey M. O'Brien, "Sports+Tech=$$$," CNNMoney.com, October 17, 2008.

The Innovation Process

The organizational innovation process consists of developing, applying, launching, growing, and managing the maturity and decline of creative ideas.[43] This process is depicted in Figure 7.4.

Innovation Development   Innovation development involves the evaluation, modification, and improvement of creative ideas. It can transform a product or service with only modest potential into a product or service with significant potential. Parker Brothers, for example, decided during innovation development not to market an indoor volleyball game but instead to sell separately the appealing little foam ball designed for the game. The firm will never know how well the volleyball game would have sold, but

Figure 7.4 The Innovation Process

Organizations actively seek to manage the innovation process. These steps illustrate the general life cycle that characterizes most innovations. Of course, as with creativity, the innovation process will suffer if it is approached too mechanically and rigidly.

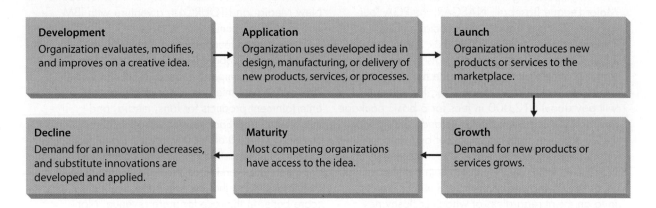

Development	**Application**	**Launch**
Organization evaluates, modifies, and improves on a creative idea.	Organization uses developed idea in design, manufacturing, or delivery of new products, services, or processes.	Organization introduces new products or services to the marketplace.

Decline	**Maturity**	**Growth**
Demand for an innovation decreases, and substitute innovations are developed and applied.	Most competing organizations have access to the idea.	Demand for new products or services grows.

the Nerf ball and numerous related products generated millions of dollars in revenues for it.

Innovation Application Innovation application is the stage in which an organization takes a developed idea and uses it in the design, manufacturing, or delivery of new products, services, or processes. At this point, the innovation emerges from the laboratory and is transformed into tangible goods or services. One example of innovation application is the use of radar-based focusing systems in Polaroid's instant cameras. The idea of using radio waves to discover the location, speed, and direction of moving objects was first applied extensively by Allied forces during World War II. As radar technology developed during the following years, the electrical components needed became smaller and more streamlined. Researchers at Polaroid applied this well-developed technology in a new way.[44]

Application Launch Application launch is the stage at which an organization introduces new products or services to the marketplace. The important question is not "Does the innovation work?" but "Will customers want to purchase the innovative product and service?" History is full of creative ideas that did not generate enough interest among customers to be successful. Some notable innovation failures include a portable seat warmer from Sony, "New" Coke, and Polaroid's SX-70 instant camera (which cost $3 billion to develop, but never sold more than 100,000 units in a year).[45] Thus, despite development and application, new products and services can still fail at the launch phase.

Application Growth Once an innovation has been successfully launched, it then enters the stage of application growth. This is a period of high economic performance for an organization because demand for the product or service is often greater than supply. Organizations that fail to anticipate this stage may unintentionally limit their growth, as Apple did by not anticipating demand for its iMac computer.[46] At the same time, overestimating demand for a new product can be just as detrimental to performance. Unsold products can sit in warehouses for years.

Innovation Maturity After a period of growing demand, an innovative product or service often enters a period of maturity. Innovation maturity is the stage at which most organizations in an industry have access to an innovation and are applying it in approximately the same way. The technological application of an innovation during this stage of the innovation process can be very sophisticated. Because most firms have access to the innovation, however, as a result of either their developing the innovation on their own or copying the innovation of others, it does not provide competitive advantage to any one of them. The time that elapses between innovation development and innovation maturity varies notably depending on the particular product or service. Whenever an innovation involves the use of complex skills (such as a complicated manufacturing process or highly sophisticated teamwork), moving from the growth phase to the maturity phase will take longer. In addition, if the skills needed to implement these innovations are rare and difficult to imitate, then strategic imitation may be delayed, and the organization may enjoy a period of sustained competitive advantage.

Innovation Decline Every successful innovation bears its own seeds of decline. Because an organization does not gain a competitive advantage from an innovation at maturity, it must encourage its creative scientists, engineers, and managers to begin looking for new innovations. This continued search for competitive advantage usually leads new products and services to move from the creative process through innovation maturity, and finally to innovation decline. Innovation decline is the stage during which demand for an innovation decreases and substitute innovations are developed and applied.

Forms of Innovation

Each creative idea that an organization develops poses a different challenge for the innovation process. Innovations can be radical or incremental, technical or managerial, and product or process.

Radical versus Incremental Innovations Radical innovations are new products, services, or technologies developed by an organization that completely replace the existing products, services, or technologies in an industry.[47] Incremental innovations are new products, services, or processes that modify existing ones. Firms that implement radical innovations fundamentally shift the nature of competition and the interaction of firms within their environments. Firms that implement incremental innovations alter, but do not fundamentally change, competitive interaction in an industry.

Over the last several years, organizations have introduced many radical innovations. For example, compact disk technology replaced long-playing vinyl records in the recording industry and now digital downloading is replacing CDs, DVDs have replaced videocassettes but are now being supplanted by Blu-ray DVDs and online downloading, and high-definition television is replacing regular television technology. Whereas radical innovations like these tend to be very visible and public, incremental innovations actually are more numerous. For instance, each new generation of the iPhone and the iPod represents relatively minor changes over previous versions.

Technical versus Managerial Innovations Technical innovations are changes in the physical appearance or performance of a product or service or of the physical processes through which a product or service is manufactured. Many of the most important innovations over the last 50 years have been technical. For example, the serial replacement of the vacuum tube with the transistor, the transistor with the integrated circuit, and the

radical innovation
A new product, service, or technology that completely replaces an existing one

incremental innovation
A new product, service, or technology that modifies an existing one

technical innovation
A change in the appearance or performance of a product or service or of the physical processes through which a product or service is manufactured

NEWSCOM

Many products today are the result of incremental innovations—new products, services, or processes that modify existing ones. Take the iPhone, for example. The first iPhone, one of the most successful new products in history, was a radical innovation. But each successive version of the iPhone has taken the existing product and made various improvements to it.

integrated circuit with the microchip has greatly enhanced the power, ease of use, and speed of operation of a wide variety of electronic products. Not all innovations developed by organizations are technical, however. **Managerial innovations** are changes in the management process by which products and services are conceived, built, and delivered to customers.[48] They do not necessarily affect the physical appearance or performance of products or services directly. In effect, reengineering, as we discussed earlier, represents a managerial innovation.

Product versus Process Innovations

Perhaps the two most important types of technical innovations are **product innovations** and process innovations. Product innovations are changes in the physical characteristics or performance of existing products or services or the creation of brand-new products or services. **Process innovations** are changes in the way products or services are manufactured, created, or distributed. Whereas managerial innovations generally affect the broader context of development, process innovations directly affect manufacturing.

The implementation of robotics is a process innovation. The effect of product and process innovations on economic return depends on the stage of the innovation process that a new product or service occupies. At first, during development, application, and launch, the physical attributes and capabilities of an innovation mostly affect organizational performance. Thus product innovations are particularly important during these beginning phases. Later, as an innovation enters the phases of growth, maturity, and decline, an organization's ability to develop process innovations, such as fine-tuning manufacturing, increasing product quality, and improving product distribution, becomes important to maintaining economic return.

Japanese organizations have often excelled at process innovation. The market for 35 mm cameras was dominated by German and other European manufacturers when, in the early 1960s, Japanese organizations such as Canon and Nikon began making cameras. Some of these early Japanese products were not very successful, but these companies continued to invest in their process technology and eventually were able to increase quality and decrease manufacturing costs.[49] The Japanese organizations came to dominate the worldwide market for 35 mm cameras, and the German companies, because they were not able to maintain the same pace of process innovation, struggled to maintain market share and profitability. And as film technology gave way to digital photography, the same Japanese firms effectively transitioned to leadership in this market as well.

The Failure to Innovate

To remain competitive in today's economy, organizations must be innovative. And yet many organizations that should be innovative are not successful at bringing out new products or services or do so only after innovations created by others are very mature. Organizations may fail to innovate for at least three reasons.

managerial innovation
A change in the management process in an organization

product innovation
A change in the physical characteristics or performance of an existing product or service or the creation of a new one

process innovation
A change in the way a product or service is manufactured, created, or distributed

CHAPTER 7 Managing Organization Change and Innovation **197**

Lack of Resources Innovation is expensive in terms of money, time, and energy. If a firm does not have sufficient money to fund a program of innovation or does not currently employ the kinds of employees it needs to be innovative, it may lag behind in innovation. Even highly innovative organizations cannot become involved in every new product or service its employees think up. For example, numerous other commitments in the electronic instruments and computer industry forestalled Hewlett-Packard (HP) from investing in Steve Jobs and Steve Wozniak's original idea for a personal computer. With infinite resources of money, time, and technical and managerial expertise, HP might have entered this market early. Because the firm did not have this flexibility, however, it had to make some difficult choices about which innovations to invest in.[50]

When Steve Jobs and his partner, Steve Wozniak, developed their initial plans to build a personal computer, they took their idea to Hewlett-Packard to see if the technology company had an interest in buying or investing in the new product. At the time, though, Hewlett-Packard was stretched financially due to other commitments and so the firm decided to pass. As a result, Jobs and Wozniak eventually decided to develop the computer on their own and launched Apple.

Failure to Recognize Opportunities Because firms cannot pursue all innovations, they need to develop the capability to carefully evaluate innovations and to select the ones that hold the greatest potential. To obtain a competitive advantage, an organization must usually make investment decisions before the innovation process reaches the mature stage. The earlier the investment, however, the greater the risk. If organizations are not skilled at recognizing and evaluating opportunities, they may be overly cautious and fail to invest in innovations that later turn out to be successful for other firms.

Resistance to Change As we discussed earlier, many organizations tend to resist change. Innovation means giving up old products and old ways of doing things in favor of new products and new ways of doing things. These kinds of changes can be personally difficult for managers and other members of an organization. Thus resistance to change can slow the innovation process.

Promoting Innovation in Organizations

A wide variety of ideas for promoting innovation in organizations has been developed over the years. Three specific ways for promoting innovation are through the reward system, through the organizational culture, and through a process called *intrapreneurship*.[51]

The Reward System A firm's reward system is the means by which it encourages and discourages certain behaviors by employees. Major components of the reward system include salaries, bonuses, and perquisites. Using the reward system to promote innovation is a fairly mechanical but nevertheless effective management technique. The idea is to provide financial and nonfinancial rewards to people and groups who develop innovative ideas. Once the members of an organization understand that they will be rewarded for such activities, they are more likely to work creatively. With this end in mind, Monsanto gives a $50,000 award each year to the scientist or group of scientists who develop the biggest commercial breakthrough.

It is important for organizations to reward creative behavior, but it is vital to avoid punishing creativity when it does not result in highly successful innovations. It is the nature of the creative and innovative processes that many new-product ideas will simply not work out in the marketplace. Each process is fraught with too many uncertainties to generate positive results every time. An individual may have prepared himself or herself to be creative, but an insight may not be forthcoming. Or managers may attempt to apply a developed innovation, only to recognize that it does not work. Indeed, some organizations operate according to the assumption that, if all their innovative efforts succeed, then they are probably not taking enough risks in research and development. At 3M, nearly 60 percent of the creative ideas suggested each year do not succeed in the marketplace.

Managers need to be very careful in responding to innovative failure. If innovative failure is due to incompetence, systematic errors, or managerial sloppiness, then a firm should respond appropriately, for example, by withholding raises or reducing promotion opportunities. People who act in good faith to develop an innovation that simply does not work out, however, should not be punished for failure. If they are, they will probably not be creative in the future. A punitive reward system will discourage people from taking risks and therefore reduce the organization's ability to obtain competitive advantages.

Organization Culture As we discussed in Chapter 2, an organization's culture is the set of values, beliefs, and symbols that help guide behavior. A strong, appropriately focused organizational culture can be used to support innovative activity. A well-managed culture can communicate a sense that innovation is valued and will be rewarded and that occasional failure in the pursuit of new ideas is not only acceptable but even expected. In addition to reward systems and intrapreneurial activities, firms such as Apple, Google, LG Electronics, Tata, Nintendo, Nokia, and HP are all known to have strong, innovation-oriented cultures that value individual creativity, risk taking, and inventiveness.[52]

Intrapreneurship in Larger Organizations In recent years, many large businesses have realized that the entrepreneurial spirit that propelled their growth becomes stagnant after they transform themselves from a small but growing concern into a larger one.[53] To help revitalize this spirit, some firms today encourage what they call *intrapreneurship*. **Intrapreneurs** are similar to entrepreneurs except that they develop a new business in the context of a large organization. There are three intrapreneurial roles in large organizations.[54] To successfully use intrapreneurship to encourage creativity and innovation, the organization must find one or more individuals to perform these roles.

The *inventor* is the person who actually conceives of and develops the new idea, product, or service by means of the creative process. Because the inventor may lack the expertise or motivation to oversee the transformation of the product or service from an idea into a marketable entity, however, a second role comes into play. A *product champion* is usually a middle manager who learns about the project and becomes committed to it. He or she helps overcome organizational resistance and convinces others to take the innovation seriously. The product champion may have only limited understanding of the technological aspects of the innovation. Nevertheless, product champions are skilled at knowing how the organization works, whose support is needed to push the project forward,

intrapreneurs
Similar to entrepreneurs except that they develop new businesses in the context of a large organization

and where to go to secure the resources necessary for successful development. A *sponsor* is a top-level manager who approves of and supports a project. This person may fight for the budget needed to develop an idea, overcome arguments against a project, and use organizational politics to ensure the project's survival. With a sponsor in place, the inventor's idea has a much better chance of being successfully developed.

Several firms have embraced intrapreneurship as a way to encourage creativity and innovation. Colgate-Palmolive has created a separate unit, Colgate Venture Company, staffed with intrapreneurs who develop new products. General Foods developed Culinova as a unit to which employees can take their ideas for possible development. S.C. Johnson & Son established a $250,000 fund to support new-product ideas, and Texas Instruments refuses to approve a new innovative project unless it has an acknowledged inventor, champion, and sponsor.

SUMMARY OF LEARNING OBJECTIVES AND KEY POINTS

1. Describe the nature of organization change, including forces for change and planned versus reactive change.

   - Organization change is any substantive modification to some part of the organization.

   - Change may be prompted by forces internal or external to the organization.

   - In general, planned change is preferable to reactive change.

2. Discuss the steps in organization change and how to manage resistance to change.

   - The Lewin model provides a general perspective on the steps involved in change.

   - A comprehensive model is usually more effective.

   - People tend to resist change because of uncertainty, threatened self-interests, different perceptions, and feelings of loss.

   - Participation, education and communication, facilitation, and force-field analysis are methods for overcoming this resistance.

3. Identify and describe major areas of organization change and discuss the assumptions, techniques, and effectiveness of OD.

   - The most common areas of change involve changing organizational structure and design, technology, and people.

   - Business process change is a more massive and comprehensive change.

   - OD is concerned with changing attitudes, perceptions, behaviors, and expectations. Its effective use relies on an important set of assumptions.

   - There are conflicting opinions about the effectiveness of several OD techniques.

4. Describe the innovation process, forms of innovation, the failure to innovate, and how organizations can promote innovation.

   - The innovation process has six steps: development, application, launch, growth, maturity, and decline.

   - Basic categories of innovation include radical, incremental, technical, managerial, product, and process innovations.

   - Despite the importance of innovation, many organizations fail to innovate because they lack the required creative individuals or are committed to too many other creative activities, fail to recognize opportunities, or resist the change that innovation requires.

   - Organizations can use a variety of tools to overcome these problems, including the reward system, organizational culture, and intrapreneurship.

DISCUSSION QUESTIONS

Questions for Review

1. What forces or kinds of events lead to organization change? Identify each force or event as a planned or a reactive change.

2. Compare planned and reactive change. What are the advantages of planned change, as compared to reactive change?

3. Identify the primary reasons people resist change, and then summarize the primary methods managers can use to overcome this resistance.

4. In a brief sentence or just a phrase, describe each of the OD techniques.

5. Consider the following list of products. Categorize each along all three dimensions of innovation, if possible (radical versus incremental, technical versus managerial, and product versus process). Explain your answers.

    *   Teaching college courses by digitally recording the instructor and then making the digital file available online.

    *   The rise in popularity of virtual organizations (discussed in Chapter 6).

    *   Checking the security of packages on airlines with the type of MRI (magnetic resonance imaging) scanning devices that are common in health care.

    *   A device such as the iPhone that combines features of a cell phone and a handheld computer with Internet capability.

    *   Robotic arms that can perform surgery that is too precise for a human surgeon's hands.

    *   Hybrid automobiles, which run on both batteries and gasoline.

    *   Using video games to teach soldiers how to plan and execute battles.

Questions for Analysis

1. What are the symptoms that a manager should look for in determining whether an organization needs to change? What are the symptoms that indicate that an organization has been through too much change?

2. Assume that you are the manager of an organization that has a routine way of performing a task and now faces a major change in how it performs that task. Using the Lewin model, tell what steps you would take to implement the change. Using the comprehensive approach, tell what steps you would take. For each step, give specific examples of actions you would take at that step.

3. Think back to a time when a professor announced a change that you, the student, did not want to adopt. What were the reasons for your resistance to change? Was the professor able to overcome your resistance? If so, tell what he or she did. If not, tell what he or she could have done that might have been successful.

4. Some people resist change, whereas others welcome it enthusiastically. To deal with the first group, one needs to overcome resistance to change; to deal with the second, one needs to overcome resistance to stability. What advice can you give a manager facing the latter situation?

5. Can a change made in one area of an organization—in technology, for instance—not lead to change in other areas? If you think that change in one area must lead to change in other areas, describe an example of an organization change to illustrate your point. If you think that change can occur in just one area without causing change in other areas, describe an example of an organization change that illustrates your point.

BUILDING EFFECTIVE DECISION-MAKING SKILLS

Exercise Overview

Decision-making skills refer to the ability to recognize and define problems and opportunities correctly and then to select an appropriate course of action for solving problems or capitalizing on opportunities. This exercise gives you some practice in making decisions about organizational innovation.

Exercise Background

You're a manager at a venture capital firm that seeks out companies with promising new ideas for technological improvements and then provides financing, advice, and expertise in exchange for part ownership. Your firm makes money when an idea is successfully brought to market and the value of your ownership shares increases. Your personal compensation—not to mention your continued employment—are therefore based on your ability to choose the right ideas and to provide entrepreneurs with the right support.

Exercise Task

1. Use the Internet to locate information about at least five promising new technologies. (*Hint:* The websites of publications that report technology news, such as *TechWeb*, are good sources, as are the corporate websites of innovative companies like 3M. Or search the term *technology venture capital* to locate firms that invest in new technologies and then find out what you can about their clients.) Then choose the new technology that interests you the most.

2. Next, describe the current status of your chosen technology in the innovation process. Explain how you arrived at your decision about where to place the technology in the process.

3. Finally, discuss the kinds of advice and expertise that this idea and its company need to grow into a successful start-up.

BUILDING EFFECTIVE DIAGNOSTIC SKILLS

Exercise Overview

Diagnostic skills, which enable a manager to visualize the most appropriate response to a situation, are especially important during periods of organizational change.

Exercise Background

You're the general manager of a hotel situated along a beautiful stretch of beach on a tropical island. One of the oldest of six large resorts in the immediate area, your hotel is owned by a group of foreign investors. For several years, it's been operated as a franchise unit of a large international hotel chain, as have all the other hotels on the island.

For the past few years, the hotel's franchisee-owners have been taking most of the profits for themselves and putting relatively little back into the hotel. They've also let you know that their business is not in good financial health and that the revenue from the hotel is being used to offset losses incurred elsewhere. In contrast, most of the other hotels on the island have recently been refurbished, and plans for two brand-new hotels have been announced for the near future.

A team of executives from franchise headquarters has just visited your hotel. They're quite disappointed in the property, particularly because it's failed to keep pace with other resorts on the island. They've informed you that if the property isn't brought up to standards, the franchise agreement, which is up for review in a year, will be revoked. You realize that this move would be a potential disaster because you can ill afford to lose the franchisor's brand name, access to its reservation system, or any other benefits of the franchise arrangement.

Sitting alone in your office, you've identified several seemingly viable courses of action:

1. Convince the franchisee-owners to remodel the hotel. You estimate that it will take $5 million to meet the franchisor's minimum standards and another $5 million to bring the hotel up to the standards of the island's top resort.

2. Convince the franchisor to give you more time and more options for upgrading the facility.

3. Allow the franchise agreement to terminate and try to succeed as an independent hotel.

4. Assume that the hotel will fail and start looking for another job. You have a pretty good reputation, but you're not terribly happy about the possibility of having to accept a lower-level position (say, as an assistant manager) with another firm.

Exercise Task

Having mulled over your options, do the following:

1. Rank-order your four alternatives in terms of probable success. Make any necessary assumptions.

2. Identify alternatives other than the four that you identified above.

3. Can more than one alternative be pursued simultaneously? Which ones?

4. Develop an overall strategy for trying to save the hotel while protecting your own interests.

SKILLS SELF-ASSESSMENT INSTRUMENT

Innovation and Learning Styles

Introduction: David Kolb, a professor at Case Western University, has described a learning model that tells about different learning styles. While individuals move through all four activities, most express a preference for either hands-on learning or learning by indirect observation and most express a preference for either learning about abstract concepts or learning about concrete experience. When these two dimensions are combined, the following learning styles are created.

	Active Experimentation	Reflective Observation
Concrete Experience	Accommodator	Diverger
Abstract Conceptualization	Converger	Assimilator

Individuals with any of these styles can be creative and innovative, although the way they will approach creativity and the contribution they can make to the innovation process differs. If you understand your learning style, you'll be better equipped to participate in innovation.

Instructions: Fill out the following tables.

			Rank from 1 to 4 1 = Least like you, 4 = Most like you
1.	a.	I want to try something out first.	
	b.	I need to feel personally involved with things.	
	c.	I focus on useful practical applications.	
	d.	I look for differences and distinctions.	

Rank from 1 to 4
1 = Least like you,
4 = Most like you

2.   a.   I work mainly by intuition.

     b.   I tend to ask myself questions.

     c.   I always try to think logically.

     d.   I am very result oriented.

Rank from 1 to 4
1 = Least like you,
4 = Most like you

3.   a.   I let everything filter through my head and think about it.

     b.   I am interested in the here and now.

     c.   I mainly have a practical nature.

     d.   I am mostly interested in the future.

Rank from 1 to 4
1 = Least like you,
4 = Most like you

4.   a.   I consider the facts, and then I act.

     b.   I act.

     c.   I ponder until I have evaluated every option, and then I act.

     d.   I would rather dream or imagine than think about the facts.

Interpretation: Add scores for 1a, 2d, 3b, and 4b. This is your Accommodator Score.

Add scores for 1b, 2a, 3d, and 4d. This is your Diverger Score.

Add scores for 1c, 2c, 3c, and 4a. This is your Converger Score.

Add scores for 1d, 2b, 3a, and 4c. This is your Assimilator Score.

While everyone uses each of the four styles at times, whichever score is higher is your preferred mode.

EXPERIENTIAL EXERCISE

Team Innovation

Purpose: To give you practice related to innovation as a team activity.

Introduction: Assume that your group is a team of professionals who are in charge of new-product design at your company.

Instructions:

Step 1: Using *only* the materials your professor will give to you, design and construct a new product. This product can be something wholly new or an improvement on an existing product.

Step 2: Present your product to the class. Explain its use, features, and appeal to consumers.

Follow-up Questions

1. How much influence did the selection of materials have on your design? What, if anything, does this suggest to you about organization resources and their effect on innovation?

2. Explain the process your group used to come up with the design. Describe the number of people participated, how they participated, how any disagreements were resolved, and so on. What, if anything, does this suggest to you about some of the potential advantages as well as the challenges of team-based innovation in organizations?

3. Describe the various roles played by members of your group. For example, did anyone function primarily as a "voice of caution"? Did anyone serve as a devil's advocate? Did anyone work as a facilitator, smoothing over feelings and resolving conflicts? Were some members better at design, or at implementation? What, if anything, does this tell you regarding the various roles that individuals take in the innovation process in organizations?

 YOU MAKE THE CALL

The Science of the Deal

1. You're an up-and-coming assistant to a mid-level manager at Roche. Your boss is being transferred to the company's newly acquired research facilities at the former Genentech headquarters in San Francisco. She's asked you to compile a brief report on Genentech's overall approach to product innovation. What will you say in your report?

2. Having hit a home run on the assignment that you were given in part 1, you're the obvious choice to draw up another brief report. This time, your boss wants an overview of Genentech's 2004 reorganization and a summary of the ways in which it's facilitated growth in the company's product pipeline and its success in rolling out new products. What will you say in your report?

3. Now that Roche chairman Franz Humer has publicly committed the parent company to sustaining Genentech's "innovative culture," he needs suggestions on how best to follow through on the promise. Not surprisingly, your boss has asked you to furnish her with two or three ideas. In particular, she wants your opinion on what to recommend about Genentech's regular Friday "Ho-Ho" beer fest. What will your suggestions be?

4. You're a top-level manager at Genentech who's amassed 250,000 shares of stock during your years with the company. What are your next career and lifestyle moves?

CHAPTER 8

HUMAN RESOURCES MANAGEMENT IN ORGANIZATIONS

LEARNING OBJECTIVES

After studying this chapter, you should be able to:

1 Describe the environmental context of human resource management, including its strategic importance and its relationship with legal and social factors.

2 Discuss how organizations attract human resources, including human resource planning, recruiting, and selecting.

3 Describe how organizations develop human resources, including training and development, performance appraisal, and performance feedback.

4 Discuss how organizations maintain human resources, including the determination of

compensation and benefits and career planning.

5 Discuss the nature of diversity, including its meaning, associated trends, impact, and management.

6 Discuss labor relations, including how employees form unions and the mechanics of collective bargaining.

7 Describe the issues associated with managing knowledge and contingent and temporary workers.

The Temptations of Temping

> **"It's a good opportunity to go in and possibly find a job you like. And it's an easy out if it's something you'd never do in a million years."**
>
> —EX-TEMP WORKER MATT DEANE

Back in 2002, New Yorker Diana Bloom logged on to Craigslist and offered her services as a tutor, editor, and translator. She's been making a living on the short-term jobs that come her way from the website ever since. She works out of her home to take care of a young son. Temp work is appealing, she says, because, "I'm not very outgoing, and getting my foot in the door to companies would have been hard."

Craigslist works in the other direction, too, with employers posting openings for jobs both permanent and temporary. Another New Yorker, Simone Sneed, scours the Craigslist "Gigs" section for jobs that last for perhaps a day, often for just a few hours. Whether as a backup singer or a grants writer, she's turned the strategy of patching together "gigs" into a convenient way to supplement the income from her full-time job. "I'll use the extra money to pay off my school loan," she says. "Every little bit helps."

In the 2010 economic climate, unfortunately, overall job postings except for short-term jobs—gigs that usually include no health benefits, sick days, or paid vacations—are down on Craigslist and everywhere else. If you're employed short term or part time for economic reasons, the Bureau of Labor Statistics (BLS) classifies you as "underemployed." You're on a list that added up to almost 10 million at the beginning of 2010—about 4 percent of the overall workforce.

Naturally, most people who are underemployed are, by definition, "overqualified": In fact, they often have years of professional experience but are willing to take jobs that don't call for their levels of training or experience. Take the case of Gloria Christ. As national project manager for an information-technology company in the Chicago area, Christ used to coordinate the installation of Wi-Fi hot spots all over the country. She has nearly 20 years of managerial experience, but today she's willing to put it to good use as a temporary office manager. "At this point in time," she says, "I think even if there was something that was temporary, it could become full time later on. . . . Sometimes, you can go in at a low level to interview just to get your foot in the door."

It may be small compensation, but during the current recession, although many companies are reluctant to add costly permanent jobs, they are increasingly willing to open up temporary positions to tide them over. Often, of course, you'll have to take a job that isn't exactly what you've trained for or set your sights on, but as one employment-services manager observes, job seekers today "are more than willing to try new

The use of temporary workers is becoming increasingly widespread. Temporary employment is also growing in popularity in other countries as well. For example, this Manpower office recently opened in Paris.

occupations—much more willing than they were even a year ago." Interestingly, for a lot of people, the adjustment to current labor-market conditions isn't necessarily as traumatic as you might think. A recent survey conducted by the temporary-staffing agency Kelly Services found that as many as 26 percent of employed American adults regarded themselves as "free agents" when it comes to the type of job they're willing to take (up from 19 percent in 2006). Of all those polled, only 10 percent said that they were doing temporary work because they'd been laid off from permanent jobs and 90 percent said that they were doing it because they liked the variety and flexibility that temping afforded them.

In fact, temping offers several work-life advantages. You can learn something not only about a given company but about the industry in which it operates. Even if the job doesn't work out, you can acquire some skills and beef up your résumé. You may also come away with better ideas about what you want in a job or a boss. These are some factors that convinced Matt Deane, when he was fresh out of college, to take a three-month job at the American National Standards Institute (ANSI). "It's a good opportunity to go in and possibly find a job you like," he says. He also enjoys the freedom to move on when and if the time comes: "It's an easy out if it's something you'd never do in a million years."

Temp work can also provide income during career transitions, and it's a good way to exercise a little control over the balance between your work and the rest of your life. In 1995, for example, when she was seven months pregnant with her first child, veteran retail manager Stacey Schick accepted a two-week data-entry job with the Orange County (New York) Association of Realtors. "I didn't know how to turn on a computer," she remembers, but "they needed bodies." Now she is still with the association as its education coordinator. "I would never had considered it," she says, if a job in her field had come up, but the job she landed in has turned out to be a much better fit with her lifestyle: "It's afforded me the opportunity to have a family and be able to have time with them."

Like Schick's, a temp job may very well lead to a full-time job. That's what happened to Deane, who stayed at ANSI for ten years. The path taken by Schick and Deane is called "temp to perm," and it offers employers several advantages as well. Companies, for instance, that are hesitant to make commitments to untested employees can

try before they buy—they get a chance to see employees in action before finalizing hiring decisions. Because there are no fees to pay when an employee goes from temp to perm, trying out temps is also cheaper than paying an agency outright to find a hire. The big savings, of course, come from benefits, which can amount to one-third of the total cost of compensating a permanent position.

For these and other reasons, according to the American Staffing Association (ASA), 72 percent of temps were offered permanent jobs with their employers in 2006. That, however, was during a hiring boom that peaked in 2007 and before the U.S. job picture changed dramatically in the wake of the credit crunch and global economic crisis that hit in 2008. Unemployment in the United States, for instance, stood at 4.5 and 4.8 percent in February of 2007 and 2008, respectively. By February 2009, it had ballooned to 8.1 percent, reflecting a loss of 3.8 million jobs over a 12-month period. During the same period, the number of people who, in BLS parlance, "worked part time for economic reasons (sometimes referred to as involuntary part-time workers)" went up by 3.7 million. In other words, although the recession is causing employers to lay off full-time workers, some are trying to compensate by turning over some of the work to temp staff. Ironically, of course, many of those who've been laid off are highly qualified, and as they hit the job market willing to accept lower-level positions, the ranks of job hunters are being joined by a substantial number of overqualified workers. "The quality of candidates," says Laura Long of Banner Personnel, "is tremendous. . . . As an employer, you can get great employees for a great price."

As a matter of fact, if you're a U.S. employer, you've always been able to get temp workers at a relatively good price. As of December 2009, according to the BLS, the average cost of a full-time worker in private industry was $21.64 per hour in wages plus $9.43 in benefits, for total compensation of $31.07. By contrast, the average wages for a temp were $12.04 and the average benefits were $3.28, for total compensation of $15.32. One of the results of this differential in cost has been a long-term increase in the number of temp workers that far outstrips the increase in jobs occupied by full-time workers. Between 1990 and 2006, for example, the number of temp jobs in the United States more than doubled, from

1.2 million to 2.6 million. Total employment in key sectors, meanwhile, went up by only 26 percent.

Vicki Smith, coauthor of *The Good Temp*, observes that "many of the problems that temporary workers experience are shared by low-wage workers in general. . . . The work conditions aren't particularly better." In February 2009, for example, software giant Microsoft announced a plan to cut the salaries of temporary employees by 10 percent. More precisely, the company announced a reduction in the amount of money that it would pay to the *temp agencies* that supply the workers. Temps at a firm like Microsoft are actually paid by staffing agencies working under contract with the employer. A staffing agency, for example, might bill Microsoft $100 an hour for a worker whom Microsoft pays $60 an hour. The extra $40 goes to cover agency expenses and profit and benefits for workers. In reality, Microsoft's 10-percent reduction applies to the $100 paid to the agency, not to the $60 that appears in the temp worker's paycheck. If the agency passes along the cut directly to the worker—as is the case with most of Microsoft's staffing agencies—then $10 comes out of the worker's paycheck, not $6. The worker, therefore, actually takes a cut of nearly 17 percent.

Microsoft had just laid off 1,400 full-time employees as part of a plan to reduce its total headcount by 5,000 over the ensuing 18 months. It isn't clear if the planned cuts will eventually include any of the company's 8,600 temp workers, but most experts agree that when the economy starts to show signs of recovery, temp workers will probably be the first to find new jobs. "You never know how strong the recovery is going to be," explains one economist, "so the last thing employers are going to want to do is bring back full-time workers only to have to let them go again." When that time comes, say many observers, the ranks of those temp workers will undoubtedly be swollen by the addition of former full-time workers forced to accept temporary status to find new jobs.[1]

The decision to enter into an employment relationship is clearly complicated for both the individual seeking a job and the organization seeking an employee. Although temporary workers have been around for a long time, the strategic use of temporary employment as a precursor to regular employment is a fairly new phenomenon. This emerging practice may become yet another of the many activities necessary to successfully manage an effective workforce. This chapter is about how organizations manage the people who comprise them. This set of processes is called *human resource management* (HRM). We start by describing the environmental context of HRM. We then discuss how organizations attract human resources. Next we describe how organizations seek to further develop the capacities of their human resources. We also examine how high-quality human resources are maintained by organizations. We conclude by discussing workforce diversity, labor relations, and new challenges in the changing workplace.

THE ENVIRONMENTAL CONTEXT OF HRM

HRM is the set of organizational activities directed at attracting, developing, and maintaining an effective workforce.[2] HRM takes place within a complex and ever-changing environmental context. Three particularly vital components of this context are HRM's strategic importance and the legal and social environments of HRM.

human resource management (HRM)
The set of organizational activities directed at attracting, developing, and maintaining an effective workforce

The Strategic Importance of HRM

Human resources are critical for effective organizational functioning. HRM (or "personnel," as it is sometimes called) was once relegated to second-class status in many organizations, but its importance has grown dramatically in the last two decades. Its new importance stems from increased legal complexities, the recognition that human resources are a valuable means for improving productivity, and the awareness today of the costs associated with poor HRM.[3] For example, Microsoft announced that it was eliminating 5,000 jobs in business areas that are expected to shrink. At the same time, though the firm began developing strategies for hiring high-talent people for jobs related to Internet search, an important growth area for the company.[4] This careful and systematic approach reducing human resources in areas where they are no longer needed and adding new human resources to key growth areas reflects a strategic approach to HRM.

Indeed, managers now realize that the effectiveness of their HR function has a substantial impact on the bottom-line performance of the firm. Poor human resource planning can result in spurts of hiring followed by layoffs—costly in terms of unemployment compensation payments, training expenses, and morale. Haphazard compensation systems do not attract, keep, and motivate good employees, and outmoded recruitment practices can expose the firm to expensive and embarrassing discrimination lawsuits. Consequently, the chief human resource executive of most large businesses is a vice president directly accountable to the CEO, and many firms are developing strategic HR plans and integrating those plans with other strategic planning activities.[5]

Even organizations with as few as 200 employees usually have a human resource manager and a human resource department charged with overseeing these activities. Responsibility for HR activities, however, is shared between the HR department and line managers. The HR department may recruit and initially screen candidates, but the final selection is usually made by managers in the department where the new employee will work. Similarly, although the HR department may establish performance appraisal policies and procedures, the actual evaluation and coaching of employees is done by their immediate superiors.

The growing awareness of the strategic significance of HRM has even led to new terminology to reflect a firm's commitment to people. **Human capital** reflects the organization's investment in attracting, retaining, and motivating an effective workforce. Hence, just as the phrase financial capital is an indicator of a firm's financial resources and reserves, so, too, does human capital serve as a tangible indicator of the value of the people who comprise an organization.[6]

The Legal Environment of HRM

A number of laws regulate various aspects of employee–employer relations, especially in the areas of equal employment opportunity, compensation and benefits, labor relations, and occupational safety and health. Several major ones are summarized in Table 8.1.

Equal Employment Opportunity Title VII of the Civil Rights Act of 1964 forbids discrimination in all areas of the employment relationship. The intent of Title VII is to ensure that employment decisions are made on the basis of an individual's qualifications rather than on the basis of personal biases. The law has reduced direct forms of discrimination (refusing to promote African Americans into management, failing to hire men as flight attendants, refusing to hire women as construction workers) as well as indirect forms of discrimination (using employment tests that whites pass at a higher rate than African Americans).

Employment requirements such as test scores and other qualifications are legally defined as having an **adverse impact** on minorities and women when such individuals meet or pass the requirement at a rate less than 80 percent of the rate of majority group members. Criteria that have an adverse impact on protected groups can be used only

human capital
Reflects the organization's investment in attracting, retaining, and motivating an effective workforce

Title VII of the Civil Rights Act of 1964
Forbids discrimination on the basis of sex, race, color, religion, or national origin in all areas of the employment relationship

adverse impact
When minority group members meet or pass a selection standard at a rate less than 80 percent of the pass rate of majority group members

Table 8.1
The Legal Environment of Human Resource Management

As much as any area of management, HRM is subject to wide-ranging laws and court decisions. These laws and decisions affect the human resource function in many areas. For example, AT&T was once fined several million dollars for violating Title VII of the Civil Rights Act of 1964.

Equal Employment Opportunity

Title VII of the Civil Rights Act of 1964 (as amended by the Equal Employment Opportunity Act of 1972). Forbids discrimination in all areas of the employment relationship.

Age Discrimination in Employment Act. Outlaws discrimination against people older than 40 years.

Various executive orders, especially Executive Order 11246 in 1965. Requires employers with government contracts to engage in affirmative action.

Pregnancy Discrimination Act. Specifically outlaws discrimination on the basis of pregnancy.

Vietnam Era Veterans Readjustment Assistance Act. Extends affirmative action mandate to military veterans who served during the Vietnam War.

Americans with Disabilities Act. Specifically outlaws discrimination against disabled persons.

Civil Rights Act of 1991. Makes it easier for employees to sue an organization for discrimination but limits punitive damage awards if they win.

Compensation and Benefits

Fair Labor Standards Act. Establishes minimum wage and mandated overtime pay for work in excess of 40 hours per week.

Equal Pay Act of 1963. Requires that men and women be paid the same amount for doing the same job.

Employee Retirement Income Security Act of 1974 (ERISA). Regulates how organizations manage their pension funds.

Family and Medical Leave Act of 1993. Requires employers to provide up to 12 weeks of unpaid leave for family and medical emergencies.

Labor Relations

National Labor Relations Act. Spells out procedures by which employees can establish labor unions and requires organizations to bargain collectively with legally formed unions; also known as the *Wagner Act.*

Labor-Management Relations Act. Limits union power and specifies management rights during a union-organizing campaign; also known as the *Taft-Hartley Act.*

Health and Safety

Occupational Safety and Health Act of 1970 (OSHA). Mandates the provision of safe working conditions.

Equal Employment Opportunity Commission
Charged with enforcing Title VII of the Civil Rights Act of 1964

Age Discrimination in Employment Act
Outlaws discrimination against people older than forty years; passed in 1967, amended in 1978 and 1986

affirmative action
Intentionally seeking and hiring qualified or qualifiable employees from racial, sexual, and ethnic groups that are underrepresented in the organization

when there is solid evidence that they effectively identify individuals who are better able than others to do the job. The **Equal Employment Opportunity Commission** is charged with enforcing Title VII as well as several other employment-related laws.

The **Age Discrimination in Employment Act**, passed in 1967, amended in 1978, and amended again in 1986, is an attempt to prevent organizations from discriminating against older workers. In its current form, it outlaws discrimination against people older than 40 years. Both the Age Discrimination in Employment Act and Title VII require passive nondiscrimination, or equal employment opportunity. Employers are not required to seek out and hire minorities, but they must treat all who apply fairly.

Several executive orders, however, require that employers holding government contracts engage in **affirmative action**—intentionally seeking and hiring employees from groups that are underrepresented in the organization. These organizations must have a written affirmative action plan that spells out employment goals for underutilized groups and how those goals will be met. These employers are also required to act affirmatively in hiring Vietnam era veterans (as a result of the Vietnam Era Veterans Readjustment Assistance Act) and qualified handicapped individuals. Finally, the Pregnancy Discrimination Act forbids discrimination against women who are pregnant.

In 1990, Congress passed the **Americans with Disabilities Act**, which forbids discrimination on the basis of disabilities and requires employers to provide reasonable accommodations for disabled employees. More recently, the **Civil Rights Act of 1991** amended the original Civil Rights Act as well as other related laws by both making it easier to bring discrimination lawsuits (which partially explains the aforementioned backlog of cases) and limiting the amount of punitive damages that can be awarded in those lawsuits.

Compensation and Benefits Laws also regulate compensation and benefits. The **Fair Labor Standards Act**, passed in 1938 and amended frequently since then, sets a minimum wage and requires the payment of overtime rates for work in excess of 40 hours per week. Salaried professional, executive, and administrative employees are exempt from the minimum hourly wage and overtime provisions. The **Equal Pay Act of 1963** requires that men and women be paid the same amount for doing the same job. Attempts to circumvent the law by having different job titles and pay rates for men and women who perform the same work are also illegal. Basing an employee's pay on seniority or performance is legal, however, even if it means that a man and woman are paid different amounts for doing the same job.

The provision of benefits is also regulated in some ways by state and federal laws. Certain benefits are mandatory—for example, worker's compensation insurance for employees who are injured on the job. Employers who provide a pension plan for their employees are regulated by the **Employee Retirement Income Security Act of 1974 (ERISA)**. The purpose of this act is to help ensure the financial security of pension funds by regulating how they can be invested. The **Family and Medical Leave Act of 1993** requires employers to provide up to 12 weeks of unpaid leave for family and medical emergencies.

In the last few years, some large employers, most notably Wal-Mart, have come under fire because they do not provide health care for all of their employees. In response to this, the state of Maryland passed a law, informally called the "Wal-Mart bill," that requires employers with more than 10,000 workers to spend at least 8 percent of their payrolls on health care or else pay a comparable amount into a general fund for uninsured workers. Wal-Mart appealed this ruling and the case is still pending; meanwhile, several other states are considering the passage of similar laws.[7]

Labor Relations

Union activities and management's behavior toward unions constitute another heavily regulated area. The **National Labor Relations Act** (also known as the Wagner Act), passed in 1935, sets up a procedure for employees to vote on whether to have a union. If they vote for a union, management is required to bargain collectively with the union. The **National Labor Relations Board (NLRB)** was established by the Wagner Act to enforce its provisions. Following a series of severe strikes in 1946, the **Labor-Management Relations Act** (also known as the Taft-Hartley Act) was passed in 1947 to limit union power. The law increases management's rights during an organizing campaign. The Taft-Hartley Act also contains the National Emergency Strike provision, which allows the president of the United States to prevent or end a strike that endangers national security. Taken together, these laws balance union and management power. Employees can be represented by a legally created and managed union, but the business can make nonemployee-related business decisions without interference.

Americans with Disabilities Act
Forbids discrimination against people with disabilities

Civil Rights Act of 1991
Amends the original Civil Rights Act, making it easier to bring discrimination lawsuits while also limiting punitive damages

Fair Labor Standards Act
Sets a minimum wage and requires overtime pay for work in excess of 40 hours per week; passed in 1938 and amended frequently since then

Equal Pay Act of 1963
Requires that men and women be paid the same amount for doing the same job

Employee Retirement Income Security Act of 1974 (ERISA)
A law that sets standards for pension plan management and provides federal insurance if pension funds go bankrupt

Family and Medical Leave Act of 1993
Requires employers to provide up to 12 weeks of unpaid leave for family and medical emergencies

National Labor Relations Act
Passed in 1935 to set up procedures for employees to vote on whether to have a union; also known as the Wagner Act

National Labor Relations Board (NLRB)
Established by the Wagner Act to enforce its provisions

Labor-Management Relations Act
Passed in 1947 to limit union power; also known as the Taft-Hartley Act

AP PHOTO/CHARLIE NEIBERGALL

The Occupational Safety and Health Act (OSHA) was passed to help protect workers from unsafe and/or unhealthy working conditions. For instance, some employees who work for popcorn-processing companies have claimed that chemical agents found in the butter flavoring used to produce microwave popcorn are harmful and may cause a rare lung disease. These claims have sparked an inquiry by OSHA investigators.

Health and Safety The **Occupational Safety and Health Act of 1970 (OSHA)** directly mandates the provision of safe working conditions. It requires that employers (1) provide a place of employment that is free from hazards that may cause death or serious physical harm and (2) obey the safety and health standards established by the Department of Labor. Safety standards are intended to prevent accidents, whereas occupational health standards are concerned with preventing occupational disease. For example, standards limit the concentration of cotton dust in the air because this contaminant has been associated with lung disease in textile workers. The standards are enforced by OSHA inspections, which are conducted when an employee files a complaint of unsafe conditions or when a serious accident occurs. Spot inspections of plants in especially hazardous industries such as mining and chemicals are also made. Employers who fail to meet OSHA standards may be fined.

Investigators have been looking into claims that chemical agents in the butter flavoring used in microwave popcorn are harmful to workers where such products are made. At least 30 workers at one plant in Jasper, Missouri, contracted a rare lung disease, and some doctors believe that it resulted from conditions on their job site. Although federal health officials point out that there is no danger to those cooking or eating microwave popcorn, research is ongoing into potential hazards to those who work in the industry.[8]

Emerging Legal Issues Several other areas of legal concern have emerged during the past few years. One is sexual harassment. Although sexual harassment is forbidden under Title VII, it has received additional attention in the courts recently, as more and more victims have decided to publicly confront the problem. Another emerging HRM issue is alcohol and drug abuse. Both alcoholism and drug dependence are major problems today. Recent court rulings have tended to define alcoholics and drug addicts as disabled, protecting them under the same laws that protect other handicapped people. Finally, AIDS has emerged as an important legal issue as well. AIDS victims, too, are most often protected under various laws protecting the disabled.

ATTRACTING HUMAN RESOURCES

With an understanding of the environmental context of HRM as a foundation, we are now ready to address its first substantive concern—attracting qualified people who are interested in employment with the organization.

Occupational Safety and Health Act of 1970 (OSHA)
Directly mandates the provision of safe working conditions

Human Resource Planning

The starting point in attracting qualified human resources is planning. HR planning, in turn, involves job analysis and forecasting the demand and supply of labor.

Job Analysis Job analysis is a systematic analysis of jobs within an organization. A job analysis is made up of two parts. The job description lists the duties of a job, the job's working conditions, and the tools, materials, and equipment used to perform it. The job specification lists the skills, abilities, and other credentials needed to do the job. Job analysis information is used in many human resource activities. For instance, knowing about job content and job requirements is necessary to develop appropriate selection methods and job-relevant performance appraisal systems and to set equitable compensation rates.

Forecasting Human Resource Demand and Supply After managers fully understand the jobs to be performed within the organization, they can start planning for the organization's future human resource needs. Figure 8.1 summarizes the steps most often followed. The manager starts by assessing trends in past human resource usage, future organizational plans, and general economic trends. A good sales forecast is often the foundation, especially for smaller organizations. Historical ratios can then be used to predict demand for employees such as operating employees and sales representatives. Of course, large organizations use much more complicated models to predict their future

job analysis
A systematized procedure for collecting and recording information about jobs within an organization

Figure 8.1   Human Resource Planning

Attracting human resources cannot be left to chance if an organization expects to function at peak efficiency. Human resource planning involves assessing trends, forecasting supply and demand of labor, and then developing appropriate strategies for addressing any differences.

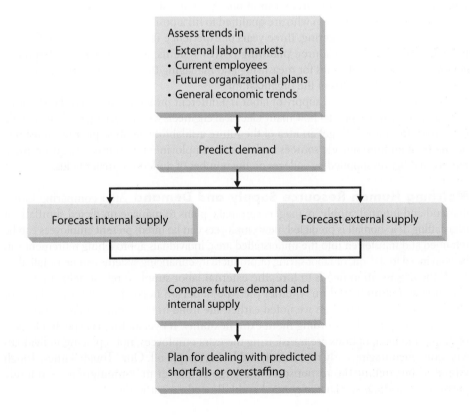

human resource needs. In 2002, Wal-Mart went through an exhaustive planning process that projected that the firm would need to hire 1 million people by 2010. Of this projected total, 800,000 are for new positions created as the firm grows, and the other 200,000 will replace current workers who leave for various reasons.[9] As time has passed, of course, Wal-Mart had adjusted these figures both up and down. But as things turned out, by the end of 2010 Wal-Mart did indeed employ about 800,000 more people than it did with the plan was first completed.

Forecasting the supply of labor is really two tasks: forecasting the internal supply (the number and type of employees who will be in the firm at some future date) and forecasting the external supply (the number and type of people who will be available for hiring in the labor market at large).[10] The simplest approach merely adjusts present staffing levels for anticipated turnover and promotions. Again, though, large organizations use extremely sophisticated models to make these forecasts. At higher levels of the organization, managers plan for specific people and positions. The technique most commonly used is the **replacement chart**, which lists each important managerial position, who occupies it, how long he or she will probably stay in it before moving on, and who (by name) is now qualified or soon will be qualified to move into the position. This technique allows ample time to plan developmental experiences for persons identified as potential successors to critical managerial jobs.[11] In 2007, Xerox CEO Anne Mulcahy essentially identified her eventual successor when she appointed Ursula Burns as president. And sure enough, when Mulcahy decided to take early retirement in 2009 Burns was quickly appointed as the new CEO. This well-managed process made the transition easy and efficient.[12]

To facilitate both planning and identifying persons for current transfer or promotion, some organizations also have an **employee information system**, or **skills inventory**, which is usually computerized and contains information on each employee's education, skills, work experience, and career aspirations. Such a system can quickly locate all the employees in the organization who are qualified to fill a position requiring, for instance, a degree in chemical engineering, three years of experience in an oil refinery, and fluency in Spanish. Enterprise resource planning (ERP) systems, as described in Chapter 7, generally include capabilities for measuring and managing the internal supply of labor in ways that best fit the needs of the organization.

Forecasting the external supply of labor is a different problem altogether. How does a manager, for example, predict how many electrical engineers will be seeking work in Georgia three years from now? To get an idea of the future availability of labor, planners must rely on information from outside sources such as state employment commissions, government reports, and figures supplied by colleges on the number of students in major fields.

Matching Human Resource Supply and Demand After comparing future demand and internal supply, managers can make plans to manage predicted shortfalls or overstaffing. If a shortfall is predicted, new employees can be hired, present employees can be retrained and transferred into the understaffed area, individuals approaching retirement can be convinced to stay on, or labor-saving or productivity-enhancing systems can be installed.

If the organization needs to hire, the external labor supply forecast helps managers plan how to recruit, based on whether the type of person needed is readily available or scarce in the labor market. As we noted earlier, the trend in temporary workers also helps managers in staffing by affording them extra flexibility. If overstaffing is expected to be a problem, the main options are transferring the extra employees, not replacing individuals who quit, encouraging early retirement, and laying people off. Our "Tough Times, Tough Choices" box details the response of one large employer to contemporary economic pressure on its strategic plans in general and HR needs in particular.

replacement chart
Lists each important managerial position in the organization, who occupies it, how long he or she will probably remain in the position, and who is or will be a qualified replacement

employee information system (skills inventory)
Contains information on each employee's education, skills, experience, and career aspirations; usually computerized

TOUGH TIMES, TOUGH CHOICES

"Negative Macroeconomic Conditions" Hit Home Depot

The news at Home Depot hasn't been good for the past few years. For instance, revenues, profits, and share price have all dropped consistently since mid-2008. Sales had fallen sharply, especially in big-ticket items such as special-order kitchens and expensive discretionary products such as cabinets, countertops, and fashion plumbing. Earnings from standard-plumbing and other hardware, as well as from repair and maintenance products, are also down, but not by as much. Consumers, who clearly weren't buying new homes, were apparently busy fixing up their old ones. "Plumbing is as basic as it can get in terms of repair," explained CFO Carol B. Tomé. "It outperformed the company average."

"The housing and home-improvement markets remain challenging," admitted CEO Frank Blake, who also promised investors that "across our entire business, we are making the adjustments necessary to respond to a tough market environment. We are focused on the things we can control with a commitment to provide value and service to our customers. I am proud of what our associates have accomplished in a very difficult sales environment." Alluding to "negative macroeconomic conditions," Home Depot executives warned that sales and profits will continue to be a challenge.

In 2009, Home Depot announced that it was closing all the stores in its Expo Design Center, YardBIRDs, and Design Center operations and a bath-remodeling business called HD Bath. The closings cut 5,000 jobs, and additional streamlining called for the elimination of about 2,000 nonstore jobs, including 500 at corporate headquarters, for a total reduction of 7,000 positions, or about 2 percent of the company's workforce. The cuts, according to Home Depot, would not affect "any customer-facing positions in Home Depot stores."

Home Depot shares went up by more than 5 percent the morning after the news was released. "We see the announcements as largely positive," confirmed one analyst, who applauded the company's decision to jettison its smaller brands instead of propping them up while trying simultaneously to "trim and optimize the core business." For 2009, revenues were $71.3 billion (down 7.8 percent from fiscal 2007), but the firm reported a net *loss* of $54 million. Why did the firm incur such a loss when sales declined by only 7.8 percent? The answer to that question takes us back to the decision to close down virtually all of the company's noncore operations and lay off 7,000 employees. The move, of course, was designed to make the company more profitable in the long run, but it came at a substantial short-term cost. In Home Depot's case, for example, many of the 7,000 laid-off workers were entitled to severance pay. In addition, the assets of the discontinued businesses were to be sold under circumstances that sharply reduced their value. The difference between fair market value and what the seller can expect to receive may be written off as an *impairment charge,* and Home Depot wrote off $387 million in impairment and other charges. That sum was added to operating expenses for the quarter, and the increase in expenses pushed (pretax) revenue into negative territory—thus the net loss of $54 million.

"We expect the home-improvement market in 2010," said CEO Blake, "will remain just as challenging as [it was in] 2009," and Home Depot forecasted a 9 percent decrease in sales and 7 percent decrease in earnings per share (EPS) for the year. On the other hand, it expects the results of the changes to boost earnings by more than $300 million. "We're very fortunate that the soundness of our company lets us live our value of taking care of our people, even in this time of

(continued)

unprecedented economic hardship," said Blake in a news release. "These changes will make us a stronger company and will allow us to continue to grow associate employment over the long term to benefit our customers."

References: Stephanie Rosenbloom, "Home Repairs Become Focus as Consumers Feel Pinched," *New York Times*, August 20, 2008, www. nytimes.com on April 13, 2009; "Home Depot Announces Third Quarter Results," *Reuters*, November 18, 2008, www.reuters.com on April 13, 2009; Rosenbloom, "Rough Quarter for Two Major Retailers," *New York Times*, November 19, 2009, www.nytimes.com on April 13, 2009; Ashley M. Heher, "Home Depot Layoffs: Will Cut 7,000 Jobs, Closing Expo Chain," *Huffington Post*, January 26, 2009, www.huffingtonpost. com on April 7, 2009; "Home Depot Exits Expo Business, Reaffirms Fiscal '08 Guidance," *Rental Equipment Register*, January 30, 2009, http:// rermag.com on April 7, 2009; "The Home Depot Announces Fourth Quarter and Fiscal 2008 Results," *iStockAnalyst*, February 24, 2009, www.istockanalyst.com on April 13, 2009; "HD: Financial Analysis through January 2009," Gauging Corporate Financial Results, February 28, 2009, www.financial-gauges.com on April 13, 2009.

Recruiting Human Resources

Once an organization has an idea of its future human resource needs, the next phase is usually recruiting new employees.[13] **Recruiting** is the process of attracting qualified persons to apply for jobs that are open. Where do recruits come from? Some recruits are found internally; others come from outside the organization.

Internal recruiting means considering present employees as candidates for openings. Promotion from within can help build morale and keep high-quality employees from leaving the firm. In unionized firms, the procedures for notifying employees of internal job change opportunities are usually spelled out in the union contract. For higher-level positions, a skills inventory system may be used to identify internal candidates, or managers may be asked to recommend individuals who should be considered. Most businesses today routinely post job openings on their internal communication network, or intranet. One disadvantage of internal recruiting is its ripple effect. When an employee moves to a different job, someone else must be found to take his or her old job. In one organization, 454 job movements were necessary as a result of filling 195 initial openings.

External recruiting involves attracting persons outside the organization to apply for jobs. External recruiting methods include advertising, campus interviews, employment agencies or executive search firms, union hiring halls, referrals by present employees, and hiring "walk-ins" or "gate-hires" (people who show up without being solicited). Increasingly, firms are using the Internet to post job openings and to solicit applicants. Of course, a manager must select the most appropriate methods, using the state employment service to find maintenance workers but not a nuclear physicist, for example. Private employment agencies can be a good source of clerical and technical employees, and executive search firms specialize in locating top-management talent. In general, "help wanted" ads in newspapers and in online job posting sites are often used because they reach a wide audience and thus allow a large number of people to find out about and apply for job openings.

One generally successful method for facilitating a good person-job fit is the so-called **realistic job preview** (**RJP**), which involves providing the applicant with a real picture of what performing the job that the organization is trying to fill would be like.[14] For example, it would not make sense for a firm to tell an applicant that the job is exciting and challenging when in fact it is routine and straightforward, yet some managers do this to hire the best people. The likely outcome will be a dissatisfied employee who will quickly be looking for a better job. If the company is more realistic about a job, though, the person hired will be more likely to remain in the job for a longer period of time.

recruiting
The process of attracting individuals to apply for jobs that are open

internal recruiting
Considering current employees as applicants for higher-level jobs in the organization

external recruiting
Getting people from outside the organization to apply for jobs

realistic job preview (RJP)
Provides the applicant with a real picture of what it would be like to perform the job that the organization is trying to fill

Selecting Human Resources

Once the recruiting process has attracted a pool of applicants, the next step is to select whom to hire. The intent of the selection process is to gather from applicants information that will predict their job success and then to hire the candidates likely to be most successful.[15] Of course, the organization can gather information only about factors that are predictive of future performance. The process of determining the predictive value of information is called **validation**.

Application Blanks The first step in selection is usually asking the candidate to fill out an application blank. Application blanks are an efficient method of gathering information about the applicant's previous work history, educational background, and other job-related demographic data. They should not contain questions about areas not related to the job, such as gender, religion, or national origin. Application blank data are generally used informally to decide whether a candidate merits further evaluation, and interviewers use application blanks to familiarize themselves with candidates before interviewing them. Unfortunately, in recent years there has been a trend toward job applicants' either falsifying or inflating their credentials to stand a better chance of getting a job. Indeed, one recent survey of 2.6 million job applications found that an astounding 44 percent of them contained some false information.[16]

Tests Tests of ability, skill, aptitude, or knowledge that is relevant to the particular job are usually the best predictors of job success, although tests of general intelligence or personality are occasionally useful. In addition to being validated, tests should be administered and scored consistently. All candidates should be given the same directions, should be allowed the same amount of time, and should experience the same testing environment (temperature, lighting, distractions).[17]

validation
Determining the extent to which a selection device is really predictive of future job performance

Interviews Although a popular selection device, interviews are sometimes poor predictors of job success. For example, biases inherent in the way people perceive and judge others at a first meeting affect subsequent evaluations by the interviewer. Interview validity can be improved by training interviewers to be aware of potential biases and by increasing the structure of the interview. In a structured interview, questions are written in advance, and all interviewers follow the same question list with each candidate they interview. This procedure introduces consistency into the interview procedure and allows the organization to validate the content of the questions to be asked.[18]

MICHAEL DELEON/ISTOCKPHOTO

Employment interviews are among the most commonly used selection techniques today. These two managers, for instance, are interviewing a potential new colleague. Unfortunately, despite its popularity, the interview is often a poor predictor of job success. Among other reasons, biases in the way people perceive and judge others may affect subsequent evaluations by the interviewer.

Assessment Centers Assessment centers are a popular method used to select managers and are particularly good for selecting current employees for promotion. The assessment center is a content-valid simulation of major parts of the managerial job. A typical center lasts two to three days, with groups of 6 to 12 persons participating in a variety of managerial exercises. Centers may also include interviews, public speaking, and standardized ability tests. Candidates are assessed by several trained observers, usually managers several levels above the job for which the candidates are being considered. Assessment centers are quite valid if properly designed and are fair to members of minority groups and women.[19] For some firms, the assessment center is a permanent facility created for these activities. For other firms, the assessment activities are performed in a multipurpose location such as a conference room. AT&T pioneered the assessment center concept. For years, the firm has used assessment centers to make virtually all of its selection decisions for management positions.

Other Techniques Organizations also use other selection techniques depending on the circumstances. Polygraph tests, once popular, are declining in popularity. On the other hand, more and more organizations are requiring that applicants in whom they are interested take physical exams. Organizations are also increasingly using drug tests, especially in situations in which drug-related performance problems could create serious safety hazards. For example, applicants for jobs in a nuclear power plant would likely be tested for drug use. And some organizations today even run credit checks on prospective employees.

DEVELOPING HUMAN RESOURCES

Regardless of how effective a selection system is, however, most employees need additional training if they are to grow and develop in their jobs. Evaluating their performance and providing feedback are also necessary.

Training and Development

In HRM, **training** usually refers to teaching operational or technical employees how to do the job for which they were hired. **Development** refers to teaching managers and professionals the skills needed for both present and future jobs. Most organizations provide regular training and development programs for managers and employees. For example, IBM spends more than $700 million annually on programs and has a vice president in charge of employee education. U.S. businesses spend more than $30 billion annually on training and development programs away from the workplace. And this figure does not include wages and benefits paid to employees while they are participating in such programs.

Assessing Training Needs The first step in developing a training plan is to determine what needs exist. For example, if employees do not know how to operate the machinery necessary to do their job, a training program on how to operate the machinery is clearly needed. On the other hand, when a group of office workers is performing poorly, training may not be the answer. The problem could be motivation, aging equipment, poor supervision, inefficient work design, or a deficiency of skills and knowledge. Only the last could be remedied by training. As training programs are being developed, the manager should set specific and measurable goals specifying what participants are to learn. The manager should also plan to evaluate the training program after employees complete it.

Common Training Methods Many different training and development methods are available. Selection of methods depends on many considerations, but perhaps the most important is training content. When the training content is factual material (such as

training
Teaching operational or technical employees how to do the job for which they were hired

development
Teaching managers and professionals the skills needed for both present and future jobs

company rules or explanations for how to fill out forms), assigned reading, programmed learning, and lecture methods work well. When the content is interpersonal relations or group decision making, however, firms must use a method that allows interpersonal contact, such as role-playing or case discussion groups. When employees must learn a physical skill, methods allowing practice and the actual use of tools and materials are needed, as in on-the-job training or vestibule training. (Vestibule training enables participants to focus on safety, learning, and feedback rather than on productivity.)

Web-based and other electronic media–based training are becoming very popular. Such methods allow a mix of training content, are relatively easy to update and revise, let participants use a variable schedule, and lower travel costs.[20] On the other hand, they are limited in their capacity to simulate real activities and facilitate face-to-face interaction. Xerox, Massachusetts Mutual Life Insurance, and Ford have all reported tremendous success with these methods. In addition, most training programs actually rely on a mix of methods. Boeing, for example, sends managers to an intensive two-week training seminar involving tests, simulations, role-playing exercises, and CD-ROM flight simulation exercises.[21]

Finally, some larger businesses have started creating their own self-contained training facility, often called a *corporate university*. McDonald's was among the first to start this practice with its so-called Hamburger University in Illinois. All management trainees of the firm attend training programs there to learn exactly how long to grill a burger, how to maintain good customer service, and so on. The cult hamburger chain In-N-Out Burger also has a similar training venue called In-N-Out University. Other firms that are using this approach include Shell Oil and General Electric.[22]

Evaluation of Training Training and development programs should always be evaluated. Typical evaluation approaches include measuring one or more relevant criteria (such as attitudes or performance) before and after the training, and determining whether the criteria changed. Evaluation measures collected at the end of training are easy to get, but actual performance measures collected when the trainee is on the job are more important. Trainees may say that they enjoyed the training and learned a lot, but the true test is whether their job performance improves after their training.

Performance Appraisal

Once employees are trained and settled into their jobs, one of management's next concerns is performance appraisal. **Performance appraisal** is a formal assessment of how well employees are doing their jobs. Employees' performance should be evaluated regularly for many reasons. One reason is that performance appraisal may be necessary for validating selection devices or assessing the impact of training programs. A second reason is administrative—to aid in making decisions about pay raises, promotions, and training. Still another reason is to provide feedback to employees to help them improve their present performance and plan future careers.[23] Because performance evaluations often help determine wages and promotions, they must be fair and nondiscriminatory.

Common Appraisal Methods Two basic categories of appraisal methods commonly used in organizations are objective methods and judgmental methods. Objective measures of performance include actual output (that is, number of units produced), scrap rate, dollar volume of sales, and number of claims processed. This may be contaminated by "opportunity bias" if some persons have a better chance to perform than others. For example, a sales representative selling snow blowers in Michigan has a

performance appraisal
A formal assessment of how well an employee is doing his or her job

greater opportunity than a colleague selling the same in Arkansas. Fortunately, adjusting raw performance figures for the effect of opportunity bias and thereby arriving at figures that accurately represent each individual's performance is often possible.

Another type of objective measure, the special performance test, is a method in which each employee is assessed under standardized conditions. This kind of appraisal also eliminates opportunity bias. For example, Verizon Southwest has a series of prerecorded calls that operators in a test booth answer. The operators are graded on speed, accuracy, and courtesy in handling the calls. Performance tests measure ability but do not measure the extent to which one is motivated to use that ability on a daily basis. (A high-ability person may be a lazy performer except when being tested.) Special performance tests must therefore be supplemented by other appraisal methods to provide a complete picture of performance.

Judgmental methods, including ranking and rating techniques, are the most common ways to measure performance. Ranking compares employees directly with one another and orders them from best to worst. Ranking has a number of drawbacks. Ranking is difficult for large groups, because the persons in the middle of the distribution may be hard to distinguish from one another accurately. Comparisons of people in different work groups are also difficult. For example, an employee ranked third in a strong group may be more valuable than an employee ranked first in a weak group. Another criticism of ranking is that the manager must rank people on the basis of overall performance, although each person likely has both strengths and weaknesses. Furthermore, rankings do not provide useful information for feedback. To be told that one is ranked third is not nearly as helpful as to be told that the quality of one's work is outstanding, its quantity is satisfactory, one's punctuality could use improvement, or one's paperwork is seriously deficient.

Rating differs from ranking in that it compares each employee with a fixed standard rather than comparison with other employees. A rating scale provides the standard. Figure 8.2 gives examples of three graphic rating scales for a bank teller. Each consists of a performance dimension to be rated (punctuality, congeniality, and accuracy) followed by a scale on which to make the rating. In constructing graphic rating scales, performance dimensions that are relevant to job performance must be selected. In particular, they should focus on job behaviors and results rather than on personality traits or attitudes.

The **Behaviorally Anchored Rating Scale (BARS)** is a sophisticated and useful rating method. Supervisors construct rating scales associated with behavioral anchors. They first identify relevant performance dimensions and then generate anchors—specific, observable behaviors typical of each performance level. Figure 8.3 shows an example of a BARS for the dimension "Inventory control."

The other scales in this set, developed for the job of department manager in a chain of specialty stores, include "Handling customer complaints," "Planning special promotions," "Following company procedures," "Supervising sales personnel," and "Diagnosing and solving special problems." BARS can be effective because it requires that management takes proper care in constructing the scales and it provides useful anchors for supervisors to use in evaluating people. It is costly, however, because outside expertise is usually needed and because scales must be developed for each job within the organization.

Errors in Performance Appraisal Errors or biases can occur in any kind of rating or ranking system.[24] One common problem is *recency error*—the tendency to base judgments on the subordinate's most recent performance because it is most easily recalled. Often a rating or ranking is intended to evaluate performance over an entire time period, such as six months or a year, so the recency error does introduce error into the judgment.

Behaviorally Anchored Rating Scale (BARS)
A sophisticated rating method in which supervisors construct a rating scale associated with behavioral anchors

Figure 8.2 **Graphic Rating Scales for a Bank Teller**

Graphic rating scales are very common methods for evaluating employee performance. The manager who is doing the rating circles the point on each scale that best reflects her or his assessment of the employee on that scale. Graphic rating scales are widely used for many different kinds of jobs.

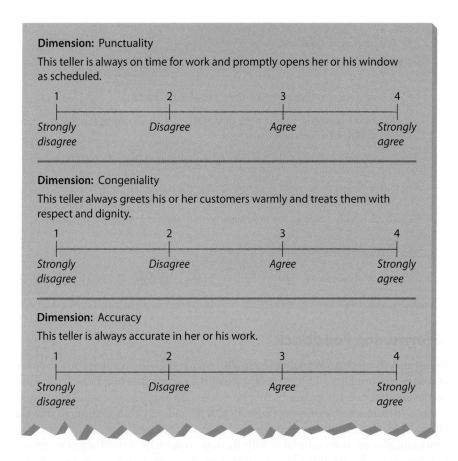

Other errors include overuse of one part of the scale—being too lenient, being too severe, or giving everyone a rating of "average." *Halo error* is allowing the assessment of an employee on one dimension to "spread" to ratings of that employee on other dimensions. For instance, if an employee is outstanding on quality of output, a rater might tend to give him or her higher marks than deserved on other dimensions. Errors can also occur because of race, sex, or age discrimination, intentionally or unintentionally. The best way to offset these errors is to ensure that a valid rating system is developed at the outset and then to train managers in how to use it.

One interesting innovation in performance appraisal used in some organizations today is called **360-degree feedback**, in which managers are evaluated by everyone around them—their boss, their peers, and their subordinates. Such a complete and thorough approach provides people with a far richer array of information about their performance than does a conventional appraisal given just by the boss. Of course, such a system also takes considerable time and must be handled so as not to breed fear and mistrust in the workplace.[25]

360-degree feedback
A performance appraisal system in which managers are evaluated by everyone around them—their boss, their peers, and their subordinates

Figure 8.3 Behaviorally Anchored Rating Scale

Behaviorally anchored rating scales help overcome some of the limitations of standard rating scales. Each point on the scale is accompanied by a behavioral anchor—a summary of an employee behavior that fits that spot on the scale.

Job: Specialty store manager
Dimension: Inventory control

7 Always orders in the right quantities and at the right time

6 Almost always orders at the right time but occasionally orders too much or too little of a particular item

5 Usually orders at the right time and almost always in the right quantities

4 Often orders in the right quantities and at the right time

3 Occasionally orders at the right time but usually not in the right quantities

2 Occasionally orders in the right quantities but usually not at the right time

1 Never orders in the right quantities or at the right time

Performance Feedback

The last step in most performance appraisal systems is giving feedback to subordinates about their performance. This is usually done in a private meeting between the person being evaluated and his or her boss. The discussion should generally be focused on the facts—the assessed level of performance, how and why that assessment was made, and how it can be improved in the future. Feedback interviews are not easy to conduct. Many managers are uncomfortable with the task, especially if feedback is negative and subordinates are disappointed by what they hear. Properly training managers, however, can help them conduct more effective feedback interviews.[26]

Some firms use a very aggressive approach to terminating people who do not meet expectations. General Electric has long used a system whereby each year the bottom 10 percent of its workforce is terminated and replaced with new employees. Company executives claim that this approach, although stressful for all employees, helps it to continuously upgrade its workforce. Other firms have started using this same approach. However, both Ford and Goodyear recently agreed to abandon similar approaches in response to age discrimination lawsuits.[27]

MAINTAINING HUMAN RESOURCES

After organizations have attracted and developed an effective workforce, they must also make every effort to maintain that workforce. To do so requires effective compensation and benefits as well as career planning.

Determining Compensation

Compensation is the financial remuneration given by the organization to its employees in exchange for their work. There are three basic forms of compensation. *Wages* are the hourly compensation paid to operating employees. The minimum hourly wage paid in the United States today is $7.25 (some states have higher minimums). *Salary* refers to compensation paid for total contributions, as opposed to pay based on hours worked. For example, managers earn an annual salary, usually paid monthly. They receive the salary regardless of the number of hours they work. Some firms have started paying all their employees a salary instead of hourly wages. For example, all employees at Chaparral Steel earn a salary, starting at $30,000 a year for entry-level operating employees. Finally, *incentives* represent special compensation opportunities that are usually tied to performance. Sales commissions and bonuses are among the most common incentives.

Compensation is an important and complex part of the organization–employee relationship. Basic compensation is necessary to provide employees with the means to maintain a reasonable standard of living. Beyond this, however, compensation also provides a tangible measure of the value of the individual to the organization. If employees do not earn enough to meet their basic economic goals, they will seek employment elsewhere. Likewise, if they believe that their contributions are undervalued by the organization, they may leave or exhibit poor work habits, low morale, and little commitment to the organization. Thus, designing an effective compensation system is clearly in the organization's best interests.[28]

A good compensation system can help attract qualified applicants, retain present employees, and stimulate high performance at a cost reasonable for one's industry and geographic area. To set up a successful system, management must make decisions about wage levels, the wage structure, and the individual wage determination system. Some firms used the 2008–2009 recession as an opportunity to refine their compensation systems. While many firms reduced their workforces through layoffs, others used targeted salary cuts to avoid layoffs. For instance, at Hewlett-Packard the CEO first cut his own salary by 20 percent. The firm's very top performers kept their same pay levels. But others were given tiered salary cuts ranging from as little as 2.5 percent to as much as 20 percent. A few firms went even further. CareerBuilder.com, for instance, not only instituted pay cuts for all employees but also told everyone they only had to work half a day on Fridays.[29]

Wage-Level Decision The wage-level decision is a management policy decision about whether the firm wants to pay above, at, or below the going rate for labor in the industry or the geographic area. Most firms choose to pay near the average, although those that cannot afford more pay below average. Large, successful firms may like to cultivate the image of being "wage leaders" by intentionally paying more than average and thus attracting and keeping high-quality employees. IBM, for example, pays top dollar to get the new employees it wants. McDonald's, on the other hand, often pays close to the minimum wage. The level of unemployment in the labor force also affects wage levels. Pay declines when labor is plentiful and increases when labor is scarce. Once managers make the wage-level decision, they need information to help set actual wage rates. Managers need to know what the maximum, minimum, and average wages are for particular jobs in the appropriate labor market. This information is collected by means of a wage survey. Area wage surveys can be conducted by individual firms or by local HR or business associations. Professional and industry associations often conduct surveys and make the results available to employers.

Wage Structure Decision Wage structures are usually set up through a procedure called **job evaluation**—an attempt to assess the worth of each job relative to other jobs.

compensation
The financial remuneration given by the organization to its employees in exchange for their work

job evaluation
An attempt to assess the worth of each job relative to other jobs

At Ben & Jerry's Homemade, company policy once dictated that the highest-paid employee in the firm could not make more than seven times what the lowest-paid employee earned. But this policy had to be modified when the company found that it was simply unable to hire a new CEO without paying more than this amount. The simplest method for creating a wage structure is to rank jobs from those that should be paid the most (for example, the president) to those that should be paid the least (for example, a mail clerk or a janitor). In a smaller firm with few jobs (like Ben & Jerry's, for example), this method is quick and practical, but larger firms with many job titles require more sophisticated methods. The next step is setting actual wage rates on the basis of a combination of survey data and the wage structure that results from job evaluation. Jobs of equal value are often grouped into wage grades for ease of administration.

Individual Wage Decisions After wage-level and wage structure decisions are made, the individual wage decision must be addressed. This decision concerns how much to pay each employee in a particular job. Although the easiest decision is to pay a single rate for each job, more typically a range of pay rates is associated with each job. For example, the pay range for an individual job might be $7.25 to $9.00 per hour, with different employees earning different rates within the range.

A system is then needed for setting individual rates. This may be done on the basis of seniority (enter the job at $7.25, for example, and increase 15 cents per hour every six months on the job), initial qualifications (inexperienced people start at $7.25; more experienced people start at a higher rate), or merit (raises above the entering rate are given for good performance). Combinations of these bases may also be used.

The Internet is also playing a key role in compensation patterns today because both job seekers and current employees can more easily get a sense of what their true market value is. If they can document the claim that their value is higher than what their current employer now pays or is offering, they are in a position to demand a higher salary. Consider the case of one compensation executive who met recently with a subordinate to discuss her raise. He was surprised when she produced data from five different websites backing up her claim for a bigger raise than he had intended to offer.[30]

Determining Benefits

Benefits are things of value other than compensation that the organization provides to its workers. (Benefits are sometimes called *indirect compensation*.) The average company spends an amount equal to more than one-third of its cash payroll on employee benefits. Thus an average employee who is paid, say, $30,000 per year averages a bit over $10,000 more per year in benefits. Benefits come in several forms. Pay for time not worked includes sick leave, vacation, holidays, and unemployment compensation. Insurance benefits often include life and health insurance for employees and their dependents. Workers' compensation is a legally required insurance benefit that provides medical care and disability income for employees injured on the job. Social security is a government pension plan to which both employers and employees contribute. Many employers also provide a private pension plan to which they and their employees contribute. Employee service benefits include extras such as tuition reimbursement and recreational opportunities.

Some organizations have instituted "cafeteria benefit plans," whereby basic coverage is provided for all employees but employees are then allowed to choose which additional benefits they want (up to a cost limit based on salary). An employee with five children might choose enhanced medical and dental coverage for dependents, a single employee

benefits
Things of value other than compensation that an organization provides to its workers

might prefer more vacation time, and an older employee might elect increased pension benefits. Flexible systems are expected to encourage people to stay in the organization and even help the company attract new employees.[31]

In response to economic pressures, some firms have reduced employee benefits in the last few years. In 2002, for example, 17 percent of employees in the United States with employer healthcare coverage saw their benefits cut; the 2008–2009 recession led to further reductions. Some employers have also reduced their contributions to employee retirement plans, cut the amount of annual leave they offer to employees, or both.[32] For instance, in 2008 16 major companies announced that they would reduce or eliminate employer contributions to employee retirement plans. Several others followed suit in 2009. Among these were Wells Fargo, Anheuser-Busch, Boise Cascade, Cooper Tire & Rubber, Kimberly-Clark, and Saks.[33]

MANAGING WORKFORCE DIVERSITY

Workforce diversity has become a very important issue in many organizations. The management of diversity is often seen as a key human resource function.

The Meaning of Diversity

Diversity exists in a community of people when its members differ from one another along one or more important dimensions. In the business world, the term *diversity* is generally used to refer to demographic differences among people—differences in gender, age, ethnicity, and so forth. For instance, the average age of the U.S. workforce is gradually increasing, and so is the number of women in the labor force. Likewise, the labor force reflects growing numbers of African Americans, Latinos, and Asians, as well as more dual-career couples, same-gender couples, single parents, and physically challenged employees.

The Impact of Diversity

There is no question that organizations are becoming ever more diverse. But how does this affect organizations? Diversity provides both opportunities and challenges for organizations.

Diversity as a Competitive Advantage   Many organizations are finding that diversity can be a source of competitive advantage in the marketplace (in addition to the fact that hiring and promoting in such a way as to enhance diversity is simply the right thing to do). For instance, organizations that manage diversity effectively often have higher levels of productivity and lower levels of turnover and absenteeism. Likewise, organizations that manage diversity effectively become known among women and minorities as good places to work. These organizations are thus better able to attract qualified employees from among these groups. Organizations with a diverse workforce are also better able to understand different market segments than are less diverse organizations. For example, a cosmetics firm such as Avon, which wants to sell its products to women and African Americans, can better understand how to create such products and effectively market them if women and African-American managers are available to provide and solicit inputs into product development, design, packaging, advertising, and so forth.[34] Finally, organizations with diverse workforces are generally more creative and innovative than other organizations.

diversity
A characteristic of a group or organization whose members differ from one another along one or more important dimensions, such as age, gender, or ethnicity

Diversity as a Source of Conflict Unfortunately, diversity in an organization can also create conflict. This conflict can arise for a variety of reasons.[35] One potential source of conflict exists when an individual thinks that someone else has been hired, promoted, or fired because of his or her diversity status. Another source of conflict is when diversity is misunderstood or misinterpreted or as a result of inappropriate interactions among people of different groups.[36] Conflict may also arise if there is an environment of fear, distrust, or individual prejudice. Members of the dominant group in an organization may worry that newcomers from other groups pose a personal threat to their own position in the organization. For example, when U.S. firms have been taken over by Japanese firms, U.S. managers have sometimes been resentful about or hostile toward Japanese managers assigned to work with them. A final source of conflict exists when people are unwilling to accept people different from themselves. Personal bias and prejudices are still very real among some people today and can lead to potentially harmful conflict.

Managing Diversity in Organizations

Because of the tremendous potential that diversity holds for competitive advantage, as well as the importance of trying to avoid the negative consequences of associated conflict, much attention has been focused in recent years on how individuals and organizations can function more effectively in diverse contexts.

Individual Strategies One important element of managing diversity and multiculturalism in an organization consists of things that individuals themselves can do. Understanding, of course, is the starting point. For instance, although people need to be treated fairly and equitably, managers must understand that differences among people do, in fact, exist. Thus any effort to treat everyone the same, without regard for their fundamental human differences, will lead only to problems. People in an organization should also try to understand the perspectives of others. Further, even though people may learn to understand others, and even though they may try to empathize with others, the fact remains that they still may not accept or enjoy some aspect of their behavior. So, tolerance is also required. Finally, communication is also required. For example, suppose that a young employee has a habit of making jokes about the age of an older colleague. Perhaps the young colleague means no harm and is just engaging in what she sees as good-natured kidding. But the older employee may find the jokes offensive. If the two do not communicate, the jokes will continue, and the resentment will grow. Eventually, what started as a minor problem may erupt into a much bigger one.

Organizational Approaches Whereas individuals are important in managing diversity and multiculturalism, the organization itself must play a fundamental role.[37] The starting point in managing diversity and multiculturalism is the policies that an organization adopts that directly or indirectly affect how people are treated. Another aspect of organizational policies that affects diversity and multiculturalism is how the organization addresses and responds to problems that arise from differences among people. For example, consider the example of a manager charged with sexual harassment. If the organization's policies put an excessive burden of proof on the individual being harassed and invoke only minor sanctions against the guilty party, it is sending a clear signal about the importance of such matters. But the organization that has a balanced set of policies for addressing questions like sexual harassment sends its employees a message that diversity and individual rights and privileges are important.

Organizations can also help manage diversity and multiculturalism through a variety of ongoing practices and procedures. Avon's creation of networks for various groups represents one example of an organizational practice that fosters diversity. In general, the idea is that, because diversity and multiculturalism are characterized by differences among people, organizations can more effectively manage that diversity by following practices and procedures that are based on flexibility rather than on rigidity. Many organizations are finding that diversity and multicultural training is an effective means for managing diversity and minimizing its associated conflict. More specifically, **diversity and multicultural training** is designed to better enable members of an organization to function in a diverse and multicultural workplace.[38] Some organizations even go so far as to provide language training for their employees as a vehicle for managing diversity and multiculturalism. Motorola, for example, provides English-language training for its foreign employees on assignment in the United States. At Pace Foods in San Antonio, with a total payroll of over 450 employees, staff meetings and employee handbooks are translated into Spanish for the benefit of the company's 200 or so Latino employees.

MANAGING LABOR RELATIONS

Labor relations is the process of dealing with employees who are represented by a union.[39] At one time, almost a third of the entire U.S. labor force belonged to a labor union. Unions enjoyed their largest membership between 1940 and 1955. Membership began to steadily decline in the mid-1950s, though, for several reasons: (1) increased standards of living made union membership seem less important, (2) traditionally unionized industries in the manufacturing sector began to decline, and (3) the globalization of business operations caused many unionized jobs to be lost to foreign workers. This downward trend continued until 2008, when union membership rose by the largest amount in over a quarter century, a gain of 428,000 members.[40] Much of this gain was attributable to fears of job insecurity due to the recession that hit that year. Managing labor relations is an important part of HRM. However, most large firms have separate labor relations specialists to handle these activities apart from other human resource functions.

diversity and multicultural training
Training that is specifically designed to better enable members of an organization to function in a diverse and multicultural workforce

labor relations
The process of dealing with employees who are represented by a union

How Employees Form Unions

For employees to form a new local union, several things must occur. First, employees must become interested in having a union. Nonemployees who are professional organizers employed by a national union (such as the Teamsters or United Auto Workers [UAW]) may generate interest by making speeches and distributing literature outside the workplace. Inside, employees who want a union try to convince other workers of the benefits of a union.

The second step is to collect employees' signatures on authorization cards. These cards state that the signer wishes to vote to determine whether the union will represent him or her. To show the

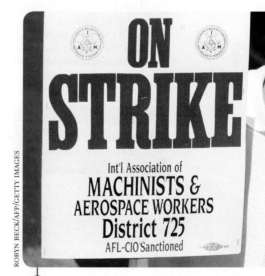

ROBYN BECK/AFP/GETTY IMAGES

A strike by a unionized workforce can be a debilitating event for any organization. Chris Langness is a machinist at the Boeing plant in Huntington Beach, California. He and 1,500 other members of the International Association of Machinists and Aerospace Workers (IAM) went on strike against Boeing when the two sides couldn't reach agreement over health insurance premiums and retirement benefits.

NLRB that interest is sufficient to justify holding an election, 30 percent of the employees in the potential bargaining unit must sign these cards. Before an election can be held, however, the bargaining unit must be defined. The bargaining unit consists of all employees who will be eligible to vote in the election and to join and be represented by the union if one is formed.

The election is supervised by an NLRB representative (or, if both parties agree, the American Arbitration Association—a professional association of arbitrators) and is conducted by secret ballot. If a simple majority of those voting (not of all those eligible to vote) votes for the union, then the union becomes certified as the official representative of the bargaining unit.[41] The new union then organizes itself by officially signing up members and electing officers; it will soon be ready to negotiate the first contract. The union-organizing process is diagrammed in Figure 8.4. If workers become disgruntled with their union or if management presents strong evidence that the union is not representing

Figure 8.4 The Union-Organizing Process

If employees of an organization want to form a union, the law prescribes a specific set of procedures that both employees and the organization must follow. Assuming that these procedures are followed and the union is approved, the organization must engage in collective bargaining with the new union.

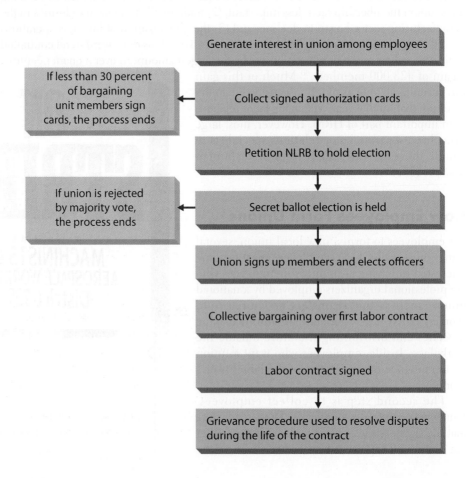

workers appropriately, the NLRB can arrange a decertification election. The results of such an election determine whether the union remains certified.

Organizations usually prefer that employees not be unionized because unions limit management's freedom in many areas. Management may thus wage its own campaign to convince employees to vote against the union. "Unfair labor practices" are often committed at this point. For instance, it is an unfair labor practice for management to promise to give employees a raise (or any other benefit) if the union is defeated. Experts agree that the best way to avoid unionization is to practice good employee relations all the time—not just when threatened by a union election. Providing absolutely fair treatment with clear standards in the areas of pay, promotion, layoffs, and discipline; having a complaint or appeal system for persons who feel unfairly treated; and avoiding any kind of favoritism will help make employees feel that a union is unnecessary. Wal-Mart strives to avoid unionization through these practices.[42]

Collective Bargaining

The intent of **collective bargaining** is to agree on a labor contract between management and the union that is satisfactory to both parties. The contract contains agreements about issues such as wages, work hours, job security, promotion, layoffs, discipline, benefits, methods of allocating overtime, vacations, rest periods, and the grievance procedure. The process of bargaining may go on for weeks, months, or longer, with representatives of management and the union meeting to make proposals and counterproposals. The resulting agreement must be ratified by the union membership. If it is not approved, the union may strike to put pressure on management, or it may choose not to strike and simply continue negotiating until a more acceptable agreement is reached. For example, Boeing's machinists union went on strike in 2008 over issues of job security and the firm's plans to outsource more jobs to foreign factories.[43]

Occasionally circumstances arise that cause management and labor to bargain over changes in existing contracts even before a new contract is needed. This is most likely to happen when unforeseen problems jeopardize the future of the business, and hence the jobs of union members. For example, when General Motors, Ford, and Chrysler were facing financial crisis in 2008–2009, the UAW agreed to contract concessions with the automakers to help give the firms the flexibility they claimed they needed to restructure their operations. Among others things, for instance, the UAW agreed to allow the companies to delay billions of dollars in payments for healthcare costs for retirees and to eliminate a controversial job bank program that allowed workers to get most of their wages even when they had been laid off.[44]

The **grievance procedure** is the means by which the contract is enforced. Most of what is in a contract concerns how management will treat employees. When employees feel that they have not been treated fairly under the contract, they file a grievance to correct the problem. The first step in a grievance procedure is for the aggrieved employee to discuss the alleged contract violation with her immediate superior. Often the grievance is resolved at this stage. If the employee still believes that she is being mistreated, however, the grievance can be appealed to the next level. A union official can help an aggrieved employee present her case. If the manager's decision is also unsatisfactory to the employee, additional appeals to successively higher levels are made until, finally, all in-company steps are exhausted. The final step is to submit the grievance to binding arbitration. An arbitrator is a labor law expert who is paid jointly by the union and management. The arbitrator studies the contract, hears both sides of the case, and renders a decision that both parties must obey. The grievance system for resolving disputes about contract enforcement prevents any need to strike during the term of the contract.

collective bargaining
The process of agreeing on a satisfactory labor contract between management and a union

grievance procedure
The means by which a labor contract is enforced

NEW CHALLENGES IN THE CHANGING WORKPLACE

As we have seen throughout this chapter, human resource managers face several ongoing challenges in their efforts to keep their organizations staffed with effective workforces. To complicate matters, new challenges arise as the economic and social environments of business change. We conclude this chapter with a look at two of the most important HRM issues facing business today.

Managing Knowledge Workers

Employees traditionally added value to organizations because of what they did or because of their experience. In the "information age," however, many employees add value because of what they know.[45]

The Nature of Knowledge Work These employees are usually called **knowledge workers**, and the skill with which they are managed is a major factor in determining which firms will be successful in the future. Knowledge workers, including computer scientists, engineers, and physical scientists, provide special challenges for the HR manager. They tend to work in high-technology firms and are usually experts in some abstract knowledge base. They often like to work independently and tend to identify more strongly with their profession than with any organization—even to the extent of defining performance in terms recognized by other members of their profession.

As the importance of information-driven jobs grows, the need for knowledge workers continues to grow as well. But these employees require extensive and highly specialized training, and not every organization is willing to make the human capital investments necessary to take advantage of these jobs. In fact, even after knowledge workers are on the job, retraining and training updates are critical to prevent their skills from becoming obsolete. It has been suggested, for example, that the "half-life" of a technical education in engineering is about three years. The failure to update such skills will not only result in the loss of competitive advantage but also increase the likelihood that the knowledge worker will go to another firm that is more committed to updating them.

Knowledge Worker Management and Labor Markets Even though overall demand for labor has slumped in recent years due to the economic downturn, the demand for knowledge workers remains strong. As a result, organizations that need these workers must introduce regular market adjustments (upward) to pay them enough to keep them. This is especially critical in areas in which demand is growing, as even entry-level salaries for these employees are high. Once an employee accepts a job with a firm, the employer faces yet another dilemma. Once hired, workers are more subject to the company's internal labor market, which is not likely to be growing as quickly as the external market for knowledge workers as a whole. Consequently, the longer an employee remains with a firm, the further behind the market his or her pay falls—unless, of course, it is regularly adjusted (upward).

Not surprisingly, strong demand for these workers has inspired some fairly extreme measures for attracting them in the first place.[46] High starting salaries and sign-on bonuses are common. BP Exploration was recently paying starting petroleum engineers with undersea platform-drilling knowledge—not experience, just knowledge—salaries in the six figures, plus sign-on bonuses of over $50,000 and immediate profit sharing. Even with these incentives, HR managers complained that, in the Gulf Coast region, they cannot retain specialists because young engineers soon leave to accept sign-on bonuses with competitors.

knowledge workers
Workers whose contributions to an organization are based on what they know

Contingent and Temporary Workers

A final contemporary HR issue of note involves the use of contingent or temporary workers. Indeed, recent years have seen an explosion in the use of such workers by organizations. The FBI, for example, routinely employs a cadre of retired agents in various temporary jobs.[47]

Trends in Contingent and Temporary Employment In recent years, the number of contingent workers in the workforce has increased dramatically. A contingent worker is a person who works for an organization on something other than a permanent or full-time basis. Categories of contingent workers include independent contractors, on-call workers, temporary employees (usually hired through outside agencies), and contract and leased employees. Another category is part-time workers. The financial services giant Citigroup, for example, makes extensive use of part-time sales agents to pursue new clients. About 10 percent of the U.S. workforce currently uses one of these alternative forms of employment relationships. Experts suggest, however, that this percentage is increasing at a consistent pace.

Managing Contingent and Temporary Workers Given the widespread use of contingent and temporary workers, HR managers must understand how to use such employees most effectively. In other words, they need to understand how to manage contingent and temporary workers. One key is careful planning. Even though one of the presumed benefits of using contingent workers is flexibility, it is still important to integrate such workers in a coordinated fashion. Rather than having to call in workers sporadically and with no prior notice, organizations try to bring in specified numbers of workers for well-defined periods of time. The ability to do so comes from careful planning.

A second key is understanding contingent workers and acknowledging both their advantages and their disadvantages. In other words, the organization must recognize what it can and cannot achieve from the use of contingent and temporary workers. Expecting too much from such workers, for example, is a mistake that managers should avoid. Third, managers must carefully assess the real cost of using contingent workers. We noted earlier, for example, that many firms adopt this course of action to save labor costs. The organization should be able to document precisely its labor-cost savings. How much would it be paying people in wages and benefits if they were on permanent staff? How does this cost compare with the amount spent on contingent workers? This difference, however, could be misleading. We also noted, for instance, that contingent workers might be less effective performers than permanent and full-time employees. Comparing employee for employee on a direct-cost basis, therefore, is not necessarily valid. Organizations must learn to adjust the direct differences in labor costs to account for differences in productivity and performance.

Finally, managers must fully understand their own strategies and decide in advance how they intend to manage temporary workers, specifically focusing on how to integrate them into the organization. On a very simplistic level, for example, an organization with a large contingent workforce must make some decisions about the treatment of contingent workers relative to the treatment of permanent, full-time workers. Should contingent workers be invited to the company holiday party? Should they have the same access to such employee benefits as counseling services and childcare? There are no right or wrong answers to such questions. Managers must understand that they need to develop a strategy for integrating contingent workers according to some sound logic and then follow that strategy consistently over time.[48]

Indeed, this last point has become part of a legal battleground in recent years as some workers hired under the rubric of contingent workers have subsequently argued that this has been a title in name only, and that their employers use this title to discriminate against them in various ways. For instance, FedEx relies on over 13,000 "contract" drivers. These individuals wear FedEx uniforms, drive FedEx trucks, and must follow FedEx rules and procedures. However, because the firm has hired them under a different employment agreement than its "regular" employees, it does not provide them with benefits. Some of those individuals are currently suing FedEx on the grounds that, for all practical purposes, they are employees and should enjoy the same benefits as other drivers.[49]

SUMMARY OF LEARNING OBJECTIVES AND KEY POINTS

1. Describe the environmental context of HRM, including its strategic importance and its relationship with legal and social factors.

   - HRM is concerned with attracting, developing, and maintaining the human resources an organization needs.

   - Its environmental context consists of its strategic importance and the legal and social environments that affect HRM.

2. Discuss how organizations attract human resources, including human resource planning, recruiting, and selecting.

   - Attracting human resources is an important part of the HRM function.

   - Human resource planning starts with job analysis and then focuses on forecasting the organization's future need for employees, forecasting the availability of employees both within and outside the organization, and planning programs to ensure that the proper number and type of employees will be available when needed.

   - Recruitment and selection are the processes by which job applicants are attracted, assessed, and hired.

   - Methods for selecting applicants include application blanks, tests, interviews, and assessment centers.

   - Any method used for selection should be properly validated.

3. Describe how organizations develop human resources, including training and development, performance appraisal, and performance feedback.

   - Organizations must also work to develop their human resources.

   - Training and development enable employees to perform their present job effectively and to prepare for future jobs.

   - Performance appraisals are important for validating selection devices, assessing the impact of training programs, deciding pay raises and promotions, and determining training needs.

   - Both objective and judgmental methods of appraisal can be applied, and a good system usually includes several methods.

   - The validity of appraisal information is always a concern, because it is difficult to accurately evaluate the many aspects of a person's job performance.

4. Discuss how organizations maintain human resources, including the determination of compensation and benefits and career planning.

   - Maintaining human resources is also important.

   - Compensation rates must be fair compared with rates for other jobs within the organization and with rates for the same or similar jobs in other organizations in the labor market.

   - Properly designed incentive or merit pay systems can encourage high performance, and a good benefits program can help attract and retain employees.

   - Career planning is also a major aspect of HRM.

5. Discuss the nature of diversity, including its meaning, associated trends, impact, and management.

   - Diversity exists in an organization when its members differ from one another along one or more important dimensions, including gender, age, and ethnicity.

- Individual strategies for managing diversity include being understanding, tolerant, and communicative with those who are different.

- Organizational strategies include having fair policies, practices, and procedures; providing diversity training; and maintaining a tolerant culture.

6. Discuss labor relations, including how employees form unions and the mechanics of collective bargaining.

   - If a majority of a company's nonmanagement employees so desire, they have the right to be represented by a union.

- Management must engage in collective bargaining with the union in an effort to agree on a contract.

- While a union contract is in effect, the grievance system is used to settle disputes with management.

7. Describe the issues associated with managing knowledge and contingent and temporary workers.

   - Two important new challenges in the workplace include

     - the management of knowledge workers

     - issues associated with the use of contingent and temporary workers

DISCUSSION QUESTIONS

Questions for Review

1. Describe the steps in the process of human resource planning. Explain the relationships between the steps.

2. Describe the common selection methods. Which method or methods are the best predictors of future job performance? Which are the worst? Why?

3. Compare training and development, noting any similarities and differences. What are some commonly used training methods?

4. Define wages and benefits. List different benefits that organizations can offer. What are the three decisions that managers must make to determine compensation and benefits? Explain each decision.

5. What are the potential benefits of diversity? How can individuals and organizations more effectively manage diversity?

Questions for Analysis

1. The Family and Medical Leave Act of 1993 is seen as providing much-needed flexibility and security for families and workers. Others think that it places an unnecessary burden on business. Yet another opinion is that the act hurts women, who are more likely to ask for leave, and shuffles them off to a low-paid "mommy track" career path. In your opinion, what are the likely consequences of the act? You can adopt one of the viewpoints expressed above or develop another. Explain your answer.

2. How do you know a selection device is valid? What are the possible consequences of using invalid selection methods? How can an organization ensure that its selection methods are valid?

3. Consider a job that you have held or with which you are familiar. Describe how you think an organization could best provide an RJP for that position. What types of information and experiences should be conveyed to applicants? What techniques should be used to convey the information and experiences?

4. How would managing nonunionized workers differ from managing workers who elected to be in a union? Which would be easier? Why?

5. In what ways would managing temporary workers be easier than managing traditional permanent employees? In what ways would it be more difficult? What differences would likely exist in your own behavior if you were in a contingent or temporary job versus a traditional permanent job?

BUILDING EFFECTIVE DECISION-MAKING SKILLS

Exercise Overview

Decision-making skills refer to the ability to recognize and define problems and opportunities correctly and then to select an appropriate course of action for solving problems or capitalizing on opportunities. For obvious reasons, these skills should be important to you in making career choices.

Exercise Background

If you're in the process of making a career choice, you need to have a firm grip on your own abilities, preferences, and limitations. This is particularly true for recent college graduates, who are often preparing to enter career fields that are largely unknown to them. Fortunately, there are many sources of helpful information out there. The BLS, for example, maintains data about occupations, employment prospects, compensation, working conditions, and many other issues of interest to job seekers. Information is available by industry, occupation, employer type, and region.

Exercise Task

1. Access a summary of the Department of Labor's *National Compensation Survey* at **http://stats.bls. gov/ncs/ocs/sp/ncbl0449.pdf**. (If the page has moved, search by the survey title.) Find detailed data related to the occupation that you regard as your most likely career choice when you graduate. Then locate detailed data about two other occupations that you might consider—one with a salary that's higher than that of your number-one career choice and one with a salary that's lower.

2. Record the hourly salary data for each of your three choices, and then use the hourly salary to project an expected annual income. (*Hint:* Full-time jobs require about 2,000 hours annually.)

3. Based *purely on salary information*, which occupation would be "best" for you?

4. Now go to **www.bls.gov/oco** and access job descriptions for various occupations. Review the description for each of the three career choices that you've already investigated.

5. Based *purely on job characteristics*, which occupation would be "best" for you?

6. Is there any conflict between your answers to questions 3 and 5? If so, how do you plan to resolve it?

7. Are there any job characteristics that you desire strongly enough to sacrifice compensation in order to get them? What are they? What are the limits, if any, on your willingness to sacrifice pay for these job characteristics?

BUILDING EFFECTIVE TECHNICAL SKILLS

Exercise Overview

Technical skills are necessary to understand or perform the specific kind of work that an organization does. In many organizations, this work includes hiring appropriate people to fill positions. This exercise will help you apply certain technical skills to the process of employee selection.

Exercise Background

You may choose either of the following exercise variations. We tend to favor Variation 1 because the exercise is usually more useful if you can relate to real job requirements on a personal level.

Variation 1. If you currently work or have worked in the past, select two jobs with which you have some familiarity. Try to select one job that entails relatively low levels of skill, responsibility, education, and pay and one job that entails relatively high levels in the same categories.

Variation 2. If you've never worked or you're not personally familiar with an array of jobs, assume that you're a manager of a small manufacturing plant. You need to hire people to fill two jobs. One job is for a plant custodian to sweep floors, clean bathrooms, empty trash cans, and so forth. The other job is for an office manager who will supervise a staff of three clerks and secretaries, administer the plant payroll, and coordinate the administrative operations of the plant.

Exercise Task

Reviewing what you've done so far, now do the following:

1. Identify the most basic skills needed to perform each of the two jobs effectively.

2. Identify the general indicators or predictors of whether a given individual can perform each job.

3. Develop a brief set of interview questions that you might use to determine whether an applicant has the qualifications for each job.

4. How important is it for you, as a manager hiring an employee to perform a job, to possess the technical skills needed to perform the job that you're trying to fill?

SKILLS SELF-ASSESSMENT INSTRUMENT

What Do Students Want from Their Jobs?

Purpose: This exercise investigates the job values held by college students at your institution. Then it asks the students to speculate about employers' perceptions of college students' job values. This will help you understand how college students can be recruited effectively. It also gives you insight into the difficulties of managing and motivating individuals with different values and perceptions.

Introduction: Employees choose careers that match their job values. Employers try to understand employee values to better recruit, manage, and motivate them. Job values are important therefore, in every HR process, from job advertisements and interviews, to performance appraisals, to compensation planning.

Instructions:

1. Complete the following Job Values Survey. Consider what you want from your future career. Using Column 1, rank the 14 job values from 1 to 14, with 1 being the most important to you and 14 being the least important.

2. In your opinion, when potential employers try to attract students, how much important do they think students give to each of the values? For Column 2, respond with a + (plus) if you think employers would rank it higher than students or with a − (minus) if you think employers would rate it lower. This is the employers' perception of students' values, not of their own values.

3. In small groups or a class, compute an average ranking for each value. Then discuss the results.

Job Values Survey

	Column 1 Your Ranking	Column 2 Employer Ranking
Working conditions		
Working with people		
Employee benefits		
Challenge		
Location of job		
Self-development		
Type of work		
Job title		
Training program		
Advancement		
Salary		
Company reputation		
Job security		
Autonomy on the job		

Discussion Questions

1. How much variation do you see in the job value rankings in Column 1? That is, are students' values quite different, moderately different, or very similar overall?

2. If there are significant differences between individuals, what impact might these differences have on the recruiting process? On the training process? On the performance evaluation and compensation process?

3. How much variation do you see in the responses for Column 2? That is, does your group or class agree on how employers perceive college students?

4. Is there a large difference between how you think employers perceive college students and your group's or class's reported job values? If there is a large difference, what difficulties might this create for job seekers and potential employers? How might these difficulties be reduced or eliminated?

EXPERIENTIAL EXERCISE

Choosing a Compensation Strategy

Purpose: This exercise helps you better understand how internal and external market forces affect compensation strategies.

Introduction: Assume that you are the head of a large academic department in a major research university. Your salaries are a bit below external market averages. For example, your assistant professors make between $45,000 and $55,000 a year, your associate professors make between $57,000 and $65,000 a year, and your full professors make between $80,000 and $90,000 a year.

Faculty who have been in your department for a long time enjoy the work environment and appreciate the low cost of living in the area. They know that they are somewhat underpaid but have tended to regard the advantages of being in your department as offsetting this disadvantage. Recently, however, external market forces have caused salaries for people in your field to escalate rapidly. Unfortunately, although your university acknowledges this problem, you have been told that no additional funds will be provided to your department.

You currently have four vacant positions that need to be filled. One of these is at the rank of associate professor and the other three are at the rank of assistant professor. You have surveyed other departments in similar universities and you realize that to hire the best new assistant professors, you will need to offer at least $60,000 a year and that to get a qualified associate professor, you will need to pay at least $70,000. You have been given the budget to hire new employees at more competitive salaries but cannot do anything to raise the salaries of faculty currently in your department. You have identified the following options:

1. You can hire new faculty from lower-quality schools. They will likely accept salaries below market rate.

2. You can hire the best people available, pay market salaries, and deal with internal inequities later.

3. You can hire fewer new faculty, use the extra money to boost the salaries of your current faculty, and cut class offerings in the future.

Instructions

Step 1: Working alone, decide how you will proceed.

Step 2: Form small groups with your classmates and compare solutions.

Step 3: Identify the strengths and weaknesses of each option.

Follow-up Questions

1. Are there other options that might be pursued?

2. Assume that you chose Option 2. How would you go about dealing with the internal inequity problems?

3. Discuss with your instructor the extent to which this problem exists at your school.

 YOU MAKE THE CALL

The Temptations of Temping

1. You're a senior manager at a growing business and you're ready to add employees. Your HR manager has recommended a temp-to-perm policy. You know the advantages of this approach, but what might be some of the disadvantages?

2. Assume that you're a prospective job seeker (which you may very well be). What do you personally see as the advantages and disadvantages of taking a temp-to-perm position? Under what circumstances are you most likely to take a temp-to-perm position?

3. What sort of challenges are likely to confront a manager who supervises a mix of temporary and

permanent employees? In what ways might these challenges differ if the temporary workers have been hired on a temp-to-perm basis rather than on a strictly temporary basis?

4. What, in your opinion, does the future hold for temp workers in the U.S. labor force? Assuming that you might one day have to accept temp work instead of a permanent job, what sort of changes would you like to see in the status and treatment of U.S. temp workers?

THE ELEMENTS OF CONTROL

LEARNING OBJECTIVES

After studying this chapter, you should be able to:

1 Explain the purpose of control, identify different types of control, and describe the steps in the control process.

2 Identify and explain the three forms of operations control.

3 Describe budgets and other tools for financial control.

4 Identify and distinguish between two opposing forms of structural control.

5 Discuss the relationship between strategy and control.

6 Identify characteristics of effective control, why people resist control, and how managers can overcome this resistance.

FIRST THINGS FIRST

Facets of Jamie Dimon's Control Strategy at J.P. Morgan Chase

In October 2006, the head of the mortgage-servicing department, which collects payments on home loans, informed J.P. Morgan CEO Jamie Dimon that late payments were increasing at an alarming rate. When Dimon reviewed the report, he confirmed not only that late payments were a problem at Morgan but also that things were even worse for other lenders. "We concluded," recalls Dimon, "that underwriting standards were deteriorating across the industry." Shortly thereafter, Dimon was informed that the cost of insuring securities backed by subprime mortgages was going up even though ratings agencies persisted in rating them *AAA*. At the time, creating securities backed by subprime mortgages was the hottest and most profitable business on Wall Street, but by the end of the year, Dimon had decided to get out of it. "We saw no profit, and lots of risk," reports Bill Winters, co-head of Morgan's investment arm. "It was Jamie," he adds, "who saw all the pieces."

Dimon's caution—and willingness to listen to what his risk management people were telling him—paid off in a big way. Between July 2007 and July 2008, when the full impact of the crisis hit the country's investment banks, Morgan re-

> **"[A large organization] can get arrogant and full of hubris and lose focus, like the Roman Empire."**
>
> —JAMIE DIMON, CEO, J. P. MORGAN CHASE

corded losses of $5 billion on mortgage-backed securities. That's a lot of money, but relatively little compared to the losses sustained by banks that didn't see the writing on the wall—$33 billion at Citibank, for example, and $26 billion at Merrill Lynch. Citi is still in business thanks to $45 billion in cash infusions from the federal government, but Merrill Lynch isn't—it was forced to sell itself to Bank of America. Morgan, though hit hard, weathered the storm and is still standing on its own Wall Street foundations. "You know," said President-Elect Barack Obama as he surveyed the damage sustained by the U.S. banking

MARIO TAMA/GETTY IMAGES

The banking crisis that swept the United States in the period 2008-2010 was partially attributable to poor control. Banks took too many risks and did not have sufficient capital to sustain their losses. These people are protesting JPMorgan Chase's mortgage practices and opposition to financial reform.

industry in 2008, ". . . . there are a lot of banks that are actually pretty well managed, J.P. Morgan being a good example. Jamie Dimon . . . is doing a pretty good job managing an enormous portfolio."

Ironically, Dimon had gotten his start at Citi, where, as a newly minted MBA, he worked closely with legendary CEO Sandy Weill for 12 years, transforming Citigroup into the largest financial institution in the United States. The relationship, however, eventually soured, and Dimon left in 1998. Taking over as CEO in 2000, he revitalized Bank One, then the country's fifth-largest bank, before selling it to J.P. Morgan Chase in 2004. In 2006, he became CEO and chairman of J.P. Morgan Chase, a financial-services institution that includes J.P. Morgan Chase Bank, a commercial-retail bank, and J.P. Morgan Trust Company, an investment bank. With assets of $2.3 trillion, J.P. Morgan Chase boasts the largest market capitalization and deposit bases in the U.S. financial industry.

Dimon came to J.P. Morgan Chase with a few ideas about how to manage an enormous portfolio. Shortly after he took over, he increased oversight and control of Bank One's operations and expenses, using cost-saving measures to free up $3 billion annually by 2007. He then used the cash to finance the expansion of Morgan Chase operations, including the installation of more ATM machines and the creation of new products. As improved fundamentals and expanded operations yielded greater revenues, the bank's stock price went up (at least until subprime crisis hit), freeing up further funds for new growth. Once the basics are right, says Dimon, "you earn the right to do a deal," and he set about building a Citi-like financial empire, relying mostly on mergers to jumpstart growth in underserved regional and international markets.

Experience had shown Dimon that a large organization "can get arrogant and full of hubris and lose focus, like the Roman Empire." In 2006, for example, J.P. Morgan Chase was enjoying high sales but spending a lot more than Dimon was used to spending at Bank One. Moreover, Dimon had inherited a company that had engineered multiple mergers without making much effort to integrate operations. The twofold result was ho-hum profits and a loose collection of incompatible structures and systems. Financial results from different divisions, for instance, were simply being combined,

and the upshot, according to CFO Michael Cavanagh, was that even though "strong businesses were subsidizing weak ones . . . the numbers didn't jump out at you. With the results mashed together, it was easy for managers to hide."

Dimon thus set out to exercise more effective operational oversight, and his control practices currently extend to virtually every aspect of J. P. Morgan Chase operations:

- Every month, managers must submit 50-page reports showing financial ratios and results, product sales, and even detailed expenses for every worker. Then Dimon and his top executives spend hours combing through the data, with the CEO asking tough questions and demanding frank answers.

- Dimon prepares a detailed to-do list every week. "I make my list by business [and] by person [in order] to think about what I might be avoiding [and] what I have to do. It's hard to see the truth," he admits, "[and] even harder to do something about it."

- One of Dimon's top priorities is slashing bloated budgets. "Waste hurt[s] our customers," he reminds his management team. "Cars, phones, clubs, perks—what's that got to do with customers?" He's also eliminated such amenities as fresh flowers, lavish expense accounts, and oversized offices and closed the in-house gym. One time, he asked a line of limousine drivers outside company headquarters for the names of the executives they were waiting for. Then he called up each one, asking, "Too good for the subway?" or "Why don't you try walking?" Dimon denies the story, but limo service at J.P. Morgan Chase is way down.

- Dimon also takes a close look at compensation. Regional bank managers at J.P. Morgan Chase once earned $2 million a year, compared with Bank One's modest salary of $400,000. "I'd tell people they were way overpaid," says Dimon, and as he suspected, "they already knew it." He cut pay for most staff by 20 to 50 percent, but most people elected to stay with the company. Today, a strict pay-for-performance formula keeps compensation in line.

- "In a big company," Dimon advises, "it's easy for people to b.s. you. A lot of them have been practicing for decades." So he gathers outcome data from every manager, various forms of information from low-level staffers, and even candid performance critiques from suppliers. "If you just want to run your business on your own and report results," warns Steve Black, co-head of investment banking, "you won't like working for Jamie."
- Finally, Dimon is convinced that IT is critical to the bank's long-term strategy and once cancelled a long-running information services contract with IBM. "When you're outsourcing," he explained, ". . . people don't care" about your performance. At J.P. Morgan Chase, "we want patriots, not mercenaries." Between 2007 and 2008, he invested $2 billion in technology developed in-house and considers it money well spent.

Dimon, however, doesn't like being thought of as a control freak. "It's offensive . . . to be called a cost cutter," he complains, and besides, his long-run goal isn't merely control—it's growth. "It's [a] thousand-mile march," observes one company analyst, "and not everyone will survive."[1]

Jamie Dimon is almost single-handedly remaking J.P. Morgan Chase. Among other things, he is bringing compensation in line with industry standards, cutting costs, streamlining operations, and slashing budgets. He is also setting clear targets for profitability and growth, and managers throughout the company are then being held accountable for meeting these targets. At the heart of all these efforts is a comprehensive control system that helps him monitor all aspects of performance. In a nutshell, effective control helps managers like Jamie Dimon decide where they want their business to go, point it in that direction, and monitor results to keep it on track. Ineffective control, on the other hand, can result in a lack of focus, weak direction, and poor overall performance.

As we discussed in Chapter 1, control is one of the four basic managerial functions that provide the organizing framework for this book. This is the first of two chapters devoted to this important area. In the first section of this chapter, we explain the purpose of control. We then look at types of control and the steps in the control process. The rest of the chapter examines the four levels of control that most organizations must employ to remain effective: operations, financial, structural, and strategic control. We conclude by discussing the characteristics of effective control, noting why some people resist control and describing what organizations can do to overcome this resistance. The other chapter in this part focuses on managing operations and managing information.

THE NATURE OF CONTROL

control
The regulation of organizational activities in such a way as to facilitate goal attainment

Control is the regulation of organizational activities so that some targeted element of performance remains within acceptable limits. Without this regulation, organizations have no indication of how well they are performing in relation to their goals. Control, like a ship's rudder, keeps the organization moving in the proper direction. At any point in time, it compares where the organization is in terms of performance (financial, productive, or otherwise) to where it is supposed to be. Like a rudder, control provides an organization with a mechanism for adjusting its course if performance falls outside of acceptable boundaries. For example, FedEx has a performance goal of delivering

99.9 percent of its packages on time. If on-time deliveries fall to, say, 99.6 percent, control systems will signal the problem to managers, so that they can make necessary adjustments in operations to regain the target level of performance.[2] An organization without effective control procedures is not likely to reach its goals—or, if it does reach them, to know that it has!

The Purpose of Control

As Figure 9.1 illustrates, control provides an organization with ways to adapt to environmental change, to limit the accumulation of error, to cope with organizational complexity, and to minimize costs. These four functions of control are worth a closer look.

Adapting to Environmental Change In today's complex and turbulent business environment, all organizations must contend with change.[3] If managers could establish goals and achieve them instantaneously, control would not be needed. But between the time a goal is established and the time it is reached, many things can happen in the organization and its environment to disrupt movement toward the goal—or even to change the goal itself. A properly designed control system can help managers anticipate, monitor, and respond to changing circumstances.[4] In contrast, an improperly designed system can result in organizational performance that falls far below acceptable levels.

For example, Michigan-based Metalloy, a 56-year-old, family-run metal-casting company, signed a contract to make engine seal castings for NOK, a big Japanese auto parts maker. Metalloy was satisfied when its first 5,000-unit production run yielded 4,985 acceptable castings and only 15 defective ones. NOK, however, was quite unhappy with this performance and insisted that Metalloy raise its standards. In short, global quality standards in most industries are such that customers demand near perfection from their suppliers. A properly designed control system can help managers like those at Metalloy stay better attuned to rising standards.

Figure 9.1 The Purpose of Control

Control is one of the four basic management functions in organizations. The control function, in turn, has four basic purposes. Properly designed control systems can fulfill each of these purposes.

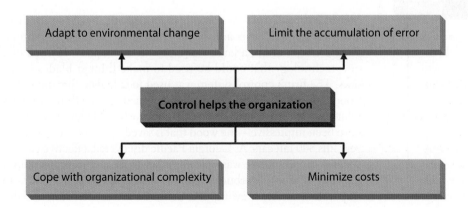

Limiting the Accumulation of Error Small mistakes and errors do not often seriously damage the financial health of an organization. Over time, however, small errors may accumulate and become very serious. For example, Whistler Corporation, a large radar detector manufacturer, was once faced with such rapidly escalating demand that quality essentially became irrelevant. The defect rate rose from 4 percent to 9 percent to 15 percent and eventually reached 25 percent. One day, a manager started paying more attention to this and realized that 100 of the plant's 250 employees were spending all their time fixing defective units and that $2 million worth of inventory was awaiting repair. Had the company adequately controlled quality as it responded to increased demand, the problem would never have reached such proportions. Similarly, in late 2008 a routine quality control inspection of a prototype of Boeing's 787 Dreamliner revealed that a fastener had not been installed correctly. Closer scrutiny then revealed that literally thousands of fasteners had been installed wrong in each prototype under construction. As a result, the entire project was delayed several months. If the inspection process had been more rigorous, the error would likely have been found and corrected much earlier, rather than accumulating into a major problem for Boeing.[5]

Coping with Organizational Complexity When a firm purchases only one raw material, produces one product, has a simple organization design, and enjoys constant demand for its product, its managers can maintain control with a very basic and simple system. But a business that produces many products from myriad raw materials and has a large market area, a complicated organization design, and many competitors needs a sophisticated system to maintain adequate control. When large firms merge, the short-term results are often disappointing. The typical reason for this is that the new enterprise is so large and complex that the existing control systems are simply inadequate. When United Airlines and Continental Airlines agreed to merge at the end of 2010 the two firms faced myriad challenges in how to merge two complex flight operations centers, their human resource practices, their frequent flyer programs, and so forth. As a result, it will take the combined firm some period of time even after the merger is complete to continue to sort out and address all of the complex issues associated with the two firms becoming a single corporate entity.

EDWARD KARAA/ALAMY

One key to Starbucks' long-term success has been effective control. For instance, Starbucks has tight specifications regarding water temperature and how long brewed coffee can set before it has to be thrown out. The firm recently realized that sales of decaffeinated coffee drop substantially after lunch. To reduce waste and maintain product freshness baristas now brew decaf in the afternoons only when a customer orders it.

Minimizing Costs When it is practiced effectively, control can also help reduce costs and boost output. For example, Georgia-Pacific Corporation, a large wood products company, learned of a new technology that could be used to make thinner blades for its saws. The firm's control system was used to calculate the amount of wood that could be saved from each cut made by the thinner blades relative to the costs used to replace the existing blades. The results have been impressive—the wood that is saved by the new blades each year fills 800 rail cars. As Georgia-Pacific discovered, effective control systems can eliminate waste, lower labor costs, and improve output per unit of input. Starbucks recently instructed its coffee shops to stop automatically brewing decaffeinated coffee after lunch. Sales of decaf plummet after lunch, and Starbucks realized that baristas were simply pouring most of it down the drain. Now, between noon and early evening they brew decaf only by the cup and only when a customer orders it.[6] Similarly, many businesses are cutting back on everything from health insurance coverage to overnight shipping to business lunches for clients in their quest to lower costs.[7]

Types of Control

The examples of control given thus far have illustrated the regulation of several organizational activities, from producing quality products to coordinating complex organizations. Organizations practice control in a number of different areas and at different levels, and the responsibility for managing control is widespread.

Areas of Control Control can focus on any area of an organization. Most organizations define areas of control in terms of the four basic types of resources they use: physical, human, information, and financial.[8] Control of physical resources includes inventory management (stocking neither too few nor too many units in inventory), quality control (maintaining appropriate levels of output quality), and equipment control (supplying the necessary facilities and machinery). Control of human resources includes selection and placement, training and development, performance appraisal, and compensation. Relatedly, organizations also attempt to control the behavior of their employees—directing them toward higher performance, for example, and away from unethical behaviors.[9] Control of information resources includes sales and marketing forecasting, environmental analysis, public relations, production scheduling, and economic forecasting.[10] Financial control involves managing the organization's financial obligations so that they do not become excessive, ensuring that the firm always has enough cash on hand to meet its obligations but does not have excess cash sitting idly in a checking account, and ensuring that receivables are collected and bills are paid on a timely basis.

In many ways, the control of financial resources is the most important area, because financial resources are related to the control of all the other resources in an organization. Too much inventory leads to storage costs; poor selection of personnel leads to termination and rehiring expenses; inaccurate sales forecasts lead to disruptions in cash flows and other financial effects. Financial issues tend to pervade most control-related activities.

The crisis in the U.S. airline industry precipitated by the terrorist attacks on September 11, 2001, the economic recession of 2009 that reduced business travel, and rising fuel costs can be fundamentally traced to financial issues. Essentially, airline revenues have dropped while their costs have increased. Because of high labor costs and other expenses, the airlines faced major problems in making appropriate adjustments. Major long-haul U.S. airlines such as American spend nearly half of their revenues on labor; in contrast, JetBlue spends only about 25 percent of its revenues on labor.

Levels of Control Just as control can be broken down by area, it can also be broken down by level within the organizational system, as shown in Figure 9.2. **Operations control** focuses on the processes the organization uses to transform resources into products or services.[11] Quality control is one type of operations control. **Financial control** is concerned with the organization's financial resources. Monitoring receivables to make sure customers are paying their bills on time is an example of financial control. **Structural control** is concerned with how the elements of the organization's structure are serving their intended purpose. Monitoring the administrative ratio to make sure staff expenses do not become excessive is an example of structural control. Finally, **strategic control** focuses

operations control
Focuses on the processes the organization uses to transform resources into products or services

financial control
Concerned with the organization's financial resources

structural control
Concerned with how the elements of the organization's structure are serving their intended purpose

strategic control
Focuses on how effectively the organization's strategies are succeeding in helping the organization meet its goals

Figure 9.2 Levels of Control

Managers use control at several different levels. The most basic levels of control in organizations are strategic, structural, operations, and financial control. Each level must be managed properly if control is to be most effective.

on how effectively the organization's corporate, business, and functional strategies are succeeding in helping the organization meet its goals. For example, if a corporation has been unsuccessful in implementing its strategy of related diversification, its managers need to identify the reasons and either change the strategy or renew their efforts to implement it. We discuss these four levels of control more fully later in this chapter.

Responsibilities for Control Traditionally, managers have been responsible for overseeing the wide array of control systems and concerns in organizations. They decide which types of control the organization will use, and they implement control systems and take actions based on the information provided by control systems. Thus, ultimate responsibility for control rests with all managers throughout an organization.

Most larger organizations also have one or more specialized managerial positions called *controller*. A **controller** is responsible for helping line managers with their control activities, for coordinating the organization's overall control system, and for gathering and assimilating relevant information. Many businesses that use an H-form or M-form organization design have several controllers: one for the corporation and one for each division. The job of controller is especially important in organizations where control systems are complex.[12]

In addition, many organizations are also beginning to use operating employees to help maintain effective control. Indeed, employee participation is often used as a vehicle for allowing operating employees an opportunity to help facilitate organizational effectiveness. For example, Whistler Corporation increased employee participation in an effort to turn its quality problems around. As a starting point, the quality control unit, formerly responsible for checking product quality at the end of the assembly process, was eliminated. Next, all operating employees were encouraged to check their own work and told that they would be responsible for correcting their own errors. As a result, Whistler has eliminated its quality problems and is now highly profitable once again.

controller
A position in organizations that helps line managers with their control activities

$\mathcal{F}igure$ 9.3   Steps in the Control Process

Having an effective control system can help ensure that an organization achieves its goals. Implementing a control system, however, is a systematic process that generally proceeds through four interrelated steps.

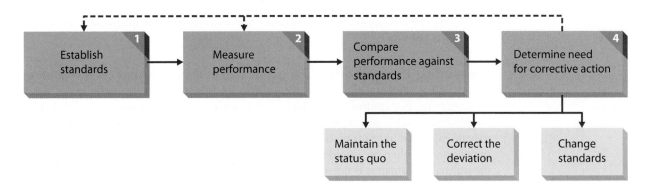

Steps in the Control Process

Regardless of the type or levels of control systems an organization needs, there are four fundamental steps in any control process.[13] These are illustrated in Figure 9.3.

Establishing Standards   The first step in the control process is establishing standards. A **control standard** is a target against which subsequent performance will be compared.[14] Employees at a Taco Bell fast-food restaurant, for example, work toward the following service standards:

1. A minimum of 95 percent of all customers will be greeted within 3 minutes of their arrival.
2. Preheated tortilla chips will not sit in the warmer more than 30 minutes before they are served to customers or discarded.
3. Empty tables will be cleaned within 5 minutes after being vacated.

Standards established for control purposes should be expressed in measurable terms. Note that standard 1 above has a time limit of 3 minutes and an objective target of 95 percent of all customers. In standard 3, the objective target of "all" empty tables is implied.

Control standards should also be consistent with the organization's goals. Taco Bell has organizational goals involving customer service, food quality, and restaurant cleanliness. A control standard for a retailer like Home Depot should be consistent with its goal of increasing its annual sales volume by 25 percent within five years. A hospital trying to shorten the average hospital stay for a patient will have control standards that reflect current averages. A university reaffirming its commitment to academics might adopt a standard of graduating 80 percent of its student athletes within five years of their enrollment. Control standards can be as narrow or as broad as the level of activity to which they apply and must follow logically from organizational goals and objectives. When Airbus introduced the A380, the world's largest passenger airplane, managers indicated that the firm needed to ship 270 planes to break even, and set a goal of delivering 18 per year. Managers also forecast that demand for very large aircraft like the A380 and Boeing's revamped 747 would exceed 1,200 planes during the next 20 years.[15]

control standard
A target against which subsequent performance will be compared

A final aspect of establishing standards is to identify performance indicators. Performance indicators are measures of performance that provide information that is directly relevant to what is being controlled. For example, suppose an organization is following a tight schedule in building a new plant. Relevant performance indicators could be buying a site, selecting a building contractor, and ordering equipment. Monthly sales increases are not, however, directly relevant. On the other hand, if control is being focused on revenue, monthly sales increases are relevant, whereas buying land for a new plant is less relevant.

Measuring Performance The second step in the control process is measuring performance. Performance measurement is a constant, ongoing activity for most organizations. For control to be effective, performance measures must be valid. Daily, weekly, and monthly sales figures measure sales performance, and production performance may be expressed in terms of unit cost, product quality, or volume produced. Employees' performance is often measured in terms of quality or quantity of output, but for many jobs measuring performance is not so straightforward.

A research and development scientist at Merck, for example, may spend years working on a single project before achieving a breakthrough. A manager who takes over a business on the brink of failure may need months or even years to turn things around. Valid performance measurement, however difficult to obtain, is nevertheless vital in maintaining effective control, and performance indicators usually can be developed. The scientist's progress, for example, may be partially assessed by peer review, and the manager's success may be evaluated by her ability to convince creditors that she will eventually be able to restore profitability.

As Airbus completed the design and manufacture of its A380 jumbo jet, managers recognized that delays and cost overruns had changed its breakeven point. New calculations indicated that the company would need to sell 420 planes before it would become profitable. Its actual annual sales, of course, remained relatively easy to measure.

Comparing Performance Against Standards The third step in the control process is comparing measured performance against established standards. Performance may be higher than, lower than, or identical to the standard. In some cases comparison is easy. The goal of each product manager at General Electric is to make the product either number one or number two (on the basis of total sales) in its market. Because this standard is clear and total sales are easy to calculate, it is relatively simple to determine whether this standard has been met. Sometimes, however, comparisons are less clear-cut. If performance is lower than expected, the question is how much deviation from standards to allow before taking remedial action. For example, is increasing sales by 7.9 percent close enough when the standard was 8 percent?

The timetable for comparing performance to standards depends on a variety of factors, including the importance and complexity of what is being controlled. For longer-run and higher-level standards, annual comparisons may be appropriate. In other circumstances, more frequent comparisons are necessary. For example, a business with a severe cash shortage may need to monitor its on-hand cash reserves daily. In its first year of production, Airbus did indeed deliver 18 A380s, just as it had forecast.

Considering Corrective Action The final step in the control process is determining the need for corrective action. Decisions regarding corrective action draw heavily on a manager's analytic and diagnostic skills. For example, as healthcare costs have risen, many firms have sought ways to keep their own expenses in check. Some have reduced benefits; others have opted to pass on higher costs to their employees.[16]

After comparing performance against control standards, one of three actions is appropriate: maintain the status quo (do nothing), correct the deviation, or change the standards. Maintaining the status quo is preferable when performance essentially matches the standards, but it is more likely that some action will be needed to correct a deviation from the standards.

Sometimes, performance that is higher than expected may also cause problems for organizations. For example, when highly anticipated new video games or game systems are first introduced the demand may be so strong that customers are placed on waiting lists. And even some people who are among the first to purchase such products immediately turn around and list them for sale on eBay for an inflated price. The manufacturer may be unable to increase production in the short term, though, and also knows that demand will eventually drop. At the same time, however, the firm would not want to alienate potential customers. Consequently, it may decide to simply reduce its advertising. This may curtail demand a bit and limit customer frustration.

Changing an established standard usually is necessary if it was set too low or too high at the outset. This is apparent if large numbers of employees routinely beat the standard by a wide margin or if no employees ever meet the standard. Also, standards that seemed perfectly appropriate when they were established may need to be adjusted if circumstances have since changed.

As the 2008–2009 global recession began to take its toll, two major Airbus customers, Qantas and Emirates, indicated that they wanted to defer delivery of some previously ordered A380s. As a result, Airbus found it necessary to reduce its production in 2009 from 18 down to only 14. It also indicated that the plane's breakeven point had increased, but would not reveal the new target.

OPERATIONS CONTROL

One of the four levels of control practiced by most organizations, **operations control** is concerned with the processes the organization uses to transform resources into products or services. As Figure 9.4 shows, the three forms of operations control—preliminary, screening, and postaction—occur at different points in relation to the transformation processes used by the organization.

Preliminary Control

Preliminary control concentrates on the resources—financial, material, human, and information—the organization brings in from the environment. Preliminary control attempts to monitor the quality or quantity of these resources before they enter the organization. Firms such as PepsiCo and General Mills hire only college graduates for their management training programs, and even then only after applicants satisfy several interviewers and selection criteria. In this way, they control the quality of the human resources entering the organization. When Sears orders merchandise to be manufactured under its own brand name, it specifies rigid standards of quality, thereby controlling physical inputs. Organizations also control financial and information resources. For example, privately held companies such as Toys "R" Us and Mars limit the extent to which outsiders can buy their stock, and television networks verify the accuracy of news stories before they are broadcast.

operations control
Focuses on the processes the organization uses to transform resources into products or services

preliminary control
Attempts to monitor the quality or quantity of financial, physical, human, and information resources before they actually become part of the system

Figure 9.4   Forms of Operations Control

Most organizations develop multiple control systems that incorporate all three basic forms of control. For example, the publishing company that produced this book screens inputs by hiring only qualified employees, typesetters, and printers (preliminary control). In addition, quality is checked during the transformation process, such as after the manuscript is typeset (screening control), and the outputs— printed and bound books—are checked before they are shipped from the bindery (postaction control).

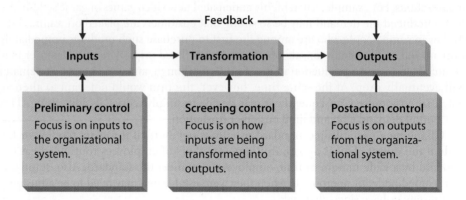

Screening Control

Screening control focuses on meeting standards for product or service quality or quantity during the actual transformation process itself. Screening control relies heavily on feedback processes. For example, in a Dell assembly factory, computer system components are checked periodically as each unit is being assembled. This is done to ensure that all the components that have been assembled up to that point are working properly. The periodic quality checks provide feedback to workers so that they know what, if any, corrective actions to take. Because they are useful in identifying the cause of problems, screening controls tend to be used more often than other forms of control.

More and more companies are adopting screening controls because they are an effective way to promote employee participation and catch problems early in the overall transformation process. For example, Corning adopted screening controls for use in manufacturing television glass. In the past, finished television screens were inspected only after they were finished. Unfortunately, over 4 percent of them were later returned by customers because of defects. Now the glass screens are inspected at each step in the production process, rather than at the end, and the return rate from customers has dropped to .03 percent.

screening control
Relies heavily on feedback processes during the transformation process

postaction control
Monitors the outputs or results of the organization after the transformation process is complete

Postaction Control

Postaction control focuses on the outputs of the organization after the transformation process is complete. Corning's old system was postaction control—final inspection after the product was manufactured. Although Corning abandoned its postaction control system, it still may be an effective method of control, primarily if a product can be manufactured in only one or two steps or if the service is fairly simple and routine. Although postaction control alone may not be as effective as preliminary or screening control, it can provide management with information for future planning. For example, if a quality check of finished goods indicates an unacceptably high defect rate, the production manager knows that he or she must identify the causes and take steps to eliminate them. Postaction control also provides a basis for rewarding employees. Recognizing that an employee has exceeded personal sales goals by a wide margin, for example, may alert the manager that a bonus or promotion is in order.

Most organizations use more than one form of operations control. For example, Honda's preliminary control includes hiring only qualified employees and specifying strict quality standards when ordering parts from other manufacturers. Honda uses numerous screening controls in checking the quality of components during assembly of cars. A final inspection and test drive as each car rolls off the assembly line is part of the company's postaction control.[17] Indeed, most successful organizations employ a wide variety of techniques to facilitate operations control.

RICHARD FREEDA/AURORA/GETTY IMAGES

Establishing standards, comparing performance against standards, and correcting deviations are central elements of the control process. This quality control inspector is testing dishwashers. The inspector is applying equal parts of cake batter to the same locations of several identical dinner plates. After the plates have gone through automatic dishwashers, the inspector will be able to judge whether or not the dishwashers are performing up to the desired level of cleanliness.

FINANCIAL CONTROL

Financial control is the control of financial resources as they flow into the organization (revenues, shareholder investments), are held by the organization (working capital, retained earnings), and flow out of the organization (pay, expenses). Businesses must manage their finances so that revenues are sufficient to cover costs and still return a profit to the firm's owners. Not-for-profit organizations such as universities have the same concerns: Their revenues (from tax dollars or tuition) must cover operating expenses and overhead. U.S. auto makers Ford and General Motors have come to realize that they have to reduce the costs of paying employees they do not need but whom they are obligated to keep due to longstanding labor agreements. Ford has offered to cover the full costs of a college education for certain of its employees if they will resign; GM, for its part, has offered lump sum payments of varying amounts to some of its workers in return for their resignations.[18] A complete discussion of financial management is beyond the scope of this book, but we will examine the control provided by budgets and other financial control tools.

Budgetary Control

A **budget** is a plan expressed in numerical terms.[19] Organizations establish budgets for work groups, departments, divisions, and the whole organization. The usual time period for a budget is one year, although breakdowns of budgets by the quarter or month are also common. Budgets are generally expressed in financial terms, but they may occasionally be expressed in units of output, time, or other quantifiable factors. When Disney launches the production of a new animated cartoon feature, it creates a budget for how much the

financial control
Concerned with the organization's financial resources

budget
A plan expressed in numerical terms

movie should cost. Several years ago, when movies such as *The Lion King* were raking in hundreds of millions of dollars, Disney executives were fairly flexible about budget overruns. But, on the heels of several animated-movie flops, such as *Atlantis: The Lost Empire* and *Treasure Planet*, the company had to take a much harder line on budget overruns.[20]

Because of their quantitative nature, budgets provide yardsticks for measuring performance and facilitate comparisons across departments, between levels in the organization, and from one time period to another. Budgets serve four primary purposes. They help managers coordinate resources and projects (because they use a common denominator, usually dollars). They help define the established standards for control. They provide guidelines about the organization's resources and expectations. Finally, budgets enable the organization to evaluate the performance of managers and organizational units.

Types of Budgets Most organizations develop and make use of three kinds of budgets—financial, operating, and nonmonetary. Table 9.1 summarizes the characteristics of each of these.

A *financial budget* indicates where the organization expects to get its cash for the coming time period and how it plans to use it. Because financial resources are critically important, the organization needs to know where those resources will be coming from and how they are to be used. The financial budget provides answers to both these questions. Usual sources of cash include sales revenue, short- and long-term loans, the sale of assets, and the issuance of new stock.

For years Exxon was very conservative in its capital budgeting. As a result, the firm amassed a huge financial reserve but was being overtaken in sales by Royal Dutch/Shell Group. But executives at Exxon were then able to use their reserves to help finance the firm's merger with Mobil, creating ExxonMobil, and to regain the number-one sales position. Since that time, the firm has become more aggressive in capital budgeting to stay ahead of its European rival.

Table 9.1
Developing Budgets in Organizations

Organizations use various types of budgets to help manage their control functions. The three major categories of budgets are financial, operating, and nonmonetary. There are several different types of budgets in each category. To be most effective, each budget must be carefully matched with the specific function being controlled.

Types of Budget	What Budget Shows
Financial Budget	*Sources and Uses of Cash*
Cash flow or cash budget	All sources of cash income and cash expenditures in monthly, weekly, or daily periods
Capital expenditures budget	Costs of major assets such as a new plant, machinery, or land
Balance sheet budget	Forecast of the organization's assets and liabilities in the event all other budgets are met
Operating Budget	*Planned Operations in Financial Terms*
Sales or revenue budget	Income the organization expects to receive from normal operations
Expense budget	Anticipated expenses for the organization during the coming time period
Profit budget	Anticipated differences between sales or revenues and expenses
Nonmonetary Budget	*Planned Operations in Nonfinancial Terms*
Labor budget	Hours of direct labor available for use
Space budget	Square feet or meters of space available for various functions
Production budget	Number of units to be produced during the coming time period

An *operating budget* is concerned with planned operations within the organization. It outlines what quantities of products or services the organization intends to create and what resources will be used to create them. IBM creates an operating budget that specifies how many of each model of its personal computer will be produced each quarter.

A *nonmonetary budget* is simply a budget expressed in nonfinancial terms, such as units of output, hours of direct labor, machine hours, or square-foot allocations. Nonmonetary budgets are most commonly used by managers at the lower levels of an organization. For example, a plant manager can schedule work more effectively knowing that he or she has 8,000 labor hours to allocate in a week, rather than trying to determine how to best spend $86,451 in wages in a week.

Developing Budgets   Traditionally, budgets were developed by top management and the controller and then imposed on lower-level managers. Although some organizations still follow this pattern, many contemporary organizations now allow all managers to participate in the budget process. As a starting point, top management generally issues a call for budget requests, accompanied by an indication of overall patterns the budgets may take. For example, if sales are expected to drop in the next year, managers may be told up front to prepare for cuts in operating budgets.

As Figure 9.5 shows, the heads of each operating unit typically submit budget requests to the head of their division. An operating unit head might be a department manager in a manufacturing or wholesaling firm or a program director in a social service agency. The division heads might include plant managers, regional sales managers, or college deans. The division head integrates and consolidates the budget requests from operating unit heads into one overall division budget request. A great deal of interaction among managers usually takes place at this stage, as the division head coordinates the budgetary needs of the various departments.

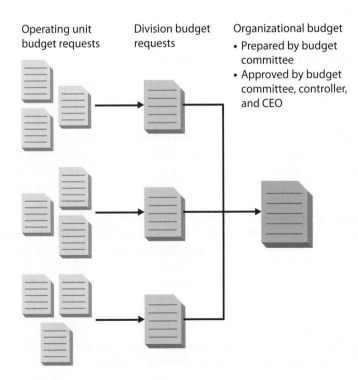

Operating unit budget requests

Division budget requests

Organizational budget
- Prepared by budget committee
- Approved by budget committee, controller, and CEO

Figure 9.5
Developing Budgets in Organizations

Most organizations use the same basic process to develop budgets. Operating units are requested to submit their budget requests to divisions. These divisions, in turn, compile unit budgets and submit their own budgets to the organization. An organizational budget is then compiled for approval by the budget committee, controller, and CEO.

Division budget requests are then forwarded to a budget committee. The budget committee is usually composed of top managers. The committee reviews budget requests from several divisions, and once again, duplications and inconsistencies are corrected. Finally, the budget committee, the controller, and the CEO review and agree on the overall budget for the organization, as well as specific budgets for each operating unit. These decisions are then communicated back to each manager.

Strengths and Weaknesses of Budgeting Budgets offer a number of advantages, but they also have weaknesses. On the plus side, budgets facilitate effective control. Placing dollar values on operations enables managers to monitor operations better and pinpoint problem areas. Budgets also facilitate coordination and communication between departments because they express diverse activities in a common denominator (dollars). Budgets help maintain records of organizational performance and are a logical complement to planning. In other words, as managers develop plans, they should simultaneously consider control measures to accompany them. Organizations can use budgets to link plans and control by first developing budgets as part of the plan and then using those budgets as part of control.

On the other hand, some managers apply budgets too rigidly. Budgets are intended to serve as frameworks, but managers sometimes fail to recognize that changing circumstances may warrant budget adjustments. Also, the process of developing budgets can be very time consuming. Finally, budgets may limit innovation and change. When all available funds have been allocated to specific operating budgets, it may be impossible to procure additional funds to take advantage of an unexpected opportunity. Indeed, for these very reasons, some organizations are working to scale back their budgeting systems. Although most organizations are likely to continue to use budgets, the goal is to make them less confining and rigid.

The *Tough Times, Tough Choices* box shows what can happen to the best-laid plans and best-prepared budgets when an organization's financial control is beyond its control.

Other Tools for Financial Control

Although budgets are the most common means of financial control, other useful tools are financial statements, ratio analysis, and financial audits.

Financial Statements A **financial statement** is a profile of some aspect of an organization's financial circumstances. There are commonly accepted and required ways that financial statements must be prepared and presented.[21] The two most basic financial statements prepared and used by virtually all organizations are a balance sheet and an income statement.

financial statement
A profile of some aspect of an organization's financial circumstances

balance sheet
List of assets and liabilities of an organization at a specific point in time

income statement
A summary of financial performance over a period of time

The **balance sheet** lists the assets and liabilities of the organization at a specific point in time, usually the last day of an organization's fiscal year. For example, the balance sheet may summarize the financial condition of an organization on December 31, 2011. Most balance sheets are divided into current assets (assets that are relatively liquid, or easily convertible into cash), fixed assets (assets that are longer term in nature and less liquid), current liabilities (debts and other obligations that must be paid in the near future), long-term liabilities (payable over an extended period of time), and stockholders' equity (the owners' claim against the assets).

Whereas the balance sheet reflects a snapshot profile of an organization's financial position at a single point in time, the **income statement** summarizes financial performance over a period of time, usually one year. For example, the income statement

TOUGH TIMES, TOUGH CHOICES

The Grift That Keeps on Giving

Established in 1955 by insurance magnate Cornelius Vander Starr, the Starr Foundation is the 16th-largest charitable foundation in the United States. Focusing on education, healthcare, and social services, the Starr Foundation helps to fund medical research, teacher training, literacy, and scholarship programs and has, in its 53 years of operation, given nearly $2 billion in grants.

As for the source of the wealth that created the Starr Foundation, Starr's company originally insured U.S. firms against risks entailed by foreign ventures, and after a series of mergers, it emerged in 1962 as American International Group, ultimately becoming the world's number-one international insurance and financial-services company. Starr's legacy included a bequest of 39 million shares of AIG stock in 1968, and from the outset, the charitable organization has been financed and managed by AIG insiders and executives. Ex-AIG CEO Maurice R. Greenberg is currently chairman of the Starr Foundation, and President Florence A. Davis was formerly general counsel of AIG. The relationship between the two organizations hasn't always been fiscally amicable, but it's kept the nonprofit foundation financially stable for more than half a century. As of December 2006, the Starr Foundation had assets of $3.3 billion, the bulk of it deriving from Starr's endowment.

At the end of 2006, AIG itself boasted assets of slightly more than $1 trillion. Shortly thereafter, however, the company's financial superstructure was washed away in the tidal wave of greed and monetary misjudgment known as the *subprime crisis*. Having invested billions in securities backed by subprime-mortgage loans, AIG was poised for crippling losses when housing prices went down, adjusted-rate mortgage payments went up, and millions of home buyers defaulted on their home loans. From a total of $14 billion in 2006, AIG's income plummeted to $6.2 billion in 2007. Its stock price, which had been at $73 a share in May 2007, dropped under $5 in October 2008.

Needless to say, these weren't good times for the Starr Foundation either. It was, however, luckier than most AIG stockholders. Between January 2006 and May 2008, the foundation had sold about 30 million shares of AIG, taking advantage of prices that still hovered between $40 and $73 a share. In mid-2008, however, it still counted 15.5 million shares of AIG among its assets, and between the end of 2006 and October of 2008, the Starr Foundation lost at least $1 billion in assets—about one-third of its 2006 value. "You will see smaller grants from us," reported Davis. "At least for the time being, some of our initiatives will be put on hold."

In the meantime, Davis and Greenberg took stock of their fiduciary responsibility to the Starr Foundation and decided to sue the corporate hand that funded them. AIG management, charged a suit filed in May 2008, had "fraudulently reassured" shareholders in February that it foresaw no more than $900 million in future losses from the subprime fiasco. The fictitious projection, argued Starr, "caused the Foundation to retain stock in AIG which it would otherwise have sold." In reality, the complaint reminded the court, AIG's losses came in at "billions more than AIG has previously acknowledged" (about $10 billion, to be more or less precise), and the foundation sought $300 million in damages.

AIG, meanwhile, was saved from bankruptcy by an $85 billion line of credit from the Federal Reserve, and U.S. taxpayers now own a 79.9 percent stake in the onetime financial giant.

References: Geraldine Fabrikant, "A Squeeze on Giving Is Expected," *New York Times*, September 30, 2008, pp. C1, C10; Philip Boroff and Ryan J. Donmoyer, "Starr Foundation Plans Smaller Grants after AIG Stock Plunge," Bloomberg.com, October 3, 2008, www.bloomberg.com on October 4, 2008; The Foundation Center, "Starr Foundation Reduces Grantmaking after AIG Stock Plunges," *Philanthropy News Digest*, September 25, 2008, http://foundationcenter.org on October 1, 2008; Lila Zuill, "Starr Foundation Sues AIG, Alleging Fraud," Reuters, May 8, 2008, www.reuters.com on October 1, 2008; Patricia Hurtado, "Starr Foundation Sues AIG Chief Sullivan for Fraud over Loss," Bloomberg.com, October 1, 2008, www.bloomberg.com on October 1, 2008; and AIG, "AIG Signs Agreement with Federal Reserve Bank of New York for $85 Billion Credit Facility," AIG website, September 23, 2008, http://ir.aigcorporate.com on October 4, 2008.

might be for the period January 1, 2011 through December 31, 2011. The income statement summarizes the firm's revenues less its expenses to report net income (profit or loss) for the period. Information from the balance sheet and income statement is used in computing important financial ratios.

Ratio Analysis Financial ratios compare different elements of a balance sheet or income statement to one another. **Ratio analysis** is the calculation of one or more financial ratios to assess some aspect of the financial health of an organization. Organizations use a variety of financial ratios as part of financial control. For example, *liquidity ratios* indicate how liquid (easily converted into cash) an organization's assets are. *Debt ratios* reflect ability to meet long-term financial obligations. *Return ratios* show managers and investors how much return the organization is generating relative to its assets. *Coverage ratios* help estimate the organization's ability to cover interest expenses on borrowed capital. *Operating ratios* indicate the effectiveness of specific functional areas rather than that of the total organization. Walt Disney is an example of a company that relies heavily on financial ratios to keep its financial operations on track.[22]

Financial Audits Audits are independent appraisals of an organization's accounting, financial, and operational systems. The two major types of financial audits are the external audit and the internal audit.

External audits are financial appraisals conducted by experts who are not employees of the organization.[23] External audits are typically concerned with determining whether the organization's accounting procedures and financial statements are compiled in an objective and verifiable fashion. The organization contracts with a certified public accountant (CPA) for this service. The CPA's main objective is to verify for stockholders, the IRS, and other interested parties that the methods by which the organization's financial managers and accountants prepare documents and reports are legal and proper. External audits are so important that publicly held corporations are required by law to have external audits regularly, as assurance to investors that the financial reports are reliable.

Unfortunately, flaws in the auditing process played a major role in the downfall of Enron and several other major firms. The problem can be traced back partially to the auditing groups' problems with conflicts of interest and eventual loss of objectivity. For instance, Enron was such an important client for its auditing firm, Arthur Andersen, that the auditors started letting the firm take liberties with its accounting systems for fear that if they were too strict, Enron might take its business to another auditing firm. In the aftermath of the resulting scandal, Arthur Andersen was forced to close its doors, Enron is a shell of its former self, indictments continue to be handed down, and the entire future of the accounting profession has been called into question.[24]

Some organizations are also starting to employ external auditors to review other aspects of their financial operations. For example, some auditing firms now specialize in checking corporate legal bills. An auditor for the Fireman's Fund Insurance Company uncovered several thousands of dollars in legal-fee errors. Other auditors are beginning to specialize in real estate, employee benefits, and pension plan investments.

Whereas external audits are conducted by external accountants, an *internal audit* is handled by employees of the organization. Its objective is the same as that of an external audit—to verify the accuracy of financial and accounting procedures used by the organization. Internal audits also examine the efficiency and appropriateness of financial and accounting procedures. Because the staff members who conduct them are a permanent part of the organization, internal audits tend to be more expensive than external audits. But employees, who are more familiar with the organization's practices, may also point out significant aspects of the accounting system besides its technical correctness. Large organizations like

ratio analysis
The calculation of one or more financial ratios to assess some aspect of the organization's financial health

audit
An independent appraisal of an organization's accounting, financial, and operational systems

Halliburton and Ford have an internal auditing staff that spends all its time conducting audits of different divisions and functional areas of the organization. Smaller organizations may assign accountants to an internal audit group on a temporary or rotating basis.

The findings of an internal auditor led to a major financial scandal at WorldCom. CEO Bernard Ebbers was ousted in early 2002 because of deteriorating performance at the firm and was replaced by John Sidgmore. Sidgmore, suspicious of the firm's public financial reporting, then gave a small auditing group the task of secretly investigating the firm's financial activity. The auditors uncovered several major problems, including the fact that the firm's chief financial officer was misapplying major expenses: Instead of treating them as current expenses, he was treating them as capital expenditures. This treatment, in turn, made the firm look much more profitable than it really was. These findings led to criminal charges against several top managers at the firm, and pushed WorldCom into bankruptcy (the largest bankruptcy in U.S. history until the collapse of Lehmann Brothers in 2008). The CFO was fired, but it will take WorldCom a long time to sort out the $3.8 billion it has so far found to have handled improperly.[25]

STRUCTURAL CONTROL

Organizations can create designs for themselves that result in very different approaches to control. Two major forms of structural control, bureaucratic control and decentralized control, represent opposite ends of a continuum, as shown in Figure 9.6.[26] The six dimensions shown in the figure represent perspectives adopted by the two extreme types of structural control. In other words, they have different goals, degrees of formality, performance expectations, organization designs, reward systems, and levels of participation. Although a few organizations fall precisely at one extreme or the other, most tend toward one end but may have specific characteristics of either.

Bureaucratic Control

Bureaucratic control is an approach to organization design characterized by formal and mechanistic structural arrangements. As the term suggests, it follows the bureaucratic model. The goal of bureaucratic control is employee compliance. Organizations that use it rely on strict rules and a rigid hierarchy, insist that employees meet minimally acceptable levels of performance, and often have a tall structure. They focus their rewards on individual performance and allow only limited and formal employee participation.

NBC television applies structural controls that reflect many elements of bureaucracy. The organization relies on numerous rules to regulate employee travel, expense accounts, and other expenses. A new performance appraisal system precisely specifies minimally acceptable levels of performance for everyone. The organization's structure is considerably taller than those of the other major networks, and rewards are based on individual contributions. Perhaps most significantly, many NBC employees have argued that they have too small a voice in how the organization is managed.

In another example, a large oil company recently made the decision to allow employees to wear casual attire to work. But a committee then spent weeks developing a 20-page set of guidelines on what was and was not acceptable. For example, denim pants are not allowed. Similarly, athletic shoes may be worn as long as they are not white. And all shirts must have a collar. Nordstrom, the department store chain, is also moving toward bureaucratic control as it works to centralize all of its purchasing in an effort to lower costs.[27] Similarly, Home Depot is moving more toward bureaucratic control to cut its costs and more effectively compete with its hard-charging rival, Lowe's.[28]

bureaucratic control
A form of organizational control characterized by formal and mechanistic structural arrangements

Figure 9.6 Organizational Control

Organizational control generally falls somewhere between the two extremes of bureaucratic and decentralized control. NBC television uses bureaucratic control, whereas Levi Strauss uses decentralized control.

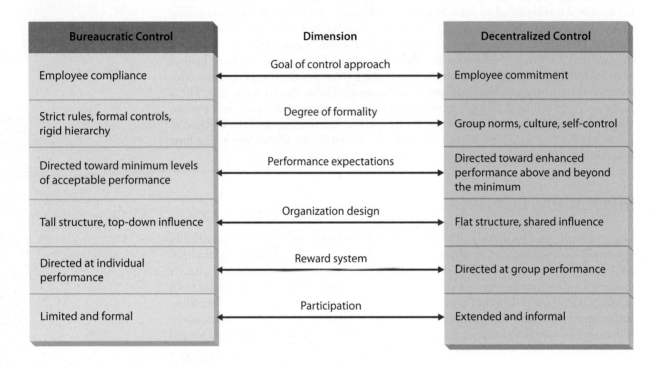

Bureaucratic Control	Dimension	Decentralized Control
Employee compliance	Goal of control approach	Employee commitment
Strict rules, formal controls, rigid hierarchy	Degree of formality	Group norms, culture, self-control
Directed toward minimum levels of acceptable performance	Performance expectations	Directed toward enhanced performance above and beyond the minimum
Tall structure, top-down influence	Organization design	Flat structure, shared influence
Directed at individual performance	Reward system	Directed at group performance
Limited and formal	Participation	Extended and informal

Decentralized Control

Decentralized control, in contrast, is an approach to organizational control characterized by informal and organic structural arrangements. As Figure 9.6 shows, its goal is employee commitment to the organization. Accordingly, it relies heavily on group norms and a strong corporate culture, and gives employees the responsibility for controlling themselves. Employees are encouraged to perform beyond minimally acceptable levels. Organizations using this approach are usually relatively flat. They direct rewards at group performance and favor widespread employee participation.

Levi Strauss practices decentralized control. The firm's managers use groups as the basis for work and have created a culture wherein group norms help facilitate high performance. Rewards are subsequently provided to the higher-performing groups and teams. The company's culture also reinforces contributions to the overall team effort, and employees have a strong sense of loyalty to the organization. Levi's has a flat structure, and power is widely shared. Employee participation is encouraged in all areas of operation.[29] Another company that uses this approach is Southwest Airlines. When Southwest made the decision to "go casual," the firm resisted the temptation to develop dress guidelines. Instead, managers decided to allow employees to exercise discretion over their attire and to deal with clearly inappropriate situations on a case-by-case basis.

decentralized control

An approach to organizational control based on informal and organic structural arrangements

STRATEGIC CONTROL

Given the obvious importance of an organization's strategy, it is also important that the organization assess how effective that strategy is in helping the organization meet its goals.[30] To do this requires that the organization integrate its strategy and control systems. This is especially true for the global organization.

Integrating Strategy and Control

Strategic control generally focuses on five aspects of organizations—structure, leadership, technology, human resources, and information and operational control systems. For example, an organization should periodically examine its structure to determine whether it is facilitating the attainment of the strategic goals being sought. Suppose a firm using a functional (*U-form*) design has an established goal of achieving a 20 percent sales growth rate per year. However, performance indicators show that it is currently growing at a rate of only 10 percent per year. Detailed analysis might reveal that the current structure is inhibiting growth in some way (for example, by slowing decision making and inhibiting innovation) and that a divisional (*M-form*) design is more likely to bring about the desired growth (by speeding decision making and promoting innovation).

In this way, strategic control focuses on the extent to which implemented strategy achieves the organization's strategic goals. If, as outlined above, one or more avenues of implementation are inhibiting the attainment of goals, that avenue should be changed. Consequently, the firm might find it necessary to alter its structure, replace key leaders, adopt new technology, modify its human resources, or change its information and operational control systems.

For several years, Pfizer, the world's largest pharmaceutical company, has invested billions of dollars in research and development. In 2009, though, the firm acknowledged that it was not getting an adequate return on its investment. Consequently, Pfizer announced that it was laying off 800 senior researchers. The firm also signaled a strategic reorientation by suggesting it would look for other drug companies to buy in order to acquire new patents and drug formulas.[31] Kohl's department stores essentially redefined how to compete effectively in the midtier retailing market and was on trajectory to leave competitors such as Sears and Dillard's in its dust. But then the firm inexplicably stopped doing many of the very things that had led to its success—such as keeping abreast of current styles, maintaining low inventories, and keeping its stores neat and clean—and began to stumble. Now, managers are struggling to rejuvenate Kohl's strategic focus and get it back on track.[32]

© PATRICE LATRON/CORBIS

Pharmaceutical giant Pfizer has long had a strategy of in-house product development and employed a staff of several thousand researchers. But the firm recently determined that it was not getting an adequate return on its investment. Senior managers decided that a more cost-effective way to acquire new drug formulas and patents might be to simply buy other, smaller firms. To help put this new plan into effect Pfizer recently announced plans to lay off 800 senior researchers.

strategic control
Control aimed at ensuring that the organization is maintaining an effective alignment with its environment and moving toward achieving its strategic goals

Because of both their relatively large size and the increased complexity associated with international business, global organizations must take an especially pronounced strategic view of their control systems. One very basic question that has to be addressed is whether to manage control from a centralized or a decentralized perspective.[33] Under a centralized system, each organizational unit around the world is responsible for frequently reporting the results of its performance to headquarters. Managers from the home office often visit foreign branches to observe firsthand how the units are functioning.

BP, Unilever, Procter & Gamble, and Sony all use this approach. They believe centralized control is effective because it allows the home office to keep better informed of the performance of foreign units and to maintain more control over how decisions are made. For example, BP discovered that its Australian subsidiary was not billing its customers for charges as quickly as were its competitors. By shortening the billing cycle, BP now receives customer payments five days faster than before. Managers believe that they discovered this oversight only because of a centralized financial control system.

Organizations that use a decentralized control system require foreign branches to report less frequently and in less detail. For example, each unit may submit summary performance statements on a quarterly basis and provide full statements only once a year. Similarly, visits from the home office are less frequent and less concerned with monitoring and assessing performance. IBM, Ford, and Shell all use this approach. Because Ford practices decentralized control of its design function, European designers have developed several innovative automobile design features. Managers believe that if they had been more centralized, designers would not have had the freedom to develop their new ideas.

MANAGING CONTROL IN ORGANIZATIONS

Effective control, whether at the operations, financial, structural, or strategic level, successfully regulates and monitors organizational activities. To use the control process, managers must recognize the characteristics of effective control and understand how to identify and overcome occasional resistance to control.[34]

Characteristics of Effective Control

Control systems tend to be most effective when they are integrated with planning and when they are flexible, accurate, timely, and objective.

Integration with Planning Control should be linked with planning. The more explicit and precise this linkage, the more effective the control system is. The best way to integrate planning and control is to account for control as plans develop. In other words, as goals are set during the planning process, attention should be paid to developing standards that will reflect how well the plan is realized. Managers at Champion Spark Plug Company decided to broaden their product line to include a full range of automotive accessories—a total of 21 new products. As part of this plan, managers decided in advance what level of sales they wanted to realize from each product for each of the next five years. They established these sales goals as standards against which actual sales would be compared. Thus, by accounting for their control system as they developed their plan, managers at Champion did an excellent job of integrating planning and control.

Flexibility The control system itself must be flexible enough to accommodate change. Consider, for example, an organization whose diverse product line requires 75 raw materials. The company's inventory control system must be able to manage and monitor current levels of inventory for all 75 materials. When a change in product line changes the number of raw materials needed, or when the required quantities of the existing materials change, the control system should be flexible enough to handle the revised requirements. The expense associated with the alternative—designing and implementing a new control system—would then be avoided. Champion's control system, for example, included a mechanism that automatically shipped products to major customers to keep the inventories of those customers at predetermined levels. The firm had to adjust this system when one of its biggest customers decided not to stock the full line of Champion products. Because its control system was flexible, though, modifying it for the customer was relatively simple.

Accuracy   Managers make a surprisingly large number of decisions based on inaccurate information. Field representatives may hedge their sales estimates to make themselves look better. Production managers may hide costs to meet their targets. Human resource managers may overestimate their minority recruiting prospects to meet affirmative action goals. In each case, the information that other managers receive is inaccurate, and the results of inaccurate information may be quite dramatic. If sales projections are inflated, a manager might cut advertising (thinking it is no longer needed) or increase advertising (to further build momentum). Similarly, a production manager unaware of hidden costs may quote a sales price much lower than desirable. Or a human resources manager may speak out publicly on the effectiveness of the company's minority recruiting, only to find out later that these prospects have been overestimated. In each case, the result of inaccurate information is inappropriate managerial action.

Timeliness   Timeliness does not necessarily mean quickness. Rather, it describes a control system that provides information as often as is necessary. Because Champion has a wealth of historical data on its sparkplug sales, it does not need information on sparkplugs as frequently as it needs sales feedback for its newer products. Retail organizations usually need sales results daily so that they can manage cash flow and adjust advertising and promotion. In contrast, they may require information about physical inventory only quarterly or annually. In general, the more uncertain and unstable the circumstances, the more frequently measurement is needed.

Objectivity   The control system should provide information that is as objective as possible. To appreciate this, imagine the task of a manager responsible for control of his organization's human resources. He asks two plant managers to submit reports. One manager notes that morale at his plant is "okay," that grievances are "about where they should be," and that turnover is "under control." The other reports that absenteeism at her plant is running at 4 percent, that 16 grievances have been filed this year (compared with 24 last year), and that turnover is 12 percent. The second report will almost always be more useful than the first. Of course, managers also need to look beyond the numbers when assessing performance. For example, a plant manager may be boosting productivity and profit margins by putting too much pressure on workers and using poor-quality materials. As a result, impressive short-run gains may be overshadowed by longer-run increases in employee turnover and customer complaints.

Resistance to Control

Managers sometimes make the mistake of assuming that the value of an effective control system is self-evident to employees. This is not always so, however. Many employees resist control, especially if they feel overcontrolled, if they think control is inappropriately

Enterprise Rent-A-Car is one of the most successful car rental businesses in the world. Standardized of work practices is sometimes cited by Enterprise's senior managers as a key to the firm's success. However, some Enterprise workers believe the company goes overboard in its employee appearance standards. For instance, there are 30 dress-code rules for women and 26 for men.

focused or rewards inefficiency, or if they are uncomfortable with accountability.

Overcontrol Occasionally, organizations try to control too many things. This becomes especially problematic when the control directly affects employee behavior. An organization that instructs its employees when to come to work, where to park, when to have morning coffee, and when to leave for the day exerts considerable control over people's daily activities. Yet many organizations attempt to control not only these but other aspects of work behavior as well. Of particular relevance in recent years is some companies' efforts to control their employees' access to private e-mail and the Internet during work hours. Some companies have no policies governing these activities, some attempt to limit it, and some attempt to forbid it altogether.

Troubles arise when employees perceive these attempts to limit their behavior as being unreasonable. A company that tells its employees how to dress, how to arrange their desks, and how to wear their hair may meet with more resistance. Employees at Chrysler who drove non-Chrysler vehicles used to complain because they were forced to park in a distant parking lot. People felt that these efforts to control their personal behavior (what kind of car to drive) were excessive. Managers eventually removed these controls and now allow open parking. Some employees at Abercrombie & Fitch argue that the firm is guilty of overcontrol because of its strict dress and grooming requirements—for example, no necklaces or facial hair for men and only natural nail polish and earrings no larger than a dime for women. Likewise, Enterprise Rent-A-Car has a set of 30 dress-code rules for women and 26 rules for men. The firm was recently sued by one former employee who was fired because of the color of her hair.[35]

Inappropriate Focus A control system may be too narrow, or it may focus too much on quantifiable variables and leave no room for analysis or interpretation. A sales standard that encourages high-pressure tactics to maximize short-run sales may do so at the expense of goodwill from long-term customers. Such a standard is too narrow. A university reward system that encourages faculty members to publish large numbers of articles but fails to consider the quality of the work is also inappropriately focused. Employees resist the intent of the control system by focusing their efforts only at the performance indicators being used. The cartoon features another example of inappropriately focused control.

Rewards for Inefficiency Imagine two operating departments that are approaching the end of their fiscal years. Department 1 expects to have $25,000 of its budget left over; department 2 is already $10,000 in the red. As a result, department 1 is likely to have its budget cut for the next year ("They had money left, so they obviously got too much to begin with"), and department 2 is likely to get a budget increase ("They obviously

In recent years, many organizations have sought ways to manage the size of their workforce more effectively, often through workforce reductions. Eliminating unnecessary or redundant jobs is indeed an effective strategy. But businesses sometimes go too far, eliminating jobs with a detrimental impact on the company. One executive noted that his firm had eliminated the fat but then cut out some muscle too! The manager shown here may also have fallen prey to that same mistake—cutting their sales force so much that their revenues have declined significantly.

"The dip in sales seems to coincide with the decision to eliminate the sales staff."

haven't been getting enough money"). Thus department 1 is punished for being efficient, and department 2 is rewarded for being inefficient. (No wonder departments commonly hasten to deplete their budgets as the end of the year approaches!) As with inappropriate focus, people resist the intent of this control and behave in ways that run counter to the organization's intent.

Too Much Accountability Effective controls allow managers to determine whether employees successfully discharge their responsibilities. If standards are properly set and performance accurately measured, managers know when problems arise and which departments and individuals are responsible. People who do not want to be answerable for their mistakes or who do not want to work as hard as their boss might, therefore, resist control. For example, American Express has a system that provides daily information on how many calls each of its customer service representatives handles. If one representative has typically worked at a slower pace and handled fewer calls than other representatives, that individual's deficient performance can now more easily be pinpointed.

Overcoming Resistance to Control

Perhaps the best way to overcome resistance to control is to create effective control to begin with. If control systems are properly integrated with organizational planning and if the controls are flexible, accurate, timely, and objective, the organization will be less likely to overcontrol, to focus on inappropriate standards, or to reward inefficiency. Two other ways to overcome resistance are encouraging employee participation and developing verification procedures.

Encourage Employee Participation Chapter 15 will explain that participation can help overcome resistance to change. By the same token, when employees are involved with planning and implementing the control system, they are less likely to resist it. For instance, employee participation in planning, decision making, and quality control at the Chevrolet Gear and Axle plant in Detroit resulted in increased employee concern for quality and a greater commitment to meeting standards.

Develop Verification Procedures Multiple standards and information systems provide checks and balances in control and allow the organization to verify the accuracy of performance indicators. Suppose a production manager argues that she failed to meet a certain cost standard because of increased prices of raw materials. A properly designed inventory control system will either support or contradict her explanation. Suppose that an employee who was fired for excessive absences argues that he was not absent "for a long time." An effective human resource control system should have records that support the termination. Resistance to control declines because these verification procedures protect both employees and management. If the production manager's claim about the rising cost of raw materials is supported by the inventory control records, she will not be held solely accountable for failing to meet the cost standard, and some action probably will be taken to lower the cost of raw materials.

SUMMARY OF LEARNING OBJECTIVES AND KEY POINTS

1. Explain the purpose of control, identify different types of control, and describe the steps in the control process.

   - Control is the regulation of organizational activities so that some targeted element of performance remains within acceptable limits.

   - Control provides ways to adapt to environmental change, to limit the accumulation of errors, to cope with organizational complexity, and to minimize costs.

   - Control can focus on financial, physical, information, and human resources and includes operations, financial, structural, and strategic levels.

   - Control is the function of managers, the controller, and, increasingly, operating employees.

     - Steps in the control process are
     - to establish standards of expected performance.
     - to measure actual performance.
     - to compare performance to the standards.
     - to evaluate the comparison and take appropriate action.

2. Identify and explain the three forms of operations control.

   - Operations control focuses on the processes the organization uses to transform resources into products or services.

   - Preliminary control is concerned with the resources that serve as inputs to the system.

   - Screening control is concerned with the transformation processes used by the organization.

   - Postaction control is concerned with the outputs of the organization.

   - Most organizations need multiple control systems because no one system can provide adequate control.

3. Describe budgets and other tools for financial control.

   - Financial control focuses on controlling the organization's financial resources.

   - The foundation of financial control is budgets, which are plans expressed in numerical terms.

- Most organizations rely on financial, operating, and nonmonetary budgets.
- Financial statements, various kinds of ratios, and external and internal audits are also important tools organizations use as part of financial control.

4. Identify and distinguish between two opposing forms of structural control.

- Structural control addresses how well an organization's structural elements serve their intended purpose.
- Two basic forms of structural control are bureaucratic and decentralized control.
- Bureaucratic control is relatively formal and mechanistic.
- Decentralized control is informal and organic.
- Most organizations use a form of organizational control somewhere between total bureaucratic and total decentralized control.

5. Discuss the relationship between strategy and control.

- Strategic control focuses on how effectively the organization's strategies are succeeding in helping the organization meet its goals.

- The integration of strategy and control is generally achieved through organization structure, leadership, technology, human resources, and information and operational control systems.
- International strategic control is generally a question of balance between centralization and decentralization.

6. Identify characteristics of effective control, why people resist control, and how managers can overcome this resistance.

- One way to increase the effectiveness of control is to fully integrate planning and control.
- The control system should also be as flexible, accurate, timely, and objective as possible.
- Employees may resist organizational controls because of overcontrol, inappropriate focus, rewards for inefficiency, and a desire to avoid accountability.
- Managers can overcome this resistance by improving the effectiveness of controls and by allowing employee participation and developing verification procedures.

DISCUSSION QUESTIONS

Questions for Review

1. What is the purpose of organizational control? Why is it important?
2. What are the different levels of control? What are the relationships between the different levels?
3. Describe how a budget is created in most organizations. How does a budget help a manager with financial control?
4. Describe the differences between bureaucratic and decentralized control. What are the advantages and disadvantages of each?
5. Why do some people resist control? How can managers help overcome this resistance?

Questions for Analysis

1. How can a manager determine whether his or her firm needs improvement in control? If improvement is needed, how can the manager tell what type of control needs improvement (operations, financial, structural, or strategic)? Describe some steps a manager can take to improve each of these types of control.
2. One company uses strict performance standards. Another has standards that are more flexible. What are the advantages and disadvantages of each system?
3. Are the differences in bureaucratic control and decentralized control related to differences in organization structure? If so, how? If not, why not? (The terms do sound similar to those used to discuss the organizing process.)

4. Many organizations today are involving lower-level employees in control. Give at least two examples of specific actions that a lower-level worker could do to help his or her organization better adapt to environmental change. Then do the same for limiting the accumulation of error, coping with organizational complexity, and minimizing costs.

5. Describe ways that the top management team, midlevel managers, and operating employees can participate in each step of the control process. Do all participate equally in each step, or are some steps better suited for personnel at one level? Explain your answer.

BUILDING EFFECTIVE TIME MANAGEMENT SKILLS

Exercise Overview

Not surprisingly, *time management skills*—which are the ability to prioritize tasks, to work efficiently, and to delegate appropriately—play a major role in performing the control function: Managers can use time management skills to control their own work activities more effectively. The purpose of this exercise is to demonstrate the relationship between time management skills and the process of controlling workplace activities.

Exercise Background

You're a middle manager in a small manufacturing plant. Today is Monday, and you've just returned from a week's vacation. The first thing you discover is that your assistant won't be in today (his aunt died, and he's out of town at the funeral). He did, however, leave you the following note:

Dear Boss:
Sorry about not being here today. I will be back tomorrow. In the meantime, here are some things you need to know:

Ms. Glinski [your boss] wants to see you today at 4:00.

The shop steward wants to see you as soon as possible about a labor problem.

Mr. Bateman [one of your big customers] has a complaint about a recent shipment.

Ms. Ferris [one of your major suppliers] wants to discuss a change in delivery schedules.

Mr. Prescott from the Chamber of Commerce wants you to attend a breakfast meeting on Wednesday to discuss our expansion plans.

The legal office wants to discuss our upcoming OSHA inspection.

Human resources wants to know when you can interview someone for the new supervisor's position.

Jack Williams, the machinist you fired last month, has been hanging around the parking lot, and his presence is making some employees uncomfortable.

Exercise Task

Review the information above, then prioritize the work that needs to be done by sorting the information into three categories: *very timely*, *moderately timely*, and *less timely*. Then address the following questions.

1. Are *importance* and *timeliness* the same thing?

2. What additional information do you need before you can begin to prioritize all of these demands on your time?

3. How would your approach differ if your assistant were in the office?

BUILDING EFFECTIVE TECHNICAL SKILLS

Exercise Overview

Technical skills are necessary to understand or perform the specific kind of work that an organization does. This exercise allows you to develop the technical skills needed to construct and evaluate the effectiveness of a budget.

Exercise Background

Although corporate budgets are obviously much more complicated, the basic processes of creating a corporate budget on the one hand and a personal budget on the other share a few important features. Both, for instance, begin with estimations of inflow and outflow. In addition, both compare actual results with estimated results, and both culminate in plans for corrective action.

Exercise Task

1. Prepare lists of your *estimated* expenditures and income for one month. Remember: You're dealing with budgeted amounts, not the amounts that you actually spend and take in. You're also dealing with figures that represent a typical month or a reasonable minimum. If, for example, you estimate that you spend $200 a month on groceries, you need to ask yourself whether that's a reasonable amount to spend on groceries for a month. If it's not, perhaps a more typical or reasonable figure is, say, $125.

   First, estimate your necessary monthly expenses for tuition, rent, car payments, childcare, food, utilities, and so on. Then estimate your income from all sources, such as wages, allowance, loans, and funds borrowed on credit cards. Calculate both totals.

2. Now write down all of your *actual* expenses and all your *actual* income over the last month. If you don't have exact figures, estimate as closely as you can. Calculate both totals.

3. Compare your *estimates* to your *actual* expenses and actual income. Are there any discrepancies? If so, what caused them?

4. Did you expect to have a surplus or a deficit for the month? Did you actually have a surplus or a deficit? What can you do to make up any deficit or manage any surplus?

5. Do you regularly use a personal budget? If yes, how is it helpful? If no, how might it be helpful?

SKILLS SELF-ASSESSMENT INSTRUMENT

Understanding Control

Introduction: Control systems must be carefully constructed for all organizations, regardless of their specific goals. The following assessment surveys your ideas about and approaches to control.

Instructions: You will agree with some of the statements and disagree with others. In some cases, making a decision may be difficult, but you should force yourself to make a choice. Record your answers next to each statement according to the following scale.

Rating Scale

4 Strongly agree
3 Somewhat agree
2 Somewhat disagree
1 Strongly disagree

____ 1. Effective controls must be unbending if they are to be used consistently.

____ 2. The most objective form of control is one that uses measures such as stock prices and rate of return on investment (ROI).

____ 3. Control is restrictive and should be avoided if at all possible.

____ 4. Controlling through rules, procedures, and budgets should not be used unless measurable standards are difficult or expensive to develop.

____ 5. Over-reliance on measurable control standards is seldom a problem for business organizations.

____ 6. Organizations should encourage the development of individual self-control.

____ 7. Organizations tend to try to establish behavioral controls as the first type of control to be used.

____ 8. The easiest and least costly form of control is output or quantity control.

____ 9. Short-run efficiency and long-run effectiveness result from the use of similar control standards.

_____ 10. Controlling by taking into account return on investment (ROI) and using stock prices in making control decisions are ways of ensuring that a business organization is responding to its external market.

_____ 11. Self-control should be relied on to replace other forms of control.

_____ 12. Controls such as return on investment (ROI) are more appropriate for corporations and business units than for small groups or individuals.

_____ 13. Control is unnecessary in a well-managed organization.

_____ 14. The use of output or quantity controls can lead to unintended or unfortunate consequences.

_____ 15. Standards of control do not depend on which constituency is being considered.

_____ 16. Controlling through the use of rules, procedures, and budgets can lead to rigidity and to a loss of creativity in an organization.

_____ 17. Different forms of control cannot be used at the same time. An organization must decide how it is going to control and stick to that method.

_____ 18. Setting across-the-board output or quantity targets for divisions within a company can lead to destructive results.

_____ 19. Control through rules, procedures, and budgets is generally not very costly.

_____ 20. Reliance on individual self-control can lead to problems with integration and communication.

Source: Exercise adapted from Chapter 12, pp. 380–395 in Charles W. Hill and Gareth R. Jones, Strategic Management, *Fourth Edition. © 1998 by Houghton Mifflin Company. Used by permission.*

EXPERIENTIAL EXERCISE

Control Systems at State U.

Purpose: This exercise offers you an opportunity to practice analyzing an organization's need for controls. You also will describe likely challenges to implementation and list ways to overcome resistance to control.

Introduction: The case below represents an organization with seriously deficient control systems, which is rather unrealistic. However, most organizations do suffer from one or more control efforts that are lacking or ineffective. In addition, implementing controls is usually more difficult than simply diagnosing the need for controls, especially when organization members resist the control.

Instructions:
Step 1: The instructor will divide the class into small groups. Read the University Control Problem short case, below.

The University Control Problem

You are committee appointed by the State University Student Council to help the new president deal with a number of problems that have plagued the campus for years. For example, the university regularly runs out of funds before the academic year ends, causing major disruptions of student services. In fact, some departments seem to have no knowledge of how much money they need or how much they have spent. Students are upset because tuition fees are constantly being changed in an effort to match the university's varying demands for money. Department chairs have no idea how many students are being admitted, so they never schedule the appropriate number of courses. Some buildings are in bad physical shape. Classrooms are assigned to departments, and some classrooms seem to sit empty while others are overcrowded. There seems to be an oversupply of research equipment but a shortage of computer equipment for students. Some schools, such as the business school, don't have enough faculty to teach their classes, while some departments in liberal arts have surplus faculty with no students to teach.

Step 2: As a small group, reach consensus about how to complete the University Control Matrix, below. Identify the different controls that might be established for each of the four resources—physical, financial, human, and information—and remember to consider each type of control. Preliminary controls focus on inputs into the university. Screening controls act upon the university's transformation processes. Postaction controls control the university's outputs.

Step 3: As a small group, develop responses to the Discussion Questions, below. Discuss your responses with the class.

The University Control Matrix

System Stages	Physical Resources	Financial Resources	Human Resources	Information Resources
Preliminary Controls				
Screening Controls				
Postaction Controls				

Discussion Questions:

1. Which of the recommended controls may be the hardest to implement? To manage?

2. Will the controls receive some form of resistance? If so, describe which organization members are likely to resist and the likely form of that resistance.

Source: Adapted from Morable, *Exercises in Management*, to accompany Griffin, *Management*, 8th edition.

YOU MAKE THE CALL

Facets of Jamie Dimon's Control Strategy at J.P. Morgan Chase

1. In what ways is Dimon's approach to management pretty much what you'd expect of a top-level manager in the financial industry? In what ways is it different from what you'd expect?

2. As a consultant hired by Dimon, you must submit a candid critique of his management of J.P. Morgan Chase. What will be your main points?

3. Under what circumstances might Dimon need to change his approach to organizational control?

4. Do you think that Dimon's approach to control would work in other industries? Why or why not?

5. Explain how Dimon has practiced each of the following levels of control at J.P. Morgan Chase: (a) operations, (b) financial, (c) structural, and (d) strategic.

6. What aspects of Dimon's approach to control were important in steering J.P. Morgan Chase through the subprime crisis that crippled or toppled other financial institutions?

CHAPTER 10

OPERATIONS, QUALITY, AND PRODUCTIVITY

LEARNING OBJECTIVES

After studying this chapter, you should be able to:

1 Describe and explain the nature of operations management.

2 Identify and discuss the components involved in designing effective operations systems.

3 Discuss organizational technologies and their role in operations management.

4 Identify and discuss the components involved in implementing operations systems through supply chain management.

5 Explain the meaning and importance of managing quality and total quality management.

6 Explain the meaning and importance of managing productivity, productivity trends, and ways to improve productivity.

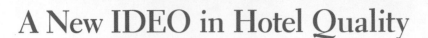

FIRST.THINGS FIRST

A New IDEO in Hotel Quality

As any experienced luxury traveler can tell you, it's not hard to find an elegant hotel in New York City. The landmark art-deco Waldorf-Astoria, the storied French Renaissance-style Plaza, and Marriott's Ritz-Carlton, heir to a legendary name in luxury brands, for example, are available for nightly rates of $500 and up. "Our clientele," says Ritz-Carlton president Simon Cooper, "is willing to pay for that quality of service," as are guests at the so-called boutique hotels—fashionable stop-overs featuring playful modern designs—that first became popular in New York in the 1990s. (At least under normal economic circumstances; right now, they only have to pay $300 and up.)

But what about travelers who aren't willing or able to pay such premium prices? Unfortunately, they may have a little trouble finding a hotel of suitable "quality" in New York. Rates are high and rooms are tiny because New York real estate is expensive. Hotel restaurants and bars may be plush, but in-room amenities such as refrigerators and even bathtubs

"[Companies are] having to think about designing from the outside in. They have to think more about the customer experience and then figure out how to make sense of that for the business."

—FRAN SAMALIONIS, HEAD OF SERVICE DESIGN AND INNOVATION AT IDEO

are scarce. In addition, new-hotel construction is limited, and high occupancy rates regularly drive up room prices. (Again, under normal economic circumstances; at present, occupancy rates are down to about 85 percent.) Perhaps most important, according to *Frommer's New York City*, "[T]here just isn't the range of properties you'd find even in other expensive markets like London and Paris. You've got fleabags, you've got palaces—and not a whole lot in

Hotel operators like Marriott are always looking for ways to attract more guests and build traveler loyalty. When Marriott was developing its chain of TownePlace Suites, researchers determined that the typical guest in the target market segment wanted a nice desk to work on, a homey lobby, and a connection to the local community. It then successfully incorporated these elements into the design of its TownePlace Suites hotels.

between." As a result, although many family and business travelers would be perfectly willing to accept as a "quality" hotel one that offers modest features such as safety, cleanliness, and comfort, they comprise a segment that's decidedly underserved in the New York hospitality market.

Granted, a few hotel operators have begun to target this segment by offering accommodations designed for people who are neither princes nor paupers. Moderately priced chain hotels such as Courtyard by Marriott and Holiday Inn Express have entered the market, as have mid-level brands. Prices for both types of hotels are under $200, a steal for pricey New York, but the number of rooms of "mid-market" quality isn't adequate to serve the needs of the so-called mid-tier customer segment.

Interestingly, some operators have actually done a little consumer research to get a more accurate idea of just what constitutes "quality" among their customers. Westin Hotels, for example, which is principally an operator of upscale hotels, found that only 6 percent of its guests wanted smoking rooms—and that, of those, 90 percent wanted to quit. So it converted all of its rooms to nonsmoking—a change requiring mainly thorough cleaning and linen replacement. Other changes prompted by research include a healthier menu and relaxing fragrances and music. "We view our hotels as a retreat from the rigor of travel," says Westin vice president Sue Brush. "At Westin, we strive to offer a spectrum of products, services, and personal touches that will help our guests walk out of our hotels feeling better than when they arrived."

But again, what about "mid-tier" customers? For what kind of "quality" are they in the market? Can the hotel industry provide "quality" rooms for these customers? It may not be the solution to the problem of supplying enough rooms over the long run, but consider the approach taken by Marriott International when it wanted to launch TownePlace Suites, a chain of extended-stay hotels catering specifically to the needs of one significant segment of mid-tier customers—guests who stay for periods longer than a few nights. To research these needs, Marriott hired IDEO, a California-based consulting firm that helps companies design products, services, and environments. The challenge, as IDEO saw it, was the fact that "tradition prevails

within many hospitality spaces and services, making improvements difficult to identify and implement across individually managed locations." Facilities, in other words, had traditionally been designed "from the inside out"—by operators who projected consumer needs and proceeded to design customer experiences catering to those projected needs. Today, however, says, IDEO's Fran Samalionis, "they're having to think about designing from the outside in. They have to think more about the customer experience and then figure out how to make sense of that for the business."

How does IDEO design a chain of hotels (or anything else) from the outside in? One of the first steps is to assemble what IDEO calls a "human-factor" team—a group of people trained in anthropology, sociology, and other social sciences who are assigned to follow customers around and observe their actual everyday behavior in conjunction with the product. They also give consumers cameras to make photo journals, ask them questions, and engage them in conversations to find out as much as they can about their product experiences.

As expected, what IDEO found out about hotel guest experiences was sometimes obvious, sometimes enlightening. Researchers learned, for example, that extended-stay guests are on the road because of work—because they have to be, not because they want to be. They have to get work done, so they prefer to have desks in their rooms but will use their beds as impromptu substitutes. Like most tourists, on the other hand, they aren't interested in food service because they want to sample local restaurants, and they have no use for sumptuous lobbies.

Once this preliminary research was done, IDEO drew up a profile of the "brand's renewed identity" and "a plan for enabling more meaningful customer relationships." For the Marriott project, the plan (or "experience blueprint") identified "five touchpoints of the guest journey" at an extended-stay hotel—the basic insights from which designers could create new sets of services, spaces, and experiences. For TownePlace Suites, the blueprint called for a lobby that conveyed more of a homelike than a hotel-like experience. There would thus be a pantry stocked with local foods, and there would also be a "map wall" featuring recommendations from other guests on the best area restaurants and other facilities, such as the best places to go jogging.

Guestrooms would be spaces for both working and living, with certain features of an office integrated into the bedroom layout.

Marriott now operates 166 TownePlace Suites around the country, but unfortunately, there are none among its more than 30 hotels in New York. And there aren't likely to be any in the near future. Industry-wide, construction is currently under way to add 20 percent more rooms to the 77,000 now available in the city, but virtually all these projects were finalized by mid-2007, and since the onset of the global credit crisis, there's been a substantial decline in both planning new projects and proceeding with those in early stages of development.

In addition, since the recession hit in earnest in the fall of 2008, New York hotel rates have suffered the steepest decline of any major U.S. city. In April 2009, the city's rates declined 26 percent to $224, down $78 from the previous year though still the highest in the country. In addition, says Fritz van Paasschen, CEO of Starwood Hotels & Resorts, which runs Westin, Sheraton, and other "quality" chains, "we'll have a hard time raising rates again. We learned after 9/11 how hard that is." On the upside, observes Stephen Joyce, head of Choice Hotels International, "extended stay is holding up as good as anything we have. It's one of the bright spots of the industry." Relatively bright, anyway: Nationwide, first-quarter revenues at extended-stay hotels declined only 14.4 percent, compared with a decline of 17.4 percent for the industry as a whole.[1]

Managers in the hotel industry are beginning to appreciate the importance of meeting customer needs—most often an optimal blend of price, location, and amenities. Indeed, as is the case in most industries, hotel managers are rethinking all aspects of their operations as they strive to improve quality and boost productivity.

In this chapter, we explore operations management, quality, and productivity. We first introduce operations management and discuss its role in general management and organizational strategy. The next three sections discuss the design of operations systems, organizational technologies, and implementing operations systems. We then introduce and discuss various issues in managing for quality and total quality. Finally, we discuss productivity, which is closely related to quality.

THE NATURE OF OPERATIONS MANAGEMENT

Operations management is at the core of what organizations do as they add value and create products and services. But what exactly are operations? And how are they managed? **Operations management** is the set of managerial activities used by an organization to transform resource inputs into products and services. When Dell Computer buys electronic components, assembles them into PCs, and then ships them to customers, it is engaging in operations management. When a Pizza Hut employee orders food ingredients and paper products and then combines dough, cheese, and tomato paste to create a pizza, he or she is engaging in operations management.

operations management
The total set of managerial activities used by an organization to transform resource inputs into products, services, or both

The Importance of Operations

Operations is an important functional concern for organizations because efficient and effective management of operations goes a long way toward ensuring competitiveness and overall organizational performance, as well as quality and productivity. Inefficient or ineffective operations management, on the other hand, will almost inevitably lead to poorer performance and lower levels of both quality and productivity.

In an economic sense, operations management creates value and utility of one type or another, depending on the nature of the firm's products or services. If the product is a physical good, such as a Harley-Davidson motorcycle, operations creates value and provides form utility by combining many dissimilar inputs (sheet metal, rubber, paint, combustion engines, and human skills) to make something (a motorcycle) that is more valuable than the actual cost of the inputs used to create it. The inputs are converted from their incoming form into a new physical form. This conversion is typical of manufacturing operations and essentially reflects the organization's technology.

In contrast, the operations activities of American Airlines create value and provide time and place utility through its services. The airline transports passengers and freight according to agreed-upon departure and arrival places and times. Other service operations, such as a Coors beer distributorship or a Gap retail store, create value and provide place and possession utility by bringing together the customer and products made by others. Although the organizations in these examples produce different kinds of products or services, their operations processes share many important features.[2]

Manufacturing and Production Operations

Because manufacturing once dominated U.S. industry, the entire area of operations management used to be called *production management*. **Manufacturing** is a form of business that combines and transforms resources into tangible outcomes that are then sold to others. The Goodyear Tire & Rubber Company is a manufacturer because it combines rubber and chemical compounds and uses blending equipment and molding machines to create tires. Broyhill is a manufacturer because it buys wood and metal components, pads, and fabric and then combines them to make furniture.

During the 1970s, manufacturing entered a long period of decline in the United States, primarily because of foreign competition. U.S. firms had grown lax and sluggish, and new foreign competitors came onto the scene with better equipment and much higher levels of efficiency. For example, steel companies in the Far East were able to produce high-quality steel for much lower prices than U.S. companies such as Bethlehem Steel and U.S. Steel (now USX Corporation). Faced with a battle for survival, many companies underwent a long and difficult period of change by eliminating waste and transforming themselves into leaner and more efficient and responsive entities. They reduced their workforces dramatically, closed antiquated or unnecessary plants, and modernized their remaining plants. In the last decade, their efforts have started to pay dividends, as U.S. businesses have regained their competitive positions in many different industries. Although manufacturers from other parts of the world are still formidable competitors, and U.S. firms may never again be competitive in some markets, the overall picture is much better than it was just a few years ago. And prospects continue to look bright.[3]

COPYRIGHT © JEFF GREENBERG / PHOTOEDIT

The service sector has grown tremendously and become a major part of the U.S. economy. Services provide utility rather than tangible manufactured goods. Banks, accounting firms, and food service operators are major components of the service sector. This banquet staff, for instance, is preparing salads for a major social function. Interestingly, one factor that has helped spur growth in the service sector is the application of operations techniques developed in the manufacturing sector. Preparation of these salads, for instance, is essentially being done with assembly line technology.

manufacturing
A form of business that combines and transforms resource inputs into tangible outcomes

Service Operations

During the decline of the manufacturing sector, a tremendous growth in the service sector kept the U.S. economy from declining at the same rate. A **service organization** is one that transforms resources into an intangible output and creates time or place utility for its customers. For example, Merrill Lynch makes stock transactions for its customers, Avis leases cars to its customers, and local hairdressers cut clients' hair. In 1947, the service sector was responsible for less than half of the U.S. gross national product (GNP). By 1975, however, this figure reached 65 percent, and by 2010 it was over 80 percent. The service sector has been responsible for almost 90 percent of all new jobs created in the United States since the early 1990s. Managers have come to see that many of the tools, techniques, and methods that are used in a factory are also useful to a service firm. For example, managers of automobile plants and hair salons both have to decide how to design their facilities, identify the best locations for them, determine optimal capacities, make decisions about inventory storage, set procedures for purchasing raw materials, and set standards for productivity and quality.

The Role of Operations in Organizational Strategy

It should be clear by this point that operations management is very important to organizations. Beyond its direct impact on factors such as competitiveness, quality, and productivity, it also directly influences the organization's overall level of effectiveness. For example, the deceptively simple strategic decision of whether to stress high quality regardless of cost, lowest possible cost regardless of quality, or some combination of the two has numerous important implications. A highest-possible quality strategy will dictate state-of-the-art technology and rigorous control of product design and materials specifications. A combination strategy might call for lower-grade technology and less concern about product design and materials specifications. Just as strategy affects operations management, operations management affects strategy. Suppose that a firm decides to upgrade the quality of its products or services. The organization's ability to implement the decision is dependent in part on current production capabilities and other resources. If existing technology will not permit higher-quality work, and if the organization lacks the resources to replace its technology, increasing quality to the desired new standards will be difficult.

DESIGNING OPERATIONS SYSTEMS

The problems, challenges, and opportunities faced by operations managers revolve around the acquisition and utilization of resources for conversion. Their goals include both efficiency and effectiveness. A number of issues and decisions must be addressed as operations systems are designed. The most basic ones are the product–service mix, capacity, and facilities.

service organization
An organization that transforms resources into an intangible output and creates time or place utility for its customers

product–service mix
How many and what kinds of products or services (or both) to offer

Determining the Product–Service Mix

A natural starting point in designing operations systems is determining the **product–service mix**. This decision flows from corporate, business, and marketing strategies. Managers have to make a number of decisions about their products and services, starting with how many and what kinds to offer.[4] Procter & Gamble, for example, makes regular, tartar control, gel, and various other formulas of Crest toothpaste and packages them in several different sizes of tubes, pumps, and other dispensers. Similarly, workers at Subway sandwich shops can combine different breads, vegetables, meats, and condiments to create hundreds of different kinds of sandwiches. Decisions have also to be made regarding the level of quality desired, the optimal cost of each product or service, and exactly how each is to be designed. GE recently reduced the number of parts in its industrial circuit breakers from 28,000 to 1,275. This whole process was achieved by carefully analyzing product design and production methods.

Capacity Decisions

The **capacity** decision involves choosing the amount of products, services, or both that can be produced by the organization. Determining whether to build a factory capable of making 5,000 or 8,000 units per day is a capacity decision. So, too, is deciding whether to build a restaurant with 100 or 150 seats, or a bank with five or ten teller stations. The capacity decision is truly a high-risk one because of the uncertainties of future product demand and the large monetary stakes involved. An organization that builds capacity exceeding its needs may commit resources (capital investment) that will never be recovered. Alternatively, an organization can build a facility with a smaller capacity than expected demand. Doing so may result in lost market opportunities, but it may also free capital resources for use elsewhere in the organization.

A major consideration in determining capacity is demand. A company operating with fairly constant monthly demand might build a plant capable of producing an amount each month roughly equivalent to its demand. But if its market is characterized by seasonal fluctuations, building a smaller plant to meet normal demand and then adding extra shifts staffed with temporary workers or paying permanent workers extra to work more hours during peak periods might be the most effective choice. Likewise, a restaurant that needs 150 seats for Saturday night but never needs more than 100 at any other time during the week would probably be foolish to expand to 150 seats. During the rest of the week, it must still pay to light, heat, cool, and clean the excess capacity. Many customer service departments have tried to improve their capacity to deal with customers while also lowering costs by using automated voice prompts to direct callers to the right representative.

Facilities Decisions

Facilities are the physical locations where products or services are created, stored, and distributed. Major decisions pertain to facilities location and facilities layout.

Location   Location is the physical positioning or geographic site of facilities and must be determined by the needs and requirements of the organization. A company that relies heavily on railroads for transportation needs to be located close to rail facilities. GE decided that it did not need six plants to make circuit breakers, so it invested heavily in automating one plant and closed the other five. Different organizations in the same industry may have different facilities requirements. Benetton uses only one distribution center for the entire world, whereas Wal-Mart has several distribution centers in the United States alone. A retail business must choose its location very carefully to be convenient for consumers.

capacity
The amount of products, services, or both that can be produced by an organization

facilities
The physical locations where products or services are created, stored, and distributed

location
The physical positioning or geographic site of facilities

layout
The physical configuration of facilities, the arrangement of equipment within facilities, or both

product layout
A physical configuration of facilities arranged around the product; used when large quantities of a single product are needed

process layout
A physical configuration of facilities arranged around the process; used in facilities that create or process a variety of products

Layout The choice of physical configuration, or the **layout**, of facilities is closely related to other operations decisions. The three entirely different layout alternatives shown in Figure 10.1 help demonstrate the importance of the layout decision. A **product layout** is appropriate when large quantities of a single product are needed. It makes sense to custom-design a straight-line flow of work for a product when a specific task is performed at each workstation as each unit flows past. Most assembly lines use this format. For example, Dell's personal computer factories use a product layout.

Process layouts are used in operations settings that create or process a variety of products. Auto repair shops and healthcare clinics are good examples. Each car and each person is a separate "product." The needs of each incoming job are diagnosed as it enters the operations system, and the job is routed through the unique sequence of workstations needed to create the desired finished product. In a process layout, each type of conversion task is centralized in a single workstation or department. All welding is done in one designated shop location, and any car that requires welding is moved to that area. This setup is in contrast to the product layout, in which several different workstations

Figure 10.1 Approaches to Facilities Layout

When a manufacturer produces large quantities of a product (such as cars or computers), it may arrange its facilities in an assembly line (product layout). In a process layout, the work (such as patients in a hospital or custom pieces of furniture) moves through various workstations. Locomotives and bridges are both manufactured in a fixed-position layout.

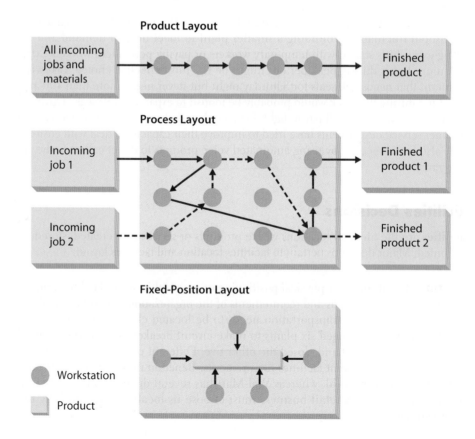

may perform welding operations if the conversion task sequence so dictates. Similarly, in a hospital, all X-rays are done in one location, all surgeries in another, and all physical therapy in yet another. Patients are moved from location to location to get the services they need.

The **fixed-position layout** is used when the organization is creating a few very large and complex products. Aircraft manufacturers like Boeing and shipbuilders like Newport News use this method. An assembly line capable of moving one of Boeing's new 787 aircraft would require an enormous plant, so instead the airplane shell itself remains stationary, and people and machines move around it as it is assembled.

The cellular layout is a relatively new approach to facilities design. **Cellular layouts** are used when families of products can follow similar flow paths. A clothing manufacturer, for example, might create a cell, or designated area, dedicated to making a family of pockets, such as pockets for shirts, coats, blouses, and slacks. Although each kind of pocket is unique, the same basic equipment and methods are used to make all of them. Hence, all pockets might be made in the same area and then delivered directly to different product layout assembly areas where the shirts, coats, blouses, and slacks are actually being assembled.

ORGANIZATIONAL TECHNOLOGIES

One central element of effective operations management is technology. In Chapter 6, we defined **technology** as the set of processes and systems used by organizations to convert resources into products or services.

Manufacturing Technology

Numerous forms of manufacturing technology are used in organizations. In Chapter 6, we discussed the research of Joan Woodward. Recall that Woodward identified three forms of technology—unit or small batch, large batch or mass production, and continuous process.[5] Each form of technology was thought to be associated with a specific type of organization structure. Of course, newer forms of technology not considered by Woodward also warrant attention. Two of these are automation and computer-assisted manufacturing.

Automation Automation is the process of designing work so that it can be completely or almost completely performed by machines. Because automated machines operate quickly and make few errors, they increase the amount of work that can be done. Thus automation helps to improve products and services, and fosters innovation. Automation is the most recent step in the development of machines and machine-controlling devices. Machine-controlling devices have been around since the 1700s. James Watt, a Scottish engineer, invented a mechanical speed control to regulate the speed of steam engines in 1787. The Jacquard loom, developed by the French inventor Joseph-Marie Jacquard, was controlled by paper cards with holes punched in them. Early accounting and computing equipment was controlled by similar punched cards.

Automation relies on feedback, information, sensors, and a control mechanism. Feedback is the flow of information from the machine back to the sensor. Sensors are the parts of the system that gather information and compare it to preset standards. The control mechanism is the device that sends instructions to the automatic machine.

fixed-position layout
A physical configuration of facilities arranged around a single work area; used for the manufacture of large and complex products such as airplanes

cellular layout
A physical configuration of facilities used when families of products can follow similar flow paths

technology
The set of processes and systems used by organizations to convert resources into products or services

automation
The process of designing work so that it can be completely or almost completely performed by machines

Figure 10.2 A Simple Automatic Control Mechanism

All automation includes feedback, information, sensors, and a control mechanism. A simple thermostat is an example of automation. Another example is Benetton's distribution center in Italy. Orders are received, items pulled from stock and packaged for shipment, and invoices prepared and transmitted, with no human intervention.

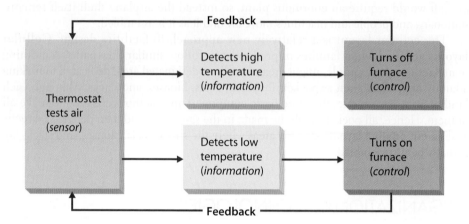

Early automatic machines were primitive, and the use of automation was relatively slow to develop. These elements are illustrated by the example in Figure 10.2. A thermostat has sensors that monitor air temperature and compare it to a preset low value. If the air temperature falls below the preset value, the thermostat sends an electrical signal to the furnace, turning it on. The furnace heats the air. When the sensors detect that the air temperature has reached a value higher than the low preset value, the thermostat stops the furnace. The last step (shutting off the furnace) is known as *feedback*, a critical component of any automated operation.

The big move to automate factories began during World War II. The shortage of skilled workers and the development of high-speed computers combined to bring about a tremendous interest in automation. Programmable automation (the use of computers to control machines) was introduced during this era, far outstripping conventional automation (the use of mechanical or electromechanical devices to control machines). The automobile industry began to use automatic machines for a variety of jobs. In fact, the term *automation* came into use in the 1950s in the automobile industry. The chemical and oil-refining industries also began to use computers to regulate production. During the 1990s, automation became a major element in the manufacture of computers and computer components, such as electronic chips and circuits. It is this computerized, or programmable, automation that presents the greatest opportunities and challenges for management today.

The impact of automation on people in the workplace is complex. In the short term, people whose jobs are automated may find themselves without a job. In the long term, however, more jobs are created than are lost. Nevertheless, not all companies are able to help displaced workers find new jobs, so the human costs are sometimes high. In the coal industry, for instance, automation has been used primarily in mining. The output per miner has risen dramatically from the 1950s on. The demand for coal, however, has decreased, and productivity gains resulting from automation have lessened the need for miners. Consequently, many workers have lost their jobs, and the industry has not been able to absorb them. In contrast, in the electronics industry, the rising demand for products has led to increasing employment opportunities despite the use of automation.[6]

Computer-Assisted Manufacturing Current extensions of automation generally revolve around **computer-assisted manufacturing**—a technology that relies on computers to design or manufacture products. One type of computer-assisted manufacturing is *computer-aided design (CAD)*—the use of computers to design parts and complete products and to simulate performance so that prototypes need not be constructed. Boeing uses CAD technology to study hydraulic tubing in its commercial aircraft. Japan's automotive industry uses CAD to speed up car design. GE used CAD to change the design of circuit breakers, and Benetton uses CAD to design new styles and products. Oneida, the table flatware firm, uses CAD to design new flatware patterns; for example, it can design a new spoon in a single day. CAD is usually combined with *computer-aided manufacturing (CAM)* to ensure that the design moves smoothly to production. The production computer shares the design computer's information and is able to have machines with the proper settings ready when production is needed. A CAM system is especially useful when reorders come in because the computer can quickly produce the desired product, prepare labels and copies of orders, and send the product out to where it is wanted.

Closely aligned with this approach is *computer-integrated manufacturing (CIM)*. In CIM, CAD and CAM are linked together, and computer networks automatically adjust machine placements and settings to enhance both the complexity and the flexibility of scheduling. In settings that use these technologies, all manufacturing activities are controlled by the computer network. Because the network can access the company's other information systems, CIM is both a powerful and a complex management control tool.

Flexible manufacturing systems (FMS) usually have robotic work units or workstations, assembly lines, and robotic carts or some other form of computer-controlled transport system to move material as needed from one part of the system to another. FMS like the one at IBM's manufacturing facility in Lexington, Kentucky, rely on computers to coordinate and integrate automated production and materials-handling facilities. And after it bought Jaguar several years ago, Ford Motor Company used FMS to transform an English factory producing low-cost Ford Escorts into a Jaguar plant making Jaguar luxury cars. Using traditional methods, the plant would have been closed, its workers laid off, and the facility virtually rebuilt from the ground up. But by using FMS, Ford was able to keep the plant open and running continuously while new equipment was being installed and its workers were being retrained in small groups.[7] Ford continues to be a pioneer in FMS as it adjusts plant capabilities to produce pickups, SUVs, or small hybrids depending on fluctuations in demand and supply.

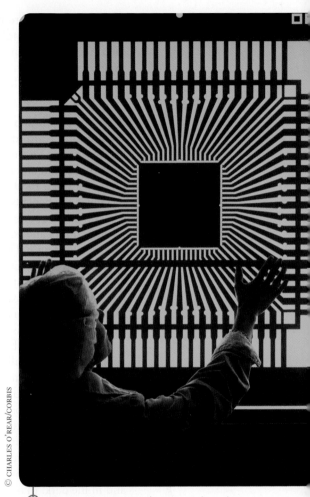

© CHARLES O'REAR/CORBIS

More and more manufacturers today rely on flexible manufacturing systems controlled by complex software algorithms. This Intel chip facility, for example, relies on flexible manufacturing systems to create most of the chips that it turns out every day. But at the end of the process, quality control inspectors like this woman check samples of the finished products to insure they have been manufactured according to the precise specifications set by both Intel and the customer.

computer-assisted manufacturing
A technology that relies on computers to design or manufacture products

These systems are not without disadvantages, however. For example, because they represent fundamental change, they also generate resistance. Additionally, because of their tremendous complexity, CAD systems are not always reliable. CIM systems are so expensive that they raise the breakeven point for firms using them. This means that the firm must operate at high levels of production and sales to be able to afford the systems.

Robotics Another trend in manufacturing technology is computerized robotics. A **robot** is any artificial device that is able to perform functions ordinarily thought to be appropriate for human beings. Robotics refers to the science and technology of the construction, maintenance, and use of robots. The use of industrial robots has steadily increased since 1980 and is expected to continue to increase slowly as more companies recognize the benefits that accrue to users of industrial robots.[8]

Welding was one of the first applications for robots, and it continues to be the area for most applications. A close second is materials handling. Other applications include machine loading and unloading, painting and finishing, assembly, casting, and machining applications such as cutting, grinding, polishing, drilling, sanding, buffing, and deburring. Daimler AG, for instance, replaced about 200 welders with 50 robots on an assembly line and increased productivity about 20 percent. The use of robots in inspection work is increasing. They can check for cracks and holes, and they can be equipped with vision systems to perform visual inspections.

Robots are also beginning to move from the factory floor to all manner of other applications. The Dallas police used a robot to apprehend a suspect who had barricaded himself in an apartment building. The robot smashed a window and reached with its mechanical arm into the building. The suspect panicked and ran outside. At the Long Beach Memorial Hospital in California, brain surgeons are assisted by a robot arm that drills into the patient's skull with excellent precision. Some newer applications involve remote work. For example, the use of robot submersibles controlled from the surface can help divers in remote locations. Surveillance robots fitted with microwave sensors can do things that a human guard cannot do, such as "seeing" through nonmetallic walls and in the dark. In other applications, automated farming (called *agrimation*) uses robot harvesters to pick fruit from a variety of trees.

Robots are also used by small manufacturers. One robot slices carpeting to fit the inside of custom vans in an upholstery shop. Another stretches balloons flat so that they can be spray-painted with slogans at a novelties company. At a jewelry company, a robot holds class rings while they are engraved by a laser. These robots are lighter, faster, stronger, and more intelligent than those used in heavy manufacturing and are the types that more and more organizations will be using in the future.

Service Technology

Service technology is also changing rapidly. And it, too, is moving more and more toward automated systems and procedures. In banking, for example, new technological breakthroughs led to automated teller machines and made it much easier to move funds between accounts or between different banks. Many people now have their paycheck deposited directly into a checking account from which many of their bills are then automatically paid. Electronic banking—where people can access their accounts, move money between accounts, and pay bills—has become commonplace. Moreover, the capabilities to do these things have been extended from personal computers to cell phones and other personal electronic communication technologies.

robot
Any artificial device that is able to perform functions ordinarily thought to be appropriate for human beings

Hotels use increasingly sophisticated technology to accept and record room reservations (other aspects of their technology are discussed in "First Things First" in this chapter). People can now, for instance, check in online and stop by the front desk only long enough to pick up their room key. Universities use new technologies to electronically store and provide access to books, scientific journals, government reports, and articles. Hospitals and other healthcare organizations use new forms of service technology to manage patient records, dispatch ambulances and emergency medical technicians (EMTs), and monitor patients' vital signs. Restaurants use technology to record and fill customer orders, order food and supplies, and prepare food. Given the increased role that service organizations are playing in today's economy, even more technological innovations are certain to be developed in the years to come.[9]

IMPLEMENTING OPERATIONS SYSTEMS THROUGH SUPPLY CHAIN MANAGEMENT

After operations systems have been properly designed and technologies developed, they must then be put into use by the organization. Their basic functional purpose is to control transformation processes to ensure that relevant goals are achieved in areas such as quality and costs. Operations management has a number of special purposes within this control framework, including purchasing and inventory management. Indeed, this area of management has become so important in recent years that a new term—*supply chain management*—has been coined. Specifically, **supply chain management** can be defined as the process of managing operations control, resource acquisition and purchasing, and inventory so as to improve overall efficiency and effectiveness.[10]

Operations Management as Control

One way of using operations management as control is to coordinate it with other functions. Monsanto Company, for example, established a consumer products division that produces and distributes fertilizers and lawn chemicals. To facilitate control, the operations function was organized as an autonomous profit center. Monsanto finds this effective because its manufacturing division is given the authority to determine not only the costs of creating the product but also the product price and the marketing program.

In terms of overall organizational control, a division like the one used by Monsanto should be held accountable only for the activities over which it has decision-making authority. It would be inappropriate, of course, to make operations accountable for profitability in an organization that stresses sales and market share over quality and productivity. Misplaced accountability results in ineffective organizational control, to say nothing of hostility and conflict. Depending on the strategic role of operations, then, operations managers are accountable for different kinds of results. For example, in an organization using bureaucratic control, accountability will be spelled out in rules and regulations. In a decentralized system, it is likely to be understood and accepted by everyone.

Within operations, managerial control ensures that resources and activities achieve primary goals such as a high percentage of on-time deliveries, low unit production cost, or high product reliability. Any control system should focus on the elements that are most crucial to goal attainment. For example, firms in which product quality is a major concern (as it is at Rolex) might adopt a screening control system to monitor the product as it is

supply chain management
The process of managing operations control, resource acquisition and purchasing, and inventory so as to improve overall efficiency and effectiveness

being created. If low-cost large-quantity is a higher priority (as it is at Timex), a postaction system might be used to identify defects at the end of the system without disrupting the manufacturing process itself.

For the past several years, Boeing has been grappling with problems in launching its latest major passenger airplane, the Boeing 787 Dreamliner. During its early development, the 787 was hailed as the most commercially successful new plane of all time. Airlines around the world preordered over 900 of the planes at a cost of $178 million each before they ever took a test flight based on its projected fuel efficiency, passenger comfort, low maintenance costs, flexibility, and other major design elements. But the first test flights for the plane were years late, largely because of supply chain issues; current projections are that the first planes will be delivered to customers in late 2010. Boeing subcontracted out the design and assembly of major components of the 787 to firms in Japan, Italy, South Carolina, and Kansas but did not impose adequate coordination across these various suppliers. As a result, subassemblies did not fit together properly, there were numerous quality and delivery issues, and myriad other problems occurred. Clearly, then, poor supply chain management can be disastrous, especially for major new products.[11]

Purchasing Management

Purchasing management, also called *procurement*, is concerned with buying the materials and resources needed to produce products and services. In many ways, purchasing is at the very heart of effective supply chain management. The purchasing manager for a retailer like Sears, Roebuck is responsible for buying the merchandise the store will sell. The purchasing manager for a manufacturer buys raw materials, parts, and machines needed by the organization. Large companies such as GE, IBM, and Siemens have large purchasing departments.[12] The manager responsible for purchasing must balance a number of constraints. Buying too much ties up capital and increases storage costs. Buying too little might lead to shortages and high reordering costs. The manager must also make sure that the quality of what is purchased meets the organization's needs, that the supplier is reliable, and that the best financial terms are negotiated.

Many firms have recently changed their approaches to purchasing as a means to lower costs and improve quality and productivity. In particular, rather than relying on hundreds or even thousands of suppliers, many companies are reducing their number of suppliers and negotiating special production delivery arrangements.[13] For example, the Honda plant in Marysville, Ohio, found a local business owner looking for a new opportunity. They negotiated an agreement whereby he would start a new company to mount car stereo speakers into plastic moldings. He delivers finished goods to the plant three times a day, and Honda buys all he can manufacture. Thus he has a stable sales base, Honda has a local and reliable supplier, and both companies benefit.

purchasing management
Buying materials and resources needed to produce products and services

inventory control
Managing the organization's raw materials, work in process, finished goods, and products in transit

Inventory Management

Inventory control, also called *materials control*, is essential for effective operations management. The four basic kinds of inventories are *raw materials*, *work in process*, *finished goods*, and *in-transit* inventories. As shown in Table 10.1, the sources of control over these inventories are as different as their purposes. Work-in-process inventories, for example, are made up of partially completed products that need further processing; they are controlled by the shop floor system. In contrast, the quantities and costs of finished-goods inventories are under the control of the overall production scheduling system,

Table 10.1
Inventory Types, Purposes, and Sources of Control

Type	Purpose	Source of Control
Raw materials	Provide the materials needed to make the product	Purchasing models and systems
Work in process	Enable overall production to be divided into stages of manageable size	Shop floor control systems
Finished goods	Provide ready supply of products on customer demand and enable long, efficient production runs	High-level production scheduling systems in conjunction with marketing
In transit (pipeline)	Distribute products to customers	Transportation and distribution control systems

which is determined by high-level planning decisions. In-transit inventories are controlled by the transportation and distribution systems.

Like most other areas of operations management, inventory management changed notably in recent years. One particularly important breakthrough is the **just-in-time (JIT) method**. JIT is a recent breakthrough in inventory management. With JIT inventory systems, materials arrive just as they are needed. JIT therefore helps an organization control its raw materials inventory by reducing the amount of space it must devote to storage.

First popularized by the Japanese, the JIT system reduces the organization's investment in storage space for raw materials and in the materials themselves. Historically, manufacturers built large storage areas and filled them with materials, parts, and supplies that would be needed days, weeks, and even months in the future. A manager using the JIT approach orders materials and parts more often and in smaller quantities, thereby reducing investment in both storage space and actual inventory. The ideal arrangement is for materials to arrive just as they are needed—or just in time.[14]

Recall our example about the small firm that assembles stereo speakers for Honda and delivers them three times a day, making it unnecessary for Honda to carry large quantities of the speakers in inventory. In an even more striking example, Johnson Controls makes automobile seats for Mercedes and ships them by small truckloads to a Mercedes plant 75 miles away. Each shipment is scheduled to arrive two hours before it is needed. Clearly, the JIT approach requires high levels of coordination and cooperation between the company and its suppliers. If shipments arrive too early, Mercedes has no place to store them. If they arrive too late, the entire assembly line may have to be shut down, resulting in enormous expense. When properly designed and used, the JIT method controls inventory very effectively.

MANAGING TOTAL QUALITY

Quality and productivity have become major determinants of business success or failure today and are central issues in managing organizations. But, as we will see, achieving higher levels of quality is not an easy accomplishment. Simply ordering that quality be improved is about as effective as waving a magic wand.[15] The catalyst for its emergence as a mainstream management concern was foreign business, especially Japanese. And nowhere was it more visible than in the auto industry. During the energy crisis in the late 1970s, many people bought Toyotas, Hondas, and Nissans because they were more fuel-efficient than U.S. cars. Consumers soon found, however, that not only were the Japanese cars more fuel-efficient, but they were also of higher quality than U.S. cars. Parts

just-in-time (JIT) method
An inventory system that has necessary materials arriving as soon as they are needed (just in time) so that the production process is not interrupted

fit together better, the trim work was neater, and the cars were more reliable. Thus, after the energy crisis subsided, Japanese cars remained formidable competitors because of their reputation for quality.

The Meaning of Quality

The American Society for Quality Control defines **quality** as the totality of features and characteristics of a product or service that bear on its ability to satisfy stated or implied needs.[16] Quality has several different attributes. Table 10.2 lists eight basic dimensions that determine the quality of a particular product or service. For example, a product that has durability and is reliable is of higher quality than a product with less durability and reliability.

Quality is also relative. For example, a Lincoln is a higher-grade car than a Mercury Marquis, which, in turn, is a higher-grade car than a Ford Focus. The difference in quality stems from differences in design and other features. The Focus, however, is considered a high-quality car relative to its engineering specifications and price. Likewise, the Marquis and Lincoln may also be high-quality cars, given their standards and prices. Thus quality is both an absolute and a relative concept.

Quality is relevant for both products and services. Although its importance for products like cars and computers was perhaps recognized first, service firms ranging from airlines to restaurants have also come to see that quality is a vitally important determinant of their success or failure. Service quality, as we will discuss later in this chapter, has thus also become a major competitive issue in U.S. industry today.[17]

The Importance of Quality

To help underscore the importance of quality, the U.S. government created the **Malcolm Baldrige Award**, named after the former secretary of commerce who championed quality in U.S. industry. The award, administered by an agency of the Commerce Department, is

quality
The totality of features and characteristics of a product or service that bear on its ability to satisfy stated or implied needs

Malcolm Baldrige Award
Named after a former secretary of commerce, this prestigious award is given annually to firms that achieve major quality improvements

Table 10.2 **Eight Dimensions of Quality**

These eight dimensions generally capture the meaning of quality, which is a critically important ingredient to organizational success today. Understanding the basic meaning of quality is a good first step to managing it more effectively.

1. *Performance.* A product's primary operating characteristic; examples are automobile acceleration and a television's picture clarity.
2. *Features.* Supplements to a product's basic functioning characteristics, such as power windows on a car.
3. *Reliability.* A probability of not malfunctioning during a specified period.
4. *Conformance.* The degree to which a product's design and operating characteristics meet established standards.
5. *Durability.* A measure of product life.
6. *Serviceability.* The speed and ease of repair.
7. *Aesthetics.* How a product looks, feels, tastes, and smells.
8. *Perceived quality.* As seen by a customer.

Source: Reprinted by permission of *Harvard Business Review*. Exhibit from "Competing on the Eight Dimensions of Quality," by David A. Garvin, November/December 1987. © 1987 by the Harvard Business School Publishing Corporation; all rights reserved.

given annually to firms that achieve major improvements in the quality of their products or services. In other words, the award is based on changes in quality, as opposed to absolute quality. In addition, numerous other quality awards have been created. For example, the Rochester Institute of Technology and *USA Today* award their Quality Cup award not to entire organizations but to individual teams of workers within organizations. Quality is also an important concern for individual managers and organizations for three very specific reasons: competition, productivity, and costs.[18]

Competition Quality has become one of the most competitive points in business today. Ford, Daimler AG, General Motors, and Toyota, for example, each implies that its cars and trucks are higher in quality than the cars and trucks of the others. And American, Delta, and United Airlines each claims that it provides the best and most reliable service. In the wake of the economic recession that started in 2008, many businesses focused even more attention on service quality as a competitive advantage during lean times. While some firms, for example, cut their staff at customer call centers, others did not. What impact might this have? One study found that cutting four representatives at a call center of three dozen people sent the number of customers put on hold for four minutes from 0 to 80. Firms with especially strong reputations for service quality include Amazon.com, USAA (an insurance firm), Lexus, Ritz-Carlton, Ace Hardware, and Apple.[19]

Productivity Managers have also come to recognize that quality and productivity are related. In the past, many managers thought that they could increase output (productivity) only by decreasing quality. Managers today have learned the hard way that such an assumption is almost always wrong. If a firm installs a meaningful quality enhancement program, three things are likely to result. First, the number of defects is likely to decrease, causing fewer returns from customers. Second, because the number of defects goes down, resources (materials and people) dedicated to reworking flawed output will be decreased. Third, because making employees responsible for quality reduces the need for quality inspectors, the organization is able to produce more units with fewer resources.

Costs Improved quality also lowers costs. Poor quality results in higher returns from customers, high warranty costs, and lawsuits from customers injured by faulty products. Future sales are lost because of disgruntled customers. An organization with quality problems often has to increase inspection expenses just to catch defective products. We noted in Chapter 9, for example, how at one point Whistler Corporation was using 40 percent of its workforce just to fix poorly assembled radar detectors made by the other 60 percent.[20]

Total Quality Management

Once an organization makes a decision to enhance the quality of its products and services, it must then decide how to implement this decision. The most pervasive approach to managing quality has been called **total quality management (TQM)** (sometimes called **quality assurance**)—a real and meaningful effort by an organization to change its whole approach to business in order to make quality a guiding factor in everything it does.[21] Figure 10.3 highlights the major ingredients in TQM.

Strategic Commitment The starting point for TQM is a strategic commitment by top management. Such commitment is important for several reasons. First, the organizational culture must change to recognize that quality is not just an ideal but also

total quality management (TQM) (quality assurance)
A strategic commitment by top management to change its whole approach to business in order to make quality a guiding factor in everything it does

Figure 10.3 **Total Quality Management**

Quality is one of the most important issues facing organizations today. Total quality management (TQM) is a comprehensive effort to enhance an organization's product or service quality. TQM involves the five basic dimensions shown here. Each is important and must be addressed effectively if the organization expects to truly increase quality.

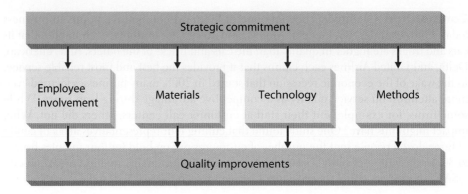

an objective goal that must be pursued.[22] Second, a decision to pursue the goal of quality carries with it some real costs—for expenditures such as new equipment and facilities. Thus, without a commitment from top management, quality improvement will prove to be just a slogan or gimmick, with little or no real change. Just a few years ago, Porsche had the lowest reliability of any automobile maker in the world. But a major commitment from top management helped turn the company around. By paying more attention to consumer preferences and using the other methods described later, Porsche shot to the top of global automobile reliability.[23]

Employee Involvement Employee involvement is another critical ingredient in TQM. Virtually all successful quality enhancement programs involve making the person responsible for doing the job responsible for making sure it is done right.[24] By definition, then, employee involvement is a critical component in improving quality. Work teams, discussed in Chapter 15, are common vehicles for increasing employee involvement.

Technology New forms of technology are also useful in TQM programs. Automation and robots, for example, can often make products with higher precision and better consistency than people. Investing in higher-grade machines capable of doing jobs more precisely and reliably often improves quality. For example, Nokia has achieved notable improvements in product quality by replacing many of its machines with new equipment. Similarly, most U.S. auto and electronics firms make regular investments in new technology to help boost quality.

Materials Another important part of TQM is improving the quality of the materials that organizations use. Suppose that a company that assembles stereos buys chips and circuits from another company. If the chips have a high failure rate, consumers will return defective stereos to the company whose nameplate appears on them, not to the company that made the chips. The stereo firm then loses in two ways: refunds back to customers and a damaged reputation. As a result, many firms have increased the quality requirements they impose on their suppliers as a way of improving the quality of their own products.

Methods   Improved methods can improve product and service quality. Methods are operating systems used by the organization during the actual transformation process. American Express Company, for example, has found ways to cut its approval time for new credit cards from 22 to just 5 days. This results in improved service quality.

TQM Tools and Techniques

Beyond the strategic context of quality, managers can also rely on several specific tools and techniques for improving quality. Among the most popular today are value-added analysis, benchmarking, outsourcing, reducing cycle times, ISO 9000:2000 and ISO 14000, statistical quality control (SQC), and Six Sigma.

Value-Added Analysis   **Value-added analysis** is the comprehensive evaluation of all work activities, materials flows, and paperwork to determine the value that they add for customers. Such an analysis often reveals wasteful or unnecessary activities that can be eliminated without jeopardizing customer service. For example, during a value-added analysis, Hewlett-Packard determined that its contracts were unnecessarily long, confusing, and hard to understand. The firm subsequently cut its standard contract form down from 20 to 2 pages and experienced an 18 percent increase in its computer sales.

Benchmarking   **Benchmarking** is the process of learning how other firms do things in an exceptionally high-quality manner. Some approaches to benchmarking are simple and straightforward. For example, Canon routinely buys copiers made by other firms and takes them apart to see how they work. This enables the firm to stay abreast of improvements and changes its competitors are using. When Ford was planning the newest version of the Taurus, it identified the 400 features customers identified as being most important to them. It then found the competing cars that did the best job on each feature. Ford's goal was to equal or surpass each of its competitors on those 400 features. Other benchmarking strategies are more indirect. For example, many firms study how L.L. Bean manages its mail-order business, how Disney recruits and trains employees, and how FedEx tracks packages for applications they can employ in their own businesses.[25]

Outsourcing   Another innovation for improving quality is **outsourcing**, which is the process of subcontracting services and operations to other firms that can perform them cheaper or better. If a business performs each and every one of its own administrative and business services and operations, it is almost certain to be doing at least some of them in an inefficient or low-quality manner. If those areas can be identified and outsourced, the firm will save money and realize a higher-quality service or operation.[26] For example, until recently Eastman Kodak handled all its own computing operations. Now, however, those operations are subcontracted to IBM, which handles all Kodak's computing. The result is higher-quality computing systems and operations at Kodak for less money than it was spending before. Firms must be careful in their outsourcing decisions, though, because service or delivery problems can lead to major complications. Boeing's new 787 aircraft, for example, has been running several months behind schedule because the firms to which Boeing has outsourced some of its production have been running late.[27] The "Ethics in Action" box discusses some of the pros and cons of IBM's reliance on outsourcing as a strategy for what's often called *global workforce optimization*.

value-added analysis
The comprehensive evaluation of all work activities, materials flows, and paperwork to determine the value that they add for customers

benchmarking
The process of learning how other firms do things in an exceptionally high-quality manner

outsourcing
Subcontracting services and operations to other firms that can perform them cheaper or better

ETHICS IN ACTION

IBM's Passage to India

IBM is perhaps the whitest of all white-collar American businesses, the one whose products are perhaps most indelibly imprinted on the global consciousness as an American brand. It's not the same company that it used to be, of course, having maneuvered itself over the last 12 or 15 years out of the manufacturing side of high tech. Today, IBM specializes in software and computer services, and for a while, this shift in focus delayed any decision on *global workforce optimization*—basically strategies for increasing labor productivity by integrating foreign workers into a company's workforce. About five years ago, however, the pressure to cut costs in a highly competitive industry convinced IBM executives that it was time to outsource its labor needs. "Our customers," explained senior vice president Robert W. Moffat Jr., "need us to put the right skills in the right place at the right time."

The right place is primarily (though not exclusively) India, and over the past six years, IBM has made substantial increases in its overseas workforce. From a staff of 9,000 in 2004, for example, IBM has increased its Indian payroll to 74,000 and is now the second-largest technical employer in India, after local outsourcing giant Wipro. It employs another 24,000 people in Brazil, Russia, and China.

The initiative, however, is about more than finding competent low-cost labor. For IBM, global workforce optimization means reorganizing an entire services workforce of 400,000 along skill lines, not merely geography. That's why the company has launched an ambitious project called Professional Marketplace, which is essentially a database of IBM's massive talent pool. Plans call for the system to identify the skills, locations, and availability of all of IBM's services, software, sales, and distribution personnel, and it's designed to ensure that the company doesn't ship an overqualified employee halfway around the world

to perform a job that could be filled by someone who costs a lot less. The system includes all of IBM's lower-cost employees in India, Brazil, and elsewhere and helps guarantee that if a job can be performed there at a lower price, it will be.

Professional Marketplace, however, doesn't automatically assign projects to staff in places such as Bangalore and Mumbai. For any project, the system relies on mathematical formulas to choose the most efficient mix of staff from any worldwide location, whether it be Tulsa, Oklahoma, where IBM maintains a pool of accounting specialists; or Yorktown Heights, New York, where it maintains a team of research scientists. Take Toronto, Canada. In the past, the process of installing software into PCs called for a single IT worker to visit each PC one at a time. Cost: $70 per PC. Today, a staff of 200 specially skilled workers in Toronto runs a software installation factory that services clients around the world. Because each installer is able to assemble complete packages for shipment over the Net, the cost is about 20 cents per PC. "Some people," explains Moffat, "think the world is centered in India, and that's it. Globalization is more than that."

Apparently, it's also Project Match, which the company announced in early 2009. In the wake of about 5,000 job cuts in January and February, IBM informed employees that "satisfactory performers who have been notified of separation from IBM U.S. or Canada" could apply for IBM jobs in India. A company spokesman explained that the offer was mainly "a vehicle for people who want to expand their life experience by working somewhere else," but there was a catch: Applicants had to be "willing to work on local terms and conditions"—that is, for local Indian wages. "Even with the lower cost of living," calculates Ron Hira, author of *Outsourcing America*, American workers "[won't] be able to save enough money to return to the U.S." "[I]t's a clear indication that IBM plans on accelerating its

Reducing Cycle Time Another popular TQM technique is reducing cycle time. **Cycle time** is the time needed by the organization to develop, make, and distribute products or services.[28] If a business can reduce its cycle time, quality will often improve. A good illustration of the power of cycle time reduction comes from GE. At one point, the firm needed six plants and three weeks to produce and deliver custom-made industrial circuit breaker boxes. By analyzing and reducing cycle time, the same product can now be delivered in three days, and only a single plant is involved. Table 10.3 identifies a number of basic suggestions that have helped companies reduce the cycle time of their operations. For example, GE found it better to start from scratch with a remodeled plant. GE also wiped out the need for approvals by eliminating most managerial positions and set up teams as a basis for organizing work. Stressing the importance of the schedule helped Motorola build a new plant and start the production of a new product in just 18 months. Nokia used to need 12 to 18 months to design new cell phone models, but can do it now in 6 months.[29]

ISO 9000:2000 and ISO 14000 Still another useful technique for improving quality is ISO 9000. **ISO 9000:2000** refers to a set of quality standards created by the International Organization for Standardization; the standards were revised and updated

cycle time
The time needed by the organization to develop, make, and distribute products or services

ISO 9000:2000
A set of quality standards created by the International Organization for Standardization and revised in 2000

Table 10.3 Guidelines for Increasing the Speed of Operations

Many organizations today are using speed for competitive advantage. Listed in the table are six common guidelines that organizations follow when they want to shorten the time they need to get things accomplished. Although not every manager can do each of these things, most managers can do at least some of them.

1. *Start from scratch.* It is usually easier than trying to do what the organization does now faster.
2. *Minimize the number of approvals needed to do something.* The fewer people who have to approve something, the faster approval will get done.
3. *Use work teams as a basis for organization.* Teamwork and cooperation work better than individual effort and conflict.
4. *Develop and adhere to a schedule.* A properly designed schedule can greatly increase speed.
5. *Do not ignore distribution.* Making something faster is only part of the battle.
6. *Integrate speed into the organization's culture.* If everyone understands the importance of speed, things will naturally get done more quickly.

Source: From *Fortune*, February 13, 1989. © 1989 Time, Inc. All rights reserved.

in 2000. These standards cover areas such as product testing, employee training, record keeping, supplier relations, and repair policies and procedures. Firms that want to meet these standards apply for certification and are audited by a firm chosen by the organization's domestic affiliate (in the United States, this is the American National Standards Institute). These auditors review every aspect of the firm's business operations in relation to the standards. Many firms report that merely preparing for an ISO 9000 audit has been helpful. Many firms today, including GE, DuPont, Eastman Kodak, British Telecom, and Philips Electronics, are urging—or in some cases requiring—that their suppliers achieve ISO 9000 certification.[30] All told, more than 159 countries have adopted ISO 9000 as a national standard, and more than 610,000 certificates of compliance have been issued. **ISO 14000** is an extension of the same concept to environmental performance. Specifically, ISO 14000 requires that firms document how they are using raw materials more efficiently, managing pollution, and reducing their impact on the environment.

Statistical Quality Control   Another quality control technique is SQC. As the term suggests, SQC is concerned primarily with managing quality.[31] Moreover, it is a set of specific statistical techniques that can be used to monitor quality. *Acceptance sampling* involves sampling finished goods to ensure that quality standards have been met. Acceptance sampling is effective only when the correct percentage of products that should be tested (for example, 2, 5, or 25 percent) is determined. This decision is especially important when the test renders the product useless. Batteries, wine, and collapsible steering wheels, for example, are consumed or destroyed during testing. Another SQC method is *in-process sampling*, which involves evaluating products during production so that needed changes can be made. The painting department of a furniture company might periodically check the tint of the paint it is using. The company can then adjust the color as necessary to conform to customer standards. The advantage of in-process sampling is that it allows problems to be detected before they accumulate.

Six Sigma   Six Sigma was developed in the 1980s for Motorola. The tool can be used by manufacturing or service organizations. The Six Sigma method tries to eliminate mistakes. Although firms rarely obtain Six Sigma quality, it does provide a challenging target. *Sigma* refers to a standard deviation, so a Six Sigma defect rate is six standard deviations above the mean rate; one sigma quality would produce 690,000 errors per million items. Obtaining three sigmas is challenging—66,000 errors per million. Six Sigma is obtained when a firm produces a mere 3.4 mistakes per million. Implementing Six Sigma requires making corrections until errors virtually disappear. At GE, the technique has saved the firm $8 billion in three years. GE is now teaching its customers, including Wal-Mart and Dell, about the approach.

ISO 14000
A set of standards for environmental performance

SQC
A set of specific statistical techniques that can be used to monitor quality; includes acceptance sampling and in-process sampling

MANAGING PRODUCTIVITY

Although the current focus on quality by U.S. companies is a relatively recent phenomenon, managers have been aware of the importance of productivity for several years. The stimulus for this attention was a recognition that the gap between productivity in the United States and productivity in other industrialized countries was narrowing. This section describes the meaning of productivity and underscores its importance. After summarizing recent productivity trends, we suggest ways that organizations can increase their productivity.

The Meaning of Productivity

In a general sense, **productivity** is an economic measure of efficiency that summarizes the value of outputs relative to the value of the inputs used to create them.[32] Productivity can be and often is assessed at different levels of analysis and in different forms.

Levels of Productivity By *level of productivity*, we mean the units of analysis used to calculate or define productivity. For example, *aggregate productivity* is the total level of productivity achieved by a country. *Industry productivity* is the total productivity achieved by all the firms in a particular industry. *Company productivity*, just as the term suggests, is the level of productivity achieved by an individual company. *Unit and individual productivity* refer to the productivity achieved by a unit or department within an organization and the level of productivity attained by a single person.

Forms of Productivity There are many different forms of productivity. *Total factor productivity* is defined by the following formula:

$$\text{Productivity} = \frac{\text{Outputs}}{\text{Inputs}}$$

Total factor productivity is an overall indicator of how well an organization uses all of its resources, such as labor, capital, materials, and energy, to create all of its products and services. The biggest problem with total factor productivity is that all the ingredients must be expressed in the same terms—dollars (it is difficult to add hours of labor to number of units of a raw material in a meaningful way). Total factor productivity also gives little insight into how things can be changed to improve productivity. Consequently, most organizations find it more useful to calculate a partial productivity ratio. Such a ratio uses only one category of resource. For example, labor productivity could be calculated by this simple formula:

$$\text{Labor productivity} = \frac{\text{Outputs}}{\text{Direct labor}}$$

PHOTODISC/GETTY IMAGES

Drive-through windows have become standard for nearly every fast food restaurant chain. Drive-throughs attract more customers because they can buy food from the convenience of their cars without having to park and come inside. For the restaurant itself, it needs fewer parking spaces and can serve customers more efficiently. As a result, labor productivity is almost always higher at fast food outlets with a drive-through window than in those without drive-throughs.

This method has two advantages. First, it is not necessary to transform the units of input into some other unit. Second, this method provides managers with specific insights into how changing different resource inputs affects productivity. Suppose that an organization can manufacture 100 units of a particular product with 20 hours of direct labor. The organization's labor productivity index is 100/20, or 5 (5 units per labor hour). Now suppose that worker efficiency is increased (through one of the ways to be discussed later in this chapter) so that the same 20 hours of labor result in the manufacture of 120 units of the product. The labor productivity index increases to 120/20, or 6 (6 units per labor hour), and the firm can see the direct results of a specific managerial action.

productivity
An economic measure of efficiency that summarizes what is produced relative to resources used to produce it

The Importance of Productivity

Managers consider it important that their firm maintains high levels of productivity for a variety of reasons. Firm productivity is a primary determinant of an organization's level of profitability and, ultimately, of its ability to survive. If one organization is more productive than another, it will have more products to sell at lower prices and have more profits to reinvest in other areas. Productivity also partially determines people's standard of living within a particular country. At an economic level, businesses consume resources and produce goods and services. The goods and services created within a country can be used by that country's own citizens or exported for sale in other countries. The more goods and services the businesses within a country can produce, the more goods and services the country's citizens will have. Even goods that are exported result in financial resources' flowing back into the home country. Thus the citizens of a highly productive country are likely to have a notably higher standard of living than the citizens of a country with low productivity.

Productivity Trends

The United States has one of the highest levels of productivity in the world. Sparked by gains made in other countries, however, U.S. business has begun to focus more attention on productivity.[33] Indeed, this was a primary factor in the decisions made by U.S. businesses to retrench, retool, and become more competitive in the world marketplace. For example, GE's dishwasher plant in Louisville cut its inventory requirements by 50 percent, reduced labor costs from 15 percent to only 10 percent of total manufacturing costs, and cut product development time in half. As a result of these kinds of efforts, productivity trends have now leveled out, and U.S. workers are generally maintaining their lead in most industries.[34]

One important factor that has hurt U.S. productivity indices has been the tremendous growth of the service sector in the United States. Although this sector grew, its productivity levels did not. One part of this problem relates to measurement. For example, it is fairly easy to calculate the number of tons of steel produced at a steel mill and divide it by the number of labor hours used; it is more difficult to determine the output of an attorney or a certified public accountant. Still, virtually everyone agrees that improving service sector productivity is the next major hurdle facing U.S. business.[35]

Figure 10.4 illustrates manufacturing productivity growth since 1970 in terms of annual average percentage of increase. As you can see, that growth slowed during the 1970s but began to rise again in the late 1980s. Some experts believe that productivity in both the United States and abroad will continue to improve at even more impressive rates. Their confidence rests on technology's potential ability to improve operations.

Productivity

How does a business or industry improve its productivity? Numerous specific suggestions made by experts generally fall into two broad categories: improving operations and increasing employee involvement.

Improving Operations One way that firms can improve operations is by spending more on research and development (R&D). R&D spending helps identify new products, new uses for existing products, and new methods for making products. Each of these

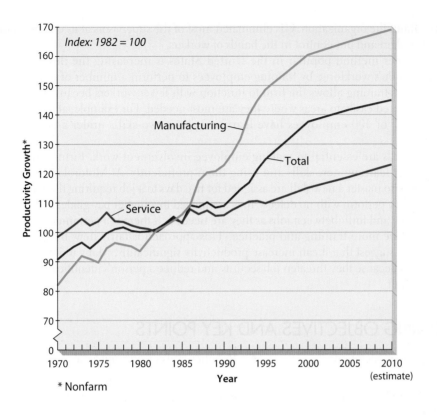

Figure 10.4
Manufacturing and Service Productivity Growth Trends

Both manufacturing productivity and service productivity in the United States continue to grow, although manufacturing productivity is growing at a faster pace. Total productivity, therefore, also continues to grow.

Source: U.S. Bureau of Labor Statistics.

contributes to productivity. For example, Bausch & Lomb almost missed the boat on extended-wear contact lenses because the company had neglected R&D. When it became apparent that its major competitors were almost a year ahead of Bausch & Lomb in developing the new lenses, management made R&D a top-priority concern. As a result, the company made several scientific breakthroughs, shortened the time needed to introduce new products, and greatly enhanced both total sales and profits—and all with a smaller workforce than the company used to employ. Even though other countries are greatly increasing their R&D spending, the United States continues to be the world leader in this area.

Another way firms can boost productivity through operations is by reassessing and revamping their transformation facilities. We noted earlier how one of GE's modernized plants does a better job than six antiquated ones. Just building a new factory is no guarantee of success, but IBM, Ford, Caterpillar, and many other businesses have achieved dramatic productivity gains by revamping their production facilities. Facilities refinements are not limited to manufacturers. Most McDonald's restaurants now have drive-through windows, and many have moved soft-drink dispensers out to the restaurant floor so that customers can get their own drinks. Each of these moves is an attempt to increase the speed with which customers can be served, and thus to increase productivity.

Increasing Employee Involvement The other major thrust in productivity enhancement has been toward employee involvement. We noted earlier that participation can enhance quality. So, too, can it boost productivity. Examples of this involvement are an individual worker being given a bigger voice in how she does her job, a formal agreement of cooperation between management and labor, and total involvement throughout the organization. GE eliminated most of the supervisors at its one new circuit breaker plant and put control in the hands of workers.

Another method popular in the United States is increasing the flexibility of an organization's workforce by training employees to perform a number of different jobs. Such cross-training allows the firm to function with fewer workers because workers can be transferred easily to areas where they are most needed. For example, at one Motorola plant, 397 of 400 employees have learned at least two skills under a cross-training program.

Rewards are essential to making employee involvement work. Firms must reward people for learning new skills and using them proficiently. At Motorola, for example, workers who master a new skill are assigned for five days to a job requiring them to use that skill. If they perform with no defects, they are moved to a higher pay grade, and then they move back and forth between jobs as they are needed. If there is a performance problem, they receive more training and practice. This approach is fairly new, but preliminary indicators suggest that it can increase productivity significantly. Many unions resist such programs because they threaten job security and reduce a person's identification with one skill or craft.

SUMMARY OF LEARNING OBJECTIVES AND KEY POINTS

1. Describe and explain the nature of operations management.

   - Operations management is the set of managerial activities that organizations use in creating their products and services.

   - Operations management is important to both manufacturing and service organizations.

   - It plays an important role in an organization's strategy.

2. Identify and discuss the components involved in designing effective operations systems.

   - The starting point in using operations management is designing appropriate operations systems.

   - Key decisions that must be made as part of operations systems design relate to the product–service mix, capacity, and facilities.

3. Discuss organizational technologies and their role in operations management.

   - Technology also plays an important role in quality.

   - Automation is especially important today.

   - Numerous CAM techniques are widely practiced.

   - Robotics is also a growing area.

   - Technology is as relevant to service organizations as it is to manufacturing organizations.

4. Identify and discuss the components involved in implementing operations systems through supply chain management.

   - After an operations system has been designed and put in place, it must then be implemented.

   - Major areas of interest during the use of operations systems are purchasing and inventory management.

   - Supply chain management is a comprehensive view of managing all these activities in a more efficient manner.

5. Explain the meaning and importance of managing quality and total quality management.

   - Quality is a major consideration for all managers today.

   - Quality is important because it affects competition, productivity, and costs.

   - TQM is a comprehensive, organization-wide effort to enhance quality through a variety of avenues.

6. Explain the meaning and importance of managing productivity, productivity trends, and ways to improve productivity.

   • Productivity is also a major concern to managers.

   • Productivity is a measure of how efficiently an organization is using its resources to create products or services.

   • The United States is a world leader in individual productivity, but firms still work to achieve productivity gains.

DISCUSSION QUESTIONS

Questions for Review

1. What is the relationship of operations management to overall organizational strategy? Where do productivity and quality fit into that relationship?

2. Describe three basic decisions that must be addressed in the design of operations systems. For each decision, what information do managers need to make that decision?

3. What are some approaches to facilities layout? How do they differ from one another? How are they similar?

4. What is total quality management? What are the major characteristics of TQM?

5. What is productivity? Identify various levels and forms of productivity.

Questions for Analysis

1. Is operations management linked most closely to corporate-level, business-level, or functional strategies? Why or in what way?

2. "Automation is bad for the economy because machines will eventually replace almost all human workers, creating high unemployment and poverty." Do you agree or disagree? Explain your answer.

3. Some quality gurus claim that high-quality products or services are those that are error free. Others claim that high quality exists when customers' needs are satisfied. Still others claim that high-quality products or services must be innovative. Do you subscribe to one of these views? If not, how would you define quality? Explain how the choice of a quality definition affects managers' behavior.

4. How can a service organization use techniques from operations management? Give specific examples from your college or university (a provider of educational services).

5. Think of a firm that, in your opinion, provides a high-quality service or product. What attributes of the product or service give you the perception of high quality? Do you think that everyone would agree with your judgment? Why or why not?

BUILDING EFFECTIVE COMMUNICATION SKILLS

Exercise Overview

Communication skills refer to the ability not only to convey information and ideas to others but also to handle information and ideas received from them. This exercise shows how you can use your communication skills in addressing issues of quality.

Exercise Background

You're the customer service manager of a large auto parts distributor. The general manager of a large auto dealer, one of your best customers, has sent the following letter, and it's your job to write a letter in response.

Dear Customer Service Manager:

On the first of last month, ABC Autos submitted a purchase order to your firm. Attached to this letter is a copy of the order. Unfortunately, the parts shipment that we received from you did not contain every item on the order. Further, that fact was not noted on the packing slip that accompanied your

shipment, and ABC was charged for the full amount of the order. To resolve the problem, please send the missing items immediately. If you are unable to do so by the end of the week, please cancel the remaining items and refund the overpayment. In the future, if you ship a partial order, please notify us at that time and do not bill for items not shipped.

I look forward to your reply and a resolution to my problem.

Sincerely,
A. N. Owner, ABC Autos
Attachment: Purchase Order 00001

Exercise Task

1. Write an answer to the customer's letter that assumes that you now have the parts available.

2. How would your answer differ if ABC Autos were not a valued customer?

3. How would your answer differ if you found out that the parts were in the original shipment but had been stolen by one of your delivery personnel?

4. How would your answer differ if you found out that the owner of ABC Autos made a mistake and that the order had been filled correctly?

5. Now review your answers to the previous questions. What are the important components of an effective response to a customer quality complaint (setting the tone, expressing an apology, suggesting a solution, and so on)? How did you use these components in your various responses?

BUILDING EFFECTIVE DIAGNOSTIC SKILLS

Exercise Overview

As we noted in this chapter, the quality of a product or service is relative to price and customer expectations. This exercise is designed to show that a manager's diagnostic skills—his or her ability to visualize the most appropriate response to a situation—can be useful in positioning a product's quality relative to price and customer expectations.

Exercise Background

Think of a recent occasion when you purchased a tangible product—say, clothing, electronic equipment, luggage, or professional supplies—which you subsequently came to feel was of especially high quality. Now think of another product that you regarded as being of appropriate or adequate quality, and then a third product that you judged to be of low or poor quality. (You should now have three separate products in mind.) Next, recall three parallel experiences involving purchases of services. Examples might include an airline, train, or bus trip; a restaurant meal; a haircut; or an oil change for your car. (Again, you should have three examples in total.)

Finally, recall three experiences involving both products and services. Perhaps you got some information about a product that you were buying or you returned a defective or broken product for a refund or warranty repair. Were there any instances in which there was an apparent disparity between product and service quality? Did a poor-quality product, for instance, receive surprisingly good service or a high-quality product receive mediocre service?

Exercise Task

Review your list of nine purchase experiences and then do the following:

1. Assess the extent to which the quality that you associated with each was a function of price and your expectations.

2. Could the quality of each product or service be improved without greatly affecting its price? If so, how?

3. Can high-quality customer service offset adequate or even poor product quality? Can outstanding product quality offset adequate or even poor customer service?

SKILLS SELF-ASSESSMENT INSTRUMENT

Defining Quality and Productivity

Introduction: *Quality* is a complex term whose meaning has no doubt changed over time. The following assessment surveys your ideas about and approaches to quality.

Instructions: You will agree with some of the statements and disagree with others. In some cases, making a decision may be difficult, but you should force yourself to make a choice. Record your answers next to each statement according to the following rating scale:

Rating Scale

4 Strongly agree
3 Slightly agree
2 Somewhat disagree
1 Strongly disagree

____ 1. Quality refers to a product's or service's ability to fulfill its primary operating characteristics, such as providing a sharp picture for a television set.

____ 2. Quality is an absolute, measurable aspect of a product or service.

____ 3. The concept of quality includes supplemental aspects of a product or service, such as the remote control for a television set.

____ 4. Productivity and quality are inversely related, so that, to get one, you must sacrifice the other.

____ 5. The concept of quality refers to the extent to which a product's design and operating characteristics conform to certain set standards.

____ 6. Productivity refers to what is created relative to what it takes to create it.

____ 7. Quality means that a product will not malfunction during a specified period of time.

____ 8. Quality refers only to products; it is immeasurable for services.

____ 9. The length of time that a product or service will function is what is known as quality.

____ 10. Everyone uses exactly the same definition of quality.

____ 11. Quality refers to the repair ease and speed of a product or service.

____ 12. Being treated courteously has nothing to do with the quality of anything.

____ 13. How a product looks, feels, tastes, or smells is what is meant by quality.

____ 14. Price, not quality, is what determines the ultimate value of service.

____ 15. Quality refers to what customers think of a product or service.

____ 16. Productivity and quality cannot both increase at the same time.

Source: Adapted from Chapter 21, especially pp. 473–474, in David D. Van Fleet and Tim O. Peterson, *Contemporary Management*, 3rd ed. © 1994 by Houghton Mifflin Company.

EXPERIENTIAL EXERCISE

Preparing the Fishbone Chart

Purpose: The fishbone chart is an excellent procedure for identifying possible causes of a problem. It provides you with knowledge that you can use to improve the operations of any organization. This skill exercise focuses on the *administrative management model*. It helps you develop the *monitor role* of the administrative management model. One of the skills of the monitor is the ability to analyze problems.

Introduction: Kaoru Ishikawa developed this technique in the 1960s and it is now considered to be one of the fundamental tools of quality management. Quality circles often use the fishbone "cause-and-effect" graphical technique to initiate the resolution of a group work problem. Quite often the causes are clustered in categories such as materials, methods, people, and machines.

The fishbone technique is usually accomplished in the following six steps:

1. Write the problem in the "head" of the fish (the large block).

2. Brainstorm the major causes of the problem and list them on the fish "bones."

3. Analyze each main cause and write in minor subcauses on bone subbranches.

4. Reach consensus on one or two of the major causes of the problem.

5. Explore ways to correct or remove the major causes.

6. Prepare a report or presentation explaining the proposed change.

Your fishbone will look something like this:

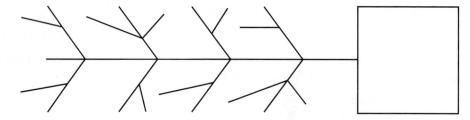

Source: Adapted from Gene R. Briton, *Exercises in Management*, 5th ed., 1996. © 1996. Houghton Mifflin Company.

 YOU MAKE THE CALL

A New IDEO in Hotel Quality

1. As a customer, what are the three quality dimensions that you consider important in a hotel room?

2. What differences in quality dimensions are likely between upscale and lower-priced hotels?

3. Given what IDEO found out about hotel guest experiences in its research for Marriott, how might these TQM components be used to improve quality at a mid-market hotel: strategic commitment, employee involvement, technology, and methods?

4. If you were the manager of either an upscale hotel or an economy hotel, which three or four quality dimensions would you examine first to improve overall quality?

5. Explore the websites of four hotel chains. Identify the specific quality dimensions used by each to promote its guest experience.

INDIVIDUAL BEHAVIOR IN ORGANIZATIONS— BASIC ELEMENTS

LEARNING OBJECTIVES

After studying this chapter, you should be able to:

1. Explain the nature of the individual–organization relationship.

2. Define personality and describe personality attributes that affect behavior in organizations.

3. Discuss individual attitudes in organizations and how they affect behavior.

4. Describe basic perceptual processes and the role of attributions in organizations.

5. Discuss the causes and consequences of stress and describe how it can be managed.

6. Describe creativity and its role in organizations.

7. Explain how workplace behaviors can directly or indirectly influence organizational effectiveness.

Is Your Boss Superficially Charming, Insincere, and Lacking in Empathy?

We'll assume that you know *something* about Bernie Madoff (and if you expect to have money to invest some day, you probably should). Madoff is the former Nasdaq chairman who turned his experience in courting investors into a second career as a con man extraordinaire. What started out as an asset management business in the 1990s gradually turned into a massive Ponzi scheme in which Madoff took money from new investors to pay off existing investors who wanted to cash out. By the time the scheme unraveled in 2008, Madoff had defrauded clients of about $50 billion over several years. Just before he was caught, Madoff was working on ways to distribute what was left (about $300 million) to his family and loyal employees, most of whom had no idea of what was going on.

How had he managed to convince so many people—including a lot of investment-savvy professionals—to give him so much money? For one thing, he was good at exploiting friends and others who trusted him, either personally or professionally. "Many of the assets he took," says one veteran market fund manager, "were from friends and family. It's almost inexplicable. Even the people I've talked to

> **"There are certainly more [psychopaths] in the business world . . . than in the general population."**
>
> —DAVID HARE, FORENSIC PSYCHOLOGIST

who've had long relationships with him are shell-shocked." Why did people who knew or worked with Madoff fail to see that the man who was soliciting their money wasn't the same man who ran a family business and contributed generously to numerous charities? "People like him," warns FBI profiler Gregg O. McCrary, "become sort of like chameleons. They are very good at impression management. They manage the impression you receive of them. They know what people want, and they give it to them."

Bernard Madoff defrauded investors out of more than $50 billion in an elaborate Ponzi scheme. His personality no doubt played a role in his willingness to steal from people as well as his ability to persuade people to allow him to manage their money.

They're a lot like serial killers, adds McCrary, likening Madoff to Ted Bundy, who confessed to murdering 30 young women between 1974 and 1978. Isn't it going a little too far to put an elderly greed-obsessed financier in the same class as a cold-blooded serial killer? "With serial killers," explains McCrary, "they have control over the life or death of people. They're playing God. . . . Madoff [was] getting the same thing [out of his criminal activity]. He was playing financial god, ruining these people and taking their money."

In fact, more and more forensic psychologists are coming to the conclusion that the behavior of people in many walks of life qualifies for a label once reserved for the acts of people like Ted Bundy. Psychologist J. Reid Meloy, for example, sees similarities between Madoff's behavior and that of many criminals he's studied: "Typically," he observes, "people with psychopathic personalities don't fear getting caught. They [also] tend to be very narcissistic with a strong sense of entitlement." Robert Hare, a forensic psychologist who consults with law enforcement agencies, agrees that perhaps we need to lower the bar when it comes to granting someone the dubious status of *psychopath*. Many criminals, explains Hare, suffer from some sort of antisocial personality disorder that causes them to act impulsively and commit violent crimes. Some of these criminals also suffer from *psychopathy*, which is evident in the absence of empathy for the people they hurt. Among this group, there's a smaller subset of people who suffer from psychopathy alone: These people exhibit no violence but appear to be indifferent to the well-being of others. Psychologist Michele Galietta calls those in this last group "white-collar psychopaths." Like Bernie Madoff, she says, "these people get real enjoyment from what they do. They feel good pulling the wool over other people's eyes."

Fortunately, your odds of encountering someone like Ted Bundy on a dark night are pretty slim. On the other hand, Hare, coauthor of *Snakes in Suits: When Psychopaths Go to Work*, suspects that your odds of encountering a psychopath in the workplace are higher than you'd think: "There are certainly more people in the business world," he says, "who would score high in the psychopathic dimension than in the general population. . . . If I wasn't studying psychopaths in prison, I'd do it at the stock exchange."

Hare, who has since expanded his research to include corporate psychopaths, has created questionnaires and other psychological testing devices to reveal an individual's psychopathic tendencies. His findings so far? Psychopaths, he says, are largely motivated by the desire to fulfill their own selfish needs regardless of the consequences to others. They're often superficially charming, insincere, prone to lying, manipulative, guilt free, lacking in empathy, ruthless, and unwilling to accept responsibility. Psychopaths in general often display two personality traits: (1) a "callous, selfish, remorseless use of others" and (2) a "chronically unstable and antisocial lifestyle." Criminal psychopaths tend to score high on both factors and are given to violent impulses that inhibit effective social performance. In contrast, psychopathic executives, who tend to score high on the first factor but low on the second, are often highly functional psychopaths. The difference, according to one team of British researchers, is between "unsuccessful psychopaths" and "successful psychopaths."

How do people like this end up in corner offices? Unfortunately, business is a very good arena in which to exercise psychopathic tendencies. Indeed, it often provides psychopaths with ample opportunity to put their particular personality traits to ostensibly good use. After all, American stockholders prefer top managers who are charismatic, visionary, and tough—characteristics that often accompany more overt psychopathic traits. Psychopathic individuals are also more comfortable with change and uncertainty. A psychopath has "no difficulty dealing with the consequences of rapid change," says industrial psychologist Paul Babiak, Hare's *Snakes in Suits* coauthor. "In fact, he or she thrives on it. . . . Organizational chaos," he explains, "provides both the necessary stimulation for psychopathic thrill seeking and sufficient cover for psychopathic manipulation and abuse."

Most corporate leaders, of course, are not psychopaths. If your boss, for example, seems inordinately insensitive or even egotistical, he or she may simply be a *narcissist*. According to psychologists, narcissists often have good intentions but won't allow themselves to see through the eyes of the people who are affected by their efforts to get what they want. They may, for example, freely criticize others while refusing to accept criticism, but that sort of behavior is a long way from the psychopathic antics of hotel magnate Leona Helmsley, who routinely shouted profanities at employees and summarily fired hundreds for trivial offenses. (Helmsley, who died in 2007, was nicknamed the "Queen of Mean" by her employees; she is perhaps best remembered for leaving $12 million to her pet dog.)

Granted, narcissists "don't have much empathy," observes psychotherapist and consultant Michael Maccoby, author of *The Productive Narcissist: The Promise and Perils of Visionary Leadership.* "They see other people as a means toward their ends. But they do have a sense of . . . improving the world," and they manipulate people in the interest of this externalized goal. "In contrast," says Maccoby, "psychopaths are only interested in self." Entrepreneurial founder-CEOs, adds Babiak, are often narcissistic. He cites successful leaders such as Apple's Steve Jobs, Microsoft's Bill Gates, and Oracle's Larry Ellison. Such people, he says, "have a vested interest: Their identity is wrapped up in the company," which is typically an extension of self. The psychopath, on the other hand, "has no allegiance to the company at all, just to self." Like Bernie Madoff, the "psychopath is playing a short-term parasitic game."

Many experts agree that a moderate share of narcissism may be helpful—even necessary—in motivating an entrepreneur to persist and excel at a difficult job in a risk-filled environment. Many people seem to accept that fact, but, unfortunately, most of us don't know how to tell the difference between a narcissist and a genuine psychopath. Indeed, we often admire highly publicized leaders who, unbeknownst to us, exhibit tendencies to cross the line. "It goes against our intuition," suggests Harvard psychologist Martha Stout, "that a small percentage of people can be so different from the rest of us—and so evil. Good people don't want to believe it" and that may be precisely why normal people are so vulnerable to psychopaths. As a rule, psychopathic tendencies eventually betray themselves in overt psychopathic behavior, but by then, to the dismay of boards and stockholders, the damage may have already been done.

Moreover, adds Babiak, lending approval to narcissistic tendencies can be dangerous because it makes us prone to overlook psychopathic tendencies: "[I]ndividuals who are really psychopaths," argues Babiak, "are often mistaken for [mere] narcissists and chosen by organizations for leadership positions." So, what *is* the best way to tell the difference? "In the case of a narcissist," says Babiak, "everything is me, me, me. With a psychopath, it's 'Is it thrilling, is it a game I can win, and does it hurt others?' My belief is a psychopath enjoys hurting others."

Can organizations manage their narcissists, especially those at the top? Maccoby suggests pairing narcissistic executives with more conscientious, control-minded executives. He cites the effective pairing of founder-chairman Bill Gates with CEO Steve Ballmer at Microsoft and attributes the remarkable success of founder Steve Jobs's second stint as Apple CEO to the steadying influence of Timothy Cook, who serves as executive vice president of sales and operations. As *BusinessWeek* magazine puts it, "Where Jobs is variously described as volatile, mercurial, and hard to please, Cook is usually described as soft-spoken, calm, and less prone to raise his voice in tense situations." (For more on Jobs, see the case for Chapter 11 at the end of the book.) As for psychopaths, Hare recommends screening them out altogether on the grounds that they're too dangerous for organizations in general and coworkers in particular.

And Bernie Madoff? For Elie Wiesel, Holocaust survivor and recipient of the Nobel Peace Prize for his lifelong effort to fight hatred and intolerance, " 'psychopath' is too nice a word for him. 'Sociopath,' 'psychopath'—it means there is a sickness, a pathology. This man knew what he was doing. I would simply call him 'thief, scoundrel, criminal.' " Wiesel, whose charitable foundation lost $15.2 million to Madoff, suggests that he be put "in a solitary cell with only a screen, and on that screen . . . every day and every night, there would be pictures of his victims, one after the other after the other, all the time a voice saying, 'Look what you have done to this old lady, look what you have done to that child, look what you have done.' "[1]

The people who populate today's business world are characterized by a wide variety of personalities and behaviors. Although most people in business have relatively healthy and constructive personalities and behave in ethical and productive ways, there are some who reflect different profiles. Indeed, myriad different and unique characteristics reside in each and every employee (and employer). These affect how they feel about the organization, how they will alter their future attitudes about the firm, and how they perform their jobs. These characteristics reflect the basic elements of individual behavior in organizations.

This chapter describes several of these basic elements and is the first of several chapters designed to develop a more complete perspective on the leading function of management. In the next section, we investigate the psychological nature of individuals in organizations. The following section introduces the concept of personality and discusses several important personality attributes that can influence behavior in organizations. We then examine individual attitudes and their role in organizations. The role of stress in the workplace is then discussed, followed by a discussion of individual creativity. Finally, we describe a number of basic individual behaviors that are important to organizations.

UNDERSTANDING INDIVIDUALS IN ORGANIZATIONS

As a starting point in understanding human behavior in the workplace, we must consider the basic nature of the relationship between individuals and organizations. We must also gain an appreciation of the nature of individual differences.

The Psychological Contract

Most people have a basic understanding of a contract. Whenever we buy a car or sell a house, for example, both buyer and seller sign a contract that specifies the terms of the agreement. A psychological contract is similar in some ways to a standard legal contract but is less formal and well defined. In particular, a **psychological contract** is the overall set of expectations held by an individual with respect to what he or she will contribute to the organization and what the organization will provide in return.[2] Thus a psychological contract is not written on paper, nor are all its terms explicitly negotiated.

The essential nature of a psychological contract is illustrated in Figure 11.1. The individual makes a variety of **contributions** to the organization—effort, skills, ability, time, loyalty, and so forth. These contributions presumably satisfy various needs and requirements of the organization. In other words, because the organization may have hired the person because of her skills, it is reasonable for the organization to expect that she will subsequently display those skills in the performance of her job.

psychological contract
The overall set of expectations held by an individual with respect to what he or she will contribute to the organization and what the organization will provide in return

contributions
What the individual provides to the organization

Figure 11.1 **The Psychological Contract**

Psychological contracts are the basic assumptions that individuals have about their relationships with their organization. Such contracts are defined in terms of contributions by the individual relative to inducements from the organization.

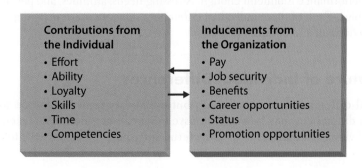

Contributions from the Individual
- Effort
- Ability
- Loyalty
- Skills
- Time
- Competencies

Inducements from the Organization
- Pay
- Job security
- Benefits
- Career opportunities
- Status
- Promotion opportunities

In return for these contributions, the organization provides **inducements** to the individual. Some inducements, like pay and career opportunities, are tangible rewards. Others, like job security and status, are more intangible. Just as the contributions available from the individual must satisfy the needs of the organization, the inducements offered by the organization must serve the needs of the individual. Thus, if a person accepts employment with an organization because he thinks he will earn an attractive salary and have an opportunity to advance, he will subsequently expect that those rewards will actually be forthcoming.

If both the individual and the organization perceive that the psychological contract is fair and equitable, they will be satisfied with the relationship and will likely continue it. On the other hand, if either party sees an imbalance or inequity in the contract, it may initiate a change. For example, the individual may request a pay raise or promotion, decrease his contributed effort, or look for a better job elsewhere. The organization can also initiate change by requesting that the individual improve his skills through training, transfer the person to another job, or terminate the person's employment altogether.[3]

A basic challenge faced by the organization, then, is to manage psychological contracts. The organization must ensure that it is getting value from its employees. At the same time, it must be sure that it is providing employees with appropriate inducements. If the organization is underpaying its employees for their contributions, for example, they may perform poorly or leave for better jobs elsewhere. On the other hand, if they are being overpaid relative to their contributions, the organization is incurring unnecessary costs.[4]

The Person–Job Fit

One specific aspect of managing psychological contracts is managing the **person–job fit**—the extent to which the contributions made by the individual match the inducements offered by the organization. In theory, each employee has a specific set of needs that he wants to be fulfilled and a set of job-related behaviors and abilities to contribute. Thus, if the organization can take perfect advantage of those behaviors and abilities and exactly fulfill his needs, it will have achieved a perfect person–job fit.

Of course, such a precise level of person–job fit is seldom achieved. There are several reasons for this. For one thing, organizational selection procedures are imperfect. Organizations can make approximations of employee skill levels when making hiring decisions and can improve them through training. But even simple performance dimensions are often hard to measure in objective and valid ways.

Another reason for imprecise person–job fits is that both people and organizations change. An individual who finds a new job stimulating and exciting may find the same job boring and monotonous after a few years of performing it. And, when the organization adopts new technology, it has changed the skills it needs from its employees. Still another reason for imprecision in the person–job fit is that each individual is unique. Measuring skills and performance is difficult enough. Assessing needs, attitudes, and personality is far more complex. Each of these individual differences serves to make matching individuals with jobs a difficult and complex process.[5]

The Nature of Individual Differences

Individual differences are personal attributes that vary from one person to another. Individual differences may be physical, psychological, or emotional. Taken together, all the individual differences that characterize any specific person serve to make that

inducements
What the organization provides to the individual

person–job fit
The extent to which the contributions made by the individual match the inducements offered by the organization

individual differences
Personal attributes that vary from one person to another

individual unique from everyone else. Much of the remainder of this chapter is devoted to individual differences. Before proceeding, however, we must also note the importance of the situation in assessing the behavior of individuals.

Are specific differences that characterize a given individual good or bad? Do they contribute to or detract from performance? The answer, of course, is that it depends on the circumstances. One person may be very dissatisfied, withdrawn, and negative in one job setting, but very satisfied, outgoing, and positive in another. Working conditions, coworkers, and leadership are all important ingredients.

Thus, whenever an organization attempts to assess or account for individual differences among its employees, it must also be sure to consider the situation in which behavior occurs. Individuals who are satisfied or productive workers in one context may prove to be dissatisfied or unproductive workers in another context. Attempting to consider both individual differences and contributions in relation to inducements and contexts, then, is a major challenge for organizations as they attempt to establish effective psychological contracts with their employees and achieve optimal fits between people and jobs. The "Ethics in Action" box takes a look inside a small business to see how independent-minded family members with different individual interests succeed in playing compatible managerial roles.

ETHICS IN ACTION

Playing Well with (and without) Others

Play is serious business. Per child, Americans spend $242 on toys each year, for a total of $21.6 billion in 2008. Most toys sold in the United States are designed here, but large-scale production typically takes place overseas, where labor costs are lower. In fact, the industry's U.S. workforce has shrunk by more than 50 percent over the last decade, and pressure from discount retail chains has accelerated the trend toward foreign manufacturing. The country's three largest toy sellers account for over one-half of all sales, with Wal-Mart commanding 30 percent of the market.

Despite cost pressures and the trend toward offshoring, however, some toy makers play by slightly different rules. One of these is BEKA, which specializes in wooden blocks, art easels, puppet theatres, and play furniture. Headed by brothers Jamie and Peter Kreisman, BEKA Inc. has been successful with an approach that adds a few creative twists to a traditional business model. BEKA has been a family-run business for more than 30 years, and the association of the family name

with quality products is essential to the BEKA approach: "Large companies," explains Jamie, "want to tell you how to cut corners to cut costs. . . . We could sell many more products, but it wouldn't be our product or what we want our name on. So we said, 'No, thank you.' "

BEKA employs expert woodworkers to craft safe custom-made toys out of durable hardwoods, and the Kreismans also pride themselves on a commitment to customer service that allows them to pay personal attention to satisfying customer needs. The company also caters to the small toy stores that, like small toy makers, are endangered by the expansion of discount chains and the proliferation of low-cost products. Indeed, many small stores prefer toys made by independent manufacturers like BEKA because their products allow them to differentiate themselves from retailers such as Wal-Mart and Toys "R" Us.

BEKA's unique business model reflects not only the Kreisman brothers' creativity, but the interplay of their contrasting temperaments and

(continued)

interests. On the one hand, they share a spirit of independence, a love of craftsmanship, and a commitment to service-oriented business practices. Jamie, however, has an MBA while Peter has a PhD in physics. Jamie explains how they integrate their respective skills into their business operations: "I'll speak with customers about a product and mock up a sample, and then Peter will work out all the details and figure out how to build it safely,

solidly, and as economically as possible. He's the scientist, and I'm the people person and the number cruncher."

References: The NPD Group, "U.S. Toy Industry Sales Generate $21.64 Billion in 2008," press release, February 12, 2009, www.npd.com on April 20, 2009; "History/About Us," BEKA website, www.bekainc.com on April 20, 2009; Erin Chambers, "How a Toy Store Plays to Win," *BusinessWeek*, November 24, 2004, www.businessweek.com on April 20, 2009; Erin Chambers, "Playing by BEKA's Rules," *BusinessWeek*, December 8, 2004, www.businessweek.com on April 20, 2009.

PERSONALITY AND INDIVIDUAL BEHAVIOR

Personality traits represent some of the most fundamental sets of individual differences in organizations. **Personality** is the relatively stable set of psychological and behavioral attributes that distinguish one person from another.[6] Managers should strive to understand basic personality attributes and the ways they can affect people's behavior in organizational situations, not to mention their perceptions of and attitudes toward the organization.

The "Big Five" Personality Traits

Psychologists have identified literally thousands of personality traits and dimensions that differentiate one person from another. But, in recent years, researchers have identified five fundamental personality traits that are especially relevant to organizations. Because these five traits are so important and because they are currently the subject of so much attention, they are now commonly referred to as the **"Big Five"** personality traits, which is illustrated in Figure 11.2.[7]

personality
The relatively stable set of psychological and behavioral attributes that distinguish one person from another

"Big Five" personality traits
A popular personality framework based on five key traits

Figure 11.2
The "Big Five" Model of Personality

The Big Five personality model represents an increasingly accepted framework for understanding personality traits in organizational settings. In general, experts tend to agree that personality traits toward the left end of each dimension, as illustrated in this figure, are more positive in organizational settings, whereas traits closer to the right are less positive.

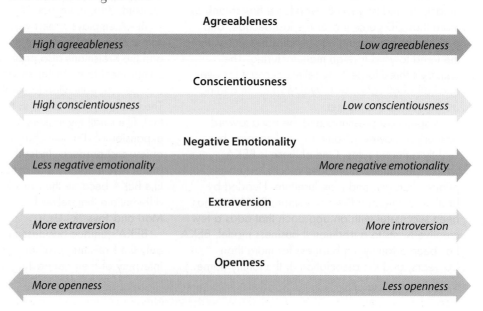

Agreeableness	
High agreeableness	Low agreeableness
Conscientiousness	
High conscientiousness	Low conscientiousness
Negative Emotionality	
Less negative emotionality	More negative emotionality
Extraversion	
More extraversion	More introversion
Openness	
More openness	Less openness

Agreeableness refers to a person's ability to get along with others. It causes some people to be gentle, cooperative, forgiving, understanding, and good-natured in their dealings with others. But it results in others' being irritable, short-tempered, uncooperative, and generally antagonistic toward other people.

Although research has not yet fully investigated the effects of agreeableness, it would seem likely that highly agreeable people will be better able to develop good working relationships with coworkers, subordinates, and higher-level managers than less agreeable people. This same pattern might also extend to relationships with customers, suppliers, and other key organizational constituents.

Conscientiousness refers to the number of goals on which a person focuses. People who focus on relatively few goals at one time are likely to be organized, systematic, careful, thorough, responsible, and self-disciplined as they work to pursue those goals. Others, however, tend to take on a wider array of goals and, as a result, are more disorganized, careless, and irresponsible, as well as less thorough and self-disciplined. Research has found that more conscientious people tend to be higher performers than less conscientious people across a variety of different jobs. This pattern seems logical, of course, because more conscientious people will take their jobs seriously and will approach the performance of their jobs in highly responsible fashions.

DAVID ROSENBERG/STONE/GETTY IMAGES

Extraverts are often attracted to jobs based on personal relationships and that involve frequent interactions with other people. Take this sales clerk, for instance. He seems genuinely friendly and is enjoying his interaction with the customer. This profile, in turn, likely plays an important role in his job performance.

The third of the Big Five personality dimensions is **negative emotionality**. People with less negative emotionality will be relatively poised, calm, resilient, and secure. But people with more negative emotionality will be more excitable, insecure, reactive, and subject to extreme mood swings. People with less negative emotionality might be expected to better handle job stress, pressure, and tension. Their stability might also lead them to be seen as more reliable than their less stable counterparts.

Extraversion refers to a person's comfort level with relationships. People who are called *extraverts* are sociable, talkative, assertive, and open to establishing new relationships. But introverts are much less sociable, talkative, assertive, and less open to establishing new relationships. Research suggests that extraverts tend to be higher overall job performers than introverts and that they are also more likely to be attracted to jobs based on personal relationships, such as sales and marketing positions.

Finally, **openness** refers to a person's rigidity of beliefs and range of interests. People with high levels of openness are willing to listen to new ideas and to change their own ideas, beliefs, and attitudes as a result of new information. They also tend to have broad interests and to be curious, imaginative, and creative. On the other hand, people with low levels of openness tend to be less receptive to new ideas and less willing to change their minds. Further, they tend to have fewer and narrower interests and to be less curious and creative. People with more openness might be expected to be better performers, owing to their flexibility and the likelihood that they will be better

agreeableness
A person's ability to get along with others

conscientiousness
The number of goals on which a person focuses

negative emotionality
Extent to which a person is poised, calm, resilient, and secure

extraversion
A person's comfort level with relationships

openness
A person's rigidity of beliefs and range of interests

accepted by others in the organization. Openness may also encompass an individual's willingness to accept change. For example, people with high levels of openness may be more receptive to change, whereas people with low levels of openness may be more likely to resist change.

The Big Five framework continues to attract the attention of both researchers and managers. The potential value of this framework is that it encompasses an integrated set of traits that appear to be valid predictors of certain behaviors in certain situations. Thus managers who can develop both an understanding of the framework and the ability to assess these traits in their employees will be in a good position to understand how and why employees behave as they do.[8] On the other hand, managers must also be careful not to overestimate their ability to assess the Big Five traits in others. Even assessment using the most rigorous and valid measures, for instance, is still likely to be somewhat imprecise. Another limitation of the Big Five framework is that it is based primarily on research conducted in the United States. Thus there are unanswered questions as to how accurately it applies to workers in other cultures. And, even within the United States, a variety of other factors and traits are also likely to affect behavior in organizations.

The Myers-Briggs Framework

Another interesting approach to understanding personalities in organizations is the Myers-Briggs framework. This framework, based on the classic work of Carl Jung, differentiates people in terms of four general dimensions. These are defined as follows:

- *Extraversion (E) versus introversion (I).* Extraverts get their energy from being around other people, whereas introverts are worn out by others and need solitude to recharge their energy.
- *Sensing (S) versus intuition (N).* The sensing type prefers concrete things, whereas intuitives prefer abstract concepts.
- *Thinking (T) versus feeling (F).* Thinking individuals base their decisions more on logic and reason, whereas feeling individuals base their decisions more on feelings and emotions.
- *Judging (J) versus perceiving (P).* People who are the judging type enjoy completion or being finished, whereas perceiving types enjoy the process and open-ended situations.

To use this framework, people complete a questionnaire designed to measure their personality on each dimension. Higher or lower scores in each of the dimensions are used to classify people into 1 of 16 different personality categories.

The Myers-Briggs Type Indicator (MBTI) is one popular questionnaire that some organizations use to assess personality types. Indeed, it is among the most popular selection instruments used today, with as many as 2 million people taking it each year. Research suggests that the MBTI is a useful method for determining communication styles and interaction preferences. In terms of personality attributes, however, questions exist about both the validity and the reliability of the MBTI.

Other Personality Traits at Work

Besides the Big Five and the Myers-Briggs framework, there are several other personality traits that influence behavior in organizations. Among the most important are locus of control, self-efficacy, authoritarianism, Machiavellianism, self-esteem, and risk propensity.

Locus of control is the extent to which people believe that their behavior has a real effect on what happens to them.[9] Some people, for example, believe that, if they work hard, they will succeed. They also may believe that people who fail do so because they lack ability or motivation. People who believe that individuals are in control of their lives are said to have an *internal locus of control*. Other people think that fate, chance, luck, or other people's behavior determines what happens to them. For example, an employee who fails to get a promotion may attribute that failure to a politically motivated boss or just bad luck, rather than to his or her own lack of skills or poor performance record. People who think that forces beyond their control dictate what happens to them are said to have an *external locus of control*.

Self-efficacy is a related but subtly different personality characteristic. It is a person's beliefs about his or her capabilities to perform a task.[10] People with high self-efficacy believe that they can perform well on a specific task, whereas people with low self-efficacy tend to doubt their ability to perform a specific task. Although self-assessments of ability contribute to self-efficacy, so, too, does the individual's personality. Some people simply have more self-confidence than do others. This belief in their ability to perform a task effectively results in their being more self-assured and more able to focus their attention on performance.

Another important personality characteristic is **authoritarianism**, the extent to which an individual believes that power and status differences are appropriate within hierarchical social systems like organizations.[11] For example, a person who is highly authoritarian may accept directives or orders from someone with more authority purely because the other person is "the boss." On the other hand, although a person who is not highly authoritarian may still carry out appropriate and reasonable directives from the boss, he or she is also more likely to question things, express disagreement with the boss, and even refuse to carry out orders if they are for some reason objectionable. A highly authoritarian manager may be autocratic and demanding, and highly authoritarian subordinates will be more likely to accept this behavior from their leader. On the other hand, a less authoritarian manager may allow subordinates a bigger role in making decisions, and less authoritarian subordinates will respond positively to this behavior.

Machiavellianism is another important personality trait. This concept is named after Niccolò Machiavelli, a sixteenth-century Italian political philosopher. In his book entitled *The Prince*, Machiavelli explained how the nobility could more easily gain and use power. *Machiavellianism* is now used to describe behavior directed at gaining power and controlling the behavior of others. Research suggests that Machiavellianism is a personality trait that varies from person to person. More Machiavellian individuals tend to be rational and nonemotional, may be willing to lie to attain their personal goals, may put little weight on loyalty and friendship, and may enjoy manipulating others' behavior. Less Machiavellian individuals are more emotional, are less willing to lie to succeed, value loyalty and friendship highly, and get little personal pleasure from manipulating others. By all accounts, Dennis Kozlowski, the indicted

INTERFOTO/ALAMY

Niccolò Machiavelli was a sixteenth-century Italian political philosopher. In his classic book entitled The Prince, *Machiavelli explained how the nobility of that era could more easily gain and use power.* Machiavellianism *is the term that is now used to describe personality-based behavior directed at gaining power and controlling the behavior of others.*

locus of control
The degree to which an individual believes that his or her behavior has a direct impact on the consequences of that behavior

self-efficacy
An individual's beliefs about his or her capabilities to perform a task

authoritarianism
The extent to which an individual believes that power and status differences are appropriate within hierarchical social systems like organizations

Machiavellianism
Behavior directed at gaining power and controlling the behavior of others

former CEO of Tyco International currently serving prison time, had a high degree of Machiavellianism. He apparently came to believe that his position of power in the company gave him the right to do just about anything he wanted with company resources.[12]

Self-esteem is the extent to which a person believes that she is a worthwhile and deserving individual.[13] A person with high self-esteem is more likely to seek high-status jobs, be more confident in her ability to achieve higher levels of performance, and derive greater intrinsic satisfaction from her accomplishments. In contrast, a person with less self-esteem may be more content to remain in a lower-level job, be less confident of his ability, and focus more on extrinsic rewards. Among the major personality dimensions, self-esteem is the one that has been most widely studied in other countries. Although more research is clearly needed, the published evidence suggests that self-esteem as a personality trait does indeed exist in a variety of countries and that its role in organizations is reasonably important across different cultures.[14]

Risk propensity is the degree to which an individual is willing to take chances and make risky decisions. A manager with a high risk propensity, for example, might be expected to experiment with new ideas and gamble on new products. She might also lead the organization in new and different directions. This manager might also be a catalyst for innovation. On the other hand, the same individual might also jeopardize the continued well-being of the organization if the risky decisions prove to be bad ones. A manager with low risk propensity might lead to a stagnant and overly conservative organization or help the organization successfully weather turbulent and unpredictable times by maintaining stability and calm. Thus the potential consequences of risk propensity to an organization are heavily dependent on that organization's environment.

Emotional Intelligence

The concept of emotional intelligence (EQ) has been identified in recent years and provides some interesting insights into personality. **EQ** refers to the extent to which people are self-aware, manage their emotions, motivate themselves, express empathy for others, and possess social skills.[15] These various dimensions can be described as follows:

- *Self-awareness.* This is the basis for the other components. It refers to a person's capacity for being aware of how they are feeling. In general, more self-awareness allows people to more effectively guide their own lives and behaviors.
- *Managing emotions.* This refers to a person's capacities to balance anxiety, fear, and anger so that they do not overly interfere with getting things accomplished.
- *Motivating oneself.* This refers to a person's ability to remain optimistic and to continue striving in the face of setbacks, barriers, and failure.
- *Empathy.* This refers to a person's ability to understand how others are feeling, even without being explicitly told.
- *Social skill.* This refers to a person's ability to get along with others and to establish positive relationships.

Preliminary research suggests that people with high EQs may perform better than others, especially in jobs that require a high degree of interpersonal interaction and that involve influencing or directing the work of others. Moreover, EQ appears to be something that is not biologically based but can be developed.[16]

self-esteem
The extent to which a person believes that he or she is a worthwhile and deserving individual

risk propensity
The degree to which an individual is willing to take chances and make risky decisions

emotional intelligence (EQ)
The extent to which people are self-aware, manage their emotions, motivate themselves, express empathy for others, and possess social skills

ATTITUDES AND INDIVIDUAL BEHAVIOR

Another important element of individual behavior in organizations is **attitudes**—complexes of beliefs and feelings that people have about specific ideas, situations, or other people. Attitudes are important because they are the mechanism through which most people express their feelings. An employee's statement that he feels underpaid by the organization reflects his feelings about his pay. Similarly, when a manager says that she likes the new advertising campaign, she is expressing her feelings about the organization's marketing efforts.

Attitudes have three components. The *affective component* of an attitude reflects feelings and emotions an individual has toward a situation. The *cognitive component* of an attitude is derived from knowledge an individual has about a situation. It is important to note that cognition is subject to individual perceptions (something we discuss more fully later). Thus one person might "know" that a certain political candidate is better than another, whereas someone else might "know" just the opposite. Finally, the *intentional component* of an attitude reflects how an individual expects to behave toward or in the situation.

To illustrate these three components, consider the case of a manager who places an order for some supplies for his organization from a new office supply firm. Suppose many of the items he orders are out of stock, others are overpriced, and still others arrive damaged. When he calls someone at the supply firm for assistance, he is treated rudely and gets disconnected before his claim is resolved. When asked how he feels about the new office supply firm, he might respond, "I don't like that company [affective component]. They are the worst office supply firm I've ever dealt with [cognitive component]. I'll never do business with them again [intentional component]."

People try to maintain consistency among the three components of their attitudes as well as among all their attitudes. However, circumstances sometimes arise that lead to conflicts. The conflict individuals may experience among their own attitudes is called **cognitive dissonance**.[17] Say, for example, that an individual who has vowed never to work for a big, impersonal corporation intends instead to open her own business and be her own boss. Unfortunately, a series of financial setbacks leads her to have no choice but to take a job with a large company and work for someone else. Thus cognitive dissonance occurs: The affective and cognitive components of the individual's attitude conflict with intended behavior. To reduce cognitive dissonance, which is usually an uncomfortable experience for most people, the individual might tell herself that the situation is only temporary and that she can go back out on her own in the near future. Or she might revise her cognitions and decide that working for a large company is more pleasant than she had expected.

Work-Related Attitudes

People in organizations form attitudes about many different things. For example, employees are likely to have attitudes about their salary, promotion possibilities, their boss, employee benefits, the food in the company cafeteria, and the color of the company softball team uniforms. Of course, some of these attitudes are more important than others. Especially important attitudes are job satisfaction or dissatisfaction and organizational commitment.[18]

Job Satisfaction or Dissatisfaction **Job satisfaction or dissatisfaction** is an attitude that reflects the extent to which an individual is gratified by or fulfilled in his or her work. Extensive research conducted on job satisfaction has indicated that personal factors, such as an individual's needs and aspirations, determine this attitude, along with group and

attitudes
Complexes of beliefs and feelings that people have about specific ideas, situations, or other people

cognitive dissonance
Caused when an individual has conflicting attitudes

job satisfaction or dissatisfaction
An attitude that reflects the extent to which an individual is gratified by or fulfilled in his or her work

organizational factors, such as relationships with coworkers and supervisors, working conditions, work policies, and compensation.[19]

A satisfied employee also tends to be absent less often, to make positive contributions, and to stay with the organization.[20] In contrast, a dissatisfied employee may be absent more often, may experience stress that disrupts coworkers, and may be continually looking for another job. Contrary to what many managers believe, however, high levels of job satisfaction do not necessarily lead to higher levels of performance. One survey has also indicated that, contrary to popular opinion, Japanese workers are less satisfied with their jobs than their counterparts in the United States.[21]

Organizational Commitment Organizational commitment is an attitude that reflects an individual's identification with and attachment to the organization itself. A person with a high level of commitment is likely to see herself as a true member of the organization (for example, referring to the organization in personal terms like "We make high-quality products"), to overlook minor sources of dissatisfaction with the organization, and to see herself remaining a member of the organization. In contrast, a person with less organizational commitment is more likely to see himself as an outsider (for example, referring to the organization in less personal terms like "They don't pay their employees very well"), to express more dissatisfaction about things, and to not see himself as a long-term member of the organization. Research suggests that Japanese workers may be more committed to their organizations than American workers.[22] As the results from Japan suggests, although job satisfaction and organizational commitment would seem to be related (and are, in most instances), there are times when a person may be very satisfied with his job but less committed to his employer and, in turn, times when a person may be less satisfied with her job but remain highly committed to the organization itself.

Research also suggests that commitment strengthens with an individual's age, years with the organization, sense of job security, and participation in decision making.[23] Employees who feel committed to an organization have highly reliable habits, plan a long tenure with the organization, and muster more effort in performance. Although there are few definitive things that organizations can do to create or promote commitment, there are a few specific guidelines available.[24] For one thing, if the organization treats its employees fairly and provides reasonable rewards and job security, those employees will more likely be satisfied and committed. Allowing employees to have a say in how things are done can also promote all three attitudes.[25]

Affect and Mood in Organizations

Researchers have recently started to focus renewed interest on the affective component of attitudes. Recall from our earlier discussion that the affective component of an attitude reflects our feelings and emotions. Although managers once believed that emotion and feelings varied among people from day to day, research now suggests that, although some short-term fluctuation does indeed occur, there are also underlying stable predispositions toward fairly constant and predictable moods and emotional states.[26]

Some people, for example, tend to have a higher degree of **positive affectivity**, which means that they are relatively upbeat and optimistic, have an overall sense of well-being,

HILL STREET STUDIOS/BLEND IMAGES/JUPITER IMAGES

Some experts believe that Japanese workers are more committed to and satisfied with their jobs than are their counterparts in the United States. These experts also claim that these higher levels of commitment and satisfaction have to productivity gains by Japanese companies. In fact, though, research evidence is mixed. One early study, for instance, found that Japanese workers may be more committed to their organizations, they are actually less satisfied with their jobs.

organizational commitment
An attitude that reflects an individual's identification with and attachment to the organization itself

positive affectivity
A tendency to be relatively upbeat and optimistic, have an overall sense of well-being, see things in a positive light, and seem to be in a good mood

and usually see things in a positive light. Thus they always seem to be in a good mood. It's recently been proposed that positive affectivity may also play a role in entrepreneurial success.[27] Other people, those with more **negative affectivity**, are just the opposite. They are generally downbeat and pessimistic, and they usually see things in a negative way. Thus they seem to be in a bad mood most of the time.

Of course, as noted above, there can be short-term variations among even the most extreme types. People with a lot of positive affectivity, for example, may still be in a bad mood if they have just received some bad news—being passed over for a promotion, getting extremely negative performance feedback, or being laid off or fired, for instance. Similarly, those with negative affectivity may still be in a good mood—at least for a short time—if they have just been promoted, received very positive performance feedback, or had other good things befall them. After the initial impact of these events wears off, however, those with positive affectivity will generally return to their normal positive mood, whereas those with negative affectivity will gravitate back to their normal bad mood.

PERCEPTION AND INDIVIDUAL BEHAVIOR

As noted earlier, an important element of an attitude is the individual's perception of the object about which the attitude is formed. Because perception plays a role in a variety of other workplace behaviors, managers need to have a general understanding of basic perceptual processes.[28] The role of attributions is also important.

Basic Perceptual Processes

Perception is the set of processes by which an individual becomes aware of and interprets information about the environment. As shown in Figure 11.3, basic perceptual processes that are particularly relevant to organizations are selective perception and stereotyping.

negative affectivity
A tendency to be generally downbeat and pessimistic, see things in a negative way, and seem to be in a bad mood

perception
The set of processes by which an individual becomes aware of and interprets information about the environment

Figure 11.3   **Perceptual Processes**

Two of the most basic perceptual processes are selective perception and stereotyping. As shown here, selective perception occurs when we screen out information (represented by the − symbols) that causes us discomfort or that contradicts our beliefs. Stereotyping occurs when we categorize or label people on the basis of a single attribute, illustrated here by color.

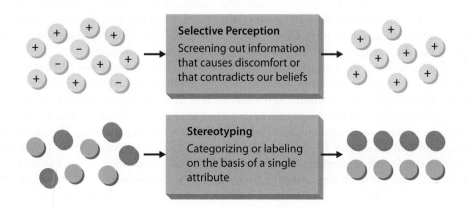

Selective Perception **Selective perception** is the process of screening out information that we are uncomfortable with or that contradicts our beliefs. For example, suppose a manager is exceptionally fond of a particular worker. The manager has a very positive attitude about the worker and thinks he is a top performer. One day the manager notices that the worker seems to be goofing off. Selective perception may cause the manager to quickly forget what he observed. Similarly, suppose a manager has formed a very negative image of a particular worker. She thinks this worker is a poor performer and never does a good job. When she happens to observe an example of high performance from the worker, she may not remember it for very long. In one sense, selective perception is beneficial because it allows us to disregard minor bits of information. Of course, this holds true only if our basic perception is accurate. If selective perception causes us to ignore important information, however, it can become quite detrimental.

Stereotyping **Stereotyping** is the process of categorizing or labeling people on the basis of a single attribute. Common attributes from which people often stereotype are race, gender, and age.[29] Of course, stereotypes along these lines are inaccurate and can be harmful. For example, suppose a manager forms the stereotype that women can perform only certain tasks and that men are best suited for other tasks. To the extent that this affects the manager's hiring practices, the manager is (1) costing the organization valuable talent for both sets of jobs, (2) violating federal law, and (3) behaving unethically. On the other hand, certain forms of stereotyping can be useful and efficient. Suppose, for example, that a manager believes that communication skills are important for a particular job and that speech communication majors tend to have exceptionally good communication skills. As a result, whenever he interviews candidates for jobs, he pays especially close attention to speech communication majors. To the extent that communication skills truly predict job performance and that majoring in speech communication does indeed provide those skills, this form of stereotyping can be beneficial.

Perception and Attribution

Perception is also closely linked with another process called **attribution**, which is a mechanism through which we observe behavior and then attribute causes to it.[30] The behavior that is observed may be our own or that of others. For example, suppose someone realizes one day that she is working fewer hours than before, that she talks less about her work, and that she calls in sick more frequently. She might conclude from this that she must have become disenchanted with her job and subsequently decide to quit. Thus she observed her own behavior, attributed a cause to it, and developed what she thought was a consistent response.

More common is attributing cause to the behavior of others. For example, if the manager of the individual described above has observed the same behavior, he might form exactly the same attribution. On the other hand, he might instead decide that she has a serious illness, that he is driving her too hard, that she is experiencing too much stress, that she has a drug problem, or that she is having family problems.

The basic framework around which we form attributions is *consensus* (the extent to which other people in the same situation behave the same way), *consistency* (the extent to which the same person behaves in the same way at different times), and *distinctiveness* (the extent to which the same person behaves in the same way in other situations). For example, suppose a manager observes that an employee is late for a meeting. The manager might further realize that he is the only one who is late (low consensus), recall that he is often late for other meetings (high consistency), and subsequently realize that he is sometimes late for work and returning from lunch (low distinctiveness). This pattern of attributions might cause the manager to decide that the individual's behavior is something that should be changed. As a result, the manager might meet with the subordinate and establish some punitive consequences for future tardiness.

STRESS AND INDIVIDUAL BEHAVIOR

Another important element of behavior in organizations is **stress**—an individual's response to a strong stimulus called a *stressor*.[31] Stress generally follows a cycle referred to as the **General Adaptation Syndrome (GAS)**,[32] shown in Figure 11.4. According to this view, when an individual first encounters a stressor, the GAS is initiated, and stage 1, alarm, is activated. He may feel panic, wonder how to cope, and feel helpless. For example, suppose a manager is told to prepare a detailed evaluation of a plan by his firm to buy one of its competitors. His first reaction may be "How will I ever get this done by tomorrow?"

If the stressor is too intense, the individual may feel unable to cope and never really try to respond to its demands. In most cases, however, after a short period of alarm, the individual gathers some strength and starts to resist the negative effects of the stressor. For example, the manager with the evaluation to write may calm down, call home to say he is working late, roll up his sleeves, order out for coffee, and get to work. Thus, at stage 2 of the GAS, the person is resisting the effects of the stressor.

In many cases, the resistance phase may end the GAS. If the manager is able to complete the evaluation earlier than expected, he may drop it in his briefcase, smile to himself, and head home tired but satisfied. On the other hand, prolonged exposure to a stressor without resolution may bring on stage 3 of the GAS—exhaustion. At this stage, the individual literally gives up and can no longer resist the stressor. The manager, for example, might fall asleep at his desk at 3:00 A.M. and never finish the evaluation.

We should note that stress is not all bad. In the absence of stress, we may experience lethargy and stagnation. An optimal level of stress, on the other hand, can result in motivation and excitement. Too much stress, however, can have negative consequences. It is also important to understand that stress can be caused by "good" as well as "bad" things.

stress
An individual's response to a strong stimulus, which is called a *stressor*

General Adaptation Syndrome (GAS)
General cycle of the stress process

Figure 11.4   **The General Adaptation Syndrome**

The GAS represents the normal process by which we react to stressful events. At stage 1—alarm—we feel panic and alarm, and our level of resistance to stress drops. Stage 2—resistance—represents our efforts to confront and control the stressful circumstance. If we fail, we may eventually reach stage 3—exhaustion—and just give up or quit.

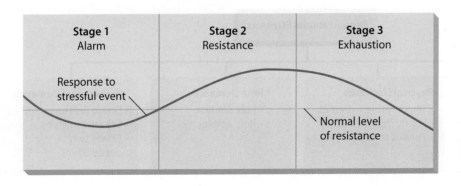

Excessive pressure, unreasonable demands on our time, and bad news can all cause stress. But even receiving a bonus and then having to decide what to do with the money can be stressful. So, too, can receiving a promotion, gaining recognition, and similar good things.

One important line of thinking about stress focuses on **Type A** and **Type B** personalities.[33] Type A individuals are extremely competitive, are very devoted to work, and have a strong sense of time urgency. They are likely to be aggressive, impatient, and very work oriented. They have a lot of drive and want to accomplish as much as possible as quickly as possible. Type B individuals are less competitive, are less devoted to work, and have a weaker sense of time urgency. Such individuals are less likely to experience conflict with other people and more likely to have a balanced, relaxed approach to life. They are able to work at a constant pace without time urgency. Type B people are not necessarily more or less successful than Type A people. But they are less likely to experience stress.

Causes and Consequences of Stress

Stress is obviously not a simple phenomenon. As listed in Figure 11.5, several different things can cause stress. Note that this list includes only work-related conditions. We should keep in mind that stress can also be the result of personal circumstances.[34]

Causes of Stress Work-related stressors fall into one of four categories—task, physical, role, and interpersonal demands. *Task demands* are associated with the task itself. Some occupations are inherently more stressful than others. Having to make fast decisions, decisions with less than complete information, or decisions that have relatively serious consequences are some of the things that can make some jobs stressful. The jobs of surgeon, airline pilot, and stockbroker are relatively more stressful than the jobs of general practitioner, baggage handler, and office receptionist. Although a general practitioner makes important decisions, he is also likely to have time to make a considered diagnosis and fully explore a number of different treatments. But, during surgery, the surgeon must make decisions quickly while realizing that the wrong one may endanger her patient's life.

Physical demands are stressors associated with the job setting. Working outdoors in extremely hot or cold temperatures, or even in an improperly heated or cooled office, can lead to stress. Likewise, jobs that have rotating work shifts make it difficult for people to have

Type A
Individuals who are extremely competitive, are very devoted to work, and have a strong sense of time urgency

Type B
Individuals who are less competitive, are less devoted to work, and have a weaker sense of time urgency

Figure 11.5 Causes of Work Stress

There are several causes of work stress in organizations. Four general sets of organizational stressors are task demands, physical demands, role demands, and interpersonal demands.

Organizational Stressors			
Task Demands	**Physical Demands**	**Role Demands**	**Interpersonal Demands**
• Quick decisions	• Temperature extremes	• Role conflict	• Group pressures
• Incomplete information for decisions	• Poorly designed office	• Role ambiguity	• Leadership styles
• Critical decisions	• Threats to health		• Conflicting personalities

stable sleep patterns. A poorly designed office, which makes it difficult for people to have privacy or promotes too little social interaction, can result in stress, as can poor lighting and inadequate work surfaces. Even more severe are actual threats to health. Examples include jobs such as coal mining, poultry processing, and toxic waste handling. Similarly, some jobs carry risks associated with higher incident rates of violence, such as those at risk of armed robberies including law enforcement officers, taxi drivers, and convenience store clerks.

Role demands can also cause stress. (Roles are discussed more fully in Chapter 15.) A role is a set of expected behaviors associated with a position in a group or organization. Stress can result from either role conflict or role ambiguity that people can experience in groups. For example, an employee who is feeling pressure from her boss to work longer hours or to travel more, while also being asked by her family for more time at home, will almost certainly experience stress as a result of role conflict.[35] Similarly, a new employee experiencing role ambiguity because of poor orientation and training practices by the organization will also suffer from stress. Excessive meetings are also a potential source of stress.[36] Although job cuts and layoffs during the 2008–2009 recession focused on the stress experienced by those losing their jobs (and appropriately so), it's also the case that many of the managers imposing the layoffs experienced stress.[37]

Interpersonal demands are stressors associated with relationships that confront people in organizations. For example, group pressures regarding restriction of output and norm conformity can lead to stress. Leadership styles may also cause stress. An employee who feels a strong need to participate in decision making may feel stress if his boss refuses to allow participation. And individuals with conflicting personalities may experience stress if required to work too closely together. For example, a person with an internal locus of control might be frustrated when working with someone who prefers to wait and just let things happen.

Consequences of Stress   As noted earlier, the results of stress may be positive or negative. The negative consequences may be behavioral, psychological, or medical. Behaviorally, for example, stress may lead to detrimental or harmful actions, such as smoking, alcohol or drug abuse, and overeating. Other stress-induced behaviors are accident proneness, violence toward self or others, and appetite disorders. Substance abuse is also a potential consequence.[38]

Psychological consequences of stress interfere with an individual's mental health and well-being.[39] These outcomes include sleep disturbances, depression, family problems, and sexual dysfunction. Managers are especially prone to sleep disturbances when they experience stress at work.[40] Medical consequences of stress affect an individual's physiological well-being. Heart disease and stroke have been linked to stress, as have headaches, backaches, ulcers and related disorders, and skin conditions such as acne and hives.

Individual stress also has direct consequences for businesses. For an operating employee, stress may translate into poor-quality work and lower productivity. For a manager, it may mean faulty decision making and disruptions in working relationships.[41] Withdrawal behaviors can also result from stress. People who are having difficulties with stress in their jobs are more likely to call in sick or to leave their positions. More subtle forms of withdrawal may also occur. A manager may start missing deadlines, for example, or taking longer lunch breaks. Employees may also withdraw by developing feelings of indifference. The irritation displayed by people under great stress can make them difficult to get along with. Job satisfaction, morale, and commitment can all suffer as a result of excessive levels of stress. So, too, can motivation to perform.

Another consequence of stress is **burnout**—a feeling of exhaustion that may develop when someone experiences too much stress for an extended period of time. Burnout results

burnout
A feeling of exhaustion that may develop when someone experiences too much stress for an extended period of time

JOE RAEDLE/GETTY IMAGES

Yoga is an increasingly popular method for controlling stress. Indeed, as unemployment spiked during the 2008–2009 recession, there was a surge in the number of people taking yoga classes. There are also reports of companies offering yoga as part of on-site wellness stress management programs.

in constant fatigue, frustration, and helplessness. Increased rigidity follows, as do a loss of self-confidence and psychological withdrawal. The individual dreads going to work, often puts in longer hours but gets less accomplished than before, and exhibits mental and physical exhaustion. Because of the damaging effects of burnout, some firms are taking steps to help avoid it. For example, British Airways provides all of its employees with training designed to help them recognize the symptoms of burnout and develop strategies for avoiding it.

Managing Stress

Given the potential consequences of stress, it follows that both people and organizations should be concerned about how to limit its more damaging effects. Numerous ideas and approaches have been developed to help manage stress. Some are strategies for individuals; others are strategies for organizations.[42]

One way people manage stress is through exercise. People who exercise regularly feel less tension and stress, are more self-confident, and feel more optimistic. Their better physical condition also makes them less susceptible to many common illnesses. People who do not exercise regularly, on the other hand, tend to feel more stress and are more likely to be depressed. They are also more likely to have heart attacks. And, because of their physical condition, they are more likely to contract illnesses.

Another method people use to manage stress is relaxation. Relaxation allows individuals to adapt to, and therefore better deal with, their stress. Relaxation comes in many forms, such as taking regular vacations. A recent study found that people's attitudes toward a variety of workplace characteristics improved significantly following a vacation. People can also learn to relax while on the job. For example, some experts recommend that people take regular rest breaks during their normal workday.

People can also use time management to control stress. The idea behind time management is that many daily pressures can be reduced or eliminated if individuals do a better job of managing time. One approach to time management is to make a list every morning of the things to be done that day. The items on the list are then grouped into three categories: critical activities that must be performed, important activities that should be performed, and optional or trivial things that can be delegated or postponed. The individual performs the items on the list in their order of importance.

Finally, people can manage stress through support groups. A support group can be as simple as a group of family members or friends to enjoy leisure time with. Going out after work with a couple of coworkers to a basketball game or a movie, for example, can help relieve stress built up during the day. Family and friends can help people cope with stress on an ongoing basis and during times of crisis. For example, an employee who has just learned that she did not get the promotion she has been working toward for months may find it helpful to have a good friend to lean on, talk to, or yell at. People may also make use of more elaborate and formal support groups. Community centers or churches, for example, may sponsor support groups for people who have recently gone through a divorce, the death of a loved one, or some other tragedy.

Organizations are also beginning to realize that they should be involved in helping employees cope with stress. One argument for this is that because the business is at least partially responsible for stress, it should also help relieve it. Another is that stress-related insurance claims by employees can cost the organization considerable sums of money. Still another is that workers experiencing lower levels of detrimental stress will be able to function more effectively. AT&T has initiated a series of seminars and workshops to help its employees cope with the stress they face in their jobs. The firm was prompted to develop these seminars for all three of the reasons noted above.

A wellness stress program is a special part of the organization specifically created to help deal with stress. Organizations have adopted stress management programs, health promotion programs, and other kinds of programs for this purpose. The AT&T seminar program noted earlier is similar to this idea, but true wellness programs are ongoing activities that have a number of different components. They commonly include exercise-related activities as well as classroom instruction programs dealing with smoking cessation, weight reduction, and general stress management.

Some companies are developing their own programs or using existing programs of this type. Johns Manville, for example, has a gym at its corporate headquarters. Other firms negotiate discounted health club membership rates with local establishments. For the instructional part of the program, the organization can again either sponsor its own training or perhaps jointly sponsor seminars with a local YMCA, civic organization, or church. Organization-based fitness programs facilitate employee exercise, a very positive consideration, but such programs are also quite costly. Still, more and more companies are developing fitness programs for employees. Similarly, some companies are offering their employees periodic sabbaticals—extended breaks from work that presumably allow people to get revitalized and reenergized. Intel and McDonald's are among the firms offering the benefit.[43]

CREATIVITY IN ORGANIZATIONS

Creativity is yet another important component of individual behavior in organizations. **Creativity** is the ability of an individual to generate new ideas or to conceive of new perspectives on existing ideas. What makes a person creative? How do people become creative? How does the creative process work? Although psychologists have not yet discovered complete answers to these questions, examining a few general patterns can help us understand the sources of individual creativity within organizations.[44]

The Creative Individual

Numerous researchers have focused their efforts on attempting to describe the common attributes of creative individuals. These attributes generally fall into three categories: background experiences, personal traits, and cognitive abilities.

Background Experiences and Creativity Researchers have observed that many creative individuals were raised in environments in which creativity was nurtured. Mozart was raised in a family of musicians and began composing and performing music at age six. Pierre and Marie Curie, great scientists in their own right, also raised a daughter, Irene, who

creativity
The ability of an individual to generate new ideas or to conceive of new perspectives on existing ideas

won the Nobel Prize in chemistry. Thomas Edison's creativity was nurtured by his mother. However, people with background experiences very different from theirs have also been creative. Frederick Douglass was born into slavery in Tuckahoe, Maryland, and had very limited opportunities for education. Nonetheless, his powerful oratory and creative thinking helped lead to the Emancipation Proclamation, which outlawed slavery in the United States.

Personal Traits and Creativity Certain personal traits have also been linked to creativity in individuals. The traits shared by most creative people are openness, an attraction to complexity, high levels of energy, independence and autonomy, strong self-confidence, and a strong belief that one is, in fact, creative. Individuals who possess these traits are more likely to be creative than those who do not have them.

Cognitive Abilities and Creativity Cognitive abilities are an individual's power to think intelligently and to analyze situations and data effectively. Intelligence may be a precondition for individual creativity—although most creative people are highly intelligent, not all intelligent people are necessarily creative. Creativity is also linked with the ability to think divergently and convergently. *Divergent thinking* is a skill that allows people to see differences among situations, phenomena, or events. *Convergent thinking* is a skill that allows people to see similarities among situations, phenomena, or events. Creative people are generally very skilled at both divergent and convergent thinking.

Interestingly, Japanese managers have come to question their own creative abilities. The concern is that their emphasis on group harmony may have stifled individual initiative and hampered the development of individual creativity. As a result, many Japanese firms, including Omron Corporation, Fuji Photo, and Shimizu Corporation, have launched employee training programs intended to boost the creativity of their employees.[45]

The Creative Process

Although creative people often report that ideas seem to come to them "in a flash," individual creative activity actually tends to progress through a series of stages. Not all creative activity has to follow these four stages, but much of it does.

Preparation The creative process normally begins with a period of *preparation*. To make a creative contribution to business management or business services, individuals must usually receive formal training and education in business. Formal education and training are usually the most efficient ways of becoming familiar with this vast amount of research and knowledge. This is one reason for the strong demand for undergraduate and master's level business education.

Formal business education can be an effective way for an individual to get "up to speed" and begin making creative contributions quickly. Experiences that managers have on the job after their formal training has finished can also contribute to the creative process. In an important sense, the education and training of creative people never really ends. It continues as long as they remain interested in the world and curious about the way things work. Bruce Roth earned a PhD in chemistry and then spent years working in the pharmaceutical industry learning more and more about chemical compounds and how they work in human beings.

Incubation The second phase of the creative process is *incubation*—a period of less intense conscious concentration during which the knowledge and ideas acquired during preparation mature and develop. A curious aspect of incubation is that it is often helped along by pauses in concentrated rational thought. Some creative people rely on physical activity such as jogging or swimming to provide a break from thinking. Others may read or listen to music. Sometimes sleep may even supply the needed pause. Bruce Roth eventually joined Warner-Lambert, an up-and-coming drug company, to help develop medication to lower cholesterol. In his spare time, Roth read mystery novels and hiked in the mountains. He later acknowledged that this was when he did his best thinking. Similarly, twice a year Bill Gates retreats to a secluded wooded cabin to reflect on trends in technology; it is during these weeks, he says, that he develops his sharpest insights into where Microsoft should be heading.[46]

Insight   Usually occurring after preparation and incubation, *insight* is a spontaneous breakthrough in which the creative person achieves a new understanding of some problem or situation. Insight represents a coming together of all the scattered thoughts and ideas that were maturing during incubation. It may occur suddenly or develop slowly over time. Insight can be triggered by some external event, such as a new experience or an encounter with new data, which forces the individual to think about old issues and problems in new ways, or it can be a completely internal event in which patterns of thought finally coalesce in ways that generate new understanding. One day Bruce Roth was reviewing some data from some earlier studies that had found the new drug under development to be no more effective than other drugs already available. But this time he saw some statistical relationships that had not been identified previously. He knew then that he had a major breakthrough on his hands.

Verification   Once an insight has occurred, *verification* determines the validity or truthfulness of the insight. For many creative ideas, verification includes scientific experiments to determine whether the insight actually leads to the results expected. Verification may also include the development of a product or service prototype. A prototype is one product or a very small number of products built just to see if the ideas behind this new product actually work. Product prototypes are rarely sold to the public but are very valuable in verifying the insights developed in the creative process. Once the new product or service is developed, verification in the marketplace is the ultimate test of the creative idea behind it. Bruce Roth and his colleagues set to work testing the new drug compound and eventually won FDA approval. The drug, named Lipitor, is already the largest-selling pharmaceutical in history. And Pfizer, the firm that bought Warner-Lambert in a hostile takeover, is expected to soon earn more than $10 billion a year on the drug.[47]

Enhancing Creativity in Organizations

Managers who wish to enhance and promote creativity in their organizations can do so in a variety of ways.[48] One important method for enhancing creativity is to make it a part of the organization's culture, often through explicit goals. Firms that truly want to stress creativity, like 3M and Rubbermaid, for example, state goals that some percentage of future revenues are to be gained from new products. This clearly communicates that creativity and innovation are valued. Best Buy recently picked four groups of salespeople in their twenties and early thirties and asked them to spend ten weeks living together in a Los Angeles apartment complex (with expenses paid by the company and still earning their normal pay). Their job was to sit around and brainstorm new business ideas that could be rolled out quickly and cheaply.[49]

Another important part of enhancing creativity is to reward creative successes, while being careful not to punish creative failures. Many ideas that seem worthwhile on paper fail to pan out in reality. If the first person to come up with an idea that fails is fired or otherwise punished, others in the organization will become more cautious in their own work. And, as a result, fewer creative ideas will emerge.

TYPES OF WORKPLACE BEHAVIOR

Now that we have looked closely at how individual differences can influence behavior in organizations, let's turn our attention to what we mean by workplace behavior. **Workplace behavior** is a pattern of action by the members of an organization that directly or indirectly influences organizational effectiveness. Important workplace behaviors include performance and productivity, absenteeism and turnover, and organizational citizenship. Unfortunately, a variety of dysfunctional behaviors can also occur in organizational settings.

Performance Behaviors

Performance behaviors are the total set of work-related behaviors that the organization expects the individual to display. Thus they derive from the psychological contract. For some jobs, performance behaviors can be narrowly defined and easily measured. For example, an assembly-line worker who sits by a moving conveyor and attaches parts to a product as it passes by has relatively few performance behaviors. He or she is expected to remain at the workstation and correctly attach the parts. Performance can often be assessed quantitatively by counting the percentage of parts correctly attached.

For many other jobs, however, performance behaviors are more diverse and much more difficult to assess. For example, consider the case of a research and development scientist at Merck. The scientist works in a lab trying to find new scientific breakthroughs that have commercial potential. The scientist must apply knowledge learned in graduate school with experience gained from previous research. Intuition and creativity are also important elements. And the desired breakthrough may take months or even years to accomplish. As we discussed in Chapter 8, organizations rely on a number of different methods for evaluating performance. The key, of course, is to match the evaluation mechanism with the job being performed.

Withdrawal Behaviors

Another important type of work-related behavior is that which results in withdrawal—absenteeism and turnover. **Absenteeism** occurs when an individual does not show up for work. The cause may be legitimate (illness, jury duty, death in the family, and so forth) or feigned (reported as legitimate but actually just an excuse to stay home). When an employee is absent, his or her work does not get done at all, or a substitute must be hired to do it. In either case, the quantity or quality of actual output is likely to suffer. Obviously, some absenteeism is expected. The key concern of organizations is to minimize feigned absenteeism and to reduce legitimate absences as much as possible. High absenteeism may be a symptom of other problems as well, such as job dissatisfaction and low morale.

Turnover occurs when people quit their jobs. An organization usually incurs costs in replacing individuals who have quit, but if turnover involves especially productive

workplace behavior
A pattern of action by the members of an organization that directly or indirectly influences organizational effectiveness

performance behaviors
The total set of work-related behaviors that the organization expects the individual to display

absenteeism
When an individual does not show up for work

turnover
When people quit their jobs

people, it is even more costly. Turnover seems to result from a number of factors, including aspects of the job, the organization, the individual, the labor market, and family influences. In general, a poor person–job fit is also a likely cause of turnover.[50] The current high levels of unemployment reduce employee-driven turnover, given that fewer jobs are available. But when unemployment is low (and there are many open jobs), turnover may naturally increase as people seek better opportunities, higher pay, and so forth.

Efforts to directly manage turnover are frequently fraught with difficulty, even in organizations that concentrate on rewarding good performers. Of course, some turnover is inevitable, and in some cases it may even be desirable. For example, if the organization is trying to cut costs by reducing its staff, having people voluntarily choose to leave is preferable to having to terminate their jobs. And, if the people who choose to leave are low performers or express high levels of job dissatisfaction, the organization may also benefit from turnover.

Organizational Citizenship

Organizational citizenship is the behavior of individuals that makes a positive overall contribution to the organization.[51] Consider, for example, an employee who does work that is acceptable in terms of both quantity and quality. However, she refuses to work overtime, will not help newcomers learn the ropes, and is generally unwilling to make any contribution to the organization beyond the strict performance of her job. Although this person may be seen as a good performer, she is not likely to be seen as a good organizational citizen.

Another employee may exhibit a comparable level of performance. In addition, however, he will always work late when the boss asks him to, take time to help newcomers learn their way around, and is perceived as being helpful and committed to the organization's success. Although his level of performance may be seen as equal to that of the first worker, he is also likely to be seen as a better organizational citizen.

The determinant of organizational citizenship behaviors is likely to be a complex mosaic of individual, social, and organizational variables. For example, the personality, attitudes, and needs of the individual will have to be consistent with citizenship behaviors. Similarly, the social context in which the individual works, or work group, will need to facilitate and promote such behaviors (we discuss group dynamics in Chapter 15). And the organization itself, especially its culture, must be capable of promoting, recognizing, and rewarding these types of behaviors if they are to be maintained. Although the study of organizational citizenship is still in its infancy, preliminary research suggests that it may play a powerful role in organizational effectiveness.[52]

Dysfunctional Behaviors

Some work-related behaviors are dysfunctional in nature. **Dysfunctional behaviors** are those that detract from, rather than contribute to, organizational performance.[53] Two of the more common ones, absenteeism and turnover, were discussed earlier. But other forms of dysfunctional behavior may be even more costly for an organization. Theft and sabotage, for example, result in direct financial costs for an organization. Sexual and racial harassment also cost an organization, both indirectly (by lowering morale, producing fear, and driving off valuable employees) and directly (through financial

organizational citizenship
The behavior of individuals that makes a positive overall contribution to the organization

dysfunctional behaviors
Those that detract from, rather than contribute to, organizational performance

liability if the organization responds inappropriately). So, too, can politicized behavior, intentionally misleading others in the organization, spreading malicious rumors, and similar activities. Incivility and rudeness can result in conflict and damage to morale and the organization's culture.[54] Workplace violence is also a growing concern in many organizations. Violence by disgruntled workers or former workers results in dozens of deaths and injuries each year.[55]

SUMMARY OF LEARNING OBJECTIVES AND KEY POINTS

1. Explain the nature of the individual–organization relationship.

   - A basic framework that can be used to facilitate this understanding is the psychological contract—the set of expectations held by people with respect to what they will contribute to the organization and what they expect to get in return.

   - Organizations strive to achieve an optimal person–job fit, but this process is complicated by the existence of individual differences.

2. Define personality and describe personality attributes that affect behavior in organizations.

   - Personality is the relatively stable set of psychological and behavioral attributes that distinguish one person from another.

   - The "Big Five" personality traits are
     - agreeableness
     - conscientiousness
     - negative emotionality
     - extraversion
     - openness

   - The Myers-Briggs framework can also be a useful mechanism for understanding personality.

   - Other important traits are
     - locus of control
     - self-efficacy
     - authoritarianism
     - Machiavellianism
     - self-esteem
     - risk propensity

   - EQ, a fairly new concept, may provide additional insights into personality.

3. Discuss individual attitudes in organizations and how they affect behavior.

   - Attitudes are based on emotion, knowledge, and intended behavior.

   - Whereas personality is relatively stable, some attitudes can be formed and changed easily. Others are more constant.

   - Job satisfaction or dissatisfaction and organizational commitment are important work-related attitudes.

4. Describe basic perceptual processes and the role of attributions in organizations.

   - Perception is the set of processes by which an individual becomes aware of and interprets information about the environment.

   - Basic perceptual processes include selective perception and stereotyping.

   - Perception and attribution are also closely related.

5. Discuss the causes and consequences of stress and describe how it can be managed.

   - Stress is an individual's response to a strong stimulus.

   - The GAS outlines the basic stress process.

   - Stress can be caused by task, physical, role, and interpersonal demands.

   - Consequences of stress include organizational and individual outcomes, as well as burnout.

   - Several things can be done to manage stress.

6. Describe creativity and its role in organizations.

   - Creativity is the capacity to generate new ideas.

- Creative people tend to have certain profiles of background experiences, personal traits, and cognitive abilities.
- The creative process itself includes preparation, incubation, insight, and verification.

7. Explain how workplace behaviors can directly or indirectly influence organizational effectiveness.
    - Workplace behavior is a pattern of action by the members of an organization that directly or indirectly influences organizational effectiveness.
    - Performance behaviors are the set of work-related behaviors that the organization expects the individual to display to fulfill the psychological contract.
    - Basic withdrawal behaviors are absenteeism and turnover.
    - Organizational citizenship refers to behavior that makes a positive overall contribution to the organization.
    - Dysfunctional behaviors can be very harmful to an organization.

DISCUSSION QUESTIONS

Questions for Review

1. What is a psychological contract? List the things that might be included in individual contributions. List the things that might be included in organizational inducements.

2. Describe the three components of attitudes and tell how the components are related. What is cognitive dissonance? How do individuals resolve cognitive dissonance?

3. Identify and discuss the steps in the creative process. What can an organization do to increase employees' creativity?

4. Identify and describe several important workplace behaviors.

Questions for Analysis

1. Organizations are increasing their use of personality tests to screen job applicants. What are the advantages and disadvantages of this approach? What can managers do to avoid some of the potential pitfalls?

2. As a manager, how can you tell that an employee is experiencing job satisfaction? How can you tell that employees are highly committed to the organization? If a worker is not satisfied, what can a manager do to improve satisfaction? What can a manager do to improve organizational commitment?

3. Managers cannot pay equal attention to every piece of information, so selective perception is a fact of life. How does selective perception help managers? How does it create difficulties for them? How can managers increase their "good" selective perception and decrease the "bad"?

4. Write the psychological contract you have in this class. In other words, what do you contribute, and what inducements are available? Ask your professor to tell the class about the psychological contract that he or she intended to establish with the students in your class. How does the professor's intended contract compare with the one you wrote? If there are differences, why do you think the differences exist? Share your ideas with the class.

5. Assume that you are going to hire three new employees for the department store you manage. One will sell shoes, one will manage the toy department, and one will work in the stockroom. Identify the basic characteristics you want in each of the people, to achieve a good person–job fit.

BUILDING EFFECTIVE INTERPERSONAL SKILLS

Exercise Overview

Interpersonal skills refer to the ability to communicate with, understand, and motivate individuals and groups. This exercise introduces you to a widely used tool for

personality assessment and shows how an understanding of personality can be of use in developing effective interpersonal relationships within organizations.

Exercise Background

Of the many different ways of interpreting personality, the widely used MBTI categorizes individual personality types along four dimensions, which were discussed earlier.

Using the MBTI, researchers use survey answers to classify individuals into 16 personality types—all the possible

combinations of the four Myers-Briggs dimensions. The resulting personality type is then expressed as a four-character code, such as *ESTP* for *Extravert-Sensing-Thinking-Perceiving*. These four-character codes are then used to describe an individual's preferred way of interacting with others.

Exercise Task

1. Use a Meyers-Briggs assessment form to determine your own personality type. You can find a form at **www.keirsey.com/scripts/newkts.cgi**, a website that also contains additional information about personality type. (*Note:* There are no fees for taking the Temperament Sorter, nor must you agree to receive e-mail.)

2. When you've determined the four-letter code for your personality type, you can get a handout from your instructor that will explain how your personal-

ity type affects not only your preferred style of working but your leadership style as well.

3. Conclude by responding to the following questions:

   • How easy is it to measure personality?

   • Do you feel that the online test accurately assessed your personality?

   • Why or why not? Share your assessment results and your responses with the class.

BUILDING EFFECTIVE TIME MANAGEMENT SKILLS

Exercise Overview

Time management skills refer to the ability to prioritize tasks, to work efficiently, and to delegate appropriately. Among other reasons, they're important because poor

time management skills may result in stress. This exercise shows you how effective time management skills can help reduce stress.

Exercise Background

List several of the major events or expectations that tend to be stressful for you. Common stressors include school (classes, exams), work (finances, schedules), and

personal circumstances (friends, romance, family). Try to be as specific as possible and try to identify at least ten different stressors.

Exercise Task

Using your list, do each of the following:

1. Evaluate the extent to which poor time management skills on your part play a role in the way each stressor affects you. Do exams cause stress, for example, because you tend to put off studying?

2. For each stressor that's affected by your time management habits, develop a strategy for using your time more efficiently.

3. Note the interrelationships among different kinds of stressors to see if they revolve around time-related

problems. For example, financial pressures may cause you to work, and work may interfere with school. Can you manage any of these interrelationships more effectively by managing your time more effectively?

4. How do you typically manage the stress in your life? Can you manage stress in a more time-effective manner?

SKILLS SELF-ASSESSMENT INSTRUMENT

Personality Types at Work

Interpersonal skills reflect the ability to communicate with, understand, and motivate individuals and groups. This exercise introduces a widely used tool for personality assessment. It shows how an understanding of personality can aid in developing effective interpersonal relationships within organizations.

Introduction: There are many different ways of viewing personality, and one that is widely used is called the MBTI According to Isabel Myers, each individual's personality type varies in four dimensions, which were discussed earlier.

On the basis of their answers to a survey, individuals are classified into 16 personality types—all the possible combinations of the four dimensions. The resulting personality type is then expressed as a four-character code, such as ESTP or INFJ. These four-character codes can then be used to describe an individual's preferred way of interacting with others.

Instructions:

___ 1. Use an online Myers-Briggs assessment form to assess your personality type. One place to find the form online is www.keirsey.com/scripts/newkts.cgi. This website also contains additional information about personality type. (*Note:* This site requires free registration, but you do *not* need to pay fees or agree to receive e-mails to take the Temperament Sorter.) Alternatively, your institution's Career Center or other organizations may offer a Myers-Briggs assessment service.

___ 2. When you have determined the four-letter code for your personality type, obtain a handout from your professor. The handout will show how your personality type affects your preferred style of working and your leadership style.

Source: Reprinted by permission of the author Margaret Hill.

EXPERIENTIAL EXERCISE

Stress Test

Job-related stress is very common in organizations—almost everyone experiences stress some of the time. Stress can also occur in nonwork settings, such as school or family life. While a moderate level of stress can have positive effects, too much stress can lead to physical and mental health problems, absenteeism and turnover, low productivity and morale, and eventually, burnout.

Investigate the demands of your Management class to assess the extent of factors that increase stress, writing down your answers individually. Discuss your perceptions with a small group of classmates. Then as a group, suggest changes that would make your class less stressing.

Step 1: Working alone, assess the task demands associated with your Management class. In this category, include items such as the extent to which you are fully informed and can therefore make informed decisions. Also consider the time pressure and the possible consequences of your actions.

Assess the physical demands associated with your Management class. In this category, include items such as the location and facilities available in the classroom. Also include lighting, heating, ventilation, seating, amount of space, flexibility of the space, and so on.

Assess the role demands associated with your Management class. In this category, consider the role you play as a student. Do you understand what is expected of you in this role? Are you comfortable in this role? Does your role as a student conflict with any of the other important roles that you play?

Assess the interpersonal demands associated with your Management class. In this category, consider your relationships with the instructor and your fellow students. Any personality conflicts or pressure to conform to group norms would tend to increase stress.

Step 2: In a small group, discuss your answers. Try to recognize patterns of similarities and differences. Then discuss changes that could be made that would reduce stress. Be sure to consider changes that could be made by your institution or department, by your instructor, and by the students.

Step 3: Discuss your conclusions with the class and your instructor.

 YOU MAKE THE CALL

Is Your Boss Superficially Charming, Insincere, and Lacking in Empathy?

1. Have you ever worked with or for someone who exhibited psychopathic or narcissistic behavior? If so, describe that behavior and explain why it indicates a diagnosis of psychopathy or narcissism.

2. About a month after starting a new job, you realize that your boss exhibits psychopathic tendencies. What will you do?

3. You work for a middle manager with narcissistic tendencies. He's just been assigned to work for a senior manager with psychopathic tendencies. What do you expect to happen?

4. You're a top manager at a large company, and you're about to be promoted. You've come to realize that the fast-track manager who's in line for your job has psychopathic tendencies. What will you do?

5. Once again, you're in the situation described in question 4. This time, however, the fast-track manager in question is a narcissist. Would you handle the case of the narcissist differently from the case of the psychopath? Be specific in explaining your answer.

6. Your unit works directly under an executive vice president of the company. She clearly exhibits narcissistic tendencies, but you just got another handsome year-end bonus. You wonder: Are narcissistic managers occasionally beneficial to organizations? On what grounds would you argue that they can be? On what grounds would you argue that they can't be?

MANAGING EMPLOYEE PERFORMANCE AND MOTIVATION

LEARNING OBJECTIVES

After studying this chapter, you should be able to:

1 Characterize the nature of motivation, including its importance and basic historical perspectives.

2 Identify and describe the major content perspectives on motivation.

3 Identify and describe the major process perspectives on motivation.

4 Describe reinforcement perspectives on motivation.

5 Identify and describe popular motivational strategies.

6 Describe the role of organizational reward systems in motivation.

FIRST THINGS FIRST

Addressing the Balance of Trade-offs

The good news is that 60 percent of HR executives are satisfied with the work–life services that their companies offer employees. The bad news is that only 16 percent of their employees agree with them. According to a study conducted in 2009 by the Corporate Executive Board (CEB), the disconnect results from the fact that HR managers tend to value different services than employees do. They tend to assume, for example, that expensive, high-profile services such as on-site gyms and healthcare options are the kinds of things that employees want in a workplace that promotes good work–life balance. In reality, only about 20 percent of employees place any value on such services.

So, what *do* employees—managers and subordinates alike—really want? *Time*—or, more precisely, more control over it. More than 60 percent of the 50,000 workers polled in the CEB study specified *flexible schedules* as the single most important work–life benefit that an employer can offer. Flexible scheduling—or *flextime*—allows employees to adjust the time and/or place for completing their work. Best Buy, for example, calls its flextime program ROWE, for Results Only Work Environment. Employees at corporate headquarters work when and where they want, and all meetings are optional. The results of this focus on Results Only? Productivity is up 35 percent, and turnover is down 90 percent. And Best Buy is by no means alone in realizing productivity gains from a systematic effort to help employees strike better balances in their

> *"In order to retain the best and the brightest, we have to be flexible in how, when, and where the work gets done."*
>
> —KRISTEN PIERSOL-STOCKTON, REGIONAL DIRECTOR OF WORKPLACE SOLUTIONS, KPMG

work and home lives. Research shows, for example, that similar initiatives have increased productivity by $195 million at Cisco Systems; Deloitte estimates that it's saved $41.5 million in turnover costs since implementing a program of flexible-work options.

Another company that's happy with the results of its flexible-work program is KPMG. KPMG is in an industry in which turnover is traditionally higher for women than for men, but the numbers in the financial industry also

Helping employees meet various needs can enhance their motivation to perform at a higher level. Chick-Fil-A provides its employees with this fitness center at the firm's corporate headquarters in Georgia. Access to the gym allows employees to maintain a higher level of fitness and to better control stress.

AP PHOTO/RIC FELD

reflect broader trends in the U.S. workforce. According to a survey reported by the *Harvard Business Review*, for instance, 24 percent of male executives take a career off-ramp at some point—that is, voluntarily leave their careers for a period of time. When it comes to women, the figure is 37 percent; for women with children, it's 43 percent. Whereas only 12 percent of men interrupt their careers to take care of children or elders, it's the reason cited by 44 percent of women.

Because of data like these, KPMG launched a campaign to transform itself into an "employer of choice" by offering employees a range of options for balancing work and home life. Family-friendly policies fall into categories such as *flexibility* (flextime, telecommuting, job sharing) and *family resources* (backup child- and eldercare, discounts at childcare centers), and according to Barbara Wankoff, director of Workplace Solutions, 70 percent of company employees now work flexible hours. "Our employees," she says, "tend to be ambitious and career oriented. They want to develop professionally and build a career, but they also have lives as parents, sons or daughters, and spouses. So at KPMG we're promoting a culture of flexibility to help them manage the complexities of work and life." In one recent year, KPMG managed to improve retention of female employees by 10 percent and to increase its total number of women in its workforce by 15 percent. KPMG also says that if it hadn't offered flexible scheduling to female employees with young children, it would have lost about two-thirds of them.

Obviously, many women choose to stay in their jobs rather than take the off-ramp when faced with home-life pressures such as raising children. And with good reason: Research shows that although women leave their careers for an average of only 2.2 years, those two-plus years cost them 18 percent of their earning power (and 38 percent if they're out of the workforce for three years or more). That's why flexibility and family resource options are so important to the third of all working women who choose to stay on the job and look for ways to balance professional and personal responsibilities. It's also one reason why companies like KPMG are willing to make concessions to women's needs for flexibility and family resources. "In order to retain the best and the brightest," says Kristen Piersol-Stockton, one of Barbara Wankoff's regional directors, "we have to be

flexible in how, when, and where the work gets done." Tammy Hunter, a partner at KPMG and mother of three, maintains that flexible scheduling is what makes work–home balance possible. "I struggled," she explains, "when I thought I could be great only if I was at home 100 percent of the time or at work. Now that I have a balance, I feel like I spend enough time at home *and* enough time at work."

Hunter, who not only keeps her own flexible schedule but also encourages her subordinates to do likewise, sees the advantages of adjustable scheduling from the perspectives of both employee and manager. For one thing, she's convinced that flextime programs work only if the company's commitment is top-down, with managers actively supporting participation by employees at all levels. She also knows firsthand what more and more studies now demonstrate: Trying to find time for children is particularly stressful for many employees. The results are increased absenteeism (which costs many companies nearly $1 million a year) and decreased productivity. Conversely, employees who manage their own schedules have lower stress levels, focus better on their tasks, and (according to the CEB study) work 21 percent harder than those who don't. It makes sense to Hunter: "When you enjoy your work environment and you aren't stressed out about getting other things done," she says, "you're more productive."

Unfortunately, for many working women, the task of juggling professional and personal responsibilities makes a lot less sense than it does to Hunter, even with innovations in corporate policy such as flextime, telecommuting, and compressed schedules. Consider the consensus results of no fewer than six major studies on happiness: As women get older, they get sicker and sadder. That's on average, of course, but it appears to hold true whether they're single or married (with or without kids), rich or poor, beautiful or ordinary, tall or short, American, Asian, or European.

Why? One theory holds that, particularly for successful working women, modern roles persist in remaining out of sync. In scientific wave theory, the phenomenon is called *destructive interference*: when two waves cancel each other out. If you compare the typical working woman's two roles—parent and professional—to two such waves, then you're liable to find a woman who doesn't feel that she's accomplishing much in either facet of her life.

Take Kathy Caprino, a self-described former "corporate VP with a lucrative, high-powered job. I was blessed," she reports, "with . . . a loving husband, two beautiful children, and a charming house in a quaint New England town. . . . But in midlife, all professional joy and satisfaction withered away, and my traumas at work began to 'bleed' into my personal world. . . . Life was becoming impossible and intolerable, and I had no idea why." She contracted a chronic illness that was "debilitating, painful [and] infuriating," and at 38, she was fired from her job "in a way that was brutal to my ego. . . . I felt depressed, disoriented, and alone," but Caprino's story ends on a positive note: She took her midlife crisis as an opportunity to shift gears, earning a degree as a therapist and starting up her own executive-coaching agency.

Needless to say, she specializes in coaching women. In the process of starting over, she says, "I was startled by the number of women I met who felt as overwhelmed and miserable as I had." "I discovered through my research," she adds, that there are "thousands of women suffering from a lack of professional empowerment." She also confirmed the long-held opinion among working women themselves that "women are not 'men in skirts.'" Their roles and values have never been the same as those of men, but because the workplace reflects a "male competitive model," the roles and values that women can contribute to the workplace environment are frequently underrated and underappreciated. Men, says Caprino, "typically value power, recognition, responsibility, and compensation," and these are values that the workplace tends to recognize and encourage. Women, on the other hand, pursue significantly different values in their efforts to build successful work lives. These include, according to Caprino, the following:

- Flexibility in their careers and schedules
- A healthy, satisfying balance between life and work
- Reasonable demands on the their time in the office and in travel
- The ability to shift time and focus when important child- and eldercare needs emerge

If these sound like the same needs that are supposed to be addressed by flexible scheduling and other workplace policies favorable to working women, that's because they are. So why do Caprino and other researchers still characterize them as *unmet* needs? Michelle Conlin, a senior editor at *BusinessWeek*, suggests that "things like flex time are the existential equivalent of duct tape and bubble gum. Women often end up feeling more inadequate by buying into the myth that work–life balance is actually achievable—if only you juggled better, faster, and prettier."

According to Caprino, women still get sicker and sadder because their efforts to balance their professional and personal lives are frustrated by more deeply ingrained problems—problems that reflect long-standing roles and behaviors that can't really be solved by more convenient work schedules. She observes, for example, that "although women now make up nearly one-half of the U.S. labor force, the majority of domestic responsibility still falls to women, as does raising and caring for children and elderly family members." In fact, economist Heather Boushey has found that women bring home the larger paychecks in 36 percent of all dual-career households but still end up handling 75 percent of all domestic tasks. According to Conlin, trying to perform such a balancing act reflects "the doing-it-all, all-at-the-same-time ethos so dominant" among women in the workplace. Caprino and other researchers suggest that it's an essentially impossible task and that having more time to perform an impossible task doesn't help much.

This dilemma is one reason why many professional women choose off-ramping instead of flexible scheduling. Of those who off-ramp, an overwhelming majority of 93 percent want to return to work. Of these, however, only 73 percent actually find jobs of any kind and only 40 percent find satisfactory full-time jobs. A big part of the problem is timing. Consider, for instance, the "male competitive model" to which Caprino alludes. It was established in the 1950s and 1960s and evolved to accommodate the life rhythms of (middle-class white) males. It rewarded linear professional development and ambition and expected men to forge career-defining opportunities in their thirties. Typically, however, the demands of bearing and rearing children are most stringent during the decade of a woman's thirties. For many women, therefore, the trajectories of their personal and professional lives are virtually destined to be out of sync. Little wonder, then, that when women return to the on-ramp at midlife, many have lost much of their professional ambition. Indeed, only 37 percent of working women at midlife say that they're ambitious, versus 53 percent of younger working women.

Because flexible-work options don't address the larger-scale issues like those facing returning professionals, some companies have created programs specifically designed to offer employees more than mere time in which to juggle the demands of their professional and personal lives. Deloitte, for example, found that despite a battery of nearly 70 flexible-work programs, employee satisfaction was still slipping. So in 2004, the company replaced the traditional corporate ladder with a corporate "lattice." Instead of having to climb up or jump off, employees can now move laterally or down as well as up depending on their life circumstances.

If you need to take care of children for a few years, you can ease up or drop out without forfeiting your chance of moving up again when you return. Likewise, when the results of a 2005 study called "On Ramps and Off Ramps" showed how hard it was for employees to reenter the workforce after a career break, Lehman Brothers initiated a program called Encore, which is designed to identify talented people who have left the financial industry but who might be lured back by the offer of retraining in new jobs that allow them to control the amount of time they spend in the office.[1]

Several different factors may cause managers to put in long hours—employer expectations, demanding workloads, or the sheer enjoyment of the work are all things that motivate some people to work nights and weekends. Likewise, a number of factors are also suggesting that change may be in the wind, factors such as a growing desire among younger people to lead more balanced lives and the recognition that long hours may not equate to higher performance. The trick is figuring out how to create a system in which employees can receive rewards that they genuinely want yet lead a balanced life while performing in ways that fit the organization's goals and objectives.

In most settings, people can actually choose how hard they work and how much effort they expend. Thus managers need to understand how and why employees make different choices regarding their own performance. The key ingredient behind this choice is motivation, the subject of this chapter. We first examine the nature of employee motivation and then explore the major perspectives on motivation. Newly emerging approaches are then discussed. We conclude with a description of rewards and their role in motivation.

Motivation is the set of forces that cause people to behave in certain ways.[2] On any given day, an employee may choose to work as hard as possible at a job, work just hard enough to avoid a reprimand, or do as little as possible. The goal for the manager is to maximize the likelihood of the first behavior and minimize the likelihood of the last. This goal becomes all the more important when we understand how important motivation is in the workplace.

Individual performance is generally determined by three things: motivation (the desire to do the job), ability (the capability to do the job), and the work environment (the resources needed to do the job). If an employee lacks ability, the manager can provide training or replace the worker. If there is a resource problem, the manager can correct it. But, if motivation is the problem, the task for the manager is more challenging.[3] Individual behavior is a complex phenomenon, and the manager may be hard pressed to figure out the precise nature of the problem and how to solve it. Thus motivation is important because of its significance as a determinant of performance and because of its intangible character.[4]

The motivation framework in Figure 12.1 is a good starting point for understanding how motivated behavior occurs. The motivation process begins with a need deficiency. For example, when a worker feels that she is underpaid, she experiences a need for more income. In response, the worker searches for ways to satisfy the need, such as working harder to try to earn a raise or seeking a new job. Next she chooses an option to pursue.

motivation
The set of forces that cause people to behave in certain ways

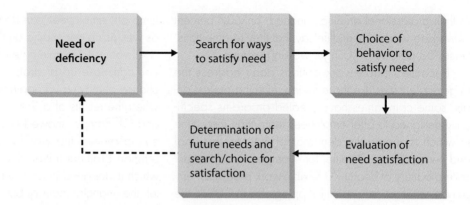

Figure 12.1
The Motivation Framework

The motivation process progresses through a series of discrete steps. Content, process, and reinforcement perspectives on motivation address different parts of this process.

After carrying out the chosen option—working harder and putting in more hours for a reasonable period of time, for example—she then evaluates her success. If her hard work resulted in a pay raise, she probably feels good about things and will continue to work hard. But, if no raise has been provided, she is likely to try another option.

CONTENT PERSPECTIVES ON MOTIVATION

Content perspectives on motivation deal with the first part of the motivation process—needs and need deficiencies. More specifically, **content perspectives** address the question "What factors in the workplace motivate people?" Labor leaders often argue that workers can be motivated by more pay, shorter working hours, and improved working conditions. Meanwhile, some experts suggest that motivation can be more effectively enhanced by providing employees with more autonomy and greater responsibility.[5] Both of these views represent content views of motivation. The former asserts that motivation is a function of pay, working hours, and working conditions; the latter suggests that autonomy and responsibility are the causes of motivation. Two widely known content perspectives on motivation are the needs hierarchy and the two-factor theory.

The Needs Hierarchy Approach

The needs hierarchy approach has been advanced by many theorists. Needs hierarchies assume that people have different needs that can be arranged in a hierarchy of importance. The two best known are Maslow's hierarchy of needs and the ERG theory.

content perspectives
Approach to motivation that tries to answer the question "What factors motivate people?"

Maslow's hierarchy of needs
Suggests that people must satisfy five groups of needs in order—physiological, security, belongingness, esteem, and self-actualization

Maslow's Hierarchy of Needs Abraham Maslow, a human relationist, argued that people are motivated to satisfy five need levels.[6] **Maslow's hierarchy of needs** is shown in Figure 12.2. At the bottom of the hierarchy are the *physiological needs*—things such as food, sex, and air, which represent basic issues of survival and biological function. In organizations, these needs are generally satisfied by adequate wages and the work environment itself, which provides restrooms, adequate lighting, comfortable temperatures, and ventilation.

Next are the *security needs* for a secure physical and emotional environment. Examples include the desire for housing and clothing and the need to be free from worry about money and job security. These needs can be satisfied in the workplace by job continuity (no layoffs), a grievance system (to protect against arbitrary supervisory actions), and an adequate insurance and retirement benefit package (for security against illness and provision of

NEEDS

General Examples   Organizational Examples

Achievement — Self-actualization — Challenging job

Status — Esteem — Job title

Friendship — Belongingness — Friends at work

Stability — Security — Pension plan

Food — Physiology — Base salary

Source: Adapted from Abraham H. Maslow, "A Theory of Human Motivation," *Psychology Review*, 1943, Vol. 50, pp. 370–396.

Figure 12.2
Maslow's Hierarchy of Needs

Maslow's hierarchy suggests that human needs can be classified into five categories and that these categories can be arranged in a hierarchy of importance. A manager should understand that an employee may not be satisfied with only a salary and benefits; he or she may also need challenging job opportunities to experience self-growth and satisfaction.

income in later life). Even today, however, depressed industries and economic decline can put people out of work and restore the primacy of security needs.

Belongingness needs relate to social processes. They include the need for love and affection and the need to be accepted by one's peers. These needs are satisfied for most people by family and community relationships outside of work and by friendships on the job. A manager can help satisfy these needs by allowing social interaction and by making employees feel like part of a team or work group.

Esteem needs actually comprise two different sets of needs: the need for a positive self-image and self-respect and the need for recognition and respect from others. A manager can help address these needs by providing a variety of extrinsic symbols of accomplishment, such as job titles, nice offices, and similar rewards as appropriate. At a more intrinsic level, the manager can provide challenging job assignments and opportunities for the employee to feel a sense of accomplishment.

At the top of the hierarchy are the *self-actualization needs*. These involve realizing one's potential for continued growth and individual development. The self-actualization needs are perhaps the most difficult for a manager to address. In fact, it can be argued that these needs must be met entirely from within the individual. But a manager can help by promoting a culture wherein self-actualization is possible. For instance, a manager could give employees a chance to participate in making decisions about their work and the opportunity to learn new things.

Maslow suggests that the five need categories constitute a hierarchy. An individual is motivated first and foremost to satisfy physiological needs. As long as they remain unsatisfied, the individual is motivated to fulfill only them. When satisfaction of physiological needs is achieved, they cease to act as primary motivational factors, and the individual moves "up" the hierarchy and becomes concerned with security needs. This process continues until the individual reaches the self-actualization level. Maslow's concept of the needs hierarchy has a certain intuitive logic and has been accepted by many managers. But research has revealed certain shortcomings and defects in the theory. Some research has found that five levels of need are not always present and that the order of the levels is not always the same, as postulated by Maslow.[7] In addition, people from different cultures are likely to have different need categories and hierarchies.

The Two-Factor Theory

Another popular content perspective is the **two-factor theory of motivation**.[8] Frederick Herzberg developed his theory by interviewing 200 accountants and engineers. He asked them to recall occasions when they had been satisfied and motivated and occasions when they had been dissatisfied and unmotivated. Surprisingly, he found that different sets of factors were associated with satisfaction and with dissatisfaction—that is, a person might identify "low pay" as causing dissatisfaction but would not necessarily mention "high pay" as a cause of satisfaction. Instead, different factors—such as recognition or accomplishment—were cited as causing satisfaction and motivation.

This finding led Herzberg to conclude that the traditional view of job satisfaction was incomplete. That view assumed that satisfaction and dissatisfaction are at opposite ends of a single continuum. People might be satisfied, dissatisfied, or somewhere in between. But Herzberg's interviews had identified two different dimensions altogether: one ranging from satisfaction to no satisfaction and the other ranging from dissatisfaction to no dissatisfaction. This perspective, along with several examples of factors that affect each continuum, is shown in Figure 12.3. Note that the factors influencing the satisfaction continuum—called *motivation factors*—are related specifically to the work content. The factors presumed to cause dissatisfaction—called *hygiene factors*—are related to the work environment.

Based on these findings, Herzberg argued that there are two stages in the process of motivating employees. First, managers must ensure that the hygiene factors are not deficient. Pay and security must be appropriate, working conditions must be safe, technical supervision must be acceptable, and so on. By providing hygiene factors at an appropriate level, managers do not stimulate motivation but merely ensure that employees are "not dissatisfied." Employees whom managers attempt to "satisfy" through hygiene factors alone will usually do just enough to get by. Thus managers should proceed to stage two—giving employees the opportunity to experience motivation factors such as achievement and recognition. The result is predicted to be a high level of satisfaction

two-factor theory of motivation
Suggests that people's satisfaction and dissatisfaction are influenced by two independent sets of factors—motivation factors and hygiene factors

Figure 12.3 **The Two-Factor Theory of Motivation**

The two-factor theory suggests that job satisfaction has two dimensions. A manager who tries to motivate an employee using only hygiene factors, such as pay and good working conditions, will likely not succeed. To motivate employees and produce a high level of satisfaction, managers must also offer factors such as responsibility and the opportunity for advancement (motivation factors).

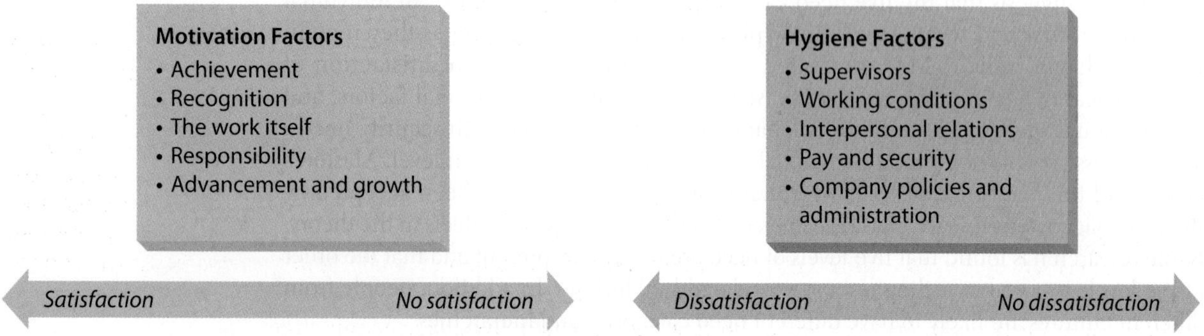

Motivation Factors
- Achievement
- Recognition
- The work itself
- Responsibility
- Advancement and growth

Hygiene Factors
- Supervisors
- Working conditions
- Interpersonal relations
- Pay and security
- Company policies and administration

Satisfaction ← → No satisfaction

Dissatisfaction ← → No dissatisfaction

and motivation. Herzberg also went a step further than most other theorists and described exactly how to use the two-factor theory in the workplace. Specifically, he recommended job enrichment, as discussed in Chapter 6. He argued that jobs should be redesigned to provide higher levels of the motivation factors.

Although widely accepted by many managers, Herzberg's two-factor theory is not without its critics. One criticism is that the findings in Herzberg's initial interviews are subject to different explanations. Another charge is that his sample was not representative of the general population and that subsequent research often failed to uphold the theory.[9] At the present time, Herzberg's theory is not held in high esteem by researchers in the field. The theory has had a major impact on managers, however, and has played a key role in increasing their awareness of motivation and its importance in the workplace.

Individual Human Needs

In addition to these theories, research has focused on specific individual human needs that are important in organizations. The three most important individual needs are achievement, affiliation, and power.[10]

The **need for achievement**, the best known of the three, is the desire to accomplish a goal or task more effectively than in the past. People with a high need for achievement have a desire to assume personal responsibility, a tendency to set moderately difficult goals, a desire for specific and immediate feedback, and a preoccupation with their task. David C. McClelland, the psychologist who first identified this need, argues that only about 10 percent of the U.S. population has a high need for achievement. In contrast, almost one-quarter of the workers in Japan have a high need for achievement.

The **need for affiliation** is less well understood. Like Maslow's belongingness need, the need for affiliation is a desire for human companionship and acceptance. People with a strong need for affiliation are likely to prefer (and perform better in) a job that entails a lot of social interaction and offers opportunities to make friends. One recent survey found that workers with one or more good friends at work are much more likely to be committed to their work. United Airlines, for instance, allows flight attendants to form their own teams; those who participate tend to form teams with their friends.[11]

The **need for power** is the desire to be influential in a group and to control one's environment. Research has shown that people with a strong need for power are likely to be superior performers, have good attendance records, and occupy supervisory positions. The need for power has also received considerable attention as an important ingredient in managerial success. One study found that managers as a group tend to have a stronger power motive than the general population and that successful managers tend to have stronger power motives than less successful managers.[12] Dennis Kozlowski, disgraced former CEO of Tyco International, clearly had a strong need for power. This was reflected in the way he routinely took control over resources and used them for his own personal gain. Indeed, the things he bought with company money were probably intended to convey to the world the extent of his power.[13]

PROCESS PERSPECTIVES ON MOTIVATION

Process perspectives are concerned with how motivation occurs. Rather than attempting to identify motivational stimuli, **process perspectives** focus on why people choose certain behavioral options to satisfy their needs and how they evaluate their satisfaction after

need for achievement
The desire to accomplish a goal or task more effectively than in the past

need for affiliation
The desire for human companionship and acceptance

need for power
The desire to be influential in a group and to control one's environment

process perspectives
Approaches to motivation that focus on why people choose certain behavioral options to satisfy their needs and how they evaluate their satisfaction after they have attained those goals

they have attained those goals. Three useful process perspectives on motivation are the expectancy, equity, and goal-setting theories.

Expectancy Theory

expectancy theory
Suggests that motivation depends on two things—how much we want something and how likely we think we are to get it

effort-to-performance expectancy
The individual's perception of the probability that effort will lead to high performance

Expectancy theory suggests that motivation depends on two things—how much we want something and how likely we think we are to get it.[14] Assume that you are approaching graduation and looking for a job. You see in the want ads that General Motors (GM) is seeking a new vice president with a starting salary of $500,000 per year. Even though you might want the job, you will not apply because you realize that you have little chance of getting it. The next ad you see is for someone to scrape bubble gum from underneath theater seats for a starting salary of $6 an hour. Even though you could probably get this job, you do not apply because you do not want it. Then you see an ad for a management trainee at a big company, with a starting salary of $45,000. You will probably apply for this job because you want it and because you think you have a reasonable chance of getting it.

Expectancy theory rests on four basic assumptions. First, it assumes that behavior is determined by a combination of forces in the individual and in the environment. Second, it assumes that people make decisions about their own behavior in organizations. Third, it assumes that different people have different types of needs, desires, and goals. Fourth, it assumes that people make choices from among alternative plans of behavior, based on their perceptions of the extent to which a given behavior will lead to desired outcomes.

Figure 12.4 summarizes the basic expectancy model. The model suggests that motivation leads to effort and that effort, combined with employee ability and environmental factors, results in performance. Performance, in turn, leads to various outcomes, each of which has an associated value, called its *valence*. The most important parts of the expectancy model cannot be shown in the figure, however. These are the individual's expectation that effort will lead to high performance, that performance will lead to outcomes, and that each outcome will have some kind of value.

WESTEND61/JUPITER IMAGES

Process perspectives on motivation, like expectancy theory, suggest that people are motivated to pursue outcomes that they want and that they think can be achieved. As more tech-savvy people enter the workforce, they are expecting to have the right to participate in social networking (such as Facebook) while they are at work. This manager, for instance, is taking a few minutes to check her Facebook status while enjoying a coffee break. Employers who can solve the dilemma of providing this access while maintaining organizational security may be at an advantage in recruiting and retaining employees.

Effort-to-Performance Expectancy The **effort-to-performance expectancy** is the individual's perception of the probability that effort will lead to high performance. When the individual believes that effort will lead directly to high performance, expectancy will be quite strong (close to 1.00). When the individual believes that effort and performance are unrelated, expectancy is very weak (close to 0). The belief that effort is somewhat but not strongly related to performance carries with it a moderate expectancy (somewhere between 0 and 1.00).

𝒯igure 12.4   The Expectancy Model of Motivation

The expectancy model of motivation is a complex but relatively accurate portrayal of how motivation occurs. According to this model, a manager must understand what employees want (such as pay, promotions, or status) to begin to motivate them.

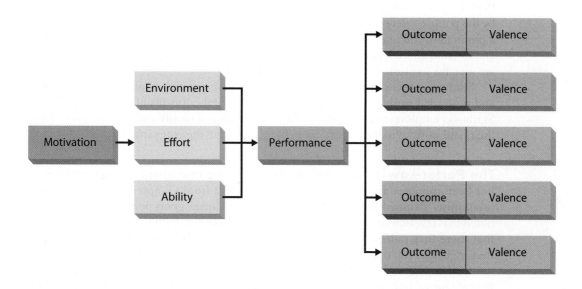

Performance-to-Outcome Expectancy The **performance-to-outcome expectancy** is the individual's perception that performance will lead to a specific outcome. For example, the individual who believes that high performance *will* result in a pay raise has a high expectancy (approaching 1.00). The individual who believes that high performance *may* lead to a pay raise has a moderate expectancy (between 1.00 and 0). The individual who believes that performance has no relationship to rewards has a low expectancy (close to 0).

Outcomes and Valences Expectancy theory recognizes that an individual's behavior results in a variety of **outcomes**, or consequences, in an organizational setting. A high performer, for example, may get bigger pay raises, faster promotions, and more praise from the boss. On the other hand, she may also be subject to more stress and incur resentment from coworkers. Each of these outcomes also has an associated value, or **valence**—an index of how much an individual values a particular outcome. If the individual wants the outcome, its valence is positive; if the individual does not want the outcome, its valence is negative; and if the individual is indifferent to the outcome, its valence is zero.

It is this part of expectancy theory that goes beyond the content perspectives on motivation. Different people have different needs, and they will try to satisfy these needs in different ways. For an employee who has a high need for achievement and a low need for affiliation, the pay raise and promotions cited above as outcomes of high performance might have positive valences, the praise and resentment zero valences, and the stress a negative valence. For a different employee, with a low need for achievement and a high need for affiliation, the pay raise, promotions, and praise might all have positive valences, whereas both resentment and stress could have negative valences.

performance-to-outcome expectancy
The individual's perception that performance will lead to a specific outcome

outcomes
Consequences of behaviors in an organizational setting, usually rewards

valence
An index of how much an individual values a particular outcome; the attractiveness of the outcome to the individual

For motivated behavior to occur, three conditions must be met. First, the effort-to-performance must be greater than 0 (the individual must believe that if effort is expended, high performance will result). The performance-to-outcome expectancy must also be greater than 0 (the individual must believe that if high performance is achieved, certain outcomes will follow). And the sum of the valences for the outcomes must be greater than 0. (One or more outcomes may have negative valences if they are more than offset by the positive valences of other outcomes. For example, the attractiveness of a pay raise, a promotion, and praise from the boss may outweigh the unattractiveness of more stress and resentment from coworkers.) Expectancy theory suggests that when these conditions are met, the individual is motivated to expend effort.

Starbucks credits its unique stock ownership program with maintaining a dedicated and motivated workforce. Based on the fundamental concepts of expectancy theory, Starbucks employees earn stock as a function of their seniority and performance. Thus their hard work helps them earn shares of ownership in the company.[15]

The Porter-Lawler Extension An interesting extension of expectancy theory has been proposed by Porter and Lawler.[16] Recall from Chapter 1 that the human relationists assumed that employee satisfaction causes good performance. We also noted that research has not supported such a relationship. Porter and Lawler suggested that there may indeed be a relationship between satisfaction and performance but that it goes in the opposite direction—that is, high performance may lead to high satisfaction. Figure 12.5 summarizes Porter and Lawler's logic. Performance results in rewards for an individual. Some of these are extrinsic (such as pay and promotions); others are intrinsic (such as self-esteem and accomplishment). The individual evaluates the equity, or fairness, of the rewards relative to the effort expended and the level of performance attained. If the rewards are perceived to be equitable, the individual is satisfied.

$\mathcal{F}igure$ **12.5**   The Porter-Lawler Extension of Expectancy Theory

The Porter-Lawler extension of expectancy theory suggests that if performance results in equitable rewards, people will be more satisfied. Thus performance can lead to satisfaction. Managers must therefore be sure that any system of motivation includes rewards that are fair, or equitable, for all.

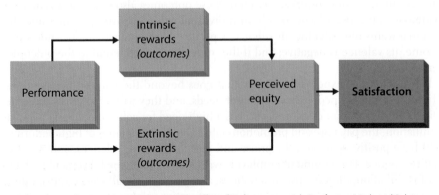

Source: Edward E. Lawler III and Lyman W. Porter, "The Effect of Performance on Job Satisfaction," *Industrial Relations,* October 1967, p. 23. Used with permission from the University of California.

Equity Theory

After needs have stimulated the motivation process and the individual has chosen an action that is expected to satisfy those needs, the individual assesses the fairness, or equity, of the resultant outcome. **Equity theory** contends that people are motivated to seek social equity in the rewards they receive for performance.[17] Equity is an individual's belief that the treatment he or she is receiving is fair relative to the treatment received by others. According to equity theory, outcomes from a job include pay, recognition, promotions, social relationships, and intrinsic rewards. To get these rewards, the individual makes inputs to the job, such as time, experience, effort, education, and loyalty. The theory suggests that people view their outcomes and inputs as a ratio and then compare it to someone else's ratio. This other "person" may be someone in the work group or some sort of group average or composite. The process of comparison looks like this:

$$\frac{\text{Outcomes (self)}}{\text{Inputs (self)}} = \frac{\text{Outcomes (other)}}{\text{Inputs (other)}}$$

Both the formulation of the ratios and comparisons between them are very subjective and based on individual perceptions. As a result of comparisons, three conditions may result: The individual may feel equitably rewarded, underrewarded, or overrewarded. A feeling of equity will result when the two ratios are equal. This may occur even though the other person's outcomes are greater than the individual's own outcomes—provided that the other's inputs are also proportionately greater. Suppose that Mark has a high school education and earns $30,000. He may still feel equitably treated relative to Susan, who earns $35,000, because she has a college degree.

People who feel underrewarded try to reduce the inequity. Such an individual might decrease her inputs by exerting less effort, increase her outcomes by asking for a raise, distort the original ratios by rationalizing, try to get the other person to change her or his outcomes or inputs, leave the situation, or change the object of comparison. An individual may also feel overrewarded relative to another person. This is not likely to be terribly disturbing to most people, but research suggests that some people who experience inequity under these conditions are somewhat motivated to reduce it. Under such a circumstance, the person might increase his inputs by exerting more effort, reduce his outcomes by producing fewer units (if paid on a per-unit basis), distort the original ratios by rationalizing, or try to reduce the inputs or increase the outcomes of the other person.

Managers today may need to pay even greater attention to equity theory and its implications. Many firms, for example, are moving toward performance-based reward systems (discussed later in this chapter) as opposed to standard or across-the-board salary increases. Hence, they must ensure that the bases for rewarding some people more than others are clear and objective. Beyond legal issues such as discrimination, managers need to be sure that they are providing fair rewards and incentives to those who do the best work.[18] Moreover, they must be sensitive to cultural differences that affect how people may perceive and react to equity and inequity.[19]

Goal-Setting Theory

The goal-setting theory of motivation assumes that behavior is a result of conscious goals and intentions.[20] Therefore, by setting goals for people in the organization, a manager should be able to influence their behavior. Given this premise, the challenge is to develop a thorough understanding of the processes by which people set goals and then work to reach them. In the original version of goal-setting theory, two specific goal characteristics—goal difficulty and goal specificity—were expected to shape performance.

equity theory
Contends that people are motivated to seek social equity in the rewards they receive for performance

Goal Difficulty *Goal difficulty* is the extent to which a goal is challenging and requires effort. If people work to achieve goals, it is reasonable to assume that they will work harder to achieve more difficult goals. But a goal must not be so difficult that it is unattainable. If a new manager asks her sales force to increase sales by 300 percent, the group may become disillusioned. A more realistic but still difficult goal—perhaps a 30 percent increase—would be a better incentive. A substantial body of research supports the importance of goal difficulty. In one study, for example, managers at Weyerhauser set difficult goals for truck drivers hauling loads of timber from cutting sites to wood yards. Over a nine-month period, the drivers increased the quantity of wood they delivered by an amount that would have required $250,000 worth of new trucks at the previous per-truck average load.[21]

Goal Specificity *Goal specificity* is the clarity and precision of the goal. A goal of "increasing productivity" is not very specific; a goal of "increasing productivity by 3 percent in the next six months" is quite specific. Some goals, such as those involving costs, output, profitability, and growth, are readily amenable to specificity. Other goals, however, such as improving employee job satisfaction, morale, company image and reputation, ethics, and socially responsible behavior, may be much harder to state in specific terms. Like difficulty, specificity has been shown to be consistently related to performance. The study of timber truck drivers mentioned above, for example, also examined goal specificity. The initial loads the truck drivers were carrying were found to be 60 percent of the maximum weight each truck could haul. The managers set a new goal for drivers of 94 percent, which the drivers were soon able to reach. Thus the goal was both specific and difficult.

Because the theory attracted so much widespread interest and research support from researchers and managers alike, an expanded model of the goal-setting process was eventually proposed. The expanded model, shown in Figure 12.6, attempts to capture more fully the complexities of goal setting in organizations.

𝒥igure 12.6 The Expanded Goal-Setting Theory of Motivation

One of the most important emerging theories of motivation is goal-setting theory. This theory suggests that goal difficulty, specificity, acceptance, and commitment combine to determine an individual's goal-directed effort. This effort, when complemented by appropriate organizational support and individual abilities and traits, results in performance. Finally, performance is seen as leading to intrinsic and extrinsic rewards that, in turn, result in employee satisfaction.

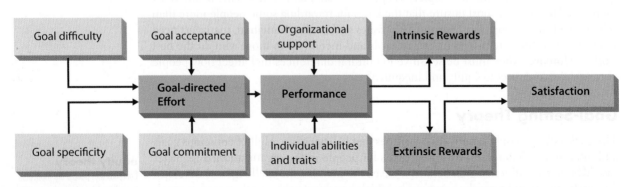

Source: Reprinted from Gary P. Latham and Edwin A. Locke, "A Motivational Technique That Works," in *Organizational Dynamics*, Autumn 1979, p. 79, © 1979 with permission from Elsevier Science.

The expanded theory argues that goal-directed effort is a function of four goal attributes: difficulty and specificity, as already discussed, and acceptance and commitment. *Goal acceptance* is the extent to which a person accepts a goal as his or her own. *Goal commitment* is the extent to which he or she is personally interested in reaching the goal. The manager who vows to take whatever steps are necessary to cut costs by 10 percent has made a commitment to achieve the goal. Factors that can foster goal acceptance and commitment include participating in the goal-setting process, making goals challenging but realistic, and believing that goal achievement will lead to valued rewards.

The interaction of goal-directed effort, organizational support, and individual abilities and traits determines actual performance. Organizational support is whatever the organization does to help or hinder performance. Positive support might mean making available adequate personnel and a sufficient supply of raw materials; negative support might mean failing to fix damaged equipment. Individual abilities and traits are the skills and other personal characteristics necessary for doing a job. As a result of performance, a person receives various intrinsic and extrinsic rewards, which in turn influence satisfaction. Note that the latter stages of this model are quite similar to the Porter and Lawler expectancy model discussed earlier.[22]

REINFORCEMENT PERSPECTIVES ON MOTIVATION

A third element of the motivational process addresses why some behaviors are maintained over time and why other behaviors change. As we have seen, content perspectives deal with needs, whereas process perspectives explain why people choose various behaviors to satisfy needs and how they evaluate the equity of the rewards they get for those behaviors. Reinforcement perspectives explain the role of those rewards as they cause behavior to change or remain the same over time. Specifically, **reinforcement theory** argues that behavior that results in rewarding consequences is likely to be repeated, whereas behavior that results in punishing consequences is less likely to be repeated.[23]

reinforcement theory
Approach to motivation that argues that behavior that results in rewarding consequences is likely to be repeated, whereas behavior that results in punishing consequences is less likely to be repeated

positive reinforcement
A method of strengthening behavior with rewards or positive outcomes after a desired behavior is performed

Kinds of Reinforcement in Organizations

There are four basic kinds of reinforcement that can result from behavior—positive reinforcement, avoidance, punishment, and extinction.[24] Two kinds of reinforcement strengthen or maintain behavior, whereas the other two weaken or decrease behavior.

Positive reinforcement, one method of strengthening behavior, is a reward or a positive outcome after a desired behavior is performed. When a manager observes an employee doing an especially good job and offers praise, the praise serves to positively reinforce the behavior of good work. Other positive reinforcers in organizations include

Many firms reward their top employees with salary increases and various other rewards. Some go further, providing them with gift cards and similar forms of tangible recognition. A few, like General Electric, go so far as to give offer a small number of annual all-expense-paid vacations to places like Disney World or Hawaii. This GE employee, for instance, is enjoying a trip to Disney's Magic Kingdom with his daughter.

DENNIS MACDONALD/ALAMY

pay raises, promotions, and awards. Employees who work at General Electric's customer service center receive clothing, sporting goods, and even trips to Disney World as rewards for outstanding performance.

The other method of strengthening desired behavior is through **avoidance**. An employee may come to work on time to avoid a reprimand. In this instance, the employee is motivated to perform the behavior of punctuality to avoid an unpleasant consequence that is likely to follow tardiness.

Punishment is used by some managers to weaken undesired behaviors. When an employee is loafing, coming to work late, doing poor work, or interfering with the work of others, the manager might resort to reprimands, discipline, or fines. The logic is that the unpleasant consequence will reduce the likelihood that the employee will choose that particular behavior again. Given the counterproductive side effects of punishment (such as resentment and hostility), it is often advisable to use the other kinds of reinforcement if at all possible. **Extinction** can also be used to weaken behavior, especially behavior that has previously been rewarded. When an employee tells an off-color joke and the boss laughs, the laughter reinforces the behavior and the employee may continue to tell off-color jokes. By simply ignoring this behavior and not reinforcing it, the boss can cause the behavior to subside and eventually become "extinct."

Providing Reinforcement in Organizations

Not only is the kind of reinforcement important, but also so is when or how often it occurs. Various strategies are possible for providing reinforcement. The **fixed-interval schedule** provides reinforcement at fixed intervals of time, regardless of behavior. A good example of this schedule is the weekly or monthly paycheck. This method provides the least incentive for good work because employees know they will be paid regularly regardless of their efforts. A **variable-interval schedule** also uses time as the basis for reinforcement, but the time interval varies from one reinforcement to the next. This schedule is appropriate for praise or other rewards based on visits or inspections. When employees do not know when the boss is going to drop by, they tend to maintain a reasonably high level of effort all the time.

A **fixed-ratio schedule** gives reinforcement after a fixed number of behaviors, regardless of the time that elapses between behaviors. This results in an even higher level of effort. For example, when Sears is recruiting new credit-card customers, salespersons get a small bonus for every fifth application returned from their department. Under this arrangement, motivation will be high because each application gets the person closer to the next bonus. The **variable-ratio schedule**, the most powerful schedule in terms of maintaining desired behaviors, varies the number of behaviors needed for each reinforcement. A supervisor who praises an employee for her second order, the seventh order after that, the ninth after that, then the fifth, and then the third is using a variable-ratio schedule. The employee is motivated to increase the frequency of the desired behavior because each performance increases the probability of receiving a reward. Of course, a variable-ratio schedule is difficult (if not impossible) to use for formal rewards such as pay because it would be too complicated to keep track of who was rewarded when.

Managers wanting to explicitly use reinforcement theory to motivate their employees generally do so with a technique called **organizational behavior modification (OB Mod)**.[25] An OB Mod program starts by specifying behaviors that are to be increased (such as producing more units) or decreased (such as coming to work late). These target behaviors are then tied to specific forms or kinds of reinforcement. Although many organizations (such as Procter & Gamble and Ford) have used OB Mod, the best-known application was at Emery Air Freight. Management felt that the containers

---

avoidance
Used to strengthen behavior by avoiding unpleasant consequences that would result if the behavior were not performed

punishment
Used to weaken undesired behaviors by using negative outcomes or unpleasant consequences when the behavior is performed

extinction
Used to weaken undesired behaviors by simply ignoring or not reinforcing them

fixed-interval schedule
Provides reinforcement at fixed intervals of time, such as regular weekly paychecks

variable-interval schedule
Provides reinforcement at varying intervals of time, such as occasional visits by the supervisor

fixed-ratio schedule
Provides reinforcement after a fixed number of behaviors regardless of the time interval involved, such as a bonus for every fifth sale

variable-ratio schedule
Provides reinforcement after varying numbers of behaviors are performed, such as the use of complements by a supervisor on an irregular basis

organizational behavior modification (OB Mod)
Method for applying the basic elements of reinforcement theory in an organizational setting

CHAPTER 12 Managing Employee Performance and Motivation **347**

used to consolidate small shipments into fewer, larger shipments were not being packed efficiently. Through a system of self-monitored feedback and rewards, Emery increased container usage from 45 percent to 95 percent and saved over $3 million during the first three years of the program.[26]

POPULAR MOTIVATIONAL STRATEGIES

Although the various theories discussed thus far provide a solid explanation for motivation, managers must use various techniques and strategies to actually apply them. Among the most popular motivational strategies today are empowerment and participation and alternative forms of work arrangements. Various forms of performance-based reward systems, discussed in the next section, also reflect efforts to boost motivation and performance.

Empowerment and Participation

Empowerment and participation represent important methods that managers can use to enhance employee motivation. **Empowerment** is the process of enabling workers to set their own work goals, make decisions, and solve problems within their sphere of responsibility and authority. **Participation** is the process of giving employees a voice in making decisions about their own work. Thus empowerment is a somewhat broader concept that promotes participation in a wide variety of areas, including but not limited to work itself, work context, and work environment.[27]

The role of participation and empowerment in motivation can be expressed in terms of both content perspectives and expectancy theory. Employees who participate in decision making may be more committed to executing decisions properly. Furthermore, the successful process of making a decision, executing it, and then seeing the positive consequences can help satisfy one's need for achievement, provide recognition and responsibility, and enhance self-esteem. Simply being asked to participate in organizational decision making may also enhance an employee's self-esteem. In addition, participation should help clarify expectancies; that is, by participating in decision making, employees may better understand the linkage between their performance and the rewards they want most.

Alternative Forms of Work Arrangements

Many organizations today are also experimenting with a variety of alternative work arrangements. These alternative arrangements are generally intended to enhance employee motivation and performance by providing employees with greater flexibility in how and when they work. Among the more popular alternative work arrangements are variable work schedules, flexible work schedules, job sharing, and telecommuting.[28]

Variable-Work Schedules Although there are many exceptions, of course, the traditional work schedule starts at 8:00 or 9:00 in the morning and ends at 5:00 in the evening, five days a week (and, of course, many managers work additional hours outside of these times). Unfortunately, this schedule makes it difficult to attend to routine personal business—going to the bank, seeing a doctor or dentist for a routine checkup, having a parent–teacher conference, getting an automobile serviced, and so forth. At a

empowerment
The process of enabling workers to set their own work goals, make decisions, and solve problems within their sphere of responsibility and authority

participation
The process of giving employees a voice in making decisions about their own work

surface level, then, employees locked into this sort of arrangement may find it necessary to take a sick day or a vacation day to handle these activities. At a more unconscious level, some people may also feel so powerless and constrained by their job schedule as to feel increased resentment and frustration.

To help counter these problems, some businesses have adopted a **compressed work schedule**, working a full 40-hour week in fewer than the traditional five days.[29] One approach involves working 10 hours a day for four days, leaving an extra day off. Another alternative is for employees to work slightly less than 10 hours a day, but to complete the 40 hours by lunchtime on Friday. And a few firms have tried having employees work 12 hours a day for three days, followed by four days off. Organizations that have used these forms of compressed workweeks include John Hancock, BP Amoco, and Philip Morris. One problem with this schedule is that when employees put in too much time in a single day, they tend to get tired and perform at a lower level later in the day.

A schedule that some organizations today are beginning to use is what they call a "nine-eighty" schedule. Under this arrangement, an employee works a traditional schedule one week and a compressed schedule the next, getting every other Friday off. In other words, they work 80 hours (the equivalent of two weeks of full-time work) in nine days. By alternating the regular and compressed schedules across half of its workforce, the organization can be fully staffed at all times, while still giving employees two full days off each month. Shell Oil and BP Amoco Chemicals are two of the firms that currently use this schedule.

Flexible-Work Schedules Another promising alternative work arrangement is **flexible-work schedules**, sometimes called *flextime*. Flextime gives employees more personal control over the times they work. The workday is broken down into two categories: flexible time and core time. All employees must be at their workstation during core time, but they can choose their own schedules during flexible time. Thus one employee may choose to start work early in the morning and leave in mid-afternoon, another to start in the late morning and work until late afternoon, and still another to start early in the morning, take a long lunch break, and work until late afternoon. Organizations that have used the flexible-work schedule method for arranging work include Hewlett-Packard, Microsoft, and Texas Instruments.

Job Sharing Yet another potentially useful alternative work arrangement is job sharing. In **job sharing**, two part-time employees share one full-time job. One person may perform the job from 8:00 A.M. to noon and the other from 1:00 P.M. to 5:00 P.M. Job sharing may be desirable for people who want to work only part time or when job markets are tight. For its part, the organization can accommodate the preferences of a broader range of employees and may benefit from the talents of more people.

Telecommuting An increasingly popular approach to alternative work arrangements is **telecommuting**—allowing employees to spend part of their time working offsite, usually at home. By using e-mail, the Internet, and other forms of information technology, many employees can maintain close contact with their organization and still get just as much work done at home as if they were in their office.

The increased power and sophistication of modern communication technology is making telecommuting easier and easier. In 2008, nearly nine out of ten (87) workers in the United States did at least a portion of their work via telecommuting. At IBM, 40 percent of the workforce has no corporate workstation or office; at AT&T, the figure is 35 percent; and at Sun Microsystems, it's 50 percent.[30]

compressed work schedule
Working a full 40-hour week in fewer than the traditional five days

flexible-work schedules
Work schedules that allow employees to select, within broad parameters, the hours they work

job sharing
When two part-time employees share one full-time job

telecommuting
Allowing employees to spend part of their time working offsite, usually at home

USING REWARD SYSTEMS TO MOTIVATE PERFORMANCE

Aside from these types of motivational strategies, an organization's reward system is its most basic tool for managing employee motivation. An organizational **reward system** is the formal and informal mechanisms by which employee performance is defined, evaluated, and rewarded. Rewards that are tied specifically to performance, of course, have the greatest impact on enhancing both motivation and actual performance.

Performance-based rewards play a number of roles and address a variety of purposes in organizations. The major purposes involve the relationship of rewards to motivation and to performance. Specifically, organizations want employees to perform at relatively high levels and need to make it worth their effort to do so. When rewards are associated with higher levels of performance, employees will presumably be motivated to work harder to achieve those awards. At that point, their own self-interests coincide with the organization's interests. Performance-based rewards are also relevant regarding other employee behaviors, such as retention and citizenship.

SULLIVAN/CORBIS

Telecommuting—allowing employees to spend part of their time working offsite—is a popular alternative to traditional work arrangements. Information technology allows people to access the information they need and to interact with others in the organization from virtually anywhere. This woman, for instance, is working from the comfort of her living room. Of course, people who telecommute may also lose the benefit of personal contact that comes with being around others in the organization.

Merit Reward Systems

Merit reward systems are one of the most fundamental forms of performance-based rewards. **Merit pay** generally refers to pay awarded to employees on the basis of the relative value of their contributions to the organization. Employees who make greater contributions are given higher pay than those who make lesser contributions. **Merit pay plans**, then, are compensation plans that formally base at least some meaningful portion of compensation on merit.

The most general form of merit pay plan is to provide annual salary increases to individuals in the organization based on their relative merit. Merit, in turn, is usually determined or defined based on the individual's performance and overall contributions to the organization. For example, an organization using such a traditional merit pay plan might instruct its supervisors to give all their employees an average pay raise of, say, 4 percent. But the individual supervisor is further instructed to differentiate among high, average, and low performers. Under a simple system, for example, a manager might give the top 25 percent of her employees a 6 percent pay raise, the middle 50 percent a 4 percent or average pay raise, and the bottom 25 percent a 2 percent pay raise.

Incentive Reward Systems

Incentive reward systems are among the oldest forms of performance-based rewards. For example, some companies were using individual piece-rate incentive plans over 100 years ago.[31] Under a **piece-rate incentive plan**, the organization pays an employee a certain

reward system
The formal and informal mechanisms by which employee performance is defined, evaluated, and rewarded

merit pay
Pay awarded to employees on the basis of the relative value of their contributions to the organization

merit pay plan
Compensation plan that formally bases at least some meaningful portion of compensation on merit

piece-rate incentive plan
Reward system wherein the organization pays an employee a certain amount of money for every unit he or she produces

amount of money for every unit he or she produces. For example, an employee might be paid $1 for every dozen units of products that are successfully completed. But such simplistic systems fail to account for facts such as minimum wage levels and rely very heavily on the assumptions that performance is totally under an individual's control and that the individual employee does a single task continuously throughout his or her work time. Thus most organizations today that try to use incentive compensation systems use more sophisticated methodologies.

Incentive Pay Plans Generally speaking, *individual incentive plans* reward individual performance on a real-time basis. In other words, rather than increasing a person's base salary at the end of the year, an individual instead receives some level of salary increase or financial reward in conjunction with demonstrated outstanding performance in close proximity to when that performance occurred. Individual incentive systems are most likely to be used in cases in which performance can be objectively assessed in terms of number of units of output or similar measures, rather than on a subjective assessment of performance by a superior.

Some variations on a piece-rate system are still fairly popular. Although many of these still resemble the early plans in most ways, a well-known piece-rate system at Lincoln Electric illustrates how an organization can adapt the traditional model to achieve better results. For years, Lincoln's employees were paid individual incentive payments based on their performance. However, the amount of money shared (or the incentive pool) was based on the company's profitability. There was also a well-organized system whereby employees could make suggestions for increasing productivity. There was motivation to do this because the employees received one-third of the profits (another third went to the stockholders, and the last share was retained for improvements and seed money). Thus the pool for incentive payments was determined by profitability, and an employee's share of this pool was a function of his or her base pay and rated performance based on the piece-rate system. Lincoln Electric was most famous, however, because of the stories (which were apparently typical) of production workers' receiving a year-end bonus payment that equaled their yearly base pay.[32] In recent years, Lincoln has partially abandoned its famous system for business reasons, but it still serves as a benchmark for other companies seeking innovative piece-rate pay systems.

Perhaps the most common form of individual incentive is *sales commissions* that are paid to people engaged in sales work. For example, sales representatives for consumer products firms and retail sales agents may be compensated under this type of commission system. In general, the person might receive a percentage of the total volume of attained sales as his or her commission for a period of time. Some sales jobs are based entirely on commission, whereas others use a combination of base minimum salary with additional commission as an incentive. Notice that these plans put a considerable amount of the salespersons' earnings "at risk." In other words, although organizations often have drawing accounts to allow the salesperson to live during lean periods (the person then "owes" this money back to the organization), if he or she does not perform well, he or she will not be paid much. The portion of salary based on commission is simply not guaranteed and is paid only if sales reach some target level.

Other Forms of Incentive Occasionally organizations may also use other forms of incentives to motivate people. For example, a nonmonetary incentive, such as additional time off or a special perk, might be a useful incentive. For example, a company might establish a sales contest in which the sales group that attains the highest level of sales increase over a specified period of time will receive an extra week of paid vacation, perhaps even at an arranged place, such as a tropical resort or a ski lodge.[33]

A major advantage of incentives relative to merit systems is that incentives are typically a one-shot reward and do not accumulate by becoming part of the individual's base salary. Stated differently, an individual whose outstanding performance entitles him or her to a financial incentive gets the incentive only one time, based on that level of performance. If the individual's performance begins to erode in the future, then the individual may receive a lesser incentive or perhaps no incentive in the future. As a consequence, his or her base salary remains the same or is perhaps increased at a relatively moderate pace; he or she receives one-time incentive rewards as recognition for exemplary performance. Furthermore, because these plans, by their very nature, focus on one-time events, it is much easier for the organization to change the focus of the incentive plan. At a simple level, for example, an organization can set up an incentive plan for selling one product during one quarter, but then shift the incentive to a different product the next quarter, as the situation requires. Automobile companies such as Ford and GM routinely do this by reducing sales incentives for models that are selling very well and increasing sales incentives for models that are selling below expectations or are about to be discontinued.

Team and Group Incentive Reward Systems

The merit compensation and incentive compensation systems described in the preceding sections deal primarily with performance-based reward arrangements for individuals. There also exists a different set of performance-based reward programs that are targeted for teams and groups. These programs are particularly important for managers to understand today, given the widespread trends toward team- and group-based methods of work and organizations.[34]

Common Team and Group Reward Systems

There are two commonly used types of team and group reward systems. One type used in many organizations is an approach called *gainsharing*. **Gainsharing programs** are designed to share the cost savings from productivity improvements with employees. The underlying assumption of gainsharing is that employees and the employer have the same goals and thus should appropriately share in incremental economic gains.[35]

In general, organizations that use gainsharing start by measuring team- or group-level productivity. It is important that this measure be valid and reliable and that it truly reflects current levels of performance by the team or group. The team or work group itself is then given the charge of attempting to lower costs or otherwise improve productivity through any measures that its members develop and its manager approves. Resulting cost savings or productivity gains that the team or group is able to achieve are then quantified and translated into dollar values. A predetermined formula is then used to allocate these dollar savings between the employer and the employees themselves. A typical formula for distributing gainsharing savings is to provide 25 percent to the employees and 75 percent to the company.

One specific type of gainsharing plan is an approach called the Scanlon plan. This approach was developed by Joseph Scanlon in 1927. The **Scanlon plan** has the same basic strategy as gainsharing plans, in that teams or groups of employees are encouraged to suggest strategies for reducing costs. However, the distribution of these gains is usually tilted much more heavily toward employees, with employees usually receiving between two-thirds and three-fourths of the total cost savings that the plan achieves. Furthermore, the distribution of cost savings resulting from the plan is given not just to the team or group that suggested and developed the ideas, but across the entire organization.

gainsharing programs
Designed to share the cost savings from productivity improvements with employees

Scanlon plan
Similar to gainsharing, but the distribution of gains is tilted much more heavily toward employees

Other Types of Team and Group Rewards Although gainsharing and Scanlon-type plans are among the most popular group incentive reward systems, there are other systems that are also used by some organizations. Some companies, for example, have begun to use true incentives at the team or group level. Just as with individual incentives, team or group incentives tie rewards directly to performance increases. And, like individual incentives, team or group incentives are paid as they are earned rather than being added to employees' base salary. The incentives are distributed at the team or group level, however, rather than at the individual level. In some cases, the distribution may be based on the existing salary of each employee, with incentive bonuses' being given on a proportionate basis. In other settings, each member of the team or group receives the same incentive pay.

Some companies also use nonmonetary rewards at the team or group level—most commonly in the form of prizes and awards. For example, a company might designate the particular team in a plant or subunit of the company that achieves the highest level of productivity increase, the highest level of reported customer satisfaction, or a similar index of performance. The reward itself might take the form of additional time off, as described earlier in this chapter, or a tangible award, such as a trophy or plaque. In any event, the idea is that the reward is at the team level and serves as recognition of exemplary performance by the entire team.

There are also other kinds of team or group level incentives that go beyond the contributions of a specific work group. These are generally organization-wide kinds of incentives. One long-standing method for this approach is *profit sharing*. In a profit-sharing approach, at the end of the year, some portion of the company's profits is paid into a profit-sharing pool that is then distributed to all employees. Either this amount is distributed at that time, or it is put into an escrow account and payment is deferred until the employee retires.

Employee stock ownership plans (ESOPs) also represent a group-level reward system that some companies use. Under the ESOP, employees are gradually given a major stake in ownership of a corporation. The typical form of this plan involves the company's taking out a loan, which is then used to buy a portion of its own stock in the open market. Over time, company profits are then used to pay off this loan. Employees, in turn, receive a claim on ownership of some portion of the stock held by the company, based on their seniority and perhaps on their performance. Eventually, each individual becomes an owner of the company.

The "Tough Times, Tough Choices" box shows how one company came up with an innovative way of motivating employees to be both more competitive and more team oriented. It also shows what happens when the best-laid motivational plans run up against harsh fiscal realities.

Executive Compensation

The top-level executives of most companies have separate compensation programs and plans. These are intended to reward these executives for their performance and for the performance of the organization.

Standard Forms of Executive Compensation Most senior executives receive their compensation in two forms. One form is a *base salary*. As with the base salary of any staff member or professional member of an organization, the base salary of an executive is a guaranteed amount of money that the individual will be paid. For example, in 2008 Kraft Foods paid its CEO, Irene Rosenfeld, $1,452,231 in base salary.[36]

TOUGH TIMES, TOUGH CHOICES

Seagate Drives Hard for a Competitive Edge

In the late 1990s, Seagate Technology, one of the world's leading makers of hard drives and storage solutions for computers and other consumer devices, was facing a motivation crisis. A merger with Conner Peripherals had produced the world's largest independent manufacturer of hard drives, but it also resulted in layoffs and unhappy survivors from both firms. President and COO Bill Watkins, who'd come over to Seagate in the merger, was in a unique position to assess the problem, which wasn't exactly bubbling beneath the surface of the corporate culture: The workforce was constantly concerned about job security and hostile toward outsiders, and as for management, according to Watkins, rewards typically went to whoever "yelled the loudest" at meetings. Watkins was convinced that the company needed to create "a different culture—one that was open, honest, and encouraged people to work together." Well known for his informal and candid style, Watkins was committed to team building as the cornerstone of the new culture, and he believed that the best way to inculcate a respect for teamwork was to "put [employees] in an environment where they have to ask for help."

So when he became CEO, Watkins initiated "Eco Seagate," which annually sends 200 employees to New Zealand, Australia, or Hawaii for a week of hiking, kayaking, biking, and rappelling. Participants are divided into teams headed by a member of top management, and everything leads up to a grueling one-day race. "It's all about the strength of the team," Watkins told an interviewer. "You're always going to have team members who are weak. How do you work together to get through it? The whole idea is to get people relating to each other." Former COO David Wickersham was most impressed by the way the offsite event engendered self-confidence and trust: "For me, the race [was] anticlimactic. You learn so much about yourself in the first four days and, personally, I'm surprised by

how much people let their guard down." Charles Pope, who's now head of Strategic Planning and Corporate Development, was initially skeptical but has since come around to the thinking behind Eco Seagate: "I don't like to schmooze for the sake of schmoozing," he says, but "I consider this an investment." In fact, it's a fairly hefty investment—about $1.8 million a year, but it's also just a fraction of the $40 million that the company spends every year on employee training.

After six years, Watkins' commitment to training and teamwork had paid off handsomely. Noting that its 2005 net profit of $925 million was triple the combined earnings of its three nearest competitors, *Forbes* magazine named Seagate its "Company of the Year" for 2006, beating out 1,000 other publicly traded companies. Revenue for the year was up 21 percent, to $7.5 billion, and analysts expected an increase to $9 billion in 2006. Watkins called the award "a tribute to the thousands of Seagate employees around the world who have made . . . Seagate not only the leader in hard drives, but now recognized as one of the . . . most innovative and most efficient companies in the world." He added that "the real story for Seagate . . . is four or five years from now. That's when I believe Seagate will really start reaching its true potential."

Three years later, Watkins confided to a reporter that he was thinking about canceling Eco Seagate 2009. For the fiscal year ending in June 2008, Seagate had reported its highest-ever sales and profits. In the first quarter of 2009 (ending in September 2008), Seagate announced profits of $60 million on revenue of $3 billion, but the effects of the global financial crisis and recession hit technology-related industries quickly and hard. December 2008, said Watkins, was the worst he'd ever seen, and the second quarter of 2009, he admitted, was "crappy." He was expecting a couple of quarters of bad news, and

(continued)

he was preparing to cut capacity to keep it in line with plunging demand. "We don't want to cut all spending," he said over the weekend of January 10, "but we don't want to spend into a disaster either."

As it turns out, Watkins never had to make the call on Eco Seagate 2009. On Monday, January 12, he was fired as CEO by the Seagate board of directors, which was apparently much more concerned about cutting costs than its top manager was. On the same day, the company announced that it was laying off 800 employees, or about 10 percent of its U.S. workforce. Two days later, management upped the figure to 3,000 employees worldwide, or 6 percent of its global workforce. In May, Seagate announced another 1,100 layoffs, another 2.5 percent of its worldwide headcount, as part of an effort to cut costs to less than $300 million per quarter and return to profitability by 2010. Having cut labor costs by 25 percent since the beginning of the year, when new CEO Stephen Luczo undertook a review of the company's entire cost structure, Seagate also closed two media facilities and a research facility in Pittsburgh and imposed companywide salary reductions.

"Things are really bad for the entire industry right now," said Jayson Noland, an analyst at Robert W. Baird & Company, but another analyst, Needham & Company's Richard Kugele, observed that Seagate had taken a few "operational missteps" under

Watkins, who could not be regarded as "completely blameless." Seagate had been losing ground to its major rival, Western Digital, for at least two years, especially in the markets for laptop and PC hard drives. It had also failed to follow through on announced plans to produce new solid-state hard drives (SSDs), which use flash memory rather than spinning disks, failing even to name an SSD supplier while competitors such as Toshiba and Samsung had developed their own flash-memory capabilities.

For the third quarter of 2009 (ending in March 2009), Seagate reported a loss of $273 million on sales of $2.1 billion. The loss, however, included $54 million in depreciation and restructuring charges (including nearly $25 million related to worldwide layoffs), and the company said that it continued to expect a return to profitability in 2010.

References: Sarah Max, "Seagate's Morale-athon," BusinessWeek, April 3, 2006, www.businessweek.com on May 14, 2009; "Seagate Named 2006 Company of the Year by Forbes Magazine," press release, Seagate website, January 9, 2006, www.seagate.com on May 14, 2009; Dean Takahasi, "Seagate to Lay off 10 Percent and Replace CEO Bill Watkins," VentureBeat, January 12, 2009, http://venturebeat.com on May 14, 2009; Ashlee Vance, "Seagate Shares Fall on Surprise Management Shift," New York Times, January 13, 2009, www.nytimes.com on May 14, 2009; Ashlee Vance, "Seagate Layoffs Grow from 800 to 3,000," New York Times, January 14, 2009, http://bits.blogs.nytimes.com on May 14, 2009; Chris Mellor, "Seagate Slashes More Jobs," The Register, May 13, 2009, www.theregister.co on May 14, 2009; "Seagate Technology Reports Fiscal Third Quarter 2009 Results," press release, Seagate website, April 21, 2009, http://media.seagate.com on May 14, 2009.

Above and beyond this base salary, however, most executives also receive one or more forms of incentive pay. The traditional method of incentive pay for executives is in the form of bonuses. Bonuses, in turn, are usually determined by the performance of the organization. Thus, at the end of the year, some portion of a corporation's profits may be diverted into a bonus pool. Senior executives then receive a bonus expressed as a percentage of this bonus pool. The CEO and president are obviously likely to get a larger percentage bonus than a vice president. The exact distribution of the bonus pool is usually specified ahead of time in the individual's employment contract. Some organizations intentionally leave the distribution unspecified, so that the board of directors has the flexibility to give larger rewards to those individuals deemed to be most deserving. Kraft Foods' Irene Rosenfeld received a cash bonus of about $4 million in 2008.[37]

Special Forms of Executive Compensation Beyond base salary and bonuses, many executives receive other kinds of compensation as well. A form of executive compensation that has received a lot of attention in recent years has been various kinds of stock options. A **stock option plan** is established to give senior managers the option to buy company stock in the future at a predetermined fixed price. The basic idea underlying stock option plans is that if the executives contribute to higher levels of organizational performance, then the company stock should increase in value. Then the executive will be able to purchase the stock at the predetermined price, which theoretically should be lower than its future market price. The difference then becomes profit for the individual. Kraft Foods awarded Irene Rosenfeld stock options with a potential value of $10 million.[38]

Stock options continue to grow in popularity as a means of compensating top managers. Options are seen as a means of aligning the interests of the manager with those of the stockholders, and given that they do not cost the organization much (other than some possible dilution of stock values), they will probably be even more popular in the future. In fact, a recent study by KPMG Peat Marwick indicates that for senior management whose salary exceeds $250,000, stock options represent the largest share of the salary mix (relative to salary and other incentives). Furthermore, when we consider all of top management (annual salary over $750,000), stock options comprise a full 60 percent of their total compensation. And the Peat Marwick report indicates that even among exempt employees at the $35,000-a-year level, stock options represent 13 percent of total compensation.

But events in recent years have raised serious questions about the use of stock options as incentives for executives. For example, several executives at Enron allegedly withheld critical financial information from the markets, cashed in their stock options (while Enron stock was trading at $80 a share), and then watched as the financial information was made public and the stock fell to less than $1 a share. Of course, these actions (if proven) are illegal, but they raise questions in the public's mind about the role of stock options and about the way organizations treat stock options from an accounting perspective. Most organizations have *not* treated stock options as liabilities, even though, when exercised, they are exactly that. There is concern that by not carrying stock options as liabilities, the managers are overstating the value of the company, which, of course, can help raise the stock price. Finally, when stock markets generally fell during the middle of 2002, many executives found that their options were worthless, as the price of the stock fell below the option price. When stock options go "underwater" in this way, they have no value to anyone.

Aside from stock option plans, other kinds of executive compensation are also used by some companies. Among the more popular are perquisites such as memberships in private clubs, access to company recreational facilities, and similar considerations. Some organizations also make available to senior executives low- or no-interest loans. These are often given to new executives whom the company is hiring from other companies and serve as an incentive for the individual to leave his or her current job to join a new organization. Kraft Food's Irene Rosenfeld received slightly more than $150,000 in other compensation during 2008 for things such as perks and payment of life insurance.[39]

stock option plan
Established to give senior managers the option to buy company stock in the future at a predetermined fixed price

Criticisms of Executive Compensation In recent years, executive compensation has come under fire for a variety of reasons. One major reason is that the levels of executive compensation attained by some managers seem simply too large for the average shareholder to understand. It is not uncommon, for instance, for a senior executive of a major corporation to earn total income from his or her job in a given year of well in excess of $1 million. Sometimes the income of CEOs can be substantially more than this. Thus, just as the typical person has difficulty comprehending the astronomical salaries paid to some movie stars and sports stars, so, too, would the average person be aghast at the astronomical salaries paid to some senior executives.

Compounding the problem created by perceptions of executive compensation is the fact that there often seems to be little or no relationship between the performance of the organization and the compensation paid to its senior executives.[40] Certainly, if an organization is performing at an especially high level and its stock price is increasing consistently, then most observers would agree that the senior executives responsible for this growth should be entitled to attractive rewards.[41] However, it is more difficult to understand a case in which executives are paid huge salaries and other forms of rewards when their company is performing at only a marginal level, yet this is fairly common today. For example, in 2008 the total compensation for Kraft Food's Irene Rosenfeld increased by 38 percent from 2007 levels, whereas the firm's stock price declined by 15 percent.[42]

Finally, we should note that the gap between the earnings of the CEO and the earnings of a typical employee is enormous. First of all, the size of the gap has been increasing in the United States. In 1980, the typical CEO earned 42 times the earnings of an ordinary worker; by 1990, this ratio had increased to 85 times the earnings of an ordinary worker; in 2007, the ratio was 344 times the earnings of a typical worker. In Japan, on the other hand, the CEO-to-worker pay ratio is 11 times; in Germany the ratio is 13 times.

New Approaches to Performance-Based Rewards

Some organizations have started to recognize that they can leverage the value of the incentives that they offer to their employees and to groups in their organization by allowing those individuals and groups to have a say in how rewards are distributed. For example, at the extreme, a company could go so far as to grant salary increase budgets to work groups and then allow the members of those groups themselves to determine how the rewards are going to be allocated among the various members of the group. This strategy would appear to hold considerable promise if everyone understands the performance arrangements that exist in the work group and if everyone is committed to being fair and equitable. Unfortunately, it can also create problems if people in a group feel that rewards are not being distributed fairly.[43]

Organizations are also getting increasingly innovative in their incentive programs. For example, some now offer stock options to all their employees, rather than just to top executives. In addition, some firms are looking into ways to purely individualize reward systems. For instance, a firm might offer one employee a paid three-month sabbatical every two years in exchange for a 20 percent reduction in salary. Another employee in the same firm might be offered a 10 percent salary increase in exchange for a 5 percent reduction in company contributions to the person's retirement account. Corning, General Electric, and Microsoft are among the firms closely studying this option.[44]

Regardless of the method used, however, it is also important that managers in an organization effectively communicate what rewards are being distributed and the basis for that distribution. In other words, if incentives are being distributed on the basis of perceived individual contributions to the organization, then members of the organization should be informed of that fact. This will presumably better enable them to understand the basis on which pay increases and other incentives and performance-based rewards have been distributed.

SUMMARY OF LEARNING OBJECTIVES AND KEY POINTS

1. Characterize the nature of motivation, including its importance and basic historical perspectives.

    • Motivation is the set of forces that cause people to behave in certain ways.

    • Motivation is an important consideration for managers because it, along with ability and environmental factors, determines individual performance.

2. Identify and describe the major content perspectives on motivation.

    • Content perspectives on motivation are concerned with what factors cause motivation.

    • Popular content theories include Maslow's hierarchy of needs, the ERG theory, and Herzberg's two-factor theory.

    • Other important needs are the needs for achievement, affiliation, and power.

3. Identify and describe the major process perspectives on motivation.

    • Process perspectives on motivation deal with how motivation occurs.

    • Expectancy theory suggests that people are motivated to perform if they believe that their effort will result in high performance, that this performance will lead to rewards, and that the positive aspects of the outcomes outweigh the negative aspects.

    • Equity theory is based on the premise that people are motivated to achieve and maintain social equity.

    • Goal setting theory assumes people are motivated by goals that are challenging and specific.

4. Describe reinforcement perspectives on motivation.

    • The reinforcement perspective focuses on how motivation is maintained.

    • Its basic assumption is that behavior that results in rewarding consequences is likely to be repeated, whereas behavior resulting in negative consequences is less likely to be repeated.

    • Reinforcement contingencies can be arranged in the form of positive reinforcement, avoidance, punishment, and extinction, and they can be provided on fixed-interval, variable-interval, fixed-ratio, or variable-ratio schedules.

5. Identify and describe popular motivational strategies.

    • Managers use a variety of motivational strategies derived from the various theories of motivation.

    • Common strategies include empowerment and participation and alternative forms of work arrangements, such as variable work schedules, flexible work schedules, and telecommuting.

6. Describe the role of organizational reward systems in motivation.

    • Reward systems also play a key role in motivating employee performance.

    • Popular methods include merit reward systems, incentive reward systems, and team and group incentive reward systems.

    • Executive compensation is also intended to serve as motivation for senior managers but has currently come under close scrutiny and criticism.

DISCUSSION QUESTIONS

Questions for Review

1. Summarize Maslow's hierarchy of needs and the two-factor theory. In what ways are they similar and in what ways are they different?

2. Compare and contrast content, process, and reinforcement perspectives on motivation.

3. Using equity theory as a framework, explain how a person can experience inequity because he or she is paid too much. What are the potential outcomes of this situation?

4. Explain how goal-setting theory works. How is goal setting different from merely asking a worker to "do your best"?

5. Describe some new forms of working arrangements. How do these alternative arrangements increase motivation?

Questions for Analysis

1. Choose one theory from the content perspectives and one from the process perspectives. Describe actions that a manager might take to increase worker motivation under each of the theories. What differences do you see between the theories in terms of their implications for managers?

2. Can factors from both the content and the process perspectives be acting on a worker at the same time? Explain why or why not. Whether you answered yes or no to the previous question, explain the implications for managers.

3. How do rewards increase motivation? What would happen if an organization gave too few rewards? What would happen if it gave too many?

4. Think about the worst job you have held. What approach to motivation was used in that organization? Now think about the best job you have held. What approach to motivation was used there? Can you base any conclusions on this limited information? If so, what are they?

5. Consider a class you have taken. Using just that one class, offer examples of times when the professor used positive reinforcement, avoidance, punishment, and extinction to manage students' behavior.

BUILDING EFFECTIVE INTERPERSONAL AND COMMUNICATION SKILLS

Exercise Overview

Interpersonal skills refer to the ability to communicate with, understand, and motivate individuals and groups, and *communication skills* refer to the ability to send and receive information effectively. This exercise is designed to demonstrate the essential roles played in employee motivation by an understanding of what motivates people and an ability to communicate that understanding.

Exercise Background

One implication of reinforcement theory is that both positive reinforcement (reward) and punishment can be effective in altering employee behavior. The use of punishment, however, may result in resentment on the employee's part, and over the long term, that resentment can diminish the effectiveness of punishment. By and large, positive reinforcement is more effective over time.

Exercise Task

Your instructor will ask for volunteers to perform a demonstration in front of the class. Consider volunteering, but if you don't want to participate, observe the behavior of the volunteers closely. When the demonstration is over, respond to the following questions:

1. Based on what you saw, which is more effective—positive reinforcement or punishment?

2. How did positive reinforcement and punishment affect the "employee" in the demonstration? How did it affect the "boss"?

3. What, in your opinion, are the likely long-term consequences of positive reinforcement and punishment?

BUILDING EFFECTIVE DECISION-MAKING SKILLS

Exercise Overview

Decision-making skills refer to the ability to recognize and define problems and opportunities correctly and then to select an appropriate course of action for solving problems or capitalizing on opportunities. This exercise allows you to build your decision-making skills while applying goal-setting theory to the task of planning your career.

Exercise Background

Lee Iacocca started his career at Ford in 1946 in an entry-level engineering job. By 1960, he was a vice president and in charge of the group that designed the Mustang, and ten years later, he was a president of the firm. After being fired from Ford in 1978, he then became a president at Chrysler and eventually rose to the CEO spot, a job he held until he retired in 1992. What's really remarkable about Iacocca's career arc—at least the upward trajectory—is the fact that he apparently had it all planned out, even before he finished college.

The story goes that, while he was still an undergraduate, Iacocca wrote out a list of all the positions that he'd like to hold during his career. Number one was "engineer at an auto maker," followed by all the career steps that he planned to take until he was a CEO. He also included a timetable for his climb up the corporate ladder. Then he put his list on a three-by-five-inch card that he folded and stowed in his wallet, and we're told that every time he took out that card and looked at it, he gained fresh confidence and drive. He apparently reached the top several years ahead of schedule, but otherwise he followed his career path and timetable faithfully.

As you can see, Iacocca used goal-setting theory to motivate himself, and there's no reason why you can't do the same.

Exercise Task

1. Consider the position that you'd like to hold at the peak of your career. It may be CEO, owner of a chain of clothing stores, partner in a law or accounting firm, or president of a university. Then again, it may be something less lofty. Whatever it is, write it down.

2. Now describe a career path that will lead you toward that goal. It may help to work "backward"—that is, starting with your final position and working backward in time to some entry-level job. If you aren't sure about the career path that will lead to your ultimate goal, do some research. Talk to someone in your selected career field, ask an instructor who teaches in it, or go online. The website of the American Institute of Certified Public Accountants, for example, has a section on "Career Resources," which includes information about career paths and position descriptions for accounting.

3. Write down each step in your path on a card or a sheet of paper.

4. If, like Lee Iacocca, you were to carry this piece of paper with you and refer to it often as you pursued your career goals, do you think it would help you achieve them? Why or why not?

SKILLS SELF-ASSESSMENT INSTRUMENT

Assessing Your Needs

Introduction: Needs are one factor that influences motivation. The following assessment surveys your judgments about some of your personal needs that might be partially shaping your motivation.

Instructions: Judge how descriptively accurate each of the following statements is about you. You may find making a decision difficult in some cases, but you should force yourself to make a choice. Record your answers next to each statement according to the following scale:

Rating Scale

5 Very descriptive of me
4 Fairly descriptive of me
3 Somewhat descriptive of me
2 Not very descriptive of me
1 Not descriptive of me at all

_____ 1. I aspire to accomplish difficult tasks and maintain high standards and am willing to work toward distant goals.

_____ 2. I enjoy being with friends and people in general and accept people readily.

_____ 3. I am easily annoyed and am sometimes willing to hurt people to get my way.

_____ 4. I try to break away from restraints or restrictions of any kind.

_____ 5. I want to be the center of attention and enjoy having an audience.

_____ 6. I speak freely and tend to act on the spur of the moment.

_____ 7. I assist others whenever possible, giving sympathy and comfort to those in need.

_____ 8. I believe in the saying that "there is a place for everything and everything should be in its place." I dislike clutter.

_____ 9. I express my opinions forcefully, enjoy the role of leader, and try to control my environment as much as I can.

_____ 10. I want to understand many areas of knowledge and value synthesizing ideas and generalization.

EXPERIENTIAL EXERCISE

Motivation at Bluefield

Bob works for a fast-growing manufacturer of cosmetics at their oldest plant in Bluefield, West Virginia. Bob has an M.B.A. from State University and began his career at Bluefield in the Human Resource Department. He got his first big chance when the company, facing increased problems with the local minority community, put Bob in charge of a new affirmative action program. Bob is proud of his success in that position. His supervisors were also impressed and promoted him to the position of Manager of Machine Operations. He managed a workforce of 74 employees through seven supervisors. He's held this job for only one year.

There is a new program to revitalize operations at Bluefield. Bob, because of his earlier success, has been assigned the task of developing a motivation plan for his seven subordinate supervisors. Bob needs to review the personnel files and try to identify the needs or motivators for each supervisor. To provide a working framework for the study, Bob decides to use both Maslow's hierarchy of needs and Herzberg's two-factor theory, as shown on the Need/Motivation Worksheet.

Bob divides the worksheet into three sections: (1) Maslow's Needs, (2) Motivation Factors, and (3) Hygiene Factors. In each category, he plans to rank the appropriate items for each supervisor, using a 1 for the top ranking, a 2 for the second ranking, and so on.

Instructions:

1. Read the following personnel files. In addition to other data, each profile contains a supervisor's Performance Measure (PM). This is a score assigned by a computer-based productivity program

developed by Industrial Engineering. The program uses a variety of cost and output figures to calculate a PM for each supervisor on a scale ranging from 0 (representing very poor performance) to 100 (nearly perfect performance).

2. Then, as a small group, use the following Need/Motivation Worksheet to rank the relative importance of each of the motivators for each supervisor. Rank within groups—1 to 5 for Maslow's Needs, then 1 to 5 for Motivation Factors, and then 1 to 6 for Hygiene Factors.

3. Present your group findings to the class and discuss.

Bluefield Plant Supervisor Profiles

JOHN MILLER is the senior supervisor with 21 years of seniority. He is 60 years old and has only a sixth-grade education. His most recent PM score is 50, which is lower than it used to be. John's past appraisals suggest that he has done an average job in the past, and Bob thinks his performance is still average and is sorry to see John's performance declining. His peers are convinced that John is too old to cut the mustard. Bob thinks that John has the easiest job in the group. John is a widower who spends a lot of time at his cabin by the lake. His current salary is $45,000.

MOHAMMAD NAJEED is 52 with 16 years with the firm. His PM is 70 and his salary is $38,000. Mohammad is a high-school graduate, and his wife is quite wealthy. Bob believes that Mohammad has the best overall experience in the group and is a very capable supervisor, although his peers rank him average, the same as his past evaluations. Mohammad supervises a group that has about average responsibilities.

TANIKA FORESTER is 36 with 10 years of seniority. She has a B.S. in Management, a PM of 80, and a salary of $31,000. Bob feels she has one of the easier jobs and is doing only a so-so job. He is surprised to find that her earlier appraisals have been very good, an evaluation shared by her peers. Tanika's husband was killed in a car accident, and she has three dependent children.

TOM WILSON is 44 with 1 year with the company. Tom has a high-school diploma, a PM of 50, and a salary of $28,000. Tom has the hardest group to supervise, but his earlier appraisals have only been average, an opinion shared by Tom's peers. Bob agrees that Tom's performance is average and is concerned that it might get worse as Tom seems to be having too many personal problems lately.

SIDNEY BENTON is 35 and has 8 years of seniority, a PM of 80, and a salary of $26,000. Sidney has a B.S. in Industrial Technology and is enrolled in State's night M.B.A. program. Sidney has a difficult job, requiring specialized skills, and he would be very hard to replace. Bob believes Sidney to be a top supervisor, an opinion shared by his peers. But Bob is troubled by past appraisals that vary from outstanding to poor.

LI TRAN is 32 with 5 years at the plant, a PM of only 30, and a salary of $22,000. She is a high-school dropout who quit school to have her first child. She is a single parent with four children and works very hard to support them. Li represents one of the affirmative action promotions that Bob arranged when he was the Affirmative Action Officer, and he is disappointed to find that her past and present appraisals are quite poor. Although her present job is perceived to require average skill, her peers consider her to be an incompetent troublemaker who constantly complains about the need for more affirmative action efforts at the plant.

LUIS FUENTES is 26, has only 2 years with the company, a PM of only 20, and a salary of $19,000. He dropped out of school to take care of his sick mother and two younger sisters. Bob hired Luis as part of the Affirmative Action Program. Luis's first appraisal was low, but Bob believes that was because he was in a job requiring too much experience. So Bob moved him to a job with more average demands. Bob thinks that Luis is doing a bit better in the new job and, in time, will be a good supervisor. Peer evaluations are somewhat mixed but above average.

Need/Motivation Worksheet

(In each category. Rank the appropriate items for each supervisor.
Top rank = 1, Second rank = 2, etc.)

Need/Factor	John Miller	Mohammed Najeed	Tanika Forester	Tom Wilson	Sidney Benton	Li Tran	Luis Fuentes
Maslow's Needs							
Physiological							
Security							
Belongingness							
Esteem							
Self-Actualization							
Motivation Factors							
Achivement							
Recognition							
Work Itself							
Responsibility							
Advancement/Growth							
Hygiene Factors							
Supervision							
Working conditions							
Interpersonal							
Pay							
Security							
Policy & Administration							

Adapted from Morable, *Exercises in Management*, to accompany Griffin, *Management*, 8th edition.

Addressing the Balance of Trade-offs

1. When you graduate and start your professional career, what factors in your work life do you expect to be your prime motivators? How do you envision these motivators changing over the course of your life?

2. Some young people today accept high-stress, high-paying jobs for what they expect will be only a short period of time. In other words, they're willing to sacrifice work–life balance in the present to get a financial head start in life. Does this approach appeal to you? Why or why not?

3. Kathy Caprino says that "role models from previous generations don't offer guidance on how to achieve a healthy, balanced, and meaningful professional and personal life." Explain what she means and whether you agree or disagree. Back up your opinion.

4. Suppose you found yourself in a job that was demanding more and more of your time. What factors would probably encourage you to stay? What factors would probably prompt you to off-ramp your career?

5. Being as realistic as possible, describe a job that you'd really like to have and explain how it might both help and hinder your efforts to strike a satisfactory work–life balance.

CHAPTER 13

LEADERSHIP AND ITS IMPACT ON INFLUENCE PROCESSES

LEARNING OBJECTIVES

After studying this chapter, you should be able to:

1 Describe the nature of leadership and relate leadership to management.

2 Discuss and evaluate the two generic approaches to leadership.

3 Identify and describe the major situational approaches to leadership.

4 Identify and describe three related approaches to leadership.

5 Describe three emerging approaches to leadership.

6 Discuss political behavior in organizations and how it can be managed.

Inside the Leadership Cycle at Intel

Intel is the largest maker of semiconductor chips in the world. It dominates its industry, producing twice as many chips as its nearest competitor and selling almost $100 million worth of them every day. For over 40 years now, one of the company's most valuable resources has been leadership. Intel has had five CEOs since it was founded in 1969, and although each has naturally brought different strengths and taken different approaches to the job, each has contributed to Intel's remarkable record of continuous success.

Bob Noyce, a physicist with an aptitude for technology, started Intel in 1969 with chemist-physicist Gordon Moore and served as its CEO until 1975. As a leader, Noyce was known as a loyal and charismatic risk taker who had a knack for knowing when his people knew what they were doing: He was general manager at Fairchild Semiconductor when its scientists invented the integrated chip in 1959, and as head of Intel, he oversaw the development of the microprocessor in the late 1960s. "The people that are supervising [a project]," he once said, "are more dependent on their ability to judge people than they are dependent on their ability to judge the work that's going on."

> *"If I had relied on [former CEO Gordon] Moore's leadership style, I would have been in deep trouble. . . . My role was to be exactly the opposite [of Gordon]."*
>
> —ANDREW GROVE, FORMER INTEL CEO

Noyce also epitomized the image of the casual California high-tech executive. He had no use for corporate jets, gaudy offices, or even reserved parking spaces and preferred a relaxed working environment in which bright employees were given the freedom to do what they were hired to do. Under his leadership, Intel developed a culture that emphasized technical proficiency over fiscal performance.

When Noyce stepped down in 1975, Gordon Moore took over as CEO and held the post

DANIEL ACKER/BLOOMBERG/GETTY IMAGES

Leadership has long played a major role in the success of chip-maker Intel. Paul Otellini, current chief executive officer at Intel, is shown here introducing a new chip designed for cell phones. Intel thinks this market holds huge potential for future growth.

until 1987, when he became chairman of the board. Back in 1965, Moore had set forth the now classic Moore's Law—the number of transistors on a microchip will double every two years—and when the new company was founded, he naturally assumed the role of chief technology innovator. From the start, Intel scientists were committed to proving the validity of Moore's Law, and they've always been fairly successful at maintaining the pace, delivering next-generation silicon technology and new processor architecture on an almost yearly basis. Today, Moore's Law is institutionalized as Intel's "tick-tock model," which is designed to put technology innovation on a reliable and predictable timetable.

Moore's leadership style was quite similar to Noyce's but—if possible—even more committed to hands-off management and the primacy of technology. According to his successor, Andy Grove, "Gordon is rational, technically based, [and] minimalist in terms of intervention. When he has something to say, it's usually worth listening to." Much of what Gordon had to say, he said to Grove, whom he promoted to president in 1979 and who actually ran the company along with Moore until the latter's retirement. "Much of [my success] is due to standing on his shoulders," says Grove, who has always extolled the value of the mentoring relationship. "If he hadn't been there," Grove adds, "I would have been a happy, productive engineer . . . but I don't think I would have ended up running the company."

At the same time, however, Grove acknowledges the conspicuous differences in leadership styles—he himself is decisive and sometimes arrogant—and makes it clear that he thinks his was the style the company needed when he took over as CEO in 1987. He likes to refer to management theorist Peter Drucker's idea that CEOs can be identified by one of three chief roles: According to Grove, Noyce was Intel's public face or "front man," and Moore was its "thought man"; he himself is a "man of action." "If I had relied on [Gordon's] leadership style," he says, "I would have been in deep trouble because [he was] not an activist. My role was to be exactly the opposite [of Gordon]."

Why had Grove decided that Intel needed a new direction? Why was he convinced that, by the late 1980s, the company needed a "man of action" to take it in that direction? The writing was writ large on the walls of company headquarters in Santa Clara, California, as early as 1985. As of 1983, Intel was still a fast-growing corporation worth $1.1 billion in annual revenues, much of the money coming, as it had since the company's founding, from sales of SRAM and DRAM memory chips. Unfortunately, Moore's Law had failed to predict that Japanese firms such as NEC and Toshiba would not only comply with Moore's Law as rigorously as Intel itself, but also in the process manage to turn the memory chip itself into a commodity. By 1985, when Intel's profits had plunged to less than $2 million—down from $198 million in 1984—Moore and Grove had agreed that the firm's future was not in memory chips. Shortly afterward, Grove announced that Intel was getting out of the memory-chip business and staking its future on a product that, ironically, it had itself introduced back in 1971—the microprocessor, which had been biding its time in applications such as timing traffic lights. At first, the changeover was extremely traumatic: In 1986, Intel lost $180 million on sales of $1.3 billion—its only loss since its earliest days as a start-up—and fired 8,000 people. But when IBM selected the Intel processor for its PC line, demand surged, and the company was set to begin an extremely profitable ten-year run. In 1992, profits topped $1 billion for the first time (on sales of $5.8 billion), and for Grove's 11-year tenure as CEO, Intel grew at a compounded annual rate of 30 percent. By the time he stepped down in 1998, Grove had overseen an increase in Intel's market capitalization from $18 billion to $197 billion—a gain of 4,500 percent.

When Craig Barrett succeeded Grove as CEO, Intel was the most valuable company in the world. A specialist in materials science, Barrett joined Intel in 1974 as a technology development manager, and in successive positions at the vice president level, he headed the company's manufacturing operations. In the 1980s, as Intel faced increasingly stiff competition from Japanese chipmakers, Barrett developed a manufacturing strategy called *copy exactly*, which called for the perfection of engineering processes at a single plant before rolling out the same method in another facility. The strategy allowed Intel to avoid costly flaws in the production process. "It wasn't until we got the Japanese competition in the mid-1980s," Barrett recalls, that "we figured out how to combine technology with manufacturing and exist as a manufacturing company, not just a technology company." When he retired as chairman in January 2009, his successor as CEO, Paul Otellini, remarked that Barrett's "legacy spans the creation of the best semiconductor manufacturing machine in the world."

How had he risen through the ranks to become CEO? "Just luck," quips Barrett, who adds that "we were able to turn manufacturing around. That caught the eye of Andy [Grove] and Gordon Moore." As COO from 1993 and the company's fourth president from 1997, Barrett had also developed a working relationship with Grove, who remained with the company as chairman and senior advisor, much like the one that Grove had enjoyed earlier with Gordon Moore. And like Grove, Barrett credits the difference in leadership styles as a critical factor in his success in the top spot: "Andy and I," says Barrett, "are very different in style. . . . Andy has a pretty instantaneous opinion. . . . I'm more of a classic engineer and a data-driven guy. Faced with a problem, I wait for the data and analyze the problem. Andy probably gets frustrated with that approach because he wants to take action. That drove me to do my part of the equation a bit faster. It was very complementary."

Barrett turned over the CEO job to Paul Otellini in 2005. With a background in finance, Otellini is the first nonengineer to lead Intel, but he's had a lot of experience in computer hardware: From 1993 to 1996, as general manager of the Peripheral Components Operation and then of the Intel Architecture Group, he was responsible for chipset operations, microprocessor and chipset business strategies, and giving technical advice to Andy Grove. He served as COO from 2002 to May 2005, when he became CEO.

Sixteen months later, Otellini presided over the largest round of layoffs in the company's history—a total of 10,500 employees (10 percent of the corporate workforce) over the course of about 18 months. Though still commanding 80 percent of the worldwide market for PC chips, Intel was under pressure from increasing competition and falling profits, and Otellini set out to save $3 billion in annual costs by 2008. He also announced that he would "restructure, repurpose, and resize" the company and has since moved to eliminate redundant jobs, simplify operations by reducing the total number of products, and selling off noncore and unprofitable businesses. He's also initiated strategies designed to bring new products to market more quickly.

In July 2008, Intel announced the highest earnings in the company's history. For the second quarter of fiscal 2008, revenues of $9.5 billion were up by 9 percent over the second quarter of 2007. Net income of $1.6 billion constituted an increase of 25 percent and operating income of $2.3 billion constituted an increase of 67 percent.[1]

The story of Intel provides several vivid examples of the roles and importance of leadership. Different circumstances call for different kinds of leadership. Intel has benefited enormously by always having just the right leader in place at just the right time. If a different leader had been in place during different stages of Intel's history, the firm might look very different (and much worse) than it does today. Likewise, had any of Intel's leaders worked for other companies, they might never have achieved the success they enjoyed at Intel.

This chapter examines people like Paul Otellini and his predecessors more carefully by focusing on leadership and its role in management. We characterize the nature of leadership and trace through the three major approaches to studying leadership—traits, behaviors, and situations. After examining other perspectives on leadership, we conclude by describing another approach to influencing others—political behavior in organizations.

THE NATURE OF LEADERSHIP

In Chapter 12, we described various models and perspectives on employee motivation. From the manager's standpoint, trying to motivate people is an attempt to influence their behavior. In many ways, leadership, too, is an attempt to influence the behavior of others. In this section, we first define leadership, then differentiate it from management, and conclude by relating it to power.

The Meaning of Leadership

Leadership is both a process and a property.[2] As a process—focusing on what leaders actually do—leadership is the use of noncoercive influence to shape the group's or organization's goals, motivate behavior toward the achievement of those goals, and help define group or organizational culture.[3] As a property, leadership is the set of characteristics attributed to individuals who are perceived to be leaders. Thus **leaders** are people who can influence the behaviors of others without having to rely on force or people whom others accept as leaders.

Leadership and Management

From these definitions, it should be clear that leadership and management are related, but they are not the same. A person can be a manager, a leader, both, or neither.[4] Some of the basic distinctions between the two are summarized by John Kotter in Table 13.1.

leadership
As a process, the use of noncoercive influence to shape the group's or organization's goals, motivate behavior toward the achievement of those goals, and help define group or organizational culture; as a property, the set of characteristics attributed to individuals who are perceived to be leaders

leaders
People who can influence the behaviors of others without having to rely on force; those accepted by others as leaders

Activity	Management	Leadership
Creating an agenda	*Planning and budgeting:* Establishing detailed steps and timetables for achieving needed results; allocating the resources necessary to make those needed results happen	*Establishing direction:* Developing a vision of the future, often the distant future, and strategies for producing the changes needed to achieve that vision
Developing a human network for achieving the agenda	*Organizing and staffing:* Establishing some structure for accomplishing plan requirements, staffing that structure with individuals, delegating responsibility and authority for carrying out the plan, providing policies and procedures to help guide people, and creating methods or systems to monitor implementation	*Aligning people:* Communicating the direction by words and deeds to everyone whose cooperation may be needed to influence the creation of teams and coalitions that understand the visions and strategies and accept their validity
Executing plans	*Controlling and problem solving:* Monitoring results versus planning in some detail, identifying deviations, and then planning and organizing to solve these problems	*Motivating and inspiring:* Energizing people to overcome major political, bureaucratic, and resource barriers by satisfying very basic, but often unfulfilled, human needs
Outcomes	Produces a degree of predictability and order and has the potential to produce consistently major results expected by various stakeholders (for example, for customers, always being on time; or, for stockholders, being on budget)	Produces change, often to a dramatic degree, and has the potential to produce extremely useful change (for example, new products that customers want, or new approaches to labor relations that help make a firm more competitive)

Table 13.1
Distinctions between Management and Leadership

Management and leadership are related, but distinct, constructs. Managers and leaders differ in how they create an agenda, develop a rationale for achieving the agenda, and execute plans, and in the types of outcomes they achieve.

Source: John P. Kotter, *A Force for Change: How Leadership Differs from Management,* 1990. © 1990 by John P. Kotter, Inc. Reprinted with permission of The Free Press, a division of Simon & Schuster Adult Publishing Group.

In the first column of the table are four elements that differentiate leadership from management. The other two columns show how each element differs when considered from a management and from a leadership point of view. For example, when executing plans, managers focus on monitoring results, comparing them with goals, and correcting deviations. In contrast, the leader focuses on energizing people to overcome bureaucratic hurdles to reach goals.

Organizations need both management and leadership if they are to be effective. Leadership is necessary to create change, and management is necessary to achieve orderly results. Management in conjunction with leadership can produce orderly change, and leadership in conjunction with management can keep the organization properly aligned with its environment. Indeed, perhaps part of the reason why executive compensation has soared in recent years is the belief that management and leadership skills reflect a critical but rare combination that can lead to organizational success.

Leadership and Power

power
The ability to affect the behavior of others

To fully understand leadership, it is necessary to understand **power**—the ability to affect the behavior of others. One can have power without actually using it. For example, a football coach has the power to bench a player who is not performing up to par. The coach seldom has to use this power because players recognize that the power exists and work hard to keep their starting positions. Managers and leaders do often have to actually use power but should only do so in ways that are ethical and appropriate. The "Ethics in Action" box tells a classic story of the manipulation of power and confirms the axiom

ETHICS IN ACTION

The Leading Edge of Corruption at Enron

The following true story, which occurred at the dawn of the century, is now a classic. The main characters, though hardly role models, are legendary in the annals of corporate leadership, and their exploits, though far from classic, are timeless enough to be recounted again here.

When the Houston-based energy-trading company Enron went bankrupt in 2001, investors lost more than $40 billion, and 15,000 employees lost $1.3 billion in pension savings. Ex-CEOs Kenneth Lay and Jeffrey Skilling were indicted for fraud and other felonies, and as their trials unfolded in early 2006, a complex saga of abused power gradually unfolded. Both Lay, who held a

PhD in economics from the University of Houston, and Skilling, who had assured Harvard Business School officials that "I'm *%#!ing smart" when he embarked on his MBA, opted for the classic "idiot" defense, each claiming that he was unaware of any problems that might be causing his $70 billion company to be collapsing around him.

Not surprisingly, most observers found claims of ignorance hard to swallow. Granted, Lay, who'd founded Enron in 1985 and headed it for the next 16 years, exercised little restraint over subordinates despite his position of power. According to Yale's Jeffrey Sonnenfeld, his trial showed that "when [Lay] sensed dangerous truths, he saw his job as one of containment, rather than showing courage or character." At one point, he insisted that the company's collapse was due to a "conspiracy" waged by short sellers, rogue executives, and the news media, and by the time the trial was over, most experts found it hard to determine whether he was a skillful liar, a self-deluded schemer, or an unimaginably incompetent executive. One thing, however, was clear: Although his company's stock was plummeting in value from more than $90 to a few pennies, Lay made $300 million on the sale of his.

Lay had hired Skilling in 1990 and promoted him to CEO in February 2001. In August, Skilling suddenly stepped down, claiming "personal" reasons for leaving the company. Lay assured analysts that there was "absolutely no accounting issue, no trading issue, no reserve issue, no previously-unknown-problem issue" behind Skilling's unexpected departure. Two months later, Enron shocked Wall Street with the announcement of $544 million in quarterly losses. Skilling had already shown signs of strange behavior, publicly referring to one Wall Street analyst as an "%#h-e" during a quarterly conference call. In April 2004, shortly after his indictment, police were summoned when Skilling was found accosting passersby on the streets of New York and accusing them of being FBI agents. His trial revealed that he had retained enough composure to sell $60 million worth of Enron stock in the months leading up to his abrupt exit from the company.

By the time the trial was over, many observers were convinced that Skilling, with Lay's support, had devised and carried out the schemes for which both men had been indicted. *Fortune* reporters

Bethany McLean and Peter Elkind, authors of *The Smartest Guys in the Room*, argue that Skilling had taken advantage of Lay's leadership deficiencies: Lay, they write, "avoided the sort of tough decisions that were certain to make others mad," preferring to "let someone else take the heat or . . . [to] throw money at the problem." Lay's ineptitude, according to McLean and Elkind, convinced Skilling and other executives that "they could do whatever they wanted and [that] Lay would never say no."

In May 2006, Lay was found guilty on ten charges of fraud and conspiracy. Two months later, three months before his scheduled sentencing, he died of heart disease, and a federal district court vacated his conviction. As if to confirm McLean and Elkind's thesis, Skilling was convicted on 19 counts of conspiracy, fraud, making false statements, and insider trading. On October 23, 2006, he was sentenced to 24 years and 4 months in prison and fined $45 million. He began serving his term in December while his case was on appeal. In January 2009, a U.S. Court of Appeals affirmed his conviction but vacated his sentence. He'll have to be resentenced, but experts don't expect him to go free anytime soon.

References: Alexei Barrionuevo and Kurt Eichenwald, "For Ken Lay, Enron's Riches Turning to Ruin," New York Times, February 26, 2006, www.nytimes.com on May 17, 2009; Anthony Bianco, "Ken Lay's Audacious Ignorance," BusinessWeek, February 6, 2006, www.businessweek.com on May 17, 2009; Michael Orey, "Something a Jury Can See," BusinessWeek, March 20, 2006, www.businessweek.com on May 17, 2009; Bethany McLean and Peter Elkind, The Smartest Guys in the Room: The Amazing Rise and Scandalous Fall of Enron (New York: Portfolio Publishing, 2004); Andrew Gumbel, "Business Analysis: Enron, the Trial," The Independent, January 31, 2006, www.independent.com on May 17, 2009; Frank Ahrens, "Skilling Sentence Vacated, but Enron Mastermind Still in Jail," Washington Post, January 6, 2009, http://voices.washingtonpost.com on May 17, 2009.

that insider trading doesn't pay. In organizational settings, there are usually five kinds of power: legitimate, reward, coercive, referent, and expert power.[5]

Legitimate Power   Legitimate power is power granted through the organizational hierarchy; it is the power defined by the organization to be accorded to people occupying a particular position. A manager can assign tasks to a subordinate, and a subordinate who refuses to do them can be reprimanded or even fired. Such outcomes stem from the manager's legitimate power as defined and vested in him or her by the organization.

legitimate power
Power granted through the organizational hierarchy; the power defined by the organization to be accorded to people occupying a particular position

Leaders can rely on several kinds of power to influence others. This supervisor, for example is directing the work of a subordinate as they develop a new advertising campaign for a client. She has legitimate power by virtue of her position as supervisor. She also controls rewards for all of her subordinates. She has expert power in terms of knowing what the client wants. Her personality and charisma may also provide her with referent power as well.

COPYRIGHT © DAVID YOUNG-WOLFF/PHOTOEDIT

reward power
The power to give or withhold rewards, such as salary increases, bonuses, promotions, praise, recognition, and interesting job assignments

coercive power
The power to force compliance by means of psychological, emotional, or physical threat

referent power
The personal power that accrues to someone based on identification, imitation, loyalty, or charisma

Legitimate power, then, is authority. All managers have legitimate power over their subordinates. The mere possession of legitimate power, however, does not by itself make someone a leader. Some subordinates follow only orders that are strictly within the letter of organizational rules and policies. If asked to do something not in their job descriptions, they refuse or do a poor job. The manager of such employees is exercising authority but not leadership.

Reward Power Reward power is the power to give or withhold rewards. Rewards that a manager may control include salary increases, bonuses, promotion recommendations, praise, recognition, and interesting job assignments. In general, the greater the number of rewards a manager controls and the more important the rewards are to subordinates, the greater is the manager's reward power. If the subordinate sees as valuable only the formal organizational rewards provided by the manager, then the manager is not a leader. If the subordinate also wants and appreciates the manager's informal rewards, such as praise, gratitude, and recognition, then the manager is also exercising leadership.

Coercive Power Coercive power is the power to force compliance by means of psychological, emotional, or physical threat. In the past, physical coercion in organizations was relatively common. In most organizations today, however, coercion is limited to verbal reprimands, written reprimands, disciplinary layoffs, fines, demotion, and termination. Some managers occasionally go so far as to use verbal abuse, humiliation, and psychological coercion in an attempt to manipulate subordinates. (Of course, most people would agree that these are not appropriate managerial behaviors.) James Dutt, a legendary former CEO of Beatrice Company, once told a subordinate that if his wife and family got in the way of his working a 24-hour day seven days a week, he should get rid of them![6] The more punitive the elements under a manager's control and the more important they are to subordinates, the more coercive power the manager possesses. On the other hand, the more a manager uses coercive power, the more likely he is to provoke resentment and hostility and the less likely he is to be seen as a leader.[7]

Referent Power Compared with legitimate, reward, and coercive power, which are relatively concrete and grounded in objective facets of organizational life, **referent power** is abstract. It is based on identification, imitation, loyalty, or charisma. Followers may react favorably because they identify in some way with a leader, who may be like them in personality, background, or attitudes. In other situations, followers might choose to imitate a leader with referent power by wearing the same kind of clothes, working the same hours, or espousing the same management philosophy. Referent power may also take the form of charisma, an intangible attribute of the leader that inspires loyalty and enthusiasm. Thus a manager might have referent power, but it is more likely to be associated with leadership.

Expert Power **Expert power** is derived from information or expertise. A manager who knows how to interact with an eccentric but important customer, a scientist who is capable of achieving an important technical breakthrough that no other company has dreamed of, and a secretary who knows how to unravel bureaucratic red tape all have expert power over anyone who needs that information. The more important the information and the fewer the people who have access to it, the greater is the degree of expert power possessed by any one individual. In general, people who are both leaders and managers tend to have a lot of expert power.

GENERIC APPROACHES TO LEADERSHIP

Early approaches to the study of leadership adopted what might be called a *universal* or *generic* perspective. Specifically, they assumed that there was one set of answers to the leadership puzzle. One generic approach focused on leadership traits, and the other looked at leadership behavior.

Leadership Traits

The first organized approach to studying leadership analyzed the personal, psychological, and physical traits of strong leaders. The trait approach assumed that some basic trait or set of traits existed that differentiated leaders from nonleaders. If those traits could be defined, potential leaders could be identified. Researchers thought that leadership traits might include intelligence, assertiveness, above-average height, good vocabulary, attractiveness, self-confidence, and similar attributes.[8]

During the first half of the twentieth century, hundreds of studies were conducted in an attempt to identify important leadership traits. For the most part, the results of the studies were disappointing. For every set of leaders who possessed a common trait, a long list of exceptions was also found, and the list of suggested traits soon grew so long that it had little practical value. Alternative explanations usually existed even for relationships between traits and leadership that initially appeared valid. For example, it was observed that many leaders have good communication skills and are assertive. Rather than those traits being the cause of leadership, however, successful leaders may begin to display those traits after they have achieved a leadership position.

Although most researchers gave up trying to identify traits as predictors of leadership ability, many people still explicitly or implicitly adopt a trait orientation.[9] For example, politicians are all too often elected on the basis of personal appearance, speaking ability, or an aura of self-confidence. In addition, honesty and integrity may very well be fundamental leadership traits that do serve an important purpose. Intelligence also seems to play a meaningful role in leadership.[10]

Leadership Behaviors

Spurred on by their lack of success in identifying useful leadership traits, researchers soon began to investigate other variables, especially the behaviors or actions of leaders. The new hypothesis was that effective leaders somehow behaved differently than less effective leaders. Thus the goal was to develop a fuller understanding of leadership behaviors.

expert power
The personal power that accrues to someone based on the information or expertise that they possess

Michigan Studies Researchers at the University of Michigan, led by Rensis Likert, began studying leadership in the late 1940s.[11] Based on extensive interviews with both leaders (managers) and followers (subordinates), this research identified two basic forms of leader behavior: job centered and employee centered. Managers using **job-centered leader behavior** pay close attention to subordinates' work, explain work procedures, and are keenly interested in performance. Managers using **employee-centered leader behavior** are interested in developing a cohesive work group and ensuring that employees are satisfied with their jobs. Their primary concern is the welfare of subordinates.

The two styles of leader behavior were presumed to be at the ends of a single continuum. Although this suggests that leaders may be extremely job centered, extremely employee centered, or somewhere in between, Likert studied only the two end styles for contrast. He argued that employee-centered leader behavior generally tends to be more effective. We should also note the similarities between Likert's leadership research and his Systems 1 through 4 organization designs (discussed in Chapter 14). Job-centered leader behavior is consistent with the System 1 design (rigid and bureaucratic), whereas employee-centered leader behavior is consistent with the System 4 design (organic and flexible). When Likert advocates moving organizations from System 1 to System 4, he is also advocating a transition from job-centered to employee-centered leader behavior.

Ohio State Studies At about the same time that Likert was beginning his leadership studies at the University of Michigan, a group of researchers at Ohio State University began studying leadership.[12] The extensive questionnaire surveys conducted during the Ohio State studies also suggested that there are two basic leader behaviors or styles: initiating-structure behavior and consideration behavior. When using **initiating-structure behavior**, the leader clearly defines the leader–subordinate role so that everyone knows what is expected, establishes formal lines of communication, and determines tasks will be performed. Leaders using **consideration behavior** show concern for subordinates and attempt to establish a warm, friendly, and supportive climate. The behaviors identified at Ohio State are similar to those described at Michigan, but there are important differences. One major difference is that the Ohio State researchers did not interpret leader behavior as being one-dimensional; each behavior was assumed to be independent of the other. Presumably, then, a leader could exhibit varying levels of initiating structure and at the same time varying levels of consideration.

At first, the Ohio State researchers thought that leaders who exhibit high levels of both behaviors would tend to be more effective than other leaders. A study at International Harvester (now Navistar International), however, suggested a more complicated pattern.[13] The researchers found that employees of supervisors who ranked high on initiating structure were high performers but expressed low levels of satisfaction and had a higher absence rate. Conversely, employees of supervisors who ranked high on consideration had low performance ratings but high levels of satisfaction and few absences from work. Later research isolated other variables that make consistent prediction difficult and determined that situational influences also occurred. (This body of research is discussed in "Situational Approaches to Leadership.")[14]

Managerial Grid Another behavioral approach to leadership is the Managerial Grid.[15] The Managerial Grid provides a means for evaluating leadership styles and then training managers to move toward an ideal style of behavior. The Managerial Grid is shown in Figure 13.1. The horizontal axis represents **concern for production** (similar to

job-centered leader behavior
The behavior of leaders who pay close attention to the job and work procedures involved with that job

employee-centered leader behavior
The behavior of leaders who develop cohesive work groups and ensure employee satisfaction

initiating-structure behavior
The behavior of leaders who define the leader–subordinate role so that everyone knows what is expected, establish formal lines of communication, and determine how tasks will be performed

consideration behavior
The behavior of leaders who show concern for subordinates and attempt to establish a warm, friendly, and supportive climate

concern for production
The part of the Managerial Grid that deals with the job and task aspects of leader behavior

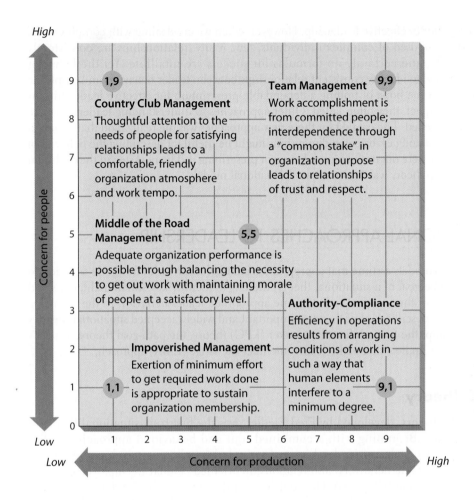

Figure 13.1
The Managerial Grid

*The Managerial Grid®
is a method of evaluating
leadership styles. The
overall objective of
an organization using
the Grid® is to train
its managers using
organization development
techniques so that they
are simultaneously more
concerned for both people
and production (9,9 style
on the Grid®).*

Source: Robert R. Blake and
Anne Adams McCanse,
*Leadership Dilemmas—Grid
Solutions* (Houston, Tex.: Gulf
Publishing Company, 1997),
p. 29. (Formerly Robert R. Blake
and Jane S. Mouton,
The Managerial Grid.) © 1997
by Grid International, Inc.
Reproduced by permission of
the owners.

job-centered and initiating-structure behaviors), and the vertical axis represents **concern for people** (similar to employee-centered and consideration behaviors). Note the five extremes of managerial behavior: the 1,1 manager (impoverished management), who exhibits minimal concern for both production and people; the 9,1 manager (authority-compliance), who is highly concerned about production but exhibits little concern for people; the 1,9 manager (country club management), who has exactly opposite concerns from the 9,1 manager; the 5,5 manager (middle-of-the-road management), who maintains adequate concern for both people and production; and the 9,9 manager (team management), who exhibits maximum concern for both people and production.

According to this approach, the ideal style of managerial behavior is 9,9. There is a six-phase program to assist managers in achieving this style of behavior. A. G. Edwards, Westinghouse, the FAA, Equicor, and other companies have used the Managerial Grid with reasonable success. However, there is little published scientific evidence regarding its true effectiveness.

The leader-behavior theories have played an important role in the development of contemporary thinking about leadership. In particular, they urge us not to be preoccupied with what leaders are (the trait approach) but to concentrate on what leaders do (their behaviors). Unfortunately, these theories also make universal generic prescriptions about

concern for people
The part of the Managerial Grid that deals with the human aspects of leader behavior

what constitutes effective leadership. However, when we are dealing with complex social systems composed of complex individuals, few, if any, relationships are consistently predictable, and certainly no formulas for success are infallible. Yet the behavior theorists tried to identify consistent relationships between leader behaviors and employee responses in the hope of finding a dependable prescription for effective leadership. As we might expect, they often failed. Other approaches to understanding leadership were therefore needed. The catalyst for these new approaches was the realization that although interpersonal and task-oriented dimensions might be useful for describing the behavior of leaders, they were not useful for predicting or prescribing it. The next step in the evolution of leadership theory was the creation of situational models.

SITUATIONAL APPROACHES TO LEADERSHIP

Situational models assume that appropriate leader behavior varies from one situation to another. The goal of a situational theory, then, is to identify key situational factors and to specify how they interact to determine appropriate leader behavior. In the following sections, we describe four of the most important and widely accepted situational theories of leadership: the least-preferred coworker (LPC) theory, the path-goal theory, Vroom's decision tree approach, and the leader–member exchange (LMX) approach.

LPC Theory

The **LPC theory**, developed by Fred Fiedler, was the first truly situational theory of leadership.[16] Beginning with a combined trait and behavioral approach, Fiedler identified two styles of leadership: task oriented (analogous to job-centered and initiating-structure behaviors) and relationship oriented (similar to employee-centered and consideration behaviors). He went beyond the earlier behavioral approaches by arguing that the style of behavior is a reflection of the leader's personality and that most personalities fall into one of his two categories—task oriented or relationship oriented by nature. Fiedler measures leadership style by means of a controversial questionnaire called the **LPC measure**. To use the measure, a manager or leader is asked to describe the specific person with whom he or she is able to work least well—the LPC—by filling in a set of 16 scales anchored at each end by a positive or negative adjective. For example, 3 of the 16 scales are as follows:

Helpful ___ ___ ___ ___ ___ ___ ___ ___ Frustrating
         8 7 6 5 4 3 2 1

Tense ___ ___ ___ ___ ___ ___ ___ ___ Relaxed
       1 2 3 4 5 6 7 8

Boring ___ ___ ___ ___ ___ ___ ___ ___ Interesting
       1 2 3 4 5 6 7 8

LPC theory
A theory of leadership that suggests that the appropriate style of leadership varies with situational favorableness

LPC measure
The measuring scale that asks leaders to describe the person with whom he or she is able to work least well

The leader's LPC score is then calculated by adding up the numbers below the line checked on each scale. Note in these three examples that the higher numbers are associated with positive qualities (helpful, relaxed, and interesting), whereas the negative qualities (frustrating, tense, and boring) have low point values. A high total score is assumed to reflect a relationship orientation, and a low score a task orientation on the part of the leader. The LPC measure is controversial because researchers disagree about its validity. Some question exactly what an LPC measure reflects and whether the score is an index of behavior, personality, or some other factor.[17]

Favorableness of the Situation The underlying assumption of situational models of leadership is that appropriate leader behavior varies from one situation to another. According to Fiedler, the key situational factor is the favorableness of the situation from the leader's point of view. This factor is determined by leader–member relations, task structure, and position power. *Leader–member relations* refer to the nature of the relationship between the leader and the work group. If the leader and the group have a high degree of mutual trust, respect, and confidence, and if they like one another, relations are assumed to be good. If there is little trust, respect, or confidence, and if they do not like one another, relations are poor. Naturally, good relations are more favorable.

Task structure is the degree to which the group's task is well defined. The task is structured when it is routine, easily understood, and unambiguous and when the group has standard procedures and precedents to rely on. An unstructured task is nonroutine, ambiguous, and complex, with no standard procedures or precedents. You can see that high structure is more favorable for the leader, whereas low structure is less favorable. For example, if the task is unstructured, the group will not know what to do, and the leader will have to play a major role in guiding and directing its activities. If the task is structured, the leader will not have to get so involved and can devote time to nonsupervisory activities.

Position power is the power vested in the leader's position. If the leader has the power to assign work and to reward and punish employees, position power is assumed to be strong. But, if the leader must get job assignments approved by someone else and does not administer rewards and punishment, position power is weak, and it is more difficult to accomplish goals. From the leader's point of view, strong position power is clearly preferable to weak position power. However, position power is not as important as task structure and leader–member relations.

Favorableness and Leader Style Fiedler and his associates conducted numerous studies linking the favorableness of various situations to leader style and the effectiveness of the group.[18] The results of these studies—and the overall framework of the theory—are shown in Figure 13.2. To interpret the model, look first at the situational factors at the top of the figure. Good or bad leader–member relations, high or low task structure, and strong or weak leader position power can be combined to yield six unique situations. For example, good leader–member relations, high task structure, and strong leader position power (at the far left) are presumed to define the most favorable situation; bad *leader–member relations*, low task structure, and weak leader power (at the far right) are the least favorable situation. The other combinations reflect intermediate levels of favorableness.

Below each set of situations are shown the degree of favorableness and the form of leader behavior found to be most strongly associated with effective group performance for those situations. When the situation is most and least favorable, Fiedler found that a task-oriented leader is most effective. When the situation is only moderately favorable, a relationship-oriented leader is predicted to be most effective.

Flexibility of Leader Style Fiedler argued that, for any given individual, leader style is essentially fixed and cannot be changed; leaders cannot change their behavior to fit a particular situation because it is linked to their particular personality traits. Thus,

Figure 13.2 The Least-Preferred Coworker Theory of Leadership

Fiedler's LPC theory of leadership suggests that appropriate leader behavior varies as a function of the favorableness of the situation. Favorableness, in turn, is defined by task structure, leader–member relations, and the leader's position power. According to the LPC theory, the most and least favorable situations call for task-oriented leadership, whereas moderately favorable situations suggest the need for relationship-oriented leadership.

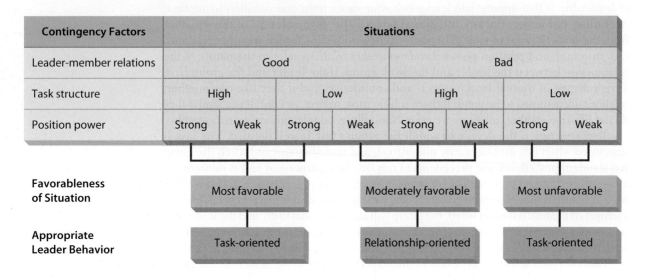

when a leader's style and the situation do not match, Fiedler argued that the situation should be changed to fit the leader's style. When leader–member relations are good, task structure low, and position power weak, the leader style that is most likely to be effective is relationship oriented. If the leader is task oriented, a mismatch exists. According to Fiedler, the leader can make the elements of the situation more congruent by structuring the task (by developing guidelines and procedures, for instance) and increasing power (by requesting additional authority or by other means).

Fiedler's LPC theory has been attacked on the grounds that it is not always supported by research, that his findings are subject to other interpretations, that the LPC measure lacks validity, and that his assumptions about the inflexibility of leader behavior are unrealistic.[19] However, Fiedler's theory was one of the first to adopt a situational perspective on leadership. It has helped many managers recognize the important situational factors they must contend with, and it has fostered additional thinking about the situational nature of leadership. Moreover, in recent years, Fiedler has attempted to address some of the concerns about his theory by revising it and adding additional elements such as cognitive resources.

path-goal theory
A theory of leadership suggesting that the primary functions of a leader are to make valued or desired rewards available in the workplace and to clarify for the subordinate the kinds of behavior that will lead to those rewards

Path-Goal Theory

The **path-goal theory** of leadership—associated most closely with Martin Evans and Robert House—is a direct extension of the expectancy theory of motivation discussed in Chapter 12.[20] Recall that the primary components of expectancy theory included the likelihood of attaining various outcomes and the value associated with those outcomes. The path-goal theory of leadership suggests that the primary functions of a leader are to make valued or desired rewards available in the workplace and to clarify for the subordinate the kinds of behavior that will lead to goal accomplishment and valued rewards—that is, the leader should clarify the paths to goal attainment.

Leader Behavior The most fully developed version of path-goal theory identifies four kinds of leader behavior. *Directive leader behavior* lets subordinates know what is expected of them, gives guidance and direction, and schedules work. *Supportive leader behavior* is being friendly and approachable, showing concern for subordinate welfare, and treating members as equals. *Participative leader behavior* includes consulting with subordinates, soliciting suggestions, and allowing participation in decision making. *Achievement-oriented leader* behavior means setting challenging goals, expecting subordinates to perform at high levels, encouraging subordinates, and showing confidence in subordinates' abilities.

In contrast to Fiedler's theory, path-goal theory assumes that leaders can change their style or behavior to meet the demands of a particular situation. For example, when encountering a new group of subordinates and a new project, the leader may be directive in establishing work procedures and in outlining what needs to be done. Next, the leader may adopt supportive behavior to foster group cohesiveness and a positive climate. As the group becomes familiar with the task and as new problems are encountered, the leader may exhibit participative behavior to enhance group members' motivation. Finally, achievement-oriented behavior may be used to encourage continued high performance.

JULIE DERMANSKY/CORBIS

One of the key premises of the path-goal theory of leadership is that leaders must adapt their own behavior to fit the situation in which they find themselves. During the BP oil leak crisis in the Gulf of Mexico during 2010, CEO Tony Hayward was widely expected to handle the situation in certain ways—being the "face" of the company, accepting responsibility for the leak on behalf of BP, and taking aggressive steps to contain the leak, for example. However, most people perceived that he had others do most of the talking, pointed fingers at other companies, and was slow to respond to the crisis. These perceptions played a large role in his ouster by BP in the summer of 2010.

Situational Factors Like other situational theories of leadership, path-goal theory suggests that appropriate leader style depends on situational factors. Path-goal theory focuses on the situational factors of the personal characteristics of subordinates and environmental characteristics of the workplace.

Important personal characteristics include the subordinates' perception of their own abilities and their locus of control. If people perceive that they are lacking in abilities, they may prefer directive leadership to help them understand path-goal relationships better. If they perceive themselves to have a lot of abilities, employees may resent directive leadership. Locus of control is a personality trait. People who have an internal locus of control believe that what happens to them is a function of their own efforts and behavior. Those who have an external locus of control assume that fate, luck, or "the system" determines what happens to them. A person with an internal locus of control may prefer participative leadership, whereas a person with an external locus of control may prefer directive leadership. Managers can do little or nothing to influence the personal characteristics of subordinates, but they can shape the environment to take advantage of these personal characteristics by, for example, providing rewards and structuring tasks.

Environmental characteristics include factors outside the subordinates' control. Task structure is one such factor. When structure is high, directive leadership is less effective than when structure is low. Subordinates do not usually need their boss to continually tell them how to do an extremely routine job. The formal authority system is another important environmental characteristic. Again, the higher the degree of formality, the less directive is the leader behavior that will be accepted by subordinates. The nature of the work group also affects appropriate leader behavior. When the work group provides the employee with social support and satisfaction, supportive leader behavior is less critical. When social support and satisfaction cannot be derived from the group, the worker may look to the leader for this support.

The basic path-goal framework as illustrated in Figure 13.3 shows that different leader behaviors affect subordinates' motivation to perform. Personal and environmental characteristics are seen as defining which behaviors lead to which outcomes. The path-goal theory of leadership is a dynamic and incomplete model. The original intent was to state the theory in general terms so that future research could explore a variety of interrelationships and modify the theory. Research that has been done suggests that the path-goal theory is a reasonably good description of the leadership process and that future investigations along these lines should enable us to discover more about the link between leadership and motivation.[21]

Vroom's Decision Tree Approach

Vroom's decision tree approach
Predicts what kinds of situations call for different degrees of group participation

The third major contemporary approach to leadership is **Vroom's decision tree approach**. The earliest version of this model was proposed by Victor Vroom and Philip Yetton and later revised and expanded by Vroom and Arthur Jago.[22] Most recently, Vroom has developed yet another refinement of the original model.[23] Like the path-goal theory,

Figure 13.3 **The Path-Goal Framework**

The path-goal theory of leadership suggests that managers can use four types of leader behavior to clarify subordinates' paths to goal attainment. Both personal characteristics of the subordinate and environmental characteristics within the organization must be taken into account when determining which style of leadership will work best for a particular situation.

this approach attempts to prescribe a leadership style appropriate to a given situation. It also assumes that the same leader may display different leadership styles. But Vroom's approach concerns itself with only a single aspect of leader behavior: subordinate participation in decision making.

Basic Premises Vroom's decision tree approach assumes that the degree to which subordinates should be encouraged to participate in decision making depends on the characteristics of the situation. In other words, no one decision-making process is best for all situations. After evaluating a variety of problem attributes (characteristics of the problem or decision), the leader determines an appropriate decision style that specifies the amount of subordinate participation.

Vroom's current formulation suggests that managers use one of two different decision trees.[24] To do so, the manager first assesses the situation in terms of several factors. This assessment involves determining whether the given factor is high or low for the decision that is to be made. For instance, the first factor is decision significance. If the decision is extremely important and may have a major impact on the organization (such as choosing a location for a new plant), its significance is high. But, if the decision is routine and its consequences are not terribly important (selecting a color for the firm's softball team uniforms), its significance is low.

This assessment guides the manager through the paths of the decision tree to a recommended course of action. One decision tree is to be used when the manager is interested primarily in making the decision as quickly as possible; the other is to be used when time is less critical and the manager is interested in helping subordinates to improve and develop their own decision-making skills.

The two decision trees are shown in Figures 13.4 and 13.5. The problem attributes (situational factors) are arranged along the top of the decision tree. To use the model, the decision maker starts at the left side of the diagram and assesses the first problem attribute (decision significance). The answer determines the path to the second node on the decision tree, where the next attribute (importance of commitment) is assessed. This process continues until a terminal node is reached. In this way, the manager identifies an effective decision-making style for the situation.

Decision-Making Styles The various decision-making styles reflected at the ends of the tree branches represent different levels of subordinate participation that the manager should attempt to adopt in a given situation. The five styles are defined as follows:

- *Decide*. The manager makes the decision alone and then announces or "sells" it to the group.
- *Consult (individually)*. The manager presents the program to group members individually, obtains their suggestions, and then makes the decision.
- *Consult (group)*. The manager presents the problem to group members at a meeting, gets their suggestions, and then makes the decision.
- *Facilitate*. The manager presents the problem to the group at a meeting, defines the problem and its boundaries, and then facilitates group member discussion as they make the decision.
- *Delegate*. The manager allows the group to define for itself the exact nature and parameters of the problem and then to develop a solution.

Vroom's decision tree approach represents a very focused but quite complex perspective on leadership. To compensate for this difficulty, Vroom has developed elaborate expert system software to help managers assess a situation accurately and quickly and then to make an appropriate decision regarding employee participation.[25] Many firms, including

Figure 13.4 — Vroom's Time-Driven Decision Tree

This matrix is recommended for situations where time is of the highest importance in making a decision. The matrix operates like a funnel. You start at the left with a specific decision problem in mind. The column headings denote situational factors that may or may not be present in that problem. You progress by selecting high or low (H or L) for each relevant situational factor. Proceed down the funnel, judging only those situational factors for which a judgment is called, until you reach the recommended process.

Decision Significance	Importance of Commitment	Leader Expertise	Likelihood of Commitment	Group Support	Group Expertise	Team Competence	Process
P R O B L E M S T A T E M E N T							
H	H	H	H	—	—	—	Decide
H	H	H	L	H	H	H	Delegate
H	H	H	L	H	H	L	Consult (group)
H	H	H	L	H	L	—	Consult (group)
H	H	H	L	L	—	—	Consult (group)
H	H	L	H	H	H	—	Facilitate
H	H	L	H	H	L	—	Consult (individually)
H	H	L	H	L	—	—	Consult (individually)
H	H	L	L	H	H	—	Facilitate
H	H	L	L	H	L	—	Consult (group)
H	H	L	L	L	—	—	Consult (group)
H	L	H	—	—	—	—	Decide
H	L	L	—	H	H	—	Facilitate
H	L	L	—	H	L	—	Consult (individually)
H	L	L	—	L	—	—	Consult (individually)
L	H	—	H	—	—	—	Decide
L	H	—	L	—	—	H	Delegate
L	H	—	L	—	—	L	Facilitate
L	L	—	—	—	—	—	Decide

Source: Victor H. Vroom and Philip W. Yetton, *Leadership and Decision-Makings*, 1973. © 1973 by University of Pittsburgh Press. Adapted and reprinted by permission of the University of Pittsburgh Press.

Halliburton Company, Litton Industries, and Borland International, have provided their managers with training in how to use the various versions of this model.

Evaluation and Implications Because Vroom's current approach is relatively new, it has not been fully scientifically tested. The original model and its subsequent refinement, however, attracted a great deal of attention and was generally supported by research.[26] For example, there is some support for the idea that individuals who make

Figure 13.5 Vroom's Development-Driven Decision Tree

This matrix is to be used when the leader is more interested in developing employees than in making the decision as quickly as possible. Just as with the time-driven tree shown in Figure 13.4, the leader assesses up to seven situational factors. These factors, in turn, funnel the leader to a recommended process for making the decision.

Problem Statement	Decision Significance	Importance of Commitment	Leader Expertise	Likelihood of Commitment	Group Support	Group Expertise	Team Competence	
P R O B L E M S T A T E M E N T	H	H	—	H	H	H	H	Decide
							L	Facilitate
						L	—	Consult (group)
					L	—	—	Consult (group)
				L	H	H	H	Delegate
							L	Facilitate
						L	—	Facilitate
					L	—	—	Consult (group)
		L	—	—	H	H	H	Delegate
							L	Facilitate
						L	—	Consult (group)
					L	—	—	Consult (group)
	L	H	—	H	—	—	—	Decide
				L	—	—	—	Delegate
		L	—	—	—	—	—	Decide

Source: Victor H. Vroom and Philip W. Yetton, *Leadership and Decision-Makings*, 1973. © 1973 by University of Pittsburgh Press. Adapted and reprinted by permission of the University of Pittsburgh Press.

decisions consistent with the predictions of the model are more effective than those who make decisions inconsistent with it. The model, therefore, appears to be a tool that managers can apply with some confidence in deciding how much subordinates should participate in the decision-making process.

The LMX Approach

Because leadership is such an important area, managers and researchers continue to study it. As a result, new ideas, theories, and perspectives are continuously being developed. The **LMX model** of leadership, conceived by George Graen and Fred Dansereau, stresses the importance of variable relationships between supervisors and each of their subordinates.[27] Each superior–subordinate pair is referred to as a *vertical dyad*. The model differs from earlier approaches in that it focuses on the differential relationship leaders often establish with different subordinates. Figure 13.6 shows the basic concepts of the LMX theory.

LMX model
Stresses that leaders have different kinds of relationships with different subordinates

Figure 13.6 The Leader–Member Exchange Model

The LMX model suggests that leaders form unique independent relationships with each of their subordinates. As illustrated here, a key factor in the nature of this relationship is whether the individual subordinate is in the leader's out-group or in-group.

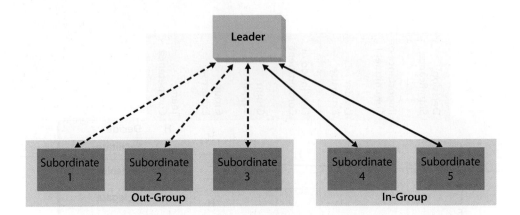

The model suggests that supervisors establish a special relationship with a small number of trusted subordinates, referred to as the *in-group*. The in-group usually receives special duties requiring responsibility and autonomy; they may also receive special privileges. Subordinates who are not a part of this group are called the *out-group*, and they receive less of the supervisor's time and attention. Note in the figure that the leader has a dyadic, or one-to-one, relationship with each of the five subordinates.

Early in his or her interaction with a given subordinate, the supervisor initiates either an in-group or an out-group relationship. It is not clear how a leader selects members of the in-group, but the decision may be based on personal compatibility and subordinates' competence. Research has confirmed the existence of in-groups and out-groups. In addition, studies generally have found that in-group members have a higher level of performance and satisfaction than do out-group members.[28]

RELATED APPROACHES TO LEADERSHIP

Because of its importance to organizational effectiveness, leadership continues to be the focus of a great deal of research and theory building. New approaches that have attracted much attention are the concepts of substitutes for leadership and transformational leadership.[29]

Substitutes for Leadership

substitutes for leadership
A concept that identifies situations in which leader behaviors are neutralized or replaced by characteristics of the subordinate, the task, and the organization

The concept of **substitutes for leadership** was developed because existing leadership models and theories do not account for situations in which leadership is not needed.[30] They simply try to specify what kind of leader behavior is appropriate. The substitutes concept, however, identifies situations in which leader behaviors are neutralized or replaced by characteristics of the subordinate, the task, and the organization. For example, when a patient is delivered to a hospital emergency room, the professionals on duty do not wait to be told what to do by a leader. Nurses, doctors, and attendants all go into action without waiting for directive or supportive leader behavior from the emergency room supervisor.

Characteristics of the subordinate that may serve to neutralize leader behavior include ability, experience, need for independence, professional orientation, and indifference toward organizational rewards. For example, employees with a high level of ability and experience may not need to be told what to do. Similarly, a subordinate's strong need for independence may render leader behavior ineffective. Task characteristics that may substitute for leadership include routineness, the availability of feedback, and intrinsic satisfaction. When the job is routine and simple, the subordinate may not need direction. When the task is challenging and intrinsically satisfying, the subordinate may not need or want social support from a leader.

Organizational characteristics that may substitute for leadership include formalization, group cohesion, inflexibility, and a rigid reward structure. Leadership may not be necessary when policies and practices are formal and inflexible, for example. Similarly, a rigid reward system may rob the leader of reward power and thereby decrease the importance of the role. Preliminary research has provided support for the concept of substitutes for leadership.[31]

Charismatic Leadership

The concept of **charismatic leadership**, like trait theories, assumes that charisma is an individual characteristic of the leader. **Charisma** is a form of interpersonal attraction that inspires support and acceptance. All else being equal, then, someone with charisma is more likely to be able to influence others than someone without charisma. For example, a highly charismatic supervisor will be more successful in influencing subordinate behavior than a supervisor who lacks charisma. Thus influence is again a fundamental element of this perspective.

Robert House first proposed a theory of charismatic leadership, based on research findings from a variety of social science disciplines.[32] His theory suggests that charismatic leaders are likely to have a lot of self-confidence, a firm conviction in their beliefs and ideals, and a strong need to influence people. They also tend to communicate high expectations about follower performance and express confidence in followers. Donald Trump is an excellent example of a charismatic leader. Even though he has made his share of mistakes and generally is perceived as only an "average" manager, many people view him as larger than life.[33]

There are three elements of charismatic leadership in organizations that most experts acknowledge today.[34] First, the leader needs to be able to envision the future, set high expectations, and model behaviors consistent with meeting those expectations. Next, the charismatic leader must be able to energize others through a demonstration of personal excitement, personal confidence, and patterns of success. And, finally, the charismatic leader enables others by supporting them, empathizing with them, and expressing confidence in them.[35]

Charismatic leadership ideas are quite popular among managers today and are the subject of numerous books and articles. Unfortunately, few studies have attempted to specifically test the meaning and impact of charismatic leadership. There are also lingering ethical issues about charismatic leadership that trouble some people. For instance, President Bill Clinton was a charismatic leader. But some of his critics argued that this very charisma caused his supporters to overlook his flaws and to minimize some of his indiscretions.

charismatic leadership
Assumes that charisma is an individual characteristic of the leader

charisma
A form of interpersonal attraction that inspires support and acceptance

3M has had a long of history of new product innovation, ranging from Scotch tape to Post-It Notes. In the last few years, though, the firm has seen its new product pipeline shrink, its profits decline, and its share price drop. New CEO George Buckley, however, is working to recapture the firm's glory days. He has overhauled the firm, modified its reward system, changed procedures, and re-energized 3M's product development teams.

KIMIMASA MAYAMA/BLOOMBERG

Transformational Leadership

Another new perspective on leadership has been called by a number of labels: charismatic leadership, inspirational leadership, symbolic leadership, and transformational leadership. We use the term **transformational leadership** and define it as leadership that goes beyond ordinary expectations by transmitting a sense of mission, stimulating learning experiences, and inspiring new ways of thinking.[36] Because of rapid change and turbulent environments, transformational leaders are increasingly being seen as vital to the success of business.[37]

A recent article in the popular press identified seven keys to successful leadership: trusting one's subordinates, developing a vision, keeping cool, encouraging risk, being an expert, inviting dissent, and simplifying things.[38] Although this list was the result of a simplistic survey of the leadership literature, it is nevertheless consistent with the premises underlying transformational leadership. So, too, are recent examples cited as effective leadership. Take the case of 3M. The firm's new CEO, George Buckley, is working to make the firm more efficient and profitable while simultaneously keeping its leadership role in new-product innovation. He has also changed the reward system, overhauled procedures, and restructured the entire firm. And so far, at least, analysts have applauded these changes.[39]

EMERGING APPROACHES TO LEADERSHIP

Recently, three potentially very important new approaches to leadership have emerged. One is called *strategic leadership*; the others deal with *cross-cultural leadership* and *ethical leadership*.

Strategic Leadership

Strategic leadership is a new concept that explicitly relates leadership to the role of top management. We define **strategic leadership** as the capability to understand the complexities of both the organization and its environment and to lead change in the organization to achieve and maintain a superior alignment between the organization and its environment. This definition reflects an integration of the leadership concepts covered in this chapter with our discussion of strategic management in Chapter 3. Its board of directors, of course, is a key element in any firm's strategic leadership.

To be effective in this role, a manager needs to have a thorough and complete understanding of the organization—its history, its culture, its strengths, and its weaknesses. In addition, the leader needs a firm grasp of the organization's environment. This understanding must encompass current conditions and circumstances as well as significant trends and issues on the horizon. The strategic leader also needs to recognize

transformational leadership
Leadership that goes beyond ordinary expectations by transmitting a sense of mission, stimulating learning experiences, and inspiring new ways of thinking

strategic leadership
The capability to understand the complexities of both the organization and its environment and to lead change in the organization to achieve and maintain a superior alignment between the organization and its environment

how the firm is currently aligned with its environment—where it relates effectively and where it relates less effectively with that environment. Finally, looking at environmental trends and issues, the strategic leader works to improve both the current alignment and the future alignment.[40]

Jeffrey Immelt (CEO of General Electric), Hector Ruiz (CEO of Advanced Micro Devices), Michael Dell (founder and CEO of Dell Computer), Anne Mulcahy (CEO of Xerox), and A. G. Lafley (CEO of Procter & Gamble) have all been recognized as strong strategic leaders. Reflecting on his dramatic turnaround at Procter & Gamble, for instance, Lafley commented, "I have made a lot of symbolic, very physical changes so people understand we are in the business of leading change." On the other hand, Raymond Gilmartin (CEO of Merck), Scott Livengood (CEO of Krispy Kreme), and Howard Pien (CEO of Chiron) have been cited as less effective strategic leaders. Under Livengood's leadership, for instance, Krispy Kreme's stock has plummeted by 80 percent, and the firm is under investigation by the SEC; moreover, most critics believe that the chain has expanded far too rapidly.[41]

Cross-Cultural Leadership

Another new approach to leadership is based on cross-cultural issues. In this context, *culture* is used as a broad concept to encompass both international differences and diversity-based differences within one culture. For instance, when a Japanese firm sends an executive to head the firm's operations in the United States, that person will need to become acclimated to the cultural differences that exist between the two countries and to change his or her leadership style accordingly. Japan is generally characterized by collectivism (the view that the group is more important than any individual within the group), whereas the United States is based more on individualism (the belief that individuals are more important than the group). The Japanese executive, then, will find it necessary to recognize the importance of individual contributions and rewards, as well as the differences in individual and group roles, that exist in Japanese and U.S. businesses.

Similarly, cross-cultural factors play a growing role in organizations as their workforces become more and more diverse. Most leadership research, for instance, has been conducted on samples or case studies involving white male leaders (until several years ago, most business leaders were white males). But, as more females, African Americans, and Latinos achieve leadership positions, it may be necessary to reassess how applicable current theories and models of leadership are when applied to an increasingly diverse pool of leaders.[42]

Ethical Leadership

Most people have long assumed that top managers are ethical people. But in the wake of recent corporate scandals, faith in top managers has been shaken. Perhaps now more than ever, high standards of ethical conduct are being held up as a prerequisite for effective leadership. More specifically, top managers are being called on to maintain high ethical standards for their own conduct, to exhibit ethical behavior unfailingly, and to hold others in their organization to the same standards.

The behaviors of top leaders are being scrutinized more than ever, and those responsible for hiring new leaders for a business are looking more and more closely at the background of those being considered. And the emerging pressures for stronger corporate governance models are likely to further increase commitment to selecting only

those individuals with high ethical standards and to hold them more accountable than in the past for both their actions and the consequences of those actions.[43]

POLITICAL BEHAVIOR IN ORGANIZATIONS

Another common influence on behavior is politics and political behavior. **Political behavior** describes activities carried out for the specific purpose of acquiring, developing, and using power and other resources to obtain one's preferred outcomes.[44] Political behavior may be undertaken by managers dealing with their subordinates, subordinates dealing with their managers, and managers and subordinates dealing with others at the same level. In other words, it may be directed upward, downward, or laterally. Decisions ranging from where to locate a manufacturing plant to where to put the company coffeemaker are subject to political action. In any situation, individuals may engage in political behavior to further their own ends, to protect themselves from others, to further goals they sincerely believe to be in the organization's best interests, or simply to acquire and exercise power. And power may be sought by individuals, by groups of individuals, or by groups of groups.[45]

Although political behavior is difficult to study because of its sensitive nature, one early survey found that many managers believed that politics influenced salary and hiring decisions in their firm. Many also believed that the incidence of political behavior was greater at the upper levels of their organization and lesser at the lower levels. More than half of the respondents felt that organizational politics was bad, unfair, unhealthy, and irrational, but most suggested that successful executives have to be good politicians and be political to get ahead.[46]

Bernard Ebbers, former CEO of WoldCom, is shown here testifying before a Congressional committee looking into a laundry list of accounting problems at the firm. Ebbers was a frequent practitioner of political behavior in order to get his way. For instance, he allowed WorldCom board members to use the corporate jet for their own personal travel and routinely agreed to invest in their pet projects. Board members, in turn, were then willing to grant just about any request that Ebbers made of them.

MARTIN H. SIMON/CORBIS

Common Political Behaviors

Research has identified four basic forms of political behavior widely practiced in organizations.[47] One form is *inducement*, which occurs when a manager offers to give something to someone else in return for that individual's support. For example, a product manager might suggest to another product manager that she will put in a good word with his boss if he supports a new marketing plan that she has developed. By most accounts, former WorldCom CEO Bernard Ebbers made frequent use of this tactic to retain his leadership position in the company. For example, he allowed board members to use the corporate jet whenever they wanted and invested heavily in their pet projects.

political behavior
The activities carried out for the specific purpose of acquiring, developing, and using power and other resources to obtain one's preferred outcomes

A second tactic is *persuasion*, which relies on both emotion and logic. An operations manager wanting to construct a new plant on a certain site might persuade others to support his goal on grounds that are objective and logical (for example, it is less expensive, taxes are lower) as well as subjective and personal. Ebbers also used this approach. For instance, when one board member attempted to remove him from his position, he worked behind the scenes to persuade the majority of board members to allow him to stay on.

A third political behavior involves the *creation of an obligation*. For example, one manager might support a recommendation made by another manager for a new advertising campaign. Although he might really have no opinion on the new campaign, he might think that by going along, he is incurring a debt from the other manager and will be able to "call in" that debt when he wants to get something done and needs additional support. Ebbers loaned WorldCom board members money, for example, but then forgave the loans in exchange for their continued support.

Coercion, a fourth political behavior, is the use of force to get one's way. For example, a manager may threaten to withhold support, rewards, or other resources as a way to influence someone else. This, too, was a common tactic used by Ebbers. He reportedly belittled any board member who dared question him, for example. In the words of one former director, "Ebbers treated you like a prince—as long as you never forgot who was king."[48]

Impression Management

Impression management is a subtle form of political behavior that deserves special mention. **Impression management** is a direct and intentional effort by someone to enhance his or her image in the eyes of others. People engage in impression management for a variety of reasons. For one thing, they may do so to further their own careers. By making themselves look good, they think they are more likely to receive rewards, to be given attractive job assignments, and to receive promotions. They may also engage in impression management to boost their self-esteem. When people have a solid image in an organization, others make them aware of it through compliments, respect, and so forth. Still another reason people use impression management is in an effort to acquire more power and hence more control.

People attempt to manage how others perceive them through a variety of mechanisms. Appearance is one of the first things people think of. Hence, a person motivated by impression management will pay close attention to choice of attire, selection of language, and use of manners and body posture. People interested in impression management are also likely to jockey for association only with successful projects. By being assigned to high-profile projects led by highly successful managers, a person can begin to link his or her own name with such projects in the minds of others.

Sometimes people too strongly motivated by impression management become obsessed with it and may resort to dishonest or unethical means. For example, some people have been known to take credit for others' work in an effort to make themselves look better. People have also been known to exaggerate or even falsify their personal accomplishments in an effort to build an enhanced image.[49] For instance, one Silicon Valley entrepreneur recently noted that "Every time I turn around, there is someone sticking their head in my office reminding me what they are doing for me."[50]

impression management
A direct and intentional effort by someone to enhance his or her image in the eyes of others

Managing Political Behavior

By its very nature, political behavior is tricky to approach in a rational and systematic way. But managers can handle political behavior so that it does not do excessive damage.[51] First, managers should be aware that, even if their actions are not politically motivated, others may assume that they are. Second, by providing subordinates with autonomy, responsibility, challenge, and feedback, managers reduce the likelihood of political behavior by subordinates. Third, managers should avoid using power if they want to avoid charges of political motivation. Fourth, managers should get disagreements out in the open so that subordinates will have less opportunity for political behavior through using conflict for their own purposes. Finally, managers should avoid covert activities. Behind-the-scenes activities give the impression of political intent, even if none really exists.[52] Other guidelines include clearly communicating the bases and processes for performance evaluation, tying rewards directly to performance, and minimizing competition among managers for resources.[53]

Of course, these guidelines are much easier to list than they are to implement. The well-informed manager should not assume that political behavior does not exist or, worse yet, attempt to eliminate it by issuing orders or commands. Instead, the manager must recognize that political behavior exists in virtually all organizations and that it cannot be ignored or stamped out. It can, however, be managed in such a way that it will seldom inflict serious damage on the organization. It may even play a useful role in some situations.[54] For example, a manager may be able to use his or her political influence to stimulate a greater sense of social responsibility or to heighten awareness of the ethical implications of a decision.

SUMMARY OF LEARNING OBJECTIVES AND KEY POINTS

1. Describe the nature of leadership and relate leadership to management.

   - As a process, leadership is the use of noncoercive influence to shape the group's or organization's goals, motivate behavior toward the achievement of those goals, and help define group or organization culture.

   - As a property, leadership is the set of characteristics attributed to those who are perceived to be leaders.

   - Leadership and management are often related but are also different.

   - Managers and leaders use legitimate, reward, coercive, referent, and expert power.

2. Discuss and evaluate the two generic approaches to leadership.

   - The trait approach to leadership assumed that some basic trait or set of traits differentiated leaders from nonleaders.

   - The leadership behavior approach to leadership assumed that the behavior of effective leaders was somehow different from the behavior of nonleaders.

   - Research at the University of Michigan and Ohio State University identified two basic forms of leadership behavior—one concentrating on work and performance and the other concentrating on employee welfare and support.

   - The Managerial Grid attempts to train managers to exhibit high levels of both forms of behavior.

3. Identify and describe the major situational approaches to leadership.

   - Situational approaches to leadership recognize that appropriate forms of leadership behavior are not universally applicable and attempt to specify situations in which various behaviors are appropriate.

- The LPC theory suggests that a leader's behaviors should be either task oriented or relationship oriented, depending on the favorableness of the situation.

- The path-goal theory suggests that directive, supportive, participative, or achievement-oriented leader behaviors may be appropriate, depending on the personal characteristics of subordinates and the environment.

- Vroom's decision tree approach maintains that leaders should vary the extent to which they allow subordinates to participate in making decisions as a function of problem attributes.

- The LMX model focuses on individual relationships between leaders and followers and on in-group versus out-group considerations.

4. Identify and describe three related approaches to leadership.

- Related leadership perspectives are as follows:
   - the concept of substitutes for leadership
   - charismatic leadership
   - the role of transformational leadership in organizations

5. Describe three emerging approaches to leadership.

- Emerging approaches include the following:
   - strategic leadership
   - cross-cultural leadership
   - ethical leadership

6. Discuss political behavior in organizations and how it can be managed.

- Political behavior is another influence process frequently used in organizations.

- Impression management, one especially important form of political behavior, is a direct and intentional effort by someone to enhance his or her image in the eyes of others.

- Managers can take steps to limit the effects of political behavior.

DISCUSSION QUESTIONS

Questions for Review

1. What activities do managers perform? What activities do leaders perform? Do organizations need both managers and leaders? Why or why not?

2. What are the two generic approaches to leadership? What can managers today learn from these approaches?

3. What are the situational approaches to leadership? Briefly describe each and compare and contrast their findings.

4. Describe the subordinate's characteristics, leader behaviors, and environmental characteristics used in path-goal theory. How do these factors combine to influence motivation?

5. In your own words, define political behavior. Describe four political tactics and give an example of each.

Questions for Analysis

1. Even though the trait approach to leadership has no empirical support, it is still widely used. In your opinion, why is this so? In what ways is the use of the trait approach helpful to those who use it? In what ways is it harmful to those who use it?

2. The behavioral theories of leadership claim that an individual's leadership style is fixed. Do you agree or disagree? Give examples to support your position. The behavioral theories also claim that the ideal style is the same in every situation. Do you agree or disagree? Again, give examples.

3. Consider the following list of leadership situations. For each situation, describe in detail the kinds of power the leader has. If the leader were the same but the situation changed—for example, if you thought of the president as the head of his family rather than of the military—would your answers change? Why?

- The president of the United States is commander in chief of the U.S. military.

- An airline pilot is in charge of a particular flight.

- Fans look up to a movie star.

- Your teacher is the head of your class.

4. Think about a decision that would affect you as a student. Use Vroom's decision tree approach to decide whether the administrator making that decision should involve students in the decision. Which parts of the model seem most important in making that decision? Why?

5. Describe a time when you or someone you know was part of an in-group or an out-group. What was the relationship between each of the groups and the leader? What was the relationship between the members of the two different groups? What was the outcome of the situation for the leader? For the members of the two groups? For the organization?

BUILDING EFFECTIVE DIAGNOSTIC SKILLS

Exercise Overview

Diagnostic skills enable a manager to visualize the most appropriate response to a situation. This exercise shows how they can be useful when a manager must decide which type of power is most appropriate in different situations.

Exercise Background

William Shakespeare's play *Henry V*, which was performed for the first time in 1599, explores the themes of war, leadership, brotherhood, and treachery in a way that remains relevant today. The play contains the famous "St. Crispin's Day" speech that, despite its brevity, many people, Shakespearean scholars and nonexperts alike, regard as one of the most inspiring speeches ever written.

First, we need to set the scene: In 1415, England, under the leadership of King Henry IV, has invaded France to regain control of some disputed lands. Bear in mind that, to Shakespeare's audience, the legitimacy of Henry's claim makes both his cause and his war "just." Having won several hard-fought battles, the English army of 6,000 have marched from the coast into the interior of France and are encamped outside the French town of Agincourt. At this point in the campaign, they are sick, cold, hungry, and dispirited, and to make matters worse, they face an army of 25,000 well-rested, well-equipped soldiers and armored knights on horse. Through a combination of courage, strategy, and plain luck, they win one of history's most renowned battles, losing only 200 men while inflicting more than 5,000 casualties on enemy.

The short scene in which Henry delivers his St. Crispin's Day speech occurs just before the Battle of Agincourt. Henry's officers are understandably disheartened and fearful of the coming battle, and Henry must motivate them. That's the purpose of his St. Crispin's Day speech.

Exercise Task

Read the transcript of the speech that your professor will provide you. Then answer the following questions:

1. What types of power does Henry exert in this speech? Give specific examples of each type.

2. Interestingly, Henry had been a notoriously wayward youth before turning his life around and living up to his royal responsibilities. In what ways might knowledge of his past tend to increase or decrease his referent power?

3. In Shakespeare's play, of course, Henry's speech inspires his soldiers to almost impossible victory. You may or may not find it inspiring, but you

should be able to see why audiences have long praised it as sufficiently stirring to account for such an improbable achievement. What elements of the speech do the most to make it inspirational? If you yourself do find it inspiring, explain why. If you don't, explain why not.

BUILDING EFFECTIVE CONCEPTUAL SKILLS

Exercise Overview

Conceptual skills require you to think in the abstract. This exercise introduces you to one approach to assessing leadership skills and relating leadership theory to practice.

Exercise Background

At any given time, there's no shortage of publications offering practical advice on management and leadership. Most business best-seller lists in 2008 included titles such as *Good to Great* by Jim Collins; *First, Break All the Rules* by Marcus Buckingham; and *The 21 Irrefutable Laws of Leadership* by John C. Maxwell. Some of these books, such as *Winning* by former General Electric CEO Jack Welch, are written by managers with years of experience. Others are written by consultants, professors, or reporters.

Granted, a lot of these books—okay, most of them—don't have much theoretical foundation, and many are basically compendiums of opinions and suggestions unsupported by scientific evidence. Even so, many touch upon ideas that may well be worth the time it takes a busy manager to read them. Thus a real issue for contemporary managers is knowing how to analyze what they read in the popular press and how to separate the practical wheat from the pop culture chaff. This exercise gives you a little practice in doing just that.

Exercise Task

1. Visit the *Fortune* magazine website at **www.fortune. com/fortune/quizzes/careers/boss_quiz.html**. Take the leadership assessment quiz devised by management expert Stephen Covey. Then look at Covey's scoring and comments.

2. Review carefully each question and each suggested answer. Do you see any correlation between Covey's questions and the theoretical models of leadership discussed in this chapter? Which model or models do you think Covey is using? What details in his questions, answers, or both led you to that conclusion?

3. Use the Internet to investigate Covey's background, training, and experience. Does the information that you've gathered give you any clues to Covey's attitudes and opinions about leadership? Do you see any connection between Covey's attitudes and the items on his quiz? Explain.

4. Based on what you've learned from this exercise, how confident are you that Covey's quiz is an accurate measure of leadership ability? Explain.

SKILLS SELF-ASSESSMENT INSTRUMENT

Managerial Leader Behavior Questionnaire

Introduction: Leadership is now recognized as consisting of a set of characteristics that is important for everyone in an organization to develop. The following assessment surveys the practices or beliefs that you would apply in a management role—that is, your managerial leadership.

Instructions: The following statements refer to different ways in which you might behave in a managerial leadership role. For each statement, indicate how you do behave or how you think you would behave. Describing yourself may be difficult in some cases, but you should force yourself to make a selection. Record your answers next to each statement according to the following scale:

Rating Scale

5 Very descriptive of me
4 Fairly descriptive of me
3 Somewhat descriptive of me
2 Not very descriptive of me
1 Not descriptive of me at all

_____ 1. I emphasize the importance of performance and encourage everyone to make a maximum effort.

_____ 2. I am friendly, supportive, and considerate toward others.

_____ 3. I offer helpful advice to others on how to advance their careers and encourage them to develop their skills.

_____ 4. I stimulate enthusiasm for the work of the group and say things to build the group's confidence.

_____ 5. I provide appropriate praise and recognition for effective performance and show appreciation for special efforts and contributions.

_____ 6. I reward effective performance with tangible benefits.

_____ 7. I inform people about their duties and responsibilities, clarify rules and policies, and let people know what is expected of them.

_____ 8. Either alone or jointly with others, I set specific and challenging but realistic performance goals.

_____ 9. I provide any necessary training and coaching or arrange for others to do it.

_____ 10. I keep everyone informed about decisions, events, and developments that affect their work.

_____ 11. I consult with others before making work-related decisions.

_____ 12. I delegate responsibility and authority to others and allow them discretion in determining how to do their work.

_____ 13. I plan in advance how to efficiently organize and schedule the work.

_____ 14. I look for new opportunities for the group to exploit, propose new undertakings, and offer innovative ideas.

_____ 15. I take prompt and decisive action to deal with serious work-related problems and disturbances.

_____ 16. I provide subordinates with the supplies, equipment, support services, and other resources necessary to work effectively.

_____ 17. I keep informed about the activities of the group and check on its performance.

_____ 18. I keep informed about outside events that have important implications for the group.

_____ 19. I promote and defend the interests of the group and take appropriate action to obtain necessary resources for the group.

_____ 20. I emphasize teamwork and try to promote cooperation, cohesiveness, and identification with the group.

_____ 21. I discourage unnecessary fighting and bickering within the group and help settle conflicts and disagreements in a constructive manner.

_____ 22. I criticize specific acts that are unacceptable, find positive things to say, and provide an opportunity for people to offer explanations.

_____ 23. I take appropriate disciplinary action to deal with anyone who violates a rule, disobeys an order, or has consistently poor performance.

Source: Reprinted from David D. Van Fleet and Gary A. Yukl, Military Leadership: An Organizational Behavior Perspective, _pp. 38–39. © 1986 with permission from Elsevier Science._

EXPERIENTIAL EXERCISE

The Leadership/Management Interview Experiment

Purpose: Leadership and management are in some ways the same, but more often they are different. This exercise offers you an opportunity to develop a conceptual framework for leadership and management.

Introduction: Most management behaviors and leadership behaviors are a product of individual work experience, so each leader/manager tends to have a unique leadership/management style. Analyzing leadership/management styles, comparing such styles, and relating them to different organizational contexts are often rewarding experiences in learning.

Instructions: *Fact-finding and Execution of the Experiment*

1. Develop a list of questions related to issues you have studied in this chapter that you want to ask a practicing manager and leader during a face-to-face interview. Prior to the actual interview, submit your list of questions to your instructor for approval.

2. Arrange to interview a practicing manager and a practicing leader. For purposes of this assignment, a manager or leader is a person whose job priority involves supervising the work of other people. The leader/manager may work in a business or in a public or private agency.

3. Interview at least one manager and at least one leader, using the questions you developed. Take good notes on their comments and on your own observations. Do not take more than one hour of each leader's/manager's time.

Oral Report

Prepare an oral report using the questions here and your interview information. Complete the following report after the interview. (Attach a copy of your interview questions.)

The Leadership/Management Interview Experiment Report

1. How did you locate the leader(s)/manager(s) you interviewed? Describe your initial contacts.

2. Describe the level and responsibilities of your leader(s)/manager(s). Do not supply names—their responses should be anonymous.

3. Describe the interview settings. How long did the interview last?

4. In what ways were the leaders/managers similar or in agreement about issues?

5. What were some of the major differences between the leaders/managers and between the ways in which they approached their jobs?

6. In what ways would the managers agree or disagree with ideas presented in this course?

7. Describe and evaluate your own interviewing style and skills.

8. How did your managers feel about having been interviewed? How do you know that?

Inside the Leadership Cycle at Intel

1. Of the five profiled Intel CEOs, whose leadership style most closely resembles your own? Which of the five profiled CEOs would you most like to work for? Which would you least like to work for?

2. Intel appears to rely heavily on mentoring and long-term leadership development from within. What are the pros and cons of such an approach? Intel also seems to have thrived on a pattern of alternating leadership styles. What are the pros and cons of this approach?

3. What factors in Intel's environment contributed to its need for a "man of action" as CEO in the 1980s?

4. You're responsible for a work unit that needs a strong-handed, task-oriented leader, and you have two candidates. Unfortunately, one is the better manager but isn't particularly task oriented, whereas the other is task oriented but not as effective as a manager. Which one will you select?

5. Would you want to work for Intel? Why or why not?

CHAPTER 14

THE ROLE OF ORGANIZATIONAL COMMUNICATION

After studying this chapter, you should be able to:

1 Describe the role and importance of communication in the manager's job.

2 Identify the basic forms of communication in organizations.

3 Describe the role of electronic communication in organizations.

4 Discuss informal communication, including its various forms and types.

5 Describe how the communication process can be managed to recognize and overcome barriers.

The Converse of In-Person Communication

Interviews are stressful. The unfamiliar dress clothes, the need to make an instant good impression, the unexpected questions that leave the job seeker grasping about for any answer. Surely phone interviews are easier, right? Wrong. Job interviews conducted on the phone have all the challenges of a face-to-face interview, and then some.

Every interview, whether in person or over the phone, requires the

"[On phone interviews,] you cannot be seen. Use this to your advantage."

—COLLEGEGRAD.COM

"Because [interviewers] don't have an image of your face to set you apart from others, you need to draw pictures with your words."

—JOB APPLICATION AND INTERVIEW ADVICE

same level and type of preparation. Candidates should sell themselves, tell interesting stories, remain poised, anticipate questions and have answers ready, and ask relevant questions. Many job seekers, however, feel that phone interviews are somehow less formal, are less thorough, or require less preparation. They couldn't be more wrong. Many corporations today conduct phone interviews

ARENA CREATIVE/ISTOCKPHOTO

Telephone interviews are becoming an increasingly common way for employers to communicate with prospective employees. This young woman is shown talking to a prospective employer on her cell phone from an outdoor coffee shop.

to prescreen applicants and many rely on phone interviews exclusively, especially for candidates located far away. Phone interviews save time and money for both the candidate and the employer. However, applicants should be aware of the communication challenges and have solutions ready.

Problem: Scheduling. The interviewer may call at a mutually agreed-upon time. Or he or she may deliberately make an unscheduled call or call at an odd time. Some want to assess a candidate's ability to think quickly and are looking for unscripted responses. Yet a call is inconvenient when the kids are screaming for dinner or a roommate is hosting an unruly party.

Solution. If the interviewer calls at a time when conversation is truly impossible, you will have to call back. Be aware, however, that some interviewers are put off by the request. If the call will be difficult but not impossible, it's best to carry on with the interview. Ask for a moment to "close the door," then do just that. Ask others to be quiet, get to a clear space, and take some deep breaths before picking up the phone again.

Problem: Preparation. Phone interviews require the same preparation, but have an added benefit. "You cannot be seen. Use this to your advantage," says CollegeGrad.com, a leading website for entry-level job seekers. Although phone interviews can help alleviate nervousness for some candidates, candidates should not relax entirely.

Solution. Prepare notes about the points you want to cover and keep them near the phone so you can look at them during the conversation. Include paper and a pen to take notes. Have a copy of your résumé too, so you can answer questions. Dress professionally. While the interviewer cannot see you, studies show that job candidates sound more articulate and more intelligent when they are appropriately dressed for work.

Problem: Noise. Phone conversations are subject to many different types of noise, including a noisy environment, a poor phone connection, and sudden loss of cell phone batteries. Gum chewing, eating, and drinking are also noisy and distracting.

Solution: Shut the door and maintain calmness. Ask the interviewer to speak up if the connection is poor. Recharge those batteries! Never eat, drink, or chew gum during an interview.

Problem: Lack of context cues. An in-person conversation contains many nonverbal context cues. Only a small portion of the conversation's meaning is carried by the words themselves. A phone interview allows for just one nonverbal element—tone of voice. Every other nonverbal element is eliminated, including gesture, body language, facial expression, and dress. Applicants must find a way to get their message across with a limited set of tools.

Solution: Even though the interviewer cannot see you, smile. Your speech will change as you do, conveying richer information and making you sound friendlier. In fact, many experts recommend that you use gestures, expression, body language, and so on, just as you would during a face-to-face interview. Many phone sales professionals stand or even walk around the room, to sound more energetic and focused. Finally, if the interviewer seems hesitant, ask if he or she has any questions or concerns. This allows you to explicitly address any weak areas and will compensate to some extent for the lack of context cues.

Job seekers list "difficulty in making phone calls" as their second-most important problem. But as *Fortune* writer Anne Fisher says, "Making these calls gets easier the more often you do it." So brush up on those communications skills, and then hit the phones![1]

Businesses continue to look for effective ways to communicate with their employees, as well as job seekers, customers, and investors. The idea of phone interviews for job seekers may seem odd to some people, but many firms are finding this method of screening prospective employees to be both efficient and effective. Of course, as noted, there are both advantages and disadvantages to phone interviews. Communication has always been a vital part of managerial work. Indeed, managers around the world agree that communication is one of their most important tasks. It is important for them to communicate with others to convey their vision and goals of the organization. And it is important for others to communicate with them so that they will better understand what is going on in their environment and how they and their organization can become more effective.

This chapter discusses communication, one of the most basic forms of interaction among people. We begin by examining communication in the context of the manager's job. We then identify and discuss forms of interpersonal, group, and organizational communication. After discussing informal means of communication, we describe how organizational communication can be effectively managed.

COMMUNICATION AND THE MANAGER'S JOB

A typical day for a manager includes doing desk work, attending scheduled meetings, placing and receiving phone calls, reading and answering correspondence (both print and electronic), attending unscheduled meetings, and making tours.[2] Most of these activities involve communication. In fact, managers usually spend over half their time on some form of communication. Communication always involves two or more people, so other behavioral processes, such as motivation, leadership, and group and team interactions, all come into play. Top executives must handle communication effectively if they are to be true leaders.

A Definition of Communication

Imagine three managers working in an office building. The first is all alone but is nevertheless yelling for a subordinate to come help. No one appears, but he continues to yell. The second is talking on the phone to a subordinate, but static on the line causes the subordinate to misunderstand some important numbers being provided by the manager. As a result, the subordinate sends 1,500 crates of eggs to 150 Fifth Street, when he should have sent 150 crates of eggs to 1500 Fifteenth Street. The third manager is talking in her office with a subordinate who clearly hears and understands what is being said. Each of these managers is attempting to communicate, but with different results.

Communication is the process of transmitting information from one person to another. Did any of our three managers communicate? The last did, and the first did not. How about the second? In fact, she did communicate. She transmitted information, and information was received. The problem was that the message transmitted and the message received were not the same. The words spoken by the manager were distorted by static and noise. **Effective communication**, then, is the process of sending a message in such a way that the message received is as close in meaning as possible to the message intended. Although the second manager engaged in communication, it was not effective.

A key element in effective communication is differentiating between data and information. **Data** are raw figures and facts reflecting a single aspect of reality. The facts that a plant has 35 machines, that each machine is capable of producing 1,000 units of output per day, that current and projected future demand for the units is 30,000 per day, and that workers sufficiently skilled to run the machines make $20 an hour are data. **Information**, meanwhile, is data presented in a way or form that has meaning.[3] Thus combining and summarizing the four pieces of data given above provides information: The plant has excess capacity and is therefore incurring unnecessary costs. Information

communication
The process of transmitting information from one person to another

effective communication
The process of sending a message in such a way that the message received is as close in meaning as possible to the message intended

data
Raw figures and facts reflecting a single aspect of reality

information
Data presented in a way or form that has meaning

has meaning to a manager and provides a basis for action. The plant manager might use the information and decide to sell four machines (perhaps keeping one as a backup) and transfer five operators to other jobs.

Characteristics of Useful Information

What characteristics make the difference between information that is useful and information that is not useful? In general, information is useful if it is accurate, timely, complete, and relevant.

Accurate For information to be of real value to a manager, it must be **accurate information.** Accuracy means that the information must provide a valid and reliable reflection of reality. One of the first major mergers between a traditional bricks-and-mortar business and a dot-com business took place in 2001 when Time Warner, an old-line media conglomerate, merged with AOL, one of the biggest dot-com businesses at the time. Unfortunately, it soon became clear that the value of AOL had been inflated by improper accounting practices and revenue overstatements. Not surprisingly, then, the new firm struggled to develop a unified strategy and culture while enduring multiple government investigations and write-downs of corporate assets. Finally, Time Warner sold its AOL division in 2009.[4]

Timely Information also needs to be **timely.** Timeliness does not necessarily mean speediness; it means only that information needs to be available in time for appropriate managerial action. What constitutes timeliness is a function of the situation facing the manager. When Marriott was gathering information for a new hotel project, managers allowed themselves a six-month period for data collection. They felt this would give them an opportunity to do a good job of getting the information they needed while not delaying things too much. In contrast, Marriott's reservation and accounting systems can provide a manager today with last night's occupancy level at any Marriott facility. In 2002, United Airlines filed for bankruptcy protection while it restructured its finances. In 2008, an error led a South Florida newspaper to post an old story about the 2002 filing on its website in a way that made it appear as a current event. The resulting panic among investors caused United Airlines' shares to drop from $12.50 a share to less than $3 a share before the error was caught and corrected.[5]

Complete Information must tell a complete story for it to be useful to a manager. If it is less than **complete information,** the manager is likely to get an inaccurate or distorted picture of reality. For example, managers at Kroger used to think that house-brand products were more profitable than national brands because they yielded higher unit profits. On the basis of this information, they gave house brands a great deal of shelf space and centered promotional activities around them. As Kroger's managers became more sophisticated in understanding their information, however, they realized that national brands were actually more profitable over time because they sold many more units than house brands during any given period of time. Hence, although a store might sell 10 cans of Kroger coffee in a day, with a profit of 50 cents per can (total profit of $5), it would sell 15 cans of Maxwell House with a profit of 40 cents per can (total profit of $6) and 10 vacuum bags of Starbucks coffee with a profit of $1 per bag (total profit of $10). With this more complete picture, managers could do a better job of selecting the right mix of Kroger, Maxwell House, and Starbucks coffee to display and promote.

accurate information Provides a valid and reliable reflection of reality

timely information Available in time for appropriate managerial action

complete information Provides the manager with all the information he or she needs

Relevant Finally, information must be relevant if it is to be useful to managers. **Relevant information**, like timely information, is defined according to the needs and circumstances of a particular manager. Operations managers need information on costs and productivity, human resource managers need information on hiring needs and turnover rates, and marketing managers need information on sales projections and advertising rates. As Wal-Mart contemplates countries as possible expansion opportunities, it gathers information about local regulations, customs, and so forth. But the information about any given country is not as relevant before a decision is made to enter that market than it is after the firm has made a decision to enter the market.

The Communication Process

Figure 14.1 illustrates how communication generally takes place between people. The process of communication begins when one person (the sender) wants to transmit a fact, idea, opinion, or other information to someone else (the receiver). This fact, idea, or opinion has meaning to the sender, whether it be simple and concrete or complex and abstract.

The next step is to encode the meaning into a form appropriate to the situation. The encoding might take the form of words, facial expressions, gestures, or even artistic expressions and physical actions. After the message has been encoded, it is transmitted through the appropriate channel or medium. The channel by which this encoded message is being transmitted to you is the printed page. Common channels in organizations include meetings, e-mails, memos, letters, reports, and phone calls. After the message is received, it is decoded back into a form that has meaning for the receiver. As noted earlier, the consistency of this meaning can vary dramatically. In many cases, the meaning prompts a response, and the cycle is continued when a new message is sent by the same steps back to the original sender.

relevant information
Information that is useful to managers in their particular circumstances for their particular needs

Figure 14.1
The Communication Process

As the figure shows, noise can disrupt the communication process at any step. Managers must therefore understand that a conversation in the next office, a fax machine out of paper, and the receiver's worries may all thwart the manager's best attempts to communicate.

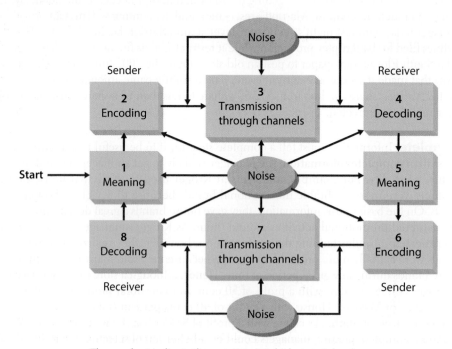

The numbers indicate the sequence in which steps take place.

"Noise" may disrupt communication anywhere along the way. Noise can be the sound of someone coughing, a truck driving by, or two people talking close at hand. It can also include disruptions such as a letter lost in the mail, a dead phone line, an interrupted cell phone call, an e-mail misrouted or infected with a virus, or one of the participants in a conversation being called away before the communication process is completed.

FORMS OF COMMUNICATION IN ORGANIZATIONS

Managers need to understand several kinds of communication that are common in organizations today.[6] These include interpersonal communication, communication in networks and work teams, organizational communication, and electronic communication.

Interpersonal Communication

Interpersonal communication generally takes one of two forms: oral and written. As we will see, each has clear strengths and weaknesses.

Oral Communication Oral communication takes place in conversations, group discussions, phone calls, and other situations in which the spoken word is used to express meaning. One study (conducted before the advent of e-mail) demonstrated the importance of oral communication by finding that most managers spent between 50 and 90 percent of their time talking to people.[7] Oral communication is so prevalent for several reasons. The primary advantage of oral communication is that it promotes prompt feedback and interchange in the form of verbal questions or agreement, facial expressions, and gestures. Oral communication is also easy (all the sender needs to do is talk), and it can be done with little preparation (though careful preparation is advisable in certain situations). The sender does not need pencil and paper, a computer, or other equipment. In another survey, 55 percent of the executives sampled felt that their own written communication skills were fair or poor, so they chose oral communication to avoid embarrassment![8]

JON FEINGERSH/PHOTOLIBRARY

Oral communication is pervasive in all organizations. It's easy and fast, doesn't require any equipment, and people can get instant feedback or answers to their questions. These two managers, for example, are discussing how to get a project that is running behind schedule back on track. By handling this in a face-to-face conversation they can get the problem solved more quickly than by relying on written communication.

However, oral communication also has drawbacks. It may suffer from problems of inaccuracy if the speaker chooses the wrong words to convey meaning or leaves out pertinent details, if noise disrupts the process, or if the receiver forgets part of the message.[9] In a two-way discussion, there is seldom time for a thoughtful, considered response or for introducing many new facts, and there is no permanent record of what has been said. In addition, although most managers are comfortable talking to people individually or in small groups, fewer enjoy speaking to larger audiences.[10]

oral communication
Face-to-face conversation, group discussions, telephone calls, and other circumstances in which the spoken word is used to transmit meaning

Written Communication "Putting it in writing" in a letter, report, memorandum, handwritten note, or e-mail can solve many of the problems inherent in oral communication. Nevertheless, and perhaps surprisingly, **written communication** is not as common as one might imagine, nor is it a mode of communication much respected by managers. One sample of managers indicated that only 13 percent of the printed mail they received was of immediate use to them.[11] Over 80 percent of the managers who responded to another survey indicated that the written communication they received was of fair or poor quality.[12]

The biggest single drawback of traditional forms of written communication is that they inhibit feedback and interchange. When one manager sends another manager a letter, it must be written or dictated, typed, mailed, received, routed, opened, and read. If there is a misunderstanding, it may take several days for it to be recognized, let alone rectified. Although the use of e-mail is, of course, much faster, both sender and receiver must still have access to a computer, and the receiver must open and read the message for it to actually be received. A phone call could settle the whole matter in just a few minutes. Thus written communication often inhibits feedback and interchange and is usually more difficult and time consuming than oral communication.

Of course, written communication offers some advantages. It is often quite accurate and provides a permanent record of the exchange. The sender can take the time to collect and assimilate the information and can draft and revise it before it is transmitted. The receiver can take the time to read it carefully and can refer to it repeatedly, as needed. For these reasons, written communication is generally preferable when important details are involved. At times it is important to one or both parties to have a written record available as evidence of exactly what took place. Julie Regan, founder of Toucan-Do, an importing company based in Honolulu, relies heavily on formal business letters in establishing contacts and buying merchandise from vendors in Southeast Asia. She believes that such letters give her an opportunity to carefully think through what she wants to say, tailor her message to each individual, and avoid later misunderstandings.

Choosing the Right Form Which form of interpersonal communication should the manager use? The best medium will be determined by the situation. Oral communication or e-mail may be preferred when the message is personal, nonroutine, and brief. More formal written communication is usually best when the message is more impersonal, routine, and longer. And, given the prominent role that e-mails have played in several recent court cases, managers should always use discretion when sending messages electronically.[13] For example, private e-mails made public during legal proceedings have played major roles in litigation involving Enron, Tyco, WorldCom, and Morgan Stanley.[14]

The manager can also combine media to capitalize on the advantages of each. For example, a quick phone call to set up a meeting is easy and gets an immediate response. Following up the call with a reminder e-mail or handwritten note helps ensure that the recipient will remember the meeting, and it provides a record of the meeting having been called. Electronic communication, discussed more fully later, blurs the differences between oral and written communication and can help each be more effective.

Communication in Networks and Work Teams

Although communication among team members in an organization is clearly interpersonal in nature, substantial research also focuses specifically on how people in networks and work teams communicate with one another. A **communication network** is

written communication
Memos, letters, reports, notes, and other circumstances in which the written word is used to transmit meaning

communication network
The pattern through which the members of a group communicate

$\mathcal{F}igure$ 14.2   Types of Communication Networks

Research on communication networks has identified five basic networks for five-person groups. These networks vary in terms of information flow, position of the leader, and effectiveness for different types of tasks. Managers might strive to create centralized networks when group tasks are simple and routine. Alternatively, managers can foster decentralized groups when group tasks are complex and nonroutine.

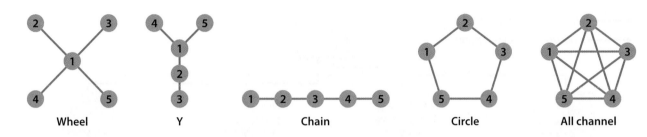

the pattern through which the members of a group or team communicate. Researchers studying group dynamics have discovered several typical networks in groups and teams consisting of three, four, and five members. Representative networks among members of five-member teams are shown in Figure 14.2.[15]

In the wheel pattern, all communication flows through one central person, who is probably the group's leader. In a sense, the wheel is the most centralized network because one person receives and disseminates all information. The Y pattern is slightly less centralized—two people are close to the center. The chain offers a more even flow of information among members, although two people (the ones at each end) interact with only one other person. This path is closed in the circle pattern. Finally, the all-channel network, the most decentralized, allows a free flow of information among all group members. Everyone participates equally, and the group's leader, if there is one, is not likely to have excessive power.

Research conducted on networks suggests some interesting connections between the type of network and group performance. For example, when the group's task is relatively simple and routine, centralized networks tend to perform with greatest efficiency and accuracy. The dominant leader facilitates performance by coordinating the flow of information. When a group of accounting clerks is logging incoming invoices and distributing them for payment, for example, one centralized leader can coordinate things efficiently. When the task is complex and nonroutine, such as making a major decision about organizational strategy, decentralized networks tend to be most effective because open channels of communication permit more interaction and a more efficient sharing of relevant information. Managers should recognize the effects of communication networks on group and organizational performance and should try to structure networks appropriately.

Organizational Communication

Still other forms of communication in organizations are those that flow among and between organizational units or groups. Each of these involves oral or written communication, but each also extends to broad patterns of communication across the organization.[16] As shown in Figure 14.3, two of these forms of communication follow vertical and horizontal linkages in the organization.

$\mathcal{F}igure$ 14.3   Formal Communication in Organizations

Formal communication in organizations follows official reporting relationships or prescribed channels. For example, vertical communication, shown here with solid lines, flows between levels in the organization and involves subordinates and their managers. Horizontal communication, shown with dashed lines, flows between people at the same level and is usually used to facilitate coordination.

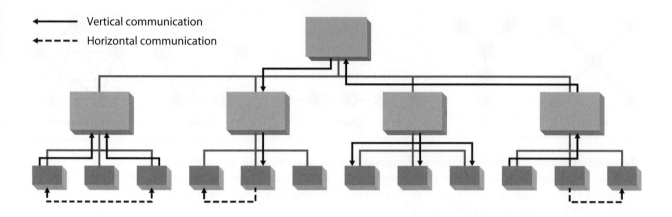

Vertical communication

Horizontal communication

Vertical Communication **Vertical communication** is communication that flows up and down the organization, usually along formal reporting lines—that is, it is the communication that takes place between managers and their superiors and subordinates. Vertical communication may involve only two people, or it may flow through several different organizational levels.

Upward communication consists of messages from subordinates to superiors. This flow is usually from subordinates to their direct superior, then to that person's direct superior, and so on up the hierarchy. Occasionally, a message might bypass a particular superior. The typical content of upward communication is requests, information that the lower-level manager thinks is of importance to the higher-level manager, responses to requests from the higher-level manager, suggestions, complaints, and financial information. Research has shown that upward communication is more subject to distortion than downward communication. Subordinates are likely to withhold or distort information that makes them look bad. The greater the degree of difference in status between superior and subordinate and the greater the degree of distrust, the more likely the subordinate is to suppress or distort information.[17] For example, subordinates might choose to withhold information about problems from their boss if they think the news will make him angry and if they think they can solve the problem themselves without his knowledge.

Downward communication occurs when information flows down the hierarchy from superiors to subordinates. The typical content of these messages is directives on how something is to be done, the assignment of new responsibilities, performance feedback, and general information that the higher-level manager thinks will be of value to the lower-level manager. Vertical communication can and usually should be two-way in nature. In other words, give-and-take communication with active feedback is generally likely to be more effective than one-way communication.[18]

vertical communication
Communication that flows up and down the organization, usually along formal reporting lines; takes place between managers and their superiors and subordinates and may involve several different levels of the organization

Horizontal Communication   Whereas vertical communication involves a superior and a subordinate, **horizontal communication** involves colleagues and peers at the same level of the organization. For example, an operations manager might communicate to a marketing manager that inventory levels are running low and that projected delivery dates should be extended by two weeks. Horizontal communication probably occurs more among managers than among nonmanagers.

This type of communication serves a number of purposes.[19] It facilitates coordination among interdependent units. For example, a manager at Motorola was once researching the strategies of Japanese semiconductor firms in Europe. He found a great deal of information that was relevant to his assignment. He also uncovered some additional information that was potentially important to another department, so he passed it along to a colleague in that department, who used it to improve his own operations. Horizontal communication can also be used for joint problem solving, as when two plant managers at Northrop Grumman got together to work out a new method to improve productivity. Finally, horizontal communication plays a major role in work teams with members drawn from several departments.

Electronic Communication

An increasingly important form of organizational communication relies on electronic communication technology. **Information technology (IT)** consists of the resources used by an organization to manage information that it needs to carry out its mission. IT may consist of computers, computer networks, telephones, fax machines, smart phones, and other pieces of hardware. In addition, IT involves software that facilitates the system's ability to manage information in a way that is useful for managers. Both formal information systems and personal information technology have reshaped how managers communicate with one another.[18] The "Management Tech" box provides some clear examples of how this reshaping has occurred.

horizontal communication
Communication that flows laterally within the organization; involves colleagues and peers at the same level of the organization and may involve individuals from several different organizational units

information technology (IT)
The resources used by an organization to manage information that it needs to carry out its mission

MANAGEMENT TECH

The Brutally Honest-Opinion Business

Cell phones and fax machines? Your grandfather's technology. Video conferencing? Been there, done that. The Internet? Old news. E-mail? Try getting away from it. PDA? Blackberry? Standard issue for today's manager.

Obviously, the explosion in digital-communication technology over the last 25 years has created many new media. Corporations now rely extensively on these new technologies, and they've changed the way we work. Virtual teams, global workforces, outsourcing, just-in-time inventory—these are just

a few of the widely accepted business tools and methods that could never have existed without new developments in communication technology. Today, yet another new technology is at the cutting edge of business-communication strategies: web logs, or *blogs*.

A *blog* is any web-based publication consisting mainly of periodically posted articles, usually in reverse chronological order. They're similar to journals in that bloggers express thoughts or opinions over a period of time, but most blogs allow

(continued)

readers to add their own comments in response to original posts. Blogs allow groups of people, whether or not they're otherwise connected, to share thoughts, and for some readers, professionally (or semiprofessionally) posted blogs actually supplement or replace traditional news media. Blogs can also function much like face-to-face grapevines to communicate information that's suppressed elsewhere.

Nowadays, organizations as disparate as General Motors, the Dallas Cowboys, Microsoft, and Stonyfield Farm (an organic dairy) maintain popular corporate blogs; Microsoft supports 237 blogs (at last count). What do corporations do with blogs? Naturally, they use them to communicate with customers and employees, but they've found a variety of other uses for them, too. A consumer-research firm called Umbria, for example, charges companies such as Electronic Arts, SAP, and Sprint $60,000 a year to conduct routine scans of 20 million blogs. The data is valuable to corporate marketers, in particular because bloggers are often early product adopters and blog opinions show up quickly. Marketers, however, should be prepared

for the kind of input they're going to get for their money: "The blogsphere," warns Umbria CEO Howard Kaushansky, "is overflowing with brutally honest opinion."

With a survey list of merely 20 million blogs and a 10 percent share, Umbria is actually a fairly small player in the blog-research market. Larger competitors in the $20 million market include Intelliseek, with about a third of the market, and BuzzMetrics, which doesn't reveal how much business it does. There appears to be room for more competitors, however. According to the search engine Technorati, there are at least 112.8 million blogs out there (not counting another 72.8 million in China), with about 175,000 new blogs popping up every day. Bloggers put up more than 1.6 million posts per day, or more than 18 updates a second.

References: Matthew Boyle, "Do's and Don'ts of Corporate Blogging," *Fortune,* February 28, 2006, http://money.cnn.com on May 25, 2009; Justin Martin, "What Bloggers Think of Your Business," *Fortune,* December 7, 2005, http://money.cnn.com on May 25, 2009; Anne Helmond, "How Many Blogs Are There? Is Someone Still Counting?" *The Blog Herald,* February 11, 2008, www.blogherald.com on May 25, 2009; Adam Thierer, "Need Help ... How Many Blogs Are There Out There?" *The Technology Liberation Front,* May 6, 2008, http://techliberation.com on May 25, 2009.

Information Systems Advances in IT have made it increasingly easy for managers to use many different kinds of information systems. In this section, we discuss the most common kinds of information systems used by businesses today.

Transaction-processing systems (TPSs) are applications of information processing for basic day-to-day business transactions. Customer order taking by online retailers, approval of claims at insurance companies, receipt and confirmation of reservations by airlines, payroll processing and bill payment at almost every company—all are routine business processes. Typically, the TPS for first-level (operational) activities is well defined, with predetermined data requirements, and follows the same steps to complete all transactions in the system.

Systems for knowledge workers and office applications support the activities of both knowledge workers and employees in clerical positions. They provide assistance for data processing and other office activities, including the creation of communications documents. Like other departments, the information systems (IS) department includes both knowledge workers and data workers. *Systems for operations and data workers* make sure that the right programs are run in the correct sequence, and they monitor equipment to ensure that it is operating properly. Many organizations also have employees who enter data into the system for processing. *Knowledge-level and office systems* are also increasingly widespread. The widespread availability of text processing, document imaging, desktop publishing, computer-aided design, simulation modeling, and similar tools has increased the productivity of both knowledge and office workers. Desktop publishing combines

transaction-processing system (TPS)
An application of information processing for basic day-to-day business transactions

graphics and word-processing text to publish professional-quality print and web documents. Document-imaging systems can scan paper documents and images, convert them into digital form, store them, retrieve them, manipulate them, and/or transmit them to workstations throughout the network, all without generating any additional paper.

Management information systems (MISs) support an organization's managers by providing daily reports, schedules, plans, and budgets. Each manager's information activities vary according to his or her functional area (say, accounting or marketing) and management level. Whereas mid-level managers focus mostly on internal activities and information, higher-level managers are also engaged in external activities. Middle managers, the largest MIS user group, need networked information to plan upcoming activities such as personnel training, materials movements, and cash flows. They also need to know the current status of the jobs and projects being carried out in their department: What stage is it at now? When will it be finished? Is there an opening so we can start the next job? Many of a firm's MIS—cash flow, sales, production scheduling, shipping—are indispensable in helping managers find answers to such questions.

Decision support systems (DSSs) are interactive systems that locate and present information needed to support the decision-making process. Whereas some DSSs are devoted to specific problems, others serve more general purposes, allowing managers to analyze different types of problems. Thus a firm that often faces decisions on plant capacity, for example, may have a capacity DSS: The manager inputs data on anticipated levels of sales, working capital, and customer delivery requirements. Then the DSS's built-in transaction processors manipulate the data and make recommendations on the best levels of plant capacity for each future time period. In contrast, a general-purpose system, such as a marketing DSS, might respond to a variety of marketing-related problems. It may be programmed to handle "what-if" questions, such as "When is the best time to introduce a new product if my main competitor introduces one in three months, our new product has an eighteen-month expected life, demand is seasonal with a peak in autumn, and my goal is to gain the largest possible market share?" The DSS can help managers make decisions for which predetermined solutions are unknown by using sophisticated modeling tools and data analysis.

An **executive support system (ESS)** is a quick-reference, easy-access application of information systems specially designed for instant access by upper-level managers. ESSs are designed to assist with executive-level decisions and problems, ranging from "What lines of business should we be in five years from now?" to "Based on forecasted developments in electronic technologies, to what extent should our firm be globalized in five years? in ten years?" The ESS also uses a wide range of both internal information and external sources, such as industry reports, global economic forecasts, and reports on competitors' capabilities. Because senior-level managers do not usually possess advanced computer skills, they prefer systems that are easily accessible and adaptable. Accordingly, ESSs are not designed to address only specific, predetermined problems. Instead, they allow the user some flexibility in attacking a variety of problem situations. They are easily accessible by means of simple keyboard strokes or even voice commands.

Artificial intelligence (AI) can be defined as the construction of computer systems, both hardware and software, to imitate human behavior—in other words, systems that perform physical tasks, use thought processes, and learn. In developing AI systems, knowledge workers (business specialists, modelers, and IT experts) try to design computer-based systems capable of reasoning, so that computers, instead of people, can perform certain business activities. One simple example is a credit evaluation system that decides which loan applicants are creditworthy and which ones are risky and then composes acceptance and rejection letters accordingly. One special form of AI, the *expert system*,

---

management information system (MIS)
An information system that supports an organization's managers by providing daily reports, schedules, plans, and budgets

decision support system (DSS)
An interactive system that locates and presents information needed to support the decision-making process

executive support system (ESS)
A quick-reference, easy-access application of information systems specially designed for instant access by upper-level managers

artificial intelligence (AI)
The construction of computer systems, both hardware and software, to imitate human behavior—that is, to perform physical tasks, use thought processes, and learn

PAUL J. RICHARDS/AFP/GETTY IMAGES

American Airlines makes extensive use of myriad information systems in every phase of its operations. When American flight 263 from Washington D.C. to Los Angeles was delayed because of thunder storms in the Washington area, its pilot used American's information systems to monitor weather along the plane's flight path, to see if he would arrive in time to make the next flight he was scheduled to work, and to see how many passengers making connections in LA were going to have to be rebooked on other flights. American systems provided him with the most current and accurate information available, helping him make better decisions.

intranet
A communication network similar to the Internet but operating within the boundaries of a single organization

extranet
A communication network that allows selected outsiders limited access to an organization's internal information system, or intranet

is designed to imitate the thought processes of human experts in a particular field. Expert systems incorporate the rules that an expert applies to specific types of problems, such as the judgments a physician makes in diagnosing illnesses. In effect, expert systems supply everyday users with "instant expertise." A system called MOCA (Maintenance Operations Center Advisor), by imitating the thought processes of a maintenance manager, schedules routine maintenance for American Airlines' entire fleet.

Intranets, or private Internet networks, are accessible only to employees via entry through electronic firewalls. Firewalls are used to limit access to an intranet. Ford's intranet connects over 100,000 workstations in Asia, Europe, and the United States to thousands of Ford websites containing private information on Ford activities in production, engineering, distribution, and marketing. Sharing such information has helped reduce the lead time for getting models into production from 36 to 24 months. Ford's latest project in improving customer service through internal information sharing is called manufacturing on demand. Now, for example, the Mustang that required 50 days' delivery time in 1996 is available in less than two weeks. The savings to Ford, of course, will be billions of dollars in inventory and fixed costs.[19]

Extranets allow outsiders limited access to a firm's intranet. The most common application allows buyers to enter the seller's system to see which products are available for sale and delivery, thus providing product availability information quickly to outside buyers. Industrial suppliers, too, are often linked into their customers' intranets so that they can see planned production schedules and make supplies ready as needed for customers' upcoming operations.

Personal Electronic Technology In recent years, the nature of organizational communication has changed dramatically, mainly because of breakthroughs in personal electronic communication technology, and the future promises even more change. It has become common, for instance, to have teleconferences in which managers stay at their own location (such as offices in different cities) but are seen on monitors as they "meet." A manager in New York can keyboard a letter or memorandum at her personal computer, point and click with a mouse, and have it delivered to hundreds or even thousands of colleagues around the world in a matter of seconds. Highly detailed information can be retrieved with ease from large electronic databanks. This has given rise to a new version of an old work arrangement—the cottage industry. In a cottage industry, people work at home (in their "cottage") and periodically bring the products of their labors in to the company. *Telecommuting* is the label given to a new electronic cottage industry. In telecommuting, people work at home on their computers and communicate with colleagues and coworkers using electronic media.

Smart phones and fax machines have made it even easier for managers to communicate with one another. Many now use cell phones to make calls while commuting to and from work and carry them in their briefcases so that they can receive calls while at lunch. Facsimile machines make it easy for people to use written communication media and get rapid feedback. And new personal computing devices such as the iPad are revolutionizing how people communicate with one another. Wi-Fi technology is further extending the impact of these devices.

Psychologists, however, are beginning to associate some problems with these communication advances. For one thing, managers who are seldom in their "real" office are likely to fall behind in their field and to be victimized by organizational politics because they are not present to keep in touch with what is going on and to protect themselves. They drop out of the organizational grapevine and miss out on much of the informal communication that takes place. Moreover, the use of electronic communication at the expense of face-to-face meetings and conversations makes it hard to build a strong culture, develop solid working relationships, and create a mutually supportive atmosphere of trust and cooperativeness.[20] Finally, electronic communication is opening up new avenues for dysfunctional employee behavior, such as the passing of lewd or offensive materials to others. For example, in 2000, the *New York Times* fired almost 10 percent of its workers at one of its branch offices for sending inappropriate e-mails at work.[21]

INFORMAL COMMUNICATION IN ORGANIZATIONS

The forms of organizational communication discussed in the previous section all represent planned and relatively formal communication mechanisms. However, in many cases some of the communication that takes place in an organization transcends these formal channels and instead follows any of several informal methods. Figure 14.4 illustrates numerous examples of informal communication. Common forms of informal communication in organizations include the grapevine, management by wandering around, and nonverbal communication.

Figure 14.4   **Informal Communication in Organizations**

Informal communication in organizations may or may not follow official reporting relationships or prescribed channels. It may cross different levels and different departments or work units and may or may not have anything to do with official organizational business.

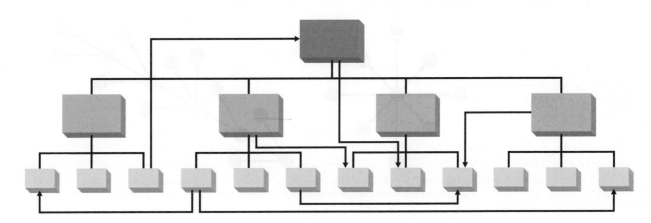

The Grapevine

The **grapevine** is an informal communication network that can permeate an entire organization. Grapevines are found in all organizations except the very smallest, but they do not always follow the same patterns as, nor do they necessarily coincide with, formal channels of authority and communication. Research has identified several kinds of grapevines.[20] The two most common are illustrated in Figure 14.5. The gossip chain occurs when one person spreads the message to many other people. Each one, in turn, may either keep the information confidential or pass it on to others. The gossip chain is likely to carry personal information. The other common grapevine is the cluster chain, in which one person passes the information to a selected few individuals. Some of the receivers pass the information to a few other individuals; the rest keep it to themselves.

There is some disagreement about how accurate the information carried by the grapevine is, but research is increasingly finding it to be fairly accurate, especially when the information is based on fact rather than speculation. One study found that the grapevine may be between 75 and 95 percent accurate.[21] That same study also found that informal communication is increasing in many organizations for two basic reasons. One contributing factor is the recent increase in merger, acquisition, and takeover activity. Because such activity can greatly affect the people within an organization, it follows that they may spend more time talking about it.[22] The second contributing factor is that as more and more corporations move facilities from inner cities to suburbs, employees tend to talk less and less to others outside the organization and more and more to one another.

Attempts to eliminate the grapevine are fruitless, but fortunately the manager does have some control over it. By maintaining open channels of communication and responding vigorously to inaccurate information, the manager can minimize the damage the grapevine can do. The grapevine can actually be an asset. By learning who the key people in the grapevine are, for example, the manager can partially control the information they receive and use the grapevine to sound out employee reactions to new ideas, such

grapevine
An informal communication network among people in an organization

---

Figure 14.5 Common Grapevine Chains Found in Organizations

The two most common grapevine chains in organizations are the gossip chain (in which one person communicates messages to many others) and the cluster chain (in which many people pass messages to a few others).

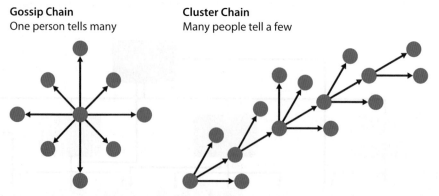

Gossip Chain
One person tells many

Cluster Chain
Many people tell a few

Source: From Keith Davis and John W. Newstrom, *Human Behavior at Work: Organizational Behavior*, 8th ed., 1989. © 1989 The McGraw-Hill Companies, Inc. Reprinted with permission.

as a change in human resource policies or benefit packages. The manager can also get valuable information from the grapevine and use it to improve decision making.[23]

Management by Wandering Around

Another increasingly popular form of informal communication is called, interestingly enough, **management by wandering around**.[24] The basic idea is that some managers keep in touch with what is going on by wandering around and talking with people—immediate subordinates, subordinates far down the organizational hierarchy, delivery people, customers, or anyone else who is involved with the company in some way. Bill Marriott, for example, frequently visits the kitchens, loading docks, and custodial work areas whenever he tours a Marriott hotel. He claims that, by talking with employees throughout the hotel, he gets new ideas and has a better feel for the entire company. And, when American Airlines CEO Gerald Arpey travels, he makes a point of talking to flight attendants and other passengers to gain continuous insights into how the business can be run more effectively.

A related form of organizational communication that really has no specific term is the informal interchange that takes place outside the normal work setting. Employees attending the company picnic, playing on the company softball team, or taking fishing trips together will almost always spend part of their time talking about work. For example, Texas Instruments engineers at TI's Lewisville, Texas, facility often frequent a local bar in town after work. On any given evening, they talk about the Dallas Cowboys, the newest government contract received by the company, the weather, their boss, the company's stock price, local politics, and problems at work. There is no set agenda, and the key topics of discussion vary from group to group and from day to day. Still, the social gatherings serve an important role. They promote a strong culture and enhance understanding of how the organization works.

Nonverbal Communication

Nonverbal communication is a communication exchange that does not use words or uses words to carry more meaning than the strict definition of the words themselves. Nonverbal communication is a powerful but little-understood form of communication in organizations. It often relies on facial expressions, body movements, physical contact, and gestures. One study found that as much as 55 percent of the content of a message is transmitted by facial expressions and body posture and that another 38 percent derives from inflection and tone. Words themselves account for only 7 percent of the content of the message.[25]

Research has identified three kinds of nonverbal communication practiced by managers—images, settings, and body language.[26] In this context, images are the kinds of words people elect to use. "Damn the torpedoes, full speed ahead" and "Even though there are some potential hazards, we should proceed with this course of action" may convey the same meaning. Yet the person who uses the first expression may be perceived as a maverick, a courageous hero, an individualist, or a reckless and foolhardy adventurer. The person who uses the second might be described as aggressive, forceful, diligent, or narrow minded and resistant to change. In short, our choice of words conveys much more than just the strict meaning of the words themselves.

The setting for communication also plays a major role in nonverbal communication. Boundaries, familiarity, the home turf, and other elements of the setting are all important. Much has been written about the symbols of power in organizations. The size and location of an office, the kinds of furniture in the office, and the accessibility of the person in the office all communicate useful information. For example, when H. Ross Perot ran Electronic Data Systems (EDS), he positioned his desk so that it is always between him

management by wandering around
An approach to communication that involves the manager's literally wandering around and having spontaneous conversations with others

nonverbal communication
Any communication exchange that does not use words or uses words to carry more meaning than the strict definition of the words themselves

and a visitor. This signaled that he was in charge. When he wanted a less formal dialogue, he moved around to the front of the desk and sat beside his visitor. Michael Dell of Dell Computer, in contrast, has his desk facing a side window so that, when he turns around to greet a visitor, there is never anything between them.

A third form of nonverbal communication is body language.[27] The distance we stand from someone as we speak has meaning. In the United States, standing very close to someone you are talking to generally signals either familiarity or aggression. The English and Germans stand farther apart than Americans when talking, whereas the Arabs, Japanese, and Mexicans stand closer together.[28] Eye contact is another effective means of nonverbal communication. For example, prolonged eye contact might suggest either hostility or romantic interest. Other kinds of body language include body and hand movement, pauses in speech, and mode of dress.

The manager should be aware of the importance of nonverbal communication and recognize its potential impact. Giving an employee good news about a reward with the wrong nonverbal cues can destroy the reinforcement value of the reward. Likewise, reprimanding an employee but providing inconsistent nonverbal cues can limit the effectiveness of the sanctions. The tone of the message, where and how the message is delivered, facial expressions, and gestures can all amplify or weaken the message or change the message altogether.

MANAGING ORGANIZATIONAL COMMUNICATION

In view of the importance and pervasiveness of communication in organizations, it is vital for managers to understand how to manage the communication process.[29] Managers should understand how to maximize the potential benefits of communication and minimize the potential problems. We begin our discussion of communication management by considering the factors that might disrupt effective communication and how to deal with them.

Barriers to Communication

Several factors may disrupt the communication process or serve as barriers to effective communication.[30] As shown in Table 14.1, these may be divided into two classes: individual barriers and organizational barriers.

Individual Barriers Several individual barriers may disrupt effective communication. One common problem is conflicting or inconsistent signals. A manager is sending conflicting signals when she says on Monday that things should be done one way, but then prescribes an entirely different procedure on Wednesday. Inconsistent signals are being sent by a manager who says that he has an "open door" policy and wants his subordinates to drop by, but keeps his door closed and becomes irritated whenever someone stops in.

Another barrier is lack of credibility. Credibility problems arise when the sender is not considered a reliable source of information. He may not be trusted or may not be perceived as knowledgeable about the subject at hand. When a politician is caught withholding information or when a manager makes a series of bad decisions, the extent to which he or she will be listened to and believed thereafter diminishes. In extreme cases, people may talk about something they obviously know little or nothing about.

Some people are simply reluctant to initiate a communication exchange. This reluctance may occur for a variety of reasons. A manager may be reluctant to tell subordinates about

Table 14.1 Barriers to Effective Communication

Numerous barriers can disrupt effective communication. Some of these barriers involve individual characteristics and processes. Others are functions of the organizational context in which communication is taking place.

Individual Barriers	Organizational Barriers
Conflicting or inconsistent signals	Semantics
Credibility about the subject	Status or power differences
Reluctance to communicate	Different perceptions
Poor listening skills	Noise
Predispositions about the subject	Overload
	Language differences

an impending budget cut because he knows they will be unhappy about it. Likewise, a subordinate may be reluctant to transmit information upward for fear of reprisal or because it is felt that such an effort would be futile.

Poor listening habits can be a major barrier to effective communication. Some people are simply poor listeners. When someone is talking to them, they may be daydreaming, looking around, reading, or listening to another conversation. Because they are not concentrating on what is being said, they may not comprehend part or all of the message. They may even think that they really are paying attention, only to realize later that they cannot remember parts of the conversation.

Receivers may also bring certain predispositions to the communication process. They may already have their minds made up, firmly set in a certain way. For example, a manager may have heard that his new boss is unpleasant and hard to work with. When she calls him in for an introductory meeting, he may go into that meeting predisposed to dislike her and discount what she has to say.

Organizational Barriers Other barriers to effective communication involve the organizational context in which the communication occurs. Semantics problems arise when words have different meanings for different people. Words and phrases such as *profit*, *increased output*, and *return on investment* may have positive meanings for managers but less positive meanings for labor.

DAVE & LES JACOBS/JUPITER IMAGES

Poor listening habits are often a major barrier to effective communication. The widespread use of electronic communication devices like smart phones has made listening even more problematic for some people. Because they are distracted by incoming emails and text messages, for instance, they may pay even less attention to someone who is talking. This manager, for example, is checking messages during a presentation about new office procedures. As a result, he will likely not fully understand the new procedures.

Communication problems may also arise when people of different power or status try to communicate with each other. The company president may discount a suggestion from an operating employee, thinking, "How can someone at that level help me run my business?" Or, when the president goes out to inspect a new plant, workers may be reluctant to offer suggestions because of their lower status. The marketing vice president may have more power than the human resource vice president and consequently may not pay much attention to a staffing report submitted by the human resource department.

If people perceive a situation differently, they may have difficulty communicating with one another. When two managers observe that a third manager has not spent much time in her office lately, one may believe that she has been to several important meetings, and the other may think she is "hiding out." If they need to talk about her in some official capacity, problems may arise because one has a positive impression and the other a negative impression.

Environmental factors may also disrupt effective communication. As mentioned earlier, noise may affect communication in many ways. Similarly, overload may be a problem when the receiver is being sent more information than he or she can effectively handle. For more than a decade, many managers have reported getting so many messages each day as to sometimes feel overwhelmed.[31] As a result, many senior executives have two e-mail accounts: one is their "public" account that is actually monitored by a subordinate who only passes along truly important messages and the other is a "private" account available only to a few critical contacts. And, when the manager gives a subordinate many jobs on which to work and at the same time the subordinate is being told by family and friends to do other things, overload may result and communication effectiveness diminishes.

Finally, as businesses become more and more global, different languages can create problems. To counter this problem, some firms are adopting an "official language." For example, when the German chemical firm Hoechst merged with the French firm Rhone-Poulenc, the new company adopted English as its official language. Indeed, English is generally considered to be the standard business language around the world.[32]

Improving Communication Effectiveness

Considering how many factors can disrupt communication, it is fortunate that managers can resort to several techniques for improving communication effectiveness.[33] As shown in Table 14.2, these techniques include both individual and organizational skills.

Individual Skills The single most important individual skill for improving communication effectiveness is being a good listener.[34] Being a good listener requires that the individual be prepared to listen, not interrupt the speaker, concentrate on both the words and the meaning being conveyed, be patient, and ask questions as appropriate.[35] So important are good listening skills that companies such as Delta, IBM, and Boeing conduct programs to train their managers to be better listeners. Figure 14.6 illustrates the characteristics of poor listeners versus good listeners.

In addition to being a good listener, several other individual skills can promote effective communication. Feedback, one of the most important, is facilitated by two-way communication. Two-way communication allows the receiver to ask questions, request clarification, and express opinions that let the sender know whether he or she has been understood. In general, the more complicated the message, the more useful two-way communication is. In addition, the sender should be aware of the meanings that different receivers might attach to various words. For example, when addressing stockholders, a manager might use the word *profits* often. When addressing labor leaders, however, she may choose to use *profits* less often.

Table 14.2   **Overcoming Barriers to Communication**

Because communication is so important, managers have developed several methods of overcoming barriers to effective communication. Some of these methods involve individual skills, whereas others are based on organizational skills.

Individual Skills	Organizational Skills
Develop good listening skills	Follow up
Encourage two-way communication	Regulate information flows
Be aware of language and meaning	Understand the richness of media
Maintain credibility	
Be sensitive to receiver's perspective	
Be sensitive to sender's perspective	

Furthermore, the sender should try to maintain credibility. This can be accomplished by not pretending to be an expert when one is not, by "doing one's homework" and checking facts, and by otherwise being as accurate and honest as possible. The sender should also try to be sensitive to the receiver's perspective. A manager who must tell a subordinate that she has not been recommended for a promotion should recognize that the subordinate will be frustrated and unhappy. The content of the message and its method of delivery should be chosen accordingly. The manager should be primed to accept a reasonable degree of hostility and bitterness without getting angry in return.[36]

Figure 14.6   **More and Less Effective Listening Skills**

Effective listening skills are a vital part of communication in organizations. There are several barriers that can contribute to poor listening skills by individuals in organizations. Fortunately, there are also several practices for improving listening skills.

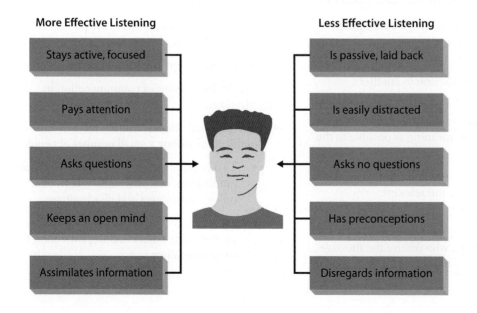

Finally, the receiver should also try to be sensitive to the sender's point of view. Suppose that a manager has just received some bad news—for example, that his position is being eliminated next year. Others should understand that he may be disappointed, angry, or even depressed for a while. Thus they might make a special effort not to take too much offense if he snaps at them, and they might look for signals that he needs someone to talk to.[37]

Organizational Skills Three useful organizational skills can also enhance communication effectiveness for both the sender and the receiver—following up, regulating information flow, and understanding the richness of different media. Following up simply involves checking at a later time to be sure that a message has been received and understood. After a manager e-mails a report to a colleague, she might call a few days later to ask whether the colleague has had an opportunity to review it or has any questions about it.

Regulating information flow means that the sender or receiver takes steps to ensure that overload does not occur. For the sender, this could mean not passing too much information through the system at one time. For the receiver, it might mean calling attention to the fact that he is being asked to do too many things at once. Many managers limit the influx of information by periodically weeding out the list of journals and routine reports they receive, or they train their assistant to screen phone calls and visitors. Indeed, some executives now get so much e-mail that they have it routed to an assistant. That person reviews the e-mails, discards those that are not useful (such as spam), responds to those that are routine, and passes on to the executive only those that require his or her personal attention.

Both parties should also understand the richness associated with different media. When a manager is going to lay off a subordinate temporarily, the message should be delivered in person. A face-to-face channel of communication gives the manager an opportunity to explain the situation and answer questions. When the purpose of the message is to grant a pay increase, written communication may be appropriate because it can be more objective and precise. The manager could then follow up the written notice with personal congratulations.

SUMMARY OF LEARNING OBJECTIVES AND KEY POINTS

1. Describe the role and importance of communication in the manager's job.

   - Communication is the process of transmitting information from one person to another.

   - Effective communication is the process of sending a message in such a way that the message received is as close in meaning as possible to the message intended.

   - For information to be useful, it must be accurate, timely, complete, and relevant.

   - The communication process consists of a sender's encoding meaning and transmitting it to one or more receivers, who receive the message and decode it into meaning.

   - In two-way communication, the process continues with the roles reversed.

   - Noise can disrupt any part of the overall process.

2. Identify the basic forms of communication in organizations.

   - Interpersonal communication focuses on communication among a small number of people.

     - Two important forms of interpersonal communication, oral and written, both offer unique advantages and disadvantages.

     - The manager should weigh the pros and cons of each when choosing a medium for communication.

- Communication networks are recurring patterns of communication among members of a group or work team.

- Vertical communication between superiors and subordinates may flow upward or downward.

- Horizontal communication involves peers and colleagues at the same level in the organization.

3. Describe the role of electronic communication in organizations.

- There are several basic levels of information systems:

  - transaction-processing systems

  - systems for various types of workers

  - basic management information systems

  - decision support systems and executive support systems

  - artificial intelligence, including expert systems

- Intranets and extranets are also growing in popularity.

- Electronic communication is having a profound effect on managerial and organizational communication.

4. Discuss informal communication, including its various forms and types.

- The grapevine is the informal communication network among people in an organization.

- Management by wandering around is also a popular informal method of communication.

- Nonverbal communication is expressed through images, settings, and body language.

5. Describe how the communication process can be managed to recognize and overcome barriers.

- Managing the communication process entails recognizing the barriers to effective communication and understanding how to overcome them.

- Barriers can be identified at both the individual and the organizational level.

- Likewise, both individual and organizational skills can be used to overcome these barriers.

DISCUSSION QUESTIONS

Questions for Review

1. Describe the difference between communication and effective communication. How can a sender verify that a communication was effective? How can a receiver verify that a communication was effective?

2. Which form of interpersonal communication is best for long-term retention? Why? Which form is best for getting across subtle nuances of meaning? Why?

3. What are the similarities and differences of oral and written communication? What kinds of situations call for the use of oral methods? What situations call for written communication?

4. What forms of electronic communication do you use regularly?

5. Describe the individual and organizational barriers to effective communication. For each barrier, describe one action that a manager could take to reduce the problems caused by that barrier.

Questions for Analysis

1. At what points in the communication process can problems occur? Give examples of how noise can interfere with the communication process. What can managers do to reduce problems and noise?

2. How are electronic communication devices (cell phones, e-mail, and websites) affecting the communication process? Describe both the advantages and the disadvantages of these three devices over traditional communication methods, such as face-to-face conversations, written notes, and phone calls.

3. What forms of communication have you experienced today? What form of communication is involved in a face-to-face conversation with a friend? A phone call from a customer? A traffic light or crossing signal? A picture of a cigarette in a circle with a slash across it? An area around machinery defined by a yellow line painted on the floor?

4. Keep track of your own activities over the course of a few hours of leisure time to determine what forms of communication you encounter. Which forms were most common? If you had been tracking your communications while at work, how would the list be different? Explain why the differences occur.

5. For each of the following situations, tell which form of communication you would use. Then ask the same question to someone who has been in the workforce for at least ten years. For any differences that occur, ask the worker to explain why his or her choice is better than yours. Do you agree with his or her assessment? Why or why not?

- Describing complex changes in how healthcare benefits are calculated and administered to every employee of a large firm

- Asking your boss a quick question about how she wants something done

- Telling customers that a new two-for-one promotion is available at your store

- Reprimanding an employee for excessive absences on the job

- Reminding workers that no smoking is allowed in your facility

BUILDING EFFECTIVE TECHNICAL SKILLS

Exercise Overview

Technical skills are the skills necessary to perform the work of the organization. This exercise will help you develop and apply technical skills involving the Internet and its potential for gathering information relevant to making important decisions.

Exercise Background

Assume that you are a manager for a large national retailer. You have been assigned the responsibility for identifying potential locations for the construction of a warehouse and distribution center. The idea behind such a center is that the firm can use its enormous purchasing power to buy many products in bulk quantities at relatively low prices. Individual stores can then order the specific quantities they need from the warehouse.

The location will need an abundance of land. The warehouse itself, for example, will occupy more than four square acres of land. In addition, it must be close to railroads and major highways because shipments will be arriving by both rail and truck, although outbound shipments will be exclusively by truck. Other important variables are that land prices and the cost of living should be relatively low and weather conditions should be mild (to minimize disruptions to shipments).

The firm's general experience is that small to midsize communities work best. Moreover, warehouses are already in place in the western and eastern parts of the United States, so this new one will most likely be in the central or south-central area. Your boss has asked you to identify three or four possible sites.

Exercise Task

With the aforementioned information as a framework, do the following:

1. Use the Internet to identify as many as ten possible locations.

2. Using additional information from the Internet, narrow the set of possible locations to three or four.

3. Again using the Internet, find out as much as possible about the potential locations.

BUILDING EFFECTIVE INTERPERSONAL SKILLS

Exercise Overview

A manager's interpersonal skills include his or her abilities to understand and to motivate individuals and groups. This in-class demonstration gives you practice in understanding the nonverbal and verbal behavior of a pair of individuals.

Exercise Background

Nonverbal communication conveys more than half of the information in any face-to-face exchange, and body language is a significant part of our nonverbal behavior. Consider, for example, the impact of a yawn or a frown or a shaking fist. At the same time, however, nonverbal communication is often neglected by managers. The result can be confusing and misleading signals.

In this exercise, you will examine interactions between two people without sound, with only visual clues to meaning. Then you will examine those same interactions with both visual and verbal clues.

Exercise Task

1. Observe the silent video segments that your professor shows to the class. For each segment, describe the nature of the relationship and interaction between the two individuals. What nonverbal clues did you use in reaching your conclusions?

2. Next, observe the same video segments, but this time with audio included. Describe the interaction again, along with any verbal clues you used.

3. How accurate were your assessments when you had only visual information? Explain why you were or were not accurate.

4. What does this exercise show you about the nature of nonverbal communication? What advice would you now give managers about their nonverbal communication?

SKILLS SELF-ASSESSMENT INSTRUMENT

Sex Talk Quiz

Introduction: Research shows that men and women sometimes have trouble communicating effectively with one another at work because they have contrasting values and beliefs about differences between the sexes. The following assessment surveys your beliefs and values about each sex.

Instructions: Mark each statement as either true or false. In some cases, you may find making a decision difficult, but you should force yourself to make a choice.

True/False Questions

_____ 1. Women are more intuitive than men. They have a sixth sense, which is typically called "women's intuition."

_____ 2. At business meetings, coworkers are more likely to listen to men than they are to women.

_____ 3. Women are the "talkers." They talk much more than men in group conversations.

_____ 4. Men are the "fast talkers." They talk much more quickly than women.

_____ 5. Men are more outwardly open than women. They use more eye contact and exhibit more friendliness when first meeting someone than do women.

_____ 6. Women are more complimentary and give more praise than men.

_____ 7. Men interrupt more than women and will answer a question even when it is not addressed to them.

_____ 8. Women give more orders and are more demanding in the way they communicate than are men.

_____ 9. In general, men and women laugh at the same things.

_____ 10. When making love, both men and women want to hear the same things from their partner.

_____ 11. Men ask for assistance less often than do women.

_____ 12. Men are harder on themselves and blame themselves more often than do women.

_____ 13. Through their body language, women make themselves less confrontational than men.

_____ 14. Men tend to explain things in greater detail when discussing an incident than do women.

_____ 15. Women tend to touch others more often than men.

_____ 16. Men appear to be more attentive than women when they are listening.

_____ 17. Women and men are equally emotional when they speak.

_____ 18. Men are more likely than women to discuss personal issues.

_____ 19. Men bring up more topics of conversation than do women.

_____ 20. Today we tend to raise our male children the same way we do our female children.

_____ 21. Women tend to confront problems more directly and are likely to bring up the problem first.

_____ 22. Men are livelier speakers who use more body language and facial animation than do women.

_____ 23. Men ask more questions than women.

_____ 24. In general, men and women enjoy talking about similar things.

_____ 25. When asking whether their partner has had an AIDS test or when discussing safe sex, a woman will likely bring up the topic before a man.

Source: Lillian Glass, Ph.D., "Sex Talk Quiz" in _He Says, She Says_, 1992. © 1992 by Lillian Glass, Ph.D. Used by permission of G. P. Putnam's Sons, a division of Penguin Putnam Inc.

EXPERIENTIAL EXERCISE

Nonverbal Communication in Groups

Purpose: The role of nonverbal communication in organizations can be just as important as oral or written communication, but is often overlooked. This activity will make you more aware of the power of nonverbal communication and give you some practice in using it.

Instructions:

Step 1: Your instructor will break your class into groups of about 20. Change your seat as needed until the group members are sitting fairly close and facing each other. Count the exact number of members and agree upon the count as a group.

Step 2: Count out loud, one at a time, from 1 up to the total number of group members. The group must do this without discussion or planning about who will say each number. Members may not use any verbal or

physical signals, for example, no pointing, nodding, or touching. Each member must say exactly one number and no number may be repeated. No two people may speak simultaneously.

Step 3: If any of the rules are violated, begin the task again from the number 1. Continue until the group successfully completes the task. Then answer the follow-up questions.

Follow-up Questions:

1. What methods of communication did you use to determine who would say each number? How effective was this method?

2. How did the group arrive at this method? For example, did the group try several methods before settling on one?

3. What does this exercise demonstrate to you about the power of nonverbal communication?

4. Can you think of examples of situations that you have experienced in which nonverbal communication played an important role?

5. Can you think of examples of situations that could occur in business organizations in which nonverbal communication might play an important role?

YOU MAKE THE CALL

The Converse of In-Person Communication

1. Experts suggest that you dress professionally for a phone interview even though the interviewer can't see you. Do you agree that this is important? Why or why not?

2. In getting ready for a phone interview for a new job, what are the three or four things for which you most want to be prepared? If you were getting ready to interview someone else for a job, what are the three or four major things that you'd expect that person to be prepared for?

3. Matt Aberham warns against simply trying to "sell yourself" during a phone interview. You agree, but you also believe that selling yourself is one of the things that you have to do as a job seeker. What sort of things do you regard as legitimate and effective in trying to sell yourself to a phone interviewer (or an in-person interviewer, for that matter)?

4. Think of one or two examples from your own life that you'd particularly like to come up in a job interview. What sort of questions might allow you to "take the initiative" in making sure that they didn't fall through the cracks? How much time do you think each incident would be worth in a 30- to 45-minute interview?

5. Linking video cameras to computers or using computers' built-in video cameras has become quite popular in setting up the complete online conversation. How might this technology be used in conjunction with phone interviews? How about other forms of communication, such as text messaging?

CHAPTER 15

TEAMS AND GROUPS

LEARNING OBJECTIVES

After studying this chapter, you should be able to:

1 Define and identify types of groups and teams in organizations, discuss reasons why people join groups and teams, and list the stages of group and team development.

2 Identify and discuss four essential characteristics of groups and teams.

3 Discuss interpersonal and intergroup conflict in organizations.

4 Describe how organizations manage conflict.

FIRST THINGS FIRST

Filling Shoes at Nike

Sometimes a successful entrepreneur gets too attached to his brainchild, identifying himself so closely with the organization, its products, and its people that it becomes almost impossible to let go. Sometimes, of course, he lets go and then grabs hold again. That's what happened at Nike when founder Phil Knight forced out CEO William Perez just 13 months after handpicking the ex-head of S.C. Johnson to take over his job. In hiring Perez, Knight was making no less than his third effort to step back from direct supervision of the world's largest sneaker and athletic–apparel company.

It's "a predictable script," says Yale professor Jeffrey Sonnenfeld, who likens this recurring corporate drama to sagas of more universal import: "It's like Shakespeare or Greek tragedy or the Bible." Business journalists have even given the familiar scenario a suitably epic title—"The Return of the Founder." Knight, who'd chosen Perez to instill the sort of organizational and managerial discipline that had never been his own strong point, put a fairly typical spin on the executive coup: Perez, he explained, had failed to grasp the company culture and to deploy the proven management teams already in place.

Since its founding in 1971, Nike's culture has been the stuff of legend. It's always

> **"The message about filling shoes is that you can't. You've got to design new shoes."**
>
> —STEPHEN MADER, EXECUTIVE HEADHUNTER

been all about athletes and top managers who compete like athletes. "Nike's early management meetings," reports *Fortune's* Daniel Roth, "were rowdy, drunken affairs. When fights broke out . . . Knight would rarely interrupt. He liked to see the passion." Today, the atmosphere at Nike is still intense and competitive. Knight is still pro-passion and, according to Roth, still cries at athletic events.

Over the years, Nike insiders have invited a few outside superstars to join in their management games, but for the most part, the company's managerial talent has always been homegrown. The promote-from-within mentality, combined with a strong cross-training program for managers, lends itself to the kind of internal

© BEN STECHSCHULTE 2005

Nike makes frequent use of teams to design new products and develop new marketing campaigns. NBA star Vince Carter is shown here working with a team of three Nike designers to develop a new basketball shoe design.

cohesiveness that Knight and Nike like. Because new executives broaden their experience by rotating through various departments, they develop connections with several senior people in the company, and Nike's matrix organization means that they're working with several ranking managers at any given time. One result of this approach to managerial indoctrination has been the development of a culture that some observers regard as a little too insular. "People who don't get the culture," advises Don Murray, a management consultant who's worked closely with Knight and Nike for many years, "don't stick around very long. They know they don't fit. That's it."

As for Knight personally, his approach has always been to hire bright, ambitious people who love sports and then give them a lot of freedom. According to insiders, he actually does and says very little, apparently preferring his executives to interpret his silences. According to company lore, Knight's instructions to one top manager who'd been tapped to start a new division consisted of the admonition "Sell shoes." "He's [not] likely to sit down and break it down for you," says former Nike executive Liz Dolan. "He believes you can figure it out." She clarifies things by adding, "He focuses more on talking to you one-on-one to get the best out of you." A number of insiders say that they look upon Knight as an inspiration, visionary, and father figure, but others report that he takes very few meetings and pays very little attention to details. He's not inclined to take stands, usually falling back on the mantra "I reserve the right to change my mind tomorrow," and he's happy to let his executives make their own decisions. "It's been 40 years that the company has grown around my idiosyncrasies," says Knight. "They don't even know that they're idiosyncrasies anymore, and of course neither do I."

And Bill Perez? He was shy and introspective (ironically, a lot like Knight), but even though he was a novice in the athletic wear and equipment industry, his experience at a giant consumer products company with diverse product lines promised to be a significant asset at Nike, which was in the process of expanding its offerings in both sports gear and apparel. Having overseen numerous acquisitions at S.C. Johnson, Perez also seemed well equipped to help Nike grow. "There will be a little bit of a bumpy period," Knight acknowledged at the time of the transition, but "I'm committed to making it work."

Unfortunately, Perez apparently ruffled feathers almost from day 1. "[He] started asking questions of 20- to 30-year veterans that [had] never been asked before," says one executive. He also irked marketing executives by questioning award-winning ads and adopting an unfamiliar approach to evaluating campaigns. "He didn't have an intuitive sense of Nike as a brand," complained one marketing manager. "He relied more on the spreadsheet, analytical approach as opposed to having a good creative marketing sense." Before long, Perez had butted heads with numerous executives, including Mark Parker and Charlie Denson, two Nike lifers who'd competed for the CEO spot before Knight decided to go with Perez.

According to Perez, Nike insiders were unreasonably resistant to change, and Knight, he adds, complicated matters by interfering with his efforts to do his job. "From virtually the day I arrived," he recalls, "Phil was as engaged in the company as he ever was. He was talking to my direct reports. It was confusing for the people and frustrating for me." Knight responded by blaming Perez for his inability to work with Nike veterans. "I think the failure to . . . get his arms around this company and this industry," he said, "led to confusion on behalf of the management team." He also cited cultural incompatibility: "Basically," Knight told analysts and journalists, "the distance between the company Bill managed in the packaged-goods business and Nike and the kind of new athletic-equipment business was too great. The cultural leap," he concluded, "was really too great."

When the dust had cleared, Parker and Denson had been anointed president and CEO, respectively. Today, Parker holds both jobs while Knight, now 71, continues to serve as chairman of the board. Many outside observers remain critical of Knight and the Nike board, particularly for perpetuating an insular culture that's apparently as inimical to fresh blood as it ever was. "It's almost like a death wish, coming into that company from outside," says Stephanie Joseph, an expert on corporate boards. Many observers also continue to fault the board of directors for being unable to envision the company without its founder and to establish a firm plan of succession. Says Stephen Mader, an executive headhunter who believes that Nike needs not only better succession planning but also an infusion of new ideas, "The message about filling shoes is that you can't. You've got to design new shoes."[1]

Under Phil Knight, Nike established a culture in which teamwork flourished and profits flowed. But when it came time (or so it seemed) to introduce some fresh blood and new ideas, the culture that had fostered such success produced interpersonal and intergroup conflict. This chapter is about the processes that lead to and follow from successes and problems like those experienced at Nike. In our last chapter, we established the interpersonal nature of organizations. We extend that discussion here by first introducing basic concepts of group and team dynamics. Subsequent sections explain the characteristics of groups and teams in organizations. We then describe interpersonal and intergroup conflict. Finally, we conclude with a discussion of how conflict can be managed.

GROUPS AND TEAMS IN ORGANIZATIONS

Groups are a ubiquitous part of organizational life. They are the basis for much of the work that gets done, and they evolve both inside and outside the normal structural boundaries of the organization. We will define a **group** as two or more people who interact regularly to accomplish a common purpose or goal.[2] The purpose of a group or team may range from preparing a new advertising campaign, to informally sharing information, to making important decisions, to fulfilling social needs.

Types of Groups and Teams

In general, three basic kinds of groups are found in organizations—functional groups, informal or interest groups, and task groups and teams.[3] These are illustrated in Figure 15.1.

Functional Groups A **functional group** is a permanent group created by the organization to accomplish a number of organizational purposes with an unspecified time horizon. The advertising department at Target, the management department at the University of North Texas, and the nursing staff at the Mayo Clinic are functional groups. The advertising department at Target, for example, seeks to plan effective advertising campaigns, increase sales, run in-store promotions, and develop a unique identity for the company. It is assumed that the functional group will remain in existence after it attains its current objectives—those objectives will be replaced by new ones.

group
Consists of two or more people who interact regularly to accomplish a common purpose or goal

functional group
A permanent group created by the organization to accomplish a number of organizational purposes with an unspecified time horizon

informal or interest group
Created by its members for purposes that may or may not be relevant to those of the organization

Informal or Interest Groups An **informal or interest group** is created by its own members for purposes that may or may not be relevant to organizational goals. It also has an unspecified time horizon. A group of employees who lunch together every day may be discussing productivity, money embezzling, or local politics and sports.[4] As long as the group members enjoy eating together, they will probably continue to do so. When lunches cease to be pleasant, they will seek other company or a different activity.

Informal groups can be a powerful force that managers cannot ignore.[5] One writer described how a group of employees at a furniture factory subverted their boss's efforts to increase production. They tacitly agreed to produce a reasonable amount of work but not to work too hard. One man kept a stockpile of completed work hidden as a backup in case he got too far behind. In another example, auto workers described how they left out gaskets and seals and put soft-drink bottles inside doors.[6] Of course, informal groups can also be a positive force, as demonstrated when Southwest Airlines employees worked

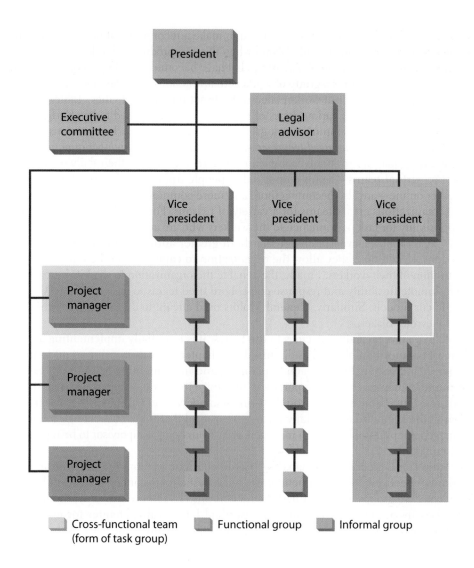

President		
Executive committee	Legal advisor	
Vice president	Vice president	Vice president
Project manager		
Project manager		
Project manager		

Cross-functional team (form of task group)   Functional group   Informal group

together to buy a new motorcycle for Herb Kelleher, the company's CEO at the time, to show their support and gratitude for his excellent leadership.

In recent years the Internet has served as a platform for the emergence of more and different kinds of informal or interest groups. Just as one example, Yahoo! includes a wide array of interest groups that bring together people with common interests. And increasingly, workers who lose their jobs as a result of layoffs are banding together electronically to offer moral support to one another and to facilitate networking as they all look for new jobs.[7]

Task Groups A task group is a group created by the organization to accomplish a relatively narrow range of purposes within a stated or implied time horizon. Most committees and task forces are task groups. The organization specifies group membership and assigns a relatively narrow set of goals, such as developing a new product or evaluating a proposed grievance procedure. The time horizon for accomplishing these purposes is

task group
A group created by the organization to accomplish a relatively narrow range of purposes within a stated or implied time horizon

either specified (a committee may be asked to make a recommendation within 60 days) or implied (the project team will disband when the new product is developed).

Teams are a special form of task group that have become increasingly popular.[8] In the sense used here, a **team** is a group of workers that functions as a unit, often with little or no supervision, to carry out work-related tasks, functions, and activities. Table 15.1 lists and defines some of the various types of teams that are being used today. Earlier forms of teams included autonomous work groups and quality circles. Today, teams are also sometimes called *self-managed teams, cross-functional teams*, or *high-performance teams*. Many firms today are routinely using teams to carry out most of their daily operations.[9] Further, **virtual teams**—teams comprised of people from remote work sites who work together online—are also becoming more and more common.[10]

Organizations create teams for a variety of reasons. For one thing, they give more responsibility for task performance to the workers who are actually performing the tasks. They also empower workers by giving them greater authority and decision-making freedom. In addition, they allow the organization to capitalize on the knowledge and motivation of their workers. Finally, they enable the organization to shed its bureaucracy and promote flexibility and responsiveness. Ford used teams to design its new Mustang and Focus models. Similarly, General Motors used a team to develop its new model of the Chevrolet Blazer.

When an organization decides to use teams, it is essentially implementing a major form of organization change, as discussed in Chapter 7. Thus it is important to follow a logical and systematic approach to planning and implementing teams in an existing organization design. It is also important to recognize that resistance may be encountered. This resistance is most likely from first-line managers, who will be giving up much of their authority to the team. Many organizations find that they must change the whole management philosophy of such managers away from being a supervisor to being a coach or facilitator.[11]

After teams are in place, managers should continue to monitor their contributions and how effectively they are functioning. In the best circumstances, teams will become very cohesive groups with high performance norms. To achieve this state, the manager can use any or all of the techniques described later in this chapter for enhancing cohesiveness. If implemented properly, and with the support of the workers themselves,

team
A group of workers that functions as a unit, often with little or no supervision, to carry out work-related tasks, functions, and activities

virtual teams
Teams comprised of people from remote work sites who work together online

Table 15.1 Types of Teams

Problem-solving team	Most popular type of team; comprises knowledge workers who gather to solve a specific problem and then disband.
Management team	Consists mainly of managers from various functions like sales and production; coordinates work among other teams.
Work team	An increasingly popular type of team; work teams are responsible for the daily work of the organization; when empowered, they are self-managed teams.
Virtual team	A new type of work team that interacts by computer; members enter and leave the network as needed and may take turns serving as leader.
Quality circle	Declining in popularity; quality circles, comprising workers and supervisors, meet intermittently to discuss workplace problems.

Source: From *Fortune*, September 5, 1994. Copyright 1994 Time Inc. All rights reserved.

performance norms will likely be relatively high. In other words, if the change is properly implemented, the team participants will understand the value and potential of teams and the rewards they may expect to get as a result of their contributions. On the other hand, poorly designed and implemented teams will do a less effective job and may detract from organizational effectiveness.[12]

Why People Join Groups and Teams

People join groups and teams for a variety of reasons. They join functional groups simply by virtue of joining organizations. People accept employment to earn money or practice their chosen professions. Once inside the organization, they are assigned to jobs and roles and thus become members of functional groups. People in existing functional groups are told, are asked, or volunteer to serve on committees, task forces, and teams. People join informal or interest groups for a variety of reasons, most of which are quite complex.[13] Indeed, the need to be a team player has grown so strong today that many organizations will actively resist hiring someone who does not want to work with others.[14]

Interpersonal Attraction One reason why people choose to form informal or interest groups is that they are attracted to one another. Many different factors contribute to interpersonal attraction. When people see a lot of each other, pure proximity increases the likelihood that interpersonal attraction will develop. Attraction is increased when people have similar attitudes, personalities, or economic standings.

Group Activities Individuals may also be motivated to join a group because the activities of the group appeal to them. Jogging, playing bridge, bowling, discussing poetry, playing war games, or flying model airplanes are all activities that some people enjoy. Many of them are more enjoyable to participate in as a member of a group, and most require more than one person. Many large firms such as Shell Oil and Apple Computer have a football, softball, or bowling league. A person may join a bowling team, not because of any particular attraction to other group members, but simply because being a member of the group allows that person to participate in a pleasant activity. Of course, if the group's level of interpersonal attraction is very low, a person may choose to forgo the activity rather than join the team.

ASIA IMAGES GROUP/GETTY IMAGES

People sometimes choose to join a group so they can engage in certain kinds of activities. Softball leagues, book clubs, and flying model airplane clubs are classic examples, while online fantasy football leagues and gaming groups are newer examples. These men all work for Shell Oil in Houston. They formed a bowling team so they could compete in the company league.

Group Goals The goals of a group may also motivate people to join. The Sierra Club, which is dedicated to environmental conservation, is a good example of this kind of interest group. Various fund-raising groups are another illustration. Members may or may not be personally attracted to the other fund-raisers, and they probably do not enjoy the activity of knocking on doors asking for money, but they join the group because they subscribe to its goal. Workers join unions such as the United Auto Workers because they support its goals.

Need Satisfaction Still another reason for joining a group is to satisfy the need for affiliation. New residents in a community may join the Newcomers Club partially as a way to meet new people and partially just to be around other people. Likewise, newly divorced people often join support groups as a way to have companionship.

Instrumental Benefits A final reason why people join groups is that membership is sometimes seen as instrumental in providing other benefits to the individual. For example, it is fairly common for college students entering their senior year to join several professional clubs or associations because listing such memberships on a résumé is thought to enhance the chances of getting a good job. Similarly, a manager might join a certain racquet club not because she is attracted to its members (although she might be) and not because of the opportunity to play tennis (although she may enjoy it). The club's goals are not relevant, and her affiliation needs may be satisfied in other ways. However, she may feel that being a member of this club will lead to important and useful business contacts. The racquet club membership is instrumental in establishing those contacts. Membership in civic groups such as the Junior League and Rotary may be solicited for similar reasons.

Stages of Group and Team Development

Imagine the differences between a collection of five people who have just been brought together to form a group or team and a group or team that has functioned like a well-oiled machine for years. Members of a new group or team are unfamiliar with how they will function together and are tentative in their interactions. In a group or team with considerable experience, members are familiar with one another's strengths and weaknesses and are more secure in their roles in the group. The former group or team is generally considered to be immature, the latter, mature. To progress from the immature phase to the mature phase, a group or team must go through certain stages of development, as shown in Figure 15.2.[15]

The first stage of development is called *forming*. The members of the group or team get acquainted and begin to test which interpersonal behaviors are acceptable and which are unacceptable to the other members. The members are very dependent on others at this point to provide cues about what is acceptable. The basic ground rules for the group or team are established, and a tentative group structure may emerge.[16] At Reebok, for example, a merchandising team was created to handle its sportswear business. The team leader and his members were barely acquainted and had to spend a few weeks getting to know one another.

The second stage of development, often slow to emerge, is *storming*. During this stage, there may be a general lack of unity and uneven interaction patterns. At the same time, some members of the group or team may begin to exert themselves to become recognized as the group leader or at least to play a major role in shaping the group's agenda. In Reebok's team, some members advocated a rapid expansion into the marketplace; others argued for a slower entry. The first faction won, with disastrous results. Because of the rush, product quality was poor and deliveries were late. As a result, the team leader was fired and a new manager placed in charge.

$\mathcal{F}igure\ 15.2$ Stages of Group Development

As groups mature, they tend to evolve through four distinct stages of development. Managers must understand that group members need time to become acquainted, accept one another, develop a group structure, and become comfortable with their roles in the group before they can begin to work directly to accomplish goals.

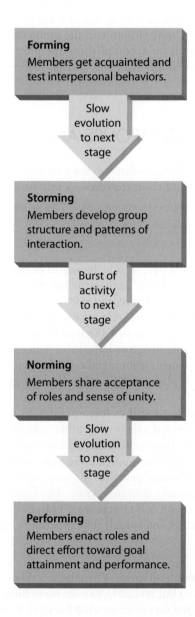

Forming
Members get acquainted and test interpersonal behaviors.

Slow evolution to next stage

Storming
Members develop group structure and patterns of interaction.

Burst of activity to next stage

Norming
Members share acceptance of roles and sense of unity.

Slow evolution to next stage

Performing
Members enact roles and direct effort toward goal attainment and performance.

The third stage of development, called *norming*, usually begins with a burst of activity. During this stage, each person begins to recognize and accept her or his role and to understand the roles of others. Members also begin to accept one another and to develop a sense of unity. There may also be temporary regressions to the previous stage. For example, the group or team might begin to accept one particular member as the leader. If this person later violates important norms or otherwise jeopardizes his or her claim to leadership, conflict might reemerge as the group rejects this leader and searches for another. Reebok's new leader transferred several people away from the team and set up a new system and structure for managing things. The remaining employees accepted his new approach and settled into doing their jobs.

Performing, the final stage of group or team development, is also slow to develop. At this stage, the team really begins to focus on the problem at hand. The members enact the roles they have accepted, interaction occurs, and the efforts of the group are directed toward goal attainment. The basic structure of the group or team is no longer an issue but has become a mechanism for accomplishing the purpose of the group. Reebok's sportswear business is now growing consistently and has successfully avoided the problems that plagued it at first.

CHARACTERISTICS OF GROUPS AND TEAMS

As groups and teams mature and pass through the four basic stages of development, they begin to take on four important characteristics—a role structure, norms, cohesiveness, and informal leadership.[17]

Role Structures

Each individual in a team has a part, or **role**, to play in helping the group reach its goals. Some people are leaders, some do the work, some interface with other teams, and so on. Indeed, a person may take on a *task specialist role* (concentrating on getting the group's task accomplished) or a *socioemotional role* (providing social and emotional support to others on the team). A few people, usually the leaders, perform both roles; a few others may do neither. The group's **role structure** is the set of defined roles and interrelationships among those roles that the group or team members define and accept. Each of us belongs to many groups and therefore plays multiple roles—in work groups, classes, families, and social organizations.[18]

Role structures emerge as a result of role episodes, as shown in Figure 15.3. The process begins with the expected role—what other members of the team expect the individual to do. The expected role gets translated into the sent role—the messages and cues that team members use to communicate the expected role to the individual. The perceived role is what the individual perceives the sent role to mean. Finally, the enacted role is what the individual actually does in the role. The enacted role, in turn, influences future expectations of the team. Of course, role episodes seldom unfold this easily. When major disruptions occur, individuals may experience role ambiguity, conflict, or overload.[19]

Role Ambiguity Role ambiguity arises when the sent role is unclear. If your instructor tells you to write a term paper but refuses to provide more information, you will probably experience role ambiguity. You do not know what the topic is, how long the paper should be, what format to use, or when the paper is due. In work settings, role ambiguity can stem from poor job descriptions, vague instructions from a supervisor, or unclear cues from coworkers. The result is likely to be a subordinate who does not know what to do. Role ambiguity can be a significant problem for both the individual who must contend with it and the organization that expects the employee to perform.

role
The parts individuals play in groups in helping the group reach its goals

role structure
The set of defined roles and interrelationships among those roles that the group members define and accept

role ambiguity
Arises when the sent role is unclear and the individual does not know what is expected of him or her

Figure 15.3   The Development of a Role

Roles and role structures within a group generally evolve through a series of role episodes. The first two stages of role development are group processes, as the group members let individuals know what is expected of them. The other two parts are individual processes, as the new group members perceive and enact their roles.

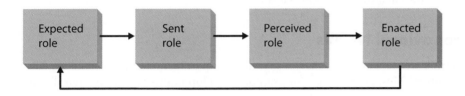

Role Conflict **Role conflict** occurs when the messages and cues composing the sent role are clear but contradictory or mutually exclusive.[20] One common form is *interrole conflict*—conflict between roles. For example, if a person's boss says that one must work overtime and on weekends to get ahead, and the same person's coworkers say that you can succeed without working nights and weekends, conflict may result. In a matrix organization, interrole conflict often arises between the roles one plays in different teams as well as between team roles and one's permanent role in a functional group.

Intrarole conflict may occur when the person gets conflicting demands from different sources within the context of the same role. A manager's boss may tell the manager that she needs to put more pressure on subordinates to follow new work rules. At the same time, her subordinates may indicate that they expect her to get the rules changed. Thus the cues are in conflict, and the manager may be unsure about which course to follow. *Intrasender conflict* occurs when a single source sends clear but contradictory messages. This might arise if the boss says one morning that there can be no more overtime for the next month but after lunch tells someone to work late that same evening. *Person–role conflict* results from a discrepancy between the role requirements and the individual's personal values, attitudes, and needs. If a person is told to do something unethical or illegal, or if the work is distasteful (for example, firing a close friend), person–role conflict is likely. Role conflict of all varieties is of particular concern to managers. Research has shown that conflict may occur in a variety of situations and lead to a variety of adverse consequences, including stress, poor performance, and rapid turnover.

Role Overload A final consequence of a weak role structure is **role overload**, which occurs when expectations for the role exceed the individual's capabilities. When a manager gives an employee several major assignments at once, while increasing the person's regular workload, the employee will probably experience role overload. Role overload may also result when an individual takes on too many roles at one time. For example, a person trying to work extra hard at work, run for election to the school board, serve on a committee in church, coach Little League baseball, maintain an active exercise program, and be a contributing member to her or his family will probably encounter role overload.

In a functional group or team, the manager can take steps to avoid role ambiguity, conflict, and overload. Having clear and reasonable expectations and sending clear and straightforward cues go a long way toward eliminating role ambiguity. Consistent

role conflict
Occurs when the messages and cues composing the sent role are clear but contradictory or mutually exclusive

role overload
Occurs when expectations for the role exceed the individual's capabilities to perform

expectations that take into account the employee's other roles and personal value system may minimize role conflict. Role overload can be avoided simply by recognizing the individual's capabilities and limits. In friendship and interest groups, role structures are likely to be less formal; hence, the possibility of role ambiguity, conflict, or overload may not be so great. However, if one or more of these problems does occur, they may be difficult to handle. Because roles in friendship and interest groups are less likely to be partially defined by a formal authority structure or written job descriptions, the individual cannot turn to those sources to clarify a role.

Behavioral Norms

Norms are standards of behavior that the group or team accepts for and expects of its members. Most committees, for example, develop norms governing their discussions. A person who talks too much is perceived as doing so to make a good impression or to get his or her own way. Other members may not talk much to this person, may not sit nearby, may glare at the person, and may otherwise "punish" the individual for violating the norm. Norms, then, define the boundaries between acceptable and unacceptable behavior.[21] Some groups develop norms that limit the upper bounds of behavior to "make life easier" for the group—for example, do not make more than two comments in a committee discussion or do not produce any more than you have to. In general, these norms are counterproductive. Other groups may develop norms that limit the lower bounds of behavior—for example, do not come to meetings unless you have read the reports to be discussed or produce as much as you can. These norms tend to reflect motivation, commitment, and high performance. Managers can sometimes use norms for the betterment of the organization. For example, Kodak has successfully used group norms to reduce injuries in some of its plants.[22] The *Ethics in Action* box goes on campus to investigate areas in which prevailing norms can affect the ethical behavior of people who are nominally working in a team-oriented environment.

norms
Standards of behavior that the group accepts for and expects of its members

ETHICS IN ACTION

How to Become a Master of Business Ambition

About 300 universities in the United States offer master of business administration (MBA) degrees. All of these institutions, which are usually called *B-schools*, emphasize the same sets of skills: business skills; quantitative, or "hard," skills; and people, or "soft," skills. This last category usually includes some study of such topics as leadership, ethics, and teamwork. After all, business today relies increasingly on groups and teams, and it would seem obvious that aspiring business leaders should learn to be team players.

Ironically, however, the educational environment in which such "people" skills are taught—the environment of B-schools—is highly competitive. According to some critics, it's actually a good environment in which to learn—and get rewarded for—various forms of self-serving and unethical behavior. Among the leaders of tomorrow, problematic behavior includes refusing to share notes, removing required readings from the library, and even spreading false rumors. One resourceful MBA student admits to a clever ruse for gaining a pre-exam tactical advantage over her classmates: "Before an exam," she explains, "I would ask [fellow] students a nonsense question like, 'What's the Dr. Seuss Method of stock valuation?' They spent their last minutes in a panic, leafing frantically through notes, while I remained confident."

Kerry Patterson, a consultant on organizational performance and leadership and an MBA professor at Brigham Young University, blames the organizational culture that predominates at most B-schools. "Teams of students are brutal to each other," he reports, adding that "calling a group of students a team doesn't make them one." Patterson is convinced that the typical university environment itself discourages team-oriented and other collaborative practices. As a rule, he points out, "professors work in a system that discourages collaboration and teamwork. . . . University faculties are just a little more cohesive than six people who just met in an elevator."

To reduce the temptation to resort to ethically questionable behavior, some B-schools don't disclose grades. Others, like Harvard, disclose only categories of achievement, such as students' standing in the top 20 percent, middle 70 percent,

and bottom 10 percent of a class. The idea is that by reducing grade pressure, schools can encourage students' willingness to practice teamwork and other collaborative behavior. Many observers and proponents of more effective training in collaborative behavior believe that such approaches to grade reporting do in fact reduce overly competitive behavior, but as yet there's no factual evidence to back them up.

Meanwhile, some educators believe that nongraded courses encourage dependence on others and diminish academic rigor. In addition, a small but growing group of experts worries that an overemphasis on teamwork may teach students to seek social acceptance and popularity over honesty and effectiveness. Some are even inclined to agree with football coach Steve Spurrier that "if people like you too much, it's probably because they're beating you."

References: Grant Allen, "Learning to Juggle," *BusinessWeek*, February 24, 2006, www.businessweek.com on May 29, 2009; Jeffrey Gangemi, "Harvard: No More Grade Secrets," *BusinessWeek*, December 16, 2005, www.businessweek.com on May 29, 2009; Gangemi, "Taking on the 'Cutthroat Culture' of B-School," *BusinessWeek*, May 17, 2006, www.businessweek.com on May 29, 2009; and Jeffrey Pfeffer, "You Don't Have to Be Well Liked to Succeed," *Business 2.0*, May 16, 2006, http://cnnmoney.com on May 29, 2009.

Norm Generalization The norms of one group cannot always be generalized to another group. Some academic departments, for example, have a norm that suggests that faculty members dress up on teaching days. People who fail to observe this norm are "punished" by sarcastic remarks or even formal reprimands. In other departments, the norm may be casual clothes, and the person unfortunate enough to wear dress clothes may be punished just as vehemently. Even within the same work area, similar groups or teams can develop different norms. One team may strive always to produce above its assigned quota; another may maintain productivity just below its quota. The norm of one team may be to be friendly and cordial to its supervisor; that of another team may be to remain aloof and distant. Some differences are due primarily to the composition of the teams.

Norm Variation In some cases, there can also be norm variation within a group or team. A common norm is that the least senior member of a group is expected to perform unpleasant or trivial tasks for the rest of the group. These tasks might be to wait on customers who are known to be small tippers (in a restaurant), to deal with complaining customers (in a department store), or to handle the low-commission line of merchandise (in a sales department). Another example is when certain individuals, especially informal leaders, may violate some norms. If the team is going to meet at 8:00 A.M., anyone arriving late will be chastised for holding things up. Occasionally, however, the informal leader may arrive a few minutes late. As long as this does not happen too often, the group probably will not do anything about it.

Norm Conformity Four sets of factors contribute to norm conformity. First, factors associated with the group are important. For example, some groups or teams may exert more pressure for conformity than others. Second, the initial stimulus that prompts behavior can affect conformity. The more ambiguous the stimulus (for example, news that the team is going to be transferred to a new unit), the more pressure there is to conform. Third, individual traits determine the individual's propensity to conform (for example, more intelligent people are often less susceptible to pressure to conform). Finally, situational factors, such as team size and unanimity, influence conformity. As an individual learns the group's norms, he can do several different things. The most obvious is to adopt the norms. For example, the new male professor who notices that all the other men in the department dress up to teach can also start wearing a suit. A variation is to try to obey the "spirit" of the norm while retaining individuality. The professor may recognize that the norm is actually to wear a tie; thus he might succeed by wearing a tie with his sport shirt, jeans, and sneakers.

The individual may also ignore the norm. When a person does not conform, several things can happen. At first the group may increase its communication with the deviant individual to try to bring her back in line. If this does not work, communication may decline. Over time, the group may begin to exclude the individual from its activities and, in effect, ostracize the person. Finally, we need to briefly consider another aspect of norm conformity—socialization. **Socialization** is generalized norm conformity that occurs as a person makes the transition from being an outsider to being an insider. A newcomer to an organization, for example, gradually begins to learn about such norms as dress, working hours, and interpersonal relations. As the newcomer adopts these norms, she is being socialized into the organizational culture. Some organizations, such as Texas Instruments, work to actively manage the socialization process; others leave it to happenstance.

Cohesiveness A third important team characteristic is cohesiveness. **Cohesiveness** is the extent to which members are loyal and committed to the group. In a highly cohesive team, the members work well together, support and trust one another, and are generally effective at achieving their chosen goals.[23] In contrast, a team that lacks cohesiveness is not very coordinated, its members do not necessarily support one another fully, and it may have a difficult time reaching goals. Of particular interest are the factors that increase and reduce cohesiveness and the consequences of team cohesiveness. These are listed in Table 15.2.

Several different factors can influence the cohesiveness of a group. For example, a manager can establish intergroup competition, assign compatible members to the group,

socialization
Generalized norm conformity that occurs as a person makes the transition from being an outsider to being an insider in the organization

cohesiveness
The extent to which members are loyal and committed to the group; the degree of mutual attractiveness within the group

Table 15.2
Factors That Influence Group Cohesiveness

Factors That Increase Cohesiveness	Factors That Reduce Cohesiveness
Intergroup competition	Group size
Personal attraction	Disagreement on goals
Favorable evaluation	Intragroup competition
Agreement on goals	Domination
Interaction	Unpleasant experiences

create opportunities for success, establish acceptable goals, and foster interaction to increase cohesiveness. Other factors can be used to decrease cohesiveness.

Factors That Increase Cohesiveness Five factors can increase the level of cohesiveness in a group or team. One of the strongest is intergroup competition. When two or more groups are in direct competition (for example, three sales groups competing for top sales honors or two football teams competing for a conference championship), each group is likely to become more cohesive. Second, just as personal attraction plays a role in causing a group to form, so, too, does attraction seem to enhance cohesiveness. Third, favorable evaluation of the entire group by outsiders can increase cohesiveness. Thus a group's winning a sales contest or a conference title or receiving recognition and praise from a superior tends to increase cohesiveness.

Similarly, if all the members of the group or team agree on their goals, cohesiveness is likely to increase.[24] And the more frequently members of the group interact with one another, the more likely the group is to become cohesive. A manager who wants to foster a high level of cohesiveness in a team might do well to establish some form of intergroup competition, assign members to the group who are likely to be attracted to one another, provide opportunities for success, establish goals that all members are likely to accept, and allow ample opportunities for interaction.[25]

Factors That Reduce Cohesiveness There are also five factors that are known to reduce team cohesiveness. First of all, cohesiveness tends to decline as a group increases in size. Second, when members of a team disagree on what the goals of the group should be, cohesiveness may decrease. For example, when some members believe the group should maximize output and others think output should be restricted, cohesiveness declines. Third, intragroup competition reduces cohesiveness. When members are competing among themselves, they focus more on their own actions and behaviors than on those of the group.

Fourth, domination by one or more persons in the group or team may cause overall cohesiveness to decline. Other members may feel that they are not being given an opportunity to interact and contribute, and they may become less attracted to the group as a consequence. Finally, unpleasant experiences that result from group membership may reduce cohesiveness. A sales group that comes in last in a sales contest, an athletic team that sustains a long losing streak, and a work group reprimanded for poor-quality work may all become less cohesive as a result of their unpleasant experiences.

Consequences of Cohesiveness In general, as teams become more cohesive, their members tend to interact more frequently, conform more to norms, and become more satisfied with the team. Cohesiveness may also influence team performance. However, performance is also influenced by the team's performance norms. Figure 15.4 shows how cohesiveness and performance norms interact to help shape team performance.

When both cohesiveness and performance norms are high, high performance should result because the team wants to perform at a high level (norms) and its members are working together toward that end (cohesiveness). When norms are high and cohesiveness is low, performance will be moderate. Although the team wants to perform at a high level, its members are not necessarily working well together. When norms are low, performance will be low, regardless of whether group cohesiveness is high or low. The least desirable situation occurs when low performance norms are combined with high cohesiveness. In this case, all team members embrace the standard of restricting performance (owing to the low performance norm), and the group is united in its efforts to maintain that standard

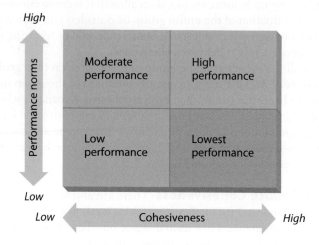

Figure 15.4 The Interaction Between Cohesiveness and Performance Norms

Group cohesiveness and performance norms interact to determine group performance. From the manager's perspective, high cohesiveness combined with high performance norms is the best situation, and high cohesiveness with low performance norms is the worst situation. Managers who can influence the level of cohesiveness and performance norms can greatly improve the effectiveness of a work group.

(owing to the high cohesiveness). If cohesiveness were low, the manager might be able to raise performance norms by establishing high goals and rewarding goal attainment or by bringing in new group members who are high performers. But a highly cohesive group is likely to resist these interventions.[26]

Formal and Informal Leadership

Most functional groups and teams have a formal leader—that is, one appointed by the organization or chosen or elected by the members of the group. Because friendship and interest groups are formed by the members themselves, however, any formal leader must be elected or designated by the members. Although some groups do designate such a leader (a softball team may elect a captain, for example), many do not. Moreover, even when a formal leader is designated, the group or team may also look to others for leadership. An **informal leader** is a person who engages in leadership activities but whose right to do so has not been formally recognized. The formal and the informal leader in any group or team may be the same person, or they may be different people. We noted earlier the distinction between the task specialist and socioemotional roles within groups. An informal leader is likely to be a person capable of carrying out both roles effectively. If the formal leader can fulfill one role but not the other, an informal leader often emerges to supplement the formal leader's functions. If the formal leader can fill neither role, one or more informal leaders may emerge to carry out both sets of functions.

Is informal leadership desirable? In many cases informal leaders are quite powerful because they draw from referent or expert power. When they are working in the best interests of the organization, they can be a tremendous asset. Notable athletes like

informal leader
A person who engages in leadership activities but whose right to do so has not been formally recognized by the organization or group

Ben Roethlisberger and Mia Hamm are classic examples of informal leaders. However, when informal leaders work counter to the goals of the organization, they can cause significant difficulties. Such leaders may lower performance norms, instigate walkouts or wildcat strikes, or otherwise disrupt the organization.

INTERPERSONAL AND INTERGROUP CONFLICT

Of course, when people work together in an organization, things do not always go smoothly. Indeed, conflict is an inevitable element of interpersonal relationships in organizations. In this section, we look at how conflict affects overall performance. We also explore the causes of conflict between individuals, between groups, and between an organization and its environment.

The Nature of Conflict

Conflict is a disagreement among two or more individuals, groups, or organizations. This disagreement may be relatively superficial or very strong. It may be short-lived or exist for months or even years, and it may be work related or personal.

© US AIR FORCE – DIGITAL VERSION c/SCIENCE FACTION/CORBIS

Conflict is inevitable in any organization. In some cases, such as the U.S. Congress, conflict plays a major role in how the organization functions. It is common, for example, for different factions within Congress to bicker over defense spending. A coalition of senators, for instance, recently blocked additional funding to build more F-22 Raptor fighter jets. Advocates for the jet argue that it is the most sophisticated and advanced jet fighter in the world and that more are needed. But critics argue that the F-22 was designed for a different kind of defense system than is currently being developed and so additional planes would be a waste of money.

Conflict may manifest itself in a variety of ways. People may compete with one another, glare at one another, shout, or withdraw. Groups may band together to protect popular members or oust unpopular members. Organizations may seek legal remedies.

Most people assume that conflict is something to be avoided because it connotes antagonism, hostility, unpleasantness, and dissension. Indeed, managers and management theorists have traditionally viewed conflict as a problem to be avoided.[27] In recent years, however, we have come to recognize that, although conflict can be a major problem, certain kinds of conflict may also be beneficial.[28] For example, when two members of a site selection committee disagree over the best location for a new plant, each may be forced to more thoroughly study and defend his or her preferred alternative. As a result of more systematic analysis and discussion, the committee may make a better decision and be better prepared to justify it to others than if everyone had agreed from the outset and accepted an alternative that was perhaps less well analyzed.

As long as conflict is being handled in a cordial and constructive manner, it is probably serving a useful purpose in the organization. On the other hand, when working relationships are being disrupted and the conflict has reached destructive levels, it has likely become dysfunctional and needs to be addressed.[29] We discuss ways of dealing with such conflict later in this chapter.

Figure 15.5 depicts the general relationship between conflict and performance for a group or an organization. If there is absolutely no conflict in the group or organization, its members may become complacent and apathetic. As a result, group or organizational

conflict
A disagreement among two or more individuals or groups

Figure 15.5 The Nature of Organizational Conflict

Either too much or too little conflict can be dysfunctional for an organization. In either case, performance may be low. However, an optimal level of conflict that sparks motivation, creativity, innovation, and initiative can result in higher levels of performance.

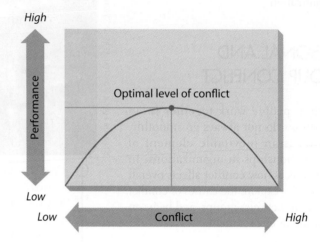

performance and innovation may begin to suffer. A moderate level of conflict among group or organizational members, on the other hand, can spark motivation, creativity, innovation, and initiative and raise performance. Too much conflict, though, can produce such undesirable results as hostility and lack of cooperation, which lower performance. The key for managers is to find and maintain the optimal amount of conflict that fosters performance. Of course, what constitutes optimal conflict varies with both the situation and the people involved.[30]

Causes of Conflict

Conflict may arise in both interpersonal and intergroup relationships. Occasionally conflict between individuals and groups may be caused by particular organizational strategies and practices. A third arena for conflict is between an organization and its environment.

Interpersonal Conflict Conflict between two or more individuals is almost certain to occur in any organization, given the great variety in perceptions, goals, attitudes, and so forth among its members. Bill Gates, founder and CEO of Microsoft, and Kazuhiko Nishi, a former business associate from Japan, once ended a lucrative long-term business relationship because of interpersonal conflict. Nishi accused Gates of becoming too political, while Gates charged that Nishi became too unpredictable and erratic in his behavior.[31]

A frequent source of interpersonal conflict in organizations is what many people call a *personality clash*—when two people distrust each other's motives, dislike each other, or for some other reason simply cannot get along.[32] Conflict may also arise between people who have different beliefs or perceptions about some aspect of their work or their organization. For example, one manager might want the organization to require that all employees use Microsoft Office software, to promote standardization. Another manager might believe that a variety of software packages should be allowed, in order to accommodate individuality.

Similarly, a male manager may disagree with his female colleague over whether the organization is guilty of discriminating against women in promotion decisions. Conflict can also result from excess competitiveness among individuals. Two people vying for the same job, for example, may resort to political behavior in an effort to gain an advantage. If either competitor sees the other's behavior as inappropriate, accusations are likely to result. Even after the "winner" of the job is determined, such conflict may continue to undermine interpersonal relationships, especially if the reasons given in selecting one candidate are ambiguous or open to alternative explanations. Robert Allen resigned as CEO of Delta Air Lines a few years ago because he disagreed with other key executives over how best to reduce the carrier's costs. After he began looking for a replacement for one of his rivals without the approval of the firm's board of directors, a conflict resulted and the ensuing controversy left him no choice but to leave.[33] Similar problems have plagued Boeing as its top executives have publicly disagreed over routine matters and sometimes gone to great lengths to make each other look bad.[34]

Intergroup Conflict Conflict between two or more organizational groups is also quite common. For example, the members of a firm's marketing group may disagree with the production group over product quality and delivery schedules. Two sales groups may disagree over how to meet sales goals, and two groups of managers may have different ideas about how best to allocate organizational resources.

Many intergroup conflicts arise more from organizational causes than from interpersonal causes. In Chapter 6, we described three forms of group interdependence— pooled, sequential, and reciprocal. Just as increased interdependence makes coordination more difficult, it increases the potential for conflict. For example, recall that in sequential interdependence, work is passed from one unit to another. Intergroup conflict may arise if the first group turns out too much work (the second group will fall behind), too little work (the second group will not meet its own goals), or poor-quality work.

At one JCPenney department store, conflict arose between stockroom employees and sales associates. The sales associates claimed that the stockroom employees were slow in delivering merchandise to the sales floor where it could be priced and shelved. The stockroom employees, in turn, claimed that the sales associates were not giving them enough lead time to get the merchandise delivered and failed to understand that they had additional duties besides carrying merchandise to the sales floor.

Just like people, different departments often have different goals. Further, these goals may often be incompatible. A marketing goal of maximizing sales, achieved partially by offering many products in a wide variety of sizes, shapes, colors, and models, probably conflicts with a production goal of minimizing costs, achieved partially by long production runs of a few items. Reebok recently confronted this very situation. One group of managers wanted to introduce a new sportswear line as quickly as possible, but other managers wanted to expand more deliberately and cautiously. Because the two groups were not able to reconcile their differences effectively, conflict arose between the two factions, which led to quality problems and delivery delays that plagued the firm for months.

Competition for scarce resources can also lead to intergroup conflict. Most organizations—especially universities, hospitals, government agencies, and businesses in depressed industries—have limited resources. In one New England town, for example, the public works department and the library battled over funds from a federal construction grant. The Buick, Pontiac, GMC, and Chevrolet divisions of General Motors frequently fought over the right to manufacture various new products developed by the company. This infighting was identified as one of many factors that led to GM's recent problems. As part of the solution, the Pontiac brand was eventually discontinued.

Conflict Between Organization and Environment Conflict that arises between one organization and another is called *interorganizational conflict*. A moderate amount of interorganizational conflict resulting from business competition is expected, of course, but sometimes conflict becomes more extreme. For example, the owners of Jordache Enterprises, Inc., and Guess?, Inc., battled in court for years over ownership of the Guess? label, allegations of design theft, and several other issues.[35] Similarly, General Motors and Volkswagen went to court to resolve a bitter conflict that spanned more than four years. It all started when a key GM executive, Jose Ignacio Lopez de Arriortua, left for a position at Volkswagen. GM claimed that he took with him key secrets that could benefit its German competitor. After the messy departure, dozens of charges and countercharges were made by the two firms, and only a court settlement was able to put the conflict to an end.[36]

Conflict can also arise between an organization and other elements of its environment. For example, an organization may conflict with a consumer group over claims it makes about its products. McDonald's faced this problem a few years ago when it published nutritional information about its products that omitted details about fat content. A manufacturer might conflict with a governmental agency such as the federal Occupational Safety and Health Administration (OSHA). For example, the firm's management may believe it is in compliance with OSHA regulations, whereas officials from the agency believe that the firm is not in compliance. Or a firm might conflict with a supplier over the quality of raw materials. The firm may think the supplier is providing inferior materials, while the supplier thinks the materials are adequate.

MANAGING CONFLICT IN ORGANIZATIONS

How do managers cope with all this potential conflict? Fortunately, as Table 15.3 shows, there are ways to stimulate conflict for constructive ends, to control conflict before it gets out of hand, and to resolve it if it does. We now look at ways of managing conflict.[37]

Table 15.3
Methods for Managing Conflict

Conflict is a powerful force in organizations and has both negative and positive consequences. Thus managers can draw on several different techniques to stimulate, control, or resolve and eliminate conflict, depending on their unique circumstances.

Stimulating Conflict
Increase competition among individuals and teams.
Hire outsiders to shake things up.
Change established procedures.

Controlling Conflict
Expand resource base.
Enhance coordination of interdependence.
Set superordinate goals.
Match personalities and work habits of employees.

Resolving and Eliminating Conflict
Avoid conflict.
Convince conflicting parties to compromise.
Bring conflicting parties together to confront and negotiate conflict.

Stimulating Conflict

In some situations, an organization may stimulate conflict by placing individual employees or groups in competitive situations. Managers can establish sales contests, incentive plans, bonuses, or other competitive stimuli to spark competition. As long as the ground rules are equitable and all participants perceive the contest as fair, the conflict created by the competition is likely to be constructive because each participant will work hard to win (thereby enhancing some aspect of organizational performance).

Another useful method for stimulating conflict is to bring in one or more outsiders who will shake things up and present a new perspective on organizational practices. Outsiders may be new employees, current employees assigned to an existing work group, or consultants or advisors hired on a temporary basis. Of course, this action can also provoke resentment from insiders who feel they were qualified for the position. The Beecham Group, a British company, once hired an executive from the United States for its CEO position, expressly to change how the company did business. His arrival brought with it new ways of doing things and a new enthusiasm for competitiveness. Unfortunately, some valued employees also chose to leave Beecham because they resented some of the changes that were made.

Changing established procedures, especially procedures that have outlived their usefulness, can also stimulate conflict. Such actions cause people to reassess how they perform their jobs and whether they perform it correctly. For example, one university president announced that all vacant staff positions could be filled only after written justification had received his approval. Conflict arose between the president and the department heads, who felt they were having to do more paperwork than was necessary. Most requests were approved, but because department heads now had to think through their staffing needs, a few unnecessary positions were appropriately eliminated.

Controlling Conflict

One method of controlling conflict is to expand the resource base. Suppose a top manager receives two budget requests for $100,000 each. If she has only $180,000 to distribute, the stage is set for conflict because each group will believe its proposal is worth funding and will be unhappy if it is not fully funded. If both proposals are indeed worthwhile, it may be possible for the manager to come up with the extra $20,000 from some other source and thereby avoid difficulty.

As noted earlier, pooled, sequential, and reciprocal interdependence can all result in conflict. If managers use an appropriate technique for enhancing coordination, they can reduce the probability that conflict will arise. Techniques for coordination (described in Chapter 6) include making use of the managerial hierarchy, relying on rules and procedures, enlisting liaison people, forming task forces, and integrating departments. At the JCPenney store mentioned earlier, the conflict was addressed by providing salespeople with clearer forms on which to specify the merchandise they needed and in what sequence. If one coordination technique does not have the desired effect, a manager might shift to another one.

Competing goals can also be a source of conflict among individuals and groups. Managers can sometimes focus employee attention on higher-level, or superordinate, goals as a way of eliminating lower-level conflict. When labor unions such as the United Auto Workers make wage concessions to ensure survival of the automobile industry, they are responding to a superordinate goal. Their immediate goal may be higher wages for members, but they realize that, without the automobile industry, their members would not even have jobs.

Finally, managers should try to match the personalities and work habits of employees so as to avoid conflict between individuals. For instance, two valuable subordinates, one a chain smoker and the other a vehement antismoker, probably should not be required to work together in an enclosed space. If conflict does arise between incompatible individuals, a manager might seek an equitable transfer for one or both of them to other units.

Resolving and Eliminating Conflict

Despite everyone's best intentions, conflict sometimes flares up. If it is disrupting the workplace, creating too much hostility and tension, or otherwise harming the organization, attempts must be made to resolve it.[38] Some managers who are uncomfortable dealing with conflict choose to avoid the conflict and hope it will go away. Avoidance may sometimes be effective in the short run for some kinds of interpersonal disagreements, but it does little to resolve long-run or chronic conflicts. Even more unadvisable, though, is "smoothing"—minimizing the conflict and telling everyone that things will "get better." Often, though, avoiding conflict may only make it worse as people continue to brood over it.

COMSTOCK/COMSTOCK IMAGES/JUPITER IMAGES

Alternative dispute resolution has become a popular method for resolving and eliminating conflict in organizations. These managers, for example, are representatives from two large businesses. One of these businesses has accused the other of violating a contract. The firms agreed that before they started legal action representatives from each firm would sit down together and attempt to hammer out their differences. Of course, if this step fails then it is likely that attorneys would then get involved and the dispute settled in court.

Compromise is striking a middle-range position between two extremes. This approach can work if it is used with care, but in most compromise situations, someone wins and someone loses. Budget problems are one of the few areas amenable to compromise because of their objective nature. Assume, for example, that additional resources are not available to the manager mentioned earlier. She has $180,000 to divide, and each of two groups claims to need $100,000. If the manager believes that both projects warrant funding, she can allocate $90,000 to each. The fact that the two groups have at least been treated equally may minimize the potential conflict.

The confrontational approach to conflict resolution—also called *interpersonal problem solving*—consists of bringing the parties together to confront the conflict. The parties discuss the nature of their conflict and attempt to reach an agreement or a solution. Confrontation requires a reasonable degree of maturity on the part of the participants, and the manager must structure the situation carefully. If handled well, this approach can be an effective means of resolving conflict. In recent years, many organizations have experimented with a technique called *alternative dispute resolution*, using a team of employees to arbitrate conflict in this way.[39] Negotiation, a closely related method, is discussed in our final section.

Regardless of the approach, organizations and their managers should realize that conflict must be addressed if it is to serve constructive purposes and be prevented from bringing about destructive consequences. Conflict is inevitable in organizations, but its negative effects can be constrained with proper attention. For example, Union Carbide sent 200 of its managers to a three-day workshop on conflict management. The managers engaged in a variety of exercises and discussions to learn with whom they were most likely to come in conflict and how they should try to resolve it. As a result, managers at the firm later reported that hostility and resentment in the organization had been greatly diminished and that people in the firm reported more pleasant working relationships.[40]

Negotiation Negotiation is the process in which two or more parties (people or groups) reach agreement on an issue even though they have different preferences regarding that issue. In its simplest form, the parties involved may be two individuals who are trying to decide who will pay for lunch. A little more complexity is involved when two people, such as an employee and a manager, sit down to decide on personal performance goals for the next year against which the employee's performance will be measured. Even more complex are the negotiations that take place between labor unions and the management of a company or between two companies as they negotiate the terms of a joint venture. The key issues in such negotiations are that at least two parties are involved, their preferences are different, and they need to reach agreement. Interest in negotiation has grown steadily in recent years. Four primary approaches to negotiation have dominated this study: individual differences, situational characteristics, game theory, and cognitive approaches.[41]

Early psychological approaches concentrated on the personality traits of the negotiators.[42] Traits investigated have included demographic characteristics and personality variables. Demographic characteristics have included age, gender, and race, among others. Personality variables have included risk taking, locus of control, tolerance for ambiguity, self-esteem, authoritarianism, and Machiavellianism. The assumption of this type of research was that the key to successful negotiation was selecting the right person to do the negotiating, one who had the appropriate demographic characteristics or personality. This assumption seemed to make sense because negotiation is such a personal and interactive process. However, the research rarely showed the positive results expected because situational variables negated the effects of the individual differences.[43]

Situational characteristics are the context within which negotiation takes place. They include such things as the types of communication between negotiators, the potential outcomes of the negotiation, the relative power of the parties (both positional and personal), the time frame available for negotiation, the number of people representing each side, and the presence of other parties. Some of this research has contributed to our understanding of the negotiation process. However, the shortcomings of the situational approach are similar to those of the individual characteristics approach. Many situational characteristics are external to the negotiators and beyond their control. Often the negotiators cannot change their relative power positions or the setting within which the negotiation occurs. So, although we have learned a lot from research on the situational issues, we still need to learn much more about the process.

Game theory was developed by economists using mathematical models to predict the outcome of negotiation situations (as illustrated in the Academy Award–winning movie *A Beautiful Mind*). It requires that every alternative and outcome be analyzed with probabilities and numerical outcomes reflecting the preferences of negotiating parties for each outcome. In addition, the order in which different parties can make choices and every possible move are predicted, along with associated preferences for outcomes. The outcomes of this approach are exactly what negotiators want: a predictive model of how negotiation should be conducted. One major drawback is that it requires the ability to describe all possible options and outcomes for every possible move in every situation before the negotiation starts. This is often very tedious, if possible at all. Another problem is that this theory assumes that negotiators are rational at all times. However, it is unlikely

negotiation
The process in which two or more parties (people or groups) reach agreement on an issue even though they have different preferences regarding that issue

negotiators will in fact always act rationally. Therefore, this approach, although elegant in its prescriptions, is usually unworkable in a real negotiation situation.

The fourth approach is the cognitive approach, which recognizes that negotiators often depart from perfect rationality during negotiation; it tries to predict how and when negotiators will make these departures. Howard Raiffa's decision analytic approach focuses on providing advice to negotiators actively involved in negotiation.[44] Bazerman and Neale have added to Raiffa's work by specifying eight ways in which negotiators systematically deviate from rationality.[45] The types of deviations they describe include escalation of commitment to a previously selected course of action, overreliance on readily available information, assuming that the negotiations can produce fixed-sum outcomes, and anchoring negotiation in irrelevant information. These cognitive approaches have advanced the study of negotiation a long way beyond the early individual and situational approaches. Negotiators can use them to attempt to predict in advance how the negotiation might take place.

SUMMARY OF LEARNING OBJECTIVES AND KEY POINTS

1. Define and identify types of groups and teams in organizations, discuss reasons why people join groups and teams, and list the stages of group and team development.

   - A group is two or more people who interact regularly to accomplish a common purpose or goal.

   - General kinds of groups in organizations are

     - functional groups.

     - task groups and teams.

     - informal or interest groups.

   - A team is a group of workers that functions as a unit, often with little or no supervision, to carry out organizational functions.

2. Identify and discuss four essential characteristics of groups and teams.

   - People join functional groups and teams to pursue a career.

   - Their reasons for joining informal or interest groups include interpersonal attraction, group activities, group goals, need satisfaction, and potential instrumental benefits.

   - The stages of team development include testing and dependence, intragroup conflict and hostility, development of group cohesion, and focusing on the problem at hand.

   - Four important characteristics of teams are role structures, behavioral norms, cohesiveness, and informal leadership.

     - Role structures define task and socioemotional specialists and may be disrupted by role ambiguity, role conflict, or role overload.

     - Norms are standards of behavior for group members.

     - Cohesiveness is the extent to which members are loyal and committed to the team and to one another.

     - Informal leaders are those leaders whom the group members themselves choose to follow.

3. Discuss interpersonal and intergroup conflict in organizations.

   - Conflict is a disagreement between two or more people, groups, or organizations.

   - Too little or too much conflict may hurt performance; an optimal level of conflict may improve performance.

   - Interpersonal and intergroup conflict in organizations may be caused by personality differences or by particular organizational strategies and practices.

4. Describe how organizations manage conflict.

- Organizations may encounter conflict with one another and with various elements of the environment.

  - Three methods of managing conflict are

  - to stimulate it.

- to control it.
- to resolve and eliminate it.

DISCUSSION QUESTIONS

Questions for Review

1. What is a group? Describe the several different types of groups and indicate the similarities and differences between them. What is the difference between a group and a team?

2. What are the stages of group development? Do all teams develop through all the stages discussed in this chapter? Why or why not? How might the management of a mature team differ from the management of teams that are not yet mature?

3. Describe the development of a role within a group. Tell how each role leads to the next.

4. Identify two examples of informal leaders. Can a person be a formal and an informal leader at the same time?

5. Describe the causes of conflict in organizations. What can a manager do to control conflict? To resolve and eliminate conflict?

Questions for Analysis

1. Individuals join groups for a variety of reasons. Most groups contain members who joined for different reasons. What is likely to be the result when members join a group for different reasons? What can a group leader do to reduce the negative impact of a conflict in reasons for joining the group?

2. Consider the case of a developed group, where all members have been socialized. What are the benefits to the individuals of norm conformity? What are the benefits of not conforming to the group's norms? What are the benefits to an organization of conformity? What are the benefits to an organization of nonconformity?

3. Do you think teams are a valuable new management technique that will endure, or are they just a

fad that will be replaced with something else in the near future?

4. Think of several groups of which you have been a member. Why did you join each? Did each group progress through the stages of development discussed in this chapter? If not, why do you think it did not?

5. Describe a case of interpersonal conflict that you have observed in an organization. Describe a case of intergroup conflict that you have observed. (If you have not observed any, interview a worker or manager to obtain examples.) In each case, was the conflict beneficial or harmful to the organization, and why?

BUILDING EFFECTIVE CONCEPTUAL SKILLS

Exercise Overview

Conceptual skills require you to think in the abstract. This exercise will allow you to practice your conceptual skills as they apply to the activities of work teams in organizations.

Exercise Background

Business organizations, of course, don't have a monopoly on effective groups. Basketball teams and military squadrons are teams, as is a government policy group such as the president's cabinet, the leadership of a church or civic organization, or even a student committee.

Exercise Task

1. Use the Internet to identify an example of a real-life team. Be sure to choose one that meets two criteria: (1) It's not part of a for-profit business, and (2) you can argue that it's highly effective.

2. Determine the reasons for the team's effectiveness. (*Hint:* You might look for websites sponsored by the group itself, review online news sources for current articles about it, or enter the group name in a search engine.) Consider team characteristics and activities, such as role structures, norms, cohesiveness, and conflict management.

3. What can a manager learn from the characteristics and activities of this particular team? How might the factors that contribute to this team's success be adopted in a business setting?

BUILDING EFFECTIVE COMMUNICATION SKILLS

Exercise Overview

Communication skills refer to the ability to not only convey information and ideas to others but also handle information and ideas received from them. They're essential to effective teamwork because teams depend on the ability of members to send and receive information that's accurate. This exercise invites you to play a game designed to demonstrate how good communication skills can lead to improved teamwork and team performance.

Exercise Background

You'll play this game in three separate rounds. In round 1, you're on your own. In round 2, you'll work in a small group and share information. You'll also work in a small group in round 3, but this time, you'll have the additional benefit of some suggestions for improving the group's performance. Typically, students find that performance improves over the course of the three rounds. In particular, they find that creativity is enhanced when information is shared.

Exercise Task

1. Play the Name Game that your professor will explain to you. In round 1, work out your answers individually and then report your individual score to the class.

2. Four round 2, you'll join a group of three to five students. Work out your answers together and write your group answers on a single sheet of paper. Now allow each group member to look at the answer sheet. If you can do so without being overheard by other groups, have each group member whisper the answers on the sheet to the group. Report your group score to the class.

3. Your professor will then ask the highest-performing individuals and groups to share their methods with the class. At this point, your professor will make some suggestions. Be sure to consider at least two strategies for improving your score.

4. Now play round 3, working together in the same small groups in which you participated in round 2. Report your group scores to the class.

5. Did average group scores improve upon average individual scores? Why or why not?

6. Did average group scores improve after methods for improvement were discussed at the end of round 2? Why or why not?

7. What has this game taught you about teamwork and effectiveness? Share your thoughts with the class.

SKILLS SELF-ASSESSMENT INSTRUMENT

Using Teams

Introduction: The use of groups and teams is becoming more common in organizations throughout the world. The following assessment surveys your beliefs about the effective use of teams in work organizations.

Instructions: You will agree with some of the statements and disagree with others. In some cases you may find making a decision difficult, but you should force yourself to make a choice. Record your answers next to each statement according to the following scale:

Rating Scale

4 Strongly agree
3 Somewhat agree
2 Somewhat disagree
1 Strongly disagree

____ 1. Each individual in a work team should have a clear assignment so that individual accountability can be maintained.

____ 2. For a team to function effectively, the team must be given complete authority over all aspects of the task.

____ 3. One way to get teams to work is simply to assemble a group of people, tell them in general what needs to be done, and let them work out the details.

____ 4. Once a team gets going, management can turn its attention to other matters.

____ 5. To ensure that a team develops into a cohesive working unit, managers should be especially careful not to intervene in any way during the initial startup period.

____ 6. Training is not critical to a team because the team will develop any needed skills on its own.

____ 7. It's easy to provide teams with the support they need because they are basically self-motivating.

____ 8. Teams need little or no structure to function effectively.

____ 9. Teams should set their own direction, with managers determining the means to the selected end.

____ 10. Teams can be used in any organization.

Source: Test: adapted from J. Richard Hackman, ed., Groups That Work (and Those That Don't), San Francisco: Jossey-Bass Publishers, 1990, pp. 493–504.

EXPERIENTIAL EXERCISE

Team Size and Performance

Purpose: Choosing the number of members in a team is an important decision that will affect team processes and outcomes. A team with too few members will have low performance because they are not receiving all of the benefits of effective teamwork. A team that is too large won't be able to develop strong cohesion and again, performance will suffer. The best team size in a particular situation depends on the members themselves, the tasks they will perform, and the nature of the interaction between them.

Instructions:

Step 1: In a small class, the class will be divided into groups of four by the instructor. In a larger class, four students may be asked to volunteer to demonstrate in front of the whole group.

Step 2: Each group will receive a regular deck of 52 playing cards from the instructor. One group member is chosen to be the "sorter." The cards should be shuffled thoroughly and placed in a stack on the desk in front of the sorter. Another group member is the timer.

Step 3: At a signal from the instructor, the sorter or sorters pick up the cards. The timer notes the starting time. They must place the cards into four stacks by suit, arranging each stack from lowest to highest card. Aces are considered to be high. The task is done when the cards are in the four stacks. The timer records the elapsed time.

Step 4: After thoroughly shuffling the cards, repeat Step 3. This time, however, the sorter will have a helper. The help may take any form—advice, encouragement, moving the cards, or anything else. After a brief discussion of the actions the helper will take to aid the sorter, begin timing and start the task. At the end, the timer notes the elapsed time.

Step 5: After thoroughly shuffling the cards, repeat Step 3. This time, however, the sorter will have three helpers. The help may take any form—advice, encouragement, moving the cards, or anything else. After a brief discus-

sion of the actions the helpers will take to aid the sorter, begin timing and start the task. At the end, the timer notes the elapsed time.

Follow-Up Questions:

1. Which of the three trials happened the most quickly? Which was the slowest? Which seemed to go the most smoothly for the sorter? Which seemed to be the most challenging for the sorter? Explain.

2. What was the impact of the help? Were three helpers better than one?

3. What types of help were effective and what types were ineffective?

4. In what ways is this exercise similar to the situation in a business organization? In what ways is it dissimilar? What lessons might managers learn from this exercise?

 YOU MAKE THE CALL

Filling Shoes at Nike

1. Judging from what you now know about Nike's managerial culture, list a few of the norms that are probably held by the company's managerial teams. What level of norm conformity seems to prevail at Nike?

2. What are some of the positive consequences that are likely to result from the highly cohesive nature of Nike managerial teams? What are some of the likely negative consequences?

3. Outsider William Perez experienced interpersonal and intergroup conflict during his short tenure at Nike. In your opinion, was the episode characterized by too much conflict, by an appropriate amount of conflict, or by too little conflict? Was the conflict handled effectively? Explain your answers.

CASES

CHAPTER 1

Jumpin' Jack Flash

Jack Armstrong doesn't have the cutest little baby face, but he has other qualifications for getting ahead despite the fact that he's still relatively young. He's smart and creative, and he combines a high-energy approach to getting things done with aggressive marketing instincts.

He's just 36 now, but Jack can already boast a breadth of management experience, largely because he's been quite adept at moving around to move up. He started out in sales for a technology company, outsold his colleagues by wide margins for two years, and was promoted to regional sales director. After a year, he began angling for a position as marketing manager, but when the job went to a senior sales director, Jack left for a job as a marketing manager with a company specializing in travel products. Though a little impatient with the tedious process of sifting through market research data, he devoted his considerable energy and creativity to planning new products. His very first pet project—a super-lightweight compact folding chair—outstripped all sales projections and provided just the impetus he needed to ask for a promotion to vice president of marketing.

When the company took too much time to make a decision, Jack moved on again, having found a suitable vice presidency at a consumer products firm. Here, his ability to spot promising items in the company's new-product pipeline—notably, a combination oral-hygiene and teeth-whitening rinse for dogs—brought him to the attention of upper management. Jack expected to go to the top of the list of candidates for president of some division within the company, but instead the president of overseas operations called Jack into his office and offered him

a yearlong special assignment: How would Jack like to head up a team to develop strategies for adapting existing company products into new products for sales in developing countries? It was the perfect opportunity, he suggested, for Jack to broaden his skills by working with managers from every area of the company. Moreover, there'd be a significant bonus if he succeeded, and promotion to a divisional presidency would be next. It was certainly an interesting opportunity, but it would sidetrack Jack's projected ascent to CEO status before the age of 40. He asked for a little time to think over the offer, which, as he well knew, would also be a stretch for him. As luck would have it, however, he didn't have to make the troublesome decision, because it was then that he was offered his current job as divisional president at a rising consumer electronics firm.

And that's where we find Jack now—with his job on the line. What happened? Jack had been in his new corner office for about six months when his marketing department came to him with an idea for a sleek high-fashion combination cell phone and music and video player. It was just the kind of product that Jack had been looking for, and he ordered his marketing people to draw up some performance specs and get them to the design department. His VP for marketing suggested that Jack assemble a project team to shepherd the product from marketing through the design, engineering, and production stages, but Jack had heard too many stories about projects getting bogged down in the endless processes of team decision making, and if there was one thing that he knew from his own experience, it was that the key to a successful new product was getting it to market as quickly as possible. Besides, he had a reputation for aggressiveness to uphold.

Determined to take the bull by the horns, he put the project on an accelerated eight-month schedule from design to rollout. He himself took charge of marketing and launched an aggressive promotional campaign designed to capture the attention of not only the market but also the company's investors. Everything went according to plan until the middle of month seven, when Jack got some bad news from the production facility in Malaysia. Tests on preliminary versions of the product revealed that the placement of the cell phone antenna inside the mouthpiece was producing a weak cellular signal. The only solution, it seems, was either to redesign for an external antenna or to provide a kit containing an antenna and adapter. In either case, the product design would be compromised and the rollout delayed by months. Electronics engineers had warned mechanical engineers of the potential glitch at an early stage of the project, but when news of the problem got back to marketing, managers had decided to proceed because the whole project was such a high priority with Jack.

As it turns out, thousands of orders were delayed, customers got mad, and when the news got out, the company's stock price began to slip.

Case Questions

1. What management skills did Jack demonstrate as a marketing manager at the travel products company? What management skills did he demonstrate as a VP at the consumer products firm?

2. Should Jack have taken the special assignment offered him by the consumer products firm? What kinds of skills was the president of overseas operations thinking about when he offered the assignment to Jack?

3. What management skills would have helped Jack avoid the catastrophe that befell his project at the consumer electronics firm?

Case References

Kerry A. Bunker, Kathy E. Kram, and Sharon Ting, "The Young and the Clueless: How to Manage Your Bad Boys," *Harvard Business School Working Knowledge*, January 20, 2003, http://hbswk.hbs.edu on December 11, 2008; Di Smith, "Young Managers Lack Communications Skills," *Internal Comms*, October 30, 2008, www.internalcommshub.com on December 12, 2008; and Kirk Shinkle, "Young Managers Take Bigger Risks," *U.S. News & World Report*, June 30, 2008, www.usnews.com on December 12, 2008.

CHAPTER 2

Is Fair Trade Really Fair?

Chocolate comes from small beans that grow on cocoa trees. It takes about 400 beans to make a pound of chocolate, and to harvest the beans, laborers have to chop them from the trees, slice them open, scoop out the beans, spread them on mats, and cover them to ferment. Once the beans are fermented, they're dried, packed in heavy bags, and carried to waiting trucks by the same laborers. At that point, they've entered the supply chain that will take them to the United States or Europe, where they'll be turned into Butterfinger candy bars and Dreyer's Double Fudge Brownie ice cream.

Over 40 percent of the world's cocoa bean supply comes from small farms scattered throughout the West African nation of Ivory Coast, which may ship as much as 47,000 tons per month to the United States. According to reports issued at the end of the 1990s by the United Nations Children's Fund and the U.S. State Department, much of the labor involved in Ivory Coast cocoa production was performed by children, mostly boys ranging in age from 12 to 16. The children—perhaps as many as 15,000 of them—work 12 hours a day, 7 days a week. They are often beaten to enforce productivity, and they sleep on bare wooden planks in cramped rooms. Most of them were tricked or sold into forced labor, many by destitute parents who couldn't feed them. In the first eight years following the initial reports of abusive conditions, efforts to alleviate the problem have met with relatively little success.

How did enslaving children become business as usual in the Ivory Coast cocoa industry? Because a full one-third of the country's economy is based on cocoa exports, Ivory Coast is heavily dependent on world market prices for cocoa. Unfortunately, cocoa is an extremely unstable commodity—global prices fluctuate significantly. Profitability in the cocoa industry, therefore, depends on prices over which farmers have no control. This problem is compounded by unpredictable natural conditions, such as drought, over which they also have no control. To improve their chances of making a profit, they look for ways to cut costs, and the use of slave labor is the most effective money saving measure.

This is where the idea of "fair trade" comes in. Fair trade refers to programs designed to ensure that export-dependent farmers in developing countries receive fair prices for their crops. Several such programs are sponsored by Fairtrade Labelling Organizations International (FLO), a global nonprofit network of fair trade groups headquartered in Germany. Here's how it works. FLO partners with cooperatives representing cocoa producers in Africa and Latin America to establish certain standards, not only for the producers' products but also for their operations and socially relevant policies (such as enforcing anti–child labor laws and providing education and health care services). In return, FLO guarantees producers a "Fairtrade Minimum Price" for their products. As of 2007, FLO guaranteed cocoa farmers a price of $1,750 per ton. If the market price falls below that level, FLO guarantees the difference. If the market price tops $1,750, FLO pays producers a premium of $150 per ton.

Where does the money come from? The cost is borne by the importers, manufacturers, and distributors who buy and sell cocoa from FLO-certified producers. These companies are in turn monitored by a network of FLO-owned organizations called Trans-Fair, which ensures that FLO criteria are met and that FLO-certified producers receive the fair prices guaranteed by FLO. Products that meet the appropriate FLO-TransFair criteria are entitled to bear labels attesting that they're "Fair Trade Certified™." At present, semifinished and branded chocolate products certified by TransFair USA can be found in more than 1,600 U.S. retail locations, including Safeway and Whole Foods stores.

What incentive encourages importers, manufacturers, and distributors not only to adopt FLO Trans-Fair standards but also to bear the costs of subsidizing overseas producers? They get the right to promote their chocolate products not only as "fair trade" but, often, as "organic" products as well—both of which categories typically command premium retail prices. In fact, FLO pays an additional premium on organically certified cocoa—$200 instead of $150 per ton—and the extra cost, of course, shows up in retail prices along with the cost of sustaining fair trade prices in general. Organic chocolate products are priced in the same range as luxury chocolates, but consumers appear to be willing to pay the relatively high asking prices—not only for organic products but also for all kinds of chocolate products bearing the Fair Trade Certified label. TransFair USA chief executive Paul Rice explains that when consumers know they're supporting programs to empower farmers in developing countries, sellers and resellers can charge "dramatically higher prices, often two to three times higher." Consumers, he says, "put their money where their mouth is and pay a little more."

A 3.5-ounce candy bar labeled "organic fair trade" may sell for $3.49, compared to about $1.50 for one that's not. Why so much? Because the fair-trade candy bar, says TransFair USA spokesperson Nicole Chettero, still occupies a niche market. "As the demand and volume of Fair Trade-certified products increase," she predicts, "the market will work itself out . . . [R]etailers will naturally start to drop prices to remain competitive." Ultimately, she concludes, "there is no reason why fair-trade [products] should cost astronomically more than traditional products."

Some critics of fair-trade practices and prices agree in principle but contend that consumers don't need to be paying such excessive prices even under *current* market conditions. They point out that, according to TransFair's own data, cocoa farmers get only 3 cents of the $3.49 that a socially conscious consumer pays for a Fair Trade-certified candy bar. "Farmers often receive very little," reports consumer researcher Lawrence Solomon. "Often fair trade is sold at a premium," he charges, "but the entire premium goes to the middlemen." Critics like Solomon suggest that sellers of fair-trade products are taking advantage of consumers who are socially but not particularly price conscious. They point out that if sellers priced that $3.49 candy bar at $2.49, farmers would still be entitled to 3 cents. The price, they charge, is inflated to $3.49 only because there's a small segment of the market willing to pay it (while farmers still get only 3 cents). Fair-trade programs, advises English economist Tim Harford, "make a promise that the producers will get a good deal. They do not promise that the consumer will get a good deal. That's up to you as a savvy shopper."

Case Questions

1. Do you think fair-trade is a viable solution to the child-labor and related problems?

2. Are you willing to pay more for fair-trade products? Why or why not?

3. What other options can you identify that might help deal with child labor and other problems in the global cocoa market?

References: "Slaves Feed World's Taste for Chocolate," Knight Ridder News Service, January 9, 2009; "Chocolate and Slavery: Child Labor in Côte d'Ivoire," TED Case Studies, No. 664 (2009), "Abolishing Child Labor on West African Cocoa Farms," SocialFunds.com, April 4, 2009; "Stop Child Labor: Cocoa Campaign," International Labor Rights Forum, 2008, www.laborrights.org on April 3, 2010; "Fair Trade Labelling Organizations International," "Cocoa," FLO International website, www.fairtrade.net on April 3, 2010; "What Is Fair Trade Certification?" and "Cocoa Program," TransFair USA website, www.transfairusa.org on April 2, 2010; and Jennifer Alsever, "Fair Prices for Farmers: Simple Idea, Complex Reality," *New York Times*, March 19, 2006, www.nytimes.com on April 3, 2010.

CHAPTER 3

Thinking Outside the Big Box

Down the hall from the CEO's office at Best Buy headquarters in Minneapolis, there's a row of hospital beds, each containing the effigy of an ailing or deceased American retailer. Bedside charts reveal dire financial results. A nearby sign reads: "This is where companies go when their strategies get sick."

As CEO of Best Buy, the world's largest consumer-electronics retailer, from 2002 to 2009, Brad Anderson saw his job as keeping the company in strategic good health, and to keep Best Buy's strategy up and functioning, Anderson regularly prescribed doses of customer focus—or, more precisely, focus on the customer's experience at Best Buy. "In our world," says Anderson, "the way you win the game isn't the price of the TV—which is about the same for all retailers—but the experience you give customers once they're in our stores." For Anderson, this principle led quite naturally to the corollary that success in retailing depends on the people who are most responsible for the customer's in-store experience—"those line-level employees who interact with our customers each and every day."

This twofold principle was at the heart of one of the first important innovations that Anderson, then right-hand man to founder and CEO Richard Schulze, implemented at Best Buy. In 1989, the company stopped paying commissions to its sales staff and put them on salary instead. The move didn't go over well with the big suppliers who expected a retailer's salespeople to push their premium products, but customers appreciated the break from high-pressure sales tactics, and revenues at Best Buy jumped by 25 percent a year in the early 1990s.

The same principle motivated one of the first moves that Anderson made after becoming CEO in June 2002. Four months later, he bought a Minneapolis start-up that specialized in installing and fixing PCs. Within a year, he had opened Geek Squad "precincts" in more than 20 Best Buy stores, and by 2005, there was a Geek Squad presence in every store in the chain. Whether working at the customer's home, in a Best Buy outlet, over the phone, or online, the Geeks constitute a first line of defense against the technological frustrations that can sap the value out of an electronics purchase and the goodwill out of a customer experience. Anderson was confident from the first that the technical-services market would continue to grow, but perhaps more importantly, he realized that competitors such as Wal-Mart and Costco would never offer the kind of customer services that Best Buy could offer through the Geek Squad. On sales of $1 billion, the Geek Squad now generates about $280 million in profits annually.

By far, however, Anderson's most ambitious strategic gambit has been the "customer-centricity"— or just plain "centricity"—initiative. The keys to centricity are demographics and segmentation. From store to store, the most valuable customers—the ones whose patronage is most lucrative—don't necessarily belong to the same group of people. At one outlet, for example, the most profitable customers might be affluent tech enthusiasts; elsewhere, they may be suburban mothers, price-conscious family guys, or youthful gadget fiends. Beginning in 2003, Anderson started "centrizing" Best Buy stores—realigning them to cater to their most profitable segments (or combination of segments). A given location, for instance, may be geared toward young gadget fiends, another toward suburban mothers. The first will have a broad range of video games and special stations for trying out accessories; the second will have a staff of personal shopping assistants to help a homemaker find the right digital camera for recording family activities. If a store caters to affluent tech enthusiasts (as about 40 percent of them do), there will be a home-theater expert on hand.

Centrized stores require specialist employees, and employees are also crucial to the success of the centricity concept because it relies on personnel who are empowered to develop the most effective in-store interactions with customers. Personal shopping assistants and home-theater experts may get weeks of training, and most line-level jobs call not only for evaluating the success of the centrized experience, but for recommending enhancements to it. "The closer you get to the customer," says Anderson, "the better your ability to see what the needs of the business are. . . . A person in a blue shirt in a store [a Best Buy associate] probably has the best single insight as to what your needs are. . . . I could take you through anything we do today . . . and all of it came from

some individual—usually a misunderstood angry individual—who was sitting there saying, 'Why won't you do this?' and was having trouble being heard."

Under Anderson, Best Buy has also implemented various other strategies to overcome the limitations inherent in being a retailer of commodity products at low prices and low profit margins. For one thing, it's begun developing relationships with small high-tech start-ups to prime flows of new products into the market. That's how Best Buy got a three-month jump on competitors with Slingbox, a device that lets users channel TV programming from their homes to their PCs. Best Buy has also introduced its own house-brand products, including an Insignia line of PCs, TVs, and DVDs. The results in established product categories have been uneven so far, but Best Buy believes that developing its own product lines will not only allow it to compete on price with competitors such as Wal-Mart and Dell, but help it build relationships with start-ups specializing in cutting-edge categories.

Perhaps most importantly, Best Buy has reengineered its supply chain—the flow of products from suppliers to end users. It was always very good at getting high volumes of products out of factories and onto its shelves, but in keeping with the priorities of customer-centricity, it's now focusing on the components of the process most closely related to the task of meeting the needs of customer segments. All stores carry products for every customer-centric segment, but as we've seen, centrized stores focus on the needs of just one or two segments. To meet shifts or peculiarities in store-level demand, for example, frontline employees may be empowered to override inventory-management plans and stock higher inventories of certain products. Suppliers, therefore, must be continuously responsive to signals that come directly from stores—agile enough to reconfigure both shipments and all the information flows related to them.

Before Brad Anderson stepped down in June 2009, he expressed his faith in the effectiveness of customer-centricity to support the company's latest— and most critical—strategic initiative: "Our customer-centric business model," he explained, "gives us the confidence to be able to grow outside of the United States. We know that we must do three seemingly simple things to succeed: gain deep insights into our customers' priorities and lifestyles; figure out how we can encourage and nurture employee ingenuity on behalf of our customers; and then offer solutions that will result in great experiences for our customers." So far, Anderson's bet on centricity appears to be paying off. "We're still figuring out how customer-centricity works in China," reports Bob Willett, CEO of Best Buy International, but after just one year, Best Buy's four-story, 87,000-square foot Shanghai store is already among the top-ten revenue-generating outlets in a 1,300-store global chain.

In a sign of the volatile times, Best Buy announced in November 2008, when fourth-quarter sales threatened to decline anywhere from 5 percent to a whopping 15 percent, that it expected revenues for fiscal 2009 (which ended in February 2009) to fall short of projections. When the smoke had cleared, however, sales had gone up 4 percent (in keeping with the company's original projections), thanks in part to another Brad Anderson gamble that had paid off: Although comparable-store sales (sales in stores that have been open for at least a year) had declined 6.8 percent, the losses were offset by revenues from 138 new stores that had been opened in the preceding 12 months. "While the environment continues to be as challenging as we expected," said Anderson, "consumers are being drawn to brands that they trust, and they are responding to our customer-centric model. In this light, we believe that the market-share gains we've been making will be sustained."

Case Questions

1. What are Best Buy's organizational strengths? Based on your response, which of Porter's generic strategies do you recommend Best Buy to adopt? Why?

2. How do Anderson's two new strategies increase Best Buy's differentiation advantage? How do they increase Best Buy's low-cost advantage?

3. The home goods retailing industry is in the maturity stage of the product life cycle. Based on that information, what industry characteristics do you expect Best Buy to face? What strategy or strategies should Best Buy use to help it compete effectively in the maturity stage of the market?

Case References

Matthew Boyle, "Best Buy's Giant Gamble," *Fortune*, April 3, 2006, http://money.cnn.com on February 18, 2009; Kristina Bell, "Q&A with Best Buy CEO Brad Anderson," *Time*, June 12, 2008, www.time.com on February 18, 2009; Matthew Boyle, "Q&A with Best Buy CEO Brad Anderson," *CNN-Money.com*, April 18, 2007, http://cnnmoney.com on February 18, 2009; "How to Break Out of Commodity Hell," *Business-Week*, March 27, 2006, www.businessweek.com on February 18, 2009; Ken Cotrill, "Best Buy's Supply Chain Transformation," *Harvard Business School Working Knowledge*, January 23, 2006, http://hbswk.hbs.edu on February 18, 2009; Adam Minter, "Best Buy Booming in China," *MinnPost.com*, February 5, 2008, www.minnpost.com on February 18, 2009; "Best Buy Reports December Revenue of $7.5 Billion, Continues Market Share Gains," Best Buy Inc., news release, January 9, 2009, www.bestbuyinc.com on February 19, 2009.

CHAPTER 4

The Art and Science of Decision Making

Is there a place for "art" in managing a business? Some researchers think so. Like Malcolm Gladwell, author of the best-selling *Blink: The Power of Thinking without Thinking*, they advocate greater reliance on certain nonrational and behavioral factors—especially intuition—in the decision-making process. Other researchers prefer to stick to the facts, measurable outcomes, and rational approaches and rely on scientifically conducted studies to improve managerial decision making. Interestingly, both approaches are leading managers to some unconventional conclusions—some rational, some intuitive—about the business of making decisions.

Intuition isn't unheard of in the business world. Few loan officers, for example, would give you the money for a house without some pertinent data at their fingertips, but many of them will also give a lot weight to personal feelings about your creditworthiness. Gladwell calls these feelings "thin slices" because they're so small and subtle, and experts have found that loan managers who draw upon both data and feelings tend to make better decisions than those who rely solely on the numbers. The same holds true in a broad array of other jobs, from art appraisers to police officers, from CEOs to physicians, in which intuition is widely accepted as a valuable supplement to fact-based decision making.

How, exactly, does intuition aid in decision making? Proponents argue that people make better and faster decisions when they select their facts—that is, when they focus on the most relevant facts while ignoring the rest. Even more important, they contend, is the fact that intuition is effective because it's based on experience. Experienced nurses, for instance, can often sense when a patient needs urgent attention. How? In such cases, they're often being responsive to subtle clues that they've learned to recognize over time and drawing the correct conclusions from them. Conversely, the intuitions of inexperienced workers are often faulty. Most of the battle casualties sustained in Iraq, for example, occur in the first 90 days of the soldier's deployment. Likewise, studies of airline crews show that 73 percent of serious mistakes happen when crews are working together for the first time.

Critics grant that intuition is particularly valuable when the situation calls for a quick decision, but they point out that most decision making in an organizational context isn't especially time sensitive. In one sense or another, of course, speed is important in just about any organizational activity, but as we've seen, when it comes to making strategic decisions, speed can be measured in days or weeks, not seconds or minutes. Except in emergencies, the context of most organizational decision making allows time for gathering information, generating alternatives, and discussing alternatives. Skeptics are also critical of the importance that the intuition approach places on the role of a single decision maker. Intuition, they argue, plays little part in group decision making, which is often highly effective and which is becoming much more prevalent in today's organizations. Finally, some critics believe that overstating the virtues of

intuition actually encourages sloppy thinking and poor decision making.

Stanford professors Jeffrey Pfeffer and Bob Sutton, authors of *Hard Facts, Dangerous Half-Truths, and Total Nonsense*, have put out a call for an increased reliance on rationality in managerial decision making—an approach that they call *evidence-based management* (EBM). "Management decisions," they argue, "[should] be based on the best evidence, managers [should] systematically learn from experience, and organizational practices [should] reflect sound principles of thought and analysis." At www. evidence-basedmanagement.com, they define EBM as "a commitment to finding and using the best theory and data available at the time to make decisions," but their "Five Principles of Evidence-Based Management" make it clear that EBM means more than just sifting through data and crunching numbers:

1. Face the hard fact and build a culture in which people are encouraged to tell the truth, even if it is unpleasant.

2. Be committed to "fact-based" decision making—which means being committed to getting the best evidence and using it to guide actions.

3. Treat your organization as an unfinished prototype—encourage experimentation and learning by doing.

4. Look for the risks and drawbacks in what people recommend—even the best medicine has side effects.

5. Avoid basing decisions on untested but strongly held beliefs, what you have done in the past, or on uncritical "benchmarking" of what winners do.

Pfeffer and Sutton are particularly persuasive when they use EBM to question the outcomes of decisions based on "untested but strongly held beliefs" or on "uncritical 'benchmarking' of what others do." Take, for instance, the popular policy of paying high performers significantly more than low performers. Pfeffer and Sutton's research shows that pay-for-performance policies get good results when employees are working solo or independently. But it's another matter altogether when it comes to collaborative teams—the kind of teams that make so many organizational decisions today. Under these circumstances, the greater the gap between highest- and lowest-paid executives, the weaker the firm's financial performance. Why? According to Pfeffer and Sutton, wide disparities in pay often weaken trust among team members as well as the social connectivity that contributes to strong team-based decision making.

Or consider another increasingly prevalent policy for evaluating and rewarding talent. Pioneered at General Electric by the legendary Jack Welch, the practice of "forced ranking" divides employees into three groups based on performance—the top 20 percent, middle 70 percent, and bottom 10 percent—and terminates those at the bottom. Pfeffer and Sutton found that, according to many HR managers, forced ranking impaired morale and collaboration and ultimately reduced productivity. They also concluded that automatically firing the bottom 10 percent resulted too often in the unnecessary disruption of otherwise effective teamwork. That's how they found out that 73 percent of the errors committed by commercial airline pilots occur on the first day that reconfigured crews work together.

Case Questions

1. Is a rational decision process likely to produce the best outcomes when a situation is risky or uncertain? Is an intuitive, behavioral process best used under risk or under certainty? Explain.

2. Consider the hypothetical case in which a company must choose one of the two promising new products to develop and introduce to the market. There are not sufficient funds for both products. How might the company make use of intuition in making this decision?

3. Reconsider the case presented in question 2. How might the company make use of EBM in making its decision?

Case References

Malcolm Gladwell, *Blink: The Power of Thinking without Thinking* (Boston: Little, Brown, 2005); Jeffrey Pfeffer and Robert I. Sutton, *Hard Facts, Dangerous Half-Truths, and Total Nonsense: Profiting from Evidence-Based Management* (Cambridge, Mass.: Harvard Business School Press, 2006); Jeffrey Pfeffer and Robert I. Sutton, "Evidence-Based Management," 2009, www.evidence-basedmanagement.com on February 21, 2009; Jena McGregor, "Forget Going with Your Gut," *BusinessWeek*, March 20, 2006, www.businessweek.com on February 21, 2009.

CHAPTER 5

JetBlue Capitalizes on the Entrepreneurial Spirit

In the challenging environment of the modern airline industry, JetBlue is a notable example of entrepreneurial success. From the start, it was conceived as a low-cost carrier to be differentiated by attention to customer service and a bundle of passenger amenities unusual at the low-cost end of the air travel market. Founded by industry veteran David Neeleman in February 1999, JetBlue began small, with just a few planes and one city pair. By the end of 2000, the new airline was flying 11 planes to 11 cities around the country and preparing to add more destinations each year. Today, JetBlue flies to 53 cities in more than 20 states and several Caribbean destinations. Routes to Latin American destinations such as Colombia and Costa Rica were added in 2009.

Meanwhile, competitors in its segment have come and gone—notably United's Ted and Delta's Song, both of which took off in 2003 and both of which were grounded by 2008. Why has JetBlue been successful where competitors have failed? Obviously, the JetBlue *idea*—a low-cost carrier differentiated by attention to service and passenger comfort—can't be patented, but as the fate of Ted and Song indicate, a good idea isn't enough to make a business work. JetBlue has succeeded, in the first place, because it boasts a number of *distinctive competencies*—organizational strengths that can't be copied quite as readily as a basic entrepreneurial idea. For one thing, JetBlue has benefited from the talent and experience of Neeleman, a crossover from big business, and a team of top managers. A one-time travel agent, Neeleman started a Utah-based discount airline, Morris Air, in 1984, when he was just 24 years old. Ten years later, he sold Morris Air to Southwest Airlines for $129 million and, after a brief executive stint at Southwest itself, left to help found Canadian-based WestJet Airlines. When he came up with the idea for JetBlue, he recruited industry veterans such as COO Dave Barger and CFO John Owen, vice presidents at Continental and Southwest Airlines, respectively.

In addition, Neeleman and his team set out from the beginning to take every advantage offered by their position as a "second mover" in a new market segment of the airline industry. Traditionally, the airline industry consisted of large international carriers and a few smaller regional airlines. Competitors in both groups differentiated themselves primarily according to routes served and charged the highest prices they could command. Southwest Airlines came along in 1971, positioning itself as a discount carrier specializing in short trips to the secondary airports of large cities, and achieved significant cost advantages by radically reducing the number of activities necessary to deliver its basic air travel service. The strategy was an immediate success (and a durable one—Southwest has posted 36 consecutive years of profitability) and spawned many imitators (including Morris Air). JetBlue is the most successful of the Southwest imitators—the airline best able to duplicate the key elements of Southwest's strategy, including reduced airport and labor costs, a single type of aircraft, and a single class of service.

JetBlue, however, is more than a mere imitator: It's a *second mover* in the market segment created by Southwest because its presence in that segment is significant. Rather than merely imitating those aspects of the first mover's strategy that met its needs, JetBlue has introduced its own innovations. Like Southwest, JetBlue is a low-cost carrier, but it has positioned itself as the low-fare airline that offers high-quality passenger service. All JetBlue aircraft, for example, feature luxurious leather seats and individual seat-back TVs. Entertainment options include 36 channels of DirecTV and 100 channels of XM satellite radio. Flyers are pampered with a selection of fine wines, a Bliss Spa kit, and Dunkin' Donuts coffee.

Such passenger amenities, of course, cost a little more, but JetBlue's success depends in part on its expertise in controlling costs. In 2006, for example, JetBlue announced that it was removing one row of seats from its A320 aircraft. Removing the seats, explained officials, not only lightened the plane by nearly 1,000 pounds (thus saving fuel) but also reduced the in-flight crew from four to three (thus offsetting any revenue lost from the missing seats). JetBlue doesn't offer expensive comforts such as lounges, full meals, or first-class seating. Its workforce is nonunionized, and many employees, such as reservation agents, work from home. JetBlue has proved equally effective on the revenue-generating side of the ledger as well: It uses its differentiation advantage to attract customers from other low-fare carriers and its own low fares to attract nonfliers, and it's also found a profitable market in underserved, high-cost routes. From 1.4 million passengers in 2000, JetBlue carried 22 million travelers in 2008. It's now the country's ninth-largest airline, with nearly 11,000 employees and nearly 150 aircraft.

"I always talk about the tripod," says Neeleman, "—low costs, a great product, and capitalization." He founded JetBlue with his own fortune (amassed from the sale of Morris Air to Southwest and the sale of an electronic ticketing system to Hewlett Packard) and $160 million in venture capital. The company went public in 2002 to raise another $158 million in capital, and in addition to being the best-funded start-up in aviation history, it's become one of the most popular stocks in aviation history.

When Neeleman started JetBlue, however, most observers didn't consider launching an airline a particularly good idea: Between 1998 and 2002, the major U.S. airlines had lost more than $7 billion. Obviously, early capitalization was crucial, not only to Neeleman's strategy of building a fast-growing airline but also to any hope he had of surviving long enough to build anything at all. He certainly wanted to avoid the fate of People Express, a no-frills British-owned carrier that started up in 1981. By 1985, it was the fifth-largest airline in the United States, but its strategy of expanding through acquisitions saddled it with an immense debt burden, and it was out of business by 1987. Chris Collins, a former People Express manager who's now a JetBlue executive, remembers what happened at People Express: "We were the best thing going. A year later, we're gone because we couldn't sustain growth. You know what keeps me up at night [now]? Figuring out what we're going to need, not next year but five years from now."

Growth at JetBlue accounted for record profits from 2000 through 2004 (it was one of the few U.S. airlines to turn a profit during the industrywide downswing following 9/11). The number of passengers carried grew by more than 25 percent annually between 2001 and 2006, and average sector length—the distance flown between two airports—increased from 825 miles in 2000 to 1,358 miles in 2005 as the airline added more routes and more distant destinations.

In October 2005, however, profit for the third quarter dropped to $2.7 million from $81 million the previous year—the result of rising fuel prices, low fares, and operational inefficiencies. Fourth-quarter losses made 2005 JetBlue's first unprofitable year since its IPO in 2002, and when losses were again projected for 2006, Neeleman, Barger, and Owen announced a "Return to Profitability" plan calling for $50 million in reduced costs and $30 million in increased revenues. When the dust had cleared, JetBlue had declared a net profit of $14 million for the second quarter of 2006 (doubling Wall Street forecasts of $7 million), and by the end of the year, the airline had announced a return to profitability.

And then came 2007—the year of what's known at JetBlue as "2/14." The inside reference is to Valentine's Day, when a massive winter storm paralyzed all activity at New York's John F. Kennedy (JFK) International Airport, home to JetBlue's busiest hub. Amid forecasts of the imminent storm, other airlines began canceling flights, but JetBlue—which boasted a goal of completing every flight no matter how long the delay—held off. "They shut it down [and] we should have," lamented Neeleman in retrospect. Passengers on no fewer than nine JetBlue planes were stranded on the tarmac at JFK for more than six hours each, and the airline's operations were snarled all across the country for days, forcing it to cancel 279 of 503

flights the next day and 217 of 562 flights the day after that. "We love our customers," affirmed Neeleman, "and we're horrified by this. There's going to be a lot of apologies." Apologies were indeed profuse, but they ended up costing JetBlue $30 million in compensation to stranded passengers and did little to prevent observers from wondering whether the airline hadn't squandered years of industry-leading customer satisfaction ratings in one very bad week.

In May, JetBlue's board of directors asked its founder to step down as CEO. (Neeleman left the company to concentrate on starting up an airline in Brazil.) David Barger, who'd been serving as both president and COO since 1998, took over. To fill his old job, Barger hired a former Federal Aviation Administration official named Russell G. Chew. Chew dumped the policy of completing every scheduled flight, but more importantly, he took a closer look at the company's cash flow. Eight quarters of declining performance had taken their toll, and in December, Chew announced the sale of a 19 percent stake in JetBlue to the German airline Lufthansa for $300 million. Later in the year, he raised another $165 million by selling convertible debt (bonds that can be converted into stock ownership).

The move to raise capital turned out to be especially forward looking when oil prices spiked in January 2008, precipitating the most recent crisis in the airline industry. Its new leadership has given JetBlue some stability, at least temporarily, although it could do little to shield it from the economic damage inflicted first by soaring fuel prices and then by a withering global economy. Worldwide, the airline industry lost $5 billion in 2008; JetBlue announced a loss of $23 million.

And times promise to remain difficult for the industry. According to the head of the International Air Transport Association, "2009 is shaping up to be one of the toughest years ever for international aviation." Barger, who's working to replace Neeleman's emphasis on aggressive growth with a more conservative strategic approach, has cut back on plans to add more aircraft to the fleet and more destinations to the schedule. He also intends to reduce flights by about 2 percent but will follow through on plans to start service from New York to Los Angeles.

Case Questions

1. How did being a second mover contribute to JetBlue's success? What difficulties did it face in entering its market with a second-mover strategy?

2. Consider the factors that generally contribute to the success of an entrepreneurial firm. Which of those factors were present in JetBlue's case?

3. Is JetBlue still an *entrepreneurial* firm? Why or why not?

4. In your opinion, what will David Barger and his management team have to do if JetBlue is to survive the most recent crisis in the airline industry?

Case References

Micheline Maynard, "At JetBlue, Growing Up Is Hard to Do," *New York Times*, October 5, 2008, www.nytimes.com on March 3, 2009; "JetBlue Airways Corporation (JBLU)," Portfolio. com, 2009, www.portfolio.com on March 2, 2009; "JetBlue's Growth Slows Dramatically in 2008," anna.aero, November 28, 2008, www.anna.aero on March 1, 2009; Jeff Bailey, "Long Delays Hurt Image of JetBlue," *New York Times*, February 17, 2007, www.nytimes.com on March 3, 2009; "World's Airlines Lost $5 Billion in 2008, Group Says," *USA Today*, January 29, 2009, www.usatoday.com on March 1, 2009; Micheline Maynard, "3 Airlines End Tough Year with Deep Losses," *New York Times*, January 30, 2009, www.nytimes.com on March 3, 2009; "JetBlue Announces Fourth Quarter and Full Year 2008 Pre-Tax Results," *PR Newswire*, January 29, 2009, http://news. moneycentral.msn.com on March 3, 2009.

CHAPTER 6

eBay Bids for Structured Change

In 1995, 28-year-old computer programmer Pierre Omidyar started up an online business to answer the kind of question that might interest both microeconomists and entrepreneurs: "He launched eBay," we're now told by the website of that very same online business, "to experiment with how equal access to information and opportunities would affect the efficiency of a marketplace." Enthusiastic response to preliminary efforts had convinced Omidyar that, somewhere, there was a buyer for every item which, somewhere, a seller might put up for sale. The next step in Omidyar's experiment consisted of a weekend spent writing software code that would support online auctions. He launched a website, called AuctionWatch, in 1995 and, two years later, changed the company's name to eBay.

Originally, Omidyar structured his company using the *U form*, or *functional*, design typical of small businesses. He set up the usual functional areas—operations, finance, legal, human resources, and so forth—and eventually gave each of them a company president. Omidyar, however, introduced a twist in the usual functional configuration: He integrated a perspective that emphasizes the importance of group and other interpersonal processes. Omidyar's personal values favored a company whose structure

sidestepped Big Business altogether and permitted individuals, wherever they may be, to function as buyers and sellers. Today, people commonly refer to eBay something like "an online auction and shopping website," but Omidyar envisioned his site as much more than an auction space. He intended eBay to create an online community—something like a small town in cyberspace—and for that, he needed an organizational model that did away with bureaucracy and fostered democratic decision making, decentralization, open communication and interactions, and relationships of trust (after all, the whole business model depended upon two strangers trusting one another).

Omidyar stepped down as CEO in 1998, although he retained his position as chairman of the board. He was replaced by Meg Whitman, a former management consultant and a veteran of Old Economy firms such as Procter & Gamble and Disney. In the same year, eBay went public, raising $60 million and committing itself to much greater pressure to realize its profit-making potential. As you probably know, eBay became wildly popular and grew rapidly. Under Whitman, revenues increased steadily, averaging 70 percent annual growth from 1998 to 2004, before year-over-year growth began to slow down to a sustainable level. Revenues for 1999 totaled $224.7 million, up a whopping 161 percent over 1998, and by 2009, revenues had grown to $7.7 billion.

Like many companies, however, eBay did not have a good year in 2008. In the fourth quarter, revenues dropped 6.6 percent from 2007—the first quarterly shrinkage in revenues in the company's history. (Profits were down 31 percent.) "Clearly," said new CEO John Donahoe, "we've been operating in an almost unprecedented external environment," but analysts have been quick to point out other, potentially long-term factors in eBay's sluggish performance. "Part of the problem," agreed *CNNMoney*'s Michael V. Copeland, "is [that] no one is spending money . . . at the moment, but compounding the issue for eBay is that a lot of people just aren't hassling with auctions anymore." A big reason for eBay's problems, he adds, "is that virtually no one cares about eBay's original business, the online auction."

Copeland goes on to argue that eBay's online business, its Marketplace unit, "is dragging down the rest of what are pretty solid businesses that eBay owns, chiefly online payments service PayPal and Internet calling company Skype." For the fourth quarter of 2008, revenue for Skype was up by 5 percent and 23 percent for PayPal. Through 2007, the core Marketplace unit, through which all the goods trading at eBay takes place, contributed about 70 percent of the company's revenues, but in March 2009, in announcing a three-year growth plan, eBay projected a much different distribution of its future income. Donahoe announced projected revenues of $10 billion to $12 billion by 2011. (That's up from 2008's $8.5 billion. If that increase doesn't seem like very much, remember that the company will probably have to make up more lost ground from 2009, for which analysts have projected another drop in revenue of 6 percent.) The company expects its future revenues to be distributed as follows:

- PayPal will generate between $4 billion and $5 billion, up from $2.4 billion in 2010.
- Skype will contribute $1 billion, up from roughly $500 million in 2010.
- Marketplace will ring up $5 billion to $7 billion, up slightly from $4.7 billion in 2010.

Not surprisingly, the meteoric rise in its financial fortunes that began in earnest with the 1998 initial public offering (IPO) has already had a profound impact on both the organizational structure and operations of eBay. One of its first major post-IPO moves was the acquisition, in April 1999, of Butterfield & Butterfield, one of the world's largest and most prestigious auction houses. Butterfield was folded into eBay's auction operations and served to open up a new marketplace category for goods selling for $500 and up. A year later, eBay purchased Half.com, an online shopping site specializing in the sale of books and media products in a nonauction or "fixed-price" format. The purpose of the acquisition was to expand not only the parent company's inventory but its format options as well. The original plan to roll Half.com into eBay.com stalled in 2002, when users objected to the pace of the changes to Half.com, and today it's still an independent site. Both Butterfield's auction operations (which have been rolled into eBay.com) and Half.com's independent fixed-price operations are managed by a unit called eBay North America, whose president reports to a president of eBay Marketplaces (who in turn reports to the CEO).

In the nearly ten years since the Half.com acquisition, eBay has purchased several other online-auction companies, most of them overseas start-ups that have been used to gain entry in foreign markets. Today, there's a unit called Marketplace Operations, whose president oversees operations at all the company's global sites (meaning North America as well as Europe and the Asia-Pacific region). This president is one of three respective presidents in charge of eBay's three divisional units, all of whom report directly to CEO Donahoe. The other two divisional units, interestingly enough, are PayPal and Skype, both of which have been built around the acquisition of independent firms and both of which focus on activities outside eBay's core Marketplace activities.

eBay purchased PayPal, an e-commerce payments system, for $1.5 billion in 2002. Essentially, PayPal is a system that allows payments and money transfers to be made through the Internet, and eBay has developed it into the number-one payments system for e-commerce in general (only direct credit-card transactions transfer more money). Skype was added to the eBay portfolio of businesses in 2005, at a cost of $2.6 billion. It was originally developed as a VoIP (*Voice-over-Internet-Protocol*) service—a transmission technology for sending voice communications over networks like the Internet—but eBay wants to turn it into a communications hub over which its buyers and sellers can transact business by voice. As we've already seen, both PayPal and Skype have emerged as important revenue generators and figure prominently in eBay's plans for the future.

Needless to say, eBay has undergone a good deal of organizational change in its brief ten-plus years of existence. Back in 2004, when she could still refer to eBay as a "unique blend of commerce and community," former CEO Whitman (who stepped down in March 2008) admitted that perhaps the pace of change at the company was a little too brisk for some members of the community. "The community right now," she said, "has seen a lot of change. We probably need to slow down that pace just a tad. It's hard for folks to adapt to so much change." Nevertheless, investor pressure to sustain profit levels, coupled with increased competition from sources such as Amazon.com, Google, and Yahoo!, continued to force change, much of it in the form of rules and regulations instituted to deal with ever-increasing numbers of buyers and sellers.

Recent changes, coupled with certain details of the announced three-year plan, suggest that the company also wants to alter its strategic focus. In January 2008, for example, a month after Amazon.com surpassed it in total U.S. traffic for the first time ever, eBay announced a change in its fee structure. Fees for listing items were slashed by up to 50 percent, but commissions for items that do sell went up. Increases in commissions for low-end items—especially goods selling for less than $25—were particularly steep at 67 percent. Some eBay sellers were understandably unhappy about the change in fee structure. "It looks like what they're trying to do with the fees," surmised one user, "is make it more difficult and expensive to sell low-end items." Many observers agreed with this assessment, adding that eBay was shifting its emphasis to higher-priced items, especially used, off-season, end-of-life-cycle, and open-box products supplied by business sellers.

In a similar move, eBay stipulated that, beginning in March 2008, all sellers who had received less than 100 percent in feedback ratings would be required to use PayPal for all transactions. This requirement followed several stipulations regarding PayPal that had already been put in place the previous year. As of January 2007, for instance, all transactions in certain categories, including "Computer>Software," "Consumer Electronics>MP3 Players," and "Mobile & Home Phones," had to be made through PayPal. Other categories were added in August, such as "Video Games" and "Health & Beauty." Such changes are clearly intended to leverage the revenue potential of PayPal, which, in March 2009, CEO Donahoe referred to as a "second core business" for eBay.

So far, the strategic effort to synergize its Marketplace and PayPal operations has been less than wholly successful. Beginning in June 2008, for example, eBay required that all transactions involving Australian buyers and sellers use PayPal as the only payment option (in addition to cash on delivery). Within a month, however, the company was forced to rescind the policy when the Australian government, acting upon a groundswell of complaints from users and petitions from bankers, informed eBay that its policy would have "an anticompetitive effect" on online commerce. eBay had promoted PayPal as a means for improving security in online transactions, but the Australian government was also unconvinced by this argument, finding "no evidence to suggest that the relative frequency of online fraud for PayPal online transactions is any less than found in general online transactions." The Australian Competition and Consumer Commission also noted that its PayPal-only plan would allow eBay to raise its fees by 45.7 percent. At this juncture, the result of the plan seems to be a few thousand annoyed users in Australia and a few thousand more in the United States, where users aren't convinced by the company's assurances that it's not planning a similar policy for its largest marketplace.

Case Questions

1. eBay started out with a U form, or functional, design. What changes in that design have already

occurred as a result of the company's growth? What kinds of changes seem likely for the future?

2. Currently, its Marketplace unit, one of its three divisional units, runs eBay's overseas operations. As the company expands into more foreign markets, what changes may take place in its organizational structure? In your opinion, what changes *should* be made to accommodate further overseas expansion?

3. In addition to its three divisional units, eBay has three functional units—finance, human resources, and legal—all of which also report directly to the CEO. As the company grows and expands into more foreign markets, what changes may affect the roles of these units in its organizational structure?

4. What changes in its external environment are likely to affect the online-auction industry in the next few years? What impact might these changes have on the organizational structure of eBay and its main competitors?

Case References

Adam Cohen, *The Perfect Store: Inside eBay* (Boston: Little, Brown, 2002), http://books.google.com on March 19, 2009; Robert D. Hof, " 'The Constant Challenge' at eBay," *BusinessWeek*, June 30, 2004, www.businessweek.com on March 18, 2009; "Total Sales of Goods at eBay in 2007 Reached $59.35 Billion," *RetaileCommerce*, February 14, 2008, www.retail-ecommerce.com on March 19, 2009; Cade Metz, "eBay Revenue Shrinks for the First Time in History," *The Register*, January 22, 2009, www.theregister.co on March 19, 2009; Michael V. Copeland, "Uninspired by eBay," *CNNMoney*, February 20, 2009, http://cnnmoney.com on March 19, 2009; "eBay Inc. Announces Three-Year Roadmap for Growth," *MarketWatch*, March 11, 2009, www.marketwatch.com on March 19, 2009; Eric J. Savitz, "New Bid for Profit at eBay, but Don't Buy It Now," *Barron's*, March 16, 2009, http://online.barrons.com on March 20, 2009; Aristotle Munarriz, "Are We There Yet, eBay?" *The Motley Fool*, March 12, 2009, www.fool.com on March 19, 2009; Aron Hsiao, "About eBay the Business," *About.com*, 2009, http://ebay.about.com on March 19, 2009; Duncan Riley, "eBay Changes Fee Structure to Drive Growth," *TechCrunch*, January 30, 2008, www.techcrunch.com on March 19, 2009; Dave Parrack, "eBay Drops Plan to Force PayPal on Customers: Australia Forces Hand," *Tech.Blorge*, July 4, 2008, http://tech.blorge.com on March 20, 2009.

CHAPTER 7

Cultivating Innovation at IKEA

Have you ever *really wanted* a couch? Enough to camp outside a furniture store for a week? That's how badly some consumers in the southeastern United States wanted a couch (or some other manifestation of euromodern furniture) when IKEA opened its Atlanta store in June 2005. Thousands lined up at the door on opening day, although the record was set when 35,000 customers visited IKEA's first Tokyo store on opening day in April 2006. Back home in West Chester, Ohio, Jen Segrest doesn't need any furniture, but "I'd walk over molten glass for my pot rack," she admits during a two-day vigil waiting for the West Chester store to open in March 2008. Segrest also runs a website called OhIkea.com. Another member of the crowd who doesn't plan to buy anything says that he's just there "paying homage."

IKEA is a sort of cult. It's certainly a darling of a consulting firm called the Cult Branding Company, which certifies that the Swedish retailer more than amply exemplifies the "Seven Golden Rules of Cult Branding":

1. Cult brands understand that consumers want to be part of a group that's different.

2. Cult-brand inventors show daring and determination.

3. Cult brands sell lifestyles.

4. Cult brands listen to the choir and create cult-brand evangelists.

5. Cult brands always create customer communities.

6. Cult brands are inclusive.

7. Cult brands promote personal freedom and draw power from their enemies.

IKEA, confirms *Business Week* magazine, "is the quintessential cult brand," and its customers belong to "a like-minded cost/design/environmentally-sensitive global tribe."

The founder of this global "cult" is a Swedish entrepreneur named Ingvar Kamprad, who started the company in his rural hometown in 1943, at the age of 17. (*IKEA* stands for *Ingvar Kamprad* plus *Elmtaryd Agunnaryd*, the names, respectively, of the farm and village where Kamprad grew up.) At first, Kamprad sold miscellaneous bargain goods (pens, wallets, picture frames, and so forth) through a catalog, delivering orders with the village milk wagon. He added furniture to his product line in 1951, started commissioning designs in 1955, and introduced the flat-pack design (for convenient storage and transport) in 1956, but he didn't open his first brick-and-mortar store until 1958. More stores followed throughout Scandinavia, and the first non-Scandinavian outlet opened in Switzerland in 1973. IKEA entered Canada in 1976 but didn't venture into the American market until 1985. As of mid-2008, IKEA operated 253 stores in 24 countries (another 32 outlets are run by franchisees). In 2008, the company added 21 stores in 11 countries; another 20 global outlets were added in 2009. There are 36 stores in the United States, and IKEA wants to increase the number to 50 by the end of 2010. Sales have risen from $8.6 billion to $28.9 billion in the decade between 1998 and 2008.

Kamprad retired in 1999, but to the faithful, he's still the spiritual father of the IKEA movement. His pronouncements on the company's mission and manner of doing business have a way of sounding like a sermon on the Seven Golden Rules of Cult Branding. He refers to his target audience—and targeted customers—as "the many," and from the outset, his plan was to bring affordable, well-designed furniture to this market composed of "the many." Bear in mind that "the many" is not really a "mass" market: In reality, it's a profitable niche consisting basically of consumers who want stylish furniture at a low cost. Today, the company says that it offers "affordable solutions for better living," with "better living" referring to a range of well-designed furniture and furnishings and "affordable" referring to the price range of consumers starting up their own homes and/or expanding their families. Although IKEA sells furniture in

more than 20 countries, its market share in each is fairly small—somewhere between 5 and 10 percent.

As we shall see, the IKEA concept depends on innovation, and the company's ability to innovate successfully depends in part on an organizational structure that encourages creativity and communication. To understand how it's all designed to work, however, we first need to break down the elements of "the IKEA way"—the factors which, *taken in combination*, have made the IKEA concept so successful. The *target market* that we've just described is the first of these factors, and we can identify four others in terms that any marketer would recognize:

- *Product.* With nearly 10,000 items, the IKEA product line is quite large, and because smaller products compliment larger products, customers can experiment with ensembles that satisfy their own needs and tastes while calculating total costs as they proceed through the store or catalog. As for product design, one German expert recalls that the first IKEA designs were "quite horrible." Fortunately, he adds, the company started paying more attention to design in the early 1990s. "Today if you go to IKEA," he admits, "you will always find some pieces which are good designs and very reasonable in pricing." IKEA also wants consumers—especially Americans—to stop thinking of furniture as durable goods. Older Americans, says one company marketing manager, "keep a sofa longer than a car" because they believe that it's going to be the long-term "icon of the living room." IKEA wants to appeal to the willingness of younger consumers to experiment with changes, and its price structure makes it possible for them to do it.

- *Price.* "Designing beautiful-but-expensive products is easy," says one Swedish executive. "Designing beautiful products that are inexpensive and functional is a huge challenge." Nevertheless, IKEA prices are typically 20 to 30 percent, and sometimes 30 to 50 percent, below those of stores selling fully assembled furniture. "When we decide about a product, we always start with the price," reports one product developer, and after starting with an original competitive price,

IKEA then proceeds to drive it even lower. The company maintains price leadership not only by purchasing in large quantities but by constantly looking for cheaper suppliers; nearly 50 percent of IKEA's outsourcing partners are located in developing economies.

- *Distribution.* Unlike manufacturing, which is outsourced, IKEA regards distribution as one of its own core competencies. So, in addition to a global network of thousands of manufacturers and nearly 1,400 suppliers in 54 countries, IKEA maintains a system of 27 distribution centers (which ship products to stores) and 11 customer-distribution centers (which ship goods to consumers) in 16 countries. About 70 percent of inventory reaches stores through distribution centers, with the remaining 30 percent coming directly from manufacturers. Its stores, too, are an important facet of IKEA's distribution strategy. A key innovation is the way they're laid out. Unlike the traditional furniture outlet, which directs customers to separate sections to view multiple versions of one product (for example, beds) or one room (for example, bedrooms), IKEA stores are laid out around a wide one-way path—the "natural path," according to the company—that carries customers directly from one section to the next. "Because the store is designed as a circle," observes one customer in Ohio, "I can see everything as long as I keep walking in one direction." That's the way it's supposed to work: The "natural path" not only exposes her to the whole range of IKEA offerings but also encourages her to extend her in-store visit.

- *Promotion.* Promotion at IKEA revolves around the near-legendary annual catalog, a 300-page compendium of color photos and blurbs for such exotic-sounding products as Extorp armchairs and Mumsig ovens. Issued every summer in 55 different editions, 27 languages, and 35 countries, the IKEA catalog boasts a circulation of 175 million copies worldwide. It consumes about 70 percent of the company's annual marketing budget, but

it's a logical medium for getting across the IKEA message: Featuring about 12,000 items, it covers the whole range of the company's new products, focuses on ideas for innovations in the customer's home, and relies on word-of-mouth publicity among the faithful. Not surprisingly, IKEA stores are arranged to accomplish essentially the same goals. First of all, they are, like the IKEA catalog, designed to encourage repeat visits by showcasing the company's regular turnover in new products (about one-third per year). They're also more colorful and attractive than the typical retail-furniture outlet—the better to suggest the wealth of product ideas contained within their walls and the better to stir the imagination of the customer's inner home decorator.

The IKEA store is also the company's most obvious and most important process innovation. Averaging around 300,000 square feet, most boxlike blue-and-yellow stores feature both the series of showrooms ranged along the "natural path" and an in-store self-serve warehouse. After choosing items from the Showroom (where product and price information is provided on large easy-to-read tags), customers collect trolleys for transporting their purchases and pass into the Market Hall, where they can pick up smaller items, such as linen, lighting, glassware, and rugs. Next along the path is the Self Serve Warehouse, where they collect their furniture purchases in flat-pack form and then proceed to the rows of cashier's stations to pay for everything. Once they've paid for their purchases, customers can arrange for delivery or roll them to the loading dock, pack them in or on their vehicles, and take them home.

The procedure, in which customers perform many of the functions performed by employees at traditional furniture stores, is a model of process optimization in a retail operation, and it's been the key to effective cost and price cutting at IKEA since Ingvar Kamprad first introduced the concept in 1953. Another major process innovation is the concept of flat-packing products—breaking down the parts and packing them in separate containers for shipping, storage, and customer self-assembly. IKEA developed the process in the mid-1950s as a logical extension of yet another important process innovation—the concept of designing its own furniture.

As important as process innovation has been to the company's success, the IKEA engine is powered by the introduction of new products and a constant stream of product innovations. We've already seen why new products are so important to the IKEA concept: The encounter with showrooms and display racks full of products that weren't there the last time around stirs the customer's impulse to make changes—"to create a better everyday life at home," as CEO Anders Dahlvig puts it on the IKEA Group website. Finding new products from outside sources, however, isn't the same thing as innovating within the company. At IKEA, innovation from within signals the company's commitment not only to respond to changes in the needs of customers all around the world, but to maintain a global brand identity and to convey an ongoing sense of excitement among the brand-loyal faithful.

At any given time, about 50 designers at the company's Swedish workshop are busy creating five to ten new products, but designers aren't the only people in the organization who are responsible for innovative ideas. "[W]ith our flat organization structure," says Bill Agee, head of marketing at IKEA U.S., "everyone contributes. Whoever you are within the IKEA organization, you're expected to contribute your ideas—your new ideas, your old ideas or whatever it may be—and every idea is welcome." The concept works, explains Agee, because "we're a very process-oriented company. . . . [W]e have three basic processes: creating, communicating, and selling the home-furnishings offer." "Each of these processes," he adds, "has a matrix structure": Working as members of what amounts to a companywide team, designers design products, marketers like Agee communicate the product message, and coworkers in the company's warehouses and stores deliver the product to the customer. "Our independence," Agee thinks, "has a lot to do with our innovation because

we don't know any better. . . . We feel that we are, to a certain extent, operating outside of standard operating procedures."

Case Questions

1. One IKEA executive says that the current global economic situation has "pushed innovation" at the company. In fact, he says, "This is a great time to be more innovative." Explain what he means.

2. You're an IKEA store manager, and corporate headquarters has instructed you to change the layout of your store. The change must be "dramatic," but the details are up to you. Wanting to make the most of the opportunity, you intend to manage the project as planned change. What steps will you take to ensure that you'll be successful?

3. There's an IKEA TV ad that features a discarded lamp, forsaken on a rainy night in some American city. A man looks at the camera and says in a sympathetic Swedish accent, "Many of you feel bad for this lamp," and then, after a well-timed pause, "That's because you're crazy." What's the message of the commercial?

4. Would you want to manage an IKEA store? Why or why not?

Case References

Zachary Lewis, "IKEA Has Inspired a Cult of Devoted Fans," *NJ.com*, May 14, 2008, www.nj.com on March 22, 2009; Kerry Capell, "Understanding IKEA: How the Swedish Company Turned into a Global Obsession," *BusinessWeek*, November 8, 2005, www.msnbc.msn.com on March 22, 2009; B. J. Bueno, "Seven Golden Rules of Cult Branding," The Cult-Branding Company, 2009, www.cult-branding.com on March 22, 2009; Colin White, "Strategic Management: The IKEA Way," *Business Innovation*, December 22, 2008, www.united-bit.com on March 23, 2009; "Key of IKEA," *The Hub Magazine*, January 1, 2009, www.hubmagazine.com on March 23, 2009; "IKEA History: How It All Began" "The IKEA Way," IKEA website, www.ikea.com on March 22, 2009; "Facts & Figures," IKEA Group website, www.ikea-group.ikea.com on March 22, 2009.

CHAPTER 8

"Still Better Off Than Most"

For the most part, 2008 was a pretty good year for Nucor, the country's largest steelmaker. In fact, net earnings hit a record $1.83 billion; net sales also set a record—$23.6 billion, up 43 percent over 2007. Unfortunately, despite such record-setting year-end numbers, the fourth quarter of 2008 was a disaster. Net earnings for the last three months of the year came to $105.9 million—down a whopping 71 percent from $364.8 million for the fourth quarter of fiscal 2007. "The record sales and earnings achieved by Nucor in 2008," said chairman and CEO Daniel R. DiMicco, "were accomplished in spite of the unprecedented economic and steel-market conditions that we experienced in the fourth quarter."

Referring again to "the unprecedented speed and magnitude of the global economy's decline," DiMicco went on to forecast an equally dismal first quarter—and beyond—for fiscal 2009. In January, with the capacity of its mills down from 95 percent to 50 percent and its stock down by more than 10 percent, Nucor management passed out one-time bonuses of $1,000 to $2,000 to all of the firm's workers, at a total cost to the company of $40 million. In March, management distributed another $270 million in profit sharing. Things had gotten bad and were looking worse, but "we're making money. We've got jobs," explained one veteran executive.

Indeed, Nucor still had *all* its jobs. Hit by a 50-percent plunge in output that had begun in September 2008, the U.S. steel industry had laid off some 10,000 workers by January 2009, and the United Steelworkers union was expecting the number to double before the recession came to an end. As of the end of March 2009, however, Nucor had refused to follow suit in laying anyone off. At its 11 U.S. facilities, Nucor employees are rewriting safety manuals, getting a head start on maintenance jobs, mowing the lawns, and cleaning the bathrooms—but they're still drawing paychecks. "Financially," says one employee at the company's facility in Crawfordsville, Indiana, "Nucor workers are still better off than most."

As far as DiMicco is concerned, the company's ability to survive the current economic crisis will depend on several factors, "most importantly, our employees and the Nucor culture." What's that culture like? It originated in the 1960s as the result of policies established by Ken Iverson, who brought a radical perspective on how to manage a company's human resources to the job of CEO. Iverson figured that workers would be much more productive if an employer went out of its way to share authority with them, respect what they accomplished, and compensate them as handsomely as possible. Today, the basics of the company's HR model are summed up in its "Employee Relations Principles":

1. *Management is obligated to manage Nucor in such a way that employees will have the opportunity to earn according to their productivity.*

2. *Employees should feel confident that if they do their jobs properly, they will have a job tomorrow.*

3. *Employees have the right to be treated fairly and must believe that they will be.*

4. *Employees must have an avenue of appeal when they believe they are being treated unfairly.*

The Iverson approach is based on motivation, and the key to that approach is a highly original pay system. Step 1, which calls for base pay below the industry average, probably doesn't seem like a promising start, but the Nucor compensation plan is designed to get better as the results of the work get better. If a shift, for example, can turn out a defect-free batch of steel, every worker is entitled to a bonus that's paid weekly and that can potentially triple his or her take-home pay. In addition, there are one-time annual bonuses and profit-sharing payouts. In 2005, for instance, Nucor had an especially good year: It shipped more steel than any other U.S. producer, and net income hit $1.3 billion, up from $311 million in 2000. The average steelworker took home $79,000 in base pay and weekly bonuses, plus a $2,000 year-end bonus and an average of $18,000 in profit-sharing money.

The system, however, cuts both ways. Take that defect-free batch of steel, for example. If there's a problem with a batch, workers on the shift obviously don't get any weekly bonus. And that's if they catch the problem before the batch leaves the plant. If it reaches the customer, they may *lose* up to three times what they would have received as a bonus. "In average-to-bad years," adds HR vice president James M. Coblin, "we earn less than our peers in other companies. That's supposed to teach us that we don't want to be average or bad. We want to be good." For the first quarter of fiscal 2009, total pay at Nucor was down by about 40 percent.

Everybody in the company, from janitors to the CEO, is covered by some form of incentive plan tied to various goals and targets. We've just described the Production Incentive Plan, which covers operating and maintenance workers and supervisors and which may boost base salaries by 80 percent to 150 percent. Bonuses for department managers are based on a return-on-assets formula tied to divisional performance, as are bonuses under the Non-Production and Non-Department–Manager Plan, which covers everyone, except senior officers, not included in either of the first two plans; bonuses under both manager plans may increase base pay by 75 percent to 90 percent. Senior officers don't work under contracts or get pension or retirement plans, and their base salaries are below industry average. In a world in which the typical CEO makes more than 400 times what a factory worker makes, Nucor CEO DiMicco makes considerably less. In the banner year of 2005, for example, his combined salary and bonus (about $2.3 million) came to 23 times the total taken home by the average Nucor factory worker. His bonus and those of other top managers are based on a ratio of net income to stockholder's equity.

Nucor needs just four incentive plans because of an unusually flat organizational structure—another Iverson innovation. There are just four layers of personnel between a janitor and senior management: general managers, department managers, line supervisors, and hourly personnel. Most operating decisions are made at the divisional level or lower, and the company is known for its tolerance of honest mistakes made in the line of decision-making duty.

The Nucor website quotes an unnamed executive as saying, "Workers excel here because they are allowed to fail," and goes on to explain that the occasional misstep is considered a good trade-off for the benefits of initiative and idea sharing: "Nucor managers at all levels encourage their employees to try out their new ideas. Sometimes the ideas work out, sometimes they don't. But this freedom to try helps give Nucor one of the most creative, get-it-done work forces in the world."

The Nucor system works not only because employees share financial risks and benefits but because, in sharing risks and benefits, they're a lot like owners. And people who think like owners are a lot more likely to take the initiative when decisions have to be made or problems solved. What's more, Nucor has found that teamwork is a good incubator for initiative as well as idea sharing. John J. Ferriola, who managed the Nucor mill in Hickman, Arkansas, before becoming chief operating officer, remembers an afternoon in March 2006 when the electrical grid at his facility went down. His electricians got on the phone to three other company electricians, one in Alabama and two in North Carolina, who dropped what they were doing and went straight to Arkansas. Working 20-hour shifts, the joint team had the plant up and running again in three days (as opposed to an anticipated full week). There was nothing in it (at least financially) for the visiting electricians, but they knew that maintenance personnel get no bonuses when equipment in their facility isn't operating. "At Nucor," says one frontline supervisor, "we're not 'you guys' and 'us guys.' It's all of us guys. Wherever the bottleneck is, we go there, and everyone works on it."

Nucor also likes to see teamwork—cooperation and idea sharing—combined with a little productive competition. Plant managers often set up contests between shifts to improve efficiency, output, or safety, but sometimes the effort of a work group to give itself a competitive edge can be taken to another level. In 2002, the Nucor plant in Crawfordsville, Indiana, was a pioneer in the development of an innovative process called thin-strip steel casting, and as of 2008, it was still setting records for continuous output from the process. The facility, however, isn't located near any major waterway and is thus at a disadvantage when it comes to transportation costs, especially when fuel prices are high. So General Manager Ron Dickerson and his employees collaborated on a plan not only to get around the problem but to increase profitability at the same time. Because it was too expensive for them to ship sheet steel as wide as that regularly made by competitors (including other Nucor-owned plants), Crawfordsville management and workers campaigned for the opportunity to shift the plant's focus to other types of steel.

It was a risky proposition, but today Crawfordsville turns out 160 different grades of steel. Some of them present manufacturing difficulties that employees have had to solve over time, but making the new processes work meant more orders for the plant and more hours for its employees. By the first quarter of 2008, the plant was setting production and shipment records. "We're continually expanding product ranges and the types of steel we make," says Dickerson, who continues to look forward, particularly to the opportunity to apply the Nucor brand of employee initiative to new technologies. "Nucor has a couple of other things going on," he notes, "and it's not yet decided where they'll make an investment. [But] Crawfordsville is known for successful startups, so I'm hoping we get some of these new technologies."

Case Questions

1. Instead of a system of individual performance appraisals, Nucor appraises employee performance according to division-wide quality, productivity, and profitability goals and targets.

What are the advantages and disadvantages of this approach?
2. Identify the incentives—both financial and nonfinancial—that Nucor uses to motivate employees.
3. How does Nucor's flat organizational structure contribute to the success of its compensation system?
4. Many firms today use temporary, part-time, or virtual workers to reduce costs and gain flexibility. Nucor has never taken this route. Should management consider it in the future? Why or why not?
5. CEO Dan DiMicco believes that when the economy turns around, Nucor will be "first out of the box" in the steel industry. What reasons does he have for being so optimistic?

Case References

Nanette Byrnes, "Pain, but No Layoffs at Nucor," *BusinessWeek*, March 26, 2009, www.businessweek.com on April 2, 2009; Byrnes with Michael Arndt, "The Art of Motivation," *BusinessWeek*, May 1, 2006, www.businessweek.com on April 2, 2009; "About Us," Nucor website, www.nucor.com on April 2, 2009; "Nucor Reports Record Results for 2008," *Reuters*, January 27, 2009, www.reuters.com on April 2, 2009; "Nucor Expects Loss in Q1," *RTTNews*, March 17, 2009, www.rttnews.com on April 2, 2009; Louis Uchitelle, "Steel Industry, In Slump, Looks to Federal Stimulus," *New York Times*, January 2, 2009, www.nytimes.com on April 2, 2009; Kathy Mayer, "Nucor Steel: Pioneering Mill in Crawfordsville Celebrates 20 Years and 30 Million Tons," *AllBusiness*, September 1, 2008, www.allbusiness.com on April 3, 2009.

CHAPTER 9

Dell Does Damage Control

Michael Dell, says Harvard's David Yoffie, "broke the paradigm about how to run a computer business." By now, the litany of innovations at Dell, one of the world's top suppliers of personal computers, is pretty familiar: direct selling to customers to avoid retail markups, flexible manufacturing for low-cost customization, and just-in-time inventory to hold down carrying costs. The nature of such innovations makes it clear that Dell's phenomenal success over the last

25 years owes much to tightly disciplined operations and vigorously applied controls.

The success of Dell's "value-priced" business model, for example, reflects effective efforts to control costs. Dell's North Carolina plant, which opened in October 2005, can produce PCs 40 percent faster and with 30 percent less downtime than its facilities in Texas and Tennessee. Unlike older factories, which must retool equipment for different types of computers, the plant in Winston-Salem can build any of Dell's 40 models at any time. "Other factories have a process-driven flow," explains factory designer Richard Komm. "[This plant] is focused on one thing: How do we get [a computer] to the customer in the shortest amount of time?"

Excellent quality control also holds down costs. At Dell, teams of three workers typically collaborate on the assembly of a PC. Because each individual is assigned a specialized set of tasks, training is simpler and quicker, assembly time is faster, and errors are less common. Each team includes a tester who performs a quick check to ensure that every completed machine is correctly wired and boots properly. Finished machines must also pass inspection and then undergo even more extensive testing, but the purpose of the quick test is to allow the assembly team to catch gross defects as early as possible. The principle, explains Komm, is quite simple: "The faster you get feedback to the operator, the fewer defects." Dell now catches most defects in 4 minutes (rather than 60, as in the past), and the overall defect rate is 30 percent lower.

On the other hand, although earnings grew by 52 percent in 2005, customer complaints doubled. During the next year, Dell acknowledged problems with customer service call transfers and wait times, promising on its corporate blog that "we're spending more than $100 million—and a lot of blood, sweat and tears of talented people—to fix this." For the year, spending on customer service reached $150 million.

In addition, competitive conditions in the PC market were a lot different in 2005 than they had been during Dell's glory days—mainly the decade from 1991 to 2001, when annual sales soared from $546 million to $32 billion. For the third quarter of fiscal 2006, Dell's growth of 3.6 percent paled against Hewlett-Packard's 15 percent, and the fourth quarter produced even more disappointing numbers: Sales had tumbled by 51 percent from the previous year, and PC shipments had declined by 8.9 percent while HP boasted an increase of 23.9 percent. (It was a dismal quarter all around: Dell also had to recall 4.1 million laptops because the batteries threatened to ignite, and the SEC announced an investigation

into the company's accounting practices.) By the end of the year, industry analysts estimated that HP had overtaken Dell in worldwide market share, 17.4 percent to 13.9 percent.

With revenues of $56 billion (good for No. 25 among the Fortune 500), Dell was in no immediate danger of going out of business, but obviously there were some problems. Ironically, it was becoming increasingly clear that Dell's troubles could be traced back to the innovative, low-cost, no-nonsense business model on which the company had prospered. For one thing, although Dell had eliminated the early competitors who'd failed to imitate its business model and meet its low prices, by 2006 it was facing a new set of rivals, particularly HP and the Chinese company Lenovo, both of which had emerged as formidable competitors by making themselves remarkably efficient.

In addition, it was clear by 2006 that the computer industry had outgrown the era of the generic box. The stylish iMac had been on the market for nearly 10 years, and HP's MediaSmart TV, which functioned as either a TV or a wireless PC monitor that could stream videos and music, had come out early in the year. Meanwhile, Dell, according to a senior editor at *Fortune*, remained "the ultimate provider of white-bread (well, gray plastic) PCs." A veteran industry consultant put it a little more bluntly: "Dell," he suggested, "is down there with food and shelter in the hierarchy of human needs."

Dell, it seems, had fallen behind in two areas that weren't adequately addressed by a business model powered principally by operations and financial control: (1) product innovation and design, and (2) customer service and consumer brand preference. "Competitors," remarked an industry marketing expert, "are selling the use, the solution, but Dell's still selling products." In other words, Dell needed to build a business model driven as much by marketing management as by operations and financial management. Michael Dell, who'd stepped down as CEO in 2004 while staying on as chairman, agreed: "[We were] managing cost instead of managing service and quality," he admitted. "We had this historical structural advantage which manifested itself in lower price and better value for customers, and I think we overemphasized the price element and did not emphasize relationship and customer experience."

The first thing Dell did was reinstate himself as CEO, replacing Kevin B. Rollins in January 2007. The next thing he did (in April) was hire a chief marketing officer—a heretofore nonexistent position at the company. "We'll be seeing radical change at Dell over the next two years," promised Mark Jarvis, an ex-CMO at software giant Oracle, and by 2008, Dell had begun turning out a stream of innovative new products:

- The Area-51 m17x from Alienware, a Dell subsidiary specializing in desktops and laptops for games, is a futuristic-looking laptop. It comes with an optional HDTV tuner and HDMI port for displaying high-definition video.
- The Studio Hybrid PC, fashionably curved and available in six translucent colors, boasts a variety of special power-saving features. With an upgrade, it can read Blu-ray discs, and an optional tuner lets users watch TV.
- The Inspiron Mini 9 netbook is intended for a range of Internet-centric tasks for which users typically rely on PCs—surfing, chatting, blogging, watching videos, and listening to music.
- Weighing less than a pound, the M109S On-the-Go pocket-sized projector combines power output and connectors into a multi-input cable, thus cutting down on the number of peripherals that the user has to pack around. It's compatible with both U.S. and European TV standards, and it's HDTV capable.
- The luxury-priced Adamo netbook is designed to compete with Apple's MacBook Air. Featuring a high-definition display with Web camera and Bluetooth, it comes in a $2,000 model (the Admire) and a $2,700 model (the Desire).

So far, however, Dell's new product and marketing initiatives have failed to pull it out of a slump that began in mid-2005, and that has worsened with the global economic crisis and recession. The problem? Dell is trying to do two things at once—keep costs down and expand its business. Expansion—which involves introducing new products and increasing sales overseas and through retail outlets—is an expensive proposition, and the two goals are hardly compatible.

During the fourth quarter of 2007 (ending February 1, 2008), income slipped 6.5 percent to 31 cents a share, continuing a slide in share price from $30 in November 2007 to $20.87 three months later. As for controlling costs, the company had cut 3,200 jobs over the previous eight months.

By the end of the second quarter of 2008, share price had hit an eight-year low of $18.24, and by December, at $11.13, it was at its lowest level since 1997. Michael Dell admitted that recent price-cutting measures had been "a bit too aggressive," but more importantly, analysts agreed that Dell's prospects for difficult economic times were dampened by its long-term failure to do what other big tech companies had done—get bigger by means of acquisitions. Dell, which had long boasted of its successful internal growth, had finally made a few strategic acquisitions, but observers pointed out that most of the prized assets had already been bought up.

As we've seen, Dell was also making heavy investments in design, and by the end of 2008, it had made moves to increase its activities in hardware and services for corporate offices and data centers. Analysts, however, remained skeptical that all of these measures would soon result in a well-rounded, well-managed company. Michael Dell tried to explain the company's efforts to rework its business model: "Here was a company," he said, "that was maniacally focused on an approach to its business which caused an enormous amount of success, and when it kind of realized that that wasn't working as well as it did in earlier periods, decided to make a number of changes. . . . It's okay," he added, "if everyone doesn't understand what we're doing."

For the first quarter of 2009 (ending on May 1), revenue dropped in all of Dell's major businesses, including declines of 34 percent and 20 percent in desktop and notebook PCs, respectively. Although share price had reached a 52-week high of $25.63 in August 2008, it had dipped as low as $8. For the quarter, income had plummeted 63 percent, to $290 million (15 cents a share) from $784 million (38 cents a share) a year earlier. Having earned 24 cents a share, Dell beat estimates by a penny, but revenues fell below forecasts, declining 23 percent from $16 billion to $12.3 billion.

Case Questions

1. Describe Dell's original innovative business model and explain the roles played in it by operations, financial, and strategic levels of control.

2. Under its original business model, what advantages did Dell gain from its tight control system? What disadvantages is the company now experiencing? Can you pinpoint two or three areas in which Dell's approach to strategic control could be more effective?

3. Describe what you think would be an effective new business model for Dell, explaining the roles played in it by operations, financial, strategic, and structural levels of control. In what ways will your new approach to control be effective in the company's current environment?

4. In your opinion, which areas of control management (integration with planning, flexibility, etc.) most need improvement at Dell?

Case References

Louise Lee, "Hanging Up on Dell?" *BusinessWeek*, October 10, 2005, www.businessweek.com on June 4, 2009; Lee, "It's Dell vs. The Dell Way," *BusinessWeek*, March 6, 2006, www.businessweek.com on June 4, 2009; Christopher Null, "Dude, You're Getting a Dell—Every Five Seconds," CNNMoney.com, December 1, 2005, http://money.cnn.com on June 4, 2009; David Kirkpatrick, "Dell in the Penalty Box," *Fortune*, September 5, 2006, http://cnnmoney.com on June 4, 2009; Matt Richtel, "Profit Falls as Dell Tries to Grow and Limit Costs," *New York Times*, February 29, 2008, www.nytimes.com on June 4, 2009; Laurie J. Flynn, "Dell's Profit Drop Surprises Investors," *New York Times*, August 29, 2008, www.nytimes.com on June 4, 2009; Ashlee Vance, "Dell Trails Rivals in the Worst of Times," *New York Times*, December 16, 2008, www.nytimes.com on June 4, 2009; and Ashlee Vance, "Dell, Its Quarterly Earnings Down 63%, Predicts Recovery," *New York Times*, May 29, 2009, www.nytimes.com on June 4, 2009.

CHAPTER 10

Amazon Rekindles Its Flair for Technology

As you probably know, selling things online—online retailing, or *e-tailing*—is the only thing that Amazon.com does. Unlike online rivals, such as Barnes&Noble.com or Walmart.com, Amazon has no roof over its head—no bricks-and-mortar presence to anchor its online presence. The seller and its customers interact by website, e-mail, or phone. Behind the website, however, is one of the largest direct-to-consumer distribution operations in the world.

Founded in 1995 as a bookseller, Amazon does pretty well these days—nearly $5 billion in sales for the second quarter of 2009—but it's had its ups and downs. Early investors believed that the promise of online business outweighed the risks associated with the new type of enterprise, but it wasn't long before giddy expectation gave way to more sober assessment, as soaring costs kept pace with expanding sales and wiped out profits. That's when Amazon diversified its range of product offerings, adding toys, music, electronics, software, and household goods. Expansion

continued to eat into profits, and the company had to make huge investments in infrastructure and IT before it finally went into the black in 2002.

Though fairly commonplace among today's online enterprises, Amazon's business model was revolutionary for its time. There was no need to open stores in high-rent shopping areas, and the company was free to choose locations for distribution centers based on cost and convenience to transportation facilities. Amazon's seven distribution centers stock thousands of popular items, but many of the goods that consumers buy through Amazon are in fact "drop-shipped" directly from the manufacturer. Amazon, therefore, can offer a multitude of products without incurring high inventory expenses, and because the middleman has been eliminated, delivery times are faster.

In addition, much of the work at Amazon facilities is automated. Workers use simple, menu-driven computer programs to access and monitor customer orders. Goods are then picked from the shelves and placed in a vast system of automated chutes and bins that bundles them appropriately. At one point, Amazon had tried to minimize shipping costs by bundling all items for shipment to a single address into one package. Now, however, the system relies on a more effective sorting algorithm that calculates optimal package size to both protect items and reduce costs. Automated scanners track the progress of every order, and automated boxers and labelers prepare goods for shipping.

Software, of course, is an important part of Amazon's operations because better systems hold down labor costs, increase accuracy and speed, enhance the customer experience, and support effective planning. Supply chain software, for example, uses a complex formula to choose which goods should be carried in distribution centers and which should be drop-shipped. Yet another algorithm constantly recalculates item popularity ratings to choose which goods to store in the most-frequented sections of warehouses.

Amazon is also a pioneer in the development of several operations technologies:

- "One-click" buying allows customers to make final purchases with a single mouse click. (The process is patented and licensed to other companies.)
- Amazon was one of the first online retailers to let customers post online product reviews, which not only boost sales but also contribute to a sense of community among users.
- Customers can review their order histories, create wish and favorites lists, share information with friends, receive personalized recommendations and gift-giving reminders, and tag items with customized category data.

Amazon's operations software is so popular with other firms that the company has launched a feature called Amazon Web Services, which allows independent programmers and merchants to access Amazon's library of software and adapt it for their own use. The library is free unless the "borrower" intends to sell through Amazon, in which case there's a 15 percent commission on each sale. The service has proven so popular that 22 percent of Amazon's sales are now conducted by other merchants. In February 2009, as part of Amazon Web Services, Amazon launched Amazon SimpleDB, a system that allows businesses to store and quickly retrieve simple data. Some companies already rely on Amazon's expertise to manage their websites. Target and Office Depot, for instance, contract their online presence to Amazon.

And now—for consumers—there's Kindle, which, ironically, hearkens back to Amazon's origins as a bookseller. Developed by an Amazon subsidiary called Lab126, Kindle is a software–hardware platform for reading electronic print material. The first-generation Kindle device came out at the very end of 2007 and was aimed primarily at readers of books, who Amazon founder and CEO Jeff Bezos promptly labeled "the last bastion of analog." "The vision [of Kindle]," he hastened to add, "is that you should be able to get any book—not just any book in print, but any book that's *ever* been in print—on this device in less than a minute."

By the end of 2008, Amazon had more than 275,000 titles available for download, but Kindle is designed to handle much more than books. With this device, which doesn't require a computer, Amazon allows you not only to download 1,500 books, but also even to subscribe to newspapers and magazines, which will automatically be downloaded as soon as new issues go to press. You can search for material through Google, follow links from blogs and other webpages, jot down notes on the page you're reading, and even capture selected passages with the equivalent of an electric highlighter. Kindle 2 and Kindle DX, each with larger displays and other new and improved features, arrived in early 2009, and there's also a Kindle for iPhone.

Eight months after its release, Amazon had sold nearly $100 million worth of Kindles, and by the end of the year, amid speculation that it was the iPod of the book world, the Kindle had sold double its projected sales figure (and equaled sales of the iPod in its first year of release). Analysts expect sales of $1.2 billion to $1.4 billion by 2010, which would amount to about 4 percent of Amazon's yearly revenue.

Case Questions

1. What types of decisions common to manufacturing firms does Amazon make? What types of decisions common to service firms? How do both types of decisions relate to the marketing of Kindle?

2. Describe Amazon's entire supply chain. From which activities in this supply chain does Amazon make money? At what points in the supply chain does Amazon outsource or contract activities to outsiders?

3. Go online to Amazon.com and select an item that comes from Amazon itself rather than from a drop shipper. What kind of purchasing decisions were necessary to make this product available at Amazon's price? What kind of inventory control decisions?

4. What facets of Amazon's operations allow it to offer a high-quality shopping experience to customers?

5. Give three or four examples of ways in which Amazon's operations contribute to high productivity.

Case References

Robert Hof, "Amazon's Brighter Horizon?" *BusinessWeek*, April 26, 2006, www.businessweek.com on June 10, 2009; Robert Hof, "Amazon's Costly Bells and Whistles," *BusinessWeek*, February 3, 2006, www.businessweek.com on June 10, 2009; Paul R. La Monica, "Consumers Keep on Clicking," CNNMoney.com, July 26, 2005, http://money.cnn.com on June 10, 2009; Jeff Cogswell, "Amazon Simple DB a Solid Choice for Simple Web-Based Data Storage," *eweek*, February 5, 2009, www.eweek.com on June 10, 2009; Steven Levy, "The Future of Reading," *Newsweek*, November 26, 2007, www.newsweek.com on June 10, 2009; Amy Martinez, "Amazon Says Kindle Sales Top Its 'Most Optimistic' Projections," *The Seattle Times*, April 17, 2009, http://seattletimes.nwsource.com on June 10, 2009; Holly Jackson, "Kindle Sales Pegged at $1 Billion by 2010," *CNET News*, August 11, 2008, http://news.cnet.com on June 10, 2009.

CHAPTER 11

Being Steve Jobs

When you hear the word *personality*, what's the first thing you think of? A high-profile person like Oprah or Bono? Or do your thoughts turn to that dynamic and organized set of characteristics that make each person different from other people? Steve Jobs, the charismatic and controversial cofounder and head of Apple Computer, could come to mind in either case. He's a personality with an interesting personality. He's the public face of an extremely successful company whom some people see as an inspiring visionary and others as an insufferable egotist. The bottom line is that a complex and often contradictory personality is clearly a factor in the remarkable success of not one but two business ventures notable for high-tech breakthroughs and marketing savvy.

Born in San Francisco in 1955 and raised in the Bay Area by adoptive parents, Jobs spent one semester at Reed College in Oregon and then worked briefly at Hewlett-Packard, where, in 1971, he met fellow electronics aficionado Steve Wozniak. After a short stint at Atari, an early videogame maker, Jobs backpacked around India in search of spiritual enlightenment. When he returned to the United States, he hooked up again with Wozniak at Atari. In 1976, 21-year-old Jobs convinced ex-electronics hacker Wozniak to commercialize a personal computer that he'd designed for his own use, and with funding from an angel investor, they started Apple Computer. Wozniak's design became the first commercially available personal computer, and by 1980, Apple's initial public offering had made millionaires of Jobs, Wozniak, and a lot of other people.

As CEO, Jobs marshaled his idealistic vision and high standards to push the company on to further success, but as rapid expansion put more and more pressure on his managerial skills, the company turned to an experienced executive, hiring PepsiCo CEO John Sculley to take over in 1983. Jobs continued to oversee the development of a new computer called the Macintosh, which, despite a series of failed designs and cost overruns, was introduced in 1984. The first small computer with a graphical user interface, the Macintosh was enormously successful. Meanwhile, however, Jobs and Sculley clashed continually, until, in May 1985, the Apple board forced Jobs to resign as head of the Macintosh unit. "People in the company had very mixed feelings about it," admits chief scientist Larry Tesler. "Everyone had been terrorized by Steve Jobs at some point or another, and so there was a certain relief that the terrorist would be gone. On the other hand, I think there was incredible respect for Steve Jobs by the very same people, and we were all very worried what would happen to this company without the visionary, without the founder, without the charisma."

Jobs protested by selling his Apple stock and, in 1985, starting up NeXT Computer to market a technologically advanced workstation. In the late 1980s, MIT computer scientist Tim Berners-Lee used the NeXTSTEP operating system to build the first web browser and editor (WorldWideWeb), but the system was too expensive for most people. Jobs continued to push NeXT products in the scientific and academic markets, but by 1993, the company had shifted exclusively to the development of software such as NeXTSTEP. Meanwhile, in 1986, Jobs paid $5 million for *Star Wars* impresario George Lucas's animation studio, called The Graphics Group, which he proceeded to manage with an uncharacteristic hands-off style.

In 1996, Apple, though hampered by a record-low stock price and crippling financial losses, purchased NeXT for $429 million, and Jobs came along with it. In July 1997, the board removed CEO Gilbert F. Amelio and named Jobs "interim CEO" (or "iCEO," as Jobs put it). Jobs focused on returning the company to profitability, and in March 1998, he announced the termination of several research-and-development projects. His predecessor had actually cut the number of such projects from 350 to 50, while Jobs's further reductions merely reduced the number from 50 to 10. Some people lost their jobs, but Amelio had presided over 4,100 layoffs (about 30 percent of the workforce). Nevertheless, rumors about further cuts—indeed, about summary firings—started to run rampant. Employees were reportedly wary about bumping into Jobs in an elevator, afraid that they might be unemployed by the time the door opened again. Apparently, it wasn't so much the reality of the situation as accounts of Jobs's abrasive personality and blunt manner that made Apple

employees apprehensive (although Jobs's profession that he intended to do more cutting than Amelio may have been a contributing factor). "When Steve attacks a problem," explained an executive at Adobe, Apple's biggest software supplier, "he attacks it with a vengeance. I think he mellowed during the NeXT years, [but] he's not so mellow anymore."

Under Jobs, Apple showed a profit in the first quarter of 1998 after substantial losses in 1997 and the first part of 1998. Analysts predicted that continued improvement would depend on a steady stream of new products, but Jobs, according to biographer Alan Deutschman, preferred to put the bulk of his energy and capital into marketing and rejuvenating the company's image as a maker of hip, cool-looking computers rather than counting on some stunning technical breakthrough to turn the company around. The result was the immensely successful "Think Different" campaign, which centered on a TV ad featuring celebrated visionaries such as Albert Einstein and Bob Dylan. The campaign marked a turning point for the company, restoring an image that had been tarnished by financial embarrassment and a flood of lackluster new brands. Jobs took a personal interest in the campaign, and according to a *Newsweek* reporter who watched it with him, he teared up when he saw the commercial for the first time. "That's what I love about him," recalls Katie Hafner. "It wasn't trumped up. Steve was genuinely moved by that stupid ad."

Meanwhile, Jobs had by no means neglected Apple's new-product pipeline. He had streamlined a process in which projects often overlapped by focusing the company's efforts on two new product lines, both of which used Apple's existing PowerPC G3 processors and Mac OS operating system: a desktop computer called the iMac and a laptop called the PowerBook G3. The iMac, which Jobs had greenlighted as a special research product shortly after he'd begun his second tour of duty as Apple CEO, featured an innovative design (an egg shape with a colorful shell of translucent plastic) and a distinctive aesthetic appeal. Supported by an energetic marketing campaign, it became what *Forbes* declared an "industry-altering success" and a piece of cultural iconography. Apple was once more a juggernaut in the computer industry. Apple, declared Jobs, "leads when it expresses its vision through its products, exciting you and making you proud to own a Mac. . . . The same focus and passion that brings these products to market has also made us a healthier company."

Fortune magazine, which has acknowledged Jobs as "one of Silicon Valley's leading egomaniacs," has also given him the entirely complimentary epithet of "master of disruption," observing that in a little over a decade after his return to Apple, Jobs enjoyed "the kind of position that most mad-genius tech wunderkinds can only fantasize about: thrilling consumers while wreaking havoc in multiple industries." Jobs, it seems, has a special talent for an approach to competing in dynamic industries that management strategists call *high-end disruption*—making moves that have allowed Apple to redefine industry rules and create significant new markets.

When, for example, Apple decided to branch out into the development of other digital appliances, it virtually hijacked the music industry with the introduction, between 2001 and 2003, of the iPod portable music player, iTunes digital music software, and the iTunes Music Store (which by 2006 would account for 10 percent of all music sales in the United States). The iPhone, a combination of cell phone, iPod, and Internet device, went on sale in June 2007, and by January 2009, Apple was the third-largest mobile-phone manufacturer in the world, behind only Nokia and Samsung.

Jobs may be (as his critics claim) an erratic self-absorbed control freak with unrealistically high standards and a bad temper, but since his return to the top spot, the value of Apple's shares has gone up more than 38-fold. By comparison, Microsoft shares have only doubled in value over the same stretch of time.

Finally, remember The Graphics Group, the animation studio that Jobs picked up back in 1986? In 1991, Jobs reached an agreement with Disney to produce three computer-animated feature films using the company's high-quality image-rendering technology. Rechristened Pixar, the studio turned out three movies (*Toy Story*, *A Bug's Life*, and *Toy Story 2*) that grossed a total of $2.5 billion—equal to the highest per-film gross in the motion-picture industry. Under a subsequent

agreement, Pixar continued to produce blockbuster hits, including *Monsters, Inc.*; *Cars*; and *Finding Nemo* (which grossed more than $800 million). In 2006, Disney bought Pixar for $7.4 billion in an all-stock transaction that made Jobs Disney's largest single shareholder and newest board member.

Fortune's Fred Vogelstein attributes Jobs's astounding success to his genius not only for developing wildly popular products, but for exploiting—indeed, fostering—conditions of turbulence in the industries in which he works: At both Apple and Pixar, says Vogelstein, "Jobs has been able to simultaneously harness technology in a way that throws the status quo into disorder and ride that chaos to the front of the pack."

Case Questions

1. Describe Steve Jobs's personality using the "Big Five" traits. Describe his personality using the Myers-Briggs framework.

2. How does Jobs's personality help him to be a better leader? How does his personality compromise his ability to lead?

3. How would you characterize the general state of affect and mood at Apple?

4. How do personality traits support entrepreneurial drive? What personality traits contribute to Jobs's success as an entrepreneur?

5. How do personality traits support a creative tendency? What personality traits contribute to Jobs's ability to be creative in an organizational context?

Case References

Peter Burrows, "An Insider's Take on Steve Jobs," *BusinessWeek*, January 30, 2006, www.businessweek.com on April 16, 2009; Peter Burrows and Ronald Grover, "Steve Jobs' Magic Kingdom," *BusinessWeek*, February 6, 2006, www.businessweek.com on April 16, 2009; Brian Caulfield, "The Sweet Revenge of Steve Jobs," *Forbes.com*, January 14, 2008, www.forbes.com on April 17, 2009; Tom Hornby, "25 Years of Macintosh," *Low End Mac*, April 9, 2007, http://lowendmac.com on April 16, 2009; Fred Vogelstein, "Mastering the Art of Disruption," *Fortune*, February 6, 2006, http://cnnmoney.com on April 16, 2009; Arik Hesseldahl, "Tim Cook: A Steady Go-To Guide for Apple," *BusinessWeek*, January 14, 2009, www.businessweek.com on April 15, 2009.

CHAPTER 12

The Law of Diminishing Motivation

At the end of *Legally Blonde*, a 2001 comedy about a sorority girl who aces Harvard Law School through a combination of hard work and valley-girl smarts, the heroine gets a marriage proposal from her Hollywood-handsome lawyer boyfriend and an invitation to join a prestigious law firm. Her life, it seems, is destined for uncontested happiness, and if she continues to practice law in romantic comedies, everything will probably turn out well. If, however, she succumbs to a blonde ambition to practice law in the real world, she'll probably find the going a little rougher.

Amanda Brown, author of the novel on which the movie was based, is a former law student and the daughter of two lawyers. Interestingly, her mother was a member of the second Harvard Law School class that included women. Harvard was about 30 years ahead of the curve, but the enrollment of women in U.S. law schools skyrocketed after 1970. It was naturally assumed that the flood of young female associates would eventually result in greatly increased numbers of female partners in law firms across the country. As it turns out, however, although female law school enrollments have been climbing for years, there are still relatively few women partners in American law firms. Currently, for example, 34.4 percent of all lawyers are women, yet only 17.8 percent of law firm partners are women, representing a modest increase from 13 percent in 1995. At this rate, women will achieve parity with male colleagues in approximately 2088.

What happens between the time women get job offers and the time firms hand out partnerships? Bettina B. Plevan, an employment law specialist and partner in the Manhattan firm of Proskauer Rose, believes that somewhere along the way, female lawyers lose the kind of motivation necessary to get ahead in a law office. "You have a given population of people," she observes, "who were significantly motivated to go through law school with a certain career goal in mind. What de-motivates them to want to continue working in the law?"

The problem, says Karen M. Lockwood, a partner in the Washington DC firm Howrey, is neither discrimination nor lack of opportunity. "Law firms," she says, "are way beyond discrimination. Problems with advancement and retention are grounded in biases, not discrimination." In part, these biases issue from institutional inertia. Lauren Stiller Rikleen, a partner in the Worcester, Massachusetts, firm of Bowditch & Dewey, points out that most law firms are "running on an institutional model that's about 200 years old." Most of them, she adds, "do a horrible job of managing their personnel, in terms of training them and communicating with them." Such problems, of course, affect men as well as women, but because of lingering preconceptions about women's attitudes, values, and goals, women bear the brunt of the workplace burden. In practical terms, they face less adequate mentoring, poorer networking opportunities, lower-grade case assignments, and unequal access to positions of committee control.

To all of these barriers to success, Lockwood adds the effect of what she calls the "maternal wall": Male partners, she says, assume that women who return to the firm after having children will be less willing to work hard and less capable of dedicating themselves to their jobs when they return. As a result, men get the choice assignments and senior positions. Jane DiRenzo Pigott, a onetime law-firm partner who now runs a consultancy firm, agrees but thinks that the issues run deeper than maternity leave. "People explain it simply as the fact that women have children," she explains,

> but so many other factors play into it. Women self-promote in a different way than men, and because women don't get their success acknowledged in the same way as men who more aggressively self-promote, it creates a high level of professional dissatisfaction for women. Saying these two words "I want" is not something women are used to doing. They're not saying, "I want the top bonus" or "I want that position.". . . [W]omen need to learn how to be comfortable saying "I want" and how to say it effectively.

The fact remains that, according to a 2009 study of "Women in Law" conducted by Catalyst, a New York research firm, 1 in 8 female lawyers work part time, compared to only 1 in 50 males. Why? According to Plevan, most female attorneys would prefer to work and raise children at the same time but find that they can't do both effectively. "I organized my personal life so I was able to move toward my goals," she says but admits that it helped to have a gainfully employed spouse (also a lawyer), dual incomes sufficient to hire household help, and nearby relatives. In most cases, of course, although dual incomes are an advantage to a household, it's difficult for either spouse to devote time to child rearing when they're both working. The Catalyst study shows that while 44 percent of male lawyers have spouses who are employed full time, nearly twice as many female lawyers—84 percent—have employed spouses who are unavailable for household duties such as attending to children.

"As long as firms are male dominated," says Plevan, "it's much less likely that firms will make changes to accept the challenges of work–life balance." She hastens to add, however, "It's not that men aren't receptive to these issues. It's that they're not aware," and this lack of awareness on the part of the men who run law firms, she suggests, accounts for the persistence of operational practices that hamper the efforts of women attorneys to strike an adequate balance between their professional and personal lives. Take, for example, the concept of billable hours. Law firms typically bill clients according to the amount of a lawyer's time that they consume. This regime not only requires lawyers to keep precise records of the time spent with clients, but also provides the firm with a convenient method of measuring each lawyer's specific contribution to the firm's bottom line. More women than men are penalized by this system, but it's becoming a source of discontent among lawyers of both sexes. "They don't like being part of a billable-hour production unit," says Rikleen. "They want more meaning out of their lives than that."

Like firms in many other industries, law firms have experimented with flexible-work options such as flexible scheduling and parental leave (see "First Things First"). More and more, however, they report that such measures have not been as effective as they'd hoped. Says Edith R. Matthai, founder with her husband of the Los Angeles firm Robie &

Matthai: "We're very accommodating with leaves and flexible schedules, and even with that we still lose women." The "pressures on women from spouses, family, peers, schools, and others is huge," she adds. The situation has improved over the last 30 years, but "we have a long way to go. . . . I think the real solution is a reassessment of the role that women play in the family. One thing we need is a sense of shared responsibilities for the household and, most importantly, shared responsibilities for taking care of the kids."

Case Questions

1. You're the managing partner in a law firm that's getting ready to hand out partnerships. You're aware that a few of the voting partners harbor somewhat old-fashioned views about the attitudes, values, and goals of working women, and you want to say a word or two to help make sure that, when it comes time to select partners, every candidate is playing on a level field. What sort of arguments would you make in a prevote partners meeting?

2. You're the managing partner in a law firm with 55 male associates and 45 female associates, and you agree with the argument that women lawyers need to "self-promote" more effectively. Which approach to motivation would you apply to encourage female associates in your firm to "self-promote" more actively? Explain your choice of approach.

3. What about your own values when it comes to balancing your home and work life? Assume that you're about to graduate from law school and about to get married to a fiancé(e) who's also about to graduate from law school. When you sit down with your future husband or wife to discuss your plans for married life, what feelings will you express about raising a family? What kind of adjustments will you propose if it turns out that your fiancé(e)'s ideas on the matter are more or less the opposite of your own? Be sure to consider factors such as the debt you've racked up while in law school and the standard of living that you'd like to achieve during your working life.

Case References

Legally Blonde (Metro-Goldwyn-Mayer, 2001); Timothy L. O'Brien, "Up the Down Staircase," *New York Times*, March 19, 2006, http://query.nytimes.com on April 29, 2009;

"Women in Law," *Catalyst*, 2009, www.catalyst.org on April 29, 2009; Andrew Zolli, "Demographics: The Population Hourglass," *Fast Company*, March 2006, www.fastcompany .com on April 29, 2009.

CHAPTER 13

When to Stand on Your Head and Other Tips from the Top

It isn't easy leading a U.S. business these days. Leaving aside the global recession (at least for a moment), the passion for "lean and mean" operations means that there are fewer workers to do more work. Globalization means keeping abreast of cross-cultural differences. Knowledge industries present unique leadership challenges requiring better communication skills and greater flexibility. Advances in technology have opened unprecedented channels of communication. Now more than ever, leaders must be able to do just about everything and more of it. As U.S. Senator and former presidential candidate John McCain puts it, "[Leadership is] a game of pinball, and you're the ball." Fortunately, a few of Corporate America's veteran leaders have some tips for those who still want to follow their increasingly treacherous path.

First of all, if you think you're being overworked—if your hours are too long and your schedule is too demanding—odds are, you're right: Most people—including executives—*are* overworked. And in some industries, they're *particularly* overworked. U.S. airlines, for example, now service 100 million more passengers annually than they did just four years ago—with 70,000 fewer workers. "I used to manage my time," quips one airline executive. "Now I manage my energy." In fact, many high-ranking managers have realized that energy is a key factor in their ability to complete tasks on tough schedules. Most top corporate leaders work 80 to 100 hours a week, and many have found that regimens that allow them to rebuild and refresh make it possible for them to keep up the pace.

Carlos Ghosn, who's currently president of Renault *and* CEO of Nissan, believes in regular breaks. "I don't bring my work home. I play with my four children and spend time with my family

on weekends," says Ghosn. "I come up with good ideas as a result of becoming stronger after being recharged." Google vice president Marissa Mayer admits that "I can get by on four to six hours of sleep," but she also takes a weeklong vacation three times a year. Many leaders report that playing racquetball, running marathons, practicing yoga, or just getting regular exercise helps them to recover from overwork.

Effective leaders also take control of information flow—which means managing it, not reducing the flow until it's as close to a trickle as you can get it. Like most executives, for example, Mayer can't get by without multiple sources of information: "I always have my laptop with me," he reports, and "I adore my cellphone." Starbucks CEO Howard Schultz receives a morning voice mail summarizing the previous day's sales results and reads three newspapers a day. Mayer watches the news all day, and Bill Gross, a securities portfolio manager, keeps an eye on six monitors displaying real-time investment data.

On the other hand, Gross stands on his head to force himself to take a break from communicating. When he's upright again, he tries to find time to concentrate. "Eliminating the noise," he says, "is critical. . . . I only pick up the phone three or four times a day. . . . I don't want to be connected—I want to be disconnected." Ghosn, whose schedule requires weekly intercontinental travel, uses bilingual assistants to screen and translate information—one assistant for information from Europe (where Renault is), one for information from Japan (where Nissan is), and one for information from the United States (where Ghosn often has to be when he doesn't have to be in Europe or Japan). Clothing designer Vera Wang also uses an assistant to filter information. "The barrage of calls is so enormous," she says, "that if I just answered calls I'd do nothing else. . . . If I were to go near e-mail, there'd be even more obliga-tions, and I'd be in [a mental hospital] with a white jacket on." Not surprisingly, Bill Gates integrates the role of his assistant into a high-tech information-organizing system:

On my desk I have three screens, synchronized to form a single desktop. I can drag items from one screen to the next. Once you have that large display area, you'll never go back, because it has a direct impact on productivity.

The screen on the left has my list of e-mails. On the center screen is usually the specific e-mail I'm reading and responding to. And my browser is on the right-hand screen. This setup gives me the ability to glance and see what new has come in while I'm working on something and to bring up a link that's related to an e-mail and look at it while the e-mail is still in front of me.

At Microsoft, e-mail is the medium of choice. . . . I get about 100 e-mails a day. We apply filtering to keep it to that level. E-mail comes straight to me from anyone I've ever corresponded with, anyone from Microsoft, Intel, HP, and all the other partner companies, and anyone I know. And I always see a write-up from my assistant of any other e-mail, from companies that aren't on my permission list or indi-viduals I don't know. . . .

We're at the point now where the challenge isn't how to communicate effectively with e-mail—it's ensuring that you spend your time on the e-mail that matters most. I use tools like "in-box rules" and search folders to mark and group mes-sages based on their content and importance.

Like most leaders of knowledge workers, Gates also knows how important it is to motivate and retain talented individuals who (at least under normal cir-cumstances) have other options for employment. In fact, he once stated that if the 20 smartest people at Microsoft left the company, it would shrivel into an insignificant dot on the corporate map. Obviously, then, executives who employ thousands of such workers are under enormous pressure to keep them productive and happy. Mayer holds office hours at a regularly scheduled time every day so that she can field employee complaints and concerns. Schultz visits at least 25 Starbucks stores each week. Jane Friedman, CEO of publisher HarperCollins, attends lots of parties. Authors, she explains, "are the most important people in our company, [and they] really appreciate it when the [publisher's] CEO turns up at events [to celebrate their books]."

At Boeing, CEO Jim McNerney has a goal of making his people 15 percent better each year. The key, he says, is a two-step process. First, you focus your attention on those people who show the greatest potential to change, generally because they're more open, appreciate teamwork, and have more courage. Second, you remove all the bureaucratic obstacles that will prevent them from doing what you're work-ing so hard to get them to do. (McNerney apparently remembers what management expert Peter Drucker once said: "Most of what we call management con-sists of making it difficult for people to get their work done.")

And what about leading in a recession? What adjustments do you have to make when money is scarce, markets are volatile, and morale needs boost-ing? The current economy, says Neiman Marcus CEO Burt Tansky, "requires all of us to pull up every leadership trait that we have." Dennis Carey, a senior partner at Korn Ferry International, an executive search firm, suggests that top managers start by ac-knowledging that leading in extreme circumstances means calling into question everything they do under normal circumstances. "You can't rely on a peace-time general to fight a war," he reminds fellow execu-tives. "The wartime CEO prepares for the worst so that his or her company can take market share away from players who haven't." Hire away your competi-tors' best people, for example, and keep them from grabbing yours. Or buy up their assets while they can be had at bargain prices.

Jack Hayhow, founder and COO of Opus Train-ing, adds that leaders need to make sure their em-ployees know why they're making changes: "Clearly state to your people that we are in a recession . . . [and that] very little of what [they've] assumed to be true in the past will be true in the future. [Tell them]: 'You must understand that this is no longer business as usual.'" Let them know if you can no longer guaran-tee their jobs. "My suggestion," says Hayhow, "would be [something like]: 'Quit worrying about the things you can't control and focus on what you can. Find ways to contribute . . . and make it really hard for the company to let you go. . . .' If you have people who argue or debate, show them the door."

Hayhow also realizes that "when things are as bad as they are [in a recession], motivation is criti-cal. . . . If you create an environment conducive to people motivating themselves," he contends, "you'll be able to motivate in these changing times." Ho do you create such an environment? "Start by matching talent with the task," says Hayhow. "Play to your employees' strengths. Figure out who does what and make sure they're spending their time where they can best utilize their talents." And don't forget to "give people some choice. . . . When people have even a little choice over what they do or how they do it, they're more committed and enthusiastic about the task." Let employees decide how to do something "or maybe even who they work with to get the job done."

Many leaders go a step further and use a time of crisis as an opportunity to rethink a company's reward system. At Boeing, for example, McNerney replaced an old bonus system based something that managers can't control (the company's stock price) with a system based on something they *can*—profit: He rewards people who improve the firm's profitability by better managing its capital. So, if a manager can figure out how to generate $10 million in profit by spending $1 million instead of $2 million, he or she now gets to keep some of the savings. One organizational psychologist adds that if you're the top person at your company, "the last thing you want is for people to perceive that you're in it for yourself." In December 2008, for example, when FedEx founder Frederick W. Smith was forced to make broad salary cuts, he started with himself, slashing his own paycheck by 20 percent.

Ex-Starbucks CEO Jim Donald makes a fairly simple recommendation: "Communicate, communicate, communicate. Especially at a time of crisis," he advises, "make sure your message reaches all levels, from the very lowest to the uppermost." Kip Tindell, who's been CEO of the Container Store since its founding in 1978, agrees. That's why his managers "run around like chickens relentlessly trying to communicate everything to every single employee at all times." He admits that it's an impossible task, but he's also convinced that the effort is more important than ever in times of crisis. He also contends that his company is in a better position to ride out the economic storm "because we're

so dedicated to the notion that communication and leadership are the same thing." At the very least, he says, "we're fortunate to be minus the paranoia that goes with employees who feel they don't know what's going on."

Case Questions

1. All the opinions expressed by leaders in this case imply certain forms of leader behavior that would be consistent with them. Of these opinions, which are most consistent with job-centered leader behavior? Which are most consistent with employee-centered leader behavior?

2. Of all the leaders cited in this story, which do you think is likely to be the most charismatic? Explain.

3. Of all the leaders cited in this case, for which would you most like to work? For which would you least like to work? Explain your answers.

4. Of all the leaders cited in this case, whose company would you be most likely to invest in? Whose company would you be least likely to invest in? Explain your answers.

5. You're the owner-manager of a [select two] small-motor manufacturer/commercial dry-cleaning service/high-end catering company/tax-preparation office. As you know, we're in a recession, and you'd like some advice on how to lead in tough times. Which of the leaders cited in this case would be your first choice as a source of advice? Explain your choices.

Case References

Geoffrey Colvin, "Catch a Rising Star," *Fortune*, February 6, 2006, http://money.cnn.com on May 18, 2009; Bill Gates, "How I Work," *Fortune*, March 20, 2006, http://money.cnn.com on May 18, 2009; Geoffrey Colvin, "Star Power," *Fortune*, February 6, 2006, http://money.cnn.com on May 18, 2009; Jerry Useem, "Making Your Work Work for You," *Fortune*, March 20, 2006, http://money.cnn.com on May 18, 2009; Peter Cohan, "Six Small Biz Tips from a CEO Who Flies Right," *BloggingStocks*, January 4, 2009, www.bloggingstocks.com on May 18, 2009; Emily Thornton, "Managing through a Crisis: The New Rules," *BusinessWeek*, January 8, 2009, www.businessweek.com on May 18, 2009; Anthony Portuesi, "Leading in a Recession: An Interview with Jack Hayhow," *Driven Leaders*, February 24, 2009, http://drivenleaders.com on May 19, 2009; Jim Donald, "Guest Post: Former Starbucks CEO's Tips for Tough Times," *Fortune*, April 1, 2009, http://postcards.

blogs.fortune.cnn.com on May 18, 2009; Ellen Davis, "Retail Execs Offer Insights on Leadership in Tough Economic Times," *NRF Annual 2009 Convention Blog*, January 15, 2009, http://annual09.nrfblogs.com on May 19, 2009.

CHAPTER 14

¿Qué Pasa *in the Ad Agency?*

- A contemporary Toyota television ad: *A father is explaining Toyota's hybrid engine to his son. "[The car] runs on gas and electricity," he says. "Mira. Mira aquí. [Look. Look here.] It uses both." The son replies, "Like you, with English and Spanish." "Sí," replies the father.*

As the makeup of U.S. society changes, organizations have realized that they need to change the ways in which they communicate with diverse customer bases. It might come as something of a surprise, but this Toyota TV spot reflects a virtually revolutionary change in the way American companies address potential buyers from different cultures. Once, for example, they assumed that Hispanics living in the United States were immigrants, spoke no English, and clung to old-world values. Today, however, they're well aware of the fact that over half of the country's 45.5 million Hispanics were born in this country. Like the father and son in Toyota's depiction of Hispanic life, most Spanish speakers know English and mix elements not only of both languages but also of both U.S. and Latino culture. "This group is not about nostalgia for the home country," says Jaime Fortuño, managing partner of Azafrán, a New York–based agency.

There was also a time when advertisers relied on mainstream ads—ads aimed at the center of the market where they expected to find the "typical" consumer. But as the purchasing power of minorities has increased, companies have put more energy into developing targeted ads—ads aimed at specific groups of consumers and often delivered through language-targeted media. Today, for example, a corporation thinks nothing of budgeting $100 million a year for Hispanic-themed ads. Since 2004, about one-third of ads targeted to Hispanics have been presented in

Spanish, and that proportion is growing—for good reason. The buying power of Hispanics is growing at a compound annual rate of 8.2 percent, compared to 4.9 percent for non-Hispanics. From $220 billion in 1990, Hispanic spending will reach nearly $1 trillion in 2009—an increase of 347 percent, compared to 148.5 percent for all consumers. (Spending by Asian Americans, incidentally, will also increase by 347 percent.)

- A contemporary Energizer battery ad: *In Spanish, a man says, "When I lost my arm, I got a new one. From a Japanese guy. Now I can't stop taking pictures." He compulsively takes pictures everywhere—of himself in the shower, in bed, in the men's room—until a fight ensues.*

Advertisers also recognize different segments of Hispanic customers, just as they've long recognized segments of the mainstream market. Another sign of the times: When it comes to offbeat, sometimes irreverent humor, ads targeted to Hispanic audiences are catching up to mainstream ads—which is to say, mainstream advertisers are getting more comfortable communicating to minority consumers.

- A contemporary Verizon ad: *A young woman is trying to download a music-video clip using a slow dial-up connection. To add to her frustration, the song, José José's "La Nave del Olvido" [The Ship of Oblivion] gets stuck on the line "espera un poco, un poquitiiiiiiiii" [wait a bit more]. In Spanish, an announcer extols the virtues of Verizon High Speed Internet.*

"A high percentage of Hispanic consumers," explains Marquita Carter, director of multicultural marketing for Verizon, "still use a dial-up connection." The spot ran on Spanish-language TV and radio in

Boston, New York, Philadelphia, Tampa, and Washington, D.C., as part of a campaign that also includes newspaper and online ads in Dallas and Los Angeles. Verizon is one of the country's top-ten advertisers in Spanish-language media, having spent $73.8 million in the first three quarters of 2008 (up 20 percent over the same period in 2007).

Other companies in the top ten include number-one Procter & Gamble ($133.2 million for the first three quarters of 2008, up 13 percent), AT&T, General Motors, McDonald's, Toyota, and Johnson & Johnson. Total spending for the period topped $4 billion, an increase of 2.7 percent over 2007.

The Association of Hispanic Advertising Agencies (AHAA) thinks it should be even more. "The Hispanic advertising industry," reported the organization's website in 2009, "is growing four times faster than all other sectors of advertising." Spending on Spanish-language advertising by 500 major U.S. companies represented 5.6 percent of the total spent in all media, but Hispanics, observes the AHAA, represent 15.1 percent of the total U.S. population.

About 9,000 members of that 15.1 percent are illegal aliens, but as far as John Gallegos is concerned, companies should direct advertising to them, too. "The guy who just came across the border with a coyote, do I want to go after him, too?" asks Gallegos, who runs Grupo Gallegos, an L.A.-area agency. "Well, he's going to get a job. He's going to work. He's going to start buying products and contributing to the economy. So while he might not be viable for a Mercedes today, I can introduce you to people who came here illegally or legally, with nothing, and are now driving a Mercedes. Advertising is aspirational. I want to aim ahead of where my audience is. Unless it's the equivalent of beef to Hindus, I always say, any product and any service should be sold to Latinos in this country."

- An old Milk Board ad: *As a grandmother is preparing tres leches cake in a crowded kitchen, a slogan appears on the screen:* "Familia, amor, y leche *[Family, love, and milk].*" A new Milk Board ad: *Commuters hold on to train steps by their teeth. The slogan says,* "Toma leche *[Have some milk]*."
Grupo Gallegos created the new Milk Board ad as well as one set in a town where gravity comes

and goes. Locals aren't the least bit surprised to find themselves floating along 30 feet in the air or suddenly plummeting to the ground with bone-crushing impact. Fortunately, they drink a lot of milk, so they have exceptionally strong bones and walk away unscathed. "You have to put something out there that hasn't been seen before," says Gallegos art director Juan Pablo Oubiña, who didn't much care for the old "*Familia, amor, y leche*" Milk Board ad on more than one level. It reminded him of what's known as "*Abuelita* advertising," after a Spanish term for "grandma." It's better than traditional advertising for Hispanics dreamed up by non-Hispanic agencies (think businessmen in sombreros), but it's steeped in its own clichés—particularly Hispanics as cheerful suburban homeowners living in warm multigenerational families. "On any team I lead," vows Oubiña, "there is never going to be a kitchen with somebody exclaiming, 'Mmmm, how delicious.'"

Grupo Gallegos, which also has accounts with companies such as Fruit of the Loom, Comcast (high-speed Internet service), and Bally fitness centers, was careful to reconsider the Spanish wording of the Milk Board's well-known "Got Milk?" slogan. To many Spanish speakers, the easiest translation—"*Tiene leche?*"—apparently came across as something like "Are you lactating?" The replacement phrase—"*Toma leche*" ("Have some milk")—seems like an obvious solution, but as one journalist pointed out on her first viewing of the ad, "I appreciated what the challenge had been. . . . I was pretty sure that asking people in Spanish whether they have milk is a bad idea, since I had once learned the regrettable way that if you use Spanish to ask a male Mexican grocer, 'Do you have eggs?' you're inquiring as to his testicles."

- An ad for Southwest Airlines: *A virile young Hispanic rollerblades up to a parked car to admire his image in the tinted window. The window unexpectedly rolls down to reveal two men inside the car who are also admiring him.* "Want to get away?" *reads the punchline, which is followed by a low airfare price.*

"In advertising," observes Oubiña, "it's not easy to be different. It takes ten times as much work." And getting the language right isn't really the hardest part of making Spanish-language ads. Like this Southwest ad from the Hispanic-owned agency Dieste Harmel & Partners, many of the latest-vintage Spanish-language ads have succeeded in appealing to Hispanic audiences by playing with and against stereotypes, but as one Hispanic marketing consultant observes, it's a tricky balancing act. "Not only are Americans comfortable with positive stereotypes as a means to be politically correct," says Jennifer Woodard, "but so are many Hispanics." The problem of stereotyping, she reminds us, is usually twofold: Advertisers tend to rely on stereotypes because they assume that they're somehow reflective of the mainstream, and the consumers being stereotyped tend to settle for stereotypes because they dominate the images of themselves that are available to them in the media.

- An ad for Fox Sports Net: *Returning home from a shopping trip, a Hispanic woman detects an unpleasant odor in the house. The camera follows her as she follows her nose from room to room until she reaches the living room, where she realizes that her husband is so thoroughly immersed in a televised soccer game that he's been watching through the open door of a nearby bathroom.*

This ad—another Grupo Gallegos creation—does a good job of playing *with and against* stereotypes because it bounces off the stereotype of the soccer-obsessed Latino in what Woodard describes as "a great example of taking a slice of life from a husband and wife, no matter the culture, and pushing the ad into entertainment." Contrast this ad, however, with the far more common appropriation of the same stereotype in TV advertising aimed at Hispanics. "[W]atch a few hours," suggests agency executive Tommy Thompson, "and count how many soccer-themed spots you see. And I'm not talking about World Cup season or during the airing of soccer matches where contextually it makes sense. It almost seems that soccer is the only way to connect with [Hispanic viewers]. What does soccer have to do with life insurance, for example? Are there really no other insights as relates to Hispanics' need for life insurance that can be communicated without soccer?"

Thompson, founder and president of Dallas-based iNSPIRE!, argues that advertisers should focus on "what makes the target [market] tick as it relates to [a] particular brand or category." It's advice that's already been put to good use in ads such as the Verizon and Energizer spots described earlier. For the Energizer ad, for example, Gallegos was originally given the task of making the brand "iconic" for Hispanic consumers—giving it immediately familiar symbolic value so that Spanish speakers would think of perpetual motion and say, "*como el conejito Energizer,*" the same way that English speakers think of perpetual motion and say "like the Energizer bunny." At Grupo Gallegos, brainstorming on a new account always starts with "Okay, *aquí está el problema que tenemos* when we really start looking at the brand," and the Gallegos team realized early on that most Hispanics don't associate batteries with perpetual motion (or anything else): For them, a battery is a battery. So Gallegos came up with an ad in which a Mexican man walks down the street and shares his realization that he's immortal—whereupon a two-story commercial sign falls on his head. Being immortal, he explains, he needs a very long-lasting battery for his camera.

- Ad for Virgin Mobile Telecoms: *A man with cocker spaniel ears flapping in the wind drives his girlfriend in a convertible. A tagline appears: "No Soy Normal" [I'm Not Normal]."*

Case Questions

1. You're assistant director of marketing for a maker of upscale furniture, and your company is preparing to enter new markets in California and the Southwest. Entering new markets, especially one of this size, is expensive, and your boss has decided to forgo Spanish-language advertising as part of the firm's market entry strategy. You're inclined to disagree. What might you say to your boss to change her mind?

2. You're a top manager in a large factory whose workforce is approximately 40 percent Hispanic. Business is down because of the recession, and you've learned that there's a rumor about layoffs circulating in the grapevine. In particular, a lot of Hispanic-speaking employees seem to think that they'll be laid off first. How should you deal with the rumor?

3. Arnold Schwarzenegger, the Austrian-born governor of California, which is home to 13.2 million Hispanics, advised Latino immigrants that if they want to learn English more quickly, "You've got to turn off Spanish[-language] television. . . . I know that when I came to this country, I very rarely spoke German to anyone." Do you agree with Schwarzenegger's advice to immigrants on learning English in the United States? Why or why not?

Case References

Cynthia Gorney, "How Do You Say 'Got Milk' en Español?" *New York Times*, September 23, 2007, www.nytimes.com on May 22, 2009; David Kiley, "Laughing Out Loud in Spanish," *BusinessWeek*, March 13, 2006, www.businessweek.com on May 22, 2009; Mark Maier, "Breaking Down Hispanic Stereotypes," *Luce Performance Group*, January 11, 2009, www.luceperformancegroup.com on May 22, 2009; "Verizon's Newest Spanish-Language Advertising Campaign Features Latin American Balladist," *Reuters*, March 6, 2008, www.reuters.com on May 22, 2009; "Spanish-Language Ads Climb, African-American Advertising Drops," *Nielsen Wire*, January 29, 2009, http://blog.nielsen.com on May 22, 2009; Carroll Trosclair, "Hispanic Advertising Trend in America," *Suite101*, April 13, 2009, http://advertising.suite101.com on May 22, 2009; Tommy Thompson, "The Problem with 'Hispanic Insights,' " *Advertising Age*, August 14, 2008, http://adage.com on May 22, 2009.

CHAPTER 15

Testosterone and Teamwork in Tampa Bay

One of the early milestones in the history of the Tampa Bay Devil Rays Major League Baseball (MLB) team occurred on April 23, 1998, when they beat the Texas Rangers 12–5 for their eleventh victory in the very first 19 games of their existence. Then they lost six games in a row to fall to 11–14 and never again reached .500 (sports parlance for winning as many games as you lose) during the season. Ultimately, they lost 99 games (out of 162) to finish in fifth and last place in their division. In fact, the Devil Rays never lost fewer than 91 games between 1998 and 2004 (posting a high of 106 in 2002) and only once managed to finish out of the division cellar (sports parlance for last place)—in 2004, when they achieved a team-best 91 losses to end up in fourth.

In that same year, Andrew Friedman, a former outfielder at Tulane University and a former analyst at Bear, Stearns, was living in New Jersey, selling securities by day and going online to play fantasy baseball by night. Two years later, he'd be living his fantasy as executive vice president of the Tampa Bay Devil Rays, part of an innovative leadership team trying to reverse the fortunes of the struggling team. The management team of which Friedman is a part is headed by a former executive at the investment bank Goldman Sachs and had recruited its key members from the rosters of Wall Street firms. It boasted a thorough grasp of financial markets and decades' of collective experience in leveraging fiscal know-how, but securities trading is one sort of game and baseball quite another. Could Wall Street smarts turn around a Major League Baseball team that didn't seem to have a clue?

It was a long shot, but to Stuart Sternberg, a onetime partner at both Goldman Sachs and the investment group Spear, Leeds & Kellogg, it looked like a good deal. "I'm a buy-low guy," said Sternberg, who'd retired from Wall Street at the age of 43, "and if you pay the right price for something, I don't care what it is, you can't go very wrong." He certainly got the Devil Rays at the right price. In 2004, the team was valued at $152 million (29th among the 30 MLB teams), and Sternberg and five former colleagues were able to get a 48 percent share of the team for $65 million. General partner Vince Naimoli, who had obtained the MLB franchise in 1995, retained 15 percent ownership and limited partners held the rest. In 2006, Naimoli stepped aside, turning over management control to the 46-year-old Sternberg.

Having gotten his chance, how did Sternberg plan to turn the Devil Rays around? "We have to start at the top and work our way down," he announced, and immediately appointed 29-year-old Matthew Silverman, a former strategist and colleague at Goldman Sachs, as team president. Sternberg recruited veteran baseball executive Gerry Hunsicker as Senior VP of Baseball Operations, and Andrew Friedman was promoted from Director of Baseball Development to Executive VP of Baseball Operations, or General Manager. Friedman, who was also 29, would now make all baseball-related decisions—trading players, negotiating contracts, and signing free agents. When asked why he'd placed two 29-year-old executives in such important jobs, Sternberg replied, "I think I have a good eye for the right people, which is why I'm so excited about Matt and Andrew and Gerry. Especially the two young guys, who I think are in a position to affect change in our business and the whole industry for a lot of years."

Even so, it wasn't going to be easy. "What makes this difficult," said Sternberg, "is that we're so anxious and eager to mold the franchise in the way we see it." What made it even more difficult were a few pressing practical problems. For one thing, the Devil Rays' home field, Tropicana Park, was located in St. Petersburg, Florida, at a considerable distance from the main population center in Tampa. And when fans did make the trip to the ballpark, they had to put up with a facility that wasn't particularly congenial either to baseball or to watching it. "The Trop" had been cheaply built and looked like a generic multipurpose building on the outside and a large warehouse on the inside—a far cry in 2006 from the new retro-style ballparks that were attracting record numbers of baseball fans around the country. Sternberg gave the field a $25 million facelift before the 2006 season, made another $10 million in improvements during the season, and put more money into enhancements prior to the 2007 season.

It didn't help much. In 1998, their first year, the Devil Rays had attracted 2.5 million fans—seventh best in the 14-team American League and just above the league average. The novelty, however, wore off quickly, with attendance dropping to 1.5 million the next year and never topping 1.45 million between 2000 and 2005—good for 14th best in the league in every year but one. When Sternberg took over prior to the 2006 season, one of the first things he did was announce that parking at the stadium would henceforth be free. The Devil Rays, however,

finished last again in 2006, both on the field and off, drawing just 1.37 million fans, or about a million below the league average. A survey conducted by the *St. Petersburg Times* revealed that fewer than 30 percent of Tampa-area baseball fans regarded the Devil Rays as their favorite team.

One major problem, however, had been addressed: At least the Devil Rays were under new management. Although the free-parking initiative didn't do much to boost consumer confidence among Tampa-area fans, it did at least signal a new approach on the part of the team that would be running the franchise. When asked how his investment-banking experience would help him in his job as president of a baseball team, Silverman cited the "corporate philosophy" of Goldman Sachs: Investment banking, he said, "is a people-centric business. Goldman prided itself on customer service [and] training and employing the best people. That's what we want to apply to the Rays organization to make it better." By 2006, many Tampa fans were apparently ready for a more "people-centric" approach from the team's management. Vince Naimoli's hard-nosed style had been critical in his ability to assemble an ownership group and bring a team to the area in the late 1990s, but by 2005, just before he turned the reins over to Sternberg, it wasn't working so well in the public relations arena. Early in the 2005 season, for example, he'd reportedly got into a profanity-laced shouting match with a fan decked out in a team jersey and hat.

Naimoli's style had also alienated the other members of his ownership team. In fact, the Sternberg group had been able to buy into the team because all five of Naimoli's disgruntled general partners had sold their shares in 2004. Thus, when Andrew Friedman was asked how *his* experience in the securities business had prepared him to be a baseball executive, he cited teamwork at the top: At both of the firms for which he'd worked, he said, "the culture was very focused on teams—you'd have four or five people per deal. That kind of problem-solving approach is what we're trying to create here. We're more top-heavy than before," he explained, "but it's about recognizing certain people's strengths and weaknesses to build a full array in the front office." From the start, the Sternberg-Silverman-Friedman trio has been the core of the front office "array." "The slap-happy ca-maraderie that binds Mr. Sternberg to his two young executives," says one *New York Times* journalist, has "a distinct boys-club feel. . . . It mixes the testosterone of the Wall Street trading floor with the geekiness of those who spend an inordinate amount of time break-ing down earned-run averages."

There was, however, one aspect of Naimoli's management strategy that Sternberg and his team weren't yet ready to change—at least not dramati-cally. From 2002 to 2005, Naimoli had managed to keep the Devil Rays' payroll the lowest among baseball's 30 teams. As we've seen, the on-field results were compatible—four straight last-place finishes—and Sternberg announced prior to the 2006 season that "our goal is to raise payroll by 10, 15, maybe as much as 20 percent a year. That's a good jump in any business." Would it be enough to compete? "I won't say I expect it to be enough," Sternberg admitted. "If we were spending $100 million, I would expect to compete." He bumped the payroll from $29.6 mil-lion in 2005 to nearly $35 million (about 18 percent) in 2006, moving the Devil Rays up a notch to the 29th-highest in baseball.

Unfortunately, the number of losses for the sea-son also went up, from 95 to 101. For 2007, Stern-berg cut payroll by more than 30 percent, or more than $10 million—from $35 million to $24 million. The Devil Rays actually won a few more games in 2007 (they lost only 96 games), but they were once again 30th in payroll. This time, however, the reduc-tion in the team's payroll had been more a matter of strategy than desperation. Sternberg and his team had decided to trade a number of veteran (higher-salaried) players during the 2006 season and go into 2007 with younger players who fit into their future plans. The team that finished last in 2007 featured the youngest starting lineup of any major league team in nearly 25 years. Nobody on the Sternberg team was sure when the Devil Rays would be ready to contend, but one thing was certain: If the Devil Rays were to become competitive, it would be with the talented prospects, underrated role-players, and one or two affordable veterans who had for the most part been acquired by General Manager Andrew Friedman.

For the 2008 season, Sternberg had given Friedman a slightly bigger budget: After some care-fully considered free-agency signings and contract extensions, the payroll had ballooned to $43 million, restoring the Devil Rays to 29th place on the MLB list. Friedman, however, figured that his $43 million was worth perhaps 40 percent more than that. How so? In an era in which a new breed of baseball execu-tives are using financial models, data mining, and statistics-based methods to arrive at both individual and team valuations, the business of trading baseball players had for some time sounded a lot like the busi-ness of trading stocks. Friedman, however, was able to bring an experienced investment-oriented mind-set to the general manager's job. His ground rule for placing value on baseball talent, for example, came straight from Wall Street. It's called *mark-to-market accounting*, and it allows a trader to value a security at its current market price, not the price that he paid for it. Take, for example, Scott Kazmir, an extremely talented left-handed pitcher whom the Devil Rays had paid $424,000 in 2007. Because he had only three full years of major league experience, the 22-year-old Kazmir, who'd made the All Star team a year earlier, was being paid at well below his market value, which Friedman calculated at somewhere around $7 million. Friedman reasons that, with a few more players like Kazmir—and the Devil Rays did in fact have a few more players like Kazmir—the disparity between his payroll and those of his higher-spending competitors isn't as wide as it seems. "I'm purely market driven," he admits. "I love players I think I can get for less than they're worth. It's positive arbitrage, the valuation asymmetry in the game."

Before the 2008 season started, Sternberg and Sil-verman made a few moves in the interest of market-ing, changing the team's colors, uniforms, and logo and dropping the *Devil* from *Devil Rays*. "We're now the 'Rays,' " he announced, "a new and improved version of the Devil Rays." Silverman was quick to add that the changes weren't merely cosmetic (or the result of pressure from Florida religious groups): "We wanted to distance ourselves from the past and really establish that the organization was different, and sometimes it takes very visible changes—uniforms and caps and even a name change—to show everyone a lot has changed." In the front office and on the field, however, patience remained the order of the day. Referring to his bosses, Manager Joe Maddon, who'd been hired in 2005, observed that "their baseball biological clock has a lot of space at the end of it. It's not running down to the very end—there's time. . . . [W]hen you talk about the future with these guys, they know there is such a thing."

As it turns out, the future was a lot closer than anyone had expected. The 2008 edition of the Tampa Bay Rays engineered one of the most stunning turnarounds in baseball history. Picked by experts to finish in fifth or (at best) fourth place, the Rays won 97 games—31 more than the previous year and 27 more than they'd ever won—and finished atop the American League's Eastern Division. They had beaten out one team with a payroll of $209 million (the New York Yankees) and another with a payroll of $133 million (the Boston Red Sox) and advanced beyond the first round of the postseason playoffs by beating a team with a payroll of $121 million (the Chicago White Sox). When they defeated the Red Sox in round two, they went to the World Series, where the bubble finally burst and they were defeated by the Philadelphia Phillies ($98 million).

Because the most obvious sign of the team's newfound success had been on the field, Friedman garnered most of the attention and the encomiums from baseball people. In truth, of course, the success of the baseball model developed by the Tampa Bay management team went hand in hand with the success of its business model. "When it comes to stretching a dollar," wrote a sports columnist for the *St. Petersburg Times* during the 2008 postseason, "the government should be on the phone asking [Friedman] for tips. There's nothing new about looking for bargains, of course. Most small-market clubs fish in the same pond. The difference is how often Friedman seems to get it right." That's true enough from a baseball standpoint, but Friedman will be the first to point out that the key to his job is not finding the right player for the right money: It's more like finding the right *asset* for the right money—the player, that is, whose value can be leveraged either on the field or on the trading block, where value can be exchanged for value. That's the front office blueprint

for organizational success in Tampa Bay, and Friedman, who prepared for his job by trading financial assets during the day and fantasy-baseball assets at night, sticks to that blueprint with the confidence of an investment analyst whose tools happen to include scouting reports as well as financial statements.

Case Questions

1. In what respects does the Sternberg-Silverman-Friedman trio function as a group? As a team? Why is it necessary that the trio functions sometimes more like a group and sometimes more like a team?

2. What factors contribute to the cohesiveness of the Sternberg-Silverman-Friedman group? What factors might affect the group's performance norms in the future? What might be the potential consequences for group cohesiveness and performance?

3. How would you characterize the role of each member of the Sternberg-Silverman-Friedman group? What possible sources of role conflict might affect group performance in the future?

4. How would you characterize Sternberg's style as leader of the group?

5. As the owner of a professional sports franchise, you've decided that you need a new executive team. What are the relative advantages and disadvantages of bringing in managers from outside the sports industry versus bringing in managers with experience in the industry?

6. If you were going to work in sports management, which situation would you prefer—working for a well-established franchise (e.g., the New York Yankees or the Dallas Cowboys) or working for a newer or less successful franchise (e.g., the Tampa Bay Devil Rays or the Houston Texans)?

Case References

Mark Hyman, "Baseball: Money Can't Buy Me Wins," *BusinessWeek*, October 4, 2005, www.businessweek.com on May 26, 2009; Chris Isidore, "Baseball Spending Spree Ahead," CNNMoney.com, October 7, 2005, http://money.cnn.com on May 26, 2009; Landon Thomas Jr., "Case Study: Fix a Baseball Team," *New York Times*, April 2, 2006, www.nytimes.com on May 26, 2009; "Tampa Bay Rays Attendance, Stadiums, and Park Factors," Baseball-Reference. com, May 26, 2009, www.baseball-reference.com on May 27, 2009; Jonah Keri, "Prospectus Q&A: Matthew Silverman and Andrew Friedman," *Baseball Prospectus*, April 19, 2006, www.baseballprospectus.com on May 26, 2009; John Beamer, "How Much Is Your Team Worth, 2008," *The Hardball Times,*

April 24, 2008, www.hardballtimes.com on May 26, 2009; Alan Schwarz, "In Rays' Plan, Success Wasn't Something to Be Rushed," *New York Times*, October 8, 2008, www.nytimes. com on May 27, 2009; and Gary Shelton, "Where He Didn't Have Salary, He Used His Savvy," *St. Petersburg Times*, October 7, 2008, www.tampabay.com on May 26, 2009.

APPENDIX

INTERPRETATIONS OF SKILLS SELF-ASSESSMENT INSTRUMENTS

CHAPTER 1: SELF-AWARENESS

Total your scores for each skill area.

Skill Area	Items	Score
Self-disclosure and openness to feedback from others	1, 2, 3, 9, 11	_____
Awareness of own values, cognitive style, change orientation, and interpersonal orientation	4, 5, 6, 7, 8, 10	_____
Now total your score:		_____

To assess how well you scored on this instrument, compare your scores to three comparison standards.

1. Compare your scores with the maximum possible (66).
2. Compare your scores with the scores of other students in your class.
3. Compare your scores to a norm group consisting of five hundred business school students. In comparison to the norm group, if you scored:

   55 or above, you are in the top quartile

   52 to 54, you are in the second quartile

   48 to 51, you are in the third quartile

   47 or below, you are in the bottom quartile

Your total numerical score suggests your perceptions of your possession of the skills of effective managers—the lower the total score, the lower the level of skills. You should examine your individual item scores for lower numbers and then to try to use your educational experiences to develop more skill in the areas identified.

CHAPTER 2: GLOBAL AWARENESS

All the statements are true. See explanations below.

Thus your score should be close to 40. The closer your score is to 40, the better you understand the global context of organizational environments. The closer your score is to 10, the less you understand the global context.

1. Slurping your soup or noodles is good manners in both public and private settings. It shows enjoyment and appreciation of the quality.
2. Korean managers use "divide-and-rule" to encourage competition among subordinates. They maintain maximum control and subordinates report directly to them, ensuring the managers know more than their subordinates.
3. Public discussions of business dealings are considered inappropriate. Many American firms have been shut out of deals with Chinese firms due to discussing negotiations in the press or with other firms.
4. Public displays of affection between men and women are unacceptable, although men often walk in public holding hands as a sign of friendship.
5. Touching one another during business encounters is common practice in much of Latin America. This is true for both same-sex and opposite-sex touches and is definitely not considered to be sexual in nature.
6. Whereas in the U.S. being late is frowned upon, being quite late is not only accepted but expected in some South American countries. Promptness may be considered rude.
7. Public praise is embarrassing because modesty is an important cultural value. This is also true in Japan and many other Asian countries. A common Japanese saying is, "A nail that sticks up gets hammered down," meaning that workers should strive not to stand out from the crowd.
8. Friendship, especially of old family friends, is more important than task competence in Iran. A wise manager will carefully investigate the work-related web of family and friendship ties when working in most Middle Eastern countries.
9. Private space is considered so important in Germany that partitions are erected to separate people from one another. Privacy screens and walled gardens are the norm.

10. Whereas in the U.S., leaders are often selected for their ability to inspire, in Germany, charisma is viewed with suspicion, and leaders are typically selected for their superior job performance.

For developmental purposes, you should note any particular items for which you had a low score and concentrate on improving your knowledge of those areas.

CHAPTER 3: YOUR WORK LIFE STRENGTHS AND WEAKNESSES

Consider your lists of strengths and skills. Clearly, the more strengths you possess and the fewer weaknesses, the better your chances of obtaining a satisfactory career. For further enhancement of your understanding of your work life strengths and weaknesses, do one or more of the following.

1. Rate each strength and weakness as A—a powerful strength or a significant weakness, B—a moderately important strength or weakness, or C—a nice strength to have but not essential or only a minor drawback. Assign ratings based on the qualities that are judged important in your specific career area. Following the rating, examine the results. The more "A" strengths you have the better, while "C" weaknesses are preferred.

2. Re-evaluate your lists of strengths and weaknesses relative to the job opportunities and threats to individuals in your chosen career field. For example, if your chosen field is rapidly growing and hiring many entry-level workers, the fact that you have little work experience may not be a significant handicap. If a credential such as CPA is essential in your field, your obtaining that credential adds significantly to your employment options. If you're unaware of events and trends in your career specialty, conduct research by interviewing professors, reading trade publications, or attending professional association meetings and viewing their websites. Your school's Career Center may also have helpful information.

3. Develop a "strategic plan" to manage your career. Think about actions that might work to strengthen strengths or might help to overcome or minimize weaknesses. The more specific you are in your assessment of strengths and weaknesses, the more specific your action plan can be. For example, if you list "shy" as one of your weaknesses, it's not clear what actions can be taken to offset that. On the other hand, if you list "nervous about public speaking" as one of your weaknesses, many solutions come to mind, including a communications course, participation in Toastmasters, or volunteering to give tours to prospective students. Again, as you search for solutions, professors, career placement staff, and friends can be helpful sources of information.

CHAPTER 4: DECISION-MAKING STYLES

Generally there are three decision-making styles: reflexive, consistent, and reflective. To determine your style, add up your score by totaling the numbers assigned to each response. The total will be between 10 and 30. A score from 10 to 16 indicates a reflexive style, a score from 17 to 23 indicates a consistent style, and a score from 24 to 30 indicates a reflective style.

Reflexive Style: A reflexive decision maker likes to make quick decisions (to shoot from the hip) without taking the time to get all the information that may be needed and without considering all alternatives. On the positive side, reflexive decision makers are decisive; they do not procrastinate. On the negative side, making quick decisions can lead to waste and duplication when the best possible alternative is overlooked. Employees may see a decision maker as a poor supervisor if he or she consistently makes bad decisions. If you use a reflexive style, you may want to slow down and spend more time gathering information and analyzing alternatives.

Reflective Style: A reflective decision maker likes to take plenty of time to make decisions, gathering considerable information and analyzing several alternatives. On the positive side, the reflective type does not make hasty decisions. On the negative side, he or she may procrastinate and waste valuable time and other resources. The reflective decision maker may be viewed as wishy-washy and indecisive. If you use a reflective style, you may want to speed up your decision making. As Andrew Jackson once said, "Take time to deliberate; but when the time for action arrives, stop thinking and go on."

Consistent Style: Consistent decision makers tend to make decisions without either rushing or wasting time. They know when they have enough information and alternatives to make a sound decision. Consistent decision makers tend to have the best record for making good decisions.

CHAPTER 5: AN ENTREPRENEURIAL QUIZ

If most of your marks are in the first column, you probably have what it takes to run a business. If most of your marks are in the second column, you are likely to have more trouble than you can handle by yourself. You should look for a partner who is strong on the points on which you are weak. If most of your marks are in the third column, not even a good partner will be able to shore you up. Now go back and answer the first question on the self-assessment.

CHAPTER 6: HOW IS YOUR ORGANIZATION MANAGED?

Bureaucratic System 1	0–9
	10–19
	20–29
	30–39
Mixed Systems 2 and 3	40–49
	50–59
	60–69
	70–79
Organic System 4	80–89
	90–100

The higher the score, the more organic and participative the organization. The lower the score, the more mechanistic and bureaucratically managed the organization.

Scores in the 0–39 range suggest that the organization is relatively bureaucratic and mechanistic. Scores above 80 suggest that the organization is relatively organic and participative. Scores in the 40–79 range suggest a mixed design. Students should compare the type of organization identified with the type of environment in which it is most likely to be successful as described in the text.

CHAPTER 7: INNOVATION AND LEARNING STYLES

According to Kolb, Accommodators learn and work by doing, Divergers learn and work through imagination, Convergers learn and work by problem solving, and Assimilators learn and work using inductive reasoning. Each of these types, then, has a specific role to play in innovation.

Accommodators would be best at innovation tasks such as designing and building prototypes or testing product features and functions. They would excel as product champions because they are energetic and enthusiastic.

Divergers would be best at brainstorming and generating new products. They would excel as inventors, whether of an entirely new product or of an improvement to an existing product.

Convergers would be best at testing products through experimentation or at developing additional features or enhancements to existing products. They would excel as technical advisors to the innovation process.

Assimilators would be best at thought experiments. They would excel at observing users and then generalizing from the specific observations to more general principles or ideas. They would excel as champions, because they enjoy organizing people and information toward a practical outcome.

For more information about Kolb's styles and their implications for learning and work, look online. One interesting site is http://www.businessballs.com/kolblearningstyles.htm.

CHAPTER 8: WHAT DO STUDENTS WANT FROM THEIR JOBS?

This survey was administered to a large group and the average results are below. Responses to this survey vary quite a bit.

If your individual scores fit the pattern of a typical student, then you will likely have an easy time explaining your job values to potential employers.

If your individual scores vary in one or more significant ways, this is not a cause for concern. Many employers seek students with job values that match those of their organizations, which can vary considerably. However, you should plan ahead about ways to effectively communicate with potential employers. Without your self-knowledge and ability to communicate your unique job values, employers would likely assume that you are typical, resulting in a poor understanding your needs and a possibly a poor person-job fit. On the other hand, good self-knowledge and communication skills can result in a superior person-job fit.

The second column of the table demonstrates that recruiters are not able to perfectly predict the relative importance of various job values to potential recruits. Again, self-knowledge and communication are the keys to finding a good person-job fit.

Job Values Survey		
Job Value	Student Average	Employer Perceptions
Working Conditions	12	—
Work with People	7	—
Employee Benefits	11	—
Challenge	2	—
Location of Job	13	—
Self-Development	3	—
Type of Work	4	—
Job Title	14	—
Training Program	9	+
Advancement	1	+
Salary	6	—
Company Reputation	10	+
Job Security	8	—
Autonomy on the Job	5	—

CHAPTER 9: UNDERSTANDING CONTROL

The odd-numbered items are all false, and the even-numbered ones are all true. Thus you should have positive responses for the even-numbered items and negative responses for the odd-numbered items. If you agreed strongly with all of the even-numbered items and disagreed strongly with all of the odd-numbered items, your total score would be zero.

Examine your responses to see which items you responded to incorrectly. Focus on learning why the answers are what they are.

CHAPTER 10: DEFINING QUALITY AND PRODUCTIVITY

The odd-numbered items are all true; they refer to eight dimensions of quality (see Table 10.2). Those eight dimensions are performance, features, reliability, conformance, durability, serviceability, aesthetics, and perceived quality. The even-numbered statements are all false. Thus you should have positive responses for the odd-numbered items and negative responses for the even-numbered items. If you agree strongly with all of the odd-numbered items and disagree strongly with all of the even-numbered items, your total score is zero.

Examine your responses to see which items you responded to incorrectly. Focus on learning why the answers are what they are. Remember that the American Society for Quality Control defines quality as the totality of features and characteristics of a product or service that bear on its ability to satisfy stated or implied needs of customers.

CHAPTER 11: PERSONALITY TYPES AT WORK

Conclude by addressing the following questions:

1. Do you feel that the online test accurately assessed your personality?
2. Is it easy to measure personality? What are some problems or limitations with personality assessments?
3. Share your assessment results and your answers with the class. Are the personality types equally represented in your class? If some types are over- or under-represented, why do you think that is so?

For more information about Myers-Briggs personality types in the workplace visit http://www.myersbriggs.org/my-mbti-personality-type/mbti-basics/the-16-mbti-types.asp; http://www.teamtechnology.co.uk/tt/t-articl/mb-simpl.htm; http://www.mbtitoday.org/typechars.html; and http://www.bbc.co.uk/science/humanbody/mind/surveys/whatamilike/index.shtml. There are a host of others available online.

While none of these sites is scientifically validated and should not be used to replace the advice of a professional, they can provide you some interesting ideas and insights.

CHAPTER 12: ASSESSING YOUR NEEDS

This set of needs was developed in 1938 by H. A. Murray, a psychologist, and operationalized by another psychologist, I. W. Atkinson. Known as Murray's Manifest Needs because they are visible through behavior, they are:

1. Achievement
2. Affiliation
3. Aggression
4. Autonomy
5. Exhibition
6. Impulsivity
7. Nurturance
8. Order
9. Power
10. Understanding

To score your results, look at each question individually—the needs correspond one-to-one to the items on the assessment questionnaire.

Although little research has evaluated Murray's theory, the different needs have been investigated. People seem to have a different profile of needs underlying their motivations at different ages. The more any one or more of these needs are descriptive of you, the more you see that particular need as being active in your motivational makeup.

For more information, see H. A. Murray, *Explorations in Personality* (New York: Oxford University Press, 1938) and J. W. Atkinson, *An Introduction to Motivation* (Princeton, NJ: Van Nostrand, 1964).

CHAPTER 13: MANAGERIAL LEADER BEHAVIOR QUESTIONNAIRE

These statements represent twenty-three behavior categories that research has identified as descriptive of managerial leadership. Not all twenty-three are important in any given situation. Typically, fewer than half of these behaviors are associated with effective performance in particular situations; thus there is no "right" or "wrong" set of responses on this questionnaire. The behavior categories are:

1. Emphasizing performance
2. Showing consideration
3. Providing career counseling
4. Inspiring subordinates
5. Providing praise and recognition
6. Structuring reward contingencies

7. Clarifying work roles
8. Setting goals
9. Training-coaching
10. Disseminating information
11. Encouraging participation in decisions
12. Delegating
13. Planning
14. Innovating
15. Problem solving
16. Facilitating the work
17. Monitoring operations
18. Monitoring the environment
19. Representing the unit
20. Facilitating cooperation and teamwork
21. Managing conflict
22. Providing criticism
23. Administering discipline

In military organizations at war, inspiring subordinates, emphasizing performance, clarifying work roles, problem solving, and planning seem most important. In military organizations during peacetime, inspiring subordinates, emphasizing performance, clarifying work roles, showing consideration, providing criticism, and administering discipline seem most important. In business organizations, emphasizing performance, monitoring the environment, clarifying work roles, setting goals, and sometimes innovating seem to be most important. In each of these instances, however, the level of organization, type of technology, environmental conditions, and objectives sought help determine the exact mix of behaviors that will lead to effectiveness. You should analyze your particular situation to determine which subset of these behavior categories is most likely to be important and then should strive to develop that subset.

CHAPTER 14: SEX TALK QUIZ

1. **False**—According to studies, there is no truth to the myth that women are more intuitive than men. However, research has shown that women pay greater attention to "detail." Linguist Robin Lakoff, in her classic book *Language and Woman's Place* (Harper Colophon, 1975), confirms this and states that women tend to use finer descriptions of colors.

2. **True**—Men are listened to more often than women. In "Sex Differences in Listening Comprehension," Kenneth Gruber and Jacqueline Gaehelein (*Sex Roles*, Vol. 5, 1979) found that both male and female audiences tended to listen more attentively to male speakers than to female speakers.

3. **False**—Contrary to popular stereotype, it is men—not women—who talk more. Studies like the one done by Linguist Lynnette Hirshman showed that men far outtalk women ("Analysis of Supportive and Assertive Behavior in Conversations." Paper presented at the Linguists Society of America, July 1974).

4. **False**—Although several studies show that women talk more rapidly than men, women don't necessarily talk extremely fast.

5. **False**—Numerous studies show that women, not men, tend to maintain more eye contact and facial pleasantries. Dr. Nancy Henley, in the chapter "Power, Sex, and Non-Verbal Communication" in *Language and Sex: Difference and Dominance* (Newbury House Publishers, 1975), shows that women exhibit more friendly behavior (such as smiles, facial pleasantries, and head nods) than men.

6. **True**—Studies show that women are more open in their praise and give more "nods of approval" than men. They also use more complimentary terms throughout their speech, according to Peter Falk in his book *Word-Play: What Happens When People Talk* (Knopf, 1973).

7. **True**—Donald Zimmerman and Candace West showed that 75 percent to 93 percent of the interruptions were made by men. ("Sex Roles, Interruptions

and Silences in Conversation," in *Language and Sex: Difference and Dominance,* edited by B. Thorne and N. Henley, Newbury House Publishers, 1975.)

8. **False**—Men use more command terms or imperatives, which makes them sound more demanding. In essence, several researchers have concluded that women tend to be more polite in their speech.

9. **False**—Men and women definitely differ in their sense of humor. Women are more likely to tell jokes when there is a small, same-sex group, and men are more likely to tell jokes in a larger, mixed-sex group.

10. **False**—In a survey conducted for the Playboy Channel, people were asked what they wanted to hear when making love. In general, women wanted to be told they were beautiful and loved, and men wanted to hear how good they were in bed and how much they pleased their women.

11. **True**—Deborah Tannen in her book *You Just Don't Understand: Women and Men in Conversation* (William Morrow, 1990), found that men usually will not solicit help by asking for directions, whereas women will.

12. **False**—Several surveys and numerous psychotherapists' observations have indicated that women tend to be more self-critical and more apt to blame themselves than men. Deborah Tannen's findings (see item 11) confirm this. She states that in their conversations, women also tend to use more "apologetic phrases," such as, "I'm sorry," "I didn't mean to," or "Excuse me."

13. **True**—Naturalist Charles Darwin stated that making oneself appear smaller by bowing the head to take up less space can inhibit human aggression. Other researchers found that women tend to make themselves smaller by crossing their legs at the ankles or knees or keeping their elbows to their sides.

14. **False**—As mentioned earlier, women tend to be more detailed and more descriptive than men in what they say and in how they explain things. As Robin Lakoff's research shows (see item 1), women tend to use more description in word choices.

15. **False**—Men tend to touch more than females. According to several researchers, women are more likely to be physically touched by men who guide them through the door, assist them with jackets and coats, and help them into cars.

16. **False**—Women, not men, appear to be more attentive when listening. Studies consistently show that women exhibit greater eye contact and express approval by smiling and head nodding as a form of attentiveness and agreement.

17. **True**—Men and women are equally emotional when they speak. However, according to researchers such as Robin Lakoff (see item 1), women sound more emotional because they use more psychological-state verbs: I *feel*, I *hope*, and I *wish*.

18. **False**—In general, men tend to bring up less personal topics than women. Women tend to discuss people, relationships, children, self-improvement, and how certain experiences have affected them. Men, on the other hand, tend to be more "outer-directed" as they originate discussions about events, news, sports, and topics related to more concrete physical tasks.

19. **False**—Even though men do not bring up as many subjects of conversation as women, men interrupt more, which ultimately gives them control of even the topics that are raised by women.

20. **False**—Even though there are many progressive and socially enlightened parents in the modern world, parents still treat their male children differently than their female children. They tend to communicate differently with their children according to their sex, which, in turn, induces sex-stereotyped behaviors.

21. **True**—Even though men make more direct statements, a recent survey indicated that women tend to confront and bring up a problem more often than men. Even though women bring up a problem more often, they tend to be more indirect and polite, as Deborah Tannen relates in her book (see item 11).

22. **False**—In several studies, it was determined that women are more animated and livelier speakers than men. Studies also show that women make more eye contact, use more body movement, use more intonation, have a more varied pitch range, and use more emotionally laden words and phrases.

23. **False**—Just as women bring up more topics of conversation, they also ask more questions. According to researchers, this is usually done to facilitate the conversation.

24. **False**—Men and women usually talk about different things. Studies indicate that women enjoy talking about diet, personal relationships, personal appearance, clothes, self-improvement, children, marriages, personalities of others, actions of others, relationships at work, and emotionally charged issues that have a personal component. Men, on the other hand, enjoy discussing sports, what they did at work, where they went, news events, mechanical gadgets, the latest technology, cars, vehicles, and music.

25. **True**—A recent Gallup poll survey commissioned for Lillian Glass, *He Says, She Says*, found that women rather than men were more likely to introduce the topics of AIDS testing and safe sex.

CHAPTER 15: USING TEAMS

Judging on the basis of research conducted by J. Richard Hackman and others, all the statements are false.

1. An emphasis on individual accountability essentially undermines any effort to develop a team.

2. Complete authority is likely to lead to anarchy. Limits should be set.

3. Teams should be kept small, should have clear boundaries, and should have an enabling structure that ensures member motivation.

4. Teams need coaching, counseling, and support at certain intervals during their functioning.

5. The start-up period is critical, which is why managers must spend time and energy coaching and counseling the team during this period. Once the team gets going, the manager should pull back until it reaches a natural break or completes a performance cycle.

6. Training is absolutely critical and should be done before the team is assembled or shortly thereafter. If the needed skills and knowledge change, management should be ready to assist in training to help the team learn the new skills and acquire the new knowledge quickly.

7. Providing support for teams is difficult. A reward system must recognize and reinforce team performance, an educational system must provide needed skills and knowledge, an information system must provide necessary information, and physical and fiscal resources must be available as needed.

8. Teams need some structure to work effectively.

9. The opposite is true. Managers should set the direction and establish wide limits on constraints, whereas the means to the end should be determined by the team.

10. Teams cannot effectively be used in organizations that have strong individualistic cultures.

NOTES

Chapter 1

1 "Corporate Information," *Google website*, www.google.com on March 25, 2010; Peter Coy, "The Secret to Google's Success," *BusinessWeek*, March 6, 2006, www.businessweek.com on December 19, 2008; Mara Der Hovanesian and Sarah Lacy, "Reality Check for the Google Boys," *BusinessWeek*, March 13, 2006, www.businessweek.com on December 19, 2008; Alan Deutschman, "Can Google Stay Google?" *Fast Company*, August 2005, www.fastcompany.com on December 19, 2008; "Apple's Market Cap Overtakes Google," *San Francisco Business Times*, August 14, 2008, http://eastbay.bizjournals.com on December 9, 2008; Don Reisinger, "Can Google Be Bested? Not Any Time Soon," *Ars Technica*, August 3, 2008, http://arstechnica.com on December 9, 2008; Alan Deutschman, "Googling for Courage," *Fast Company*, September 2004, www.fastcompany.com on December 19, 2008; Burt Helm, "Google Shows Surfers the Money," *BusinessWeek*, March 1, 2006, www.businessweek.com on December 19, 2008; and Adi Ignatius, "In Search of the Real Google," *Time*, February 20, 2006, www.time.com on December 19, 2009.

2 Fred Luthans, "Successful vs. Effective Real Managers," *Academy of Management Executive*, May 1988, Vol. 2, No. 2, pp. 127–132. See also "The Best Performers," *BusinessWeek*, Spring 2006 Special Issue, pp. 61–140.

3 See "The Best (& Worst) Managers of the Year," *BusinessWeek*, January 10, 2005, pp. 55–86.

4 See "Executive Pay," *BusinessWeek*, April 15, 2002, pp. 80–100. See also Jim Collins, "The Ten Greatest CEO's of All Times," *Fortune*, July 21, 2003, pp. 54–68.

5 "Executive Compensation for 50 of the Largest U.S. Companies," *USA Today*, May 4, 2009, p. 3B.

6 Rosemary Stewart, "Middle Managers: Their Jobs and Behaviors," in Jay W. Lorsch (ed.), *Handbook of Organizational Behavior* (Englewood Cliffs, N.J.: Prentice Hall, 1987), pp. 385–391. See also Rosabeth Moss Kanter, "The Middle Manager as Innovator," *Harvard Business Review*, July–August 2004, pp. 150–161; and Bill Woolridge, Torsten Schmid, and Steven W. Floyd, "The Middle Management Perspective on Strategy Process: Contributions, Synthesis, and Future Research," *Journal of Management*, 2008, Vol. 34, No. 6, pp. 1190–1221.

7 John P. Kotter, "What Effective General Managers Really Do," *Harvard Business Review*, March–April 1999, pp. 145–155. See also Peter Drucker, "What Makes an Effective Executive," *Harvard Business Review*, June 2004, pp. 58–68.

8 See Robert L. Katz, "The Skills of an Effective Administrator," *Harvard Business Review*, September–October 1974, pp. 90–102, for a classic discussion of several of these skills. For a recent perspective, see J. Brian Atwater, Vijay R. Kannan, and Alan A. Stephens, "Cultivating Systemic Thinking in the Next Generation of Business Leaders," *Academy of Management Learning & Education*, 2008, Vol. 7, No. 1, pp. 9–25.

9 See Mark Gottfredson, Steve Schaubert, and Hernan Saenz, "The New Leader's Guide to Diagnosing the Business," *Harvard Business Review*, February 2008, pp. 63–72, for an interesting application.

10 See "The Real Reasons You're Working So Hard . . . and What You Can Do about It," *BusinessWeek*, October 3, 2005, pp. 60–68; and "I'm Late, I'm Late, I'm Late," *USA Today*, November 26, 2002, pp. 1B, 2B.

11 For a thorough discussion of the importance of time management skills, see David Barry, Catherine Durnell Cramton, and Stephen J. Carroll, "Navigating the Garbage Can: How Agendas Help Managers Cope with Job Realities," *Academy of Management Executive*, May 1997, pp. 26–42.

12 Gary Hamel and C. K. Prahalad, "Competing for the Future," *Harvard Business Review*, July–August 1994, pp. 122–128; see also Joseph M. Hall and M. Eric Johnson, "When Should a Process Be Art, Not Science?" *Harvard Business Review*," March 2009, pp. 58–65.

13 James Waldroop and Timothy Butler, "The Executive as Coach," *Harvard Business Review*, November–December 1996, pp. 111–117.

14 Terence Mitchell and Lawrence James, "Building Better Theory: Time and the Specification of When Things Happen," *Academy of Management Review*, 2001, Vol. 26, No. 4, pp. 530–547.

15 Peter F. Drucker, "The Theory of the Business," *Harvard Business Review*, September–October 1994, pp. 95–104.

16 "Why Business History?" *Audacity*, Fall 1992, pp. 7–15. See also Alan L. Wilkins and Nigel J. Bristow, "For Successful Organization Culture, Honor Your Past," *Academy of Management Executive*, August 1987, Vol. 1, No. 3, pp. 221–227.

17 Daniel Wren, *The Evolution of Management Thought*, 5th ed. (New York: Wiley, 2005); and Page Smith, *The Rise of Industrial America* (New York: McGraw-Hill, 1984).

18 Martha I. Finney, "Books That Changed Careers," *HRMagazine*, June 1997, pp. 141–145. See also "Leadership in Literature," *Harvard Business Review*, March 2006, pp. 47–55.

19 See Harriet Rubin, *The Princessa: Machiavelli for Women* (New York: Doubleday/Currency, 1997). See also Nanette Fondas, "Feminization Unveiled: Management Qualities in Contemporary Writings," *Academy of Management Review*, January 1997, Vol. 22, No. 1, pp. 257–282.

20 Alan M. Kantrow (ed.), "Why History Matters to Managers," *Harvard Business Review*, January–February 1986, pp. 81–88.

21 Wren, *The Evolution of Management Thought* (Hoboken, N.J.: Wiley).

22 Wren, *The Evolution of Management Thought* (Hoboken, N.J.: Wiley).

23 Frederick W. Taylor, *Principles of Scientific Management* (New York: Harper and Brothers, 1911).

24 Charles D. Wrege and Amedeo G. Perroni, "Taylor's Pig-Tale: A Historical Analysis of Frederick W. Taylor's Pig-Iron Experiment," *Academy of Management Journal*, March 1974, Vol. 17, No. 1, pp. 6–27; Charles D. Wrege and Ann Marie Stoka, "Cooke Creates a Classic: The Story behind F.W. Taylor's Principles of Scientific Management," *Academy of Management Review*, October 1978, Vol. 3, No. 4, pp. 736–749.

25 Robert Kanigel, *The One Best Way* (New York: Viking, 1997); Oliver E. Allen, "'This Great Mental Revolution,'" *Audacity*, Summer 1996, pp. 52–61; and Jill Hough and Margaret White, "Using Stories to Create Change: The Object Lesson of Frederick Taylor's 'Pig-Tale,'" *Journal of Management*, 2001, Vol. 27, pp. 585–601.

26 Henri Fayol, *General and Industrial Management*, trans. J. A. Coubrough (Geneva: International Management Institute, 1930).

27 Max Weber, *Theory of Social and Economic Organizations*, trans. T. Parsons (New York: Free Press, 1947); and Richard M. Weis, "Weber on Bureaucracy: Management Consultant or Political Theorist?" *Academy of Management Review*, April 1983, Vol. 8, No. 2, pp. 242–248.

28 "The Line Starts Here," *Wall Street Journal*, January 11, 1999, pp. R1, R25.

29 Hugo Munsterberg, *Psychology and Industrial Efficiency* (Boston: Houghton Mifflin, 1913).

30 Wren, *The Evolution of Management Thought*, pp. 255–264 (Hoboken, N.J.: Wiley).

31 Elton Mayo, *The Human Problems of an Industrial Civilization* (New York: Macmillan, 1933); and Fritz J. Roethlisberger and William J. Dickson, *Management and the Worker* (Cambridge, Mass.: Harvard University Press, 1939).

32 Abraham Maslow, "A Theory of Human Motivation," *Psychological Review*, July 1943, pp. 370–396.

33 Douglas McGregor, *The Human Side of Enterprise* (New York: McGraw-Hill, 1960).

34 Sara L. Rynes and Christine Quinn Trank, "Behavioral Science in the Business School Curriculum: Teaching in a Changing Institutional Environment," *Academy of Management Review*, 1999, Vol. 24, No. 4, pp. 808–824.

35 See Ricky W. Griffin and Gregory Moorhead, *Organizational Behavior*, 10th ed. (Cincinnati, Ohio: Cengage, 2011), for a recent review of current developments in the field of organizational behavior.

36 Wren, *The Evolution of Management Thought*, pp. 255–264. (Hoboken, N.J.: Wiley).

37 "Math Will Rock Your World," *BusinessWeek*, January 23, 2006, pp. 54–61.

38 "Quantitative Analysis Offers Tools to Predict Likely Terrorist Moves," *Wall Street Journal*, February 17, 2006, p. B1.

39 For more information on systems theory in general, see Ludwig von Bertalanffy, C. G. Hempel, R. E. Bass, and H. Jonas, "General Systems Theory: A New Approach to Unity of Science," I–VI *Human Biology*, 1951, Vol. 23, pp. 302–361. For systems theory as applied to organizations, see Fremont E. Kast and James E. Rosenzweig, "General Systems Theory: Applications for Organizations and Management," *Academy of Management Journal*, December 1972, pp. 447–465. For a recent update, see Donde P. Ashmos and George P. Huber, "The Systems Paradigm in Organization Theory: Correcting the Record and Suggesting the Future," *Academy of Management Review*, October 1987, pp. 607–621.

40 See Robert S. Kaplan and David P. Norton, "Mastering the Management System," *Harvard Business Review*, January 2008, pp. 63–72.

41 "Gillette's New Edge," *BusinessWeek*, February 6, 2006, p. 44.

42 Kathleen M. Eisenhardt and D. Charles Galunic, "Coevolving—At Last, a Way to Make Synergies Work," *Harvard Business Review*, January–February 2000, pp. 91–103.

43 Fremont E. Kast and James E. Rosenzweig, *Contingency Views of Organization and Management* (Chicago: Science Research Associates, 1973).

44 "There Is No More Normal," *BusinessWeek*, March 23–30, 2009, pp. 30–34.

45 "The BusinessWeek Best-Seller List," *BusinessWeek*, November 4, 2002, p. 26.

46 See Phanish Puranam and Bart S. Vanneste, "Trust and Governance: Untangling a Tangled Web," *Academy of Management Review*, January 2009, Vol. 34, No. 1, pp. 11–31.

47 "Yes, We'll Still Make Stuff," *Time*, May 25, 2009, p. 49.

48 "The Way We'll Work," *Time*, May 25, 2009, pp. 39–51.

49 Patricia L. Nemetz and Sandra L. Christensen, "The Challenge of Cultural Diversity: Harnessing a Diversity of Views to Understand Multiculturalism," *Academy of Management Review*, 1996, Vol. 21, No. 2, pp. 434–462; and Frances J. Milliken and Luis L. Martins, "Searching for Common Threads: Understanding the Multiple Effects of Diversity in Organizational Groups," *Academy of Management Review*, 1996, Vol. 21, No. 2, pp. 402–433.

50 "When Gen X Runs the Show," *Time*, May 25, 2009, p. 48.

51 Craig L. Pearce and Charles P. Osmond, "Metaphors for Change: The ALPS Model of Change Management," *Organizational Dynamics*, Winter 1996, pp. 23–35.

Chapter 2

1 Cora Daniels, "Mr. Coffee," *Fortune*, April 14, 2003, pp. 139–143; Kevin Helliker and Shirley Leung "Despite the Jitters, Most Coffeehouses Survive Starbucks," *Wall Street Journal*, September 24, 2002, pp. A1, A11 (*quote p. A1); "Planet Starbucks," *BusinessWeek*, September 9, 2008, pp. 100–110; "Not a Johnny-Come-Latte," *USA Today*, September 9, 2009, p. 3B; Andy Serwer, "Hot Starbucks To Go," *Fortune*, January 26, 2009, pp. 60–74; *Hoover's Handbook of American Business 2010* (Austin Tex.: Hoover's Business Press, 2010), 793–794; "Starbucks Plans to Stir Up Coffee Market," CNN.com, May 26, 2010.

2 See Jay B. Barney and William G. Ouchi (eds.), *Organizational Economics* (San Francisco: Jossey-Bass, 1986), for a detailed analysis of linkages between economics and organizations.

3 See, for example, "Political Pendulum Swings toward Stricter Regulation," *Wall Street Journal*, March 24, 2008, pp. A1, A11; see also "Changing Safety Rules Perplex and Polarize," *USA Today*, February 5, 2009, pp. 1B, 2B; and Nina Easton and Telis Demos, "The Business Guide to Congress," *Fortune*, May 11, 2009, pp. 72–75.

4 For example, see Susanne G. Scott and Vicki R. Lane, "A Stakeholder Approach to Organizational Identity," *Academy of Management Review*, 2000, Vol. 25, No. 1, pp. 43–62.

5 Richard N. Osborn and John Hagedoorn, "The Institutionalization and Evolutionary Dynamics of Interorganizational Alliances and Networks," *Academy of Management Journal*, April 1997, pp. 261–278. See also "More Companies Cut Risk by Collaborating with Their 'Enemies,'" *Wall Street Journal*, January 31, 2000, pp. A1, A10.

6 The Best & Worst Boards," *BusinessWeek*, October 7, 2002, pp. 104–114. See also Amy Hillman and Thomas Dalziel, "Boards of Directors and Firm Performance: Integrating Agency and Resource Dependence Perspectives," *Academy of Management Review*, 2003, Vol. 23, No. 3, pp. 383–396.

7 "The Wild New Workforce," *BusinessWeek*, December 6, 1999, pp. 38–44.

8 "Temporary Workers Getting Short Shrift," *USA Today*, April 11, 1997, pp. 1B, 2B.

9 "Curves Ahead," *Wall Street Journal*, March 10, 1999, pp. B1, B10.

10 See Norman Barry, *Business Ethics* (West Lafayette, IN: Purdue University Press, 1999).

11 Thomas Donaldson and Thomas W. Dunfee, "Toward a Unified Conception of Business Ethics: An Integrative Social Contracts Theory," *Academy of Management Review*, Vol. 19, No. 2, 1994, pp. 252–284.

12 "Chains' Ties Run Deep on Pharmacy Boards," *USA Today*, December 31, 2008, pp. 1B, 2B.

13 Jeremy Kahn, "Presto Chango! Sales Are Huge," *Fortune*, March 20, 2000, pp. 90–96; "More Firms Falsify Revenue to Boost Stocks," *USA Today*, March 29, 2000, p. 1B.

14 "U.S. Probes Hilton over Theft Claims," *Wall Street Journal*, April 22, 2009, pp. B1, B4.

15 William Dill, "Beyond Codes and Courses," *Selections*, Fall 2002, pp. 21–23.

16 See "Restoring Trust in Corporate America," *BusinessWeek*, June 24, 2002, pp. 30–35.

17 "How to Fix Corporate Governance," *BusinessWeek*, May 6, 2002, pp. 68–78. See also Catherine Daily, Dan Dalton, and Albert Cannella, "Corporate Governance: Decades of Dialogue and Data," *Academy of Management Review*, 2003, Vol. 28, No. 3, pp. 371–382.

18 "Is It Rainforest Crunch Time?" *BusinessWeek*, July 15, 1996, pp. 70–71; "Yo, Ben! Yo, Jerry! It's Just Ice Cream," *Fortune*, April 28, 1997, p. 374.

19 Andrew Singer, "Can a Company Be Too Ethical?" *Across the Board*, April 1993, pp. 17–22.

20 "Legal But Lousy," *Fortune*, September 2, 2002, p. 192.

21 Lynn Sharp Paine, "Managing for Organizational Integrity," *Harvard Business Review*, March–April 1994, pp. 106–115.

22 "To Give, or Not to Give," *Time*, May 11, 2009, p. 10.

23 "Battling 'Donor Dropsy,'" *Wall Street Journal*, July 19, 2002, pp. B1, B4.

24 "A New Way of Giving," *Time*, July 24, 2000, pp. 48–51. See also Michael Porter and Mark Kramwe, "The Competitive Advantage of Corporate Philanthropy," *Harvard Business Review*, December 2002, pp. 57–66.

25 "To Give, or Not to Give," *Time*, May 11, 2009, p. 10.

26 David M. Messick and Max H. Bazerman, "Ethical Leadership and the Psychology of Decision Making," *Sloan Management Review*, Winter 1996, pp. 9–22.

27 "Ethics in Action: Getting It Right," *Selections*, Fall 2002, pp. 24–27.

28 See Janet P. Near and Marcia P. Miceli, "Whistle-Blowing: Myth and Reality," *Journal of Management*, 1996, Vol. 22, No. 3, pp. 507–526, for a recent review of the literature on whistle blowing. See also Michael

Gundlach, Scott Douglas, and Mark Martinko, "The Decision to Blow the Whistle: A Social Information Processing Framework," *Academy of Management Review*, 2003, Vol. 28, No.1, pp. 107–123.

29 For instance, see "The Complex Goals and Unseen Costs of Whistle-Blowing," *Wall Street Journal*, November 25, 2002, pp. A1, A10.

30 "He Blew a Whistle for 9 Years," *USA Today*, February 13, 2009, pp. 1B, 2B.

31 "SEC Announces a Whistle-Blower Overhaul Plan," *USA Today*, March 6, 2009, p. 1B.

32 "The Fortune Global 500—World's Largest Corporations," *Fortune*, July 27, 2008, pp. 85–104.

33 "The Fortune Global 500 Ranked within Industries," *Fortune*, July 27, 2008, pp. 85–104.

34 *Hoover's Handbook of American Business 2010*, pp. 116–117, 334–335.

35 See "Spanning the Globe," *USA Today*, April 30, 2002, pp. 1C, 2C.

36 "Creating a Worldwide Yen for Japanese Beer," *Financial Times*, October 7, 1994, p. 20.

37 Kenichi Ohmae, "The Global Logic of Strategic Alliances," *Harvard Business Review*, March–April 1989, pp. 143–154.

38 "What If There Weren't Any Clocks to Watch?" *Newsweek*, June 30, 1997, p. 14.

39 "Main Street, H.K.—Disney Localizes Mickey to Boost Its Hong Kong Theme Park," *Wall Street Journal*, January 23, 2008, p. B1, B2.

40 For an excellent discussion of the effects of NAFTA, see "In the Wake of Nafta, a Family Firm Sees Business Go South," *Wall Street Journal*, February 23, 1999, pp. A1, A10.

41 Terrence E. Deal and Allan A. Kennedy, *Corporate Cultures: The Rights and Rituals of Corporate Life* (Reading, MA: Addison-Wesley, 1982).

42 Jay B. Barney, "Organizational Culture: Can It Be a Source of Sustained Competitive Advantage?" *Academy of Management Review*, July 1986, pp. 656–665.

43 For example, see Carol J. Loomis, "Sam Would Be Proud," *Fortune*, April 17, 2000, pp. 131–144.

44 *Hoover's Handbook of American Business 2009* (Austin Tex.: Hoover's Business Press, 2009), pp. 277–278.

Chapter 3

1 Eric-Jon Rossel Waugh, "A Short History of Electronic Arts," *BusinessWeek*, August 25, 2006, www.businessweek.com on February 13, 2009; Peter C. Beller, "Activision's Unlikely Hero," *Forbes*, February 2, 2009, www.forbes.com on February 12, 2009; Matt Richtel, "Vivendi to Acquire Activision," *New York Times*, December 3, 2007, www.nytimes.com on February 13, 2009; "Activision Beats EA as Top Third Party Publisher in U.S.," *Gamasutra*, July 24, 2007, www.gamasutra.com on February 13, 2009; "Activision Posts 92% Revenue Increase in Record Year," *Gamasutra*, May 8, 2008, www.gamasutra.com on February 13, 2009; "Activision's 'Focus' Drives Revenue Past Estimates," *Gamasutra*, February 12, 2009, www.gamasutra.com on February 13, 2009; Burt Helm, "Electronic Arts: A Radical New Game Plan," *BusinessWeek*, March 20, 2006, www.businessweek.com on February 12, 2009; Seth Schiesel, "A Company Looks to Its Creative Side to Regain What It Had Lost," *New York Times*, February 19, 2008, www.nytimes.com on February 12, 2009.

2 See Peter J. Brews and Michelle R. Hunt, "Learning to Plan and Planning to Learn: Resolving the Planning School/Learning School Debate," *Strategic Management Journal*, 1999, Vol. 20, pp. 889–913.

3 Max D. Richards, *Setting Strategic Goals and Objectives*, 2nd ed. (St. Paul, Minn.: West, 1986).

4 Jim Collins, "Turning Goals into Results: The Power of Catalytic Mechanisms," *Harvard Business Review*, July–August 1999, pp. 71–81.

5 "GE, No. 2 in Appliances, Is Agitating to Grab Share from Whirlpool," *Wall Street Journal*, July 2, 1997, pp. A1, A6. See also "A Talk with Jeff Immelt," *BusinessWeek*, January 28, 2002, pp. 102–104.

6 Kenneth R. Thompson, Wayne A. Hochwarter, and Nicholas J. Mathys, "Stretch Targets: What Makes Them Effective?" *Academy of Management Executive*, August 1997, pp. 48–58.

7 "A Methodical Man," *Forbes*, August 11, 1997, pp. 70–72.

8 "FDA Not Meeting Its Audit Goals," *USA Today*, May 7, 2009, p. 1B.

9 John A. Pearce II and Fred David, "Corporate Mission Statements: The Bottom Line," *Academy of Management Executive*, May 1987, p. 109.

10 See Charles Hill and Gareth Jones, *Strategic Management*, 6th ed. (Boston: Houghton Mifflin, 2004).

11 For early discussions of strategic management, see Kenneth Andrews, *The Concept of Corporate Strategy*, rev. ed. (Homewood, Ill.: Dow Jones–Irwin, 1980); and Igor Ansoff, *Corporate Strategy* (New York: McGraw-Hill, 1965). For more recent perspectives, see Michael E. Porter, "What Is Strategy?" *Harvard Business Review*, November–December 1996, pp. 61–78; Kathleen M. Eisenhardt, "Strategy as Strategic Decision Making," *Sloan Management Review*, Spring 1999, pp. 65–74; and Sarah Kaplan and Eric Beinhocker, "The Real Value of Strategic Planning," *Sloan Management Review*, Winter 2003, pp. 71–80.

12 *Hoover's Handbook of American Business 2010* (Austin, Tex.: Hoover's Business Press, 2010), pp. 29–30.

13 T. R. Holcomb, R. M. Holmes Jr., and B. L. Connelly, "Making the Most of What You Have: Managerial Ability as a Source of Resource Value Creation," *Strategic Management Journal*, 2009, Vol. 30, No. 5, pp. 457–486.

14 Jay Barney, "Firm Resources and Sustained Competitive Advantage," *Journal of Management*, June 1991, pp. 99–120. See also T. Russell Crook, David J. Ketchen Jr., James G. Combs, and Samuel Y. Todd, "Strategic Resources and Performance: A Meta-Analysis," *Strategic Management Journal*, 2008, Vol. 29, pp. 1141–1154.

15 Michael Porter, *Competitive Strategy* (New York: Free Press, 1980). See also Colin Campbell-Hunt, "What Have We Learned About Generic Competitive Strategy? A Meta-Analysis," *Strategic Management Journal*, 2000, Vol. 21, pp. 127–154. See also Michael E. Porter, "The Five Competitive Forces That Shape Strategy," *Harvard Business Review*, January 2008, pp. 79–90, for a recent update.

16 Ian C. MacMillan and Rita Gunther McGrath, "Discovering New Points of Differentiation," *Harvard Business Review*, July–August 1997, pp. 133–136.

17 "In a Water Fight, Coke and Pepsi Try Opposite Tacks," *Wall Street Journal*, April 18, 2002, pp. A1, A8.

18 "Abercrombie Fights Discount Tide," *Wall Street Journal*, December 8, 2008, p. B1.

19 "When Service Means Survival," *BusinessWeek*, March 2, 2009, pp. 26–40.

20 "Recession Puts Hershey in Sweet Spot," *Wall Street Journal*, January 28, 2009, p. B1.

21 "P&G, Colgate Hit by Consumer Thrift," *Wall Street Journal*, May 1, 2009, pp. B1, B8.

22 Alfred Chandler, *Strategy and Structure: Chapters in the History of the American Industrial Enterprise* (Cambridge, Mass.: MIT Press, 1962); Richard Rumelt, *Strategy, Structure, and Economic Performance* (Cambridge, Mass.: Division of Research, Graduate School of Business Administration, Harvard University, 1974); Oliver Williamson, *Markets and Hierarchies* (New York: Free Press, 1975).

23 "Mars's Takeover of Wrigley Creates a Global Powerhouse," *Wall Street Journal*, April 29, 2009, p. 1A.

24 K. L. Stimpert and Irene M. Duhaime, "Seeing the Big Picture: The Influence of Industry, Diversification, and Business Strategy on Performance," *Academy of Management Journal*, 1997, Vol. 40, No. 3, pp. 560–583.

25 See Chandler, *Strategy and Structure: Chapters in the History of the American Industrial Enterprise* (Cambridge, Mass.: The MIT Press, 1962). Yakov Amihud and Baruch Lev, "Risk Reduction as a Managerial Motive for Conglomerate Mergers," *Bell Journal of Economics*, 1981, pp. 605–617.

26 Chandler, *Strategy and Structure: Chapters in the History of the American Industrial Enterprise* (Cambridge, Mass.: The MIT Press, 1962). Williamson, *Markets and Hierarchies*. (New York: Free Press, 1975).

27 For a discussion of the limitations of unrelated diversification, see Jay Barney and William G. Ouchi, *Organizational Economics* (San Francisco: Jossey-Bass, 1986).

28 See Barry Hedley, "A Fundamental Approach to Strategy Development," *Long Range Planning*, December 1976, pp. 2–11; Bruce Henderson, "The Experience Curve-Reviewed: IV. The Growth Share Matrix of the Product Portfolio," *Perspectives*, No. 135 (Boston: Boston Consulting Group, 1973).

29 Michael G. Allen, "Diagramming G.E.'s Planning for What's WATT," in Robert J. Allio and Malcolm W. Pennington (eds.), *Corporate Planning: Techniques and Applications* (New York: AMACOM, 1979). Limits of this approach are discussed in R. A. Bettis and W. K. Hall, "The Business Portfolio Approach: Where It Falls Down in Practice," *Long Range Planning*, March 1983, pp. 95–105.

30 "Unilever to Sell Specialty-Chemical Unit to ICI of the U.K. for About $8 Billion," *Wall Street Journal*, May 7, 1997, pp. A3, A12; "For Unilever, It's Sweetness and Light," *Wall Street Journal*, April 13, 2000, pp. B1, B4.

31 "Unprofitable Businesses Getting Axed More Often," *Wall Street Journal*, February 17, 2009, pp. B1, B2.

32 James Brian Quinn, Henry Mintzberg, and Robert M. James, *The Strategy Process* (Englewood Cliffs, N.J.: Prentice Hall, 1988).

33 Vasudevan Ramanujam and N. Venkatraman, "Planning System Characteristics and Planning Effectiveness," *Strategic Management Journal*, 1987, Vol. 8, No. 2, pp. 453–468.

34 "Coca-Cola May Need to Slash Its Growth Targets," *Wall Street Journal*, January 28, 2000, p. B2. See also "Pepsi and Coke Roll Out Flavors to Boost Sales," *Wall Street Journal*, May 7, 2002, pp. B1, B4.

35 "Finally, Coke Gets It Right," *BusinessWeek*, February 10, 2003, p. 47.

36 K. A. Froot, D. S. Scharfstein, and J. C. Stein, "A Framework for Risk Management," *Harvard Business Review*, November–December 1994, pp. 91–102.

37 "How the Fixers Fended Off Big Disasters," *Wall Street Journal*, December 23, 1999, pp. B1, B4.

38 "At Wal-Mart, Emergence Plan Has Big Payoff," *Wall Street Journal*, September 12, 2005, pp. B1, B3.

39 "Next Time," *USA Today*, October 4, 2005, pp. 1B, 2B. See also Judith A. Clair and Ronald L. Dufresne, "How Companies Can Experience Positive Transformation from a Crisis," *Organizational Dynamics*, 2007, Vol. 36, No. 1, pp. 63–77.

40 Michael Watkins and Max Bazerman, "Predictable Surprises: The Disasters You Should Have Seen Coming," *Harvard Business Review*, March 2003, pp. 72–81.

Chapter 4

1 Eric Dash and Julie Creswell, "Citigroup Saw No Red Flags Even as It Made Bolder Bets," *New York Times*, November 23, 2008, www.nytimes.com on February 10, 2009; Marcia Vickers, "The Unlikely Revolutionary," *Fortune*, February 27, 2006, http://cnnmoney.com on February 9, 2009; "SEC Examinations Find Shortcomings in Credit Rating Agencies' Practices and Disclosure to Investors," *U.S. Securities and Exchange Commission*, press release, July 8, 2008, www.sec.gov on February 10, 2009; Richard Tomlinson and David Evans, "The Ratings Charade," *Bloomberg Markets*, July 2007, www.bloomberg.com on February 10, 2009; Jenny Anderson and Eric Dash, "Citigroup Raises Anxiety over Economy," *New York Times*, January 16, 2008, www.nytimes.com on February 10, 2009; Floyd Norris, "An Effort to Stem Losses at Citigroup Produces a Renewed Focus on Risk," *New York Times*, January 16, 2008, www.nytimes.com on February 10, 2009; Eric Dash, "Citigroup Reports Big Loss and a Breakup Plan," *New York Times*, January 17, 2009, www.nytimes.com on February 10, 2009.

2 Richard Priem, "Executive Judgment, Organizational Congruence, and Firm Performance," *Organization Science*, August 1994, pp. 421–432. See also R. Duane Ireland and C. Chet Miller, "Decision-Making and Firm Success," *Academy of Management Executive*, 2004, Vol. 18, No. 4, pp. 8–12.

3 "Disney Buys Marvel Entertainment for $4 Billion," *Forbes*, August 31, 2009, p. 45.

4 Paul Nutt, "The Formulation Processes and Tactics Used in Organizational Decision Making," *Organization Science*, May 1993, pp. 226–240.

5 For a review of decision making, see E. Frank Harrison, *The Managerial Decision Making Process*, 5th ed. (Boston: Houghton Mifflin, 1999). See also Elke U. Weber and Eric J. Johnson, "Mindful Judgment and Decision Making," in Susan T. Fiske, Daniel L. Schacter, and Robert Sternberg (eds.), *Annual Review of Psychology 2009* (Palo Alto, Calif.: Annual Reviews, 2009), pp. 53–86.

6 George P. Huber, *Managerial Decision Making* (Glenview, Ill.: Scott, Foresman, 1980).

7 For an example, See Paul D. Collins, Lori V. Ryan, and Sharon F. Matusik, "Programmable Automation and the Locus of Decision-Making Power," *Journal of Management*, 1999, Vol. 25, No. 1, pp. 29–53.

8 George P. Huber, *Managerial Decision Making* (Glenview, Ill.: Scott, Foresman, 1980). See also David W. Miller and Martin K. Starr, *The Structure of Human Decisions* (Englewood Cliffs, N.J.: Prentice Hall, 1976); and Alvar Elbing, *Behavioral Decisions in Organizations*, 2nd ed. (Glenview, Ill.: Scott, Foresman, 1978).

9 Rene M. Stulz, "Six Ways Companies Mismanage Risk," *Harvard Business Review*," March 2009, pp. 86–94.

10 "Ford Lays Bet on New Truck by Rehiring 1,000 Workers," *Wall Street Journal*, October 31, 2008, pp. B1, B2.

11 See Alex Taylor III, "Porsche's Risky Recipe," *Fortune*, February 17, 2003, pp. 90–94; "This SUV Can Tow an Entire Carmaker," *BusinessWeek*, January 19, 2004, pp. 40–41. See also "Porsche's Road to Growth Has Real Hazards," *Wall Street Journal*, December 8, 2005, pp. B1, B2.

12 Gerard P. Hodgkinson, Nicola J. Bown, A. John Maule, Keith W. Glaister, and Alan D. Pearman, "Breaking the Frame: An Analysis of Strategic Cognition and Decision Making under Uncertainty," *Strategic Management Journal*, 1999, Vol. 20, No. 10, pp. 977–985.

13 "Andersen's Fall from Grace Is a Tale of Greed and Miscues," *Wall Street Journal*, June 7, 2002, pp. A1, A6.

14 Glen Whyte, "Decision Failures: Why They Occur and How to Prevent Them," *Academy of Management Executive*, August 1991, pp. 23–31. See also Jerry Useem, "Decisions, Decisions," *Fortune*, June 27, 2005, pp. 55–154.

15 Jerry Useem, "Boeing vs. Boeing," *Fortune*, October 2, 2000, pp. 148–160; "Airbus Prepares to 'Bet the Company' as It Builds a Huge New Jet," *Wall Street Journal*, November 3, 1999, pp. A1, A10.

16 Robert C. Litchfield, "Brainstorming Reconsidered: A Goal-Based View," *Academy of Management Review*, 2008, Vol. 33, No. 3, pp. 649–668.

17 Paul Nutt, "Expanding the Search for Alternatives During Strategic Decision-Making," *Academy of Management Executive*, 2004, Vol. 18, No. 4, pp. 13–22.

18 See Paul J. H. Schoemaker and Robert E. Gunther, "The Wisdom of Deliberate Mistakes," *Harvard Business Review*, June 2006, pp. 108–115.

19 "Airbus Clips Superjumbo Production," *Wall Street Journal*, May 7, 2009, p. B1.

20 "Accommodating the A380," *Wall Street Journal*, November 29, 2005, p. B1; "Boeing Roars Ahead," *BusinessWeek*, November 7, 2005, pp. 44–45; "Boeing's New Tailwind," *Newsweek*, December 5, 2005, p. 45.

21 "The Wisdom of Solomon," *Newsweek*, August 17, 1987, pp. 62–63.

22 "Making Decisions in Real Time," *Fortune*, June 26, 2000, pp. 332–334. See also Eugene Sadler-Smith and Erella Shefy, "The Intuitive Executive: Understanding and Applying 'Gut Feel' in Decision-Making," *Academy of Management Executive*, 2004, Vol. 18, No. 4, pp. 76–91; and Don A. Moore and Francis J. Flynn, "The Case of Behavioral Decision Research in Organizational Behavior," in James P. Walsh and Arthur P. Brief (eds.), *The Academy of Management Annals*, Vol. 2 (London: Routledge, 2008), pp. 399–432.

23 Herbert A. Simon, *Administrative Behavior* (New York: Free Press, 1945). Simon's ideas have been refined and updated in Herbert A. Simon, *Administrative Behavior*, 3rd ed. (New York: Free Press, 1976); and Herbert A. Simon, "Making Management Decisions: The Role of Intuition and Emotion," *Academy of Management Executive*, February 1987, pp. 57–63.

24 Patricia Corner, Angelo Kinicki, and Barbara Keats, "Integrating Organizational and Individual Information Processing Perspectives on Choice," *Organization Science*, August 1994, pp. 294–302.

25 "Lessons from Saturn's Fall," *BusinessWeek*, March 2, 2009, p. 25.

26 Kimberly D. Elsbach and Greg Elofson, "How the Packaging of Decision Explanations Affects Perceptions of Trustworthiness," *Academy of Management Journal*, 2000, Vol. 43, No. 1 pp. 80–89.

27 Kenneth Brousseau, Michael Driver, Gary Hourihan, and Rikard Larsson, "The Seasoned Executive's Decision-Making Style," *Harvard Business Review*, February 2006, pp. 111–112. See also Erik Dane and Michael G. Pratt,

"Exploring Intuition and Its Role in Managerial Decision Making," *Academy of Management Review*, 2007, Vol. 32, No. 1, pp. 33–54.

28 Charles P. Wallace, "Adidas—Back in the Game," *Fortune*, August 18, 1997, pp. 176–182.

29 Barry M. Staw and Jerry Ross, "Good Money after Bad," *Psychology Today*, February 1988, pp. 30–33; D. Ramona Bobocel and John Meyer, "Escalating Commitment to a Failing Course of Action: Separating the Roles of Choice and Justification," *Journal of Applied Psychology*, 1994, Vol. 79, No. 3, pp. 360–363.

30 Mark Keil and Ramiro Montealegre, "Cutting Your Losses: Extricating Your Organization When a Big Project Goes Awry," *Sloan Management Review*, Spring 2000, pp. 55–64.

31 "Closing Time for a Rock Theme Park," *Wall Street Journal*, January 7, 2009, p. B1.

32 Gerry McNamara and Philip Bromiley, "Risk and Return in Organizational Decision Making," *Academy of Management Journal*, 1999, Vol. 42, No. 3, pp. 330–339.

33 For an example, see Brian O'Reilly, "What It Takes to Start a Startup," *Fortune*, June 7, 1999, pp. 135–140.

34 Martha I. Finney, "The Catbert Dilemma—the Human Side of Tough Decisions," *HRMagazine*, February 1997, pp. 70–78.

35 See Ann E. Tenbrunsel and Kristen Smith-Crowe, "Ethical Decision Making: Where We've Been and Where We're Going," in J. Walsh and A.P. Brief (eds.), *The Academy of Management Annals*, pp.545–607.

36 Edwin A. Locke, David M. Schweiger, and Gary P. Latham, "Participation in Decision Making: When Should It Be Used?" *Organizational Dynamics*, Winter 1986, pp. 65–79; Nicholas Baloff and Elizabeth M. Doherty, "Potential Pitfalls in Employee Participation," *Organizational Dynamics*, Winter 1989, pp. 51–62.

37 "The Art of Brainstorming," *BusinessWeek*, August 26, 2002, pp. 168–169.

38 Andre L. Delbecq, Andrew H. Van de Ven, and David H. Gustafson, *Group Techniques for Program Planning* (Glenview, Ill.: Scott, Foresman, 1975); Michael J. Prietula and Herbert A. Simon, "The Experts in Your Midst," *Harvard Business Review*, January–February 1989, pp. 120–124.

39 See Kevin P. Coyne, Patricia Gorman Clifford, and Renee Dye, "Breakthrough Thinking from Inside the Box," *Harvard Business Review*, December 2007, pp. 71–80, for an extension of the nominal group method.

40 Norman P. R. Maier, "Assets and Liabilities in Group Problem Solving: The Need for an Integrative Function," in J. Richard Hackman, Edward E. Lawler III, and Lyman W. Porter (eds.), *Perspectives on Business in Organizations*, 2nd ed. (New York: McGraw-Hill, 1983), pp. 385–392.

41 Anthony L. Iaquinto and James W. Fredrickson, "Top Management Team Agreement about the Strategic Decision Process: A Test of Some of Its Determinants and Consequences," *Strategic Management Journal*, 1997, Vol. 18, No. 1, pp. 63–75.

42 Tony Simons, Lisa Hope Pelled, and Ken A. Smith, "Making Use of Difference: Diversity, Debate, and Decision Comprehensiveness in Top Management Teams," *Academy of Management Journal*, 1999, Vol. 42, No. 6, pp. 662–673.

43 Richard A. Cosier and Charles R. Schwenk, "Agreement and Thinking Alike: Ingredients for Poor Decisions," *Academy of Management Executive*, February 1990, pp. 69–78.

44 Irving L. Janis, *Groupthink*, 2nd ed. (Boston: Houghton Mifflin, 1982).

45 Irving L. Janis, *Groupthink*, 2nd ed. (Boston: Houghton Mifflin, 1982).

Chapter 5

1 David Kushner, "The Web's Hottest Site: Facebook.com," *Rolling Stone*, April 7, 2006, www.rollingstone.com on February 26, 2009; Brad Stone, "Microsoft Buys Stake in Facebook," *New York Times*, October 25, 2007, www.nytimes.com on February 26, 2009; Brad Stone, "Facebook Expands into MySpace's Territory," *New York Times*, May 25, 2007, www.nytimes.com on February 27, 2009; Michael Arrington, "Social Networking: Will Facebook Overtake MySpace in the U.S. in 2009?" *Tech Crunch*, January 13, 2009, www.techcrunch.com on February 27, 2009; Debra Aho

Williamson, "Social Network Revenues Down: Here's Why," *eMarketer*, December 23, 2008, www.emarketer.com on February 26, 2009; Brian Stelter, "MySpace Might Have Friends, but It Wants Ad Money," *New York Times*, June 16, 2008, www.nytimes.com on February 27, 2009; Brad Stone, "In Facebook, Investing in a Theory," *New York Times*, October 4, 2007, www.nytimes.com on February 27, 2009; Louise Story, "Facebook Is Marketing Your Brand Preferences (with your permission)," *New York Times*, November 7, 2007, www.nytimes.com on February 27, 2009; Louise Story, "Apologetic, Facebook Changes Ad Program," *New York Times*, December 6, 2007, www.nytimes.com on February 27, 2009; C. T. Moore, "The Future of Facebook Revenues," *ReveNews*, February 15, 2009, www.revenews.com on February 26, 2009.

2 Bro Uttal, "Inside the Deal That Made Bill Gates $350,000,000," *Fortune*, July 21, 1986, pp. 23–33.

3 "The Richest People in America," *Forbes*, May 25, 2009.

4 Murray B. Low and Ian MacMillan, "Entrepreneurship: Past Research and Future Challenges," *Journal of Management*, June 1988, pp. 139–159.

5 U.S. Bureau of the Census, *Statistical Abstract of the United States: 2009* (Washington, D.C.: Government Printing Office, 2009).

6 "Small Business 'Vital Statistics,' " www.sba.gov/aboutsba on May 24, 2009.

7 "Small Business 'Vital Statistics.' " www.sba.gov/aboutsba on May 24, 2009.

8 "Small Business 'Vital Statistics.' " www.sba.gov/aboutsba on May 24, 2009.

9 "A World That's a-Twitter," *USA Today*, May 26, 2009, pp. 1B, 2B.

10 "Heaven on Wheels," *Forbes*, April 13, 2009, pp. 74–75.

11 Amar Bhide, "How Entrepreneurs Craft Strategies That Work," *Harvard Business Review*, March–April 1994, pp. 150–163.

12 "Three Men and a Baby Bell," *Forbes*, March 6, 2000, pp. 134–135.

13 *Hoover's Handbook of American Business 2010* (Austin, Tex.: Hoover's Business Press, 2010), pp. 896–897; "Peace, Love, and the Bottom Line," *BusinessWeek*, December 7, 1998, pp. 79–82.

14 Nancy J. Lyons, "Moonlight over Indiana," *Inc.*, January 2000, pp. 71–74.

15 F. M. Scherer, *Industrial Market Structure and Economic Performance*, 2nd ed. (Boston: Houghton Mifflin, 1980).

16 "Three Biker-Entrepreneurs Take on Mighty Harley," *New York Times*, August 20, 1999, p. F1.

17 The importance of discovering niches is emphasized in Charles Hill and Gareth Jones, *Strategic Management: An Integrative Approach*, 7th ed. (Boston: Houghton Mifflin, 2007).

18 D. Kirsch, B. Goldfarb, and A. Gera, "Form or Substance: The Role of Business Plans in Venture Capital Decision Making," *Strategic Management Journal*, Vol. 30, No. 5, 2009, pp. 487–516.

19 "Cheap Tricks," *Forbes*, February 21, 2000, p. 116.

20 U.S. Bureau of the Census, *Statistical Abstract of the United States*, May 24, 2009 (Washington, D.C.: Government Printing Office, 2009). See also "Too Much Ventured, Nothing Gained," *Fortune*, November 25, 2002, pp. 135–144.

21 "This Recession Isn't Being Kind to Entrepreneurs," *USA Today*, June 8, 2009, p. 1B.

22 "Up-and-Comers," *BusinessWeek*, May 15, 2000, pp. EB70–EB72.

23 "High-Tech Advances Push C.I.A. into New Company," *New York Times*, September 29, 1999, p. A14.

24 "Women Increase Standing as Business Owners," *USA Today*, June 29, 1999, p. 1B.

25 Norman M. Scarborough and Thomas W. Zimmerer, *Effective Small Business Management: An Entrepreneurial Approach*, 6th ed. (Upper Saddle River, N.J.: Prentice Hall, 2000), pp. 412–413.

26 See Robert A. Baron, "The Role of Affect in the Entrepreneurial Process," *Academy of Management Review*, 2008, Vol. 33, No. 2, pp. 328–340. See also Keith M. Hmieleski and Robert A. Baron, "Entrepreneurs' Optimism and New Venture Performance: A Social Cognition Perspective," *Academy of Management Journal*, 2009, Vol. 52, No. 3, pp. 540–572.

27 "Expert Entrepreneur Got Her Show on the Road at an Early Age," *USA Today*, May 24, 2000, p. 5B.

28 "Flush Times for Liquidators," *Wall Street Journal*, January 20, 2009, p. B1.

Chapter 6

1 Robert Berner, "Flip-Flops, Torn Jeans—and Control," *BusinessWeek*, May 30, 2005, www.businessweek.com on March 16, 2009; Benoit Denizet-Lewis, "The Man behind Abercrombie & Fitch," *Salon.com*, January 24, 2006, www.salon.com on March 16, 2009; "Abercrombie & Fitch to Open Paris Flagship Store," *FashionUnited USA*, November 18, 2008, www.fashionunited.com on March 17, 2009; Steve Stone, "Virginia Beach Police Seize Photos from Abercrombie Store," *The Virginian-Pilot*, February 3, 2008, http://hamptonroads.com on March 17, 2009; "Abercrombie & Fitch," *Snopes.com*, November 27, 2007, www.snopes.com on March 17, 2009; Paul Carton, "Too Much Sex Hurts Abercrombie & Fitch (ANF)," *BloggingStocks*, November 11, 2008, www.bloggingstocks.com on March 16, 2009; Andria Cheng, "Abercrombe & Fitch Clothed in Green," *MarketWatch*, February 13, 2009, www.marketwatch.com on March 17, 2009; "Abercrombie Refuses to Discount, Stock Plunges," *New York Magazine*, November 8, 2008, http://nymag.com on March 16, 2009.

2 Ricky W. Griffin, *Task Design* (Glenview, Ill.: Scott Foresman, 1982).

3 Anne S. Miner, "Idiosyncratic Jobs in Formal Organizations," *Administrative Science Quarterly*, September 1987, pp. 327–351.

4 Maurice D. Kilbridge, "Reduced Costs through Job Enlargement: A Case," *Journal of Business*, 1960, Vol. 33, No. 4, pp. 357–362.

5 Ricky W. Griffin and Gary C. McMahan, "Motivation through Job Enrichment," in Jerald Greenberg (ed.), *Organizational Behavior: State of the Science* (New York: Lawrence Erlbaum and Associates, 1994), pp. 23–44.

6 Maurice D. Kilbridge, "Reduced Costs through Job Enlargement: A Case," *Journal of Business*, 1960, Vol. 33, No. 4, pp. 357–362.

7 Frederick Herzberg, *Work and the Nature of Man* (Cleveland, Ohio: World Press, 1966).

8 J. Richard Hackman and Greg R. Oldham, *Work Redesign* (Reading, Mass.: Addison-Wesley, 1980).

9 Jerry Useem, "What's That Spell? Teamwork!" *Fortune*, June 12, 2006, pp. 64–66.

10 Richard L. Daft, *Organization Theory and Design*, 10th ed. (Cincinnati, Ohio: South-Western, 2009).

11 David D. Van Fleet and Arthur G. Bedeian, "A History of the Span of Management," *Academy of Management Review*, 1977, pp. 356–372.

12 James C. Worthy, "Factors Influencing Employee Morale," *Harvard Business Review*, January 1950, pp. 61–73.

13 Dan R. Dalton, William D. Todor, Michael J. Spendolini, Gordon J. Fielding, and Lyman W. Porter, "Organization Structure and Performance: A Critical Review," *Academy of Management Review*, January 1980, pp. 49–64.

14 "Cadbury Gives Its CEO More Control," *Wall Street Journal*, October 15, 2008, p. B2.

15 See Jerry Useem, "Welcome to the New Company Town," *Fortune*, January 10, 2000, pp. 62–70, for a related discussion. See also "Wherever You Go, You're on the Job," *BusinessWeek*, June 20, 2005, pp. 87–90.

16 See Richard L. Daft, *Organization Theory and Design*, 10th ed. (Cincinnati, Ohio: South-Western, 2009).

17 William Kahn and Kathy Kram, "Authority at Work: Internal Models and Their Organizational Consequences," *Academy of Management Review*, 1994, Vol. 19, No. 1, pp. 17–50.

18 Carrie R. Leana, "Predictors and Consequences of Delegation," *Academy of Management Journal*, December 1986, pp. 754–774.

19 Jerry Useem, "In Corporate America It's Cleanup Time," *Fortune*, September 16, 2002, pp. 62–70.

20 "New Shell CEO Begins Shake-Up," *Wall Street Journal*, May 28, 2009, p. B4.

21 "Yahoo CEO to Install Top-Down Management," *Wall Street Journal*, February 23, 2009, p. B1.

22 Kevin Crowston, "A Coordination Theory Approach to Organizational Process Design," *Organization Science*, March–April 1997, pp. 157–166.

23 James Thompson, *Organizations in Action* (New York: McGraw-Hill, 1967). For a recent discussion, see Bart Victor and Richard S. Blackburn, "Interdependence: An Alternative Conceptualization," *Academy of Management Review*, July 1987, pp. 486–498.

24 Jay R. Galbraith, *Designing Complex Organizations* (Reading, Mass.: Addison-Wesley, 1973) and *Organizational Design* (Reading, Mass.: Addison-Wesley, 1977).

25 Paul R. Lawrence and Jay W. Lorsch, "Differentiation and Integration in Complex Organizations," *Administrative Science Quarterly*, March 1967, pp. 1–47.

26 Max Weber, *Theory of Social and Economic Organizations*, trans. T. Parsons (New York: Free Press, 1947).

27 Paul Jarley, Jack Fiorito, and John Thomas Delany, "A Structural Contingency Approach to Bureaucracy and Democracy in U.S. National Unions," *Academy of Management Journal*, 1997, Vol. 40, No. 4, pp. 831–861.

28 See N. Anand and Richard L. Daft, "What Is the Right Organization Design?" *Organizational Dynamics*, 2007, Vol. 36, No 4, pp. 329–344, for a recent review.

29 Joan Woodward, *Industrial Organization: Theory and Practice* (London: Oxford University Press, 1965).

30 Joan Woodward, *Management and Technology, Problems of Progress Industry*, Series no. 3 (London: Her Majesty's Stationery Office, 1958).

31 For example, see Michael Russo and Niran Harrison, "Organizational Design and Environmental Performance: Clues from the Electronics Industry," *Academy of Management Journal*, 2005, Vol. 48, No. 4, pp. 582–593. See also Sebastian Raisch and Julian Birkinshaw, "Organizational Ambidexterity: Antecedents, Outcomes, and Moderators," *Journal of Management*, 2008, Vol. 34, No. 3, pp. 375–409.

32 Tom Burns and G. M. Stalker, *The Management of Innovation* (London: Tavistock, 1961).

33 Paul R. Lawrence and Jay W. Lorsch, *Organization and Environment* (Homewood, Ill.: Irwin, 1967).

34 Edward E. Lawler III, "Rethinking Organization Size," *Organizational Dynamics*, Autumn 1997, pp. 24–33. See also Henrich R. Greve, "A Behavioral Theory of Firm Growth: Sequential Attention to Size and Performance Goals," *Academy of Management Journal*, 2008, Vol. 51, No. 3, pp. 476–494.

35 Derek S. Pugh and David J. Hickson, *Organization Structure in Its Context: The Aston Program I* (Lexington, Mass.: D. C. Heath, 1976).

36 "Can Wal-Mart Get Any Bigger?" *Time*, January 13, 2003, pp. 38–43.

37 Robert H. Miles and Associates, *The Organizational Life Cycle* (San Francisco: Jossey-Bass, 1980). See also "Is Your Company Too Big?" *BusinessWeek*, March 27, 1989, pp. 84–94.

38 Douglas Baker and John Cullen, "Administrative Reorganization and Configurational Context: The Contingent Effects of Age, Size, and Change in Size," *Academy of Management Journal*, 1993, Vol. 36, No. 6, pp. 1251–1277. See also Kevin Crowston, "A Coordination Theory Approach to Organizational Process Design," *Organization Science*, March–April 1997, pp. 157–168.

39 Oliver E. Williamson, *Markets and Hierarchies* (New York: Free Press, 1975).

40 Oliver E. Williamson, *Markets and Hierarchies* (New York: Free Press, 1975).

41 Michael E. Porter, "From Competitive Advantage to Corporate Strategy," *Harvard Business Review*, May–June 1987, pp. 43–59.

42 Oliver E. Williamson, *Markets and Hierarchies* (New York: Free Press, 1975).

43 Jay B. Barney and William G. Ouchi (eds.), *Organizational Economics* (San Francisco: Jossey-Bass, 1986); Robert E. Hoskisson, "Multidivisional Structure and Performance: The Contingency of Diversification Strategy," *Academy of Management Journal*, December 1987, pp. 625–644. See also Bruce Lamont, Robert Williams, and James Hoffman, "Performance during 'M-Form' Reorganization and Recovery Time: The Effects of Prior Strategy and Implementation Speed," *Academy of Management Journal*, 1994, Vol. 37, No. 1, pp. 153–166.

44 Stanley M. Davis and Paul R. Lawrence, *Matrix* (Reading, Mass.: Addison-Wesley, 1977).

45 "Martha, Inc.," *BusinessWeek*, January 17, 2000, pp. 63–72.

46 Stanley M. Davis and Paul R. Lawrence, *Matrix* (Reading, Mass.: Addison-Wesley, 1977).

47 See Lawton Burns and Douglas Wholey, "Adoption and Abandonment of Matrix Management Programs: Effects of Organizational Characteristics and Interorganizational Networks," *Academy of Management Journal*, 1993, Vol. 36, No. 1, pp. 106–138.

48 See Michael Hammer and Steven Stanton, "How Process Enterprises Really Work," *Harvard Business Review*, November–December 1999, pp. 108–118.

49 Raymond E. Miles, Charles C. Snow, John A. Mathews, Grant Miles, and Henry J. Coleman, Jr., "Organizing in the Knowledge Age: Anticipating the Cellular Form," *Academy of Management Executive*, November 1997, pp. 7–24.

50 John Mathieu, Travis M. Maynard, Tammy Rapp, and Lucy Gibson, "Team Effectiveness 1997-2007: A Review of Recent Advancements and a Glimpse into the Future," *Journal of Management*, 2008, Vol. 34, No. 3, p. 410–476.

51 "Management by Web," *BusinessWeek*, August 28, 2000, pp. 84–96.

52 Peter Senge, *The Fifth Discipline* (New York: Free Press, 1993). See also David Lei, John W. Slocum, and Robert A. Pitts, "Designing Organizations for Competitive Advantage: The Power of Unlearning and Learning," *Organizational Dynamics*, Winter 1999, pp. 24–35.

53 Amy C. Edmondson, "The Competitive Imperative of Learning," *Harvard Business Review*, July–August 2008, pp. 60–70.

Chapter 7

1 Daniel S. Levine, "Firm Turns up Pace of Business Development," *San Francisco Business Times*, May 27, 2005, http://sanfrancisco.bizjournals.com on March 24, 2009; "Genentech's Joe McCracken Is on the Hunt," *The Burrill Report*, May 7, 2007, www.tjols.com on March 24, 2009; "OSI Pharmaceuticals Announces Second Quarter 2008 Financial Results," *iStockAnalyst*, July 23, 2008, www.istockanalyst.com on March 27, 2009; Querida Anderson, "OSI Pharma Needs to Expand Pipeline," *Genetic Engineering & Biotechnology News*, June 15, 2007, www.genengnews.com on March 27, 2009; Trista Morrison, "Phase III/Avastin Trial Hits Goal in NSCLC Maintenance," *BioWorld*, February 4, 2009, www.bioworld.com on March 27, 2009; Christopher P. Singer, "Seattle Genetics Earns Milestone Payment from Genentech for Initiation of Clinical Trial," *Patent Docs*, January 10, 2008, www.patentdocs.com on March 28, 2009; "Genentech Announces Organizational Changes," press release, March 9, 2004, www.gene.com on March 26, 2009; "Roche and Genentech Reach a Friendly $46.8 Billion Agreement," *Bioresearch Online*, March 12, 2009, www.bioresearchonline.com on March 24, 2009.

2 For an excellent review of this area, see Achilles A. Armenakis and Arthur G. Bedeian, "Organizational Change: A Review of Theory and Research in the 1990s," *Journal of Management*, 1999, Vol. 25, No. 3, pp. 293–315.

3 For additional insights into how technological change affects other parts of the organization, see P. Robert Duimering, Frank Safayeni, and Lyn Purdy, "Integrated Manufacturing: Redesign the Organization before Implementing Flexible Technology," *Sloan Management Review*, Summer 1993, pp. 47–56.

4 Joel Cutcher-Gershenfeld, Ellen Ernst Kossek, and Heidi Sandling, "Managing Concurrent Change Initiatives," *Organizational Dynamics*, Winter 1997, pp. 21–38.

5 Michael A. Hitt, "The New Frontier: Transformation of Management for the New Millennium," *Organizational Dynamics*, Winter 2000, pp. 7–15. See also Michael Beer and Nitin Nohria, "Cracking the Code of Change," *Harvard Business Review*, May–June 2000, pp. 133–144; and Clark Gilbert, "The Disruption Opportunity," *MIT Sloan Management Review*, Summer 2003, pp. 27–32.

6 See Warren Boeker, "Strategic Change: The Influence of Managerial Characteristics and Organizational Growth," *Academy of Management Journal*, 1997, Vol. 40, No. 1, pp. 152–170.

7 Alan L. Frohman, "Igniting Organizational Change from Below: The Power of Personal Initiative," *Organizational Dynamics*, Winter 1997, pp. 39–53.

8 Nandini Rajagopalan and Gretchen M. Spreitzer, "Toward a Theory of Strategic Change: A Multi-Lens Perspective and Integrative Framework," *Academy of Management Review*, 1997, Vol. 22, No. 1, pp. 48–79.

9 Anne Fisher, "Danger Zone," *Fortune*, September 8, 1997, pp. 165–167.

10 "Kodak to Cut Staff up to 21% Amid Digital Push," *Wall Street Journal*, January 22, 2005, pp. A1, A7.

11 John P. Kotter and Leonard A. Schlesinger, "Choosing Strategies for Change," *Harvard Business Review*, March–April 1979, p. 106.

12 Clayton M. Christensen and Michael Overdorf, "Meeting the Challenge of Disruptive Change," *Harvard Business Review*, March–April 2000, pp. 67–77.

13 "To Maintain Success, Managers Must Learn How to Direct Change," *Wall Street Journal*, August 13, 2002, p. B1.

14 See Eric Abrahamson, "Change without Pain," *Harvard Business Review*, July–August 2000, pp. 75–85. See also Gib Akin and Ian Palmer, "Putting Metaphors to Work for Change in Organizations," *Organizational Dynamics*, Winter 2000, pp. 67–76.

15 Erik Brynjolfsson, Amy Austin Renshaw, and Marshall Van Alstyne, "The Matrix of Change," *Sloan Management Review*, Winter 1997, pp. 37–54.

16 Kurt Lewin, "Frontiers in Group Dynamics: Concept, Method, and Reality in Social Science," *Human Relations*, June 1947, pp. 5–41.

17 Michael Roberto and Lynne Levesque, "The Art of Making Change Initiatives Stick," *MIT Sloan Management Review*, Summer 2005, pp. 53–62.

18 "Time for a Turnaround," *Fast Company*, January 2003, pp. 55–61.

19 See Connie J. G. Gersick, "Revolutionary Change Theories: A Multilevel Exploration of the Punctuated Equilibrium Paradigm," *Academy of Management Review*, January 1991, pp. 10–36. See also John P. Kotter and Leonard A. Schlesinger, "Choosing Strategies for Change," *Harvard Business Review*, July–August 2008, pp. 130–141.

20 See Mel Fugate, Angelo J. Kinicki, and Gregory E. Prussia, "Employee Coping with Organizational Change: An Examination of Alternative Theoretical Perspectives and Models," *Personnel Psychology*, 2008, Vol. 61, No. 1, pp. 1–36. See also Jeffrey D. Ford and Laurie W. Ford, "Decoding Resistance to Change," *Harvard Business Review*, April 2009, pp. 99–104.

21 See Clark Gilbert and Joseph Bower, "Disruptive Change," *Harvard Business Review*, May 2002, pp. 95–104.

22 "RJR Employees Fight Distraction amid Buy-out Talks," *Wall Street Journal*, November 1, 1988, p. A8.

23 Arnon E. Reichers, John P. Wanous, and James T. Austin, "Understanding and Managing Cynicism about Organizational Change," *Academy of Management Executive*, February 1997, pp. 48–59.

24 For a classic discussion, see Paul R. Lawrence, "How to Deal with Resistance to Change," *Harvard Business Review*, January–February 1969, pp. 4–12, 166–176. For a more recent discussion, see Jeffrey D. Ford, Laurie W. Ford, and Angelo D'Amelio, "Resistance to Change: The Rest of the Story," *Academy of Management Review*, 2008, Vol. 33, No. 2, pp. 362–377.

25 Lester Coch and John R. P. French, Jr., "Overcoming Resistance to Change," *Human Relations*, August 1948, pp. 512–532.

26 Benjamin Schneider, Arthur P. Brief, and Richard A. Guzzo, "Creating a Climate and Culture for Sustainable Organizational Change," *Organizational Dynamics*, Spring 1996, pp. 7–19.

27 "Troubled GM Plans Major Tuneup," *USA Today*, June 6, 2005, pp. 1B, 2B.

28 Paul Bate, Raza Khan, and Annie Pye, "Towards a Culturally Sensitive Approach to Organization Structuring: Where Organization Design Meets Organization Development," *Organization Science*, March–April 2000, pp. 197–211.

29 David Kirkpatrick, "The New Player," *Fortune*, April 17, 2000, pp. 162–168.

30 Jeffrey A. Alexander, "Adaptive Change in Corporate Control Practices," *Academy of Management Journal*, March 1991, pp. 162–193.

31 "Mr. Ryder Rewrites the Musty Old Book at Reader's Digest," *Wall Street Journal*, April 18, 2000, pp. A1, A10.

32 "Struggling Saks Tries Alterations in Management," *Wall Street Journal*, January 10, 2006, pp. B1, B2.

33 Thomas A. Stewart, "Reengineering—the Hot New Managing Tool," *Fortune*, August 23, 1993, pp. 41–48.

34 "Old Company Learns New Tricks," *USA Today*, April 10, 2000, pp. 1B, 2B.

35 Richard Beckhard, *Organization Development: Strategies and Models* (Reading, Mass.: Addison-Wesley, 1969), p. 9.

36 W. Warner Burke, "The New Agenda for Organization Development," *Organizational Dynamics*, Summer 1997, pp. 7–20.

37 Wendell L. French and Cecil H. Bell, Jr., *Organization Development: Behavioral Science Interventions for Organization Improvement*, 2nd ed. (Englewood Cliffs, N.J.: Prentice Hall, 1978).

38 "Memo to the Team: This Needs Salt!" *Wall Street Journal*, April 4, 2000, pp. B1, B14.

39 Roger J. Hower, Mark G. Mindell, and Donna L. Simmons, "Introducing Innovation through OD," *Management Review*, February 1978, pp. 52–56.

40 "Is Organization Development Catching On? A Personnel Symposium," *Personnel*, November–December 1977, pp. 10–22.

41 For a recent discussion on the effectiveness of various OD techniques in different organizations, see John M. Nicholas, "The Comparative Impact of Organization Development Interventions on Hard Criteria Measures," *Academy of Management Review*, October 1982, pp. 531–542.

42 Constantinos Markides, "Strategic Innovation," *Sloan Management Review*, Spring 1997, pp. 9–24. See also James Brian Quinn, "Outsourcing Innovation: The New Engine of Growth," *Sloan Management Review*, Summer 2000, pp. 13–21.

43 L. B. Mohr, "Determinants of Innovation in Organizations," *American Political Science Review*, 1969, pp. 111–126; G. A. Steiner, *The Creative Organization* (Chicago: University of Chicago Press, 1965); R. Duncan and A. Weiss, "Organizational Learning: Implications for Organizational Design," in B. M. Staw (ed.), *Research in Organizational Behavior*, Vol. 1 (Greenwich, Conn.: JAI Press, 1979), pp. 75–123; J. E. Ettlie, "Adequacy of Stage Models for Decisions on Adoption of Innovation," *Psychological Reports*, 1980, Vol. 46, pp. 991–995.

44 See Alan Patz, "Managing Innovation in High Technology Industries," *New Management*, September 1986, Vol. 4, No. 1, pp. 54–59.

45 "Flops," *BusinessWeek*, August 16, 1993, pp. 76–82.

46 "Apple Can't Keep up with Demand for Newest iMac," *USA Today*, August 26, 2002, p. 3B.

47 See Willow A. Sheremata, "Centrifugal and Centripetal Forces in Radical New Product Development under Time Pressure," *Academy of Management Review*, 2000, Vol. 25, No. 2, pp. 389–408. See also Richard Leifer, Gina Colarelli O'Connor, and Mark Rice, "Implementing Radical Innovation in Mature Firms: The Role of Hobs," *Academy of Management Executive*, 2001, Vol. 15, No. 3, pp. 102–113.

48 See Julian Birkinshaw, Gary Hamel, and Michael J. Mol, "Management Innovation," *Academy of Management Review*, 2008, Vol. 33, No. 4, pp. 825–845.

49 See "Amid Japan's Gloom, Corporate Overhauls Offer Hints of Revival," *Wall Street Journal*, February 21, 2002, pp. A1, A11.

50 See Clayton M. Christensen, Stephen P. Kaufman, and Willy C. Shih, "Innovation Killers," *Harvard Business Review*, January 2008, pp. 98–107.

51 Dorothy Leonard and Jeffrey F. Rayport, "Spark Innovation through Empathic Design," *Harvard Business Review*, November–December 1997, pp. 102–115.

52 "The 50 Most Innovative Companies," *BusinessWeek*, April 25, 2010, pp. 34–42.

53 Geoffrey Moore, "Innovating within Established Enterprises," *Harvard Business Review*, July–August 2004, pp. 87–96. See also David A. Garvin and Lynne C. Levesque, "Meeting the Challenge of Corporate Entrepreneurship," *Harvard Business Review*, October 2006, pp. 102–113.

54 See Gifford Pinchot III, *Intrapreneuring* (New York: Harper & Row, 1985).

Chapter 8

1 "For Some, a Patchwork of Jobs Pays the Bills," *Boston.com*, March 27, 2009, www.boston.com on March 31, 2009; Kristin Kridel, "Overqualified Applying for Temporary Work," *Spokesman.com*, March 4, 2009, www.spokesman.com on March 31, 2009; Anne Fisher, "Be a Manager and a Temp?" *CNNMoney.com*, March 16, 2009, http://cnnmoney.com on March 31, 2009; Tanya Mohn, "A Way to Try a Job on for Size before Making a Commitment," *New York Times*, March 12, 2006, http://query.nytimes.com on March 31, 2009; Sital Patel, "Skill Level of Temp Workers Rises amid Recession," *Fox Business*, February 27, 2009, www.foxbusiness.com on April 1, 2009; U.S. Bureau of Labor Statistics (BLS), "Employment Situation Summary," news release, March 6, 2009, http://data.bls.gov on March 31, 2009; BLS, "Table 12. Private Industry, by Industry Group and Full-Time and Part-Time Status," news release, March 12, 2009, www.bls.gov on April 1, 2009; Candice Novak, "Behind the Rise of Temp Work: Q&A with Vicki Smith, Coauthor of 'The Good Temp,'" *U.S. News & World Report*, July 15, 2008, www.usnews.com on April 1, 2009; Benjamin J. Romano, "Microsoft Temps Take Pay Hit as Staffing Firms Agree to Cut Fees," *Seattle Times*, February 27, 2009, http://seattletimes.nwsource.com on April 2, 2009; M. Liedtke, "Temps—Recession's Hidden Jobless," Medford (Oregon) *Mail Tribune*, February 1, 2009, www.mailtribune.com on April 2, 2009.

2 For a complete review of HRM, see Angelo S. DeNisi and Ricky W. Griffin, *Human Resource Management*, 4th ed. (Cincinnati, Ohio: Cengage, 2011).

3 Patrick Wright and Gary McMahan, "Strategic Human Resources Management: A Review of the Literature," *Journal of Management*, June 1992, pp. 280–319. See also Peter Cappelli, "Talent Management for the Twenty-First Century," *Harvard Business Review*, March 2008, pp. 74–84, and Edward E. Lawler III, "Make Human Capital a Source of Competitive Advantage," *Organizational Dynamics*, January–March 2009, Vol. 38, No. 1, pp. 1–7.

4 "From the Ashes, New Tech Start-Ups Can Bloom," *USA Today*, February 17, 2009, p. 1B.

5 Augustine Lado and Mary Wilson, "Human Resource Systems and Sustained Competitive Advantage: A Competency-Based Perspective," *Academy of Management Review*, 1994, Vol. 19, No. 4, pp. 699–727.

6 David Lepak and Scott Snell, "Examining the Human Resource Architecture: The Relationships among Human Capital, Employment, and Human Resource Configurations," *Journal of Management*, 2002, Vol. 28, No. 4, pp. 517–543. See also Wayne F. Cascio and Herman Aguinis, "Staffing Twenty-First Century Organizations," in James P. Walsh and Arthur P. Brief (eds.), *The Academy of Management Annals*, Vol. 2 (London: Routledge, 2008), pp. 133–166.

7 "Maryland First to OK 'Wal-Mart Bill,'" *USA Today*, January 13, 2006, p. 1B.

8 "Is Butter Flavoring Ruining Popcorn Workers' Lungs?" *USA Today*, June 20, 2002, pp. 1A, 8A.

9 "While Hiring at Most Firms Chills, Wal-Mart's Heats Up," *USA Today*, August 26, 2002, p. 1B.

10 Peter Cappelli, "A Supply Chain Approach to Workforce Planning," *Organizational Dynamics*, January–March 2009, Vol. 38, No. 1, pp. 8–15.

11 John Beeson, "Succession Planning," *Across the Board*, February 2000, pp. 38–41.

12 "Xerox Names Burns Chief as Mulcahy Retires Early," *Wall Street Journal*, May 22, 2009, pp. B1, B2.

13 "Star Search," *BusinessWeek*, October 10, 2005, pp. 66–78. See also Claudio Fernandez-Araoz, Boris Groysberg, and Nitin Nohria, "The Definitive Guide to Recruiting in Good Times and Bad," *Harvard Business Review*, May 2009, pp. 74–85.

14 James A. Breaugh and Mary Starke, "Research on Employee Recruiting: So Many Studies, So Many Remaining Questions," *Journal of Management*, 2000, Vol. 26, No. 3, pp. 405–434.

15 See Paul R. Sackett and Filip Lievens, "Personnel Selection," in Susan T. Fiske, Daniel L. Schacter, and Robert Sternberg (eds.), *Annual Review of Psychology 2008* (Palo Alto, Calif.: Annual Reviews, 2008), pp. 419–450.

16 "Pumping up Your Past," *Time*, June 10, 2002, p. 96.

17 Frank L. Schmidt and John E. Hunter, "Employment Testing: Old Theories and New Research Findings," *American Psychologist*, October 1981, pp. 1128–1137.

18 Robert Liden, Christopher Martin, and Charles Parsons, "Interviewer and Applicant Behaviors in Employment Interviews," *Academy of Management Journal*, 1993, Vol. 36, No. 2, pp. 372–386.

19 Paul R. Sackett, "Assessment Centers and Content Validity: Some Neglected Issues," *Personnel Psychology*, 1987, Vol. 40, No. 1, pp. 13–25.

20 Renee DeRouin, Barbara Fritzsche, and Eduardo Salas, "E-Learning in Organizations," *Journal of Management*, 2005, Vol. 31, No. 6, pp. 920–940. See Fred Luthans, James B. Avey, and Jaime L. Patera, "Experimental

Analysis of a Web-Based Training Intervention to Develop Positive Psychological Capital," *Academy of Management Learning & Education*, 2008, Vol. 7, No. 2, pp. 209–221, for a recent illustration.

21 " 'Boeing U': Flying by the Book," *USA Today*, October 6, 1997, pp. 1B, 2B. See also "Is Your Airline Pilot Ready for Surprises?" *Time*, October 14, 2002, p. 72.

22 "The Secret Sauce at In-N-Out Burger," *BusinessWeek*, April 20, 2009, pp. 68–69; "Despite Cutbacks, Firms Invest in Developing Leaders," *Wall Street Journal*, February 9, 2009, p. B4.

23 See Paul Levy and Jane Williams, "The Social Context of Performance Appraisal: A Review and Framework for the Future," *Journal of Management*, 2004, Vol. 30, No. 6, pp. 881–905.

24 See Michael Hammer, "The 7 Deadly Sins of Performance Measurement (and How to Avoid Them)," *MIT Sloan Management Review*, Spring 2007, pp. 19–30.

25 See Angelo S. DeNisi and Avraham N. Kluger, "Feedback Effectiveness: Can 360-Degree Appraisals Be Improved?" *Academy of Management Executive*, 2000, Vol. 14, No. 1, pp. 129–139.

26 Barry R. Nathan, Allan Mohrman, and John Milliman, "Interpersonal Relations as a Context for the Effects of Appraisal Interviews on Performance and Satisfaction: A Longitudinal Study," *Academy of Management Journal*, June 1991, Vol. 34, No. 2, pp. 352–369.

27 "Goodyear to Stop Labeling 10% of Its Workers as Worst," *USA Today*, September 12, 2002, p. 1B.

28 Jaclyn Fierman, "The Perilous New World of Fair Pay," *Fortune*, June 13, 1994, pp. 57–64. See also "The Best vs. the Rest," *Wall Street Journal*, January 30, 2006, pp. B1, B3.

29 "Pay Cuts Made Palatable," *BusinessWeek*, May 4, 2009, p. 67. See also "The Right Way to Pay," *Forbes*, May 11, 2009, pp. 78–80, and "Do Pay Cuts Pay Off?" *Time*, April 27, 2009, p. Global 6.

30 Stephanie Armour, "Show Me the Money, More Workers Say," *USA Today*, June 6, 2000, p. 1B.

31 "To Each According to His Needs: Flexible Benefits Plans Gain Favor," *Wall Street Journal*, September 16, 1986, p. 29.

32 See "Companies Chisel away at Workers' Benefits," *USA Today*, November 18, 2002, pp. 1B, 2B. See also "The Benefits Trap," *BusinessWeek*, July 19, 2004, pp. 64–72.

33 "More Companies Freeze Pensions," *USA Today*, May 11, 2009, p. 1A.

34 For an example, see "A Female Executive Tells Furniture Maker What Women Want," *Wall Street Journal*, June 25, 1999, pp. A1, A11.

35 Patricia L. Nemetz and Sandra L. Christensen, "The Challenge of Cultural Diversity: Harnessing a Diversity of Views to Understand Multiculturalism," *Academy of Management Review*, 1996, Vol. 21, No. 2, pp. 434–462. See also "Generational Warfare," *Forbes*, March 22, 1999, pp. 62–66.

36 Christine M. Riordan and Lynn McFarlane Shores, "Demographic Diversity and Employee Attitudes: An Empirical Examination of Relational Demography within Work Units," *Journal of Applied Psychology*, 1997, Vol. 82, No. 3, pp. 342–358.

37 Sara Rynes and Benson Rosen, "What Makes Diversity Programs Work?" *HR Magazine*, October 1994, pp. 67–75.

38 Karen Hildebrand, "Use Leadership Training to Increase Diversity," *HR Magazine*, August 1996, pp. 53–59.

39 Barbara Presley Nobel, "Reinventing Labor," *Harvard Business Review*, July–August 1993, pp. 115–125.

40 "Big Gains for Unions," *New York Times*, January 29, 2009, p. C1.

41 John A. Fossum, "Labor Relations: Research and Practice in Transition," *Journal of Management*, Summer 1987, Vol. 13, No. 2, pp. 281–300.

42 "How Wal-Mart Keeps Unions at Bay," *BusinessWeek*, October 28, 2002, pp. 94–96.

43 "Outsourcing at Crux of Boeing Strike," *Wall Street Journal*, September 8, 2008, p. B1, B4.

44 "UAW Gives Concessions to Big Three," *Wall Street Journal*, December 4, 2008, pp. B1, B2.

45 Max Boisot, *Knowledge Assets* (Oxford, U.K.: Oxford University Press, 1998).

46 Thomas Stewart, "In Search of Elusive Tech Workers," *Fortune*, February 16, 1998, pp. 171–172.

47 "FBI Taps Retiree Experience for Temporary Jobs," *USA Today*, October 3, 2002, p. 1A.

48 "When Is a Temp Not a Temp?" *BusinessWeek*, December 7, 1998, pp. 90–92.

49 "Drivers Deliver Trouble to FedEx by Seeking Employee Benefits," *Wall Street Journal*, January 7, 2005, pp. A1, A8.

Chapter 9

1 Felix Salmon, "Dimon in the Rough: How JP Morgan's CEO Manages Risk," *Seeking Alpha*, September 3, 2008, www.seekingalpha.com on June 3, 2009; Shawn Tully, "How J. P. Morgan Steered Clear of the Credit Crunch," *CNNMoney.com*, September 2, 2008, http://cnnmoney.com on June 3, 2009; Mara Der Hovanesian, "Dimon in the Rough," *BusinessWeek*, March 28, 2005, www.businessweek.com on June 3, 2009; "Dimon's Grand Design," *BusinessWeek*, March 28, 2005, www.businessweek.com on June 3, 2009; "Jamie Dimon, In His Own Words," *BusinessWeek*, March 28, 2005, www. businessweek.com on June 3, 2009; and Tully, "The Contender: Jamie Dimon, the New CEO of J. P. Morgan Chase," *Fortune*, April 3, 2006, pp. 54–66.

2 For a complete discussion of how FedEx uses control in its operations, see "The FedEx Edge," *Fortune*, April 3, 2006, pp. 77–84. Note also the Management *Tech* box elsewhere in this chapter.

3 Thomas A. Stewart, "Welcome to the Revolution," *Fortune*, December 13, 1993, pp. 66–77.

4 William Taylor, "Control in an Age of Chaos," *Harvard Business Review*, November–December 1994, pp. 64–70.

5 "Fastener Woes to Delay Flight of First Boeing 787 Jets," *Wall Street Journal*, November 5, 2008, p. B1.

6 "Starbucks Brews Up New Cost Cuts By Putting Lid on Afternoon Decaf," *Wall Street Journal*, January 28, 2009, p. B1.

7 "An Apple a Day," *BusinessWeek*, October 14, 2002, pp. 122–125; "More Business People Say: Let's Not Do Lunch," *USA Today*, December 24, 2002, p. 1B; and David Stires, "The Breaking Point," *Fortune*, March 3, 2003, pp. 107–114; see also Shawn Coyne and Edward Coyne, Sr., "When You've Got to Cut costs—Now," *Harvard Business Review*, May 2010, pp. 74–83.

8 Mark Kroll, Peter Wright, Leslie Toombs, and Hadley Leavell, "Form of Control: A Critical Determinant of Acquisition Performance and CEO Rewards," *Strategic Management Journal*, 1997, Vol. 18, No. 2, pp. 85–96.

9 See Donald Lange, "A Multidimensional Conceptualization of Organizational Corruption Control," *Academy of Management Review*, 2008, Vol. 33, No. 3, pp. 710–729 for an example.

10 See Karynne Turner and Mona Makhija, "The Role of Organizational Controls in Managing Knowledge," *Academy of Management Review*, 2006, Vol. 31, No. 1, pp. 197–217.

11 Sim Sitkin, Kathleen Sutcliffe, and Roger Schroeder, "Distinguishing Control from Learning in Total Quality Management: A Contingency Perspective," *Academy of Management Review*, 1994, Vol. 19, No. 3, pp. 537–564.

12 Robert Lusch and Michael Harvey, "The Case for an Off-Balance-Sheet Controller," *Sloan Management Review*, Winter 1994, pp. 101–110.

13 Edward E. Lawler III and John G. Rhode, *Information and Control in Organizations* (Pacific Palisades, Calif.: Goodyear, 1976).

14 Charles W. L. Hill, "Establishing a Standard: Competitive Strategy and Technological Standards in Winner-Take-All Industries," *Academy of Management Executive*, 1997, Vol. 11, No. 2, pp. 7–16.

15 "Airbus Clips Superjumbo Production," *Wall Street Journal*, May 7, 2009, p. B1.

16 "Shifting Burden Helps Employers Cut Health Costs," *Wall Street Journal*, December 8, 2005, pp. B1, B2.

17 "An Efficiency Guru Refits Honda to Fight Auto Giants," *Wall Street Journal*, September 15, 1999, p. B1.

18 See "To Shed Idled Workers, Ford Offers to Foot Bill for College," *Wall Street Journal*, January 18, 2006, pp. B1, B3; and "GM's Employees Buyout Offer," *Fast Company*, May 2006, p. 58.

19 See Belverd E. Needles, Jr., Henry R. Anderson, and James C. Caldwell, *Principles of Accounting*, 2002 ed. (Boston: Houghton Mifflin, 2002).

20 "At Disney, String of Weak Cartoons Leads to Cost Cuts," *Wall Street Journal*, June 18, 2002, pp. A1, A6.

21 Needles, Anderson, and Caldwell, *Principles of Accounting*, 2002 ed. (Boston: Houghton Mifflin, 2002).

22 "Mickey Mouse, CPA," *Forbes*, March 10, 1997, pp. 42, 43.

23 Needles, Anderson, and Caldwell, *Principles of Accounting*, 2002 ed. (Boston: Houghton Mifflin, 2002).

24 Jeremy Kahn, "Do Accountants Have a Future?" *Fortune*, March 3, 2003, pp. 115–117.

25 "Inside WorldCom's Unearthing of a Vast Accounting Scandal," *Wall Street Journal*, June 27, 2002, pp. A1, A12.

26 William G. Ouchi, "The Transmission of Control Through Organizational Hierarchy," *Academy of Management Journal*, June 1978, Vol. 21, No. 2, pp. 173–192; and Richard E. Walton, "From Control to Commitment in the Workplace," *Harvard Business Review*, March–April 1985, pp. 76–84.

27 "Nordstrom Cleans Out Its Closets," *BusinessWeek*, May 22, 2000, pp. 105–108.

28 "Best Managed Companies in America," *Forbes*, January 9, 2006, p. 118.

29 See "In Bow to Retailers New Clout, Levi Strauss Makes Alterations," *Wall Street Journal*, June 17, 2005, pp. A1, A15.

30 Peter Lorange, Michael F. Scott Morton, and Sumantra Ghoshal, *Strategic Control* (St. Paul, Minn.: West, 1986). See also Joseph C. Picken and Gregory G. Dess, "Out of (Strategic) Control," *Organizational Dynamics*, Summer 1997, Vol. 26, No. 1, pp. 35–45.

31 "Pfizer Plans Layoffs in Research," *Wall Street Journal*, January 14, 2009, p. B1.

32 "Kohl's Works to Refill Consumers' Bags," *USA Today*, April 8, 2005, pp. B1, B7.

33 See Hans Mjoen and Stephen Tallman, "Control and Performance in International Joint Ventures," *Organization Science*, May–June 1997, Vol. 8, No. 3, pp. 257–265.

34 For a recent study of effective control, see Diana Robertson and Erin Anderson, "Control System and Task Environment Effects on Ethical Judgment: An Exploratory Study of Industrial Salespeople," *Organization Science*, November 1993, Vol. 4, No. 4, pp. 617–629.

35 "Enterprise Takes Idea of Dressed for Success to a New Extreme," *Wall Street Journal*, November 20, 2002, p. B1.

Chapter 10

1 Lisa Chamberlain, "Going Off the Beaten Path for New Design Ideas," *New York Times*, March 12, 2006, www.nytimes.com on June 5, 2009; Roger O. Crockett, "Keeping Ritz-Carlton at the Top of Its Game," *BusinessWeek*, May 29, 2006, www.businessweek.com on June 5, 2009; Holly Hughes, *Frommer's New York City with Kids*, 9th ed. (New York: Wiley, 2005); Alison Gregor, "Finding the Middle Ground," *New York Times*, April 16, 2006, http://travel.nytimes.com on June 5, 2009; John Holusha, "Where All the Rooms Are Nonsmoking," *New York Times*, February 19, 2006, http://query.nytimes.com on June 5, 2009; Charlie Devereux, "The Spirit of Design: Designing the Perfect Consumer," *CNN.com*, December 19, 2008, http://edition.cnn.com on June 6, 2009; "Marriott TownePlace Suites," IDEO website, 2009, www.ideo.com on June 6, 2009; "Hotel Construction Down, But New York Has Large Pipeline," *The Real Deal*, October 23, 2008, http://therealdeal.com on June 6, 2009; Lisa Fickenscher, "NYC Hotel Rates Fall Furthest in Nation," *Crain's New York Business.com*, June 5, 2009, www.crainsnewyork.com on June 6, 2009.

2 Paul M. Swamidass, "Empirical Science: New Frontier in Operations Management Research," *Academy of Management Review*, October 1991, Vol. 16, No. 4, pp. 793–814.

3 See Anil Khurana, "Managing Complex Production Processes," *Sloan Management Review*, Winter 1999, pp. 85–98.

4 For an example, see Robin Cooper and Regine Slagmulder, "Develop Profitable New Products with Target Costing," *Sloan Management Review*, Summer 1999, pp. 23–34.

5 Joan Woodward, *Industrial Organization: Theory and Practice* (London: Oxford University Press, 1965).

6 See "Tight Labor? Tech to the Rescue," *BusinessWeek*, March 20, 2000, pp. 36–37.

7 "New Plant Gets Jaguar in Gear," *USA Today*, November 27, 2000, p. 4B.

8 "Thinking Machines," *BusinessWeek*, August 7, 2000, pp. 78–86.

9 James Brian Quinn and Martin Neil Baily, "Information Technology: Increasing Productivity in Services," *Academy of Management Executive*, 1994, Vol. 8, No. 3, pp. 28–37.

10 See Charles J. Corbett, Joseph D. Blackburn, and Luk N. Van Wassenhove, "Partnerships to Improve Supply Chains," *Sloan Management Review*, Summer 1999, pp. 71–82; and Jeffrey K. Liker and Yen-Chun Wu, "Japanese Automakers, U.S. Suppliers, and Supply-Chain Superiority," *Sloan Management Review*, Fall 2000, pp. 81–93. See also Mark Pagell and Zhaohui Wu, "Building a More Complete Theory of Sustainable Supply Chain Management Using Case Studies of 10 Exemplars," *Journal of Supply Chain Management*, 2009, Vol. 45, No. 2, pp. 37–56.

11 "Fastener Woes to Delay Flight of First Boeing 787 Jets," *Wall Street Journal*, November 5, 2008.

12 See "Siemens Climbs Back," *BusinessWeek*, June 5, 2000, pp. 79–82.

13 See M. Bensaou, "Portfolios of Buyer-Supplier Relationships," *Sloan Management Review*, Summer 1999, pp. 35–44.

14 "Just-in-Time Manufacturing Is Working Overtime," *BusinessWeek*, November 8, 1999, pp. 36–37.

15 Rhonda Reger, Loren Gustafson, Samuel DeMarie, and John Mullane, "Reframing the Organization: Why Implementing Total Quality Is Easier Said Than Done," *Academy of Management Review*, 1994, Vol. 19, No. 3, pp. 565–584.

16 Ross Johnson and William O. Winchell, *Management and Quality* (Milwaukee, Wis.: American Society for Quality Control, 1989). See also Carol Reeves and David Bednar, "Defining Quality: Alternatives and Implications," *Academy of Management Review*, 1994, Vol. 19, No. 3, pp. 419–445; and C. K. Prahalad and M. S. Krishnan, "The New Meaning of Quality in the Information Age," *Harvard Business Review*, September–October 1999, pp. 109–120.

17 "Quality Isn't Just for Widgets," *BusinessWeek*, July 22, 2002, pp. 72–73.

18 W. Edwards Deming, *Out of the Crisis* (Cambridge, Mass.: MIT Press, 1986).

19 "When Service Means Survival," *BusinessWeek*, March 2, 2009, pp. 26–40. See also "Customer Service Champs," *Bloomberg BusinessWeek*, March 1, 2010, pp. 40–46.

20 Joel Dreyfuss, "Victories in the Quality Crusade," *Fortune*, October 10, 1988, pp. 80–88.

21 Thomas Y. Choi and Orlando C. Behling, "Top Managers and TQM Success: One More Look after All These Years," *Academy of Management Executive*, 1997, Vol. 11, No. 1, pp. 37–48.

22 James Dean and David Bowen, "Management Theory and Total Quality: Improving Research and Practice through Theory Development," *Academy of Management Review*, 1994, Vol. 19, No. 3, pp. 392–418.

23 See "Porsche Figures Out What Americans Want," *USA Today*, June 28, 2006, p. 4B.

24 Edward E. Lawler, "Total Quality Management and Employee Involvement: Are They Compatible?" *Academy of Management Executive*, 1994, Vol. 8, No. 1, pp. 68–79.

25 Jeremy Main, "How to Steal the Best Ideas Around," *Fortune*, October 19, 1992, pp. 102–106.

26 See James Brian Quinn, "Strategic Outsourcing: Leveraging Knowledge Capabilities," *Sloan Management Review*, Summer 1999, pp. 8–22.

27 "Global Gamble," *Forbes*, April 17, 2006, pp. 78–82.

28 Thomas Robertson, "How to Reduce Market Penetration Cycle Times," *Sloan Management Review*, Fall 1993, pp. 87–96.

29 "Speed Demons," *BusinessWeek*, March 27, 2006, pp. 68–76.

30 Ronald Henkoff, "The Hot New Seal of Quality," *Fortune*, June 28, 1993, pp. 116–120. See also Mustafa V. Uzumeri, "ISO 9000 and Other Metastandards: Principles for Management Practice?" *Academy of Management Executive*, 1997, Vol. 11, No. 1, pp. 21–28.

31 Paula C. Morrow, "The Measurement of TQM Principles and Work-Related Outcomes," *Journal of Organizational Behavior*, July 1997, Vol. 18, No. 4, pp. 363–376.

32 John W. Kendrick, *Understanding Productivity: An Introduction to the Dynamics of Productivity Change* (Baltimore: Johns Hopkins University Press, 1977).

33 "Study: USA Losing Competitive Edge," *USA Today*, April 25, 1997, p. 9D.

34 "Why the Productivity Revolution Will Spread," *BusinessWeek*, February 14, 2000, pp. 112–118. See also "Productivity Grows in Spite of Recession," *USA Today*, July 29, 2002, pp. 1B, 2B; and "Productivity's Second Wind," *BusinessWeek*, February 17, 2003, pp. 36–37.

35 Michael van Biema and Bruce Greenwald, "Managing Our Way to Higher Service-Sector Productivity," *Harvard Business Review*, July–August 1997, pp. 87–98.

Chapter 11

1 Stephen Gandel, "Wall Street's Latest Downfall: Madoff Charged with Fraud," *Time*, December 12, 2008, www.time.com on April 14, 2009; Jeffrey Kluger, "Putting Bernie Madoff on the Couch," *Time*, December 31, 2008, www.time.com on April 14, 2009; Henry Blodget, "Madoff: The Ted Bundy of Money," *The Business Insider*, January 24, 2009, www.businessinsider.com on April 14, 2009; Andy Serwer, " 'Financial Psychopaths' Wreak Havoc," *CNNMoney.com*, http://cnnmoney.com on April 14, 2009; Paul Babiak and Robert D. Hare, *Snakes in Suits: When Psychopaths Go to Work* (New York: Regan, 2006), http://books.google.com on April 14, 2009; Alan Deutschman, "Is Your Boss a Psychopath?" *Fast Company*, July 2005, www.fastcompany.com on April 14, 2009; Stephanie Strom, "Elie Wiesel Levels Scorn at Madoff," *New York Times*, February 27, 2009, www.nytimes.com on April 14, 2009; James Bandler and Nicholas Varchaver, "How Bernie Did It," *Fortune*, May 11, 2009, pp. 50–71.

2 Lynn McGarlane Shore and Lois Tetrick, "The Psychological Contract as an Explanatory Framework in the Employment Relationship," in C. L. Cooper and D. M. Rousseau (eds.), *Trends in Organizational Behavior* (London: Wiley, 1994). See also Jacqueline Coyle-Shapiro and Neil Conway, "Exchange Relationships: Examining Psychological Contracts and Perceived Organizational Support," *Journal of Applied Psychology*, 2005, Vol. 90, No. 4, pp. 774–781.

3 For an illustration, see Zhen Xiong Chen, Anne Tsui, and Lifeng Zhong, "Reactions to Psychological Contract Breach: A Dual Perspective," *Journal of Organizational Behavior*, 2008, Vol. 29, No. 5, pp. 527–548.

4 Elizabeth Wolfe Morrison and Sandra L. Robinson, "When Employees Feel Betrayed: A Model of How Psychological Contract Violation Develops," *Academy of Management Review*, January 1997, Vol. 22, No.1, pp. 226–256.

5 See Arne Kalleberg, "The Mismatched Worker: When People Don't Fit Their Jobs," *Academy of Management Perspectives*, 2008, Vol. 22, No. 1, pp. 24–40.

6 See Dan McAdams and Bradley Olson, "Personality Development: Continuity and Change over the Life Course," in Susan Fiske, Daniel Schacter, and Robert Sternberg (eds.), *Annual Review of Psychology*, Vol. 61 (Palo Alto, Calif.: Annual Reviews, 2010), pp. 517–542.

7 L. R. Goldberg, "An Alternative 'Description of Personality': The Big Five Factor Structure," *Journal of Personality and Social Psychology*, 1990, Vol. 59, pp. 1216–1229.

8 Michael K. Mount, Murray R. Barrick, and J. Perkins Strauss, "Validity of Observer Ratings of the Big Five Personality Factors," *Journal of Applied Psychology*, 1994, Vol. 79, No. 2, pp. 272–280; Timothy A. Judge, Joseph J. Martocchio, and Carl J. Thoreson, "Five-Factor Model of Personality and Employee Absence," *Journal of Applied Psychology*, 1997, Vol. 82, No. 5, pp. 745–755.

9 J. B. Rotter, "Generalized Expectancies for Internal vs. External Control of Reinforcement," *Psychological Monographs*, 1966, Vol. 80, pp. 1–28. See also Simon S. K. Lam and John Schaubroeck, "The Role of Locus of Control in Reactions to Being Promoted and to Being Passed Over: A Quasi Experiment," *Academy of Management Journal*, 2000, Vol. 43, No. 1, pp. 66–78.

10 Marilyn E. Gist and Terence R. Mitchell, "Self-Efficacy: A Theoretical Analysis of Its Determinants and Malleability," *Academy of Management Review*, April 1992, pp. 183–211.

11 T. W. Adorno, E. Frenkel-Brunswick, D. J. Levinson, and R. N. Sanford, *The Authoritarian Personality* (New York: Harper & Row, 1950).

12 "The Rise and Fall of Dennis Kozlowski," *BusinessWeek*, December 23, 2002, pp. 64–77.

13 Jon L. Pierce, Donald G. Gardner, and Larry L. Cummings, "Organization-Based Self-Esteem: Construct Definition, Measurement, and Validation," *Academy of Management Journal*, 1989, Vol. 32, No. 3, pp. 622–648.

14 Michael Harris Bond and Peter B. Smith, "Cross-Cultural Social and Organizational Psychology," in Janet Spence (ed.), *Annual Review of Psychology*, Vol. 47 (Palo Alto, Calif.: Annual Reviews, 1996), pp. 205–235.

15 See Daniel Goleman, *Emotional Intelligence: Why It Can Matter More Than IQ* (New York: Bantam, 1995).

16 Daniel Goleman, "Leadership That Gets Results," *Harvard Business Review*, March–April 2000, pp. 78–90. See also Kenneth Law, Chi-Sum Wong, and Lynda Song, "The Construct and Criterion Validity of Emotional Intelligence and Its Potential Utility for Management Studies," *Journal of Applied Psychology*, 2004, Vol. 87, No. 3, pp. 483–496; Joseph C. Rode, Christine H. Mooney, Marne L. Arthaud-Day, Janet P. Near, Timothy T. Baldwin, Robert S. Rubin, and William H. Bommer, "Emotional Intelligence and Individual Performance: Evidence of Direct and Indirect Effects," *Journal of Organizational Behavior*, 2007, Vol. 28, No. 4, pp. 399–421; and John D. Mayer, Richard D. Roberts, and Sigal G. Barsade, "Human Abilities: Emotional Intelligence," in Susan T. Fiske, Daniel L. Schacter, and Robert Sternberg (eds.), *Annual Review of Psychology 2008* (Palo Alto, Calif.: Annual Reviews, 2008), pp. 507–536.

17 Leon Festinger, *A Theory of Cognitive Dissonance* (Palo Alto, Calif.: Stanford University Press, 1957).

18 See John J. Clancy, "Is Loyalty Really Dead?" *Across the Board*, June 1999, pp. 15–19.

19 Patricia C. Smith, L. M. Kendall, and Charles Hulin, *The Measurement of Satisfaction in Work and Behavior* (Chicago: Rand-McNally, 1969). See also Steven Currall, Annette Towler, Tomothy Judge, and Laura Kohn, "Pay Satisfaction and Organizational Outcomes," *Personnel Psychology*, 2005, Vol. 58, pp. 613–640.

20 "Companies Are Finding Real Payoffs in Aiding Employee Satisfaction," *Wall Street Journal*, October 11, 2000, p. B1.

21 James R. Lincoln, "Employee Work Attitudes and Management Practice in the U.S. and Japan: Evidence from a Large Comparative Study," *California Management Review*, Fall 1989, pp. 89–106.

22 Lincoln, "Employee Work Attitudes and Management Practice in the U.S. and Japan."

23 Richard M. Steers, "Antecedents and Outcomes of Organizational Commitment," *Administrative Science Quarterly*, 1977, Vol. 22, pp. 46–56.

24 See Timothy R. Clark, "Engaging the Disengaged," *HR Magazine*, April 2008, pp. 109–115.

25 Omar N. Solinger, Woody van Olffen, and Robert A. Roe, "Beyond the Three-Component Model of Organizational Commitment," *Journal of Applied Psychology*, 2008, Vol. 93, No. 1, pp. 70–83. See also Steven M. Elias, "Employee Commitment in Times of Change: Assessing the Importance of Attitudes Toward Organizational Change," *Journal of Management*, 2009, Vol. 35, No. 1, pp. 37–55.

26 For research work in this area, see Jennifer M. George and Gareth R. Jones, "The Experience of Mood and Turnover Intentions: Interactive Effects of Value Attainment, Job Satisfaction, and Positive Mood," *Journal of Applied Psychology*, 1996, Vol. 81, No. 3, pp. 318–325; and Larry J. Williams, Mark B. Gavin, and Margaret Williams, "Measurement and Nonmeasurement Processes with Negative Affectivity and Employee Attitudes," *Journal of Applied Psychology*, 1996, Vol. 81, No. 1, pp. 88–101.

27 See Robert A. Baron, "The Role of Affect in the Entrepreneurial Process," *Academy of Management Review*, 2008, Vol. 33, No. 2, pp. 328–340.

28 Kathleen Sutcliffe, "What Executives Notice: Accurate Perceptions in Top Management Teams," *Academy of Management Journal*, 1994, Vol. 37, No. 5, pp. 1360–1378.

29 Richard A. Posthuma and Michael A. Campion, "Age Stereotypes in the Workplace: Common Stereotypes, Moderators, and Future Research Directions," *Journal of Management*, 2009, Vol. 35, No. 1, pp. 158–188.

30 For a classic treatment of attribution, see H. H. Kelley, *Attribution in Social Interaction* (Morristown, N.J.: General Learning Press, 1971). For a recent application, see Edward C. Tomlinson and Roger C. Mayer, "The Role of

Causal Attribution Dimensions in Trust Repair," *Academy of Management Review*, January 2009, Vol. 34, No. 1, pp. 85–104.

31 For a recent overview of the stress literature, see Frank Landy, James Campbell Quick, and Stanislav Kasl, "Work, Stress, and Well-Being," *International Journal of Stress Management*, 1994, Vol. 1, No. 1, pp. 33–73.

32 Hans Selye, *The Stress of Life* (New York: McGraw-Hill, 1976).

33 M. Friedman and R. H. Rosenman, *Type A Behavior and Your Heart* (New York: Knopf, 1974).

34 "Work & Family," *BusinessWeek*, June 28, 1993, pp. 80–88.

35 Richard S. DeFrank, Robert Konopaske, and John M. Ivancevich, "Executive Travel Stress: Perils of the Road Warrior," *Academy of Management Executive*, 2000, Vol. 14, No. 2, pp. 58–67.

36 Steven Rogelberg, Desmond Leach, Peter Warr, and Jennifer Burnfield, " 'Not Another Meeting!' Are Meeting Time Demands Related to Employee Well Being?" *Journal of Applied Psychology*, 2006, Vol. 91, No. 1, pp. 86–96.

37 "Those Doing Layoffs Can Feel the Pain," *USA Today*, April 23, 2009, p. 5D.

38 Michael R. Frone, "Are Work Stressors Related to Employee Substance Abuse? The Importance of Temporal Context in Assessments of Alcohol and Illicit Drug Use," *Journal of Applied Psychology*, 2008, Vol. 93, No. 1, pp. 199–296.

39 Thomas Wright, Much More than Meets the Eye: "The Role of Psychological Well-Being in Job Performance, Employee Retention, and Cardiovascular Health," *Organizational Dynamics*, January–March 2010, Vol. 39, No. 1, pp. 13–23.

40 "Breaking Point," *Newsweek*, March 6, 1995, pp. 56–62. See also "Rising Job Stress Could Affect Bottom Line," *USA Today*, July 28, 2003, p. 18.

41 See Christopher M. Barnes and John R. Hollenbeck, "Sleep Deprivation and Decision-Making Teams: Burning the Midnight Oil or Playing with Fire?" *Academy of Management Review*, January 2009, Vol. 34, No. 1, pp. 56–66.

42 John M. Kelly, "Get a Grip on Stress," *HRMagazine*, February 1997, pp. 51–58. See also Marilyn Macik-Frey, James Campbell Quick, and Debra Nelson, "Advances in Occupational Health: From a Stressful Beginning to a Positive Future," *Journal of Management*, 2007, Vol. 33, No. 6, pp. 809–840.

43 "Nice Work if You Can Get It," *BusinessWeek*, January 9, 2006, pp. 56–57. See also "Wellness," *Time*, February 23, 2009, pp. 78–79.

44 See Richard W. Woodman, John E. Sawyer, and Ricky W. Griffin, "Toward a Theory of Organizational Creativity," *Academy of Management Review*, April 1993, pp. 293–321. See also Beth Henessey and Teresa Amabile, "Creativity," in Susan Fiske, Daniel Schacter, and Robert Sternberg (eds.), *Annual Review of Psychology*, Vol. 61 (Palo Alto, Calif.: Annual Reviews, 2010), pp. 569–598.

45 Emily Thornton, "Japan's Struggle to be Creative," *Fortune*, April 19, 1993, pp. 129–134.

46 "In Secret Hideaway, Bill Gates Ponders Microsoft's Future," *Wall Street Journal*, March 28, 2005, pp. A1, A13.

47 John Simons, "The $10 Billion Pill," *Fortune*, January 20, 2003, pp. 58–68.

48 Christina E. Shalley, Lucy L. Gilson, and Terry C. Blum, "Matching Creativity Requirements and the Work Environment: Effects on Satisfaction and Intentions to Leave," *Academy of Management Journal*, 2000, Vol. 43, No. 2, pp. 215–223. See also Filiz Tabak, "Employee Creative Performance: What Makes It Happen?" *Academy of Management Executive*, 1997, Vol. 11, No. 1, pp. 119–122, and Giles Hirst, Daan van Knippenberg, and Jing Zhou, "A Cross-Level Perspective on Employee Creativity: Goal Orientation, Team Learning Behavior, and Individual Creativity," *Academy of Management Journal*, 2009, Vol. 52, No. 2, pp. 280–293.

49 "Real Life Imitates *Real World*," *BusinessWeek*, March 23/30, 2009, p. 42.

50 See Ryan D. Zimmerman, "Understanding the Impact of Personality Traits on Individuals' Turnover Decisions: A Meta-Analytic Path Model," *Personnel Psychology*, 2008, Vol. 61, 309–348. See also Jean Martin and Conrad Schmidt, "How to Keep Your Top Talent," *Harvard Business Review*, May 2010, pp. 54–61.

51 For recent findings regarding this behavior, see Philip M. Podsakoff, Scott B. MacKenzie, Julie Beth Paine, and Daniel G. G. Bacharah, "Organizational Citizenship Behaviors: A Critical Review of the Theoretical and Empirical Literature and Suggestions for Future Research," *Journal of Management*, 2000, Vol. 26, No. 3, pp. 513–563.

52 Dennis W. Organ "Personality and Organizational Citizenship Behavior," *Journal of Management*, 1994, Vol. 20, No. 2, pp. 465–478; Mary Konovsky and S. Douglas Pugh, "Citizenship Behavior and Social Exchange," *Academy of Management Journal*, 1994, Vol. 37, No. 3, pp. 656–669; Jacqueline A.–M. Coyle-Shapiro, "A Psychological Contract Perspective on Organizational Citizenship," *Journal of Organizational Behavior*, 2002, Vol. 23, pp. 927–946.

53 Ricky Griffin and Yvette Lopez, " 'Bad Behavior' in Organization: A Review and Typology for Future Research," *Journal of Management*, 2005, Vol. 31, No. 6, pp. 988–1005.

54 For an illustration, see Sandy Lim, Lilia M. Cortina, and Vicki J. Magley, "Personal and Workgroup Incivility: Impact on Work and Health Outcomes," *Journal of Applied Psychology*, 2008, Vol. 93, No. 1, pp. 95–107. See also Christine Porath and Christine Pearson, "The Cost of Bad Behavior," *Organizational Dynamics*, January–March 2010, Vol. 39, No. 1, pp. 64–71.

55 See Anne O'Leary-Kelly, Ricky W. Griffin, and David J. Glew, "Organization-Motivated Aggression: A Research Framework," *Academy of Management Review*, January 1996, Vol. 21, No. 1, pp. 225–253. See also Ricky W. Griffin and Anne M. O'Leary-Kelly, *The Dark Side of Organizational Behavior* (San Francisco: Jossey-Bass, 2004), and Scott C. Douglas, Christian Kiewitz, Mark J. Martinko, Paul Harvey, Younhee Kim, and Jae Uk Chun, "Cognitions, Emotions, and Evaluations: An Elaboration Likelihood Model for Workplace Aggression, "*Academy of Management Review*, 2008, Vol. 33, No. 2, pp. 425–451.

Chapter 12

1 Corporate Executive Board, "The Increasing Call for Work-Life Balance," *BusinessWeek*, March 27, 2009, www.businessweek.com on April 27, 2009; Lori K. Long, "How to Negotiate a Flexible Work Schedule," *CIO.com*, August 29, 2007, www.cio.com on April 27, 2009; Network of Executive Women, "Balancing Acts: People-Friendly Policies That Build Productivity," *The Center for Workforce Excellence*, 2007, http://workforceexcellence.com on April 27, 2009; Emily Schmitt, "How a Flexible Work Schedule Can Help You Strike the Balance," *Forbes*, March 16, 2009, www.forbes.com on April 27, 2009; Michelle Conlin, "Career Women at Midlife: Sadder and Sicker," *BusinessWeek*, March 27, 2009, www.businessweek.com on April 27, 2009; Kathy Caprino, *Breakdown, Breakthrough: The Professional Woman's Guide to Claiming a Life of Passion, Power, and Purpose* (San Francisco: Barrett-Koehler, 2008), http://books.google.com on April 27, 2009; Center for Work–Life Policy, "Cherie Blair and Michelle Obama," *Off-Ramps and On-Ramps*, June 29, 2007, www.offrampsandonramps.org on April 27, 2009; Barbara Rose, "Forget Career Ladder; They're on the Lattice," *The Seattle Times*, November 11, 2007, http://seattletimes.nesource.com on April 28, 2009; Jessica Titlebaum, "Return to the Work Force Programs: Spotlight on Lehman Brothers," *The Glass Hammer*, December 18, 2007, www.theglasshammer.com on April 28, 2009.

2 Richard M. Steers, Gregory A. Bigley, and Lyman W. Porter, *Motivation and Leadership at Work*, 7th ed. (New York: McGraw-Hill, 2002). See also Maureen L. Ambrose and Carol T. Kulik, "Old Friends, New Faces: Motivation Research in the 1990s," *Journal of Management*, 1999, Vol. 25, No. 3, pp. 231–292; Edwin Locke and Gary Lartham, "What Should We Do about Motivation Theory? Six Recommendations for the Twenty-First Century," *Academy of Management Review*, 2004, Vol. 29, No. 3, pp. 388–403; and Robert Lord, James Diefendorff, Aaron Schmidt, and Rosalie Hall, "Self-Regulation at Work," in Susan Fiske, Daniel Schacter, and Robert Sternberg (eds.), *Annual Review of Psychology*, Vol. 61 (Palo Alto, Calif.: Annual Reviews, 2010), pp. 543–568.

3 See Nigel Nicholson, "How to Motivate Your Problem People," *Harvard Business Review*, January 2003, pp. 57–67. See also Hugo Kehr, "Integrating Implicit Motives, Explicit Motives, and Perceived Abilities: The Compensatory Model of Work Motivation and Volition," *Academy of Management Review*, 2004, Vol. 29, No. 3, pp. 479–499.

4 See Jeffrey Pfeffer, *The Human Equation* (Cambridge, Mass.: Harvard Business School Press, 1998). See also Nitin Nohria, Boris Groysberg, and Linda-Eling Lee, "Employee Motivation—A Powerful New Model,"

Harvard Business Review, July–August 2008, pp. 78–89, and Adrienne Fox, "Raising Engagement," *HR Magazine*, May 2010, pp. 35–40.

5 For a recent discussion of these questions, see Eryn Brown, "So Rich So Young—But Are They Really Happy?" *Fortune*, September 18, 2000, pp. 99–110. See also Teresa Amabile and Steven Kramer, "What Really Motivates Workers," *Harvard Business Review*, January–February 2010, pp. 44–45.

6 Abraham H. Maslow, "A Theory of Human Motivation," *Psychological Review*, 1943, Vol. 50, pp. 370–396; Abraham H. Maslow, *Motivation and Personality* (New York: Harper & Row, 1954). Maslow's most recent work is Abraham H. Maslow and Richard Lowry, *Toward a Psychology of Being* (New York: Wiley, 1999).

7 For a review, see Craig Pinder, *Work Motivation in Organizational Behavior*, 2nd ed. (Upper Saddle River, N.J.: Prentice Hall, 2008).

8 Frederick Herzberg, Bernard Mausner, and Barbara Snyderman, *The Motivation to Work* (New York: Wiley, 1959); Frederick Herzberg, "One More Time: How Do You Motivate Employees?" *Harvard Business Review*, January–February 1987, pp. 109–120 (reprinted in *Harvard Business Review*, January 2003, pp. 87–98).

9 Robert J. House and Lawrence A. Wigdor, "Herzberg's Dual-Factor Theory of Job Satisfaction and Motivation: A Review of the Evidence and a Criticism," *Personnel Psychology*, Winter 1967, Vol. 20, No. 4, pp. 369–389; Victor H. Vroom, *Work and Motivation* (New York: Wiley, 1964). See also Pinder, *Work Motivation in Organizational Behavior*, 2nd ed. (Upper Saddle River, N.J.: Prentice Hall, 2008).

10 David C. McClelland, *The Achieving Society* (Princeton, N.J.: Van Nostrand, 1961); David C. McClelland, *Power: The Inner Experience* (New York: Irvington, 1975).

11 "Best Friends Good for Business," *USA Today*, December 1, 2004, pp. 1B, 2B.

12 David McClelland and David H. Burnham, "Power Is the Great Motivator," *Harvard Business Review*, March–April 1976, pp. 100–110 (reprinted in *Harvard Business Review*, January 2003, pp. 117–127).

13 See "The Rise and Fall of Dennis Kozlowski," *BusinessWeek*, December 23, 2002, pp. 64–77.

14 Victor H. Vroom, *Work and Motivation* (New York: Wiley, 1964).

15 "Starbucks' Secret Weapon," *Fortune*, September 29, 1997, p. 268.

16 Lyman W. Porter and Edward E. Lawler III, *Managerial Attitudes and Performance* (Homewood, Ill.: Dorsey, 1968).

17 J. Stacy Adams, "Towards an Understanding of Inequity," *Journal of Abnormal and Social Psychology*, November 1963, Vol. 67, No. 5, pp. 422–436.

18 "The Best vs. the Rest," *Wall Street Journal*, January 30, 2006, pp. B1, B3.

19 Mark C. Bolino and William H. Turnley, "Old Faces, New Places: Equity Theory in Cross-Cultural Contexts," *Journal of Organizational Behavior*, 2008, Vol. 29, pp. 29–50.

20 See Edwin A. Locke, "Toward a Theory of Task Performance and Incentives," *Organizational Behavior and Human Performance*, 1968, Vol. 3, pp. 157–189.

21 Gary P. Latham and J. J. Baldes, "The Practical Significance of Locke's Theory of Goal Setting," *Journal of Applied Psychology*, 1975, Vol. 60, pp. 187–191.

22 For a recent extension of goal-setting theory, see Yitzhak Fried and Linda Haynes Slowik, "Enriching Goal-Setting Theory with Time: An Integrated Approach," *Academy of Management Review*, 2004, Vol. 29, No. 3, pp. 404–422.

23 B. F. Skinner, *Beyond Freedom and Dignity* (New York: Knopf, 1971).

24 Fred Luthans and Robert Kreitner, *Organizational Behavior Modification and Beyond: An Operant and Social Learning Approach* (Glenview, Ill.: Scott, Foresman, 1985).

25 Luthans and Kreitner, *Organizational Behavior Modification and Beyond*; W. Clay Hamner and Ellen P. Hamner, "Behavior Modification on the Bottom Line," *Organizational Dynamics*, Spring 1976, pp. 2–21.

26 "At Emery Air Freight: Positive Reinforcement Boosts Performance," *Organizational Dynamics*, Winter 1973, pp. 41–50; for a recent update, see Alexander D. Stajkovic and Fred Luthans, "A Meta-Analysis of the Effects of Organizational Behavior Modification on Task Performance, 1975–95," *Academy of Management Journal*, 1997, Vol. 40, No. 5, pp. 1122–1149.

27 David J. Glew, Anne M. O'Leary-Kelly, Ricky W. Griffin, and David D. Van Fleet, "Participation in Organizations: A Preview of the Issues and Proposed Framework for Future Analysis," *Journal of Management*, 1995, Vol. 21, No. 3, pp. 395–421.

28 Baxter W. Graham, "The Business Argument for Flexibility," *HRMagazine*, May 1996, pp. 104–110.

29 A. R. Cohen and H. Gadon, *Alternative Work Schedules: Integrating Individual and Organizational Needs* (Reading, Mass.: Addison Wesley, 1978).

30 "The Easiest Commute of All," *BusinessWeek*, December 12, 2005, pp. 78–80.

31 Daniel Wren, *The Evolution of Management Theory*, 4th ed. (New York: Wiley, 1994).

32 C. Wiley, "Incentive Plan Pushes Production," *Personnel Journal*, August 1993, p. 91.

33 "When Money Isn't Enough," *Forbes*, November 18, 1996, pp. 164–169.

34 Jacquelyn DeMatteo, Lillian Eby, and Eric Sundstrom, "Team-Based Rewards: Current Empirical Evidence and Directions for Future Research," in L. L. Cummings and Barry Staw (eds.), *Research in Organizational Behavior*, Vol. 20 (Greenwich, Conn.: JAI, 1998), pp. 141–183.

35 Theresa M. Welbourne and Luis R. Gomez-Mejia, "Gainsharing: A Critical Review and a Future Research Agenda," *Journal of Management*, 1995, Vol. 21, No. 3, pp. 559–609.

36 "Executive Compensation Form 50 of the Largest U.S. Companies," *USA Today*, May 4, 2009, p. 4B.

37 "Executive Compensation Form 50 of the Largest U.S. Companies." *USA Today*, May 4, 2009, p. 4B.

38 "Executive Compensation Form 50 of the Largest U.S. Companies." *USA Today*, May 4, 2009, p. 4B.

39 "Executive Compensation Form 50 of the Largest U.S. Companies." *USA Today*, May 4, 2009, p. 4B.

40 Harry Barkema and Luis Gomez-Mejia, "Managerial Compensation and Firm Performance: A General Research Framework," *Academy of Management Journal*, 1998, Vol. 41, No. 2, pp. 135–145.

41 Rajiv D. Banker, Seok-Young Lee, Gordon Potter, and Dhinu Srinivasan, "Contextual Analysis of Performance Impacts of Outcome-Based Incentive Compensation," *Academy of Management Journal*, 1996, Vol. 39, No. 4, pp. 920–948.

42 Rajiv D. Banker, Seok-Young Lee, Gordon Potter, and Dhinu Srinivasan, "Contextual Analysis of Performance Impacts of Outcome-Based Incentive Compensation." *Academy of Management Journal*, 1996, Vol. 39, No. 4, pp. 920–948.

43 Steve Kerr, "The Best-Laid Incentive Plans," *Harvard Business Review*, January 2003, pp. 27–40.

44 "Now It's Getting Personal," *BusinessWeek*, December 16, 2002, pp. 90–92.

Chapter 13

1 Leslie Berlin, *The Man behind the Microchip: Robert Noyce and the Invention of Silicon Valley* (New York: Oxford University Press, 2005), http://books.google.com on May 15, 2009; Cliff Edwards, "Inside Intel," *BusinessWeek*, January 9, 2006, www.businessweek.com on May 15, 2009; "Corporate Timeline: Our History of Innovation," "Moore's Law," "Intel's Tick-Tock Model," *Intel website*, 2009, www.intel.com on May 15, 2009; Richard S. Tedlow, "The Education of Andy Grove," *Fortune*, December 12, 2005, http://money.cnn.com on May 15, 2009; Dean Takahashi, "Exit Interview: Retiring Intel Chairman Craig Barrett on the Industry's Unfinished Business," *VentureBeat*, May 8, 2009, http://venturebeat.com on May 15, 2009; Cliff Edwards, "Craig Barrett's Mixed Record at Intel," *BusinessWeek*, January 23, 2009, www.businessweek.com on May 15, 2009; Adam Lashinsky, "Is This the Right Man for Intel?" *Fortune*, April 18, 2005, http://money.cnn.com on May 15, 2009; "Intel Announces Layoffs, Reorganization," *IDG News Service*, September 6, 2006, www.itworld.com on May 16, 2009; "Intel Posts Record Second-Quarter Revenue of $9.5 Billion," *Intel Corporation*, press release, July 15, 2008, www.intc.com on May 16, 2009.

2 See Ronald A. Heifetz and Donald L. Laurie, "The Work of Leadership," *Harvard Business Review*, January–February 1997, pp. 124–134. See also Arthur G. Jago, "Leadership: Perspectives in Theory and Research," *Management Science*, March 1982, pp. 315–336; and Arthur G. Jago, "The New Leadership," *BusinessWeek*, August 28, 2000, pp. 100–187.

3 Gary A. Yukl, *Leadership in Organizations*, 3rd ed. (Englewood Cliffs, N.J.: Prentice Hall, 1994), p. 5. See also Gregory G. Dess and Joseph C.

Pickens, "Changing Roles: Leadership in the 21st Century," *Organizational Dynamics*, Winter 2000, pp. 18–28.

4   John P. Kotter, "What Leaders Really Do," *Harvard Business Review*, May–June 1990, pp. 103–111 (reprinted in *Harvard Business Review*, December 2001, pp. 85–93). See also Daniel Goleman, "Leadership That Gets Results," *Harvard Business Review*, March–April 2000, pp. 78–88; and Keith Grints, *The Arts of Leadership* (Oxford, UK: Oxford University Press, 2000).

5   John R. P. French and Bertram Raven, "The Bases of Social Power," in Dorwin Cartwright (ed.), *Studies in Social Power* (Ann Arbor, Mich.: University of Michigan Press, 1959), pp. 150–167.

6   Hugh D. Menzies, "The Ten Toughest Bosses," *Fortune*, April 21, 1980, pp. 62–73.

7   Bennett J. Tepper, "Consequences of Abusive Supervision," *Academy of Management Journal*, 2000, Vol. 43, No. 2, pp. 178–190. See also Bennett J. Tepper, "Abusive Supervision in Work Organizations: Review, Synthesis, and Research Agenda," *Journal of Management*, 2007, Vol. 33, No. 3, pp. 261–289.

8   Bernard M. Bass, *Bass & Stogdill's Handbook of Leadership*, 3rd ed. (Riverside, N.J.: Free Press, 1990).

9   Shelley A. Kirkpatrick and Edwin A. Locke, "Leadership: Do Traits Matter?" *Academy of Management Executive*, May 1991, Vol. 5, No. 2, pp. 48–60. See also Robert J. Sternberg, "Managerial Intelligence: Why IQ Isn't Enough," *Journal of Management*, 1997, Vol. 23, No. 3, pp. 475–493.

10 Timothy Judge, Amy Colbert, and Remus Ilies, "Intelligence and Leadership: A Quantitative Review and Test of Theoretical Propositions," *Journal of Applied Psychology*, 2004, Vol. 89, No. 3, pp. 542–552.

11 Rensis Likert, *New Patterns of Management* (New York: McGraw-Hill, 1961); Rensis Likert, *The Human Organization* (New York: McGraw-Hill, 1967).

12 The Ohio State studies stimulated many articles, monographs, and books. A good overall reference is Ralph M. Stogdill and A. E. Coons (eds.), *Leader Behavior: Its Description and Measurement* (Columbus, Ohio: Bureau of Business Research, Ohio State University, 1957).

13 Edwin A. Fleishman, E. F. Harris, and H. E. Burt, *Leadership and Supervision in Industry* (Columbus, Ohio: Bureau of Business Research, Ohio State University, 1955).

14 See Timothy Judge, Ronald Piccolo, and Remus Ilies, "The Forgotten One? The Validity of Consideration and Initiating Structure in Leadership Research," *Journal of Applied Psychology*, 2004, Vol. 89, No. 1, pp. 36–51.

15 Robert R. Blake and Jane S. Mouton, *The Managerial Grid* (Houston, Tex.: Gulf Publishing, 1964); Robert R. Blake and Jane S. Mouton, *The Versatile Manager: A Grid Profile* (Homewood, Ill.: Dow Jones-Irwin, 1981).

16 Fred E. Fiedler, *A Theory of Leadership Effectiveness* (New York: McGraw-Hill, 1967).

17 Chester A. Schriesheim, Bennett J. Tepper, and Linda A. Tetrault, "Least Preferred Co-Worker Score, Situational Control, and Leadership Effectiveness: A Meta-Analysis of Contingency Model Performance Predictions," *Journal of Applied Psychology*, 1994, Vol. 79, No. 4, pp. 561–573.

18 Fiedler, *A Theory of Leadership Effectiveness*; Fred E. Fiedler and M. M. Chemers, *Leadership and Effective Management* (Glenview, Ill.: Scott, Foresman, 1974).

19 For recent reviews and updates, see Lawrence H. Peters, Darrell D. Hartke, and John T. Pohlmann, "Fiedler's Contingency Theory of Leadership: An Application of the Meta-Analysis Procedures of Schmidt and Hunter," *Psychological Bulletin*, Vol. 97, 2002, pp. 274–285; Fred E. Fiedler, "When to Lead, When to Stand Back," *Psychology Today*, September 1987, pp. 26–27.

20 Martin G. Evans, "The Effects of Supervisory Behavior on the Path-Goal Relationship," *Organizational Behavior and Human Performance*, May 1970, pp. 277–298; Robert J. House and Terence R. Mitchell, "Path-Goal Theory of Leadership," *Journal of Contemporary Business*, Autumn 1974, pp. 81–98. See also Yukl, *Leadership in Organizations* 3rd ed. (Englewood Cliffs, N.J.: Prentice Hall, 1994), p. 5.

21 For a recent review, see J. C. Wofford and Laurie Z. Liska, "Path-Goal Theories of Leadership: A Meta-Analysis," *Journal of Management*, 1993, Vol. 19, No. 4, pp. 857–876.

22 See Victor H. Vroom and Philip H. Yetton, *Leadership and Decision Making* (Pittsburgh, Pa.: University of Pittsburgh Press, 1973); and Victor H. Vroom and Arthur G. Jago, *The New Leadership* (Englewood Cliffs, N.J.: Prentice Hall, 1988).

23 Victor Vroom, "Leadership and the Decision-Making Process," *Organizational Dynamics*, 2000, Vol. 28, No. 4, pp. 82–94.

24 Victor H. Vroom and Arthur G. Jago, *The New Leadership* (Englewood Cliffs, N.J.: Prentice Hall, 1988).

25 Victor H. Vroom and Arthur G. Jago, *The New Leadership* (Englewood Cliffs, N.J.: Prentice Hall, 1988).

26 See Madeline E. Heilman, Harvey A. Hornstein, Jack H. Cage, and Judith K. Herschlag, "Reaction to Prescribed Leader Behavior as a Function of Role Perspective: The Case of the Vroom-Yetton Model," *Journal of Applied Psychology*, February 1984, Vol. 69, No. 1, pp. 50–60; and R. H. George Field, "A Test of the Vroom-Yetton Normative Model of Leadership," *Journal of Applied Psychology*, February 1982, Vol. 67, No. 5, pp. 523–532.

27 George Graen and J. F. Cashman, "A Role-Making Model of Leadership in Formal Organizations: A Developmental Approach," in J. G. Hunt and L. L. Larson (eds.), *Leadership Frontiers* (Kent, Ohio: Kent State University Press, 1975), pp. 143–165; Fred Dansereau, George Graen, and W. J. Haga, "A Vertical Dyad Linkage Approach to Leadership within Formal Organizations: A Longitudinal Investigation of the Role-Making Process," *Organizational Behavior and Human Performance*, 1975, Vol. 15, pp. 46–78.

28 See Kathryn Sherony and Stephen Green, "Coworker Exchange: Relationships Between Coworkers, Leader-Member Exchange, and Work Attitudes," *Journal of Applied Psychology*, 2002, Vol. 87, No. 3, pp. 542–548.

29 See Bruce J. Avolio, Fred O. Walumbwa, and Todd J. Weber, "Leadership: Current Theories, Research, and Future Directions," in Susan T. Fiske, Daniel L. Schacter, and Robert Sternberg (eds.), *Annual Review of Psychology 2009* (Palo Alto, Calif.: Annual Reviews, 2009), pp. 421–450.

30 Steven Kerr and John M. Jermier, "Substitutes for Leadership: Their Meaning and Measurement," *Organizational Behavior and Human Performance*, December 1978, Vol. 22, No. 3, pp. 375–403.

31 See Charles C. Manz and Henry P. Sims, Jr., "Leading Workers to Lead Themselves: The External Leadership of Self-Managing Work Teams," *Administrative Science Quarterly*, March 1987, Vol. 32, No. 1, pp. 106–129. See also "Living Without a Leader," *Fortune*, March 20, 2000, pp. 218–219.

32 See Robert J. House, "A 1976 Theory of Charismatic Leadership," in J. G. Hunt and L. L. Larson (eds.), *Leadership: The Cutting Edge* (Carbondale, Ill.: Southern Illinois University Press, 1977), pp. 189–207. See also Jay A. Conger and Rabindra N. Kanungo, "Toward a Behavioral Theory of Charismatic Leadership in Organizational Settings," *Academy of Management Review*, October 1987, Vol.12, No. 4, pp. 637–647.

33 Stratford P. Sherman, "Donald Trump Just Won't Die," *Fortune*, August 13, 1990, pp. 75–79.

34 David A. Nadler and Michael L. Tushman, "Beyond the Charismatic Leader: Leadership and Organizational Change," *California Management Review*, Winter 1990, Vol. 32, No. 2, pp. 77–97.

35 Jane Howell and Boas Shamir, "The Role of Followers in the Charismatic Leadership Process: Relationships and Their Consequences," *Academy of Management Review*, 2005, Vol. 30, No. 1, pp. 96–112.

36 James MacGregor Burns, *Leadership* (New York: Harper & Row, 1978). See also A. N. Pieterse, D. van Knippenberg, M. Schippers, and D. Stam, "Transformational and Transactional Leadership and Innovative Behavior: The Role of Psychological Empowerment," *Journal of Organizational Behavior*, May 2010, Vol. 32, No. 4, pp. 609–623.

37 Robert Rubin, David Munz, and William Bommer, "Leading from Within: The Effects of Emotion Recognition and Personality on Transformational Leadership Behaviors," *Academy of Management Journal*, 2005, Vol. 48, No. 5, pp. 845–858.

38 Kenneth Labich, "The Seven Keys to Business Leadership" *Fortune*, October 1988, pp. 97–104.

39 Jerry Useem, "Tape + Light Bulbs = ?" *Fortune*, August 12, 2002, pp. 127–132.

40 Dusya Vera and Mary Crossan, "Strategic Leadership and Organizational Learning," *Academy of Management Review*, 2004, Vol. 29, No. 2, pp. 222–240. See also Cynthia A. Montgomery, "Putting Leadership Back into Strategy," *Harvard Business Review*, January 2008, pp. 54–63.

41 "The Best & Worst Managers of the Year," *BusinessWeek*, January 19, 2005, pp. 55–84.

42 Tamara Erickson, "The Leaders We Need Now," *Harvard Business Review*, May 2010, pp. 62–67.

43 See Kurt Dirks and Donald Ferrin, "Trust in Leadership," *Journal of Applied Psychology*, 2002, Vol. 87, No. 4, pp. 611–628. See also Russell A. Eisenstat, Michael Beer, Nathanial Foote, Tobias Fredberg, and Flemming Norrgren, "The Uncompromising Leader," *Harvard Business Review*, July–August 2008, pp. 51–59; and Christopher Meyer and Julia Kirby, "Leadership in the Age of Transparency," *Harvard Business Review*, April 2010, pp. 38–46.

44 Jeffrey Pfeffer, *Power in Organizations* (Marshfield, Mass.: Pitman, 1981), p. 7.

45 Timothy Judge and Robert Bretz, "Political Influence Behavior and Career Success," *Journal of Management*, 1994, Vol. 20, No. 1, pp. 43–65.

46 Victor Murray and Jeffrey Gandz, "Games Executives Play: Politics at Work," *Business Horizons*, December 1980, pp. 11–23; Jeffrey Gandz and Victor Murray, "The Experience of Workplace Politics," *Academy of Management Journal*, June 1980, Vol. 23, No. 2, pp. 237–251.

47 Don R. Beeman and Thomas W. Sharkey, "The Use and Abuse of Corporate Power," *Business Horizons*, March–April 1987, pp. 26–30.

48 "How Ebbers Kept the Board in His Pocket," *BusinessWeek*, October 14, 2002, pp. 138–139.

49 See William L. Gardner, "Lessons in Organizational Dramaturgy: The Art of Impression Management," *Organizational Dynamics*, Summer 1992, Vol. 21, No. 1, pp. 51–63; Elizabeth Wolf Morrison and Robert J. Bies, "Impression Management in the Feedback-Seeking Process: A Literature Review and Research Agenda," *Academy of Management Review*, July 1991, pp. 522–541; and Mark C. Bolino, K. Michele Kacmar, William H. Turnley, and J. Bruce Gilstrap, "A Multi-Level Review of Impression Management Motives and Behaviors," *Journal of Management*, 2008, Vol. 34, No. 6, pp. 1080–1109.

50 *BusinessWeek*, April 13, 2009, p. 54.

51 See Chad Higgins, Timothy Judge, and Gerald Ferris, "Influence Tactics and Work Outcomes: A Meta-Analysis," *Journal of Organizational Behavior*, 2003, Vol. 24, pp. 89–106; and Gerald R. Ferris, Darren C. Treadway, Pamela L. Perrewe, Robyn L. Brour, Ceasar Douglas, and Sean Lux, "Political Skill in Organizations," *Journal of Management*, 2007, Vol. 33, No. 3, pp. 290–320.

52 Murray and Gandz, "Games Executives Play: Politics at Work," *Business Horizons*, December 1980, pp. 11–23.

53 Beeman and Sharkey, "The Use and Abuse of Corporate Power." *Business Horizons*, March–April 1987, pp. 26–30.

54 Stefanie Ann Lenway and Kathleen Rehbein, "Leaders, Followers, and Free Riders: An Empirical Test of Variation in Corporate Political Involvement," *Academy of Management Journal*, December 1991, Vol. 34, No. 4, pp. 893–905.

Chapter 14

1 Hugh Anderson, "Phone-Interview Tips for Savvy Candidates," *Wall Street Journal*, executive career website, www.careerjournal.com on May 2, 2006; Anne Fisher, "Fear of Phoning," *Fortune*, September 6, 2005, www.fortune.com on May 2, 2006; Anne Fisher, "How Can I Survive a Phone Interview?" *Fortune*, April 19, 2004, www.fortune.com on May 2, 2006; "Phone Interview Success," CollegeGrad.com website, May 2, 2006.

2 Henry Mintzberg, *The Nature of Managerial Work* (New York: Harper & Row, 1973).

3 See Michael H. Zack, "Managing Codified Knowledge," *Sloan Management Review*, Summer 1999, Vol. 40, No. 4, pp. 45–58.

4 "It's Now Official: AOL, Time Warner to Split," *Wall Street Journal*, May 29, 2009, p. B1.

5 "UAL Shares Dive as Old News Surfaces on Net," *Wall Street Journal*, September 2008, pp. B1, B10.

6 Bruce Barry and Ingrid Fulmer, "The Medium and the Message: The Adaptive Use of Communication Media in Dyadic Influence," *Academy of Management Review*, 2004, Vol. 29, No. 2, pp. 272–292.

7 Mintzberg, *The Nature of Managerial Work* (New York: Harper & Row, 1973).

8 Reid Buckley, "When You Have to Put It to Them," *Across the Board*, October 1999, pp. 44–48.

9 " 'Did I Just Say That?!' How to Recover from Foot-in-Mouth," *Wall Street Journal*, June 19, 2002, p. B1.

10 "Executives Who Dread Public Speaking Learn to Keep Their Cool in the Spotlight," *Wall Street Journal*, May 4, 1990, pp. B1, B6.

11 Henry Mintzberg, *The Nature of Managerial Work* (New York: Harper & Row, 1973).

12 Reid Buckley, "When You Have to Put It to Them." *Across the Board*, October 1999, pp. 44–48.

13 See "Watch What You Put in That Office Email," *BusinessWeek*, September 30, 2002, pp. 114–115.

14 Nicholas Varchaver, "The Perils of E-mail," *Fortune*, February 17, 2003, pp. 96–102; "How a String of E-Mail Came to Haunt CSFB and Star Banker," *Wall Street Journal*, February 28, 2003, pp. A1, A6; "How Morgan Stanley Botched a Big Case by Fumbling Emails," *Wall Street Journal*, May 16, 2005, pp. A1, A10.

15 A. Vavelas, "Communication Patterns in Task-Oriented Groups," *Journal of the Accoustical Society of America*, 1950, Vol. 22, pp. 725–730; Jerry Wofford, Edwin Gerloff, and Robert Cummins, *Organizational Communication* (New York: McGraw-Hill, 1977).

16 Nelson Phillips and John Brown, "Analyzing Communications in and around Organizations: A Critical Hermeneutic Approach," *Academy of Management Journal*, 1993, Vol. 36, No. 6, pp. 1547–1576.

17 Walter Kiechel III, "Breaking Bad News to the Boss," *Fortune*, April 9, 1990, pp. 111–112.

18 Mary Young and James Post, "Managing to communicate, communicating to manage: How Leading Companies Communicate with Employees," *Organizational Dynamics*, Summer 1993, pp. 31–43.

19 For one example, see Kimberly D. Elsbach and Greg Elofson, "How the Packaging of Decision Explanations Affects Perceptions of Trustworthiness," *Academy of Management Journal*, 2000, Vol. 43, No. 1, pp. 80–89.

20 Keith Davis, "Management Communication and the Grapevine," *Harvard Business Review*, September–October 1953, pp. 43–49.

21 "Spread the Word: Gossip Is Good," *Wall Street Journal*, October 4, 1988, p. B1.

22 See David M. Schweiger and Angelo S. DeNisi, "Communication with Employees Following a Merger: A Longitudinal Field Experiment," *Academy of Management Journal*, March 1991, Vol. 34, No. 1, pp. 110–135.

23 Nancy B. Kurland and Lisa Hope Pelled, "Passing the Word: Toward a Model of Gossip and Power in the Workplace," *Academy of Management Review*, 2000, Vol. 25, No. 2, pp. 428–438.

24 See Tom Peters and Nancy Austin, *A Passion for Excellence* (New York: Random House, 1985).

25 Albert Mehrabian, *Non-verbal Communication* (Chicago: Aldine, 1972).

26 Michael B. McCaskey, "The Hidden Messages Managers Send," *Harvard Business Review*, November–December 1979, pp. 135–148.

27 David Givens, "What Body Language Can Tell You That Words Cannot," *U.S. News & World Report*, November 19, 1984, p. 100.

28 Edward J. Hall, *The Hidden Dimension* (New York: Doubleday, 1966).

29 For a detailed discussion of improving communication effectiveness, see Courtland L. Bovee, John V. Thill, and Barbara E. Schatzman, *Business Communication Today*, 7th ed. (Upper Saddle River, N.J.: Prentice Hall, 2003).

30 See Otis W. Baskin and Craig E. Aronoff, *Interpersonal Communication in Organizations* (Glenview, Ill.: Scott, Foresman, 1980).

31 See "You Have (Too Much) E-Mail," *USA Today*, March 12, 1999, p. 3B.

32 Justin Fox, "The Triumph of English," *Fortune*, September 18, 2000, pp. 209–212.

33 Joseph Allen and Bennett P. Lientz, *Effective Business Communication* (Santa Monica, Calif.: Goodyear, 1979).

34 See "Making Silence Your Ally," *Across the Board*, October 1999, p. 11.

35 Boyd A. Vander Houwen, "Less Talking, More Listening," *HRMagazine*, April 1997, pp. 53–58.

36 For a discussion of these and related issues, see Eric M. Eisenberg and Marsha G. Witten, "Reconsidering Openness in Organizational Communication," *Academy of Management Review*, July 1987, Vol. 12, No. 3, pp. 418–426.

37 For a recent illustration, see Barbara Kellerman, "When Should a Leader Apologize—and When Not?" *Harvard Business Review*, April 2006, pp. 72–81.

Chapter 15

1 Stanley Holmes, "Nike: Can Perez Fill Knight's Shoes?" *BusinessWeek,* November 19, 2004, www.businessweek.com on June 1, 2009; Holmes, "Inside the Coup at Nike," *BusinessWeek,* February 6, 2006, www.businessweek.com on May 31, 2009; Holmes, "Nike's CEO Gets the Boot," *BusinessWeek,* January 24, 2006, www.businessweek.com on May 31, 2009; and Daniel Roth, "Can Nike Still Do It without Phil Knight?" *Fortune,* April 4, 2005, http://money.cnn.com on June 1, 2009.

2 For a review of definitions of groups, see Gregory Moorhead and Ricky W. Griffin, *Organizational Behavior,* 9th ed. (Boston: Houghton Mifflin, 2010).

3 Dorwin Cartwright and Alvin Zander, eds., *Group Dynamics: Research and Theory,* 3rd ed. (New York: Harper & Row, 1968).

4 See Willem Verbeke and Stefan Wuyts, "Moving in Social Circles—Social Circle Membership and Performance Implications," *Journal of Organizational Behavior,* 2007, Vol. 28, pp. 357–379, for an interesting extension of these ideas.

5 Rob Cross, Nitin Nohria, and Andrew Parker, "Six Myths About Informal Networks—and How to Overcome Them," *Sloan Management Review,* Spring 2002, pp. 67–77. See also Richard McDermott and Douglas Archibald, "Harnessing Your Staff's Informal Networks," *Harvard Business Review,* March 2010, pp. 82–89.

6 Robert Schrank, *Ten Thousand Working Days* (Cambridge, Mass.: MIT Press, 1978); Bill Watson, "Counter Planning on the Shop Floor," in Peter Frost, Vance Mitchell, and Walter Nord (eds.), *Organizational Reality,* 2nd ed. (Glenview, Ill.: Scott, Foresman, 1982), pp. 286–294.

7 "After Layoffs, More Workers Band Together," *Wall Street Journal,* February 26, 2002, p. B1.

8 Bradley L. Kirkman and Benson Rosen, "Powering Up Teams," *Organizational Dynamics,* Winter 2000, pp. 48–58.

9 John Mathieu, M. Travis Maynard, Tammy Rapp, and Lucy Gibson, "Team Effectiveness 1997–2007: A Review of Recent Advancements and a Glimpse Into the Future," *Journal of Management,* 2008, Vol. 34, No. 3, pp. 410–476.

10 Arvind Malhotra, Ann Majchrzak, and Benson Rosen, "Leading Virtual Teams," *Academy of Management Perspectives,* 2007, Vol. 21, No. 1, pp. 60–70.

11 "Why Teams Fail," *USA Today,* February 25, 1997, pp. 1B, 2B.

12 Brian Dumaine, "The Trouble with Teams," *Fortune,* September 5, 1994, pp. 86–92. See also Susan G. Cohen and Diane E. Bailey, "What Makes Teams Work: Group Effectiveness Research from the Shop Floor to the Executive Suite," *Journal of Management,* 1997, Vol. 23, No. 3, pp. 239–290; and John Mathieu, Lucy Gilson, and Thomas Ruddy, "Empowerment and Team Effectiveness: An Empirical Test of an Integrated Model," *Journal of Applied Psychology,* 2006, Vol. 91, No. 1, pp. 97–108.

13 Marvin E. Shaw, *Group Dynamics: The Psychology of Small Group Behavior,* 4th ed. (New York: McGraw-Hill, 1985).

14 "How to Avoid Hiring the Prima Donnas Who Hate Teamwork," *Wall Street Journal,* February 15, 2000, p. B1.

15 See Connie Gersick, "Marking Time: Predictable Transitions in Task Groups," *Academy of Management Journal,* June 1989, Vol. 32, No. 2, pp. 274–309. See also Avan R. Jassawalla and Hemant C. Sashittal, "Building Collaborative Cross-Functional New Product Teams," *Academy of Management Review,* 1999, Vol. 13, No. 3, pp. 50–60.

16 See Gilad Chen, "Newcomer Adaptation in Teams: Multilevel Antecedents and Outcomes," *Academy of Management Journal,* 2005, Vol. 48, No. 1, pp. 101–116.

17 For a review of other team characteristics, see Michael Campion, Gina Medsker, and A. Catherine Higgs, "Relations Between Work Group Characteristics and Effectiveness: Implications for Designing Effective Work Groups," *Personnel Psychology,* Winter 1993, pp. 823–850.

18 David Katz and Robert L. Kahn, *The Social Psychology of Organizations,* 2nd ed. (New York: Wiley, 1978), pp. 187–221. See also Greg L. Stewart and Murray R. Barrick, "Team Structure and Performance: Assessing the Mediating Role of Intrateam Process and the Moderating Role of Task Type," *Academy of Management Journal,* 2000, Vol. 43, No. 2, pp. 135–148; and Michael G. Pratt and Peter O. Foreman, "Classifying Managerial Responses to Multiple Organizational Identities," *Academy of Management Review,* 2000, Vol. 25, No. 1, pp. 18–42.

19 See Travis C. Tubre and Judith M. Collins, "Jackson and Schuler (1985) Revisited: A Meta-Analysis of the Relationships Between Role Ambiguity, Role Conflict, and Job Performance," *Journal of Management,* 2000, Vol. 26, No. 1, pp. 155–169.

20 Robert L. Kahn, D. M. Wolfe, R. P. Quinn, J. D. Snoek, and R. A. Rosenthal, *Organizational Stress: Studies in Role Conflict and Role Ambiguity* (New York: Wiley, 1964).

21 Daniel C. Feldman, "The Development and Enforcement of Group Norms," *Academy of Management Review,* January 1984, Vol. 9, No. 1, pp. 47–53.

22 "Companies Turn to Peer Pressure to Cut Injuries as Psychologists Join the Battle," *Wall Street Journal,* March 29, 1991, pp. B1, B3.

23 James Wallace Bishop and K. Dow Scott, "How Commitment Affects Team Performance," *HRMagazine,* February 1997, pp. 107–115.

24 Anne O'Leary-Kelly, Joseph Martocchio, and Dwight Frink, "A Review of the Influence of Group Goals on Group Performance," *Academy of Management Journal,* 1994, Vol. 37, No. 5, pp. 1285–1301.

25 See Anat Drach-Zahavy and Anat Freund, "Team Effectiveness Under Stress: A Structural Contingency Approach," *Journal of Organizational Behavior,* 2007, Vol. 28, pp. 423–450, for an interesting application of these ideas.

26 Philip M. Podsakoff, Michael Ahearne, and Scott B. MacKenzie, "Organizational Citizenship Behavior and the Quantity and Quality of Work Group Performance," *Journal of Applied Psychology,* 1997, Vol. 82, No. 2, pp. 262–270.

27 Suzy Wetlaufer, "Common Sense and Conflict," *Harvard Business Review,* January–February 2000, pp. 115–125.

28 Kathleen M. Eisenhardt, Jean L. Kahwajy, and L. J. Bourgeois III, "How Management Teams Can Have a Good Fight," *Harvard Business Review,* July–August 1997, pp. 77–89.

29 Thomas Bergmann and Roger Volkema, "Issues, Behavioral Responses and Consequences in Interpersonal Conflicts," *Journal of Organizational Behavior,* 1994, Vol. 15, pp. 467–471; see also Carsten K. W. De Dreu, "The Virtue and Vice of Workplace Conflict: Food for (Pessimistic) Thought," *Journal of Organizational Behavior,* 2008, Vol. 29, pp. 5–18.

30 Robin Pinkley and Gregory Northcraft, "Conflict Frames of Reference: Implications for Dispute Processes and Outcomes," *Academy of Management Journal,* 1994, Vol. 37, No. 1, pp. 193–205.

31 "How 2 Computer Nuts Transformed Industry Before Messy Breakup," *Wall Street Journal,* August 27, 1996, pp. A1, A10.

32 Bruce Barry and Greg L. Stewart, "Composition, Process, and Performance in Self-Managed Groups: The Role of Personality," *Journal of Applied Psychology,* 1997, Vol. 82, No. 1, pp. 62–78.

33 "Delta CEO Resigns After Clashes with Board," *USA Today,* May 13, 1997, p. B1.

34 "Why Boeing's Culture Breeds Turmoil," *BusinessWeek,* March 21, 2005, pp. 34–36.

35 "A 'Blood War' in the Jeans Trade," *BusinessWeek,* November 13, 1999, pp. 74–81.

36 Peter Elkind, "Blood Feud," *Fortune,* April 14, 1997, pp. 90–102.

37 See Patrick Nugent, "Managing Conflict: Third-Party Interventions for Managers," *Academy of Management Executive,* 2002, Vol. 16, No. 1, pp. 139–148.

38 See Kristin J. Behfar, Randall S. Peterson, Elizabeth A. Mannix, and William M. K. Trochim, "The Critical Role of Conflict Resolution in Teams: A Close Look at the Links Between Conflict, Conflict Management Strategies, and Team Outcomes," *Journal of Applied Psychology,* 2008, Vol. 93, No. 1, pp. 170–188.

39 "Solving Conflicts in the Workplace Without Making Losers," *Wall Street Journal,* May 27, 1997, p. B1.

40 "Teaching Business How to Cope with Workplace Conflicts," *BusinessWeek,* February 18, 1990, pp. 136, 139.

41 See Kimberly Wade-Benzoni, Andrew Hoffman, Leigh Thompson, Don Moore, James Gillespie, and Max Bazerman, "Barriers to Resolution in Ideologically Based Negotiations: The Role of Values and Institutions," *Academy of Management Review,* 2002, Vol. 27, No. 1, pp. 41–57.

42 J. Z. Rubin and B. R. Brown, *The Social Psychology of Bargaining and Negotiation* (New York: Academic Press, 1975).

43 R. J. Lewicki and J. A. Litterer, *Negotiation* (Homewood, Ill.: Irwin, 1985).

44 Howard Raiffa, *The Art and Science of Negotiation* (Cambridge, Mass.: Belknap, 1982).

45 K. H. Bazerman and M. A. Neale, *Negotiating Rationally* (New York: Free Press, 1992).

ORGANIZATION AND PRODUCT INDEX

Note: Page numbers in italics refer to tables or figures

Note: Page numbers in italics refer to tables or figures